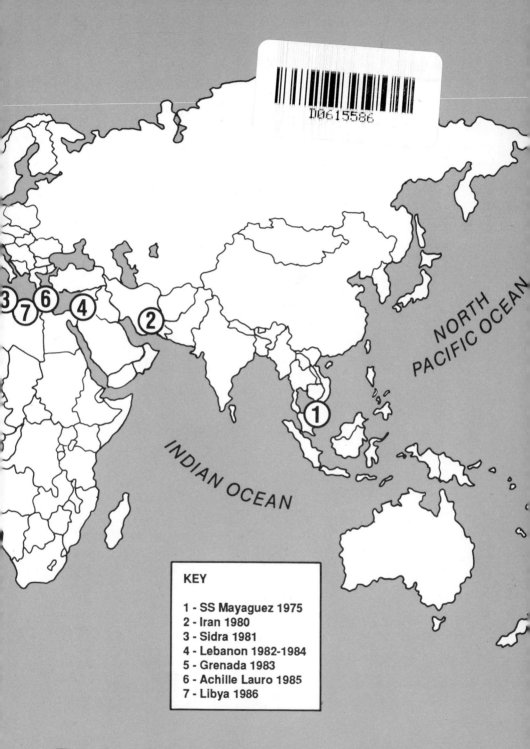

KEY

1 - SS Mayaguez 1975
2 - Iran 1980
3 - Sidra 1981
4 - Lebanon 1982-1984
5 - Grenada 1983
6 - Achille Lauro 1985
7 - Libya 1986

U.S. Expeditions, 1975-1986

AT WAR

AMERICANS AT WAR

1975–1986,
AN ERA OF VIOLENT PEACE

Daniel P. Bolger

PRESIDIO

The views expressed herein are those of the author and do not purport
to reflect the position of the United States Military Acadamy,
Department of the Army, or Department of Defense.

Published by Presidio Press
31 Pamaron Way, Novato CA 94949

LIBRARY OF CONGRESS
Library of Congress Cataloging-in-Publication Data

Bolger, Daniel P., 1957–
    Americans at war, 1975–1986: an era of violent peace/Daniel P.
Bolger.
      p. cm.
    Bibliography: p. 454
    Includes index.
    ISBN 0–89141–303–0:
    1. United States—History, Military—20th century. 2. United
States—History—1945   I. Title.
E745.B57 1988
973.92—dc19   88–4144
                                          CIP

Cartography by Jaeger and Associates

Photo credits: All photographs courtesy of the U.S. Department of
Defense, except where otherwise noted.

Printed in the United States of America

This book is dedicated to the soldiers, sailors, airmen, and marines who made the supreme sacrifice, 1975–1986.

CONTENTS

ACKNOWLEDGMENTS

Although I am a professional soldier, I have yet to see combat, expeditionary or otherwise. But I knew something was wrong with a lot of the things I read about recent American combat experiences. The stories in the papers or on the television did not always quite square with my own knowledge of the military and how it operates. "Media bias" was not the problem; there was no ideological slant to most defense reporting. To be blunt, what seemed to be amiss was an articulate understanding of how armed forces actually work. The era of Hanson Baldwin and Drew Middleton is definitely over.

This is not to say that the public organs suffer from a lack of experts. Indeed, an entire galaxy of military reformers has sprung up, most of whom have never worn this nation's uniform. They base their authority upon a conventional wisdom supposedly derived from their analyses of U.S. military actions since 1975, and they enjoy wide access to the American public. But the more I heard from these people, the more I became certain that they were focusing on the wrong things. Combat successes sometimes were converted into defeats in a search for troubles in the American defense establishment, and very real problems were often unnoticed.

Still, in the absence of other information, certain ideas have become fixtures in the popular media. Here are a few typical shibboleths: bad maintenance and lack of spare parts doomed the Iran raid, crafty terrorists killed the defenseless marines in Beirut, the Grenada operation was flawed and bungled, and "interservice rivalry" has ruined most U.S. combat undertakings since World War II. Given that scholars, journalists, and even legislators are making judgments and decisions based upon such ideas, I wondered if it was not about time to examine the evidence and evaluate the conventional wisdom. Could a professional soldier's viewpoint, tempered by historical research methods, help clear the air?

I approached these recent events as an historian, concentrating on primary sources. "Contemporary history" seems a contradiction in terms, and although I have been careful, I am not at all convinced that I have figured out exactly what happened in each engagement. But these accounts are fuller than most, offering a panorama of America's armed forces as they dealt with a dangerous world over the last decade. If I have shed a bit more light and a lot less heat on the continuing debate over the effectiveness of the national defenses, this book will have accomplished its purpose.

Fortunately, I found many primary sources to aid my investigation. Those who have come under fire have left an ample (and largely untapped) written record in the plethora of U.S. military publications available to the general researcher. The superb collections of the U.S. Military Academy and University of Chicago Library provided invaluable troves of such matter, without which this book would have been impossible.

The photographs in this book are courtesy of the Department of Defense, in particular the Navy and Air Force media relations agencies. Various defense public relations officials rendered yeoman service in the choice and captioning of pictures. Some of the Lebanon photographs are from Jim Breckenridge, who commanded the Army unit there in 1983.

No account or picture is complete without a human touch and a bit of on-scene expertise. These outstanding soldiers deserve special thanks for their honesty and valuable assistance: Jim Breckenridge, Chuck Jacoby, Frank Kearney, Dave Lamm, Dave Petraeus, and Tim Sayers.

Finally, a word of gratitude is due to the fine staff of Presidio Press, in particular Colonel Robert Kane and the most understanding editor in the world, Joan Griffin.

PROLOGUE
AN ERA OF VIOLENT PEACE

"War is peace."

George Orwell, *1984*

Captain Arthur Mallano looked out from the cockpit window as the last few passengers ambled aboard his C-130 Hercules transport. He checked his watch: 0358, 29 April 1975. Soon he would be out of this eerie place, this city with a noose around its throat, waiting only for the rope to snap tight. Mallano noticed that the predicted squall line seemed to be rolling in right on schedule. The sky flickered along the horizon, illuminating banked, somber clouds. "Gee, that thunderstorm is getting a little closer. It's moving toward the field," said the pilot to his deputy. Mallano watched the lightning flare up—white, red, blue, and green.[1] That seemed odd. But it was not an act of nature. This storm came from men.

The clutch of 122-mm rockets arced in from the muggy, overcast night faster than sound, splitting the darkness over Tan Son Nhut Air Base and roaring down to erupt among the concrete aprons and buildings of the American Defense Attaché Office, the former home of Military Assistance Command, Vietnam. One rocket impacted below the high wing of a hapless U.S. Air Force C-130. The plane carried a 15,000-pound BLU-82 bomb, and the runway brightened with a searing white light as the brilliant fireball engulfed the doomed plane. A wing cartwheeled crazily skyward, silhouetted by the blazing wreckage. Another hostile shot crashed into a fuel truck, which split open in a geyser of yellow-white heat. Fires brewed up in the shattered hulks of buildings

1

all over the compound, and the dancing flames cast a lurid light on the frantic, running men and careening vehicles and aircraft that raced to and fro under the murderous surprise attack.

Captain Mallano raced his engines and ordered his remaining passengers to get aboard or stand clear. The loadmaster slammed the cargo hatches and began to elevate the ramp as Mallano started to roll down the cluttered, broken runway. Rockets peppered the straightaway in front, behind, and beside the Hercules, but the American flier did not hesitate. Mallano slammed his four throttles forward and roared over the runway, skirting an embattled antiaircraft emplacement as he urged the laden plane off the deadly runway.

As Mallano took off, rocket casing fragments and jagged debris whirred through the air. Impact flashes lit the compound like maniacal strobe beacons. Thunderous cracks of explosives splitting cement marked the sites where the big rockets sighed to earth. Smoking, torn pieces of damaged American and South Vietnamese airplanes blocked the runways and burned on the parking areas. Two South Vietnamese Air Force (VNAF) C-130s struggled down the cratered, littered runways, with panicked passengers pushing frenzied soldiers out of the overloaded craft as the transports waddled and lurched out of the blazing madhouse. A VNAF twin-engine C-7 Caribou tried to leave on only one motor and flipped off the shattered tarmac to explode on the grass strip beyond. Meanwhile, the North Vietnamese gunners continued to rain 122-mm rockets onto the stricken base, augmenting the initial barrage with 130-mm rounds from the big M-46 field guns south of Saigon.[2] The final agony of Vietnam had begun.

One of the first projectiles screamed directly into security post number four, erasing the two young marines who had been manning the sandbagged position. Corporals Wilson Judge and Charles McMahon died instantly. American army Capt. Stuart A. Herrington described what he saw: "The twisted motor of a 122-mm rocket lay in the center of a charred hole. A few meters away, a pile of twisted and smoking motorcycles and other vehicles gave mute testimony to the force of the explosion that killed the two men. Bits of uniform and flesh hung from the chain-link fence."[3]

Although the two marines were the only U.S. dead, the havoc, fires, and physical devastation at the air base and the loss of military discipline among the South Vietnamese rendered the facility unusable.

In the words of Army of the Republic of Vietnam (ARVN) Gen. Cao Van Vien, the Vietnamese Air Force was "no longer in control of its personnel." [4] Needless to say, the American fixed-wing evacuation airlift from Tan Son Nhut was over.

Since 1 April 1975, United States civil and military planes had been pulling Americans, American allies, and selected South Vietnamese out of the crumbling Republic of Vietnam. Americans had abandoned beleaguered Phnom Penh, Cambodia, on 12 April 1975 in the sad, yet flawlessly executed and unopposed Operation EAGLE PULL. By 19 April, 5,000 Vietnamese had departed aboard a steady series of Military Airlift Command (MAC) and charter civilian flights. Continuing North Vietnamese pressure, to include a daring air attack in captured A-37 Dragonfly light attack planes, ended C-141 Starlifter jet sorties and most civilian flights by 28 April. American pilots reported fire from both North and South Vietnamese positions and interceptions by enemy planes, but they brought out 18,400 more people. On 28 April, only eighteen of fifty-eight planned C-130 flights landed; after the vicious, sustained barrage on the early morning of 29 April, any hope for further Hercules arrivals vanished in gouts of exploding fuel and mobs of rampaging, despairing ARVN and VNAF troops.[5]

Nobody ever dreamed that things could have gone so sour so quickly. Only three months earlier, all had seemed so normal, or what passed for it in Vietnam after the January 1973 cease-fire. Everything had gone crazy back in March 1975, when the smoldering half-peace burst into a major conventional North Vietnamese attack in the Central Highlands. On 10 March 1975 the northerners struck the fortified town of Ban Me Thuot. ARVN counterattacks failed miserably, and the victorious Communists pushed eastward across the narrow republic. The North Vietnamese thrust threatened to slice South Vietnam in two.

President Nguyen Van Thieu made the fateful decision on 14 March to withdraw from the highlands. Thieu hoped to trade space for time, and perhaps pull the enemy advance far beyond its supply bases. If only the ARVN held on a bit longer, maybe the May monsoon rains would slow down the enemy. Thieu also guessed that the battlefield disaster would provide clear evidence to American President Gerald R. Ford that it was time for the United States to intervene with massive deliveries of new equipment, selected use of air power (B-52 Stratofortress bombers in particular), and perhaps even a few U.S. ground units. Richard

Nixon had promised as much, in secret letters written on 14 November 1972 and 5 January 1973. But President Nixon was gone, a victim of the Watergate scandal. President Ford chose to wait before he acted.

While the new American president wrestled with a surly, isolationist Congress and the unfamiliar strictures of the new War Powers Resolution, Thieu's country disintegrated. Danang and the northern provinces slipped away amidst a chaotic succession of military reverses, heavy losses, desertions, and unit mutinies. Even supposedly good outfits, like the elite 1st ARVN Division, suffered from the general collapse of morale and degenerated into a nervous, unruly rabble. Of 85,000 effectives, only 16,000 disarmed, confused ARVN troops escaped the North Vietnamese noose. Four infantry divisions, an armored regiment, four Ranger groups, an air division, and numerous militia units ceased to exist.[6] Thieu's men could not halt the relentless Communist offensives.

The North Vietnamese turned south to complete their work. They had not expected the south to collapse so swiftly; in fact, they originally envisioned victory some time in 1976. As of 9 April, nine Communist divisions moved to surround Saigon. Only a few organized ARVN troops remained to stop them.

For twelve days, brave ARVN soldiers of the 18th Division (previously regarded as average at best), ARVN paratroopers, Rangers, and every plane the VNAF could fly held the line east of Saigon, at Xuan Loc. At first, the southerners stunned the North Vietnamese and threw them back in disarray. But by 16 April, the Communists had elected to isolate the tough garrison and press on toward the South Vietnamese capital. On 20 April, ARVN units had to withdraw toward Saigon in a vain attempt to relieve pressure on that city.[7] Xuan Loc fell, and with this, South Vietnam was finished. The time had come to play out the grim final act.

President Nguyen Van Thieu found his capital of Saigon surrounded, his army in revolt, in hiding, or fighting desperately in a doomed cause. He knew that he had failed, and he believed that America had failed him. Thieu quit on 21 April, after an impassioned final speech. He accused the United States of irresponsibility and selfishness, saying that "refusing to aid an ally and abandoning it is an inhumane act." [8] After a brief interregnum, Gen. Duong Van "Big" Minh took over on 27 April. Minh hoped to strike a bargain with the Communists, but it was far too late for that.

In America, the realization dawned that there would be no resurrection in Saigon. The final Vietnamese crisis had come, not by guerrilla raids and booby traps, but in the form of an overt, conventional attack. This was the sort of war, with tanks and howitzers and fronts, that American soldiers could understand and fight well. But the U.S. commanders had squandered their public support years before, thrashing aimlessly through the jungles and rice paddies. On 23 April President Gerald Ford decided that "America can regain the sense of pride that existed before Vietnam. But it cannot be achieved by refighting a war that is finished as far as America is concerned." [9] It was time to leave.

The end would be worse than anyone could imagine. America's last twenty-four hours in Saigon resembled a full-scale, living recreation of Dante's hell. There is never much dignity in a rout, and despite a truly competent extraction effort, the images still haunt America. Again and again the scenes repeated themselves: desperate South Vietnamese pleading and clawing for the American helicopters, a ragtag flotilla of crowded little fishing boats swirling around the great gray American ships, VNAF Huey choppers being tossed over the side of U.S. vessels to make room for more fugitive craft, and grim-faced marine infantry holding back frenzied mobs of Vietnamese civilians and defrocked soldiers as the last few Americans scrambled up unceremoniously onto the embassy helipad.

United States Ambassador Graham Martin hoped it would not come to this, but it did. At sunrise on 29 April, Martin drove from the embassy to the battered defense attaché compound at Tan Son Nhut. He found the place a shambles, with fires burning, random sniper firing, and the air base in an uproar. Martin still wanted to try to land a flight of inbound C-130s. His military attaché, army Maj. Gen. Homer D. Smith, received reports from marine officers on the scene. The briefing building rocked with desultory explosions, and word came that rebellious ARVN and VNAF troops had overrun much of the parking and loading area. General Smith advised the ambassador that C-130 landings were "just not in the cards."

Martin assented reluctantly, and President Ford approved Operation FREQUENT WIND at 1051 Saigon time, 29 April 1975. This plan called for a complete withdrawal by helicopter. Americans all over Saigon, who had been tuned to American Service Radio waiting for news, heard the incongruous Bing Crosby record "I'm Dreaming of a White Christmas'' play several times. This was the agreed signal.[10] The helicopters that symbolized America's Southeast Asian war would remove the last American participants.

During late March and early April, the U.S. Navy, Marines, and Air Force assembled a significant armada to conduct the withdrawal. Rear Admiral Donald Whitmire commanded Task Force 77, the biggest armed contingent collected off Vietnam since 1972. The aircraft carriers USS *Coral Sea,* USS *Midway,* USS *Enterprise,* and USS *Hancock,* along with the amphibious carrier USS *Okinawa* and 40 other vessels steamed offshore, protected by more than 150 navy aircraft and 120 USAF planes. Eighty-one helicopters, principally marine CH-53 Sea Stallions and CH-46 Sea Knights plus 10 armed USAF CH-53 Knife and HH-53 Jolly Green Giant choppers, formed up on the carrier flight decks to execute FREQUENT WIND.

Twelve of the big whirlybirds carried 840 marines inland about 1500 on 29 April. These men constituted the withdrawal security force. Brigadier General Richard Carey, USMC, commanded this component, built around 2nd Battalion of the 4th Marines.[11] The first wave of marines veered off to land at gutted Tan Son Nhut, where they debarked and assumed a rough perimeter around the defense attaché buildings. The Americans and lucky Vietnamese evacuees at the attaché area broke into applause when the rescue force arrived. Despite some M-16 rifle fire from the sullen packs of dejected ARVN deserters roaming Saigon, the helicopters loaded their first groups and lifted off within six minutes of landing. The other waves of marine and air force craft soon arrived to continue the flow behind the watchful, ready ring of marine riflemen. Marine snipers and grenadiers fired warning shots to keep back the curious, the anxious, and the vengeful.

Air force Maj. John F. Guilmartin piloted one of the helicopters involved at Tan Son Nhut. His experiences are quite representative. As he turned toward the landing zone, he saw dirt and concrete chips thrown up by artillery shells striking the airfield. Muzzle flashes dotted his flight path across the crowded streets and rooftops of nervous Saigon. When Guilmartin's radar warning system identified a North Vietnamese surface to air missile device locking on his USAF helicopter, he radioed an orbiting F-105 Thunderchief. The jet launched an antiradar homing missile and the warning indicators ceased. Guilmartin completed his pickup and returned to the *Midway.*

Major Guilmartin refueled and headed back in. One of his three gunners engaged rooftop snipers as the big HH-53 banked over the long shadows darkening late afternoon Saigon. North Vietnamese antiaircraft crews laced the skies with tracers, but the air force crew made it in and out without damage.

Guilmartin's last mission typified the final wild night in the doomed city. The USAF helicopter came in low across the city, clearing its way with all guns blazing. Tracers and rocket fire bloomed up from dying Saigon. It was fully dark as the big HH-53 settled into the attaché compound. Frightened Vietnamese refugees rushed at the helicopter. Although most of the departing people gradually calmed down and formed into orderly columns, one persistent woman resisted the strenuous attempts of the gunners and flight mechanic to keep her in line. She jumped out of her place once and got shoved back into the row. A second time, the jabbering little woman came into the helicopter cabin. When the USAF gunner swung his rifle butt at her, she fell back. Grabbing wildly, she seized an aircraft machine gun handle. Realizing what she had done, the woman swung the barrel toward the crowd in fury and pressed the trigger. The USAF gunner heard the drive motor engage on the Gatling-style minigun and knew that 2,000 rounds per minute would spit forth in seconds. Luckily, the wicked gun jammed, and the airman dragged away the distraught woman. The loading continued. Ninety-seven passengers boarded Guilmartin's helicopter, which was double the usual capacity. He took off anyway.

Even as the big helicopter strained for altitude, an alert flight mechanic spotted real trouble rising from the eastern suburbs of Saigon. Some enterprising North Vietnamese missile crew had loosed a swift little SA-7 Grail infrared homing round. It rose like a spiteful meteor, tearing directly for Guilmartin's lurching HH-53. Thinking quickly, the USAF flight crewman leaned into the hellish night sky and shot a safety flare from his Very pistol. The enemy homer followed the flare, and Guilmartin's laden craft escaped. Offshore, the overloaded helicopter broke a landing strut as it settled onto the flight deck of the busy *Midway*. Guilmartin's contribution had ended.[12] By 2330, Tan Son Nhut was clear. The marines blew up the sensitive communications installations and left. More than 2,500 people had been removed. Now only the embassy remained to be evacuated.

Throughout the night, the procession of helicopters continued, all bound for the embassy. Head counts went out to the fleet on a regular basis, but these proved wildly inaccurate—guesses at best. The only firm number was 256: 181 marines and 75 other Americans. But there always seemed to be more Vietnamese to pick up. As Admiral Whitmire later said, it seemed "a bottomless pit of refugees."

In fact, American marines and military attachés carefully screened the Vietnamese to insure that only authorized people departed. Commitments made had to be honored, said Ambassador Graham Martin. He stretched a plan that had been designed to withdraw 150 people from his embassy roof and parking lot to include more than 2,000. Hour after hour, through black skies, under fire, with little respite, the choppers came and went, came and went.

By midnight on 29 April, the helicopter lift was reaching its limit. Fatigue took its toll on men and machines. Near the fleet, one CH-53 smacked into the water, killing a marine pilot and gunner. Almost half of the choppers, flown over and over well beyond performance limits, were out of commission for maintenance failures. On the embassy landing pad, an exhausted helicopter controller walked right off the edge and fell one story to a ledge below. Fortunately, only a few bones broke.[13]

Martin kept requesting helicopters and sending out refugees. Meanwhile, President Ford in Washington and the naval officers offshore kept asking him, "How many more people?" Cabled Martin, "726." Weary, overstressed, and determined to keep the flow going, he had made up the number. In fact, Martin underestimated by about 420 people. The bedraggled helicopter units pressed to send in the requisite number of craft, and almost did it. By 0415, only six more sorties would clear the embassy of all who had been promised evacuation. Martin knew that, as did his subordinates. Admiral Whitmire and President Ford did not; they feared Martin was shoveling out random refugees as fast as he could, without regard for time. Gerald Ford wanted no more U.S. casualties. He wanted it to end.

For the last time, the Americans faced numbers in Vietnam that did not add up. Instant satellite communications could not iron out the discrepancy. So with his tired ambassador saying one thing, his concerned admiral saying another, North Vietnamese tanks and infantry driving into Saigon's suburbs, South Vietnamese allies turning uglier by the minute, and Americans still in the embassy, the president made his decision to pull the plug. Martin was ordered out. All Americans were directed to follow immediately. No more Vietnamese could leave. Despite promises, despite reassurances by American army officers and State Department officials, 420 people waiting calmly at the embassy would be left.

Captain Stuart Herrington described the scene as his helicopter lifted off. In the parking lot, he saw the loyal Vietnamese embassy firemen, the West German priest, and a dozen South Korean diplomats, all waiting patiently for helicopters that would never come. Herrington said, "If I tried to talk I would have cried. I know of no words in any language that are adequate to describe the sense of shame that swept over me during that flight." [14]

The final two or so hours passed quickly, as a small band of marines worked their way up to the helipad on the roof. The marines surrendered the compound walls as the rest of the security unit pulled out, and Vietnamese looters and rowdies spilled over. Glass crashed in the lobby, and hundreds of running feet pursued the final group of marines as they ascended through the empty multistory embassy. The marines bolted doors on each floor and piled furniture up behind each portal. As the surging, shrieking mob howled its way through the building, the marines braced themselves on the roof helipad for the expected hostile push. America's hold on Vietnam had been shrinking since January 1973, smaller and smaller until now. Like turning off an old television, America prepared to wink out.

The last marines used fists and tear gas to beat back angry Vietnamese fighting to get onto the pad. They ducked sniper shots and waited for that all-important final helicopter. The sky brightened, clear and gray-white, turning robin's egg blue as the tropical sun ascended out of the Pacific. No American would see this sight again except as a guest of the new Communist government of all Vietnam. At last, a single Sea Knight rattled in, escorted by six Cobra gunships. The CH-46 collected eleven marines and bounded off the tiny rooftop pad.[15] It was 0749 on 30 April 1975. America's Vietnam War was over.

The Cold War continued as before.

The tragic conclusion of a limited intervention that became a major war did not signal the end of combat for the United States of America. Indeed, less than two weeks later, Americans faced hostile fire again. But the *Mayaguez* incident, like the series of vicious little actions that followed over the next decade, was part of a bigger war, one that predated the carnage in Indochina and might well continue for some time. Vietnam, like Korea before it, represented an aberration. It was the exception to the general pattern of limited but deadly serious superpower competition that characterizes the post-1945 world. Admiral James D. Watkins rightly labeled this uneasy condition an "era of violent peace." [16]

The Soviets and Americans routinely use armed forces to deter each other, to demonstrate resolve, to support shaky allies, to suppress defiant enemies, and to show the flag in a global struggle that shows no sign of abating. Plato said that only the dead have seen the end of war; George Orwell warned of a grim world where war was peace. The Soviets and Americans have proven the Greek philosopher and British author to be prophets indeed.

Two agreed-upon rules have developed in this relentless Cold War. First, and rather obviously, neither side wants to employ their apocalyptic hoards of nuclear munitions. The results of a full-scale exchange are too horrific to contemplate, but it is evident that the irradiated slag left in each homeland would be unrecognizable to any people lucky (or unlucky) enough to survive the crashing detonations of the thermonuclear thunderbolts. So Americans and Soviets, natural rivals and enemies only too akin to many similar doomed pairs in history, have no recourse to the usual arena of armed conflict. Any real clash between the two giants could unleash a train of unforeseen events that might spark the plutonium powder kegs and immolate the modern world.

Thus, the second rule of the Cold War proceeds from the first. Neither country can directly fight the other. Besides the nuclear factor, the general balance of conventional forces discourages direct confrontations between the Union of Soviet Socialist Republics and the United States. The U.S. Navy, U.S. Air Force, the amphibious fighters of the U.S. Marine Corps, and strong American allies like Britain, France, and West Germany represent the American military advantage; the numerous, tank-heavy Land Forces provide the Soviet Union's main power. Even without hydrogen warheads, both nations possess means more than capable of bludgeoning each other into the Neolithic era.

Well-trained, dedicated American military personnel provide and service the armed might that compels the Soviet Union to play by these rules. Every day, a relatively few dedicated airmen and sailors keep the American long-range bombers, intercontinental ballistic missiles, and fleet ballistic missile submarines ready to execute the dread orders that will unleash their fearsome charges. Many other soldiers, sailors, airmen, and marines man the ships, planes, and battalions that guard and support the troubled demilitarized zone in Korea, the quieter but no less threatened inter-German border, and the web of sea and air routes and bases that link these fronts with the American homeland. Other sizable American components educate allied foreign troops, protect trade lanes, and train under harsh conditions. American servicemen have been hurt and killed performing these vital daily tasks. Although critical to the prevention of World War III, such missions rarely result in actual armed conflict. As such, they form a necessary yet routine background for the dramatic dispatch of American expeditions in support of national objectives.

The two superpowers use the undeveloped and underdeveloped regions of the globe as a "neutral arena" to continue the vigorous, inevitable competition truncated by nuclear arms. This is how the Americans and Soviets compete. So the probing, the needling, the skirmishes, and the interventions continue throughout Latin America, Africa, and Asia.

Fortunately, most of the time the two giants contend with words, examples, economic assistance, military sales and advice, naval port calls, and in the American case, with the many diverse voices and resources of a free and open society. Despite a lot of superficial "anti-Americanism" in the Third World, the USA does quite well in this type of effort. When small nations get into trouble, they can turn to the Soviets, who can barely (and often cannot) feed themselves and who have a consumer economy akin to Pakistan, or they can ask for aid from the mightiest economic engine in human history. Soviet help always has long strings attached; most American assistance comes free of political prices, even to nominal U.S. "enemies" like Mozambique, India, and Yugoslavia. Sometimes, as in Egypt, the locals recognize a better deal when they see it. America's Egyptian allies used to be firm Soviet clients. Other troubled Third World nations have taken the same course. It is hard to eat "revolutionary solidarity."

Neither the Soviets nor the Americans, however, place their complete faith in propaganda, foreign aid, or cultural exchanges. Both countries "project power" into the Third World in direct support of their interests. America and its allies depend much more on foreign imports than does the Soviet Union. The United States must be able to project power to safeguard its foreign concerns. Not surprisingly, the Americans require and possess the sort of potent air, ground, naval, and amphibious units necessary to conduct expeditionary operations. With the exception of their bloody cross-border incursion into unfriendly Afghanistan, the Soviets content themselves with large advisory contingents and a lot of naval and air posturing and surveillance. In the decade since Vietnam, the Americans have had strong expeditionary forces on hand or en route when trouble erupts.

What is expeditionary combat? It is the deployment of a small military force into a hostile area to accomplish certain definite objectives. Expeditions are temporary in nature and normally of brief duration. Often, they respond to a unique, urgent threat. These operations fall outside the usual regimen of American defense missions, hence the military sometimes characterizes these missions as "contingencies." Most are "joint," in that they involve more than one armed service. With little time available and in an unexpected situation, expeditionary forces face particular challenges in intelligence analysis, communications, and coordination. Expeditionary combat falls within the mainstream of the American military heritage. Since Vietnam, this type of fighting allows U.S. presidents to use armed power without paying heavy political prices.

Expeditionary combat operations have typified American military engagements since 1975. Indeed, they have characterized the entire Cold War era, including Quemoy-Matsu (1954–55, 1958), Lebanon (1958), and the Dominican Republic (1965), among others. Americans have a long history of engaging in these sorts of actions, ranging from the punitive raids on the Barbary pirates in 1803–1805 ("the shores of Tripoli") through the gunboat diplomacy of William McKinley, Theodore Roosevelt, and Woodrow Wilson to the 1920s Marine Corps "Banana Wars" in Haiti and Nicaragua. Since the promulgation of the 1823 Monroe Doctrine, the Americans have found it in their interest to intervene (some say to interfere) in the Western Hemisphere and, eventually, around the world to protect U.S. citizens, property, business interests, and allies. Long overseas ground wars, especially indecisive ones, are a rather recent development in the American military tradition. Like the British Empire in the nineteenth century, the United States in the twentieth century maintains its power by a regular series of patrols, garrisons, and punitive strikes. When enemies oppose these activities, expeditionary combat results.

After the drawn-out debacle in Vietnam, quick expeditionary actions have suited American public opinion, especially as reflected in the Congress. Disgust over the undeclared quagmire in Southeast Asia produced the 1973 War Powers Resolution. This law limits the president to ninety days of unrestricted use of American military forces without congressional consent, and establishes a process of reports and legislative reviews to mitigate against another Gulf of Tonkin–style "blank check." To fight even a minor war, the commander in chief must consult Congress. Since 1973, presidents have tended to avoid the constitutional question inherent in this controversial statute, mainly by reverting to limited expeditions rather than requesting formal declarations of war. So there are strong political incentives to adhere to brief and limited operations.

Most United States expeditions go unchallenged. Few Third World nations desire a showdown with feared American units. Thus, the mere appearance of American ground troops, ships, or aircraft can quell many disturbances (real or potential) without a shot being fired. In April 1982, an American paratrooper battalion assumed duties as the key element in the Sinai Multinational Force, providing an armed barrier between nervous Egyptians and Israelis. American F-15 Eagle fighters and E-3A Sentry airborne warning and control system (AWACS) aircraft deployed to Egypt from February to August 1983 to support the Sudanese government against Libyan threats. July 1983 saw the aircraft carrier USS *Ranger* and her escorts and the USS *New Jersey* battleship surface action group stationed off the Pacific coast of Nicaragua; almost simultaneously, the USS *Coral Sea* carrier battle group steamed along Nicaragua's Caribbean coast to discourage Soviet supply efforts. During March 1986, U.S. Army helicopters moved Honduran battalions to block a Nicaraguan border incursion. These are just four well-known examples of many in which Americans executed successful military operations without provoking opposition.

But some American expeditions do cause a very violent reaction, often anticipated. When these American expeditions go "in harm's way," they usually find their path barred by determined men using Soviet weapons. Some of these are true Soviet allies, like the Cubans in Grenada. Others, like the Syrians, Libyans, or Palestinian terrorists, find the USSR a good source of arms and combat doctrine. The Khmer Rouge thought that way in 1975, although today Pol Pot's radicals regret that connection. Unlike the Cubans, these other nations and factions tend to display unpredictable (indeed erratic) behavior, not always in line with Soviet dictates or interests. In addition, Americans have already faced Iranian enemies armed and trained by U.S. methods. There may well be more of this as time goes on. The Third World opponents rarely match the Americans in troop quality or cohesion, but such hostile units often outnumber the intervention forces. Many of these enemies possess very sophisticated weapons.

How have the Americans overcome the challenges of the "era of violent peace"? In general, American expeditions succeed or fail based upon mass, flexibility, and especially command and control. In this regard, these small campaigns are not all that different from conventional warfare. The biggest discriminator is the short time frame generally associated with expeditions. Commanders only have time to get it right once.

To defeat the more numerous enemy quickly, U.S. expeditions must concentrate their small amount of powerful forces against the key objectives. In a military sense, mass equals force times speed. Often, expeditions sacrifice unit strength in order to get into action quickly. The alternative is to collect a mighty outfit that arrives too late. Achieving mass is a delicate balance, based upon the mission, the enemy situation, terrain considerations, troops available, and time. In expeditions, time and mission factors predominate.

During contingency situations, America can only gather forces at the expense of time. Even with the vast resources of the air force's Military Airlift Command (MAC), the Military Sealift Command (MSC), and naval amphibious shipping, the United States rarely can transport enough forces to the threatened area to achieve a preponderant numerical advantage in any reasonable time span. Other than nuclear forces, most American components cannot move "instantly," due to ongoing training, equipment maintenance, and prior commitments (such as NATO or Korean deployments). Elements can and are collected from around the globe, but at some point, preparations must stop and the fighting start.

American commanders choose their units rapidly from those available, then direct these elements where they can do the most good. Ordinarily, U.S. units mass armed strength to exploit enemy weaknesses, but mission requirements (hostage recovery, for example) or poor intelligence might pit American fighting men directly against enemy strong points. In either case, American forces gather the maximum combat power to crush the enemy and rapidly fulfill the assigned missions. Mass not only implies speed, it necessitates it. Mass without speed is mass times zero; it gains nothing in a contingency.

Even maximum mass will falter if employed under an overly complicated organization or a rigid plan. As expeditions are generally joint in nature, each service component contributes certain capabilities and liabilities. The commander should have the good sense to use the right units for the appropriate tasks. It is also a good idea to allow for the friction and fog of war that are certain to inhibit even beautifully crafted plans. Successful expeditions overcome adversity because the commanders anticipate troubles and leave themselves time, forces, and operational space to address the unexpected. Given the fact that intelligence can never be perfect and that enemies are unpredictable, an expeditionary force ought to be alert for unrecognized pitfalls and be ready to capitalize on unanticipated opportunities.

Command and control is the most important aspect of all. A good man in charge, with a clearly stated, simple concept and a willingness to get up front to smell the battle, can remedy a multitude of planning sins. Expeditions that serve under such a forceful leader can surmount major difficulties.

But the commander is only as good as the authority he can impose; control is as critical as leadership. Knowing how much or how little control to employ distinguishes good commanders from mediocre officers. Lower echelon commanders need room to exercise initiative. These subordinates must understand the commander's concept well enough to carry out his intent in the absence of orders. Equally important, the competent commander has to be able to recognize those few dire circumstances that require drastic personal action by the commander, regardless of subordinate prerogatives. This kind of perception is hard to master; the commander must be near the fighting to influence such crises. Many officers avoid the challenge and resort to the two easier extremes: allowing junior commanders total license (which may work, depending on the lower ranking men) or tightening up the reins into a centralized choke hold (made easier by modern technology). In short, the good commander must control things enough to exercise his will without unduly interfering in subordinate operations.

In modern times, control can become an actual impediment to command. The same wonderful satellite terminals that allow solid, "failsafe" supervision of America's nuclear arsenal now reach to every conventional unit as well. The signal network can greatly expedite preparations. High-technology communications assist in assembling forces in time and space and in speeding the flow of intelligence. The satellite links might even convey last-minute updates to embattled frontline units. As long as the control system is used to help the fighters, there is no problem.

But this direct line to the battlefield could well be misused to direct operations from the White House, the Pentagon, or another distant, air-conditioned headquarters. Such remote supervision requires a lot of input from the combat forces to permit the isolated, insulated commander to make decisions. Equipped with secure burst transmitters and an insatiable desire for information, the chain of command can wrap up and strangle a combat unit.

During expeditionary actions, time is precious. Combat commanders cannot afford to waste crucial minutes answering well-meaning but distracting requests for situation reports from far-off command posts and interested civilian and military officials. A sensible expeditionary mission includes distinct goals, clearly enunciated rules of engagement and limitations, and enough trust to let the assigned commander execute his mission. If higher commanders insist on leading squads from afar, the on-scene commander can probably do everyone a favor by having the gumption to turn off his satellite receivers. The political and military leaders who dispatch expeditions should develop patience and faith in the men they have selected.

Some of America's engagements since 1975 have been much discussed yet little understood, like the raid into Iran, the marine deployment into Lebanon, the Grenada campaign, and the actions off Libya in 1986. Others, such as the *Mayaguez* recapture, the 1981 air clash over the Gulf of Sidra, or the interception of the *Achille Lauro* hijackers, have already faded into oblivion. Taken in the aggregate, the seven events described in this book reflect the resurgence of American expeditionary capability after the end of the Southeast Asian war. Not all of these operations succeeded, but the lessons learned in failures contributed to later triumphs.

Expeditionary fighting since 1975 has exacted a significant toll: 337 dead and missing and nearly 400 wounded. Americans killed in small wars are just as dead as those who fall in big ones. As reporter Michael Herr noted, every dead man tells the same tale: "Put yourself in my place." [17] In an era of violent peace, any information that prevents that story from recurring is worth knowing.

Prologue Notes

1. Edward Doyle, Samuel Lipsman, and the editors of Boston Publishing Company, *The Vietnam Experience: Setting the Stage* (Boston, MA: Boston Publishing Co., 1981), 26.
2. Ray L. Bowers, *United States Air Force in Southeast Asia: Tactical Airlift* (Washington, D.C.: U.S. Government Printing Office, 1983), 643; Clark Dougan, David Fulghum, and the editors of Boston Publishing Company, *The Vietnam Experience: The Fall of the South* (Boston, MA: Boston Publishing Co., 1985), 158; David Butler, *The Fall of Saigon* (New York: Simon and Schuster, 1985), 379, 380.
3. Lt. Col. Stuart Herrington, *Peace with Honor?* (Novato, CA: Presidio Press, 1983), 204, 205.
4. Gen. Cao Van Vien, *Indochina Monographs: The Final Collapse* (Washington, D.C.: U.S. Government Printing Office, 1983), 152.
5. Bowers, *Tactical Airlift,* 641–43.
6. Dougan, Fulghum, et al., *The Fall of the South,* 28, 53–56, 63.
7. Ibid., 116–18, 130, 131.
8. Herrington, *Peace with Honor?* 189.
9. Dougan, Fulghum, et al., *The Fall of the South,* 148.
10. Frank Snepp, *Decent Interval* (New York: Random House, 1977), 488, 489; Bowers, *Tactical Airlift,* 643.
11. Doyle, Lipsman, et al., *Setting the Stage,* 26, 27; Dougan, Fulghum, et al., *The Fall of the South,* 161–64.
12. Earl H. Tilford, *Search and Rescue in Southeast Asia, 1961–1975* (Washington, D.C.: U.S. Government Printing Office, 1980), 143–45.
13. Butler, *The Fall of Saigon,* 441; Snepp, *Decent Interval,* 545, 549, 555, 556.
14. Herrington, *Peace with Honor?* 229.
15. Butler, *The Fall of Saigon,* 450–52.
16. Adm. James D. Watkins, "The Maritime Strategy" in James A. Barber, executive director, *The Maritime Strategy* (Annapolis, MD: U.S. Naval Institute Press, 1986), 5.
17. Michael Herr, *Dispatches* (New York: Avon Books, 1978), 31.

CHAPTER 1

"MARINES OVER THE SIDE!": THE RECOVERY OF SS *MAYAGUEZ*

MAY 1975

"At some point, the United States must draw the line. This is not our idea of the best such situation. It is not our choice. But we must act upon it now, and act firmly."
Secretary of State Henry Kissinger, 12 May 1975

"Even though you Navy officers do come in to about a thousand yards, I remind you that you have a little armor. I want you to know that Marines are crossing that beach with bayonets, and the only armor they will have is a khaki shirt."
Maj. Gen. Julian C. Smith, USMC, before the Tarawa landing, November 1943

With Saigon renamed Ho Chi Minh City and the first echelon of pathetic boat people already fleeing from the new socialist workers' paradise, the second Indochina war seemed over at last. America certainly tried to turn its back on the harsh, indeed horrific aftermath. But in mid-May 1975, the confusion and bluster of the new rulers of sad Cambodia produced a final spasm, a bizarre postscript to the American intervention that sprang from, of all things, an old-fashioned bit of piracy on the high seas.

Nobody would have expected a death struggle for the unsightly, undistinguished SS *Mayaguez*. Born in 1944 as a typical product of the great American arsenal of democracy, *Mayaguez* at various times sailed as SS *White Falcon,* SS *Sea,* and SS *Santa Eliana.* Even in 1975, her engine room remained essentially unaltered from the original plant. This ugly duckling resembled many of the other nondescript ships that carry the world's ocean commerce above their tired keels.

By 1965, Sea-Land Services Incorporated, a subsidiary of R. J. Reynolds Industries, had reactivated *Santa Eliana* for service in support of the American war effort in Southeast Asia. Sea-Land renamed the vessel *Mayaguez,* after the coastal city in Puerto Rico. Able to carry 274 thirty-five-foot containers and load and unload them with two large on-board cranes, the ship transferred cargo rapidly in crowded Asian ports. *Mayaguez* ran a regular Hong Kong to Singapore shuttle, with an interim stop at Sattahip, Thailand. The 10,485-ton containership cruised this route throughout the Vietnam War.[1]

On the morning of 7 May 1975, SS *Mayaguez* left Hong Kong on her usual path. But this trip was destined to be far different from her many previous uneventful travels. In appearance, *Mayaguez* was 504 feet long, with a dull black, dented hull and a few rusty patches. The hull ran flush from bow to stern, topped by a white superstructure housing the bridge, radar and communications masts, plus a single funnel. Five double layers of silver Sea-Land containers lay forward of the bridge; three more such arrays were aft. The rest of the freight boxes rested below decks.

There was nothing unusual about the cargo. Of 274 containers, 77 included food, beverages, clothing, parcel post materials, automobile parts, fertilizers, various chemicals, and paint for Sattahip concerns. Another 96 carried items for Singapore customers, such as food, industrial raw materials, and miscellaneous commercial consumer products. More than a third of the containers remained empty.[2] It was all rather routine.

The old ship steamed at a moderate 12.5 knots, passing well off the coast of troubled Vietnam on Sunday, 11 May 1975. Captain Charles T. Miller, master of the vessel, commanded a crew of thirty-nine licensed American mariners. These men knew the Gulf of Siam quite well, and as they made their way toward Sattahip, they noticed an unusual number of small craft under way and adrift throughout the area. These little boats represented the jetsam of the American war in Southeast Asia. Less than two weeks had elapsed since the surrender of the Saigon government.

Miller observed some unusual nautical activity in the early afternoon of 12 May, just as he passed about six and a half miles south of Poulo

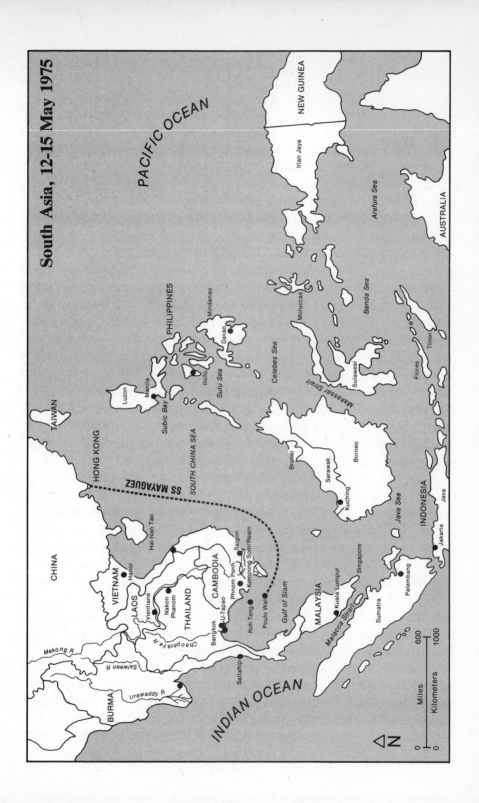

South Asia, 12-15 May 1975

Wai Island. Although Poulo Wai lies a good sixty miles south of Cambodia and even farther from Thailand to the northwest and Vietnam to the east, all three nations claimed the island. Rumors of oil deposits on Poulo Wai created particular interest. Evidently, the new Khmer Rouge government of Cambodia elected to enforce their contention. Miller and his men watched with curiosity as a few Khmer Rouge gunboats emerged from behind the disputed island and headed toward *Mayaguez*.

Unknown to Miller, this little Khmer Rouge flotilla had seen action already. These American-manufactured PCF Swift boats had fallen into Khmer hands when Cambodia collapsed in mid-April. The PCFs had gone to work immediately. They seized seven Thai fishing boats and twenty-seven crewmen on 2 May, shot at a South Korean freighter on 4 May, took over seven escaping South Vietnamese vessels on 6 May, and held a Panamanian ship for thirty-five hours on 7–8 May. The militant Khmer Rouge regime made noises about a ninety-mile limit for territorial waters and threatened to intercept and detain foreign ships that violated this sanctuary. Somehow, in the general confusion following the U.S. withdrawal from Southeast Asia, American intelligence agencies and the Department of State had neglected to pass information about this important series of incidents to the Defense Mapping Agency Hydrographic Center for broadcast to Pacific Ocean shipping. Even if a warning had gone out, there was no guarantee that *Mayaguez* would be listening. As a private vessel, Captain Miller's containership had no requirement to monitor the warning channel anyway; only about half of the American-flag commercial ships did so. Miller's radioman tuned to a British navigational station in Hong Kong.[3]

About 1410, one of the Khmer gunboats fired a 76-mm shot across Miller's bow. *Mayaguez* slowed as Miller ordered his engines to idle and told his radio operator to broadcast an urgent distress signal to any station that would answer. The American crew possessed no means of resistance, but Miller shrewdly stalled and feigned ignorance as his Cambodian-speaking captors closed to board. Since none of the Khmer Rouge sailors spoke English, these delays were not wholly contrived.

Meanwhile, Miller's radio room blared messages. Oil survey employee John Neal of Delta Exploration Company in Jakarta, Indonesia, received this alarming transmission at 1418: "Have been fired upon and boarded by Cambodian armed forces at 9 degrees 48 minutes north/ 102 degrees 53 minutes east. Ship is being towed to unknown Cambodian port." Neal maintained intermittent contact with the beleaguered container craft, finally losing touch about 1600. During these subsequent transmissions, Neal learned that *Mayaguez* was slowly following a gunboat north toward Kompong Som (Sihanoukville) under its own power, there had been no casualties, the crew felt no immediate danger, and the Khmer Rouge boarders spoke no English. Neal notified the U.S. Embassy in Jakarta as soon as he recognized that he had lost touch with the captured ship.[4] By 1554, the diplomats in Jakarta sent Washington the first of six top-priority communications detailing the unfolding situation in the Gulf of Siam.

Even as Neal struggled to keep *Mayaguez* broadcasting, the American Defense Attaché Office in Singapore picked up a slightly garbled repetition of Miller's initial Mayday, courtesy of a diligent tugboat. The Defense Attaché Office in Manila, the Philippines, also heard a rebroadcast of the original message. By 1612, the National Military Command Center (NMCC) in Washington, D.C., received the U.S. Embassy's transmission, followed shortly by the two attaché office communiques. It was 0512 Washington time.

With *Mayaguez* gone silent, the American officers on duty in the Washington command center began efforts to gather information on the captured ship. By 1720 Cambodian time, the staff phoned United States Pacific Command (PACOM), with a warning order for an air search effort. The men also notified Gen. David C. Jones, USAF, acting chairman of the Joint Chiefs of Staff (JCS), about the incident. Because Gen. George Brown, USAF, was away in Europe on a routine tour, Jones stepped up from his usual role as air force chief of staff to take charge of the military side of the situation. With operations around Southeast Asia heavily hamstrung by the wary Congress, Jones insured he had full approval from Secretary of Defense James Schlesinger before introducing any U.S. forces into this sensitive area. By 1830 (0730 in Washington), the acting JCS chairman issued orders to Adm. Noel Gayler, commander in chief of PACOM. Jones directed Gayler to dispatch reconnaissance flights to locate the *Mayaguez*. Shortly thereafter, President Gerald R. Ford heard the first reports about the boarding incident during his usual morning intelligence update. Ford approved the military actions in progress.

Over the next two hours, the NMCC began to shift naval forces toward Cambodian waters. With their relatively long transit times, the warships had to be moved early. As yet, these surface combatants had received no definite missions. Admiral Gayler sent the destroyer escort

USS *Harold E. Holt,* the guided-missile destroyer USS *Henry B. Wilson,* and the supply ship USS *Vega* toward the Kompong Som area. USS *Holt* would be in Cambodian waters late on 14 May.[5]

As for an aerial search, the orders to Gayler included a directive "to obtain a photographic, visual, or radar fix on the ship and its armed escort." The PACOM staff clarified the rules of engagement with NMCC between 1910 and 1932. PACOM planes gained authorization to employ illumination flares and searchlights. The Washington center cautioned Pacific Command to respect Cambodia's twelve-mile territorial waters limit. Again, the officers at both ends moved carefully, cognizant of congressional strictures on operations in and around Indochina. NMCC concluded their remarks with the prod "get aircraft airborne."

The reconnaissance orders percolated down from PACOM through Seventh Fleet to Task Group 72.3, a long-range patrol force built around fourteen P-3B Orion four-engine turboprop antisubmarine warfare (ASW) planes. Commander J. A. Messegee's Patrol Squadron 4, supplemented by additional aircraft from Patrol Squadrons 17 and 46, received a telephonic warning order at 2000 on 12 May. Messegee faced a bit of a problem. Like most of Seventh Fleet, his big ASW planes had seen heavy service during the FREQUENT WIND evacuation. The Orions had just settled back into their normal pattern, flying a long leg to U-Tapao Royal Thai Air Force Base, refueling, and then going westward to Diego Garcia, out across the broad expanse of the Indian Ocean. Messegee kept one alert P-3 on duty at all times at his Cubi Point Naval Air Station headquarters, and his deputy, Lt. Comdr. J. Le Doux, had an aircraft on four-hour standby at U-Tapao. This created a quandary. The Cubi plane could not reach Poulo Wai for four hours; the U-Tapao plane was forty minutes away but would take four hours to prepare. Messegee readied both P-3s, resigning himself to a four-hour delay before the big airplanes entered Cambodian waters.

But Messegee did not reckon with Le Doux's determination. The U-Tapao Orion was alerted at 2000, and Messegee's subordinate commander promised to have his plane ready to go within forty minutes. Considering it took twenty minutes merely to fuel, let alone check for takeoff and brief a crew, this seemed extremely optimistic. When Task Group 72.3 received launch orders at 2030, the U-Tapao pilot lifted off first, at 2057. By 2115, the Cubi aircraft took off. The P-3 sent by Le Doux reached Poulo Wai airspace by 2128.

The lumbering sub hunters disposed no defensive armament. Their normal enemies hid beneath the waves and did not return fire. There were two potential threats: ground fire and enemy air interception. The first seemed much more likely. Having seen a P-3 shot to pieces in South Vietnam by heavy machine guns and cannons similar to those on the Khmer PCF gunboats, Messegee took no chances. The patrol squadron commander warned his pilots to stay above 6,000 feet and outside a one-mile radius of any armed craft or military installations encountered.

Messegee worried about the lack of friendly air cover, although he was fairly certain that his men could outrun the obsolete T-28 Trojan trainers that constituted the commandeered holdings of the Khmer Rouge Air Force. More ominously, the Orion crews "did not know if the Vietnamese were involved in this caper." Communist Vietnam possessed modern MiG-21 jet fighters, plus whatever U.S. aircraft they had captured in the south. Messegee hoped that Hanoi's planes stayed home. He cautioned his men: "Play heads up!"

The lead P-3 began to search systematically among the myriad of tiny to medium-sized boats within sixty miles of Poulo Wai. As the last message reflected the *Mayaguez* steaming for Kompong Som, no large radar returns could be ignored. The Orion moved slowly across the stygian Gulf of Siam, dropping flares over every boat and ship sighted, and broadcasting course, speed, and description back to the Cubi Point Operational Control Center. It would be after 0100 before the other Orion came on station.[6]

Even as the first navy patrol plane started to sort through the many floating items on the dark waters between Cambodia and Poulo Wai, President Gerald Ford convened his National Security Council to consider the situation (1200 Washington time, 2300 Cambodian time). Central Intelligence Agency director William Colby outlined available details on the seizure of *Mayaguez*.

According to President Ford, Secretary of State Henry Kissinger talked next, leaning forward and speaking "with emotion." He emphasized that a failure to act decisively, following so closely upon the humiliating evacuation from Vietnam, would be "a serious blow to our prestige around the world." Kissinger ended by stating that the *Mayaguez* situation was far from ideal, but that America had to "draw the line." Kissinger concluded: "But we must act upon it now, and act firmly."

President Ford agreed and started asking questions. Was diplomacy a viable option? It appeared that it was not; nobody even knew who was really in charge in Phnom Penh. Ford directed the State Department to try to enlist Chinese help, but he placed little hope in this approach. How about the military? Ford heard about PACOM's ongoing air search and ship movements; Colby mentioned that all intelligence services had turned their attention to the so-recently neglected Cambodian region. Any serious military option required a day or more to assemble forces. President Ford faced the standard dilemma of expeditionary combat: how much is enough versus how fast can it get there? Ford pronounced the military situation "discouraging" in his memoirs.

Nevertheless, the forty-five-minute conclave produced some meaningful decisions. Sensibly, a general warning went out to all U.S. mariners describing the dangerous situation off Cambodia. Although diplomatic overtures would be attempted, military preparations took center stage. Ford, like Kissinger, figured that the Khmer Rouge had asked for a showdown and was about to get one. The president outlined a series of reconnaissance missions, ship and troop movements, and rules of engagement to be executed by the armed forces.

Ford ordered continuous P-3 reconnaissance over Poulo Wai, with special emphasis on tracking Khmer naval craft. He directed the military to conduct photographic reconnaissance of Kompong Som, Phnom Penh, and Poulo Wai, to include "high altitude coverage" (presumably SR-71 Blackbird or satellite imagery) of Poulo Wai. The military listed reconnaissance priorities as: identification of merchant ships (especially *Mayaguez,* obviously), naval craft, and potential helicopter landing zones (LZs) or paratrooper drop zones (DZs). This level of information collection necessitated extensive use of air bases in sovereign Thailand.

The president asked the navy to divert the aircraft carrier USS *Coral Sea* and her escorts to Poulo Wai. The carrier was on the way to Australia. Additionally, Ford wanted the navy to collect an amphibious readiness group around the helicopter assault ship USS *Okinawa* for movement to Poulo Wai. These ships lay off Taiwan. The carrier battle group and transports full of marines provided flexibility and strength for any eventual rescue operation. USAF planes in Thailand would be involved in air cover over *Mayaguez* as the U.S. ships steamed toward Poulo Wai.

Ford also issued specific rules of engagement, guided by General Jones as to military capabilities and needs. The president authorized the armed forces to employ munitions in the vicinity of *Mayaguez* to prevent the ship's departure, and even okayed the preparation of sea mines for possible use as barriers to movement. Jet fighters could make low passes and fire near any small craft in the seizure area. Riot control gas (CS agent) was approved for use in any recovery efforts. This guidance could and would be modified as the situation changed.

. One staff member warned that the Thais would not be happy about the unapproved use of their airstrips and airspace. The Thai government had already complained about the American units remaining in Thailand after the second Indochina war. Ford had no qualms in that regard. "Until the *Mayaguez* and her crew were safe," said the president, "I didn't give a damn about offending their sensibilities." [7] So the president and his men already leaned toward the hard line. The expedition began to come together.

But where was the *Mayaguez?* And more importantly, was the crew still with the ship? The answers to those questions rode with a few big, slow turboprops out over the blackened Gulf of Siam.

The American political and military leaders desperately hoped that the air patrols located the containership quickly. Many leaders feared that the ship had already reached mainland Cambodia. President Ford and his advisers recalled the shameful loss of the U.S. Navy intelligence ship USS *Pueblo* in January 1968. In that fiasco, aggressive North Korean patrol craft rapidly prodded the captive crew and their unarmed ship from just outside the twelve-mile limit into heavily defended Wonsan harbor. U.S. pleas gained the release of the unlucky sailors after almost a year of degrading imprisonment. America did not respond in time to prevent the debacle. As Ford said, "I was determined not to allow a repetition of that incident." [8]

Of course, there were two significant differences in the *Mayaguez* case. First, the Khmer Rouge gunboats intercepted the U.S. merchant vessel more than sixty miles south of the coastline, whereas *Pueblo* had been taken very close to North Korea. This gave some valuable time, which Capt. Charles T. Miller increased by his imaginative stalling, insistence on slow speeds, and exploitation of his captors' inability to speak English. Second, Miller's Mayday reached competent listeners almost immediately, and the military officers involved responded with fair speed. Admittedly, however, the delay between the seizure and the dispatch of search planes gave the Khmer Rouge enough time to bring *Mayaguez* to Kompong Som, had they been so inclined. Evidently, the Khmer sailors decided to take their time.

What caused the lag between notification and commencement of a search? Perception and recognition of a contingency situation can only move so quickly; it is easy in retrospect to complain that nobody sent out reconnaissance elements fast enough. Unlike the USS *Pueblo*, American merchant shipping was not (and is not) regularly monitored and covered by American naval and air components. It took almost two hours to get the initial distress call to the military authorities, and, after the Vietnam fiasco, they were justifiably reluctant to expose any Americans to the Indochina maelstrom without specific guidance from civilian leaders. After another two and a half hours spent explaining the boarding event to higher officials, the necessary permissions were secured, and orders went out. Within the next two and a half hours, planes in varying degrees of alert prepared and took off. Given that nobody was anticipating such an event, and that the American armed forces were involved in routine peacetime activities, this appears to be an impressive response.

If requested, could reconnaissance planes have gone out more quickly? Allowing for minimum briefing times, message transmission, and confirmations, it appears that 1700 Cambodian time represented the absolute earliest instance that orders could have been sent to PACOM. Possibly, Admiral Gayler's headquarters could have gotten the word out to his naval patrol task group or Seventh Air Force in Thailand within a half hour, allowing for the usual amplification and cross-checks. So the fact that orders arrived within an hour and a half of the outright best time indicates that coordination delays were not excessive. The first P-3 took off at 2057 after a 2000 warning order. Perhaps an aircraft could have taken off as soon as 1830. The U-Tapao Orion needed thirty-five minutes to reach the last known position of *Mayaguez*. Unfortunately, it got dark around 1915, so the earlier takeoff time would not have done much at all to increase visibility.

Were other search planes more suitable? The P-3B Orions normally hunted submarines, not errant merchantmen. P-3s lacked speed, and it did take a while to get them ready at U-Tapao and Cubi Point. Perhaps 7th Air Force jet reconnaissance aircraft could have been used. Some 7th Air Force planes were on alert the evening of 12 May. The big discriminators here involved duration and scope. An Orion was built for endurance, and so could wander about a large area, examining many items of interest. An RF-4C Phantom II was designed for speed but not loitering. These unarmed jets flew to specific targets or along determined routes, shot film, and then returned home, all at high speed. To keep such jets on station required employment of fuel tankers and compli-cated nighttime couplings. Since nobody knew where *Mayaguez* was, a long period of observation over many square miles might be necessary.

The P-3 could report its findings as the ten crewmen continued to observe. The two busy fliers in a flashing Phantom might not notice one dark shape among many. Checking the jet's discoveries may have required development of onboard camera film after landing. Even then, questionable information could not be immediately confirmed. But a P-3 with a good pilot, a sharp-eyed crew, full fuel tanks, and a powerful radio could perform admirably as a search plane. This role perfectly suited the big, plodding P-3s.[9]

By 0115 on 13 May, the Cubi Orion joined its U-Tapao cousin. The two four-engined aircraft worked deliberately around Poulo Wai, finally picking out two possible suspects from among the huge variety of things afloat below. The Orion crews agreed that the vessel dead in the water seven miles off Poulo Wai was probably *Mayaguez*, but their swaying, electric-bright USN illumination flares cast deep shadows. Com-bined with the mandated 6,000-foot altitude and one-mile standoff, this made it hard to read the lettering on the stopped ship. The two planes received authorization to close in to 300 feet above and 1,000 yards abeam, but it was still too dark to be sure.

Finally, at 0816 on 13 May, a Patrol Squadron 17 Orion, which had replaced the overnight pair, dropped down low to check the likely-looking ship off Poulo Wai. The P-3 fliers read the name in white block letters, bow and stern: *MAYAGUEZ*. Two PCF Swift boats stood alongside the containership, and the sky filled with antiaircraft fire from the gun-boats. Khmer infantry shot small arms from the white upper works of the captured U.S. ship. One heavy machine gun slug punched through the navy patrol plane's high tail, but the pilot climbed out of range before suffering further abuse. The P-3 reported the find to an excited Commander Messegee at Cubi Point, who relayed the good news to Pacific Command and the National Military Command Center in Wash-ington.

But the successful end to the long night's search seemed almost immediately imperiled when the Orion reported that SS *Mayaguez* had hoisted anchor and begun steaming north again around 0843. Without any suitable ordnance to drop, and unsure of a clearance to do so, the navy men watched the black, white, and silver ship head slowly toward

Kompong Som. The aviators guessed that *Mayaguez* would reach the mainland within six hours. A thunderstorm line moved through to frustrate American surveillance.

The P-3 trailed behind the containership and its two Khmer patrol escorts, finding them still underway at 1037. On direction from Adm. Noel Gayler of PACOM, Lt. Gen. John J. Burns diverted Seventh Air Force aircraft from training into the area. Two unarmed F-111A "Aardvarks" from 347th Tactical Fighter Wing up in Korat, Thailand, arrived from the north around 1300. Major Roger Bogard and his wingman found *Mayaguez* on their radars, halted north of a small island about halfway to Kompong Som. The swing wing jets made about twenty minutes of screaming low passes to verify their supposition. Simultaneously, the Orion in the vicinity identified the *Mayaguez* and its escorts anchoring about a mile off the north coast of Koh Tang Island.[10] American luck held; unlike *Pueblo,* this ship stopped well short of the mainland. A military rescue operation became a real possibility.

The American aircraft began to circle, and the Orion pilot and his men breathed easier as fully armed American F-4E Phantom II, F-111A, and A-7D Corsair II jets arrived to replace Major Bogard's toothless two-ship flight. Any Khmer or North Vietnamese air interference would face a warm reception from this point onward. The P-3 passed direct observation of the ship to the air force, and under Messegee's radio guidance, pulled off to monitor Khmer gunboats and local fishing craft.

A minor flurry erupted around 1545 when two A-7 pilots noticed smoke curling up from *Mayaguez*'s stack. Following the announced rules of engagement, the sleek little attack planes spun down and strafed across the front of the containership, pumping 20-mm Gatling gun shells into the clear tropical water. The string of white gouts evidently convinced the Khmer Rouge to alter their plans. The smoke stopped rising from the funnel, and no further shooting was necessary.

Although *Mayaguez* gave no further indication of movement, her decks, the water around her, and the nearby Koh Tang coast bustled with activity as the afternoon dragged on. Small boats came and went, watched by three layers of American fliers: low A-7Ds, high F-111As, and a distant P-3 Orion. F-4E fighters provided local air defense and supplemented the observation effort. The resultant series of reports made it hard to tell exactly what was going on between the ship and the Koh Tang beach.

At 1654, an Aardvark pilot saw a ladder over the side of *Mayaguez* and noted that small boats had tied up beneath the ladder. In fact, about this time, Khmer troops moved Charles Miller and his crew into two small fishing boats, which then tied up about seventy-five yards off the northeastern Koh Tang beach. The watching P-3 crew also noted this development and identified what looked to be Caucasian men aboard the fishing craft.

These particular reports encouraged the Joint Chiefs of Staff in Washington to direct Admiral Gayler (and through him, General Burns and the aircraft over Koh Tang) to prevent *Mayaguez* from sailing again. The JCS allowed the pilots to fire around (but not at) any small boats moving toward Cambodia to make the Khmer sailors think twice, and Washington specifically told its men on the scene to ignore the niceties of the twelve-mile territorial limit near Cambodia.[11] As the JCS said in a follow-up explanatory communique, "Key immediate objective is to prevent *Mayaguez* from sailing toward mainland."

The carefully drawn rules on firing were not intended to spare the Khmer Rouge but to avoid injuring the American mariners. Was the crew on the ship, on a gunboat, on a fishing boat, or already on the island? Descriptions of the traffic around the anchored vessel made it hard to be sure. Fortunately, most of the night passed without further tests of air force marksmanship. Instead, the American observers flew around and around, trying to figure out exactly where the U.S. civilians had gone.

Above the scene, the Phantoms and Corsairs left as the sun went down, to be replaced by a "night shift," consisting of a couple of high-flying, night-capable Aardvarks high overhead and a low-flying 388th Tactical Fighter Wing AC-130H Spectre gunship packed with night vision devices and hung with 7.62-mm Gatling guns, 20-mm cannons, 40-mm cannons, and a massive 105-mm tube. Off in the distance, one of Messegee's P-3s stayed on station, picking out Khmer naval vessels among the slew of meandering fishing craft on the Gulf of Siam.

The American planes sent in a regular stream of reports. Just before sunset, one A-7D sighted two small fishing boats (with Miller's crew, as it later turned out) moving away from the black hull of *Mayaguez*. One boat flew a red flag and appeared to hold Caucasians. Five minutes later, about 1730, the flier observed people disembarking on the beach, although his report did not specify from which boat these individuals came. When he slid down for a closer look, heavy antiaircraft fire blasted up from along the northeastern beach.

By nightfall, the Spectre reported people moving from small boats into the island's heavily forested interior. At 1835, another message indicated, "Crew on island but it cannot be ascertained how many men have been moved." Things only got murkier as the night dragged on, and every low pass brought on a fusillade of tracers.

After darkness was complete, the American fliers dropped random flares to illuminate the area. During a lull, the Khmer Rouge commander took Charles Miller back out to SS *Mayaguez,* ostensibly to inspect cargo containers for "weapons and spy equipment." According to Captain Miller, a few well-placed flares brightened the deck just after the small party reached the U.S. vessel. This scared the Khmers into near-panic, and they hustled Miller off the containership and back onto their patrol boat. Spectre noted at 2050, "Two 50–60-foot boats departed *Mayaguez* and tied up to three vessels anchored at beach and 5–6 people then went ashore near where antiaircraft fire had been observed." This probably was the return of Miller's shortened inspection trip.

The captured Americans later said that they never set foot on Koh Tang, but stayed on the two fishing boats that left *Mayaguez* just prior to sunset. This contradicted several air spottings. In the bad light and in between dodging a poorly directed but vigorous barrage of gunfire, these mistakes were understandable. Although the planes could not be sure where the crew had gone, or if all were together, the fliers insisted (quite correctly at this point) that no boats had left the island. The crew could only be on their merchant ship, an anchored boat, or Koh Tang. Afterward, Miller remarked that the whine of the aircraft engines provided some comfort to his exhausted, worried men.[12]

Meanwhile, the first tentative P-3 sightings in the wee hours of 13 May started serious preparations for a military rescue. Admiral Gayler made three decisions that shaped the eventual nature of the recovery effort. First, he alerted all of his western Pacific bases, ships, air units, and marine outfits about 0800 on 13 May, Cambodian time. Second, Gayler specifically told the 1st Battalion, 4th Marines at Subic Bay, the Philippines, to "prepare their men for immediate embarkation." Finally, the Pacific Command admiral designated Lt. Gen. John J. Burns of Seventh Air Force (also the commander of United States Support Activities Group) as on-scene commander. Burns received command of all of the inbound ships and planes, with full authority to call on more.

Each step had ramifications. The western Pacific alert, in tandem with earlier ship movements, affected a substantial amount of naval and amphibious power. Off Taiwan, at Subic Bay, and in waters adjacent to the Gulf of Siam, Gayler's orders backed up USS *Holt*, USS *Wilson*, and USS *Coral Sea* and her escorts with two more strong task forces, built around the helicopter carrier USS *Okinawa* and the attack carrier USS *Hancock*. Each additional group carried a marine battalion landing team (BLT). It took time to gather the ships, men, and equipment, but they were ready to steam toward Cambodia by 14 May. Still, *Hancock* and its marines would not reach Cambodia until 16 May at the earliest; *Okinawa* would not arrive until early on 18 May.

Gayler's 0800 message to Subic Bay affected 1/4 Marines, including Capt. Walter J. Wood's Company D. By 1100, Wood had his men ready to deploy, and most connected their increased readiness with news about the *Mayaguez*. The marines rested on their gear, wondering what would happen next. They had been activated repeatedly for different phases of the Vietnam evacuation, but never left. This time would be different.

At 1830, as air force and navy planes sent confusing messages describing the captured ship and its wandering crew near Koh Tang, Wood's commander ordered him to ready two platoons and a headquarters section for air movement by 2300. Wood picked two of his three rifle platoons and repacked his equipment for transport by aircraft. The marines were ready by 2100.

At 2130, Captain Wood and two of his platoon commanders attended a classified orders session at 1/4 headquarters. Battalion staff officers told the marine leaders that they had been chosen to conduct the assault to retake SS *Mayaguez*. Major Raymond E. Porter, 1/4 Marines executive officer, assumed command of the seizure effort, assisted by Capt. J. P. Feltner of the battalion staff. Wood and his lieutenants exchanged glances: this was it. The briefers told the men that they would be leaving by C-141 Starlifter Military Airlift Command jet transports after midnight. The boarding party could expect detailed guidance upon arrival in Thailand. The marine officers left the building to move their men to the airstrip, draw live ammunition, and ponder their odd assignment. The last time United States Marines took a ship at sea by assault had been back in 1826, so Company D faced an interesting assignment.[13]

Admiral Gayler's decision to appoint General Burns as his local commander paid immediate benefits. With his headquarters at Nakhon Phanom, the air force commander was the senior American combat leader in the area. Burns's Seventh Air Force fighters and Spectre gunships protected and watched the ship and its captors; Burns's connections to vital MAC airlifters expedited the movement of marines. Burns himself took some prudent actions, dispatching reconnaissance jets to learn more about Koh Tang and activities along the Cambodian coast, readying heavy-lift helicopters for a possible rescue effort, assembling a provisional assault team made up of armed air force security police, and eventually strengthening his small boarding party with an entire marine battalion.

Burns's four photographic flights on 13 May provided some details on SS *Mayaguez* and its Khmer guards, but these swift runs did not coincide with the perplexing boat and personnel transfers late that afternoon. The first RF-4C delivered excellent pictures of Poulo Wai Island, which proved useless once the containership moved to Koh Tang. Additionally, a high-altitude platform (presumably an SR-71 Blackbird or possibly a satellite) also surveyed Poulo Wai. So Burns found himself with great photographs of the wrong island. Luckily, the other three RF-4Cs flew a general track across Poulo Wai, Koh Tang, Kompong Som, and Ream.[14] These photographs would be very useful as military planners wrestled with the terrain and enemy situation on Koh Tang and the Cambodian coast.

General Burns knew that any rescue force needed a way to get to SS *Mayaguez,* and that meant USAF heavy-lift helicopters. The prospect of parachuting a force onto the *Mayaguez* looked bleak. It was just too small for army paratroopers to be certain of landing, although navy sea-air-land (SEAL) teams or army Special Forces (Green Berets) scuba experts might pull it off. Getting those lightly armed teams past the Khmer gunboats and onto a defended ship looked too daunting to attempt. Landing army paratroopers (the marines had very few, mostly Force Reconnaissance troops) on lush Koh Tang would not be possible, because the jumpers faced dangling snags and bone-breaking injuries in the large trees. The only open drop zones included a few narrow beaches. One realistic alternative to the use of USAF helicopters would be to wait until 16 May, when the first of the two amphibious groups arrived in the area with their USMC choppers and landing craft. That might well be too late; already, the Americans had been very lucky. But the U.S. could not count on the Khmer leadership to hesitate forever.

So the Seventh Air Force headquarters turned to the 56th Special Operations Wing (with its 21st Special Operations Squadron), and the 3rd Aerospace Rescue and Recovery Group (higher command of the 40th Aerospace Rescue and Recovery Squadron, 40th ARRS), both at

Nakhon Phanom. The 21st operated the twin-engine CH-53C "Knife," with armor, three 7.62-mm Gatling-type miniguns, and form-fitted fuel tanks for additional range. The similar HH-53C Super Jolly Green Giant, which carried a bit more armor, the same minigun array, external fuel tanks, and an air to air refueling boom, was used by 40th ARRS. Each squadron had eight helicopters ready to go, and the choppers and crews had seen heavy service in the Phnom Penh and Saigon evacuations.[15] Burns ordered the experienced units with these valuable aircraft to stand by for orders.

Finally, General Burns needed an emergency rescue force, just in case things went completely haywire and it became necessary to mount an immediate recovery effort. He directed the formation of a 125-man air force security police team, made up of men normally trained and equipped for air base defense. These airmen knew how to fight and had infantry weapons, but conducting an opposed helicopter assault, let alone on a containership, would certainly have strained their combat capabilities. They waited with the big choppers at Nakhon Phanom, just in case.[16]

General Burns's last orders did not go to air force units, but to the 2nd Battalion, 9th Marines. The Seventh Air Force commander wanted some added muscle, and he wanted it ready to move to Thailand aboard MAC Starlifters. Preliminary notification went out around 1300 on 13 May 1975. As in the Philippines, these Okinawa marines had been through false alarms during the Indochina evacuations, but unlike 1/4 Marines, the men of 2/9 remained largely unaware of the *Mayaguez* capture. In fact, the initial message found Lt. Col. Randall W. Austin's four rifle companies out in central Okinawa carrying out tactical exercises. Major John B. Hendricks took the call from 9th Marine Regiment, which featured the comment that 2/9 needed to get ready "to go somewhere and do something." If necessary, 3/9 Marines would follow.

Hendricks had no idea what was going on, but he informed his commander and began bringing the rifle companies back to Camp Schwab. By 2030, Seventh Air Force headquarters seemed fairly certain that some of the captured U.S. seamen had gone ashore at Koh Tang, and it looked like it might take more than a couple of marine platoons to secure the ship and its men. As his line units feverishly readied equipment, Lieutenant Colonel Austin received concrete orders: prepare an air-transportable battalion landing team to depart from Kadena air base by dawn on 14 May.[17] The final mission remained in question, but by this time,

United States Forces Order of Battle
12–15 May 1975

U.S. Seventh Air Force/United States Support Activities Group
  C-130E Hercules Airborne Battlefield Command and Control Center
U.S. Army elements
  U-21A Ute utility aircraft
  Cambodian linguists
U.S. Navy/Marine units
  Carrier Battle Group
    USS *Coral Sea* (CVA-43) with Carrier Air Wing 15 (CVW-15), USS
      Gridley (DLG-21), USS *Bausell* (DD-845), USS *Lang* (DE-970)
  Destroyer Squadron 23
    USS *Harold E. Holt* (DE-1074), USS *Henry B. Wilson* (DDG-7)
  Underway Replenishment Group
    USS *Vega* (AF-59), USS *Ashtabula* (AO-51)
  Task Group 72.3
    Patrol Squadron 4 (+)*
  Provisional Amphibious Readiness Group: USS *Hancock* (CVA-19) and es-
    corts;
    Battalion Landing Team 1/4 Marines (−) embarked**
  Amphibious Readiness Group: USS *Okinawa* (LPH-3) and escorts;
    Battalion Landing Team 2/4 Marines embarked**
  Marine Task Group 79.9
    Battalion Landing Team 2/9 Marines (BLT 2/9)#
      Company E, Company G, 81mm Platoon (−), BLT Command
      Group A
    Company D, 1/4 Marines (−)
U.S. Air Force units
  Seventh Air Force elements
    Combat Security Police Squadron (provisional)**
    56th Special Operations Wing
      21st Special Operations Squadron
    3rd Aerospace Rescue and Recovery Group
      40th Aerospace Rescue and Recovery Squadron
      56th Aerospace Rescue and Recovery Squadron
    374th Tactical Airlift Wing
    347th Tactical Fighter Wing
    388th Tactical Fighter Wing
      16th Special Operations Squadron
    432nd Tactical Fighter Wing
  Military Airlift Command
    Military Airlift Wings: 60th, 62nd, 63rd

United States Forces Order of Battle
12–15 May 1975
(continued)

Strategic Air Command
  Strategic Wings: 43rd, 307th, 376th**
  9th Strategic Reconnaissance Wing

* Reinforced by aircraft from Patrol Squadron 17 (3) and Patrol Squadron 46 (1).
** These forces were alerted for action but not committed.
# Majority of unit deployed to Thailand but not committed.

Sources: Comdr. J. B. Finkelstein, "Naval and Maritime Events January 1975–June 1975" in *Proceedings* (May 1976), 60; Comdr. J. Michael Rodgers, "Mayday for the *Mayaguez:* The Guided-Missile Destroyer Skipper" in *Proceedings* (November 1976), 108; Comptroller General, "The Seizure of the *Mayaguez*" in U.S. Congress, House of Representatives, Committee on International Affairs, *Seizure of the Mayaguez: Part IV,* 94th Congress, 2nd Session, 4 October 1976, 84–88.

---

rumors about the *Mayaguez* had reached Camp Schwab. Just what part Austin's marines would play remained to be seen.

Thus, by 2130 Cambodian time on 13 May, the components of a potential rescue force had been designated, although many details remained unresolved. The captured ship lay at anchor near a small, virtually unknown island (it was a tiny blank smudge on most U.S. maps, if indicated at all). The crew remained in the vicinity, but nobody could be sure of their exact whereabouts or condition. Admiral Gayler of PACOM had turned matters over to a competent local commander, who set up continuous observation, took steps to insure that the ship and crew remained at Koh Tang, and began to collect rescue forces. Some rescue capability (using air force security troops) would exist by dawn on 14 May, supplemented by two marine platoons shortly thereafter and with BLT 2/9 around 1400 on 14 May. By dawn on 15 May, Burns anticipated the help of USS *Holt,* USS *Wilson,* and the carrier USS *Coral Sea.* He expected a full marine amphibious group (including the carrier *Hancock*) before noon on 16 May; the other group with *Okinawa* would be on hand by 18 May. Undoubtedly, the key to any U.S. plans revolved around one task: keeping the *Mayaguez* and her men at Koh Tang. If the Khmer Rouge moved the ship or her crew, any U.S. military intervention became unlikely. But without more time to prepare and bring in forces, the results might not be pretty even at Koh Tang.

At 1022 Washington time (2122 at Koh Tang) on 13 May, President Ford convened his second meeting of the National Security Council in as many days. At issue, of course, was the *Mayaguez*. After a brief summary of the situation, Ford asked about the diplomatic efforts. The answers provided no assistance. In Washington, People's Republic of China representatives utterly refused to accept any messages for the Khmer Rouge and declined to discuss the matter with State Department officials. In Peking, U.S. Liaison Office personnel delivered notes to the Cambodian Embassy and Chinese foreign ministry, but nothing had been heard as yet.

The Thais, however, said plenty. Prime Minister Kukrit Pramoj announced a categorical prohibition on U.S. use of Thai bases for operations against the Khmer Rouge. Faced with a diplomatic black hole in Phnom Penh and the likely need to use military power, Ford ignored Pramoj's pronouncement: "I sensed that this was more political rhetoric than anything else; the Thais knew we had no alternative but to use the base at U-Tapao."

The U.S. did not completely ignore diplomacy. The Voice of America radio system broadcast complete news bulletins about the ship seizure and related U.S. announcements regularly into Cambodia, beginning as early as 0500 on 13 May. Many National Security Council (NSC) members believed that the shadowy Phnom Penh party cadre tuned to these programs, and there were valid suspicions that the Chinese communicated the contents of the messages they refused. But as of 13 May, no response had come from the mysterious Khmers.

With the State Department frustrated, talk turned to military options. Seven specific recommendations came up in discussion: a show of force, seizure of a Cambodian island in retaliation, a helicopter landing on the *Mayaguez,* a sea assault from the *Holt,* a marine assault on Koh Tang, bombing Kompong Som with *Coral Sea* aircraft, or bombing Kompong Som with B-52s. The first two ideas seemed pointless. A significant show of force had already occurred. American planes thundered overhead at Koh Tang. As for taking another island, this might cause the Khmer Rouge to execute their American prisoners. But Ford reserved his decision on the other operations. In broadest outline, the eventual *Mayaguez* recovery would employ parts of the remaining five concepts.

Instead, the president authorized PACOM to direct Seventh Air Force to implement movement of Burns's air force helicopters and security police to a forward base on the coast. Ford okayed dispatch of the small 1/4 Marines boarding team from the Philippines and the full BLT 2/9 from Okinawa. Finally, the president insisted that all boat traffic in and out of Koh Tang be intercepted and turned back, although he retained permission to fire or drop killing ordnance at such craft.[18] Again, no blood had been spilled, and as long as *Mayaguez* stayed put, time worked in favor of the rescue force.

The meeting ended at 1118 (2218 in Cambodia). Now it was up to the air force, the navy, and the marines. Across the dark Pacific, messages flashed, teletypes clattered, and men and machines moved inexorably toward their rendezvous with a tired old ship.

The presidential directives activated General Burns's tentative deployment orders. Burns selected U-Tapao Royal Thai Air Force Base on the coastline as the assembly area for the rescue force. Needless to say, the air force units in Thailand could reach the base first, before dawn on 14 May. Seventh Air Force planners expected the small Company D, 1/4 Marines force, about 0500, and BLT 2/9 Marines by 1400. Only the BLT offered the sort of combat power necessary to attack and hold Koh Tang, where Burns's staff believed most of the U.S. civilians had been transferred and imprisoned.

The air force helicopters and the security police contingent at Nakhon Phanom reacted almost immediately after President Ford's approval. They lifted off shortly before midnight. A long string of rotary-wing aircraft swung wide west of Nakhon Phanom, heading south toward U-Tapao. Once again, as they had done for days on end during the sad April evacuations, the air force fliers took their big craft up into the night.

About thirty-seven miles west of Nakhon Phanom, a CH-53C Knife staggered out of formation with mechanical trouble. Something important broke, although nobody on hand knew exactly what had gone wrong. The Knife plummeted into a thickly wooded area and blew up. A trailing HH-53C Jolly Green Giant clattered up, landed, and dismounted airmen to recover survivors, but the intense heat of burning fuel and exploding ammunition kept the rescuers seventy-five feet away from the wreckage. Five aircrewmen and eighteen security policemen died in the accident.

The rest of the air police arrived at U-Tapao along with the fifteen remaining helicopters. By 0545, this emergency rescue force stood ready to go, but General Burns recommended delaying any recovery operation until his staff had fully briefed the two Company D, 1/4 Marine platoons.

Burns estimated that his force could lift off at 0750 on 14 May.[19] Seventh Air Force headquarters advised their general that the marine infantry greatly increased the chances of any insertion effort. Marines, after all, trained for assaults. Air force security police trained to defend base perimeters.

Major Porter and his marine boarding party landed at 0505, only to be told to be ready for launch at 0610. While the young marines ate a hasty breakfast at a nearby air force mess hall, Porter, Captain Wood, and Captain Feltner went back to a building near the U-Tapao runway to receive orders. Here, for the first time, the officers found themselves "instructed and questioned as to the feasibility of a helo assault directly onto the deck of the *Mayaguez*." The marines and air force men devised a quick plan, based on aerial photography and reports from orbiting aircraft.

The Company D infantry got a simple mission: retake the *Mayaguez*. Porter heard that about thirty Khmer Rouge soldiers might be aboard, armed with automatic weapons, machine guns, and antitank weapons. The ship offered odd "terrain," although helicopter landings might be possible on the big silver containers fore and aft of the white superstructure. American captives appeared to be off the *Mayaguez*, but this could not be verified. Aside from his own men, Porter also commanded four attachments: six civilian mariners from USNS *Greenville Victory*, six sailors from USS *Duluth*, two USAF explosive ordnance disposal (bomb squad) sergeants, and an army officer who spoke Cambodian. In addition, the boarding commanders met Capt. Paul L. Jacobs, flight leader for the six large USAF choppers chosen to ferry the marines 224 miles to their objective.

As for the time available to get ready, the vital explanatory and planning session began to eat that away. 0610 and 0750 came and went without launch orders. Because the marines and air force commanders had yet to tell their men the details of the proposed plan, even the 0910 lift-off time announced in the meeting seemed patently optimistic. By the time the conclave separated, Seventh Air Force set takeoff at 1230. Given that the *Mayaguez* power system had gone "cold," the vessel could not move anywhere for at least three hours, so the planning delays did not endanger the mission.

But the infrared photos that indicated an inert engineering plant also created trouble. Without power, the marines needed daylight to seize, search, and clear the dark recesses of the containership and allow their navy and civilian technicians to restart the vessel. The *Mayaguez* crew might not be in any condition or position to assist. Major Porter estimated a minimum of three hours for the assault and subsequent securing actions. Given the two-hour-and-fifteen-minute flight duration, 1415 U-Tapao time represented the absolute latest launch opportunity on 14 May.[20] Even that deadline pushed nightfall, which would certainly occur around 1915 regardless of Porter's operational needs. The changing situation on and around Koh Tang rendered these lighting considerations irrelevant.

Even as Porter and his officers struggled to piece together an air assault plan, events at Koh Tang Island began to affect the operation. The night had been rather busy, with boats and people coming and going steadily under cover of darkness. Between 0205 and 0220 on 14 May, the AC-130H Spectre dove down to check out some suspicious activity near the dark merchant ship. Spectre took heavy fire from a gunboat and returned the shots, being careful not to hit the slowly moving craft. Instead, the Khmer PCF ran aground on a reef just off the northeastern beach. So far, reliance on warning shots had worked.

This changed shortly after dawn, as the "day shift" came on the scene. For an hour or so after 0630, F-111As, A-7Ds, F-4Es, and the slow but lethal Spectre stacked up over Koh Tang. The AC-130 acted as the airborne coordinator for the bevy of planes. But this flying firepower did not scare the Khmer Rouge. After a few false starts dissuaded by more of the usual near-misses, about 0712, one PCF gunboat headed out from the island, clearly moving to Kompong Som. The gauntlet had been thrown.

The air force pilots responded rapidly. Captain John Palm brought down his F-111 Aardvark over the target boat, sped across it, and then unloaded two 2,000-pound bombs about a mile out. The PCF roared on. Palm dumped two more bombs a half mile away. Again, the Khmers did not even hesitate. The pilots noticed but ignored a somewhat nondescript fishing trawler following behind. Their quarry remained the elusive, determined PCF. Spectre rippled the water ahead of the patrol boat; still, the Khmers pressed ahead. Khmer gunners returned fire against the four-engine AC-130.

A quick check with Seventh Air Force headquarters (who had patched through to Washington) okayed direct action against the running gunboat. Lieutenant Colonel Don Rebotoy's 388th Tactical Fighter Wing A-7D rolled down to strafe the fleeing craft. Rebotoy's wingmen followed.

They hoped to damage the engine in the stern. Instead, their concentrated 20-mm cannon fire blasted out the whole back end, flooding the hapless PCF. It sank so fast that an inbound RF-4C photo plane did not even catch the event.

Now attention turned to the wallowing forty-foot fishing boat. This obviously unarmed craft also pressed forward to Kompong Som, and the U.S. jets slipped as low as 100 feet and flirted with minimum safe airspeeds (450 miles an hour) at these dangerous altitudes, all in an attempt to determine the fishing vessel's cargo and passengers. The A-7D Corsairs and F-111A Aardvarks got only brief looks at the pitching deck and passed their impressions to Spectre. Ominously, one flier reported "30–40 possible Caucasians huddled in the bow." [21] Were the pilots watching the transfer of the *Mayaguez* crew?

Yes, they were, but nobody in the air knew that for sure. Miller and his men had spent the night on the boat, and now Khmer guards held AK-47s to the frightened Thai sailors and urged the trawler toward Kompong Som. All the pilots above could tell was that the wooden boat refused to stop, regardless of numerous low passes. Captain Charles Miller, aboard the small vessel, described what it was like to come under a near-attack by his own country's planes: "We were bombed [sic] a hundred times by our jets. Ten feet forward of our bow light. Rockets and machine gun fire. You have to give our pilots credit. They can thread the eye of the needle from a mile away. They did everything that was possible without blowing us out of the water to try to get this boat to turn around and take us back to the ship. When they saw it wasn't going to work, two jets overflew the boat from bow to stern and tear-gassed us."

Despite numerous near-misses and a dusting of choking CS, the little fishing boat did not turn back. It entered Kompong Som harbor about 1015, followed by its air pursuit. General Burns waved off his planes before they crossed the Cambodian coast. A fleeting glimpse of "possible Caucasians" did not justify risking fighters over the mainland. Perhaps the trawler was a decoy, pulling USAF planes into an ambush. If so, Burns did not bite. Even as the little boat ducked into the crowded anchorage, one of the 432nd Tactical Fighter Wing's RF-4C reconnaissance jets was on a course from Poulo Wai through Koh Tang to Kompong Som and Ream. The photos might show if the excited fliers' report of Caucasian passengers had any real substance.

In any event, the air force choked off all further attempts to reach or depart Koh Tang. Another PCF went under, and four suffered immobilizing injury.[22] F-4E Phantom IIs sank two smaller patrol craft. Counting the Swift boat grounded before dawn, a quarter of the Khmers' purloined fleet had been knocked out.

But the one "leaker" continued to raise questions. General Burns received postflight interrogations from the flight crews involved in the failed interception. Only one pair of 347th Tactical Fighter Wing F-111A pilots submitted a written report. Looking down from their two-man cockpit, the men recognized "30–40 people on decision thought to be Caucasian." All the fliers saw a few dozen people on deck, but there were substantial disagreements on how many, if any, were possible U.S. civilians. The few crews who suspected some Americans mentioned their larger size and atypical clothes for Thai or Cambodian fishermen: a man in a black turtleneck, some wearing yellow rain slickers, and some in brightly colored or white dress shirts. After assessment, Seventh Air Force intelligence officers passed an estimate of eight or nine Caucasians aboard the escaped ship. This analysis reached Washington shortly after 2240 on 13 May (0940 on 14 May in Cambodia), along with the unconfirmed flight crew report.[23]

The one that got away concerned President Ford and his National Security Council, because the news arrived just as they convened at 2240 on 13 May (Washington time) to consider the developing situation. As Ford observed, "Our efforts to solve the crisis diplomatically had failed." The Chinese in Peking returned all notes intended for the Khmer Rouge, but one official hinted that China would take no action in the event of a U.S. military operation. Maybe the Chinese told the Khmers about the notes, but thus far, there were no indications of a response from Phnom Penh.

With diplomacy dead (except for a faint trust in the ongoing Voice of America broadcasts in Cambodia), Ford and his men made the key decision to proceed with a military rescue operation. They agreed on an H hour of first light, 15 May, Cambodia time. The operation proposed retaking the ship, securing the crew from Koh Tang, and bombing the Kompong Som area to cut off reinforcements. The simultaneous *Mayaguez* and island assaults required the use of 2/9 Marines, still staging to U-Tapao. They would not be completely deployed until the midafternoon of 14 May, Cambodia time, let alone briefed and informed for a challenging air assault. The ship recovery required daylight, and BLT 2/9 could not meet a 14 May launch time that also gave Major Porter the light he needed. Additionally, B-52s from Guam and attack jets from the *Coral Sea* planned to cooperate in the air raids against the mainland, and the carrier group commander expected to be in range very early on 15 May. Thus, 15 May was D day.

As a final push for a peaceful solution, Ford directed that Ambassador John Scali at the United Nations ask for help from Secretary General Kurt Waldheim. There would be time for this. So Ford made use of the marines' preparation time to give peace one more chance.[24]

Along with 2/9 Marines, III Marine Amphibious Force (III MAF) picked Col. John M. Johnson to command both the boarders and BLT 2/9 for the coming operation. Johnson and his five staff officers received the designation "Marine Amphibious Task Group 79.9" (TG 79.9) and left Okinawa for U-Tapao at 0430 on 14 May. Johnson served as III MAF liaison officer at General Burns's Seventh Air Force headquarters throughout the Saigon withdrawal, and he judged himself "intimately familiar" with Seventh Air Force helicopter and tactical air operations. When Johnson and his staff arrived at U-Tapao around 0900, they found a great deal to be done. Immediately, Seventh Air Force officers assigned Johnson the mission of recovering the *Mayaguez*. These air planners directed the marine colonel into the ongoing boarding mission conference.

The commander of TG 79.9 found Major Porter involved in his operations briefing, and the Seventh Air Force forward staff heavily strained trying to sort out the results of the fight to contain the Khmer patrol boats. Rumors about the fleeing fishing craft complicated matters. Johnson discovered that Porter's marines and their six helicopters were on a thirty-minute alert status, just in case the situation around *Mayaguez* required immediate action.[25] So Company D had responsibility for the ship. But what about the crew?

That question represented the major uncertainty of 14 May. In truth, the Khmer Rouge guards on the fishing trawler had carried Captain Miller and all thirty-nine of his unhappy men from just outside Kompong Som harbor to nearby Koh Rong Som Lem, where the Americans went ashore at gunpoint around 1300 on 14 May. The Khmer commander held several long conversations with his deputies, and gunboat traffic went back and forth all afternoon. Miller suspected that his more senior captors spent much of this time engaged in heavy radio traffic. The guards looked worried and seemed to be looking up a lot more than

United States Command Organization
12–15 May 1975

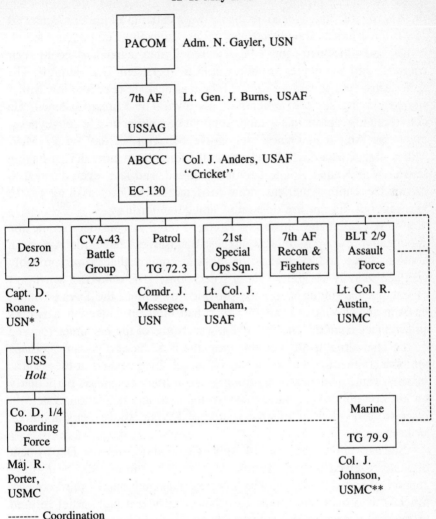

-------- Coordination

* Destroyer Squadron 23 also included USS *Henry B. Wilson*.

** Marine TG 79.9 exercised a planning role before the assault began. Colonel Johnson had been expected to control both marine units during the execution of the attack, but changes in helicopter availability and the combat situation removed the TG 79.9 headquarters from the operational chain of command. Colonel Johnson did provide valuable advice to 7th Air Force throughout the conduct of the operation.

usual at the F-111A Aardvarks flashing overhead. Something funny appeared to be transpiring.

The guard officers had probably been talking to Phnom Penh. At 1900, the Khmers announced new orders from the Cambodian capital. Miller and nine men would be released if they agreed to go to their containership and request withdrawal of the persistent U.S. aircraft. The Americans went aboard a PCF Swift boat as dusk descended. Now Miller started making some comments of his own. The Khmers listened. He convinced his captors that a gunboat might be a rather unsafe conveyance, given the American planes' aggressive behavior all day on 14 May. Miller suggested a daylight release in the familiar, unarmed Thai fishing trawler. The Khmer Rouge nervously agreed, and later even decided to permit the entire American crew to depart at 0600, "as long as the U.S. aircraft did not fire or bomb Cambodian territory."

What caused the blustering Khmer Rouge to consider freeing the Americans? Two possibilities suggest themselves. First, the American show of force and evident willingness to employ that power probably weighed heavily in Phnom Penh's decisions. It is unknown what sort of intelligence might have been provided by China, the Soviet Union, or Communist Vietnam, all of which had built up collection networks still in place from the late Indochina war. Some of these sources focused on the Thai airfields and possibly even the B-52 bases at Guam. Perhaps the Khmers themselves had agents or surveillance devices at these sites. In any event, evidence of a strong U.S. military response, particularly by air, certainly would have been available to any collection system in place to observe. Was this the source of Khmer Rouge fears about air strikes?

Second, about 1600 on 14 May (Cambodia time) the Department of State received a report from a U.S. embassy in a "Middle Eastern country" (probably Israel). The message indicated that a "third country official" had understood that a certain country that had earlier refused to relay messages to the Khmer Rouge "was using its influence with Cambodia and expected the *Mayaguez* to be released soon." Apparently, the Chinese were acting to influence their unruly clients, although Peking's rationale remains unknown.[26]

For either reason (or a combination of both), Charles Miller and his crew were promised freedom before the start of the U.S. rescue effort. But nobody in the U.S. chain of command, from Washington down to U-Tapao, knew any of this, nor could they. Intelligence teams at Seventh Air Force, PACOM, and the various Washington agencies had diligently attempted to track the crew since their containership dropped anchor off Koh Tang. The weight of opinion leaned toward a view that most of the crewmen could be found on Koh Tang. A few (nine at most) might have been taken to Kompong Som aboard the single fishing boat that successfully evaded the USAF blockade. None appeared to be on the merchant ship, which lay utterly inactive off the island. Infrared imagery revealed a steadily decreasing stack temperature, and after the night of 13–14 May, no activity occurred around the ship.

Aircraft sightings from 1654 on 13 May until 0604 on 14 May formed the basis for the intelligence officers' assessment concerning the likely location of the *Mayaguez* crew. Eight spot reports to Seventh Air Force described various numbers of people moving on and off the ship, the island, gunboats, and fishing boats. Five of these messages reflected observations before sunset. Aerial photographs revealed nothing conclusive beneath the island greenery. Once ship-to-shore motion stopped, the intelligence staffs assumed the U.S. prisoners had been incarcerated in a camouflaged location. Photo interpreters had difficulty pinpointing any enemy positions, although they marked "a possible anti-aircraft site" near the northeastern beach. Considering how active the air defense effort had been on Koh Tang, this reflects a very great concern with camouflage among the Khmer Rouge defenders. Hiding their captives certainly fit the pattern.

Unfortunately, although the aircrews had seen people moving, they were not Americans. Their observations proved erroneous—natural mistakes in poor light, at high speeds, and under fire. Nevertheless, the observations were wrong. But it all seemed reasonable and relatively verifiable, and it fit a pattern. Three independent intelligence echelons (Seventh Air Force, Pacific Command, and the several Washington agencies) all reached the same inaccurate conclusion.

Against this sensible but flawed assessment, Seventh Air Force and the other intelligence staffs weighed the sighting of thirty to forty "possible Caucasians" by a two-man F-111A crew, contradicted in part or in whole by other pilots who also saw the escaping fishing craft. Another report of suspicious patrol boat movements around Koh Rong Som Lem meant very little. Finally, close scrutiny of film taken by the RF-4C overhead at the end of the small vessel's run indicated, on one frame, a boat of similar construction with "29 possible people on deck." This key frame was not examined until long after the close of the *Mayaguez* affair because photo interpreters had not been told to look for such a craft.[27] Intelligence officers sifted all of this and guessed, splitting the difference of conflicting reports to place a maximum of nine crewmen on the Cambodian mainland. The U.S. commanders in Thailand knew this and feared that some crewmen had slipped beyond their reach as they planned their assaults. It only added to the urgency, in order to save the rest.

President Ford, through PACOM, designated three strategic objectives for the *Mayaguez* recovery: securing the captured crew, securing the SS *Mayaguez,* and preventing Khmer Rouge reinforcement. Lieutenant General Burns organized his available units to accomplish the operational tasks that flowed from these requirements. He planned to stay at his Nakhon Phanom headquarters, relaying orders through an EC-130 airborne battlefield command and control center (ABCCC, code-named "Cricket") under Col. J. J. Anders, USAF. Anders held the same post during the Southeast Asia evacuations.

Rescuing the crew was the task of BLT 2/9 Marines, flown in by the USAF CH-53 and HH-53 helicopters. Burns's Seventh Air Force fighters and fighter-bombers would continue to isolate the island and stand by to support the marines. Burns and Anders picked air mission commander Lt. Col. John H. Denham, commander of 21st Special Operations Squadron, to lead the assault. Once the marines landed, control on the island would revert to TG 79.9. Burns wanted the infantry to seize, search, and clear Koh Tang, securing the American civilians in the process.

Colonel Johnson's TG 79.9 would also secure SS *Mayaguez,* landing the Company D, 1/4 boarders by helicopter aboard the containership. In this case, Capt. Paul L. Jacobs, USAF, acted as air mission commander. Again, Johnson's TG headquarters intended to assume control once the helicopters landed.

The third mission, preventing Khmer Rouge reinforcement of Koh Tang, included a continuation of ongoing Seventh Air Force interdiction against Khmer patrol craft. Burns also anticipated using B-52 bombers from Guam and carrier attack jets from the USS *Coral Sea* to strike naval and air targets near Kompong Som and Ream.

Burns did not originally specify the role of the USS *Holt* and the USS *Wilson,* but both of these ships were integrated into the final plan of operations as 14 May went on. There could be little argument that,

---

**United States Strategic and Operational Objectives for
the *Mayaguez* Recovery**

1. STRATEGIC OBJECTIVE: Secure crew of SS *Mayaguez*.
   OPERATIONAL OBJECTIVES:
   1) Prevent the crew from leaving the Koh Tang vicinity.
   2) Seize, search, and clear Koh Tang.
   3) Secure and evacuate crew.
2. STRATEGIC OBJECTIVE: Secure SS *Mayaguez*.
   OPERATIONAL OBJECTIVES:
   1) Prevent SS *Mayaguez* from leaving the Koh Tang vicinity.
   2) Seize SS *Mayaguez* intact and remove it from contested waters.
3. STRATEGIC OBJECTIVE: Prevent Khmer Rouge reinforcement.
   OPERATIONAL OBJECTIVES:
   1) Blockade Koh Tang.
   2) Destroy reinforcements attempting to reach Koh Tang.
   3) Conduct air strikes on military targets at Ream and Kompong Som.

---

although air patrols and strikes were by no means simple, the marines
and their air force pilots had drawn the toughest assignments.

Colonel Johnson received his final mission about noon, as BLT 2/9
continued to fly in aboard MAC C-141s. Johnson recorded it as: "to
seize, occupy, and defend the island of Koh Tang, hold the island indefi-
nitely (for a minimum of forty-eight hours) and to rescue any of the
crew members of *Mayaguez* found on the island; simultaneously seize
Mayaguez and remove it from its location."

Johnson realized that he had two unique tasks. Major Porter's boarding
team had to land on the *Mayaguez,* seize the ship, clear it, and get it
underway, while BLT 2/9 air assaulted onto Koh Tang.

Porter already had a good idea of what he was doing, and Johnson
noted with satisfaction that the Company D team had designed a two-
step plan to execute their helicopter boarding. The marines had divided
into five assault teams, one per helicopter, plus a sixth helicopter carrying
the civilian and navy engineering experts. In the first phase, four heliteams
intended landing on the forward portion of the *Mayaguez* to seize key
areas—first the bridge, then the interior of the superstructure, next the
main deck, and finally the engine room. A fifth team provided a reserve.
In phase two, Porter hoped to search and clear the vessel. At that time,

he wanted technicians aboard the last chopper to land and help get the ship underway. Since the containers could not hold the weight of the HH-53s, the marines rigged rope ladders to clamber down onto the silver boxes. The young men fabricated portable bridges to lay between the cargo containers. They rehearsed, with the participation of the 40th ARRS pilots. It would not be easy, but it could be done.

Koh Tang looked much more troublesome. Colonel Johnson borrowed an available army U-21 Ute twin-engine plane for an overflight of the island by Lieutenant Colonel Austin and the key BLT 2/9 leaders. This reconnaissance took place from 1500 to 1730 on 14 May, and it confirmed initial forebodings.

The basic mission, a "vertical" amphibious operation, certainly fit right into marine training. But instead of marine aviators and a concurrent "horizontal" (seaborne) attack, BLT 2/9 had to rely on unfamiliar air force fliers (admittedly superb, but nevertheless not fully prepared for such a role) and a single mode of assault. Marines preferred to pin hostile forces with the sea landing and then envelop the enemy using a helilift to his rear. Here, the helicopters represented the only way in and out. Equal concern revolved around a lack of a surreptitious beach surveillance, normally provided by SEAL teams or marine Force Reconnaissance elements. The overflight, some photographs, and pilots' spot reports constituted the marines' main sources of information.

The mission to search for and recover the *Mayaguez* crew denied BLT 2/9 the usual pre-assault bombardment and use of riot-control agents on Koh Tang itself, for fear of injuring the prisoners. Burns okayed the use of USAF air power once the marines came ashore, and both *Holt* and *Wilson* had the ability to provide naval gunfire support. But none of this could occur until BLT observers reached the island to adjust fire. So the air force helicopter assault planned to go in cold and rely on surprise.

Enemy strength also remained in doubt. In U-Tapao, one Cambodian refugee, a former naval officer, stated that he had seen only twenty to thirty people on the island, with "no organized regular units." A PACOM analysis predicted about ninety to a hundred infantry, reinforced by ten to fifteen men with heavy weapons. The Defense Intelligence Agency agreed, and said the number of Khmer Rouge might be up to two hundred, armed with rocket-propelled grenades, 82-mm mortars, 75-mm recoilless rifles, and 12.7-mm heavy machine guns, along with lesser weaponry. The PACOM report reached Seventh Air Force at Nakhon Phanom about

2200 on 14 May, but never went to the marines at U-Tapao. Despite the refugee's remarks, Austin and his reconnaissance party planned on facing at least a hundred Khmers, based upon the flyover and aircraft spot reports. Better intelligence about the enemy should have reached the marines and their USAF associates; what they did not know could and did hurt them. But even so, the assault would have to go in.

The terrain looked difficult. Koh Tang is shaped like a four-and-a-half-mile-long dog bone, with the long axis north to south. Almost the entire island is flat, with one low ridge just south of the northern swelling. Thick, leaf-topped trees, dense secondary growth, and creeper vines cut visibility to ten feet on the average and hid most enemy activity from air observation. The marines had only photographs to use for navigation on Koh Tang. They had no properly gridded map sheets. This later made it hard to control supporting fires.

Khmer Rouge Armed Forces Order of Battle
12–15 May 1975

Khmer Rouge garrison, Koh Tang
  Infantry Company (+)
Khmer Rouge forces, Kompong Som
  Naval Patrol Squadron: 24 to 28 PCF Swift gunboats
Khmer Rouge forces, Ream
  12 T-28 Trojan trainer aircraft
  Antiaircraft battalion (23-mm, 37-mm)
Khmer Rouge forces, Kompong Som/Ream area
  Infantry Regiment

Source: Comptroller General, "The Seizure of the *Mayaguez*" in U.S. Congress, House of Representatives, Committee on International Affairs, *Seizure of the Mayaguez: Part IV*, 94th Congress, 2nd Session, 4 October 1976, 90, 91.

The *Mayaguez* floated about a mile off the northern tip of the island. Almost every enemy and U.S. prisoner sighting related to the northern lobe of the island, and coincidentally, the eastern and western beaches there constituted the only usable landing zones. A small encampment with temporary structures (a major source of antiaircraft fire) lay at the edge of the eastern beach. This seemed a likely site for any U.S. prisoners, certainly a supposition justified by the heavy volume of gunfire that

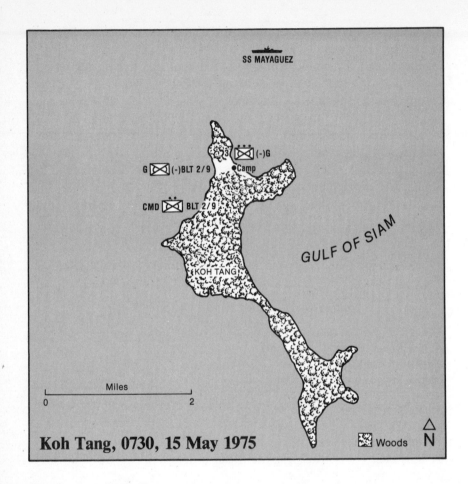

Koh Tang, 0730, 15 May 1975

rose every time U.S. planes flew over this area. Only 340 meters separated the wider eastern beach from the narrow western beach. Khmer soldiers had linked the beaches by clearing a 100-meter-wide strip of major trees, although stumps and underbrush remained in the rough lane.[28]

The key consideration for marine planners revolved around available troops and equipment, specifically helicopters. Of eight 40th ARRS choppers on hand, six HH-53C Jolly Green Giant aircraft waited for orders. One had broken down, and one would stay at U-Tapao for search and rescue duties (a reasonable precaution given the volume of planned air strikes and the continuing interdiction effort around Koh Tang). Only five CH-53C Knife choppers stood ready to go; two suffered maintenance difficulties. Four and a half hours represented the minimum turnaround time between lifts, and Anders hoped that USAF mechanics could provide a twelfth helo by the second lift. But for the first wave, Colonel Anders delivered only eleven helicopters for Colonel Johnson's marines.

Time was short (as always), with the beginning of morning twilight at 0542 on 15 May. So the mission aimed to reach Koh Tang and the ship at that gray time, hoping for surprise. The officers used the night of 14–15 May to iron out the last details, go over the plans with their men, and check equipment. There was not much time for sleep; a few airmen and marines napped, but most men stayed awake. Nerves stretched tightly.

At the 1900 final planning conference, the principals at U-Tapao gathered together for a marathon. Helicopters had to be reallocated. Johnson, Anders, Austin, Denham, Porter, and Jacobs attended, along with other staff officers and deputies. Three decisions came from the meeting.

Battalion Landing Team 2/9 Assault on Koh Tang

	PLANNED	EXECUTED

1st Wave	0542 on 15 May
	2 helicopters to West Beach
	  1st Plt., Co. G
		0607 on 15 May
		4 helicopters to West Beach
		  Co. G (−)

	6 helicopters to East Beach
	  Co. G (−), 81-mm Sec.
	  BLT Comd. Grp.
		1 helicopter to East Beach
		  3rd Plt. (−), Co. G
		
		1 helicopter to south of West Beach
		  BLT Cmd. Grp., 81-mm Sec.

WAVE TOTAL	180 marines	131 marines

2nd Wave	1000 on 15 May
	12 helicopters to Koh Tang
	  Co. E
		1130 on 15 May
		4 helicopters to West Beach
		  Co. E (−)

WAVE TOTAL	250 marines	100 marines
GRAND TOTAL	430 marines	225 marines*

* Six wounded marines withdrawn at conclusion of second wave landings.

First, the boarders found themselves reduced to only three aircraft, in order to give the 2/9 Marines enough first wave combat power to establish a lodgement at Koh Tang. Major Porter realized that there could be no alternative, and began to figure out how to do more with less.

Second, the group finalized BLT 2/9's Koh Tang scheme of maneuver. Lieutenant Colonel Austin intended to execute an envelopment, drawing enemy attention west and then descending from the east in the main effort. The first wave directed 1st Platoon, Company G to the west beach aboard two helicopters, with Capt. James H. Davis in command, to push across to east beach. They represented the fixing force. The enveloping element—the rest of Company G, a section of four 81-mm mortars, and Lieutenant Colonel Austin's Command Group A—planned to land in six choppers at east beach. Davis and his 1st Platoon wanted to drive east to link with the larger group, which would have already taken the key encampment. Four and a half hours later, Company E under Capt. Mykle E. Stahl hoped to land aboard twelve helicopters (the original eight, the three from the boarders, and one repaired craft). Additional waves could come in if needed, drawing from the rest of the BLT at U-Tapao, which waited under Maj. Lawrence R. Moran, the battalion executive officer.

The ground attack plan rested upon the belief that the marines on east beach could rapidly secure American prisoners trapped in the suspicious camp area, freeing the USMC units to call for available fire support against the certain Khmer Rouge counterattacks. A medical team, to include a navy physician, accompanied the lead units to aid any wounded American mariners. Naturally, his skills stood ready to help wounded marines and airmen as well. As a precaution, Austin (like Porter) received an army captain expert in the Cambodian tongue. He might help rescue the trapped Americans by negotiating with nervous guards, or assist the marines by interrogating Khmer Rouge prisoners of war.

Once the marines came ashore and secured the Americans, restrictions on fire support would end. Then, marine observers could make full use of USAF air strikes and naval gunfire. Marine commanders asked for and received authority to employ the 15,000-pound BLU-82 landing zone munition, an immense blockbuster capable of blowing clearings out of the densest jungle. Aside from opening another LZ, this bomb generated powerful concussion effects that might prove helpful in ground combat.

The final decision proved painful but unavoidable. The helicopter shortage left TG 79.9 high and dry. Having planned and sweated and screamed into the phone to Nakhon Phanom, Colonel Johnson and his small staff could not fit onto the first wave without robbing Austin of desperately needed fighting power. Johnson hoped to land with the second wave, so he did not fly to Nakhon Phanom or take off in Colonel Anders's ABCCC. He knew that by doctrine, the air force retained command until the marines touched down. As it turned out, Johnson was reduced to providing long-distance advice to Nakhon Phanom and the orbiting ABCCC.

When the scheme went to General Burns at 2300, he approved the details. Burns informed Anders and Johnson about the USS *Coral Sea* air strikes planned to block Khmer reinforcements from the port of Kompong Som and the Ream airfield and naval base. At that hour, the B-52 Stratofortresses in Guam remained on standby, although targets had been designated for them. At 0030 on 15 May, Seventh Air Force sent Admiral Gayler at PACOM a copy of the operations plan.

Gayler made one change, making use of USS *Holt,* which had almost reached Koh Tang. He decided against a simultaneous ship and island assault. The PACOM commander worried about the potential risk as his half-sized boarding party tried to climb down out of hovering helicopters over a potentially defended ship. Enemy snipers might well pick several heavily laden marines off the swaying rope ladders, and Porter's party had few men to spare. In order to give the reduced landing team a fighting chance against any Khmer soldiers on SS *Mayaguez,* Gayler directed that Company D, 1/4 Marines disembark first on the *Holt.* About an hour after the main attack, USS *Holt* proposed to bring the marines alongside, and could of course supplement marine manpower and firepower with her own considerable ship's company and weaponry.[29] Now the plan was complete. All that *Holt* lacked were the cutlasses necessary to give the operation an authentic flair.

As his armed forces made last-minute preparations, President Gerald Ford convened his fourth and final National Security Council session on the *Mayaguez.* At 1552 on 14 May (0252 on 15 May Cambodia time), the president opened the meeting with a review of the situation. The Waldheim initiative had borne no fruit; indeed, the Khmer Rouge did not even acknowledge the United Nations message until 19 May. The ship remained at Koh Tang. The crew—well, most seemed to be at Koh Tang, but who really knew? So Ford turned to the military.

General David Jones explained the three military operations underway (Koh Tang, ship boarding, air strikes) and then mentioned that the operation could be delayed, if so decided. Jones stressed that the men in Thailand already had awoken and were waiting for execution orders. A final ''go'' was needed within the hour to allow a dawn attack.

The recovery operations gained quick assent, but the air bombardment created controversy. At one point, General Jones stated that the planned air strikes might be considered as ''punishing'' Cambodia. Ford and Kissinger really favored this aspect of the interdiction effort: ''We wanted them to know we meant business.'' Secretary of Defense James Schlesinger disagreed; he just wanted to rescue the Americans and the ship. Risking aircraft over Cambodia to make an example for world opinion did not concern Schlesinger. The secretary of defense thought the aerial blockade around Koh Tang was strong enough to block enemy reinforcements.

At this point, official photographer David Kennerly boldly piped up. He was not an NSC member, but he had both guts and common sense. ''Has anyone considered,'' he asked, ''that this might be the act of a local Cambodian commander who has just taken it into his own hands to halt any ship that comes by? Has anyone stopped to think that he might not have gotten his orders from Phnom Penh?'' The leaders sat in silence, listening to this brash but thoughtful young interloper.

''Everyone here has been talking about Cambodia as if it were a traditional government. Like France. We have trouble with France, we just pick up the telephone and call. We know who to talk to. But I was in Cambodia just two weeks ago, and it's not that kind of government at all. We don't even know who the leadership is. Has anyone considered that?''

If not, they did now. After a pause, discussion resumed. The bombing talk grew more reasonable. Ford decided that ''massive strikes would constitute overkill''; instead, he opted for naval attack jets in ''surgical strikes'' (as if those were truly possible). The president specifically authorized four attacks, beginning at 0745 Cambodia time, to coincide with the estimated recovery of the captured ship. To cover his bets, Ford kept the Stratofortresses on alert just in case. The other proposed military actions went into effect.[30]

A half a world away, the marines and airmen boarded their rotary wing aircraft as the word came: ''Go!'' The *Holt* waited about twelve miles offshore in the darkness. Watching aircraft reported all quiet at Koh Tang. The great rescue began.

Three distinct operations commenced in the predawn darkness of 15 May 1975. From Thailand, the Koh Tang and *Mayaguez* seizure elements started their two-hour flight toward the island. This helicopter armada expected to divide about 12 miles northwest of Koh Tang, where the destroyer escort USS *Holt* waited to pick up the boarding force. Finally, 350 miles southeast of Kompong Som, USS *Coral Sea* prepared to launch her interdiction missions over the Cambodian mainland.

The USAF/USMC assault wave left U-Tapao at 0415, breaking into three elements. In the lead, Captain Jacobs's three HH-53Cs (Jolly 11, 12, and 13), carrying Major Porter's ship seizure team, clattered toward

Mayaguez/Koh Tang Helicopter Assault Waves

Waves	Helicopters	Planned Landing Zone	Actual Landing Zone	Damage	Troops Delivered
1	Jolly 11	USS *Holt*	USS *Holt*	—	Boarding Force
	Jolly 12	USS *Holt*	USS *Holt*	—	from
	Jolly 13	USS *Holt*	USS *Holt*	Severe	Co. D (−), 1/4
1	Knife 21	West Beach	West Beach	Crashed	1 Plt. (−), Co. G, 2/9
	Knife 22	West Beach	West Beach	Severe	None
1	Knife 23	East Beach	East Beach	Crashed	3 Plt. (−), Co. G, 2/9
	Knife 31	East Beach	East Beach	Crashed	None
	Knife 32	East Beach	West Beach	Severe	3 Plt. (−), Co. G, 2/9
	Jolly 41	East Beach	West Beach	Major	2 Plt. (−), Co. G, 2/9
	Jolly 42	East Beach	West Beach	Major	2 Plt. (−), Co. G, 2/9
	Jolly 43	East Beach	south of West Beach	—.	Cmd. Grp., 81mm Sec.
2	Jolly 11	West Beach	West Beach	—	Plt. (−), Co. E, 2/9
	Jolly 12	West Beach	West Beach	—	Plt. (−), Co. E, 2/9
2	Jolly 43	East Beach	West Beach	—	Plt. (−), Co. E, 2/9
	Knife 51	East Beach	West Beach	—	Plt. (−), Co. E, 2/9
	Knife 52	East Beach	East Beach	Severe	None
3	Jolly 11	East Beach	East Beach	Major	None
	Jolly 12	East Beach	East Beach	Major	None
	Knife 51	East Beach	East Beach	—	25 men withdrawn
3	Jolly 43	West Beach	West Beach	Major	54 men withdrawn
	Jolly 44	West Beach	West Beach	Major	76 men withdrawn
	Knife 51	West Beach	West Beach	—	70 men withdrawn

the darkened USS *Holt*. Next, two CH-53Cs (Knife 21 with Lieutenant Colonel Denham and Knife 22) ferried the west beach force. To the rear, three more CH-53Cs (Knife 23, 31, 32) transported the first part of the east beach units. They were accompanied by the last three HH-53Bs (Jolly 41, 42, 43), which bore Austin's command group and the rest of the east beach marines. At the same time, Colonel Anders's EC-130 "Cricket" ABCCC took up station ninety miles off Koh Tang, along with a beefed-up tactical air contingent of Phantoms, Corsairs, Aardvarks, and a Spectre. As the planes came on station, the overnight Spectre crew announced the destruction of another Khmer Rouge PCF about 0100. No other Khmer craft had tested the U.S. cordon.

Aboard the strung-out column of helicopters, marine Maj. John B. Hendricks of BLT 2/9 recalled watching marines sprawled uneasily on the floor plates as watchful airmen rested against their loaded miniguns. He found the trip across the black Gulf of Siam surprisingly long and cold. No moon lit the mysterious waters below, and the helicopters breasted scudding cloud layers as they headed south. In Knife 21, Lieutenant Colonel Denham heard little conversation among his veteran crew: "We had been through Saigon and Phnom Penh together, the same crew; we pretty well knew what each man would do. We didn't have much to discuss going into the island." [31] The men of the assault wave wondered what would greet them.

Aboard Captain Jacobs's three helicopters, the men of Major Porter's trimmed-down Company D, 1/4 Marines boarding outfit had more to say. They faced a real challenge. Half of their combat power remained at U-Tapao, although Porter had loaded the choppers to maximum capacity. The planned two-squad assault and search elements had been cut to one squad apiece, but Porter kept the same basic five teams. He retained his command group, one assault element, an army linguist and two USAF bomb-disposal men in the lead helo. The major placed two assault units and six USS *Duluth* sailors in the second. The third helicopter carried the last assault squad, the reserve squad, and six civilians from Military Sealift Command (MSC).[32] The loadings served no tactical purpose, considering that these HH-53s had no assault role anymore. But the arrangements facilitated last-minute discussion and explanation. The marines and airmen shouted over the engine roar as they adjusted their rehearsed plan into an over-the-rail attack from the deck of USS *Holt*.

Meanwhile, off to the southeast, activity aboard the flight deck of

USS *Coral Sea* intensified. Carrier Air Wing 15 readied for its first combat action since the hectic days of 1972. The Screaming Eagles of Fighter Squadron 51 and the Sundowners of Fighter Squadron 111 prepared to fly escort and protect the carrier group, just in case the Khmers or Vietnamese opposed the raids. Each plane in their combined force of two dozen F-4N Phantom II fighters carried four Sparrow radar missiles and four short-range Sidewinder infrared homing missiles, and many of the aviators had cut their teeth over Hanoi and Haiphong. Ordnance handlers rigged laser-guided Paveway Mark 82 (500-pound) and Mark 83 (1,000-pound) bombs onto the racks of Attack Squadron 95 A-6A Intruder medium bombers and Attack Squadron 22 and 94 A-7E Corsair II light attack planes. Although these airplanes were tactical aircraft, their bomb loads were substantial. A6-As could bear up to 15,000 pounds of munitions; A-7Es normally carried a bit less. Considering that a huge B-17G Flying Fortress delivered 6,000 pounds back in 1944, the much smaller navy jets packed quite a punch.

A maximum of ten VA-95 Green Lizard Intruders, twelve VA-22 Fighting Redcock Corsairs, and twelve VA-94 Mighty Shrike Corsairs planned to launch, divided into four waves. USS *Coral Sea* had authority to bomb vessels in Kompong Som harbor, Ream airfield, Ream naval base, and Kompong Som port facilities during the four cyclic strikes. It would take about ninety minutes for each evolution.

In each cycle, seven or eight bomb-laden attack planes comprised the core of a larger effort. Two other forces accompanied the bombers. First in and last out, a suppression group hoped to destroy or confuse the ground-based Khmer radars, surface to air missiles, and air defense gun batteries. A few Intruders and Corsairs carried Shrike and Standard antiradiation missiles (ARMs) to kill enemy emitters; four EA-6B Prowler electronic warfare planes packed jamming avionics designed to baffle enemy tracking systems. Following suppression activities, an escort of swift Phantom fighters would clear away any enemy interceptors, remain on station as the bombers struck, and then cover their withdrawal. The bombers came next. Since the missions employed laser bombs, some attack aircraft carried target "illuminators." These laser planes planned to designate the targets, and the following bombers then dropped their loads. Theoretically, the smart bombs flew right down the laser track. All of this allowed for President Ford's "surgical strikes." Commander I. Carmichael expected to lead his Carrier Wing 15 aviators over

Cambodia.[33] USS *Coral Sea* steamed north, pushing for a takeoff time of 0705.

All the pieces were on the board.

Faint bands of color streaked the eastern horizon as the first three big Jolly Green Giants slipped away from the approaching chopper formation. At 0550, 1st Lt. Donald R. Backlund swung his Jolly 11 over USS *Holt,* only to find what marine Capt. Walter Wood charitably called an "incredibly small helo pad." In the predawn gloom, Backlund maneuvered his rear wheels onto the pad, lowered his cargo ramp, and let the marines get off. The other helicopters executed the same tricky routine, and Major Porter's men made some use of their rope ladders. USNS *Greenville Victory* First Officer Clinton J. Harriman led his civil service sailors aboard the *Holt* about 0624 to conclude the slow, nerve-wracking process. Jollies 11, 12, and 13 flew off to refuel at a nearby HC-130P King search and rescue control plane.[34] By that time, the sun cracked the eastern skyline. It was going to be another bright, warm, beautifully clear day in the Gulf of Siam.

Commander Robert A. Peterson, skipper of the *Holt,* and his executive officer, Lt. Comdr. John Todd, met Major Porter almost immediately and outlined the plan for the boarding. Just as the air mission commander took charge of his assault force passengers until they landed, so Peterson held sway over the Company D marines until they actually jumped aboard *Mayaguez.* Peterson's simple plan cleared up many marine concerns about the modified operation.

The destroyer escort captain intended to bring his ship against the side of *Mayaguez* away from the island. In this way, the *Holt* could avoid enemy fire from Koh Tang, and put those island defenders wishing to disrupt the boarding in the uncomfortable position of having to shoot through any Khmer security units on the containership. Peterson explained how Destroyer Squadron 23 commander Capt. D. P. Roane, USN (aboard *Holt* for a routine inspection voyage when the crisis arose, and commander of the inbound USS *Wilson* as well) arranged for air force A-7D Corsair jets to drop CS gas across the containership when *Holt* was ten minutes away. Then, Roane wanted to let the USAF planes strafe the anchored ship five minutes prior to the boarding. Captain Roane's coordination effort freed Commander Peterson to handle the difficult converging movement toward the container vessel. Even as the briefing went on, *Holt* headed east for Koh Tang, into the rising sun. The destroyer escort gradually swung around, to approach the island from the east.

Porter's marines took up stations to reinforce Lieutenant Commander Todd's well-rehearsed sailor fire teams, as the boarding team leaders briefed their men. Near *Holt*'s port bow, Captain Wood stood ready with Cpl. Carl R. Coker's bridge assault squad. By 0700, all hands could see Koh Tang, with the inactive merchant ship silhouetted off the north tip. Peterson knew that without line handlers and with *Mayaguez* swinging freely around its bow anchor, the approach must be handled carefully. The captain of the *Holt* expected only one chance.

At 0705, Roane contacted Cricket to request the CS dusting. Two A-7Ds responded at 0710, and as Peterson watched the acrid gas spread across the merchantman, he realized that the wind was blowing from the south. *Holt* could anticipate a full dose as it closed in. Peterson ordered all men to don protective masks. The marines had already done so, since they expected to find CS trapped in the *Mayaguez* compartments.

Commander Peterson sweated under his gas mask as he slowed his ship for the final approach. The heat and humidity in the closed pilothouse, with hatches battened for action, only added to the discomfort. The mask muffled Peterson's commands. By 0715, *Holt* lay only 200 meters astern. Peterson called for the strafing run, then immediately canceled it. They were already too close. The *Mayaguez* loomed near, silent, wreathed in whitish wisps of hanging tear gas. *Holt* eased alongside.

Once the destroyer-escort got within a few feet, Lt. Comdr. John Todd had the honors. He shouted an order unheard since 1826: "Marines over the side!"

So it began. The energetic Cpl. Carl R. Coker and Capt. Walter Wood leaped across the gap near the containership's white upper works. Snorting in their protective masks, Coker and his company commander caught lines thrown across by sailors on the *Holt*. Wood described what happened next: "As we moved forward, I turned to check the positions of my other Marines but, much to my surprise, I discovered that no one else had boarded, for as we had jumped, the two ships had drifted apart, and indeed the two ships were now some 25 feet apart. Motivated partially out of loneliness, Corporal Coker and I worked feverishly at the lines and the two ships were made fast."

Holt was more than a hundred feet shorter than *Mayaguez*, although both ships' decks lined up closely. This met expectations, because the night before, special RF-4C flights verified *Mayaguez*'s deck arrangements. Within minutes, all the marines scrambled aboard. Coker and Wood led a squad to the bridge. Although these marines found open food canisters up there, Wood stated that "contrary to many reports, the food was not warm." Meanwhile, Captain Feltner and his men searched the rest of the superstructure. Another squad raced fore and aft along the rows of silver Sea-Land containers on the main deck, checking for resistance. Sergeant William J. Owens brought his rifle squad down through several eerie, gas-filled dark compartments toward the engine room. The marines used flashlights as they poked around the abandoned compartments. Two air force sergeants checked for booby traps, but none were found. The mysterious Khmer Rouge were nowhere to be found. To their dismay, the marines did not locate any U.S. crew members, either.

By 0800, the *Greenville Victory* volunteers went aboard to try to get the ship running, accompanied by the six sailors from USS *Duluth* and men from USS *Holt* as well. Porter reported all secure at 0822, sixty-two minutes after the boarding order. When the marines raised the flag at 0825, Peterson commanded "attention to port." [35] So although difficult in a technical sense, the unopposed ship recovery had gone very well.

But SS *Mayaguez* was a ghost ship. What had happened to the crew? As the sailors down in the fetid engine room labored to restore the ship to life, battling poor light, high heat, and lingering CS gas that necessitated masks for hours after the initial assault, marines on deck turned their eyes toward Koh Tang. The crashing of explosions and steady rattle of gunfire drifted across the sparkling tropical waters. Frantic, erratic helicopters bobbed and swarmed, jets flashed across the bright green island, and forbidding black smoke towered off the eastern beach. Unlike Company D, BLT 2/9 had found the Khmer Rouge.

At 0607, Lt. Col. John Denham in Knife 21 and Capt. Terry Ohlmeier in Knife 22 turned in toward Koh Tang. The gray light of dawn was changing to the golds and rosy pinks of early morning. Denham saw that the landing zone did not have enough room for both choppers; in fact, it did not allow enough space for one. Denham led in and had to swing his aircraft's nose over the surf and let the marines out across the CH-53's cargo ramp, not unlike Jolly 11's technique aboard USS

Holt. Ohlmeier waited just offshore. So far, the verdant woods remained quiet.

Denham settled his big helicopter onto the thin LZ, unloading 2nd Lt. James McDaniel and half of his 1st Platoon, Company G. Suddenly, as Denham looked up, he watched the tree line erupt in gunfire. He commented later: "They [Khmers] were very disciplined. They waited until we were down and Ohlmeier was close by before they cut loose on us. There was lots of noise from ammunition impacting on the aircraft and waterspouts in front of the nose. We were getting destroyed. The plane just came down around my ears." The marines ran for cover, emptying the big chopper. Denham tried to take off, with one engine blown open and useless. Various transmission indicators showed serious malfunctions, and Knife 21 set down on the sand, barely hovering, pieces flaking off under the drumfire of enemy bullets.

Nearby, Ohlmeier moved in to let his minigunners spray the enemy positions. The Knife 22 pilot thought the blazing tracers and muzzle flashes at the base of the green brush "looked like a string of Christmas tree lights." As Ohlmeier's helicopter covered, Denham coaxed his battered Knife off the surf line, bounced once, and then skipped out to the west. The single working engine sputtered, and the damaged drivetrain could barely keep Denham up. Knife 21 kept striking the clear warm water, more and more often as the helo struggled away from the eastern LZ. Each drop gulped water into the cockpit and cargo area, through holes and jammed hatches. Spray flew up and fouled the tortured engine. Finally, only three-quarters of a mile out, the engine quit. Knife 21 plopped into the Gulf of Siam, well within range of heavier Khmer Rouge machine guns and mortars. Knife 22 stayed overhead, its marines still aboard, as Ohlmeier tried to insure that Denham and his crew escaped the sinking CH-53. The flight engineer freed the unconscious copilot, then disappeared into churning waves around the hissing wreckage. He was later declared killed in action.

Overhead, Ohlmeier's 7.62-mm Gatling gunners shot back at the active Khmer defenders. The air force pilot was disquieted to see two more loaded choppers come around from the north. Knife 32 and Jolly 41 should have gone to the east beach, but Ohlmeier did not have time to find out why they had flown to the west. Instead, he turned over the rescue chores to these new arrivals and heeled over to try a landing at west beach. In Knife 22's cargo compartment, Capt. James Davis of

Company G and the rest of 1st Platoon wanted to join their hard-pressed comrades.

Knife 22 leveled off and bored in, taking heavy fire all the way. The Khmer gunners concentrated their efforts on the big, armored CH-53, and Ohlmeier tried to jink and bob as his own gunners returned the murderous fire. Several 12.7-mm slugs punched big holes in Knife 22's fuel tanks, and fragments of mortar rounds and bits of the U.S. helicopter itself flew across the pitching interior of the big aircraft. Another burst blew out part of the nose fairing. The controls bucked and shivered from the beating, and Ohlmeier had to break off to avoid a hard crash into the thick foliage. Streaming fuel from his main reservoirs, he aborted the landing. With him went Company G's commander and half of 1st Platoon. Knife 22 barely made the Thai coast, and its badly holed hull and emergency landing rendered it useless for the rest of the operation. Having off-loaded their own men, the refueled Jolly 11 and 12 followed the injured Knife to Thailand, just in case of an accident over water.[36]

As bad as the assault had gone in the west, the situation on the eastern beach was even worse. Knife 23, flown by 1st Lt. John Shramm, endured the same fate as Knife 21. Shramm pulled up to land on the wider eastern beach when the Khmer Rouge opened up. The first rounds snapped off pieces of the main rotor assembly and then tore holes in the armored hull. To his left rear, the flier glimpsed a fireball that could only contain hapless Knife 31. The Khmer shooting intensified. Knife 23 lost an engine, then staggered under a heavy blow. Shramm dropped his ramp and manhandled the vibrating, disintegrating chopper to the sand. The whole tail boom cracked off as Shramm's chopper hit hard. Second Lieutenant Michael A. Cicere and half of his 3rd Platoon stormed out, followed by the five airmen, one of whom was an air force photographer. All of the USAF men grabbed M-16 rifles as they left their ruined helicopter.

As for Knife 31, its end had been swift and dramatic. The other helos had been nicked and slashed to death, but a Khmer rocket-propelled grenade (RPG) launcher eliminated the CH-53 with one shot. The disaster occurred after a few small arms rounds found the vulnerable fuel supply. Major Howard A. Corson tried to pull his crumbling aircraft off the beach, but his torn port fuel tank split and burst into flame. A brace of 12.7-mm bullets rippled across the burning hull. Knife 31 did not react much to Corson's urgings, and despite the spreading blaze, the crew continued to return shots. The miniguns rasped and the copilot, 2nd

Lt. Richard Vandegeer, leaned out of his window to fire his M-16 rifle.

Had it gotten over deeper water, Knife 31 might have survived the creeping fire. The marines in the cargo compartment rolled and jumped, trying to fight the flames and avoid screaming enemy bullets and speeding chunks of helicopter. Just as Corson backed off the sand and reached about forty feet in altitude, the competent Khmer RPG gunner fired. His shot detonated directly on the windscreen, blowing off the nose of the Knife, killing Vandegeer, and forcing a blast of air into the burning hull to create an inferno. Corson's chopper incinerated in a white-hot explosion. Its carcass spun around violently, then crashed unceremoniously into the surf line. The broken nose sank into the surf; the flaming rear end faced the trees. Khmer machine guns, RPGs, and mortars zeroed on the crackling wreckage. It looked like few would survive this holocaust.

Those who made it had flight mechanic S. Sgt. Jon D. Harston, USAF, to thank. Most of the marines remained trapped in the burning chopper. Although shot in the leg, Harston got out of the craft quickly, and thought immediately that he needed a rifle to return the tremendously heavy Khmer fire. As he entered the half-submerged helo, he found excited marines trying to punch out windows or struggling through the flaming rear ramp area. Harston grabbed an M-16 and led the confused, injured marines to safety. He also saved Corson, who awoke to see a very determined Harston trying to open the cockpit door. As the major figured out what had happened, he waved off the resolute sergeant, and instead exited through the gaping hole that used to be the nose of Knife 31. Harston tried to save the limp, bloody, smoldering Vandegeer, helped by a marine, until flames drove them off. The copilot burned with his helo.

A group of survivors assembled in the waist-deep water near the shattered front end of Knife 31. There were ten marines and three fliers. Ten men died in the crash; three marines pitched into the surf, riddled by Khmer infantrymen. Three more could not be found. Bullets spattered the water, and RPG shots continued to career crazily off the flaming lump of twisted helicopter. Harston fired his rifle and his personal pistol until both ran out of ammunition. Going to the beach looked uninviting. Knife 23 stood empty and obviously wrecked, and its passengers could not be seen. Although only Harston, Corson, and the other USAF man had life jackets, they gathered up the wounded, shocked, and unarmed marines and began swimming for deep water. They could do nothing on the beach.

As they swam away, they left behind BLT 2/9's tactical air control party radios in the burning aircraft. Nevertheless, marine forward air controller 1st Lt. Terry Tonkin knew that he had to get in touch with tactical aircraft or the other marines on the beach could never make it. Tonkin had been blown across Knife 31 in the explosion, and he had no radio. So he borrowed an air force survival radio from Corson. The lieutenant intentionally separated himself from the rest, as the survival radio aerial attracted serious Khmer attention. As the men paddled slowly from shore, Tonkin began to call for tactical aircraft.

Overhead, three A-7D Corsair IIs of 388th Tactical Fighter Wing watched the developing crisis below. Anders's ABCCC had sent them in as soon as Knife 31's black cloud rose from the island. At first, Capt. Scott Ralston and his wingmen thought that Knife 23 was a rescue helo, sent in to pull people out of blazing Knife 31. After a low pass, they realized that Knife 23 had no tail assembly and showed huge rents across its hull. Ralston's flight picked up Tonkin's call. The Corsairs trained with the Aerospace Rescue and Recovery Service as on-scene tactical response planes, so Ralston and his fellow pilots loitered to help with what they expected next—a search and rescue mission. Instead, after about ten minutes of understandable babble and repeated calls of "Mayday," Tonkin settled down and began bringing down the Corsairs to strafe the Khmer bunkers. Ralston thought Tonkin did "a most fantastic job . . . just like we were at the target range." The strikes worked; Khmer fire subsided enough to let the swimmers pull off.

Unknown to Tonkin, he had markedly improved the chances of Lieutenant Cicere, trapped in a small rocky gully just past stricken Knife 23. The Knife 23 copilot, 1st Lt. John P. Lucas, turned on his own survival radio and picked up on Tonkin's idea. As the marine air controller slowly swam away, Lucas continued to direct air strikes.

Ralston did see something strange on one of his runs. The hulk of Knife 31 leaked a massive stain of bright crimson marker dye, which spread slowly in the crystalline water just off the white beach. It took Ralston a while to determine that the "marker dye" was human blood. He nearly retched. As another pilot later remarked: "It was amazing how such a beautiful South Seas–type island could hold such death." [37]

Colonel Anders in his ABCCC made a decision to divert the remaining eastern beach helos to the west beach. At the time Anders chose that course, Denham's struggling Knife 21 was still puttering along toward its watery grave. By comparison with the murderous eastern beach, the west LZ looked better. At least no RPG gunners had yet appeared in the west. So Knife 32, Jolly 41, Jolly 42, and Jolly 43 banked away from the deadly east LZ. Jolly 43 passenger Major Hendricks remembered looking out the small square windows with Lieutenant Colonel Austin: "We could see a column of dark smoke rising from the eastern zone. At first we were encouraged because we thought the ban against pre-assault airstrikes had been lifted." News of their change in destination convinced the two marine officers of the fatal significance of the towering smoke pillar.

As a result, Knife 32 and Jolly 41 came overhead just as Knife 21 rolled into the warm Gulf of Siam less than a mile offshore. Their arrival freed Knife 22 for its ill-fated landing attempt. Meanwhile, 1st Lt. Michael Lackey and Knife 32 descended to pick up Denham's crew. With the rest of 3rd Platoon, Company G aboard, Lackey had to dump precious fuel in order to accommodate the survivors. He picked up Denham and two others; the flight mechanic could not be found. The three fuel-soaked, waterlogged airmen enjoyed only the briefest respite.

Motivated by the critical situation ashore, Cricket ordered Lackey to head immediately for the west LZ. Knife 32 picked up speed and droned toward the beach. Right on cue, the Khmer buzz saw cranked up. Machine gun bullets walked across the waters and up the helo fuselage. Mortar bursts raised white geysers in the surf. Lieutenant Colonel Denham, tired of being shot at, snatched an M-16 rifle and began firing out a minigun portal. Khmer rifle shots reached into that same opening to wound the USAF sergeant manning the Gatling weapon. The sergeant dropped aside, gushing arterial blood and the telltale foam of a punctured lung from the chasm in his shattered chest. A nearby marine also lurched and crumpled. But Lackey reached the beach.

Staff Sergeant Francis L. Burnett urged his men off the beleaguered helo and onto the strange, deadly sand. They had planned for the other side, but the plan had blown up with Knife 31. As the marines ran for cover, a Khmer RPG man blew a two-foot hole through the side of Lackey's CH-53. Fortunately, the fuel tanks did not blow. Lackey pulled off the LZ, with hydraulic fluid dripping and more than seventy-five holes in his crippled aircraft. Knife 32 barely made it back to U-Tapao, although the wounded sergeant and Denham's shaken Knife 21 men survived the ordeal.[38] Lackey's chopper was out of action.

By about 0700, the last three helicopters tried to make the death ride into the west LZ. The refuelable HH-53Cs had topped off while the Knifes tried their luck, and now they, too, pressed toward Koh Tang. Jolly 41 went first and had to stagger away, with damage to the right fuel tank and ramp hydraulics. Jolly 42 tried an alternate site 1,200 meters south of the beach but could not land due to a violent reaction from the Khmers. Jolly 43's movement toward the actual LZ met a similar response. All three helos circled a few minutes, then tried again.

This time, Jolly 42 went for the main beach and managed to unload its half of 2nd Platoon, Company G. Mortar rounds ravaged the HH-53 as it made the landing, and it limped back to U-Tapao for another in a continuing series of controlled crashes by USAF choppers. Captain Roland Purser of Jolly 43 inserted Austin's BLT command group and a section of four 81-mm mortars in the small sand and rock patch more than a kilometer south of the main LZ. He escaped without major damage and returned to U-Tapao for the second wave. Unlucky Jolly 41 failed in two more approaches due to active enemy mortar barrages across the landing zone, and went to refill its leaking fuel tanks.[39]

The situation at Koh Tang by 0730 looked bleak. American forces on the island huddled in three separate locations: Cicere's outpost in the east, pieces of all three Company G platoons to the west, and Austin's command and mortar sections well south of Company G. Only Cicere's portion of 3rd Platoon and McDaniel's half of 1st Platoon were in the right places. Company G's executive officer, 1st Lt. James Keith, commanded the men on the west beach; his commander had returned to Thailand, an unwilling victim of Knife 22's abort. Of 180 expected infantrymen, 109 arrived, although Jolly 41 still flew offshore waiting to unload another 27 marines. A well-prepared Khmer Rouge infantry company occupied the 340 meters of jungle between the two beaches, deployed in concealed bunkers and trenches that hemmed in both LZs. Neither marines nor airmen saw any evidence of *Mayaguez* crewmen; indeed, no marine units had yet approached the key encampment near the east LZ. If the American captives were on Koh Tang, the vicious firefight in progress certainly menaced their safety. Aerial strafing only magnified this problem.

But what else could the assault wave do? The heavy opposition necessitated an early resort to fire support. Obviously, the three disjointed groups of marines had run into a numerically superior, dug-in enemy. Air power stepped in to even the odds. Standard ground to air radios failed or burned in the downed aircraft, and lack of properly gridded maps made coordination of air strikes difficult. Regardless, determined air force pilots and equally innovative men on the ground like Lucas and Tonkin soon ironed out the problem. Air support improved as the pilots gained familiarity with the enemy deployment, but because USAF forward air controllers (FACs) employed fast-moving A-7Ds rather than their usual slow-flying propeller planes, the fuel-guzzling jet FACs switched often. Each arriving air controller discovered the complex situation anew. Considering that a Khmer company, a marine company, and possible U.S. prisoners were all intermixed in a square kilometer or so of thick jungle, the USAF pilots had to be careful.[40] This explained why Captain Ralston and his fellow fliers restricted their runs to more easily directed 20-mm cannon fire.

The biggest worry after that first hour at Koh Tang must have been the status of helicopters. By 0730, only three airworthy helicopters—a far cry from the promised twelve—had sped back to U-Tapao to pick up the second wave. On-scene commander Colonel Anders retained Jolly 41 for another try at west beach, and Jolly 13 for an attempt to withdraw the Knife 23 marines and crew holed up north of the fatal eastern LZ. About 0800, 1st Lt. Charles Greer turned Jolly 13 toward the debris-strewn beach.

Greer's big HH-53C began to take fire right from the start of his approach. Heavy machine gun bullets pumped into the helicopter, increasing in intensity and supplemented by lighter automatic rifle fire as Greer pulled up north of the derelict Knife 23. The chopper rocked and shook with each impact, although Greer's gunners did their best to suppress the Khmers. Jolly 13 landed successfully, and Greer even glimpsed Cicere's embattled band in their nearby rock cut. The Khmers pinned the marines to the ground, and Greer realized that he could not get them out. His halted helo absorbed continuing punishment. A bullet shattered part of the instrument panel. Simultaneously, the cockpit filled with fumes and choking smoke as two fires broke out aboard the buffeted aircraft. Greer took off while he still could.

As the chopper gained speed and altitude, the more dangerous fire, in an auxiliary fuel pod, blew out. A bold crewman tossed out a burning rescue flare box to extinguish the other conflagration. But Jolly 13 was through, with rotor blades cracked and holed; thirty-five punctures in the hull; and major fuel, oil, and hydraulic leaks. Greer barely made the Thai coast, flopping ashore not far from Ohlmeier's crippled Knife 22.

But Jolly 13's purgatory did expose some of the key Khmer positions to the patient A-7D FAC, who confidently directed other Corsairs down to shoot up the enemy sites with cannon and rocket fire. The FAC used 388th Tactical Fighter Wing F-4E Phantoms to drop bombs, and then followed up by unleashing the heavy cannon array on the nearby Spectre gunship.[41] These strikes muted Khmer pressure against Cicere's men.

Cricket asked the Corsair FAC to duplicate this effort near the west LZ, to permit Jolly 41 to land his marines. First Lieutenant Thomas Cooper's HH-53C waited offshore while the FAC tried to sort out where the marines stopped and the Khmers started.

Meanwhile, Lieutenant Keith had organized his perimeter around the western LZ. The bulk of the Company G marines took up positions in a half circle right near the man-made cut that connected the two beaches, with the 1st Platoon (−) to the south, 2nd Platoon (−) in the center, and 3rd Platoon (−) to the north. The northern two platoons took out two enemy bunkers upon landing and kept up a lively fire on another pesky Khmer machine gun emplacement. But the marines needed more men to break the enemy ring. There were only two sources for more marines: Jolly 41 or the BLT command group a kilometer south.

The Khmer Rouge antiaircraft fire seemed heaviest just south of the Company G position, between Keith and Lieutenant Colonel Austin. Any pressure south of the western beach might help effect a linkup with Austin and remove some of the treacherous enemy machine gun bunkers. So a push in that direction facilitated both of Keith's options to gain combat power.

Working quickly, the Company G executive officer told Lieutenant McDaniel to send a reinforced squad south to do something about the string of active Khmer automatic weapons sites. The 1st Platoon commander led his men boldly forward, right into a punishing Khmer ambush just beyond the marine front line. The heavy foliage blocked visibility as Khmer AK-47s, machine guns, and command-detonated mines staggered the marine patrol. Five marines, including the lieutenant, fell wounded. One marine died in the initial burst of gunfire.

Despite the devastating reception, McDaniel's men stood their ground and returned a vigorous fire of their own. Keith ordered the patrol to pull back. The marines managed to withdraw skillfully, carrying their wounded and killing aggressive Khmers who tried to follow. In the confusion, they left behind the body of the dead marine.

First Platoon had little time to notice, because the Khmers took advantage of their successful ambush to launch a platoon-strength counterattack. This thrust hit the weakened southern U.S. flank just as McDaniel's bloodied patrol came back. The marines could barely see ten feet through the bright green vegetation, but the enemy attackers exposed themselves by their advance. Despite his wounds, McDaniel joined S. Sgt. Seferino Bernal to repulse the Khmers. The enraged marines ravaged the Khmer platoon, which stumbled back in utter disarray and with considerable losses. Even so, the marines and their enemies remained tightly interlocked, separated by a few meters along the perimeter.

With a little breathing room, Keith gained contact with the airborne FAC, who had prudently turned over to the marine BLT tactical operations net. By paying attention during McDaniel's patrol, the air force controller found all the U.S. locations. Together, he and Keith began to walk in air support from the mighty Spectre. The slowly orbiting gunship identified the U.S. forces, with the FAC's help, and opened up on the enemy with 20-mm and 40-mm cannon fire. At times, these shells impacted scant meters from the marines. But Keith knew his business and took his time. Khmer fire slackened to the south.

The abortive marine attack and stout defensive effort, combined with Spectre, cleared the way for Jolly 41. Lieutenant Cooper flew in again, only to pull up as his torn engine cowling flapped open and his rotor blades splintered. The tough fire did not come from the southern coastal bunkers this time.

Austin's command group now joined the air control effort, and reported that most of the enemy gunnery came from a hut and bunker complex to their northeast. Austin and his men correctly identified the key enemy antiaircraft site, all right: the fire emanated from the same encampment that had shot at every U.S. aircraft on 13 and 14 May. But this was also the area thought to contain the U.S. prisoners. Aerial suppression had to be perfectly precise; the USAF must hit only the enemy gun sites and not the buildings.

With this in mind, the A-7D FAC turned again to his most exact weapon, the ungainly AC-130 gunship. The air controller did not want Spectre's 20-mm and 40-mm capability. Instead, he desired a few well-placed, killing shots. Spectre employed its carefully aligned, powerful 105-mm cannon to batter the fortified area and choke off the enemy air defense. The AC-130 then switched back to its lighter guns and addressed the tree line between Keith and Austin, smothering much of the Khmer fire. Jolly 41 tried again.

This time, Cooper made his landing and disembarked all but five of his men. Jolly 41 came under a mortar barrage. The enemy walked five rounds closer and closer to their large target as the marines ran out the back ramp. The sixth landed ten feet behind the tail rotor and sprinkled fragments into the fuselage. Cooper popped up a few feet and drifted to throw off the Khmer mortar crew. As he touched sand again, a mortar shell dropped right through the rotating main rotor blades, bursting just off the side of the aircraft and scattering fragments against the armored hull. Cooper pulled up, and another mortar projectile fell directly into the spot he had just left. This round blew open Jolly 41's belly armor and damaged the cargo ramp. Cooper withdrew to refuel without unloading the last five marines. Anders in the ABCCC ordered Jolly 41 to return to U-Tapao. He, too, barely brought his damaged aircraft home. Jolly 41 flew no more on 15 May.[42] With this, at 0900, the first wave ended.

On west beach, Keith sent newly landed 2nd Lt. Richard H. Zales and his half of 2nd Platoon to back up the endangered southern side of the marine position. To his south, Austin and Hendricks tried to figure out what was going on. They had to head north to link up with Company G (−), consolidate on west beach, bring in the second wave, and then try to find the *Mayaguez* crewmen. Khmer resistance bordered on the fanatic, lending credence to the belief that the enemy held something worth keeping. Overhead, Anders faced the dismal prospect of flying in the second wave with only a handful of helicopters.

With SS *Mayaguez* under the American flag once more and the marines ashore, if not comfortably, at Koh Tang, the location of the captured American mariners began to worry U.S. commanders. Where were they? If on Koh Tang, had they survived the brutal engagement underway?

An indication that something had changed in Phnom Penh came at 0607, just as Lieutenant Colonel Denham took his helicopter over Koh Tang. The Khmer Rouge national radio station broadcast a nineteen-minute harangue by Hu Nim, minister of information and propaganda. At the very end, Hu Nim promised to release the ship with a warning against "further espionage or provocative activities." The crew went unmentioned.

In Washington, President Ford heard of the Khmer Rouge announcement at 2028 on 14 May (0728 on 15 May in Cambodia). Since the crew had not been included in the arrangement (although they were not excluded, either), Ford did not suspend the operations around Koh Tang. Indeed, Major Porter took the ship while Ford read the text of Hu Nim's remarks, and Lieutenant Colonel Austin's men struggled to expand their small enclaves on the island. But the announcement had an immediate effect on USS *Coral Sea*'s aircraft.

Commander Carmichael's first deckload launched at 0705 (2005 Washington time), and the jets formed up and headed for Kompong Som. They planned to be over the harbor by 0745 (2045 Washington time). President Ford sent a flash message to PACOM at 0728: hold the air strike. The president wanted the naval aviators to orbit in place while he made a response to the Khmer message.

Ford's response assured the Khmer Rouge that "as soon as you issue a statement that you are prepared to release the crew members you hold unconditionally and immediately, we will promptly cease military operations." Of course, he and his military chain of command could not possibly know that the Khmer Rouge had released Captain Miller about 0620, and that the Americans and their Thai comrades were en route to Koh Tang even as Ford sent his reply.

For nineteen minutes, Carmichael's jets swung in circles over the Gulf of Siam, burning valuable fuel. *Coral Sea*'s four KA-6D tankers tried to keep the suppression group, fighter escort, and strike element topped off, but this took time. At 0747 (2047 Washington), Ford ordered the strike to proceed immediately. He decided that a radio message did not reflect a wholly credible Khmer Rouge decision.

The delay hobbled the strike. It cost enough fuel to make a full-ordnance attack impossible, yet the hiatus did not allow sufficient opportunity to refuel all of the planes. So the mission of the first wave changed to "armed reconnaissance," with special emphasis on the Khmer Rouge gunboats, aircraft, and merchant fleet around Kompong Som. These planes jettisoned their ordnance at sea. They did find an additional target, the Kompong Som oil refinery. Carrier Air Wing 15 completed this reduced initial mission at 0830.

The next two waves went in on schedule. The second launched at 0845 and struck Ream airfield at 0957, destroying five of twelve Khmer propeller-driven T-28 Trojans and cratering the runway. The attack damaged the hangars as well. The third wave took off at 1020 and attacked the Kompong Som harbor area and the Ream naval station at 1050. These planes battered the naval barracks at Ream, tore up the fuel storage area near the Kompong Som refinery, blew open two dockside warehouses, and wrecked a building in the nearby railroad marshaling yard. The rationale for striking the rail yard and warehouses had to do with their relationship to Khmer naval piers. This wave returned to USS *Coral Sea* by 1120. During the second and third cyclic operations, a total of fifteen attack planes dropped bombs.[43]

Carrier Air Wing 15's results certainly prevented any Khmer Rouge reinforcement of Koh Tang, ruining the pathetic little Khmer air squadron and doing major damage to the Khmer naval patrol flotilla's shore facilities. Enemy opposition proved negligible. Poststrike analysis inflated things at first, in that USS *Coral Sea* originally reported seventeen aircraft destroyed at Ream, and the base only deployed twelve. The use of laser-guided bombs limited collateral damage, but a few laser bombs wandered off-course nevertheless. Still, the *Coral Sea* attacks concentrated on specific military targets. They probably helped convince Phnom Penh that the release of the U.S. merchant mariners represented a good choice, and the damage inhibited the Khmer Rouge gunboats' ability to conduct similar boarding attempts in the future.

Why had the fourth cycle not gone in? The appearance of a small Thai fishing boat at 0949 changed everything.

The Orions of Patrol Squadron 4 continued to switch on and off station as the Koh Tang assault began. The P-3 crews found the captured U.S. ship on 13 May, but since then, they had been reduced to the dull routine of monitoring Khmer Rouge and civilian watercraft around Koh Tang. At 0923 Cricket told the Orion aviators to check out a small patrol boat approaching from Kompong Som. The four-engine Orion heeled over to take a look.

Others also noticed the moving vessel. USS *Wilson* came on scene about 0700 and got involved in recovering the drifting survivors of Knife 31. When lookouts onboard *Holt* saw an unknown boat approaching from the north, Captain Roane, Destroyer Squadron 23 commander (still aboard USS *Holt*), ordered *Wilson* to intercept the forty-foot boat. Roane suspected that the approaching vessel could be a Khmer gunboat. With *Holt* tied up (quite literally), Roane wanted Comdr. J. Michael Rodgers of *Wilson* to block the inbound craft. Unsure of its intentions, Rodgers brought all missiles and guns to bear on the potential target. Was this a Khmer effort to break up the U.S. recovery of the ship? Based upon the furious reaction on the beach, Roane and Rodgers took no chances. But a quick look through *Wilson*'s low-light television system gave Rodgers pause. He thought it looked like a fishing craft, not a warship.

At 0935, Patrol Squadron 4 made the last important find of the *Mayaguez* incident. The aircraft commander reported to Colonel Anders on Cricket: "30 Caucasian persons on board waving white flags." Anders immediately contacted Captain Roane to vector the guided missile destroyer USS *Wilson* to the fishing trawler. Roane told the ABCCC colonel that the U.S. destroyer was already on its way.

At 0949, Rodgers came up even with the small boat. He was amazed to see more than thirty Americans aboard. Like everyone else, he assumed that most of them had been on Koh Tang, on their containership, or maybe on the mainland. Rodgers used his loudspeakers: "Are you the crew of the *Mayaguez?*"

"Yes!"

"Are you all there?"

"Yes!"

"Lay alongside. You are safe now."

USS *Wilson* secured the small boat and the Americans came aboard. Captain Charles Miller reported that all his men were with him, and expressed interest in returning to his own ship. Rodgers allowed his hospital corpsmen to check the crew, and *Wilson*'s intelligence officer debriefed the merchant ship captain. Rodgers signaled Captain Roane, Colonel Anders, and Washington itself using his sophisticated communications devices. By 1000 (2300 in Washington), President Ford had the good news. The crew was free.[44]

This knowledge had some immediate effects. USS *Coral Sea* proceeded with its second cyclic attack and readied its third, awaiting possible cancellation orders. General Burns in Thailand directed Anders to reposition the marines on Koh Tang for maximum air and naval gunfire support. At 1155, the Joint Chiefs ceased all offensive actions off Cambodia. USS *Coral Sea* suspended its fourth raid. Now, extracting the marines became the priority.

On Koh Tang, Lieutenant Colonel Austin did not have the sort of high-powered radios necessary to monitor the news about the *Mayaguez* crew. He had been told that Company D took the ship. At 0935, he requested that Anders prepare to shift part of Major Porter's force back to the *Holt,* to position them to reinforce BLT 2/9 on the island. This had been done, although the helicopter shortage prevented pickup of those marines.

Between 0900 and 1000, the shrunken second wave of helicopters took off from Thailand with part of Capt. Mykle E. Stahl's Company E aboard. Even Capt. James Davis of Company G made the trip, having been retrieved by a search and rescue helicopter from battered Knife 22 at its remote emergency landing site on the Thai coast. USAF mechanics slaved to launch two more CH-53Cs—Knife 51 and Knife 52. Along with Jolly 11, Jolly 12, and Jolly 43, this gave Cricket five helos. At 1000 Austin told Colonel Anders that he needed "an additional rifle company" immediately. This plea was made just as news about the *Mayaguez* crew arrived.

By 1015, General Burns ordered "the termination of assault operations against Koh Tang." Anders responded by turning around the second wave. He figured that those five helos could off-load, then return to pick up the engaged marines. In the process, he did not tell Austin that the crew of *Mayaguez* had been recovered.

Austin, meanwhile, heard the helos turn around, as did Colonel Johnson and his moribund TG 79.9. Johnson sat in frustration most of the morning, hearing the bitter news and watching the battered choppers limp in. The beating taken by the USAF helos left the marine colonel in Thailand, along with much of Company E.

Now Johnson entered the fray, at least by radio. He told Burns and Anders in no uncertain terms: Austin needed the additional troops to stabilize his perimeter and unite his forces. Without the extra marines, successful withdrawal might prove impossible. The USAF officers agreed and turned around the second wave again.[45]

Still, none of the higher commanders had told Austin about the *Mayaguez* crew. So the BLT commander continued his mission. He and his twenty-eight radio operators, mortar men, clerks, and staff officers, including two navy medical corpsmen, pressed north along the coast. As Major Hendricks later recounted, they "advanced aggressively" to hide their small numbers. The headquarters and mortar men rolled up the Khmer positions, using grenades and rifle fire and capturing automatic weapons, a 57-mm recoilless rifle, and a 60-mm mortar on the way. They used these items to expedite their push. By about 1200, Austin's and Keith's elements could see each other. The two officers devised a linkup plan by radio.

Basically, Lieutenant Keith intended to send Lieutenant Zales's 2nd Platoon south to ease the entry of the command section into the perimeter. An 81-mm barrage and close air support would prepare the way.

Now things got tricky. Second Lieutenant I. I. McMenamin's 81-mm section opened fire, shooting its small stock of rounds that the men had lugged more than a kilometer under fire. The mortars used an estimation method not found in any field manuals, as McMenamin plunked the first round out to sea and then adjusted off the fall of shot. The second round burst right on the enemy bunker line. Major Hendricks saw the 81-mm shells strike "scant yards in front of Lieutenant Keith's Marines." But that was where the explosions belonged.

As the 81-mm section started to fire for effect, desperate Khmers rose up and assaulted Keith's southern flank. Both marine elements halted their linkup attack and allowed mortars and close air support to pummel the hapless Khmers in the gap between the two forces. Air force Corsairs merely lined one wing over Company G and the other over the command group and bombed away. As the last A-7 peeled off, the marines executed their linkup.

Marine mortars chugged out rounds, silencing a Khmer 82-mm mortar, blowing aside an enemy recoilless rifle, and caving in a series of bunker roofs. As the mortar men fired their last few shots out of smoking tubes, McDaniel's 1st Platoon opened up a murderous suppressive fire to pin the enemy, and Zales charged forward with his men.

Zales's excited marines scrambled forward to the south, crunching through the debris of the enemy fighting positions and dispatching resilient Khmers. McMenamin used his last 81-mm rounds to cover the platoon's eastern flank, which lay exposed to the man-made lane that ran to the other beach. Out of projectiles, McMenamin and his mortar crew joined the action, counterattacking a Khmer squad moving down the open logging cut. By 1221, the two western marine units joined up.

At almost the same time, four of the five helicopters of the second wave landed on the western LZ, discharging a hundred Company E marines, including Captain Davis and his Company G command element. Once again, some of these helos diverted from the horrific fire on the east LZ. Knife 52 did not even try to land in the west; it had been shot to pieces trying to land on the east beach, and it headed slowly back to U-Tapao. Knife 51 and Jolly 43 aborted their runs on the dangerous east side and tried the west with success. Indeed, the four landings just before 1300 were the most "normal" so far; the USAF choppers even removed six critically wounded marines. Although four helicopters took fire and suffered minor damage, the damage caused by the marines' violent linkup attacks and heavy air attacks had greatly weakened the Khmer defenses.

As welcome as these successful deliveries were, the news they brought exceeded even the importance of their fresh marines. Captain Stahl told Austin that *Wilson* picked up the entire *Mayaguez* crew, and that the next helicopters that came would be for withdrawal of the BLT (−).

The marines consolidated their enlarged perimeter, dug in, and prepared to hold until relieved. Austin thought that "there was little doubt" he could hold overnight if required. Major Hendricks noted that other than a need for more fresh water, the marines were "in good condition to hold." Austin asked permission of the ABCCC to move overland to secure Lieutenant Cicere, but he was told to wait. Helicopters would try first. General Burns told Anders to make sure Austin realized that all would be pulled out by nightfall, "provided the eastern zone could be evacuated first." [46]

Why this stipulation? If the air evacuation failed in the east, Austin would probably have been told to punch overland to pick up the beleaguered half platoon. But Burns had no desire to start a bloody, time-consuming drive through the Khmer-held jungle now that the *Mayaguez* and its crew had been secured. He wanted to let the USAF helicopters try again.

By 1300 on 15 May, Colonel Anders had four working helicopters and six hours of daylight left to pull the plug on his Koh Tang operations. Thanks to the recovery of the crew and ship, he could use whatever firepower he needed. USS *Coral Sea*'s pounding eliminated any serious threat of Khmer Rouge aid from the mainland.

The local Seventh Air Force and navy planes dealt with Khmer craft already in the area. Off Koh Tang, vigilant USAF Phantom jets sank a suspicious barge about noon. *Coral Sea* Corsairs destroyed a small patrol craft with 20-mm fire at 1240. Finally, two more patrol vessels approached Koh Tang. The 388th Tactical Fighter Wing Phantoms dropped bombs and fired rockets without effect. A swing wing Aardvark from the 347th Tactical Fighter Wing finished off one elusive boat with eight 2,000-pound bombs. None hit, but the thunderous concussions stove in the Khmer boat's hull.[47] By 1300, no Khmer naval elements challenged the U.S. air blockade. Anders was free to begin his withdrawal.

About 1415, the Cricket staff sent the refueled, empty Jolly 11 and Jolly 43 to the treacherous eastern LZ, backed by the two 127-mm guns of USS *Wilson*. The big navy ship transferred the happy *Mayaguez* crew back to their merchantship around noon, leaving *Wilson* free to help cover the extraction effort. Commander Rodgers hoped the close approach of his guided missile destroyer might intimidate the enemy. He began to fire in support of Cicere almost as soon as the destroyer came opposite the eastern beach. As with the airplanes, Rodgers's gunnery plotters found themselves limited by maddeningly inexact charts that showed Koh Tang as a featureless, amorphous blotch bearing little resemblance to the real island. *Wilson* shot its first 127-mm projectile intentionally well out in the surf, then the competent air force pilots walked subsequent naval cannon rounds directly onto troublesome Khmer positions.

While *Wilson* punished the Khmers, the two big HH-53Cs waited offshore as an A-7D Corsair ripped across the east beach, dumping tear gas. As the choppers banked for their run, the wind blew the chemical cloud harmlessly out to sea. Captain Roland Purser's Jolly 43 went in first, suffering the by now familiar beating. A minigun jammed, and the rear gunner spun aside, peppered with shell fragments. Despite Jolly 11's covering fire, Purser's helo took major hits. Hot mortar fragments ruptured a fuel line, and raw aviation fuel spurted into the crew cabin. An engine ground to a screeching stop. Jolly 11 Gatling gunners spat bullets back at the Khmer ground troops as Purser pulled his shot-up helo off the fire-swept beach. Leaking fuel sprayed the interior of the chopper. Purser headed directly for USS *Coral Sea,* about seventy miles to the southeast and closing steadily.

But once again, the truncated landing tipped off a Khmer position. In the tiny marine perimeter, grounded Knife 23 copilot Lucas called the A-7D FAC to report that Khmer antiaircraft teams lay hidden on the seemingly abandoned PCF stuck on the reef. Spectre had forced this gunboat aground early on 14 May, but it remained intact. Evidently, the Khmer Rouge machine gun teams emerged only when helicopters were over the beach. Their pop-up shooting coordinated with the beach defenders to lock American helos in a lattice of heavy fire. Before any other extraction, the gunboat would have to go. So the FAC sent in other Corsairs. The small attack jets strafed the stranded gunboat repeatedly, but no Khmer soldiers emerged.[48] Although showing tatters and wrecked deck work, the PCF still squatted out there.

Just before 1600, two slow-flying OV-10A "Nail" propeller air-control planes came over Koh Tang to take control of the evacuation effort. These twin-engine aircraft each carried four internally mounted 7.62-mm machine guns and pods of marker rockets. The high FAC briefed inbound tactical aircraft and checked their ordnance loadings. The low FAC, Maj. Robert Undorf, took charge of the actual strike direction. Colonel Anders in Cricket appointed Undorf to handle the "on-scene command responsibility" to execute the withdrawal. For the first time all day, the marines could talk to an unchanging source of air support. Unlike the various A-7D FACs, Undorf possessed a plane with real endurance. The Nails were built for FAC work.

While changing over with the jet FAC, Major Undorf learned of the stubborn gunboat out on the reef. Once Undorf identified the target, he cleared USS *Wilson* to engage the boat. Commander Rodgers closed and his gunnery teams took aim. A few ranging rounds flushed about six Khmers, who disappeared in a fiery blast when *Wilson* scored a direct hit. The gunboat heeled over on its perch and coughed up secondary explosions as ammunition and fuel supplies blew up. An oily black smoke column marked the end of the PCF antiaircraft nest.

Even as *Wilson* finished off the enemy vessel, Undorf surveyed the friendly positions. Austin's dug-in western defenses stretched well across the narrow island neck, with advanced listening posts reaching the middle of the cleared lane. Undorf drew especially heavy fire from the east beach troop compound, where marines so long ago had expected to find the *Mayaguez* crew. Although Spectre 105-mm shots had knocked out a few bunkers, the observant FAC noticed that the heaviest machine guns now fired from the previously avoided buildings and temporary structures. The low Nail decided to solve this problem once and for all.

Just before 1700, Undorf increased his pace of activities due to two urgent radio transmissions. On the ground, Lieutenant Cicere spotted Khmers maneuvering to the north to surround the compressed marine defensive pocket. He started taking regular fire from his north flank. In the air, Lieutenant Backlund aboard Jolly 11 finished refueling. He had been flying steadily since 0415, with one break to pick up part of Company E. Backlund reminded Undorf in harsh terms that darkness was a mere two hours away. The Jolly 11 pilot recommended heavy suppressive bombing and strafing, followed by another attempt. He spoke directly:

"It's time to get the action going!" Undorf realized that he had the man for the job.

The FAC brought in 388th Tactical Fighter Wing Phantoms and Corsairs to plaster the enemy encampment buildings, stifling gunfire with explosives. Undorf swooped down and saw corpses sprawled out. It was time to try the extraction.

Undorf mustered his forces. In the air, he had Jolly 12, with a fresh crew and reloaded ammunition. Lieutenant Richard C. Brims's Knife 51 also arrived from U-Tapao. Finally, USS *Wilson* provided eight experienced "brown-water" sailors and two M-60 7.62-mm machine guns aboard Black Velvet 1, the destroyer's gig. When Backlund made his move, these other elements would cover.

In addition, Colonel Anders of Seventh Air Force suspended a huge hammer over the island. Five 374th Tactical Airlift Wing C-130 cargo planes rumbled over Koh Tang. One carried supplies; the other four carried massive BLU-82 15,000-pound landing zone excavation bombs, the largest conventional munitions in the U.S. arsenal. The planes planned on using their adverse weather cargo delivery systems for some makeshift bombardier work. Anders's ABCCC directed the lead C-130 to drop its immense load as Jolly 11 tried its run. To avoid hurting marines, the ABCCC designated an impact point well south of the U.S. forces. Khmer Rouge reinforcements had been sighted moving north to menace the withdrawal. Although Colonel Johnson at U-Tapao thought that Lieutenant Colonel Austin should employ the big bombs as he needed, the Seventh Air Force EC-130 passed control of the mighty implements to Major Undorf. Undorf intended to use one.

Backlund brought Jolly 11 in very fast and low, aiming directly at the marines' marking smoke grenade. Even though Jolly 12, Knife 51, and Black Velvet 1 battered the Khmer fighting positions, Backlund's helicopter bucked and jumped as enemy bullets thunked against the armored skin. With the tide up, it was a tight fit. Backlund shoved his tail right into the marines' rocky hideout and hovered his nose out over the surf. Backlund described the scene as the men fought their way aboard: "I guess the Marines and crew of Knife 23 knew this was the last train out of town, because they came right out. It was an orderly withdrawal. They came out firing their weapons behind them and each man emptied his M-16 into the treeline before scrambling up the ramp."

But the Khmers did not give up so easily. One brave enemy rifleman ran out to throw a hand grenade into the open ramp; air force S. Sgt. Harry W. Cash cut him apart with the blazing minigun. The grenade exploded just beyond the whirling tail rotor. A USAF photographer on Jolly 11, like his compatriot from Knife 23, found himself shooting rifle slugs, not pictures. As Jolly 12, Knife 51, and Black Velvet 1 moved broadside to the beach and unleashed a particularly heavy fusillade, Jolly 11 lifted with all aboard. A big 12.7-mm Khmer machine gun opened up, popping white fountains of water after the departing HH-53C. Undorf himself rolled in to strafe and silence the large weapon. With many wounded men among its thankful passengers, Jolly 11 headed directly for the nearby USS *Coral Sea*. Backlund's exhausted, bone-weary crew and disintegrating aircraft had completed their contribution to the effort.

As Jolly 11 loaded, Capt. Ronald Edmiston dumped his BLU-82 out the back ramp of his trundling cargo plane. The bomb tumbled down, exploded, and threw trees like matchsticks. It punched an area the size of a football field into smoking flatness. Any Khmers within fifty meters died instantly as the blast overpressure ruptured their internal organs. It might have drawn off enemy attention; it certainly ended the Khmer movement from the south end of the island.

Once Jolly 11 accelerated out of the deadly LZ, Undorf brought in Spectre to smash the enemy sites exposed by the extraction. Then, he sent A-7Ds to bomb the pugnacious enemy unit once again. Finally, he sent in Jolly 12, now under Capt. Barry Walls, to search Knife 23 for an injured Knife 31 marine believed to be sheltering in the hulk. Knife 51 supported by fire. No one could be found, and Jolly 12 received crippling damage in the effort. It barely made it to the *Coral Sea;* days later, sailors used a crane to remove the shattered chopper.[49]

Undorf still retained Knife 51, which he sent to the west beach. Incredibly, air force and navy mechanics on *Coral Sea* were able to tape together Jolly 43's broken fuel line. The chopper, too, returned to the island. From the north, Jolly 44, which had been left out of action all day for repairs on the mainland, now entered the action. So Undorf deployed three helicopters to evacuate 200 marines.

Fortunately, he also possessed landing platforms in close proximity. USS *Coral Sea* had already accepted limping helicopters during the afternoon. Just offshore, USS *Holt* took up station. Commander Peterson's ship had been released at last from towing, assisting, and finally escorting the freed *Mayaguez*. Now the containership was steaming for Singapore under her own power, guided by her own crew. *Holt* stood ready to receive choppers from the western beach.

Darkness began to draw its curtain over the island. In the failing light, about 1830, Knife 51 headed for the western beach. Major Hendricks and his marine infantry at first thought it was a resupply chopper, and watched it weather "an almost unbelievable hail of small arms and automatic weapons fire. . . . Tracers streamed into the perimeter and bounced around like flaming popcorn."

The exact pullout time had not been arranged beforehand, but Austin's men had a plan. All the marine commander requested was that the operation go swiftly. As marines left the defense line, the opportunity might arise for a crushing Khmer counterattack. Given the ferocity of the day's combat, Austin's plea made sense. Major Undorf agreed; provided no more helos went out of action, he thought the USAF could do the job.

As Knife 51 loaded, patched-up Jolly 43 and Jolly 44 loitered off the coast, just out of range. Black Velvet 1 delivered accurate machine gun bursts. In a pinch, the USN gig might itself become an alternative means of extraction. Knife 51 lifted in the last shreds of daylight, attracting a terrific barrage, including a near-miss by an RPG. It appeared that the Khmers were redeploying forces from the east beach. Braving the vicious fire, Knife 51 picked up the forty-one marines of the BLT (−) reserve and headed directly for the *Coral Sea*.

About 1900, Undorf tried to call in tactical jets, but it was already too dim to bring them in so close to the embattled marines. He allowed the choppers to go in without suppression. Jolly 43 and Jolly 44 nearly collided, because enemy bullets had destroyed Jolly 44's landing lights. Captain Purser packed fifty-four marines into Jolly 43 and limped to the *Coral Sea* with his overloaded, shot-up aircraft barely above the dark tropical water.

As Jolly 43 lifted off with the command group, Major Hendricks looked down from the laboring chopper. The view stayed with him as his battered transportation struggled away from the hellish scene. "The last thing I saw of the island," he said, "was the half circle of the perimeter blazing away at the larger circle of fire surrounding it." Captain James Davis of Company G took charge of the shrinking marine bastion.

Jolly 44 wriggled in after an abort, and as it loaded, Davis moved his forces to within fifty meters of the beach LZ. With this in mind, Undorf rolled in and strafed the enemy with his own OV-10A, supplemented by the energetic gun teams on Black Velvet 1 offshore. Helped by this supporting fire, Lt. Robert Blough on Jolly 44 ascended slowly off the beach with thirty-two marines, avoiding most of a blizzard of green enemy tracers. But at this juncture, about 1930, things reached an impasse. All three helos were gone to drop their passengers, Khmer pressure was building, and the moonless tropical night made navigation impossible. Davis told his men to set up a strobe light to guide in the next choppers, and the shrunken American perimeter braced for the next round of enemy attacks.

As he pulled up and gathered speed, Blough in Jolly 44 heard the marines' radio net go dead. Gravely concerned, he elected to cut his turnaround time by diverting to USS *Holt* just offshore. He banked hard toward the tiny helicopter platform on the destroyer escort, and after careful maneuvering without the aid of his broken lighting system, he discharged the men and clattered back into the fire-swept landing zone.

At about 1945, Major Undorf began to fear the worst. He was low on fuel and busy briefing his replacement when communications with Captain Davis shut down. To allay his worries, Undorf swooped over the beach with his bright landing lights shining in order to verify that the marines were still there. A fountain of green dots reached for the nimble Nail, but the air force FAC saw that the marines' position remained very much intact, albeit hotly engaged. Satisfied, Undorf and his high FAC departed to refuel.

Captain Seth Wilson assumed duties as low FAC and on-scene commander. The Spectre over Koh Tang also gave way to an inbound AC-130H gunship, which quickly detected the marine positions on its night vision and infrared sensing devices. Within a few minutes, the new Spectre began laying a curtain of steady fire to protect the men on the ground.

At the beach, Captain Davis realized that the crisis had come. After feverish work, he reestablished radio communications with the Nail plane overhead. Davis told Captain Wilson that the marines faced heavy probes and fire, and the Khmers appeared to be maneuvering for a major attack, even though Spectre pounded away. Wilson advised Davis that Jolly 44 and Knife 51 were inbound. Two minutes later, the marine captain told Wilson: "Go for broke!"

Jolly 44 got there first, shoveled forty-four tired marines aboard, and scuttled off for the *Coral Sea,* skimming the wave tops as it went.

Saltwater ruined the HH-53C's overstrained engines, and the big chopper made it to *Coral Sea* but no farther. It was 2005.

Knife 51 arrived at this juncture, with the twenty-nine remaining marines clinging to a small slice of Koh Tang. Captain Wilson shot his marking rockets; Spectre let loose with a steady, deafening broadside; and Knife 51 cleared its own way with roaring miniguns. But the fireworks confused the fliers, and Knife 51 had to back off. It took five tries to land the helicopter, and that occurred only after Lt. Richard C. Brims boldly illuminated his brilliant white landing lights. Twenty-seven marines deliberately pulled back to the helo, firing as they went. The glaring white lights, ripping Spectre guns, chattering miniguns, and barking M-16s mixed with the cracks and stutters of Khmer shooting. The enemy fire intensified as Brims turned off his lights. But two marines were not yet aboard.

Captain Davis and Gunnery Sgt. Lester A. McNemar of the marines, with T. Sgt. Wayne Fisk of the air force, crouched low as they rushed about the littered sand. Angry bullets snapped and whizzed around them. They found the last two marines, still hotly exchanging rifle shots, and hustled them to Knife 51. At about 2015, Brims took off, chased by the fiery green tracers of 12.7-mm enemy machine guns.

The Khmers fruitlessly expended massive amounts of ammunition as Spectre withdrew and Captain Wilson pulled offshore. Then the enemy guns ceased firing, after a few last pops. Wilson banked his OV-10A and departed about 2030.[50] The operation was over.

Behind, fires crackled in the rubble of the eastern encampment. In the center of the black, finally silent western beach, the single white eye of the marines' strobe blinked on and on, vainly calling for helicopters that need never return.

The successful recovery of the SS *Mayaguez* brought about immediate positive reaction in America, especially given the trauma associated with the April evacuations from Phnom Penh and Saigon. Democratic Congressman Carroll Hubbard of Kentucky summarized the national mood: "It's good to win one for a change."[51] President Ford's decisive action had saved the ship and its forty crewmen from the clutches of the Khmer Rouge. A few dissenting voices spoke up, especially after the final casualty list came out.

The *Mayaguez* operation worked, but at a cost. Of 231 marines who had set foot on Koh Tang, more than a quarter suffered wounds. The U.S. lost 68 killed, missing, and wounded. Some "Monday morning quarterbacks" added in the 23 unlucky victims of the 13 May Nakhon Phanom crash to bring the American losses to 91 men. No matter how one counted, the mission took its toll. Conservative U.S. estimates of Khmer casualties amounted to 102 enemy killed and wounded.

What caused the heavy losses? Facile analysis blamed two factors: an "intelligence failure" and the resultant "ill-conceived, hasty attack" on Koh Tang. Supposedly, it all could have (and should have) been avoided. An October 1976 General Accounting Office after-action review concentrated on these particular issues. But such contentions do not really explain anything.

Comparative Loss Summary
Personnel

	KIA	MIA	WIA	PW	Nonbattle Deaths
U.S. Army	0	0	0	0	0
U.S. Navy/USMC	13	3	44	0	0
U.S. Air Force	2	0	6	0	23
U.S. MILITARY TOTAL	15	3	50	0	23
Khmer Rouge	47	?	55	0	0

Equipment

U.S. Military: 3 USAF helicopters destroyed; 4 USAF helicopters severely damaged; 6 USAF helicopters damaged.

Khmer Rouge: 4 PCF Swift patrol gunboats sunk; 4 PCF Swift gunboats damaged; 1 barge sunk; 5 patrol boats sunk; 5 aircraft destroyed; Kompong Som refinery fuel storage damaged; Ream naval station damaged; Ream airfield cratered.

Sources: Comptroller General, "The Seizure of the *Mayaguez*" in U.S. Congress, House of Representatives, Committee on International Affairs, *Seizure of the Mayaguez: Part IV*, 94th Congress, 2nd Session, 4 October 1976, 65, 116–26; Capt. Thomas D. Des Brisay, "Fourteen Hours at Koh Tang" in *USAF Southeast Asia Monograph Series, Volume 3* (Washington, D.C.: U.S. Government Printing Office, 1977), 149, 152–54.

The "intelligence failure" argument represents twenty-twenty hindsight. According to this logic, intelligence officers should have intuitively "known" that the few inconclusive shards of evidence suggesting the movement of the U.S. prisoners away from Koh Tang were far more important than the greater weight of reports, patterns, and observations to the contrary. Given the short time available and the nature of on-scene surveillance, the intelligence assessments make sense. Any assumption that the crew departed Koh Tang represented a risky shot in the dark; the safe bet placed most of the American captives on the island. The intelligence system functioned well under pressure, but the men running it demonstrated their humanity by guessing wrong. But who could have predicted the Khmer decision to grant the crew an unconditional release?

The *Mayaguez* operation certainly may have gone better, but not without significant changes in the available time, resources, and information. To rescue the supposed American prisoners, the marines had to fly in close and take their lumps. They might have limited their losses, but not avoided them.

Given that the Koh Tang attack seemed a sound action, what caused the heavy casualties on the island? To answer that question truthfully, one must consider the more serious mistakes of omission and commission, and then isolate those that magnified the human toll. Allowing the danger-ous nature of the mission itself, five problems hobbled recovery operations in the Gulf of Siam: incomplete communication of known information, some interference from Washington, poor beach reconnaissance, the in-nate weaknesses of helicopters, and fierce Khmer Rouge resistance. Each of these contributed to the difficulty of executing an already challenging mission, but only the last two factors directly cost lives and limbs.

The quick assembly of a mixed, ad hoc USAF/USMC/USN force without time for full face-to-face coordination created an environment that limited the easy flow of important news. In some cases, such as the work of Major Porter and Commander Peterson in planning the boarding from USS *Holt* or the employment of air, mortar, and naval fire support, modification of known plans or procedures bridged the gap. The biggest "black hole" yawned between the Seventh Air Force and the marines. Colonel Johnson's TG 79.9 was supposed to bridge that chasm, but did not. The marines ashore were too busy; they needed someone else to prod Seventh Air Force regularly for the sort of data vital to the marines. In general, the marines gained much of their informa-tion from the better-informed USAF helo pilots.

As a result, Lieutenant Colonel Austin missed out on some vital messages known to Seventh Air Force, including a fairly accurate PACOM estimate of Khmer strength, the news of the U.S. prisoners' safety, and the exact timing of the helicopter withdrawal. The first piece of data did not even reach the helicopter pilots, although they heard of the second two points well before the marines on the island. TG 79.9's planning activity proved invaluable, but the impotence of this headquarters during the execution phase created real trouble.

Had Colonel Johnson deployed on schedule with the second wave, perhaps some of this might have been avoided. The marine colonel and his staff complained bitterly about being ''left out,'' but Johnson did some of this to himself. His personal insistence on trying to accompany the assault wave and then, when helicopters ran short, the second wave, shows that Colonel Johnson knew that he should set the example and see the situation first hand. But commanders have staffs to be where they cannot be. Although Johnson controlled five staff officers, he assigned no TG 79.9 officers to the ABCCC, nor did he fly any to Seventh Air Force headquarters at Nakhon Phanom. Instead, he gambled everything on helicopters. As a marine familiar with rotary wing operations, he might have covered his bets a bit better.

High-level intervention also influenced the operation. Unfortunately, Washington leaders made some use of instant communications to direct actions that might have been better left to General Burns and his subordinates. Most of Washington's requests for information or authorizations to fire were not especially critical and had little effect on military actions under way. But USS *Coral Sea*'s air wing felt the effects of such activity when the first wave dropped its bombs at sea during a delay. Certainly, diplomatic initiatives necessitated this action, and the naval aviators could understand that.

Interestingly, in his memoirs, President Gerald Ford excoriated ''high-level bumbling'' in the Pentagon, blaming the military for the failure of the first and fourth carrier cycles to bomb targets. The annoyed chief executive thought somebody had disobeyed orders: ''I was anxious to find out who had contravened my authority. The explanations I received from the Pentagon were not satisfactory at all, and direct answers kept eluding me. Perhaps I should have pursued my inquiry, but since we had achieved our objective, I let the matter drop.'' [52]

The president said that he specifically directed four attacks, and indeed, he had. But he also altered those original orders. Ford held up the first wave while he considered the Khmer broadcast that promised to release the U.S. ship unharmed; then, nineteen minutes later, the president ordered the first cycle to proceed immediately. The president evidently did not realize that carrier wings do not have enough tanker aircraft to "mark time" in midair and then fly off on a moment's notice. The naval officers took reasonable action; they jettisoned ordnance and continued the mission as an armed reconnaissance. As for the fourth strike, the president himself suspended offensive operations, an order duly passed at 1155 hours. As a result, the fourth attack wave, scheduled to hit Kompong Som around 1205, did not conduct their offensive operations. So President Ford "contravened" his own earlier decisions. Evidently, the military staff was a little too respectful and indirect in trying to suggest this situation to Ford.

But the president was not stupid; he had served on the aircraft carrier USS *Monterey* during World War II. He was tired and very concerned when he issued his contradictory orders, and he probably did not intend to confuse his commanders. But the temptation to second guess and "micro-manage" distant efforts can be strong, and having the president on the telephone is not something a general can ignore. Everyone wants to "do something"; the nation's commander in chief naturally wants to command. Professional soldiers learn the hard way that one must often wait hours while things develop. Often the best solution means doing nothing. Even the energetic General Patton recommended giving military operations sufficient time to get going before jumping in.[53] It is usually better to assign missions and let the men on the scene decide how to execute them, then give them enough time to do so. Long-distance squad leading adds to the fog of war. Fortunately, only the navy aviators really felt the effects of such behavior, and the direct repercussions for the entire recovery effort were insignificant. But it is a good example of the problem.

One seemingly small point that loomed very large concerned beach reconnaissance. A pass over Koh Tang in an army airplane represented a poor substitute for a thorough reconnaissance by SEALs or Marine Force Reconnaissance men in small boats. A battalion landing team afloat almost always has such men attached; it is not clear if Lieutenant Colonel Austin possessed these vital units. Had they been present, they may have been inserted on the night of 14–15 May. These small teams had the capabilities to save BLT 2/9 a great deal of trouble on 15 May. Skilled scouts could have located Khmer units and pinpointed air defense weapons; perhaps these highly trained men might have determined that the *Mayaguez* crew was not present on the island. In any event, when the marines next crossed an opposed surf line in Grenada, they employed beach surveillance teams.

The marines' conveyance caused a major problem. Indeed, the combat assault on Koh Tang subjected the big air force helicopters to a hellish gauntlet of ground fire. Despite armor and miniguns, thirteen of fourteen choppers sustained significant damage, although only three actually crashed. Of the eighteen dead and missing on the island, all but one died in or around beleaguered helicopters. Many of the wounded sustained their injuries onboard or near the helos as well. The twenty-three men lost in the pre-assault mishap also reflect the perils of helicopter missions, particularly at low level and in limited lighting.

The argument that somehow all would have gone better with more prelanding suppression seems specious. First, such a bombardment threatened the American captives the marines wanted to secure. Second, one should not forget that the later lifts featured vigorous coordinated use of Spectre gunship cannons, mortar fire, naval gunnery, air strafing, and aerial bombing. Yet those helos still took tremendous damage, and not all accomplished their missions.

Given all of this, why were USAF CH-53s and HH-53s employed? Was this a mistake? It appears not. Helicopters are superbly versatile machines, perfect for entering and leaving small areas. They can hover, they can drop directly down, and they can lift straight upward. The skilled, resourceful USAF pilots could not have been better. Almost all were veterans of the grueling April 1975 evacuation efforts, and many had flown combat missions during the height of the Vietnam War. Their competence encouraged planners to risk the dicey helicopter assault. As bad as losses were, most happened right off, with the Knife 31 disaster accounting for sixteen of eighteen dead and missing. Of course, there really was no alternative, at least not until 16 May when USS *Hancock* arrived with landing craft in company. USAF helos offered the only transportation available on 15 May. Without the long-range air force choppers, no rescue attempt could have occurred.

Rotary wing aircraft, especially big ones, work well with surprise and the use of a landing zone that allows a mass disembarkation of infantry to inundate the enemy defenses quickly. With surprise blown for all but the lead helos and with tiny landing zones, there was sure to be trouble on Koh Tang. Normally, chopper units mitigate such difficulties by using heavy supporting fires to smother enemy antiaircraft sites and concurrent ground or seaborne operations to spread enemy attentions thin. The nature of the American mission precluded such options. Certainly, the USAF pilots expected to take a beating; their determination and courage overcame the limitations of their strained airframes.

Helicopters by nature are slow, mechanically finicky, and vulnerable to enemy fire. Dangling them in enclosed spaces in front of determined gunners begs for disaster. The large size of the USAF choppers only magnified their attraction for Khmer Rouge gunners. Worse, as the choppers fell out of action, the marine position on Koh Tang became precarious. The big helos represented their only ticket in and out of the island. With but fourteen rotary wing aircraft on hand, the marines really gambled that the choppers would hang in there. Certainly, the BLT could have held on until the next day if necessary. But reliance on a limited number of helicopters alone to get on and off Koh Tang directly affected the eventual heavy losses, and added an element of unpleasant desperation to the operation. The Khmer Rouge marksmen knew where to aim for maximum damage; the marines had no choice but to swarm around their vulnerable transportation.

Finally, the stiff Khmer Rouge resistance cannot be discounted. The enemy used camouflage brilliantly, and Khmer units proved well-shielded from heavy U.S. fires. The enemy infantry achieved maximum effects from their light weapons; the Khmers did their damage without anything bigger than mortars, RPGs, and heavy machine guns. Their supply of ammunition seemed inexhaustible. Somebody on Koh Tang knew the business of combat, prepared to fight, and challenged the marines and air force crews with ferocity. Undaunted by the U.S. ships and planes, the Khmer Rouge fought furiously right to the end.

Given these problem areas, especially the casualties attributable to the reliance on vulnerable rotary wing craft and the violent Khmer Rouge response, could the marines have saved the American sailors on Koh Tang, had these prisoners in fact been ashore in the eastern camp site? A successful rescue seems very doubtful. No marines even approached the eastern beach buildings; indeed, Lieutenant Cicere's battered half platoon on the east LZ barely saw more of Koh Tang than the thirty feet or so around them. By the time Austin's diverted western units could have forced their way across to the suspected holding area, the Khmers might easily have killed all of the U.S. captives. Had the Americans not been recovered by 0630, they would have been dead men, barring some bizarre Khmer Rouge decision. Fortunately, the Khmers made a different choice under strong American duress, and released the *Mayaguez* crew unharmed.

The Khmers caved in because, despite some planning and execution mistakes, President Gerald Ford and his chain of command massed and used multicapable armed forces decisively. America gathered a formidable combat contingent quickly, which provided General Burns of Seventh Air Force with enough power to carry out a series of related operations, plus sufficient uncommitted strength (like USS *Wilson*) to deal with unexpected events. The U.S. did not pin all hopes to a single operation. Burns orchestrated a powerful air blockade, a ship seizure, naval actions, the Koh Tang assault, and mainland strikes over a few days. Any or all of these varied, interrelated operations could have compelled the Khmers into releasing their captives. A setback in one area (such as at Koh Tang) did not imperil the entire effort; in fact, it proved irrelevant in a strategic sense. The successful *Mayaguez* recovery effort demonstrated the virtues of mass and flexibility in planning and execution.

The quick-arriving USAF air blockaders probably made the most significant contribution to eventual victory. According to Captain Miller, the strong American air response on 13 and 14 May worried his captors and evidently impressed the Phnom Penh ruling clique with American resolve. The nervous Khmer Rouge watched the well-armed USAF planes circle and released the crew even before the U.S. retook the *Mayaguez* or bombed Cambodia.

Besides massing a flexible array of combat power, the president and his subordinate generals and admirals decided quickly and did not waver in their resolve. The military designed the operations and conducted them as soon as possible. Other than some troubles with USS *Coral Sea*'s air strikes, President Ford left military matters to military men. Given the domestic sensitivity to American actions around Southeast Asia that existed in May 1975, the early choice to rely on a military solution truly appears courageous. Dithering about would have likely produced another *Pueblo* episode. Instead, the American leadership acted rapidly; by late on 14 May, the U.S. seized the initiative. The Khmers reacted by backing down.

Finally, the American marines, airmen, and sailors displayed tremendous bravery and ability, influenced by strong tactical leadership. Men like Lieutenant Colonel Austin and Lieutenant Colonel Denham led the way in person. At sea, the unopposed boarding effort went off like

Mayaguez Recovery Time Line
(Local Cambodian Time)
12–15 May 1975

12 May—(1418)—SS *Mayaguez* fired upon and boarded by Khmer Rouge forces.

(1612)—National Military Command Center received notification of incident.

(1830)—Joint Chiefs directed Pacific Command to commence reconnaissance.

(1840)—President Ford notified.

(2037)—PACOM ordered USS *Holt* toward Cambodian waters.

(2057)—Patrol aircraft launched.

(0112)—USS *Coral Sea* battle group diverted toward Cambodia.

(0816)—SS *Mayaguez* located off Poulo Wai Island.

(1325)—SS *Mayaguez* anchored off Koh Tang Island.

(1724)—Patrol aircraft reported Caucasian people being moved from SS *Mayaguez* to Koh Tang.

13 May—(2310)—Joint Chiefs ordered USAF Security Police to prepare for a possible rescue; helicopter crashed during staging.

14 May—(0720)—Cambodian gunboat sunk while running for mainland.

(0745)—Fishing boat with "possible Caucasians" moved to mainland.

15 May—(0345)—President Ford approved U.S. military action.

(0550)—USS *Holt* received boarding party.

(0607)—Assault began on Koh Tang. Khmer Rouge broadcast an offer to release the ship; the crew is not mentioned.

(0725)—SS *Mayaguez* seized in boarding action.

(0745)—USS *Coral Sea* launched an armed reconnaissance against Kompong Som.

(0949)—USS *Wilson* recovered *Mayaguez* crew from fishing boat.

(0957)—Second *Coral Sea* strike attacked Ream targets.

(1050)—Third *Coral Sea* strike bombed Kompong Som and Ream targets.

(1155)—Joint Chiefs ordered suspension of offensive actions and preparations for withdrawal.

(1230)—Second wave of marines landed.

(2015)—All marines evacuated.

clockwork, without a full dress rehearsal or much margin for error. Navy and air force fliers found the U.S. vessel, sealed the ocean and air around the containership and the island, and flew day and night into the teeth of ferocious antiaircraft fire. On Koh Tang, intrepid pilots made crippled machines do the impossible and a lot more, and junior marine officers and sergeants mastered exceptional adversity to take charge of their beachhead by 1300 on 15 May. The marines could have reinforced, pushed out, and gained control of the island, had that still been necessary. As the otherwise highly critical General Accounting Office report admitted, "The performance of U.S. forces was inspiring." [54]

Strangely, in 1975 few Americans thought that the *Mayaguez* incident represented anything but an unusual, hopeful epilogue to the long, painful U.S. war in Indochina. The names of the eighteen marines, sailors, and airmen who died on that sunny day in the Gulf of Siam can be found on the grim black granite wall of the Vietnam Veterans' Memorial. The seizure and recovery of SS *Mayaguez* did not reflect the final chapter of a closed book, however, but the harbinger of things to come.

Chapter 1 Notes

Epigraphs come from Gerald R. Ford, *A Time to Heal* (New York: Harper & Row, 1979), 276, and William Manchester, *Goodbye Darkness* (Boston: Little, Brown & Co., 1979), 223.

1. Richard G. Head, Frisco W. Short, and Robert C. McFarlane, *Crisis Resolution: Presidential Decision Making in the Mayaguez and Korean Confrontations* (Boulder, CO: Westview Press, 1978), 104; Comptroller General, "The Seizure of the *Mayaguez*" in U.S. Congress, House of Representatives, Committee on International Affairs, *Seizure of the Mayaguez: Part IV,* 94th Congress, 2nd Session, 4 October 1976, 62, 127.
2. Comptroller General, "Seizure of the *Mayaguez*," 127.
3. Comptroller General, "System to Warn U.S. Mariners of Potential Political/Military Hazards" in U.S. Congress, House of Representatives, Committee on International Affairs, *Seizure of the Mayaguez: Part IV,* 94th Congress, 2nd Session, 4 October 1976, 12, 17–19.
4. Ibid., 25; Comptroller General, "Seizure of the *Mayaguez*," 115, 116; Head et al., *Crisis Resolution,* 104–06.
5. Comptroller General, "Seizure of the *Mayaguez*," 87, 88, 116, 117.
6. Ibid., 72, 73, 117; Comdr. J. A. Messegee, USN, "Mayday for the *Mayaguez:* The Patrol Squadron Skipper" in *Proceedings* (November 1976), 94, 95.
7. Head et al., *Crisis Resolution,* 110, 111; Comptroller General, "Seizure of the *Mayaguez*," 76, 87, 112, 117; Ford, *A Time to Heal,* 276, 277.
8. Ford, *A Time to Heal,* 277.
9. Comptroller General, "Seizure of the *Mayaguez*," 72, 73.
10. Messegee, "The Patrol Squadron Skipper," 95, 96; Capt. John B. Taylor, USAF, "Air Mission *Mayaguez*" in *Airman* (February 1976), 40; Capt. Thomas D. Des Brisay, USAF, "Fourteen Hours at Koh Tang" in *USAF Southeast Asia Monograph Series, Volume 3* (Washington, D.C.: U.S. Government Printing Office, 1977), 95.
11. Messegee, "The Patrol Squadron Skipper," 96; Comptroller General, "Seizure of the *Mayaguez*," 118, 119; Taylor, "Air Mission *Mayaguez*," 40.
12. Messegee, "The Patrol Squadron Skipper," 96; Comptroller General, "Seizure of the *Mayaguez*," 73, 74, 76, 119; Taylor, "Air Mission *Mayaguez*," 40.
13. Capt. Walter J. Wood, USMC, "Mayday for the *Mayaguez:* The Company Commander" in *Proceedings* (November 1976), 100, 101; Comptroller General, "Seizure of the *Mayaguez*," 86–88, 120.
14. Comptroller General, "Seizure of the *Mayaguez*," 76, 77.
15. Earl H. Tilford, *The United States Air Force Search and Rescue in Southeast*

Asia (Washington, D.C.: U.S. Government Printing Office, 1981), 147.

16. "Ship, Iran Incidents Cost 27 Lives" in *Air Force Times* (4 June 1975), 22.

17. Maj. John B. Hendricks, USMC, "Mayday for the *Mayaguez:* The Battalion Operations Officer" in *Proceedings* (November 1976), 104; Col. John M. Johnson, USMC, Lt. Col. Randall W. Austin, USMC, and Maj. D. A. Quinlan, USMC, "Individual Heroism Overcame Awkward Command Relationships, Confusion, and Bad Information Off the Cambodian Coast" in *Marine Corps Gazette* (October 1977), 26; Comptroller General, "Seizure of the *Mayaguez*," 88.

18. Comptroller General, "Seizure of the *Mayaguez*," 112, 113, 117, 118; Ford, *A Time to Heal*, 277; Head et al., *Crisis Resolution*, 114–116.

19. Tilford, *The USAF Search and Rescue in Southeast Asia*, 147; Ray L. Bowers, *United States Air Force in Southeast Asia: Tactical Airlift* (Washington, D.C.: U.S. Government Printing Office, 1983), 645; Taylor, "Air Mission *Mayaguez*," 40; "Ship, Iran Incidents Cost 27 Lives," 22; Hendricks, "The Battalion Operations Officer," 104; Comptroller General, "The Seizure of the *Mayaguez*," 88, 119, 120.

20. Wood, "The Company Commander," 100, 101.

21. Des Brisay, "Fourteen Hours at Koh Tang," 98; Comptroller General, "Seizure of the *Mayaguez*," 120; Tilford, *The USAF Search and Rescue in Southeast Asia*, 147.

22. Comptroller General, "Seizure of the *Mayaguez*," 74, 75, 77, 121; Taylor, "Air Mission *Mayaguez*," 40, 41.

23. Comptroller General, "Seizure of the *Mayaguez*," 74, 75, 113, 114.

24. Ibid., 113, 114, 121; Ford, *A Time to Heal*, 278, 279; Head, et al., *Crisis Resolution*, 116–18.

25. Johnson et al., "Individual Heroism," 26, 27, 29.

26. Comptroller General, "Seizure of the *Mayaguez*," 69, 94, 95, 121, 122.

27. Ibid., 73–78, 89, 110; Johnson et al., "Individual Heroism," 27.

28. Johnson et al., "Individual Heroism," 27, 28; Hendricks, "The Battalion Operations Officer," 104; Woods, "The Company Commander," 101; Comptroller General, "Seizure of the *Mayaguez*," 89–92; Howard L. Rosenberg, "Six Brave Men" in *Sealift* (July 1975), 6.

29. Comptroller General, "Seizure of the *Mayaguez*," 89, 90, 97, 122; Hendricks, "The Battalion Operations Officer," 104; Johnson et al., "Individual Heroism," 28, 29.

30. Ford, *A Time to Heal*, 279, 280; Comptroller General, "Seizure of the *Mayaguez*," 66, 67, 114, 115; Head et al., *Crisis Resolution*, 122, 123, 131.

31. Hendricks, "The Battalion Operations Officer," 105; Comptroller General,

"Seizure of the *Mayaguez*," 123; Johnson et al., "Individual Heroism," 29; Taylor, "Air Mission *Mayaguez*," 41, 42.

32. Rosenberg, "Six Brave Men," 6.

33. Comptroller General, "Seizure of the *Mayaguez*," 96, 97; Ray Bonds, ed., *The U.S. War Machine* (New York: Crown Publishers, Inc., 1983), 180, 204, 242; "Air Wing Deployment to Selected Aircraft Carriers" in *Strategy and Tactics,* No. 63 (July/August 1977), 22; "People, Planes, and Places," *Naval Aviation News* (August 1975), 26; Michael Skinner, *USN* (Novato, CA: Presidio Press, Inc., 1986), 46, 130, 131.

34. Rosenberg, "Six Brave Men," 6; Wood, "The Company Commander," 103; Taylor, "Air Mission *Mayaguez*," 42; Comdr. Robert A. Peterson, "Mayday for the *Mayaguez:* The Destroyer Escort's Skipper," *Proceedings* (November 1976), 97, 99.

35. Peterson, "The Destroyer Escort's Skipper," 97, 99; Johnson et al., "Individual Heroism," 29; Wood, "The Company Commander," 101–04; Rosenberg, "Six Brave Men," 7.

36. Taylor, "Air Mission *Mayaguez*," 42; Des Brisay, "Fourteen Hours at Koh Tang," 106, 107; Johnson et al., "Individual Heroism," 30.

37. Johnson et al., "Individual Heroism," 29, 30; Des Brisay, "Fourteen Hours at Koh Tang," 111–15; Taylor, "Air Mission *Mayaguez*," 43; Capt. John B. Taylor, USAF, "For Extraordinary Heroism," *Airman* (February 1976), 44.

38. Johnson, et al., "Individual Heroism," 30, 33; Taylor, "Air Mission *Mayaguez*," 42, 43; Hendricks, "The Battalion Operations Officer," 105; Des Brisay, "Fourteen Hours at Koh Tang," 107–11.

39. Taylor, "Air Mission *Mayaguez*," 44; Des Brisay, "Fourteen Hours at Koh Tang," 119, 120.

40. Johnson et al., "Individual Heroism," 30–31, 33; Des Brisay, "Fourteen Hours at Koh Tang," 120.

41. Taylor, "Air Mission *Mayaguez*," 44; Des Brisay, "Fourteen Hours at Koh Tang," 120–22; "Aircraft Play Major Role in Ship Incident," *Aviation Week and Space Technology* (19 May 1986), 23.

42. Des Brisay, "Fourteen Hours at Koh Tang," 123–30; Taylor, "Air Mission *Mayaguez*," 44; Johnson et al., "Individual Heroism," 30–33; Tilford, *The USAF Search and Rescue in Southeast Asia,* 152; "Mayaguez Toll:68," *Navy Times* (4 June 1975), 3.

43. Comptroller General, "The Seizure of the *Mayaguez*," 67, 96, 97, 124, 125; Ford, *A Time to Heal,* 282, 283; Head et al., *Crisis Resolution,* 133, 138.

44. Messegee, "The Patrol Squadron Skipper," 97; Comptroller General, "The Seizure of the *Mayaguez*," 125; Taylor, "Air Mission *Mayaguez*," 45; Head et al., *Crisis Resolution,* 138, 140; Ford, *A Time to Heal,* 283;

Comdr. J. Michael Rodgers, "Mayday for the *Mayaguez:* The Guided-Missile Destroyer's Skipper," *Proceedings* (November 1976), 109.

45. Comptroller General, "Seizure of the *Mayaguez*," 125; Wood, "The Company Commander," 104; Johnson et al., "Individual Heroism," 32, 34; Des Brisay, "Fourteen Hours at Koh Tang," 130.

46. Johnson et al., "Individual Heroism," 32–34; Hendricks, "The Battalion Operations Officer," 105–07; Des Brisay, "Fourteen Hours at Koh Tang," 134; Taylor, "Air Mission *Mayaguez*," 46.

47. Comptroller General, "Seizure of the *Mayaguez*," 125, 126; Taylor, "Air Mission *Mayaguez*," 46.

48. Rodgers, "The Guided-Missile Destroyer's Skipper," 110, 111; Des Brisay, "Fourteen Hours at Koh Tang," 135, 137, 138; Bonds, *The U.S. War Machine*, 200, 201.

49. "Undorf Wins MacKay Trophy," *Air Force Times* (25 October 1976), 31; Bowers, *Tactical Airlift*, 646; Des Brisay, "Fourteen Hours at Koh Tang," 139–46; Taylor, "Air Mission *Mayaguez*," 46; Hendricks, "The Battalion Operations Officer," 107; Rodgers, "The Guided-Missile Destroyer's Skipper," 111; Tilford, *The USAF Search and Rescue in Southeast Asia*, 153; Comptroller General, "Seizure of the *Mayaguez*," 94; Maj. John F. Guilmartin, USAF, "Rescue: Yesterday, Today, and Tomorrow," *MAC Flyer* (September 1975), 6.

50. Peterson, "The Guided-Missile Destroyer Skipper," 100; Des Brisay, "Fourteen Hours at Koh Tang," 146–49; Johnson et al., "Individual Heroism," 34; Hendricks, "The Battalion Operations Officer," 107; Taylor, "Air Mission *Mayaguez*," 46, 47; Guilmartin, "Rescue: Yesterday, Today, and Tomorrow," 6.

51. Ford, *A Time to Heal*, 284.

52. Ibid.

53. Gen. George S. Patton, USA, *War As I Knew It* (New York: Pyramid Books, 1970), 299.

54. Comptroller General, "Seizure of the *Mayaguez*," 100.

CHAPTER 2

DUST AND ASHES: THE IRANIAN HOSTAGE RESCUE

APRIL 1980

> *Akbar: "Carter has also threatened additional economic sanctions against us, and he says if that does not lead to your release, he may use military force."*
>
> *Colonel Scott: "I'm surprised that hasn't been done already. Any other American president would have given you a deadline for our release, then blasted hell out of your country."*
>
> *Akbar: "But then all of you would be killed."*
>
> *Colonel Scott: "That's right, but the crisis would be over and people like you would think twice before pulling a stunt like this the next time."*

Conversation in the captured U.S. Embassy, Tehran, early April 1980

> *"The mission on which they were embarked was a humanitarian mission. It was not directed against Iran; it was not directed against the people of Iran. It was not undertaken with any feeling of hostility toward Iran or its people. It has caused no Iranian casualties."*
>
> President James Earl Carter, 25 April 1980

> *"I don't understate the value of military knowledge, but if men make war in slavish obedience to rules, they will fail."*
>
> Ulysses S. Grant

Broad April skies deepened to purple as the sinking golden sun lit the distant western horizon. The calm waters of the Gulf of Oman sparkled and rippled in the failing light. Aboard the aircraft carrier USS *Nimitz*, the roar of turbine engines blasted at the scurrying deckhands and mechanics while they made final checks on the eight large, sand-colored RH-53D Sea Stallions spotted along the wide flight deck. Beyond the horizon, USS *Coral Sea* sailed into the warm evening wind, launching F-4N Phantom II jet fighters to cover the grim gray warships of Task Force 70. The American sailors performed their duties with special vigilance, because these were not friendly waters, nor were these friendly times. The region already bore wry nicknames, "Camel Station" or "Gonzo Station," echoing the Vietnam War's aircraft carrier concentrations at Yankee Station and Dixie Station. War threats hung in the humid evening air.

Half a hundred miles north of the U.S. Navy ships lay implacably hostile Iran, where fifty unlucky American diplomats, military attaches, marine guards, and embassy staff personnel endured their sixth month of squalid imprisonment in the captured American Embassy in Tehran. The senior American diplomat, *charge d'affaires* L. Bruce Laingen, and two others languished a few blocks south at the foreign ministry building. In the phrase of their noisy, well-armed young captors, the Americans were "guests of the revolution."

It had happened before, but unlike a brief takeover in February 1979, this occupation did not end quickly. The unfortunate Americans became the focus for years of pent-up Iranian frustration against the ousted Shah Mohammed Reza Pahlavi. The shah had ruled for years, financed by oil dollars; protected by his sizable army and dreaded SAVAK secret police; and backed by American arms, technology, and advisers. The shah policed the restive Persian Gulf for America, and America gave and sold the shah the implements and knowledge necessary to create a modern industrial state from old Persia. Although the shah dragged his nation far along the road to progress, many Iranians objected to the breakdown of traditional ways. Shah Mohammed Reza could not quell increasingly violent outbursts among Shiite Islamic fundamentalists. These religious fanatics were unimpressed with westernization, modernity, and the "Great Satan"—America. They wanted Iran administered as a traditional Islamic country, for and by Iranians. If that meant staying in the medieval era, so be it. Encouraged by America to loosen his iron-fisted rule in the name of human rights, the hapless shah lost his grip completely in late 1978. His army failed him, his SAVAK crumbled, and the United States could offer no succor. So Mohammed Reza Pahlavi

United States Forces Order of Battle

United States Joint Task Force 1-79
U.S. Army units
  1st Special Forces Operations Detachment—Delta (+)
    A Squadron (+) "Red Element" (48 men)
    B Squadron (−) "Blue Element" (32 men)
    HQ, Selection, and Training Section "White Element" (13 men)
    Volunteer Drivers (12 men)
    Translators/guides (2 men)
    Special Assault Team, 10th Special Forces Group (13 men)
  Company C, 1-75 Airborne Rangers

U.S. Navy/U.S. Marine Corps units
  Helicopter Force*
    Helicopters and pilots, Helicopter Mine Countermeasures Squadron 16
    Pilots, Marine Air Groups 16 and 26
  Python Force (90 marines)
  Task Force 70
    USS *Nimitz* (CVN-68) with Carrier Air Wing 8 (CVW-8), USS *Virginia* (CGN-36), USS *Texas* (CGN-39)
    USS *Coral Sea* (CV-43) with Carrier Air Wing 14 (CVW-14), USS *Halsey* (CG-23), USS *William H. Standley* (CG-32), USS *John Paul Jones* (DDG-32), USS *Schofield* (FFG-3)
  Marine Amphibious Readiness Group (Marine Amphibious Unit embarked)**
    USS *Okinawa* (LPH-3), USS *San Bernardino* (LST-1189), USS *Alamo* (LSD-33), USS *Mobile* (LKA-115)

U.S. Air Force Units
  1st Special Operations Wing (−): 8th & 16th Special Operations Squadrons
    Combat Control Team
    Road Watch Team#
  Detachments, Strategic Air Command (SAC): tankers only
  Detachments, 552nd Airborne Warning and Control Wing##
  Detachments, Military Airlift Command (MAC)

* This element included thirteen marines, two U.S. Navy aviators, and one air force pilot.
** The marines were available but not assigned to JTF 1-79.
# This unit contained Rangers and Delta support personnel.
EC-130Es converted as fuel tankers came from 7th Airborne Command and Control Squadron. E-3A Sentry AWACS also participated.

Sources: Comdr. Brent Baker, "Naval and Maritime Events 1980," *Proceedings* (May 1981), 49, 50; Journalists' Mate 1st Class Ken Cronk, "100 Days," *Naval Aviation News* (July 1980), 31.

abdicated his throne during the January–February 1979 Iranian Revolution.

Shiite Muslim madman Ayatollah Ruhollah Khomeini, who had exhorted the revolutionaries from his exile in Paris, returned in triumph and took over. He and his Islamic Revolutionary Party demanded the shah's head and the shah's money, but the former monarch fled to Egypt, where tough Anwar Sadat ignored Khomeini's pleas. Outbreaks of random violence occurred at anti-American demonstrations, and Khomeini charged that America was instigating diabolical plans to sunder Islamic revolutionary solidarity. A weak civil government in Tehran maintained a semblance of normal authority, restoring order at the U.S. Embassy in February and promising to do likewise in the event of future mob action. But a single American decision, made to help the cancer-ridden, doomed shah, created a groundswell of Iranian resentment so great that the weak Tehran officialdom could not effect matters.

United States President James Earl Carter allowed former Shah Mohammed Reza Pahlavi to enter America for cancer treatment on 22 October 1979. The Iranian Provisional Government reacted with moderate disapproval and the Tehran police controlled the resultant protest demonstrations. The U.S. legation reported a 3,500-strong rally on 1 November as "peaceful and controlled," and noted that the Iranian officials "cooperated fully" in keeping things orderly. But this was merely the calm before the storm. In the workers' neighborhoods and student quarters of Tehran, Khomeini's minions stoked inchoate rage among many Iranians into a snarling but focused frenzy, aimed at the hated Americans who now sheltered the despised shah. The nearly defenseless American diplomatic compound in downtown Tehran offered a tempting target for public outrage.

On Sunday, 4 November 1979, hundreds of rabid, armed Iranian militants stormed and seized the U.S. Embassy. The Iranian college students and militiamen wanted the return of their ex-ruler for a revolutionary trial and brutal "Islamic justice." They also insisted on return of the shah's "stolen" fortune. To emphasize these desires, the occupying factions announced that their sixty-six American prisoners would serve as hostages. Dark hints of spy trials, "war crimes" hearings for Vietnam veterans on the American staff, and public executions emanated from the boisterous student sentinels. Chanting crowds filled the streets around the captured U.S. buildings: "Death to Carter! Death to America!" These violent mobs burned American flags and hung effigies of Carter and Uncle Sam. American citizens at home saw all of it in vivid color on nightly television news programs, often live via satellite.

The Iranian civil government, despite previous guarantees to President Carter and international law regarding diplomatic immunities, did nothing. Several Iranian political leaders resigned. Although the guards released thirteen black and female Americans within two weeks, it became obvious that the real power in Iran, Khomeini, endorsed the militants' seizure and their inordinate demands. Such a policy suited his own political purposes, uniting his fractious, fratricidal revolutionary party. So it had gone, for six months, as America tried diplomacy, approached Iranian moderates, imposed various economic sanctions, appealed for help from allies, turned to the Red Cross, requested United Nations' assistance, and finally cut diplomatic relations.[1] Now it was 24 April 1980, and the American armed forces would take their turn at resolving this difficult situation.

About 1905, USS *Nimitz* swung into the breeze, placing the bloated evening sun astern. On deck, the helicopters ran up their engines, facing the coming night to the east. *Nimitz*'s wide turn also allowed the American air element to avoid a Soviet surveillance trawler in the Strait of Hormuz. About twelve minutes later, Lt. Col. Edward R. Seiffert, USMC, increased power on his twin-engined Sea Stallion, hovered, and tilted forward. Although Col. Charles H. Pitman, USMC (aboard number five) selected, trained, and commanded the helicopter element, Seiffert served as lead pilot. Pitman would give the key orders, but the highly capable Seiffert led the formation in the air.

Within minutes, the other seven choppers joined Seiffert's number one in a loose orbit near the *Nimitz*. Each carried extra fuel tanks and special combat equipment, to include a pair of .50-caliber machine guns, but no passengers except their own tense crews. They would pick up their riders later. The slab-sided craft banked and assumed a rough diamond formation, two in the lead, two in the trail, and an element of two draped on both flanks. By 1930, the rotary wing group headed to the north.

Seiffert lowered his force to the surface of the darkening waves, and the pilots turned on their AN/PVS-5 night vision goggles as daylight faded. They saw the other ghostly, unlit aircraft around them, as if through a greenish fog. Pilots looking through these devices could not make out their own cockpit instruments, so their copilots did not wear goggles. The ungoggled fliers monitored the control panels, watched the warning systems, and read the maps. About every thirty minutes, the aviators switched these taxing roles. They had flown many hours like this across the American southwestern deserts, practicing for this opportunity. Now it was for real. Seiffert pointed his chopper's blunt nose toward the Iranian coast.

Meanwhile, off to the west, six four-engine turboprop transports also flew toward the enemy shore. They had begun taking off at 1800, from Oman's Masirah Island. These planes, three MC-130E Combat Talons with troops and equipment and three EC-130E Hercules carrying two 3,000-gallon fuel "blivets" (collapsible rubber reservoirs) apiece, leveled off at about two thousand feet as they crossed the Gulf of Oman. The lead Combat Talon, with transport commander Col. James H. Kyle, USAF, and ground force commander Col. Charles A. Beckwith, USA, aboard, preceded the other five aircraft by about one hour. Along with the two colonels rode the thirty-two men of Blue Element (from B Squadron, 1st Special Forces Operations Detachment—Delta, commanded by Maj. Logan Fitch), the small USAF combat control team, and a twelve-man road watch team (six army rangers and six Delta men) with their gun jeep and motorcycles. One trailing MC-130E carried Red Element (forty-eight men of A Squadron, Delta, reinforced); the other held White Element (thirteen other Deltas), twelve drivers, two Farsi language translators/guides, and a separate special assault team (thirteen non-Delta Green Berets trained to recover the three hostages at the foreign ministry building). Like the helicopters, the heavily loaded C-130s dropped low as they neared the Iranian shoreline.

It was nearly dark when the helicopters entered Iran at 100 feet, skirting between the unalerted Iranian radars at Jask to the west and Chah Bahar to the east. Although chopper number eight's pilot noted an indicator of trouble in the rotor gearbox, he pressed on. No messages were passed; Seiffert intended to conduct his low-level intrusion under absolute radio silence. The marine aviator planned to bring his machines through a gap in the 5,400-foot Makran Mountains, then turn northwest toward Tehran. The helo commander hoped to run along the northern rim of the Zagros Mountain chain, his path covered by this 4,000-foot range with its irregularly spaced 9,000-foot peaks. Each Sea Stallion carried sophisticated OMEGA and PINS (palletized inertial navigation system) equipment, but Seiffert spoke for his team when he said: "Our primary means of navigation, even with OMEGA and PINS, is still dead reckoning." In other words, the pilots used their maps, their identifi-

United States Command Organization
24 April 1980

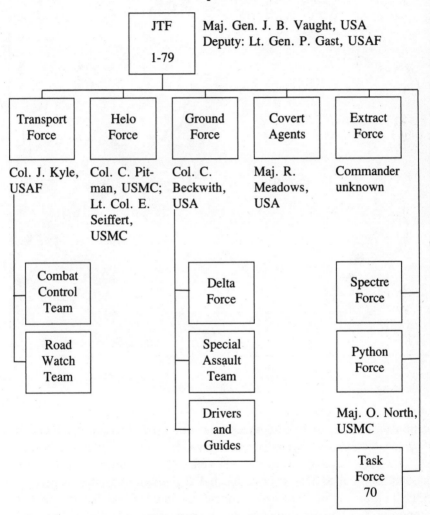

Aircraft from USN Task Force 70 were available to cover the extraction. General Vaught intended to accompany the extraction force.

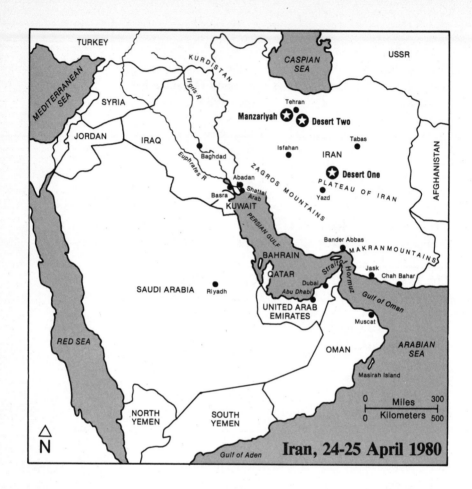

Iran, 24-25 April 1980

cation of terrain, their compasses, and time and distance calculations. The aviators trusted eyeballs and brains, not temperamental avionics.

Seiffert's destination was not yet Tehran but a carefully chosen intermediate site called Desert One, located at the extreme limit of the RH-53Ds' range, about 600 miles inland on the Dasht-e-Kavir salt flats along the Yazd-Tabas highway. Here, the helos would rendezvous with Colonel Kyle's transports, refuel from the EC-130Es, embark the Delta Force, and then continue on to the vicinity of the Iranian capital. The air force turboprops were to return to Masirah Island once they offloaded.

As the eight RH-53Ds sped north at 120 knots, Seiffert observed that winds and weather conformed to the preflight briefing. According to confirming weather photography from satellite NOAA 6, transmitted at 1903 local time on 24 April, the only thunderstorm cells in Iran lay on the other side of the Zagros.[2] The route looked clear. Seiffert anticipated arrival at Desert One by 2345, a bit behind schedule but well within the timetable.

Colonel Kyle's black Combat Talon made landfall west of Chah Bahar and the chopper diamond, dropping to 400 feet as it crossed the surf line. Colonel Beckwith recalled hot air inundating the plane as it descended, and he saw the Makran Mountains loom out of the descending night. The careful air force pilots swerved and banked, climbed and dipped, following the savage landscape and avoiding the spotty Iranian radar coverage. In the rear, some of the roadwatch team Rangers suffered motion sickness in all the bucking, but most of the men sat patiently in the dim, red-lit cabin. Some slept, or at least tried to do so. Aside from the unexpected jolts, rattling climbs, and intermittent turns, the flight was uneventful. Colonel Kyle told Beckwith he had monitored the news that Seiffert's helos successfully left the *Nimitz*. Both men smiled: so far, so good.

Shortly after 2100, Kyle's transport entered a "fog bank" that turned out to be a vast cloud of suspended dust (known as a haboob). Since the Combat Talon's forward looking infrared (FLIR) scanners and inertial navigation systems could handle the great reduction in visibility, Colonel Kyle did not break radio silence to report the unexpected phenomenon to the overall U.S. Joint Task Force 1-79 headquarters at Qena, Egypt. Kyle judged that the need to make an undetected incursion into Iran also precluded a transmission to the slower helicopter contingent. Iran possessed some radio direction–finding capacities, and it did not seem wise to test their true mettle as yet.

About 2200, the MC-130E swung around for its approach to Desert One. Tense fliers had already donned AN/PVS-5 night vision goggles and the radar navigator was directing the slow descent. A few miles out, the pilot activated a set of telltale remote-controlled beacon lights that outlined a segment of hard, unimproved shoulder paralleling the east-west Yazd to Tabas road. The flight crew would not have found these little indicators without knowing exactly where to look on the dark desert floor. The lights were courtesy of a 31 March landing by a small Central Intelligence Agency aircraft. Three operatives, including the USAF major in command of the combat control team, had landed on the Posht-e Badam salt hardpan, taken soil samples, and planted the vital lighting system. While on this hour-long foray, the Americans had noticed six vehicles motoring along the nearby road. But the passing traffic had not noticed them. Thus Posht-e Badam became Desert One.

The U.S. plane veered off from its first approach to avoid a vehicle humming slowly along the road. After a circle and another missed landing attempt, the Combat Talon bounced to a landing on its third approach, rolling east and moving off to the south of the touchdown area. Engines remained running as the rear ramp opened. Colonel Kyle's combat control team quickly left the aircraft to set up the Desert One command post, only to discover that the jouncing of the flight or landing had ruined the secure voice component on their radio. If Kyle used his radio, the Iranians (or even the Soviets) might well understand his clear voice transmissions. Hopefully, no such talk would be needed; besides, a backup would arrive on the third transport.

Beckwith's men also ran into an immediate problem. A chartered Mercedes bus, with headlights shining and forty-four Iranians aboard, lumbered up just as the MC-130E turned off the impromptu runway. The ground force's road watch team drove their machine gun jeep and two motorcycles down the MC-130E's ramp and moved off to block the highway, only to run smack into the oblivious Iranian bus travelers.

Colonel Beckwith fired a warning shot, as did a Ranger. The vehicle motored on. Major Fitch's Blue Element ran up to assist. His men shot to disable, punching a hole in the radiator and blowing out a tire. The wayward bus stopped with a screech of brakes.

The headlights were shut off, and forty-four very frightened Iranians, mostly old people and children, walked down the narrow steps at gunpoint. In accord with Delta's premission orders, they were searched, interrogated, and guarded. Beckwith intended to return these innocent civilians to Masirah with Colonel Kyle's six aircraft. But for now, they were kept clear of the area. The Delta soldiers smartly moved the bus aside. It all seemed rather routine; nobody worried about a possible compromise of security at the hands of bedraggled Iranian bus passengers. As Beckwith later boasted: "I wasn't going to worry until we stopped ten buses. Then we'd have a parking problem."

With these strange interlopers accounted for, the road watch team moved out to its distant blocking positions well east and west of the Desert One landing and parking areas. The small but potent security teams would stop any further visitors well short of the landing strip. Their pair of snorting bikes mounted headlights on spacer bars; at a distance, they would look like stalled trucks. Since Beckwith expected most unwitting intruders from the east (toward Tabas), he deployed a jeep and motorcycle team there first. Instead, trouble arose at the other end.

Motorcycle-riding Capt. Wade Ishimoto barely got his men to their designated western position when he and his Ranger passenger encountered a speeding gasoline tank truck. The big fuel carrier blew right by Ishimoto's other men, and Ishimoto's Ranger partner unleashed an M72A2 light antitank weapon, an unguided rocket that smashed into the speeding truck and created a terrific explosion. The vehicle lurched aside and halted, blazing wildly. Ishimoto dismounted from his motorcycle and tried to approach the burning tanker's cab. He was amazed to see a small Iranian leap out and run madly around the back of the brightly flaming wreck. Ishimoto gave chase, only to see a small pickup truck just behind the conflagration. Another Iranian helped the panicked driver in, then spun about and roared off toward Yazd, crashing off the road surface to head cross-country. Ishimoto returned to his cycle on the run, but he could not get it kick-started in the excitement. The Iranians escaped.

Beckwith did not allow the truck episode to upset him. He presumed (and U.S. intelligence agencies later agreed) that the men were gasoline smugglers who probably mistook Beckwith's men for local police or militiamen. The Delta team wore a decidedly unmilitary uniform: scuffed combat boots, blue jeans, flak vests, army field jackets dyed black, dark flannel shirts, and navy watch caps (small dark blue woolen toques), with tape-covered U.S. flags sewn on the upper sleeves. The tape would be removed during the embassy assault. But for now, the rough-hewn Delta troops would not be mistaken for American soldiers. Many had long hair and shaggy mustaches, and the blond-haired men had dyed their hair black. Whatever the gasoline truckers saw, they made no known report.[3] Beckwith's calm reaction was well-founded.

He would have been much more nervous if he had known of the perilous state of the approaching helicopter force. After clearing the Makran range, Lieutenant Colonel Seiffert's eight aircraft skimmed northwest behind the towering black Zagros crags, popping and dropping across the rough Iranian topography. About 2130, the pilot of helo number six received an ominous cockpit warning light, which signified possible loss of nitrogen pressure in a rotor blade. If the light were correct, the blade might have experienced a crack. Continued flight, particularly strenuous low-altitude maneuvers, could cause the spar to break off, resulting in a catastrophic loss of control. The only way to be sure was to check an instrument on the blade itself. So number six broke formation, landed, and shut down. Crew evaluation confirmed the worst: the blade inspection method (BIM) gauge showed a "black BIM." Taking off in number six seemed to risk rotor disintegration.

Without orders, in radio silence, helicopter number eight landed nearby. In accord with previously arranged procedures, the number six flight crew collected all classified materials and boarded number eight. The flight crews did not have any reliable means to destroy the downed helo, and left it intact, fearful that an explosion could alert any Iranians in the area. It was disappointing, but not disastrous.

After the successful pickup, number eight took off to catch up with the other six choppers. Radio silence remained intact; neither Colonel Pitman nor Lieutenant Colonel Seiffert heard of the incident as they pressed on through the starlit Iranian desert. Because their vision was limited by the green-soup view of their night goggles, the marine commanders probably could see only their own wingmen. With both number six and its wing craft missing, nobody noticed that the diamond had become an arrowhead.

At 2230, Seiffert and his flock entered a dust "fog bank," the same one Kyle's MC-130E had encountered earlier. The hanging talc cloud, typical to Iranian deserts and not unknown in the United States, extended many miles from side to side and thousands of feet up. But whereas the American variety normally persisted just a few minutes, an Iranian powder blanket might hang for hours in the still air. The fliers had already pressed themselves and their machines to the very limits of their capabilities; now they steeled themselves to go beyond those limits.

The choppers did not have enough fuel to avoid the haboob, and fear of Iranian radar kept them from flying above the mess. Kyle's planes had crossed Iran at 400 feet, but the helos remained as close to 100 feet as possible, where the cloud was much thicker. Seiffert and his fellows recalled an offhand comment in their training about the low-level technical features of Iranian radars. Despite the torturous conditions, the helicopter crews hugged the uneven ground. One aviator recalled this grueling experience as "flying in a bowl of milk." Vertigo became a real problem as the world turned gray above, below, and around the choppers; apprehension about unseen boulders and hillocks certainly played a part. The fine dust coated the open cockpits, filmed over instruments, raised temperatures to a sweltering 93 degrees, and rendered the night viewing devices nearly useless. Seiffert in number one proceeded for a while, then reversed course to clear the hanging curtain of dust. He landed to assess the situation; shadowy number two followed. The rest of the struggling formation, including an uninformed Colonel Pitman, continued.

Seiffert considered this strange, unnerving development. He recalled nothing about it in the preflight briefing. After several minutes, Seiffert contacted the Joint Task Force (JTF) commander, Maj. Gen. James B. Vaught, USA, and advised him of the cloud. The marine could make out enough of the desert floor to navigate. He wanted very much to press onward, and Vaught agreed. But the rest of the aircraft could not pick up this particular secure net. They droned on in a spreading gaggle, two pairs of helicopters drifting apart as they clattered along above the rocks of central Iran. Seiffert and his mate inadvertently took up the trailing position on the disintegrating formation. Even number eight, with its unreported guests aboard, had passed the grounded flight leader.

Needless to say, all of the pilots were immensely relieved when they left the dust. The crews could only see their blacked-out wingmen, and radio silence rules obviated transmission to regather the dispersed force. Within an hour, the exhausted fliers saw the ominous form of a second haboob looming ahead. Split up, tired, suffering from severe eyestrain, dehydration, muscle cramps, and mental fatigue, the broken formation plunged gamely into the second, much larger and denser cloud. The intent pilots clenched their teeth, only to grind on hard little particles. The damn stuff was everywhere—not blowing, just floating, making a sweaty flight even hotter.

This time, the heating effect of the grit took its toll. Colonel Pitman's number five experienced several brownouts of its OMEGA and PINS devices. Instruments wavered erratically or blinked on and off in a bizarre rhythm of their own. The problems grew worse as the smothering, blinding, baking dust became thicker. Later investigation found a flak vest and duffel bag over an air cooling vent, but this gear might have shifted during the rest of Pitman's flight. In any event, while battling the balky avionics, Pitman lost track of the other four rotary wing craft. With the inertial system out, and approaching a 9,000-foot ridge, Pitman hoped that his chopper's omnidirectional radio receiver could pick up an Iranian station on the ridge line. But either the Iranians were not transmitting or Pitman's receiver failed. He tried to go lower, but even with his belly nearly scraping the unforgiving stones, he could not make out any landmarks. Unsure of his position, uncertain of how much dust remained ahead (less than twenty-five minutes), unclear on how far it was to Desert One (about an hour), silenced by the transmission restrictions, and unaware that number six was down, Pitman aborted back to the *Nimitz*. Ironically, the navigation systems steadied a bit on the way back. The faulty helo barely made the carrier, and then only after some nervous radio calls and a high-speed run toward the coast by the U.S. ship.

Pitman's abort was more than a bitter disappointment. His departure reduced the number of Sea Stallions to six, an amount that General Vaught, Colonel Beckwith, and Colonel Pitman agreed represented the minimum essential force size for continuing the mission.[4] But the communications blackout kept that knowledge from Colonel Kyle and Colonel Beckwith. They would find out when the string of dust-beaten helicopters arrived at Desert One.

After the initial flurry of activity, things at Desert One settled down. Colonel Kyle commanded operations at this interim fuel site, and he and his combat control team quickly organized the parking area for the aircraft soon to arrive. The lead Combat Talon turned and took off, leaving the small group of Americans alone for a short time.

By 2300, the rest of the air force planes began to arrive. The MC-130E flight crews were surprised to see an unexpected beacon—the roaring bonfire of the stricken Iranian fuel vehicle. At least one inbound crew experienced some disorientation due to the brilliant, leaping blaze, but the competent pilots landed without incident. Red Element came in on the second Combat Talon, which unloaded the Deltas and a huge consignment of camouflage netting, then took off. The Americans planned to use the nets to hide the helicopters during a later part of the mission. Once the plane was empty, and the runway cleared of other traffic, this black transport would leave for Masirah.

The last MC-130E, with White Element, the foreign ministry assault force, and the other attachments, landed next. It disgorged its charges, then taxied slowly to a holding area south of the road under the guidance of Colonel Kyle's airmen. The road watch team, combat control team, and, apparently, forty-four bewildered Iranians would leave for Masirah on this aircraft when the activities wrapped up at Desert One. Kyle's team quickly grabbed a backup secure voice radio set off this third Combat Talon, which allowed automatically encrypted satellite communications with the JTF headquarters.

The first EC-130E fuel plane came down, and it, too, went south of the roadside "runway," about two hundred meters west of the MC-130E. The final two Hercules parked north of the road. By 2315, both troop carriers and three fuel aircraft had all landed safely, and the Red Element's transport had departed for Masirah. Delta troops deployed to await their choppers, and airmen rolled thick rubberized fuel hoses out of the blivet-carrying EC-130Es. The helicopters were expected within fifteen minutes.

Although the fiercely burning gasoline truck cast lurid, wavering light across the dim salt flat, it was not easy to tell who was who. Figures seemed shadowy and indistinct. The dark uniforms, lack of insignia, and the howling dust and noise of sixteen running engines made observation, speech, and radio messages difficult, and men spent precious time looking for key places and leaders. One Delta soldier, for example, walked to what he believed to be his assembly point. "Is this helo load number six?" he asked a group of calm, huddled figures. There was no answer, at least not in English. He had been talking to the Iranian bus passengers.

The transports did not shut down their engines for fear of troubles on start-up. What if an emergency came up, such as the arrival of an Iranian Army unit? Taking off from a salt desert with full loads on three or less out of four engines was not a pleasant prospect. So the transport turboprops kept turning.

The real problems at Desert One stemmed from the lack of a full dress rehearsal. This was the first time that Colonel Kyle attempted to coordinate the complicated ground refueling and reorganization, although portions of the exercise had been practiced once about two weeks prior. Only a few officers knew for sure where to find Colonel Kyle, Colonel Beckwith, or their principal assistants. Kyle had no runners or special markers for his position. The leaders wore no distinguishing clothing. Admittedly, the Americans knew their own units by sight. Delta men knew Delta men; aircrews knew aircrews. Beckwith and Kyle and their key officers knew each other, but counting on facial recognition in a dusty, raucous desert at night was a chancy matter. In the dust and gloom, one needed to get very close to identify a person. The engine blast required a speaker to move within a few inches and speak face to face for certain communications.[5] Fortunately, the professional airmen and soldiers pulled it off quite well, at least until the helicopters arrived to add to the complexity.

While awaiting the helos, Kyle and Beckwith used their superb radio links to pass a status report to General Vaught in Egypt and to verify some critical preparations in Tehran. Beckwith reported the encounters with Iranian vehicles, and his recommendation to backload the civilians to Masirah. Vaught approved. Back in Washington, President Carter and his advisers followed the developing mission. Thanks to Vaught's JTF headquarters, the president also knew of Seiffert's problems with the haboob. Beckwith and Kyle did not.[6]

The Delta commander next contacted two Department of Defense agents at Desert Two, about sixty miles outside Tehran. Beckwith wanted to get in touch with retired army Maj. Richard J. Meadows, known to the Iranians as Irish auto executive "Richard H. Keith" and to the CIA as "Esquire." Meadows controlled the clandestine American agent network in Tehran that had gathered firsthand information and laid the groundwork for the hostage rescue raid. Major Meadows had commanded the assault element during the November 1970 Son Tay raid to free American prisoners of war held outside Hanoi. Although intelligence sources had missed the July 1970 transfer of the U.S. prisoners to another camp, and Meadows's men found a North Vietnamese military garrison instead of grateful prisoners of war (PWs), the raid featured superb tactical and operational execution. If any American knew what a rescue mission required, especially in the realm of target area intelligence, it was Richard Meadows.

The embassy seizure imprisoned all (or at least most) American intelligence agents inside Iran, effectively denying the sort of in-depth knowledge needed to mount a thousand-mile venture into the center of a hostile city of almost three million. Meadows volunteered to assist. By January 1980, Meadows had arrived in Tehran via a civilian airliner, passing easily through disorganized Mehrabad Airport. He joined at least six other operatives (two Irano-American servicemen, two German-speaking Green Berets to assist the foreign ministry assault unit, a retired CIA agent brought back for this mission, and a wealthy Iranian exile). These men provided an exquisitely detailed picture of the situation in Tehran, to include the routines of the Pasdaran militia (Iranian Revolutionary Guards) at the embassy and foreign ministry. They isolated four buildings out of the fourteen on the twenty-seven-acre U.S. Embassy grounds as the likely locations for the fifty hostages held there.

Just as importantly, the CIA operative and his rich Iranian partner had rented a warehouse thirteen miles to the southeast of the beleaguered legation compound, bought six Mercedes trucks, a Datsun pickup truck, and a Volkswagen minibus. They stored the vehicles in the leased warehouse and fabricated facades representing stocks of construction materials to conceal the trucks' true cargo.

Meadows had confirmed all of these preparations, personally reconnoitering the embassy block. Then, he went southeast of Iran to select the exact site for Desert Two, where the RH-53Ds could deposit Delta force before dawn on 25 April. Meadows verified an excellent, isolated landing zone near Garmsar. Next, the Son Tay veteran chose a cool wadi five miles away, near an abandoned salt mine, to shelter the Deltas. Finally, Meadows scouted a well-covered helicopter laager about fifteen miles away on a hillside. Delta and the helos would hide out all day on Friday, 25 April. The Americans planned to rescue the hostages about 2400 on 25 April, as the Muslim Iranians settled down for their weekly Saturday holy day. When Beckwith called from Desert One, Meadows answered the radio at Desert Two: "All the groceries are on the shelf." He was waiting for the raiding force. Unlike Son Tay, or even parts of the rapid-fire *Mayaguez* episode, the intelligence in Tehran was nearly perfect.

Indeed, a final valuable piece to the puzzle had come in as Beckwith and Kyle staged through Qena, Egypt, en route to Masirah on 23 April. On 21 April, careless Iranian guards had released a Pakistani national who cooked at the U.S. Embassy and had been seized on 4 November 1979. In an amazingly fortuitous encounter, the cook took a flight out of Tehran and sat down next to a deep-cover CIA agent. The American operative immediately realized the value of his seat mate's knowledge and within a few hours of their landing, CIA interrogators and analysts pinpointed the locations of all fifty U.S. hostages. Every American was held in the three-floor chancellery building; the Pakistani precisely identified guard posts and hostage room locations.[7] Beckwith modified his assault plans to accommodate these vital details. So all seemed ready in Tehran.

All seemed off-schedule at Desert One. As the four transports continued to roar away in their parking spots, Kyle and Beckwith waited for the Sea Stallions; 2330 came and went, then 2400. By 0010, Beckwith called General Vaught at Qena. "I need some choppers," he reminded the JTF commander. Vaught had some good news; the craft were only ten minutes away. Kyle continued to listen for updates as Beckwith stepped aside to ponder the possible effects of the delays. Given an estimated hour or so necessary for refueling, plus more than two hours flight time and two hours for Delta to hike the five miles to its wadi hideout, Beckwith doubted he could reach his covered position near Desert Two by dawn at 0530 on 25 April. Nevertheless, Beckwith elected to go ahead, in his words, "no matter when the choppers arrived—and no matter when we arrived at the hidesite."

The Delta colonel looked up from his musings to hear the throaty "whop-whop" of approaching rotary-wing aircraft. Out of the starry vault of the Iranian night came a spectral, sand-colored, dusty Sea Stallion. Beckwith watched it land and hurried over. He expected to meet Seiffert. The pilot slowly emerged, wearing goggles. But it was not Seiffert.

Instead, it was Maj. James Schaefer, USMC, pilot of number three. When the army officer welcomed the marine, the weary major merely shrugged. "It's been a hell of a trip," said Schaefer. The disgusted pilot mumbled something about abandoning the helicopters in the desert and leaving on the air force C-130s. Beckwith, who did not understand the stress of Schaefer's harrowing flight, backed off, confused. The marine positioned his RH-53D at the easternmost Hercules north of the road and started refueling. It was 0015.

Within a few minutes, number four spiraled down onto the salt flat. It came from a slightly different direction than the first helo. Again, Col. Charles Beckwith went over to welcome the crew. The aircraft commander dismounted, obviously in a highly nervous state. He appeared to stagger in the fresh night air, and had a lot to say as he tried to settle down after the grim struggle with the haboobs: "You have no idea what I've been through. The damndest sandstorm I've ever seen hit us. I'm not really sure we can make it." He returned to his chopper and placed it behind the same EC-130E used by number three.

Like Major Schaefer, the pilot of number four enjoyed a reputation among the rescue force as a skillful, tough, no-nonsense flier. Evidently, something very bad had happened to shake up these men. The ground force commander and his subordinates began to worry about their helicopter pilots. But what could Beckwith and his men do?

Sea Stallions number seven and eight came in separately, and Colonel

Kyle assigned them to tanker planes. He ordered number seven to the single Hercules tanker south of the road, and sent number eight to join Schaefer at the first fuel carrier north of the strip. Finally, about 0110, Lieutenant Colonel Seiffert and his wingman arrived with numbers one and two. Colonel Kyle's efficient controllers dispatched Seiffert to the as yet unused second northern EC-130E, and sent number two to fuel alongside number seven.[8]

That was it; the other two aircraft obviously were not coming. Still, six was enough. The operation was more than an hour and a half behind schedule, but the mission remained a "go." Delta loaded their equipment. In the distance, the sullen busload of Iranians watched the screaming, bustling scene. Sixteen turboprops and twelve helicopter turbines thundered and threw up a haze of dirt and salty grit.

And then came the bad news. As the ground force boarded, a pilot approached Colonel Beckwith, who was crossing the road/runway, headed for the southern tanker. "The skipper told me to tell you we have only five flyable helicopters," said the unidentified man. Beckwith swore, then found Colonel Kyle. He asked the air force commander to speak to Seiffert, because "you understand this bloody flying lingo." Kyle obliged. He came back in a few minutes, his features clouded. He spoke in a measured tone: "Let's go to the radio. Helicopter number two has hydraulic problems and Seiffert feels it's unsafe to go with it." The two colonels walked in dejection to the satellite transmitter. They called General Vaught.

Helicopter number two had lost its second-stage hydraulic fluid through a cracked nut on the second-stage pump. The crew identified the problem about two hours into the mission, but hoped that it was an instrument malfunction. At Desert One, inspection revealed loss of most of the vital fluid from this backup hydraulic system. The helicopter could fly on the primary system alone, but if that failed, the chopper would certainly crash. Considering the likely overloading and expected strains of anticipated operations, the RH-53D's primary hydraulics might blow unexpectedly. Repairs were out of the question. The proper replacement parts were not on hand, although helicopters number one, three, and seven were carrying some other spares in special kits. It did not matter. Replacement would have taken at least forty-five minutes, followed by a complete flushing of the restored system and refilling with new fluid. This intricate procedure could have easily taken until dawn or longer.

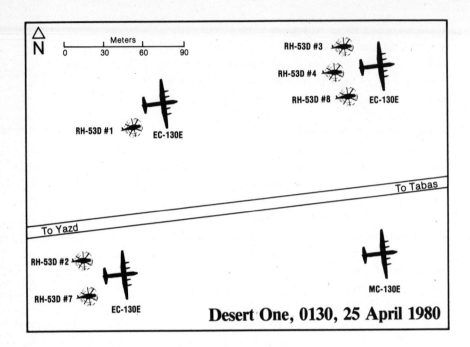

Desert One, 0130, 25 April 1980

Beckwith and Kyle briefly talked about proceeding with five helos. But the Delta leader rejected that possibility. He did not believe he could trim his assault teams or toss out equipment. The choppers needed the heavy camouflage nets and Redeye air defense missiles to survive at their hide location. Vaught heard Kyle's explanation, then responded: "Ask Eagle [Beckwith] to consider going on with five."

Beckwith exploded: "Shit no!" As Beckwith later recorded: "I lost respect right there for General Vaught. Damn, I thought, how in the hell can the boss ask me that!" The army colonel told Vaught unequivocally that all the commanders had agreed long before the mission that six operational rotary-wing aircraft must depart Desert One, so termination and withdrawal were mandatory with only five. Vaught and the men in Washington agreed. At 0157, the Americans aborted the rescue. Later, the volatile Delta commander went so far as to state that if Vaught or even President Carter himself had ordered the mission to continue, he would have replied: "I can't hear you; we're coming out." [9]

Aside from Beckwith's rather colorful insistence on sticking with the plan (although he certainly had modified Delta's scheme before leaving Egypt to account for the Pakistani cook's disclosures and again when Seiffert was delayed), the abort decision made sense to the men involved. The rescue attempt depended on secrecy, which still seemed intact. Given this, the participants (and especially President Carter and his advisers) thought that they could terminate the plan at any stage, pull out, and try again later. In the words of Maj. Logan Fitch, "Temporarily returning from Desert One might be better than getting stranded on that number-six [actually number two] chopper somewhere in the desert. It *would* be better if we could get out cleanly and come back in a few days." [10] Even if that was a realistic possibility, events following the abort decision choked off such an option.

Just after the depressing conference, preparations got underway to withdraw. Although procedures were known for handling individual air-craft failures, this sort of mass abort had not been practiced. Delta and its attachments moved to reboard the air force transports, with many hoping to ride out to Masirah on the half-empty rubber fuel containers. Colonel Kyle ordered the Sea Stallions to return to USS *Nimitz,* and he intended to drag the useless number two out of the area and destroy it. But the pilots needed more fuel for one idling RH-53D, number four. At 0222, Kyle okayed this aviator's request to reposition next to Seiffert's number one on the other northern fuel plane. To do this, Kyle told Major Schaefer to move his number three aside.

Schaefer gunned his motors, and the big helo lifted, tilting slightly to its left to clear the Hercules tanker. Tremendous sand billows wafted up, and to the horror of watching spectators, the chopper spun back right, slowly crossing the left wing of its EC-130E. The sand swirled about, the helicopter dipped shakily, and then the desert flashed with searing electric-white light. Men on the ground froze and looked as two terrific rending cracks sounded, and mangled metal fragments flew up, silhouetted in the harsh whiteness. A huge fireball boiled into the night. Helo number three's main blades severed the cockpit from the rest of the parked transport, which Delta's Blue Element had boarded minutes before the accident.

Aboard the stricken Hercules, Major Fitch watched in shock while "a spray of sparks lit up the entrance to the cockpit and the bulkhead, where most of the avionics were stored. The electrical fire, combined with one fed by aviation fuel, was turning the front of the plane into a murderous oven. I grabbed my weapon. We were obviously under attack."

As frantic Deltas grabbed for arms, acrid fumes and drifting smoke filled the cargo space. Flames licked greedily at the half-filled fuel blivet. Any moment, the volatile liquid might well erupt into a massive billow of fire. Fearing Iranian action, confused, and panicky, the Americans clawed and stumbled toward the single rear troop door that yawned open. The vicious stampede threatened to stall their escape and leave them in the clutches of the steadily approaching fuel detonation. But one leader took charge. Sergeant Major Don Linkey bellowed, "Don't panic! Don't panic!" and physically manhandled the troopers back to a semblance of order. Thanks to his forceful example, Blue Element exited smoothly from the blazing wreck, crouching to avoid the shower of bullets, grenades, and demolitions that shot, careened, and ripped out of the innards of the dying aircraft. With relief, the shaken men discovered that a mistake, not Iranians, had generated the inferno.

The next few minutes reeled by in a nightmare. Wounded, shocked, blistered men emerged from the holocaust. Some brave soldiers plunged into the flames to drag out two burned marines, including Schaefer, and three badly injured airmen. Five air force fliers died in the melting inferno of their crumpling cockpit; two marine gunners and their crew chief roasted in the cargo area of number three. Machine gun ammunition on the disintegrating Sea Stallion began to cook off, sending half-inch slugs crazily out of the disintegrating fuselage.

Around the towering flames of the exploding wreckage, some of the helicopter pilots shut down their craft. All of them scrambled to get clear. Seiffert's number one shook as pieces of the erupting EC-130E crashed into his helo. Colonel Kyle ordered all men to board the remaining three aircraft and prepare to leave. The fliers in choppers number two and seven were safe across the road, and they took their classified flight maps and frequency charts as they left. The crews north of the highway abandoned the secret materials in their helos and even left their turbines roaring away. The marines were trying to get clear of their parked RH-53Ds before they became part of the expanding blaze.

Colonel Kyle's departure orders allowed Beckwith and Seiffert to account for their men. Other than the eight dead men trapped in the fiery skeletons of the fused airplane and helicopter, the other Americans survived. Equipment littered the desert floor; many of the Blue Element troops did not have their personal weapons anymore.

The remaining three transports swung out from the silent helicopters, rolling for takeoff in the stark light of the flaming accident. Kyle told Beckwith that he recommended an air strike to demolish the deserted helicopters. The two commanders agreed on this. They hoped that navy jets from *Nimitz* and *Coral Sea* could eradicate the remaining classified matter at Desert One.

The last American plane lifted off at 0255, after being forced to run off the chosen runway to avoid the bright conflagration. After a bone-rattling, violent crossing of a three-foot embankment, the Americans were gone.[11] Behind them, the gasoline truck smoldered, almost out; the aircraft crash continued to burn until well after daybreak. The dazed Iranian bus passengers remained behind, uncomprehending witnesses to the debacle.

President Carter's concern for these civilians precluded the naval air strike. Iran finally learned of the U.S. raid when Carter announced its failure at 0100, Washington time (1000 on 25 April, Iran time). Later on 25 April, Iranian aircraft strafed and bombed the hollow choppers

---

Comparative Loss Summary
Personnel *

	KIA	MIA	WIA	PW	Nonbattle **
U.S. Army	0	0	0	0	0
U.S. Navy/USMC	3	0	2	0	0
U.S. Air Force	5	0	3	0	0
U.S. MILITARY TOTAL	8	0	5	0	0
IRANIAN TOTAL	0	0	0	0	0

Equipment

U.S. Military: 7 U.S. Navy helicopters; 1 U.S. Air Force transport airplane
Iranian Military: None

* KIW = killed in action; MIA = missing in action; WIA = wounded in action; PW = prisoner of war; Nonbattle = noncombat accidents, illnesses.

** All U.S. losses officially classified as noncombat.

Sources: Jimmy Carter, "Remarks at San Antonio, Texas, 28 April 1980" in *Public Papers of the Presidents: Jimmy Carter, 1980/81, Book I* (Washington, D.C.: U.S. Government Printing Office, 1981), 786; "Iran Rescue Attempt," *Air Force Times,* 12 May 1980, 4; "In Memoriam," *Armed Forces Journal* (June 1980), 6, 8, 9.

at Desert One, mainly out of spite. The militants frantically dispersed their American captives to other cities. Some went as far as Tabriz and Isfahan, cities more than two hundred miles from Tehran. Another rescue try seemed impossible.

Instead of the joyous return of their hostages, Americans watched a somber President Carter describe the catastrophic ending of Operation EAGLE CLAW. Television journalists in Iran treated their American audiences to the grim sight of the shattered aircraft carcasses at Desert One, close-ups of secret maps found in the debris, and the ghoulish antics of Ayatollah Khalkali holding up charred pieces of dead American marines and airmen like big-game hunting trophies.[12] The hostages remained incarcerated until 20 January 1981, for a total of 444 days of national humiliation. Not surprisingly, America had a different president by then.

Before considering what went wrong with the U.S. hostage rescue mission, it is worthwhile to describe Operation EAGLE CLAW as it might have proceeded. For this fictional speculation, assume that helicopter number two experienced a false hydraulic trouble light and remained fully operational. . . .

The hard-working aircrews on the tanker planes moved with real purpose, trying desperately to make up some of the time lost in the haboobs. Beckwith's Delta teams double-checked their gear, and Delta officers went from helo to helo inspecting arrangements. By 0200, all was in order. Beckwith told Kyle face to face: "We're locked and cocked." The air force colonel shook his hand: "Good luck and Godspeed."

Lieutenant Colonel Seiffert waited until the Delta commander reboarded number one, then gently pulled the laden chopper off the salt flat. Sand blossomed as he rose up and away from the refueling plane. In the distance, the hulk of the destroyed gasoline tanker flickered. Within a few minutes, the other five RH-53Ds joined their flight leader in a low orbit over Desert One. The stars shone brightly. Gunners worked the bolt handles on the .50 calibers, brushing off the dust. The choppers assumed a wedge of pairs and clattered northwest, toward Desert Two. This time, they flew at 400 feet, thanks to Colonel Kyle's clarification of the enemy radar threat.

Behind the departing Sea Stallions, Kyle and his teams cleaned up Desert One, obscured some of the numerous footprints and wheel ruts, secured the clandestine landing light set, and prodded forty-four Iranians aboard an EC-130E. By 0300, the four transports were en route to Masirah, leaving behind a gutted gas truck, an abandoned bus, and a lot of curious tracks and tire marks.

At Desert Two, sixty miles or so southeast of Tehran, "Esquire" scanned the southern skies. Although a line of the Iranian State Railroad ran nearby, no unexpected trains rumbled through. Major Richard Meadows and his associate were the only people for miles around.

The helicopters were late, and it became obvious that Delta could not march to its hide site until dawn. Meadows and his assistant did not worry; Kyle had notified them of the problem. Finally, at 0413, about an hour and a half behind the timetable, the thrumming vibrations of approaching rotary-wing craft began to wash over Desert Two.

Emerging from the stygian horizon like sand-colored wraiths, the six weary choppers flared up to land. This leg of the flight had been easy, by comparison with the purgatory en route to Desert One. The aircraft met two more small areas of suspended talc, but by staying at 400 feet, the aviators avoided the heaviest dust concentrations.

As soon as the big choppers touched down, spread widely in the darkness and drifting sand, Beckwith's Delta men dismounted. They dragged out heavy rucksacks full of ammunition and demolitions, saddled up, and formed for the hike to their hide site. Within a few minutes, Beckwith's hardened soldiers, the foreign ministry team, the twelve drivers, and the two Iranian translators were gone, tromping rapidly through the cool desert. They reached their wadi den, not far from a hard-surfaced road, just after first light.

As Beckwith and his men moved off, Seiffert's choppers increased power. One by one, they edged into the night air, gained height, and headed northeast into a small opening shielded by a rugged hillside, code-named Figbar. After a short hop, the Sea Stallions set down in a fairly tight formation. For the first time since leaving the deck of USS *Nimitz,* the screaming helicopters ground to a stop. The next time they started, it would be to pick up the freed hostages from Tehran.

In the stillness at Figbar, pilots, navigators, crew chiefs, and gunners climbed out of the big aircraft. Officers and men worked together to unroll and erect camouflage nets. A few marines unlimbered Redeye antiaircraft missiles and took up concealed posts on the nearby hillsides, ready to destroy any Iranian Air Force intruders. Finally, with camouflage and security established, aviators and crew chiefs returned to conduct preventive maintenance on their temperamental charges. Given the troubles with numbers five and six, the exhausted fliers gave special attention to their checklists and adjustments. Two army radio operators remained with Seiffert's flight, to allow Delta to call the helos into downtown Tehran. With all in order, the RH-53D crews hunkered down to rest and hide during the day of 25 April.

With Delta and the helos safely squirreled away, Richard Meadows and his deputy got into their Volkswagen bus and headed for the truck warehouse on the outskirts of Tehran. Behind them, the sky began to grow gray as dawn approached.

Friday, 25 April, passed quietly at the hide sites. At Figbar, the spent aviators slept around their shaded helicopters. In Delta's gulley, many men also slept under the careful watch of sentinels. While waiting at the two laagers, many men talked through their upcoming duties in hushed tones. Finally, as the shadows grew long and the daylight faded, both places sprang to life.

Major Richard Meadows arrived punctually about 1915, not long after the final rays of sunlight disappeared from the western mountains. With Meadows came the Volkswagen van and the Datsun pickup. Colonel Charles Beckwith climbed into the Datsun with Meadows and headed into Tehran for a leaders' reconnaissance. Meanwhile Meadows's agent gathered the twelve drivers (eight Iranian exiles and four Farsi-speaking Americans, including Capt. John Butterfield, USN, a volunteer from the Naval Academy faculty). These men boarded the Volkswagen bus and returned to the warehouse. Under Beckwith's deputy, Delta prepared for the return of the trucks; fifteen miles to the north, Lieutenant Colonel Seiffert's men peeled back and discarded their protective netting.

Colonel "Chargin' Charlie" Beckwith observed carefully as he rolled into Tehran, noting the various turns and landmarks. Naturally, he paid particular attention to the situation around the embassy. The embassy lay at the corner of two wide streets, Roosevelt (north-south) and Talleghani (east-west). They seemed relatively clear of traffic. Most important of all, the critical Amjadieh soccer stadium seemed empty. Everything looked good.

Around the compound, the Pasdaran militia and their college student fringe looked utterly relaxed. About half dozed at their posts. Many of the others stood talking in ramshackle sandbag emplacements, with head and shoulders exposed and G-3 German-made rifles leaning against the bags. A few people gathered laughing and joking around a warming fire in a trash can. The embassy windows showed slivers of light; apparently most were painted black. Farsi banners, revolutionary graffiti, pictures of Khomeini, tattered effigies of Carter, defaced shreds of U.S. flags, and English signs reading "Death to Carter—Death to Shah" festooned the embassy walls. The laxity around the U.S. legation confirmed Beckwith's low opinion of his adversaries.

While their commander took a look at the target area, Beckwith's men boarded their trucks and motored to the rented warehouse. The

---

Iranian Armed Forces
24 April 1980

Army: 150,000 men
    3 armored divisions
        1 regiment garrisoned near U.S. Embassy, Tehran
    4 infantry "divisions" (two understrength)
    1 airborne brigade
    4 surface to air missile battalions (Improved Hawk)
    Antiaircraft Corps (1,800 assorted guns)
Revolutionary Guard Corps: 150,000 men (Pasdaran militia)
    25–50 guards, U.S. Embassy, Tehran
National Police: 40,000 (armored cars and automatic weapons)
    Several units in Tehran
Gendarmerie: 75,000 (paramilitary)
    Tabas force
    Yazd force
Air Force: few aircraft actually operational
    10 fighter/attack squadrons (193 F-4D/E)
        2 F-4Es on strip alert at Mehrabad Airport, Tehran
    8 fighter/attack squadrons (174 F-5E/F)
    4 interceptor squadrons (77 F-14A)
Navy:
    3 old destroyers
    4 frigates
    26 patrol boats

Sources: International Institute for Strategic Studies, "The Military Balance, 1983/84," *Air Force* (December 1983), 97, 98; Richard F. Nyrop, ed. *Iran: A Country Study* (Washington, D.C.: American University, 1978), 368–72, 401–08; U.S. Congress, Senate Armed Services Committee, *FY 1979 Supplemental Military Authorization,* 96th Congress, 1st Session, 3 April 1979, 243.

---

thirteen Special Forces men assigned to attack the foreign ministry followed behind in the ubiquitous Volkswagen minibus. The vehicles moved with casual sloppiness, interspersed with the few other cars, trucks, and buses driving toward Tehran.

Meanwhile, four AC-130H Spectres raced across Iran at low level, heading for Tehran. Not far behind, three C-141 Starlifters roared across the Persian Gulf, bound for a deserted Iranian Air Force field at Manzariyeh, thirty-five miles southwest of Tehran. The lead jet transport carried Major General Vaught and eighty-three tense Rangers of Company C, 1-75 Infantry, followed by two aircraft carefully prepared to tend sick and wounded hostages and troopers. The Rangers planned to assault air-land and establish an extraction base. In the eastern Turkish highlands, Maj. Oliver L. North, USMC, waited with Python Force, ninety Force Reconnaissance marines trained as a backup extraction element. If the Ranger mission went awry, or any RH-53Ds went down, North's marines would go into Tehran, Manzariyeh, or wherever by helicopter to retrieve the hostages and the Delta men.

In the Gulf of Oman, USS *Nimitz* and USS *Coral Sea* sent their fighters and attack planes aloft, to link up with air force KC-135 tankers and prepare to run in toward Tehran. Out over the dark Persian Gulf, an air force E-3A Sentry airborne warning and control system (AWACS) jet circled, ready to direct the air cover.

But the key mission revolved around Delta. About 2230, Beckwith met his men at the warehouse. He reviewed his impressions and finalized the route. For the last time, he went over the broad details of the attack plan. "It's all up to us now, guys," said the emotional commander. "Let's kick some ass!"

Slowly, the ragged file of heavy trucks moved out of the warehouse, weaving among the light flow of Iranian traffic headed into the dark city. Delta radio operators contacted their chopper support. It was time to start the six Sea Stallions.

At Figbar, Seiffert's RH-53Ds cranked their engines. Normally, this required an auxiliary power unit, but on the quiet hillside, the pilots employed an alternative method. Each helo carried two compressed air containers, which the crews bled into the start-up hydraulic system to spin the turbines. These blades drove the generators that delivered the voltage needed to start the fuel burning. But there was only so much air in the canisters; Seiffert's men had to get it right, quickly. Despite justified concerns, every chopper motor turned over. By 2355, the big craft raced their turbines and lifted off, sliding across the empty desert to their holding orbit five miles north of Tehran. Marine gunners loaded their heavy .50 calibers, jacking the bolt handles twice to place the wicked rounds into the well-oiled chambers.

Simultaneously, the carefully staggered Delta truck column drove slowly into the city. The Special Forces assault team turned off early, taking a separate route to the foreign ministry. The Delta carriers spread out into a convoy of several miles. As each truck had a different civilian paint pattern, one would have been hard-pressed to connect these six cargo vehicles among the several others driving through Tehran.

On the way, the Mercedes trucks encountered a previously spotted two-man checkpoint. The drivers all bluffed their way through successfully. Things grew tense at one juncture, when the scruffy Iranian soldiers halted the third truck to ask for cigarettes. Fortunately, both drivers smoked and had brought an ample supply of Turkish brands to sustain them during their nerve-racking tasks. The Iranian exile and his close-mouthed American assistant gladly shared their stockpile, and the happy guards waved them on.

After clearing these sentries, the column slowly tightened into three pairs of trucks. The loose convoy meandered north of the U.S. compound, then turned south onto four-lane Roosevelt Street.

The Delta commander led the way. Beckwith remained in the Datsun pickup, driven by Meadows. In the bed, two White Element sharpshooters lay under a tarpaulin, holding .22-caliber pistols with silencers.

At 0005 on 25 April, the vehicles slowly pulled over and stopped, opposite the soccer arena. Every man wore a tiny headset radio to permit split-second reporting and orders, along with up to ninety-five pounds of ammunition, grenades, and other battle gear. The keyed-up troops had finally pulled the tape off their American flag patches.

Major Fitch's Blue Element dismounted and edged a few men near the northeastern corner of the embassy wall. They placed padded aluminum ladders and began dropping over the nine-foot-high wall. Within seconds, they were over, headed for the motor pool and power plant in the southwestern corner. Blue Element would cut all power, destroy the guard posts in that area, and establish security facing west on wide Talleghani Street. Red Element followed with their own ladders; they intended to seize and clear the critical chancellery building. White Element spread slowly along Roosevelt Street, dropping an M-60 machine gun team to cover the north approach and an HK-21 (German-made) machine

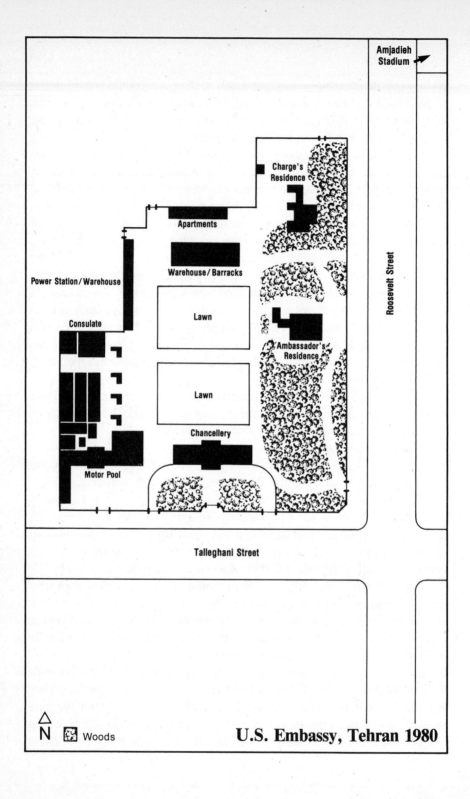

Amjadieh Stadium

Charge's Residence

Apartments

Warehouse / Barracks

Power Station / Warehouse

Lawn

Consulate

Ambassador's Residence

Lawn

Chancellery

Motor Pool

Roosevelt Street

Talleghani Street

N
Woods

U.S. Embassy, Tehran 1980

gun to face south. A demolition team prepared to blast out a chunk of wall; the rest of White readied to cross the broad street and secure the soccer field.

At 0009, the Datsun pulled in along the Roosevelt Street wall, racing its engine as it rolled. Beckwith's two concealed pistol men popped up, firing swiftly. The revving motor covered the eight rapid, muffled metallic snaps. Two Iranian Pasdaran militiamen crumpled in their guard posts. One walking guard slid down the wall, two holes in his skull. Another, sleeping against the enclosure, never woke up. The pickup halted and the Delta commander and Meadows got out (armed with a weapon brought by Beckwith) and slid quickly to the side of the demolition team. Major Fitch of Blue Element radioed he was in position. Red also reported ready. All looked at their watches: 0010.

With a gout of flame, a tremendous window-shattering roar, and a shower of flying masonry bits, the wall ripped open, leaving a gap big enough for a good-sized truck. White Element's machine gunners deployed to their chosen spots, and the rest of the White group quickly took the empty Amjadieh Stadium and established a second M-60 team to cover the entrance. Leaving their trucks, the drivers followed the Deltas into the stadium to await pickup. Beckwith radioed General Vaught, who had just touched down at Manzariyeh: "Hammer, this is Eagle. Drumbeat, I say again, drumbeat!" It was underway.

The noise of the explosion echoed across the grounds as Major Fitch and his Blues cut the power to the compound. Every light went out. Four more Pasdaran and college student sentinels, plus three unidentified civilian women, died in quick bursts of gunfire. A volley of arcing 40-mm grenades hit the main gate, blowing aside three wounded guards and their shaky enclosures. Fitch's teams systematically cleared the motor pool area, eliminating another eleven Pasdaran guardsmen scrambling for weapons in their filthy temporary barracks. Snipers killed the few dazed Iranians still moving near the main gate.

As the explosion thundered and the lights cut out, the forty-eight-strong Red Element moved swiftly against the chancellery. One four-man team smashed down the eastern staff door. While one Delta, using night vision goggles, tracked and swiftly dispatched a startled Iranian sleeping in the hall, the other three ran down the hall and knocked open the main doors. Nine seconds later, the huge southern entrance was open and Delta men streamed in, heading for their assigned rooms.

These goggled men carried Heckler and Koch German MP-5 9-mm

submachine guns, American AR-15 automatic rifles, M-16A1s, and even a few heavy M-3A1 "grease guns." In each room, they ran through the same practiced sequence: gain entry, identify the guards, kill the hostiles with two head shots, and evacuate the hostages. Since only a few doors had to be blown open, they averaged seven seconds per room. Within four minutes of the initial entry, all sixteen Iranian sentries in the building were dead, along with one unlucky marine hostage who had grabbed an Uzi automatic rifle from his terrified captor. Delta operators automatically eliminated any armed men.

Beckwith had trained his men very hard for room-clearing. In fact, his brutally tough live-fire practices often included himself or his officers as hostages among Iranian dummy targets. As he explained to President Carter's chief of staff, Hamilton Jordan, after the mission: "Me and my boys have made a career of busting down doors and saving folks. I was prepared for the worst in Tehran: a highly trained badnik sitting by each hostage with a gun to his head. But I knew what we were going to find was Joe Shit, the raghead, sitting there picking his nose with a rifle he had never cleaned and maybe never fired. When I bust down the door and go in, what is that man with the rifle going to do? Aim it at the hostage or aim it at me? You bet your ass he's going to aim it at me because I'm going to bleed him with mine."

With the guards dead, the Red Element hustled the confused hostages out of the structure and onto the open field just north of the ringing, bloody chancellery building. Designated Red Element soldiers placed luminous headbands on the recovered Americans; force medics calmed the nervous and counted heads. Others pulled down the haphazard swatch of poles erected on the clear areas to frustrate U.S. helicopter landings. Red Element reported to the Delta commander: "All items accounted for; four-niner warm, one cold." Beckwith responded by calling in the helos with the prearranged code word "dynamo."

So far, Blue Element and White Element reported no Iranian military reaction, although the city crackled with gunfire, vehicle noises, and distant shouting. Curious Iranians could be seen collecting on distant street corners. One small car ran by at high speed on Talleghani, heading east. The HK-21 gunner opened up, blowing out the tires and sending the Renault careening into a building facade. The driver did not get out.

To the west, the sky reverberated with ragged explosions, and a steady stream of bright tracer fire snapped on and off. Above the glow, a slowly banking Spectre gunship chewed up the two Iranian Air Force strip alert aircraft and most of the other Iranian fighters at Mehrabad Airport. Another AC-130H spun over the embassy, ready to assist if necessary. Two more waited off to the south. Farther up, navy F-14A Tomcats and F-4N Phantoms rode shotgun, vectored by the watchful AWACS. Finally, out at Manzariyeh, the Rangers had landed and taken the airdrome unopposed at 0011. All that remained was to extract the hostages and their rescuers.

Overhead, the sky filled with the clattering noise of helicopters, echoing off the city buildings. Beckwith stood on Roosevelt Street, checking his watch: 0025. He ordered Lieutenant Colonel Seiffert to bring the first chopper directly into the open space north of the chancellery. Major James Schaefer's number three landed at 0027. Within minutes the forty-nine living hostages, the corpse of the dead one, and three Delta medics boarded. Wary marine door gunners scanned the empty streets of Tehran, and the RH-53D lifted off. By 0030, Schaefer was en route to Manzariyeh.

With the former hostages on their way, Beckwith withdrew his own men to the soccer arena. Red went first, to be followed by Blue. The Red Element used the gaping rent in the Roosevelt Street wall to move to the pickup zone. Chopper number four already waited there, having eased in between the high grandstands. Sea Stallion number eight was en route to Manzariyeh, having already picked up the foreign ministry hostages and raiders without incident. But the confused Iranians were starting to react at last.

An Iranian police van screeched up just as Major Fitch started to pull out. The Delta grenadiers fired two 40-mm rounds into the vehicle, detonating the gas tank. Incredibly, three Iranians escaped the flames, and one wounded a Blue soldier with a panicky burst from his Uzi. More ominously, the Spectre overhead reported some activity at an Iranian mechanized regiment garrison a few blocks away, to include movement of armored vehicles in the Iranian motor park. Beckwith stood in the wall breach, urging his men across the street. Red Element and the drivers took off and within two minutes, Sea Stallion number seven landed in the stadium. Blue Element rushed across Roosevelt, carrying their wounded comrade. To the south, two Iranian national police scout cars cautiously poked their way up Roosevelt Street. The White Element

HK-21 engaged, but the Iranian armored cars accelerated. The police started firing their mounted machine guns, killing the HK-21 gunner and wounding his partner.

White Element repositioned to meet the advancing vehicles, and Beckwith called for Spectre. The Delta colonel realized that he must destroy the approaching scout cars before the Iranians could use their .50 calibers against the vulnerable helicopters. As helo number seven pulled up and hovered, the black form of Spectre blotted out the faint stars visible overhead. Three quick 40-mm shots tipped over one of the armored vehicles. The other one began to pull back, but the gunship was faster. With a sharp crack, a burst of yellow fire, and a boiling geyser of black smoke, the second scout car blew up.

White Element soldiers retrieved their dead and injured comrades and crossed Roosevelt Street. Working quickly, they boarded Seiffert's number one. Beckwith counted heads: all were present. ''That's it, let's get the hell out of here!'' he hollered to Seiffert. The pilot nodded and brought up the nose. They cleared the stadium enclosure and gained altitude, then swung southwest, toward Manzariyeh. On the wing, empty chopper number two followed. It had not been needed. It was 0055.

Beneath them, the military end of Mehrabad Airport blazed away. Beckwith signaled the AC-130H behind him: ''Spectre, this is Eagle. Close the store, out.'' In accord with the original mission orders, the big Spectre descended, assumed a left-turn orbit, and began to pound the abandoned U.S. Embassy to rubble. The smoking residue would yield few clues for enraged Iranians the next day.

The unopposed withdrawal from Manzariyeh was anticlimactic. All helicopters arrived unmolested, and the pilots climbed out of their craft after whirling to one last touchdown. The RH-53Ds stayed at Manzariyeh, but nothing remained intact by the time confused Iranian pursuers arrived. Delta troopers placed thermite grenades to help Seiffert's aviators destroy the Sea Stallions. Forty-four confused Iranian bus travelers remained behind near the burning navy choppers. They had spent more than a day en route from Desert One to Egypt and then back to Iran, only to be deposited in this madhouse. Khomeini later charged that these unfortunates had been held as ''hostages'' by ''bloodthirsty American Rangers.''

By 0245 on 26 April, the Starlifters left for Egypt, with fifty-two very happy ex-hostages and all U.S. military personnel, to include Meadows and his intrepid team of agents. Total American casualties amounted to one dead, two wounded, plus one hostage accidentally killed. Iranian losses at Mehrabad and around the embassy block were estimated at ninety-six dead and one hundred eighty-three wounded. As President Carter told the nation in announcing the operation: "This attempt became a necessity and a duty. The readiness of our team to undertake the rescue made it completely practicable." [13]

Of course, in reality EAGLE CLAW never got past first base, and the demanding Tehran embassy assault and subsequent extraction phases of the plan were not attempted. Considering the extremely difficult, complicated nature of the projected operation, perhaps the above description of "what might have been" constitutes not just fiction, but fantasy.

The American hostage rescue mission was an utter failure. Why? To establish the causes for the debacle, President Carter appointed a distinguished Special Operations Review Group headed by Adm. James L. Holloway, former chief of naval operations and an experienced naval aviator. The Holloway group received a broad charter to examine the tragic operation, but the public version of their findings addressed matters only up to the point at which the mission aborted. The investigators released their report in August 1980, while the hostages still languished in Iran. Considering the extremely sensitive nature of the Iran raid, and the ongoing hostage crisis, the forthright disclosure of the great majority of the special review group's work was truly remarkable. If nothing else, Carter's willingness to discuss the failed raid in detail demonstrated the relative hopelessness attached to thoughts of a second rescue. The general impression seemed to be that America's military had taken their gamble and lost.

The Holloway group's public report, however, did not directly address a fundamental question: was the raid the only military option available, and if not, was it the best of those conceived? In short, why did President Carter knowingly embark on what the Holloway group called a "high risk operation"? [14]

It is easy to chastise the president for his seeming reluctance to employ America's overwhelming military power against the truculent Iranians. The seizure of an embassy and its diplomatic staff is an act of war, and America had intervened strongly in response to similar incidents in the past (the 1900 Boxer Rebellion in China, for example). President Carter never seriously considered a declaration of war, although he weighed military responses from the outset.

Carter avoided a declaration of war for four reasons. First, the president had rapidly developed an immense sense of personal responsibility for the hostages. He dreaded harming them and had insisted from the beginning that their safety came first. As he wrote later: "Although I was acting in my official capacity as President, I also had deep private feelings that were almost overwhelming. The hostages sometimes seemed like part of my own family." With this in mind, a declaration of war might prove tantamount to a blank check for Iranian executioners to do their worst.

Second, Carter and his advisers assumed for at least the first month that the crisis would be short-lived. Khomeini's decision to release thirteen female and black Americans about two weeks after the takeover encouraged some hope. About the same time, a secret U.S. missive bluntly promised a strong military reaction if Iran carried out its threats to try or execute the hostages. These Iranian threats grew weaker and less frequent, and no attempts were made to carry them out. Carter announced policies of restraint and adherence to international law in the face of Iranian barbarism. This marshaled much diplomatic support around the world, admittedly just empty verbiage in most cases. By the time it became obvious that the hostage crisis would last months rather than days, Carter and his administration had advanced too far along nonbelligerent paths to reverse course and sound the war tocsin.

The third reason related to the second. Domestically, the best time to ask for a war vote was at the beginning, yet neither Carter nor his principal assistants wanted to take that opportunity in November 1979. Although American popular opinion throughout the 444 days continued to reflect a longing for presidential "action," with an emphasis on military efforts, unquestioned approval of a declaration of war grew less likely with each passing week. In the months after November, and especially after the Soviets invaded Iran's neighbor Afghanistan in December 1979, many U.S. political leaders moved beyond their initial outrage and reflected on the potential ramifications of protracted American-Iranian combat.

The hearings and congressional floor debates preceding an assent to hostilities would certainly revolve around the likely casualties, American intrusion into the Middle Eastern quagmire, possible confrontation with the Soviets, the abrogation of congressional controls granted by the constitutionally questionable but as yet unchallenged War Powers Resolution, and the possibly drastic domestic actions of a president granted full wartime authorities (such as reinstituting conscription or censoring the press, for example). The intense controversy over imposition of mere draft registration pointed to the potential for dissent at home. As Carter's National Security Council adviser on Iran, Capt. Gary Sick, USN, summarized: "It was feared in the White House that a declaration of war would be met with a burst of initial enthusiasm, followed by severe second doubts and internal debate, which would not only fail to strengthen the President's hand but conceivably could even splinter the spirit of national unity that had prevailed throughout the ordeal."

Finally, and perhaps most important of all, America needed Iran as a roadblock to USSR expansion into the oil-rich Persian Gulf. The Soviet Union in 1980 did not import oil. America used some, but European and Japanese industries depended very heavily on the exports from the gulf. Geographically, the power that controls Iran controls the Strait of Hormuz and hence, the flow of petroleum. The shah functioned as America's frontline ally, the shield for the industrialized West's oil reservoir. Of course, by 1980 the shah was a memory. But U.S. objectives in the gulf still involved containing the Soviets. A pro-American Iran would be better, but the key for the United States involved an anti-Soviet Iran. Under no circumstances could America permit the Soviet Union to choke off the Hormuz jugular.

The invasion of Afghanistan in December 1979 demonstrated hostile Soviet intentions in the Persian Gulf region. To some extent, it also reinforced common Iranian and American distrust of the USSR. Both the U.S. and Iran vigorously protested; for example, both nations boycotted the 1980 Olympics. An Iranian mob rushed the Soviet Embassy in Tehran, and Khomeini denounced Moscow's military move.

For all Khomeini's hatred of the "Great Satan America," his antipathy for his northern neighbor was often no less passionate. The Shiite Muslims despised atheistic communists almost instinctively; Iranians disliked Russians based on centuries of border skirmishing. Soviet-backed Communist party agitation, particularly among the Kurdish and Azerbaijani minorities, challenged Khomeini's Islamic fundamentalists. So even as he held his American hostages, Iran's religious ruler served American policy by opposing the USSR.

But Iran occasionally wavered in its opposition to Soviet offers. An unrevoked 1921 agreement authorized the Soviets to intervene militarily to "defend" Iranian independence, and the Iranian Army under the shah included antiaircraft guns, armored personnel carriers, and artillery made in the USSR. The ayatollah, too, accepted Soviet assistance on occasion, if only because Moscow joined him in opposing America. In

January 1980, the USSR conveniently vetoed a United Nations Security Council resolution imposing economic sanctions on Iran. Definite precedents existed for Soviet "aid" to ward off any large-scale U.S. attack on revolutionary Iran, and knowing the USSR, that help might have been massive and preemptive. Afghanistan offered an unpleasant example of how it could happen.

Indeed, an unannounced Soviet exercise along the Soviet-Iranian border in August-September 1980 looked a lot like the preparatory stages of "brotherly assistance." At that time, America did not have much to use in any proposed military intervention, but President Carter was determined to prevent or defeat a Soviet attack. Carter aide Jody Powell recalled the serious concern in the White House: "There was a lot of discussion about putting ground forces into Iran. The debate I recall was 'If you put them in, you're likely to lose them; put 'em in to draw a line, a quickly positioned trip wire' versus 'Would threatening the use of tac nukes [small nuclear weapons] make the Soviets back off?' " Fortunately, the Soviets demobilized without further action.

Although nothing came of the curious buildup, it highlighted America's odd relationship with Iran. Even as Iran imprisoned American diplomats, Carter's advisers implicitly, and probably accurately, assumed that the threatened ayatollah would accept U.S. help against a Soviet invasion. But had Carter attacked Iran in force, the Soviets could have ridden to the rescue. Iran's proximity to the USSR and erratic dealings with the Communist superpower hindered U.S. military options. If Carter declared war at any point in the hostage crisis, he might have soon found himself fighting both Iranians and Russians.[15] So he shunned war.

To be fair, it is possible to see some virtue in a quick resort to an ultimatum linked to a promised declaration of war. For example, Carter could have given Iran seventy-two hours to restore order at the embassy or face aerial bombardment. Threatening heavy air strikes might have garnered some Iranian concessions, particularly if the United States promptly began gathering forces to conduct this series of bombings.

Tougher language and brandishing of armed power evidently affected the eventual conclusion of the hostage crisis. In a widely publicized remark, President-Elect Ronald Reagan called the Iranians "barbarians" in early January 1981, darkly hinting of the consequences in store if Iran held their American prisoners after he took over. Khomeini wrapped up a very quick deal in January 1981 rather than face Reagan's wrath.

Any U.S. resort to an ultimatum would have amounted to a bluff. As long as Ayatollah Khomeini knuckled under, all would be well. But what if Khomeini and his fanatics called the American hand? Either American bombers would drop their ordnance and the Iranians would kill their captives, or the U.S. would back down and admit that intimidation failed. In either case, what next?

Visceral desires aside, such a bellicose approach necessitated a careful delineation of U.S. goals, especially if Iran rejected the American demand and executed the hostages. Barring a major shift in U.S. Persian Gulf strategy, it would make sense to keep the war limited and short. But given the popular American reaction to a hostage massacre, especially if it occurred before television cameras, keeping hostilities restrained could well prove politically impossible. Domestic American clamor might require a major ground invasion and a fight to the finish, presumably followed by the restoration of the Pahlavi royal family or some other pro-American faction over the battered, sullen remnants of Iran. Would the cure be worse than the disease?

Other than punishing Iran, what could war accomplish? Aside from writing off the unfortunate hostages, America might have destroyed a strong anti-Soviet buffer state, suffered heavy losses, and alienated much of the Islamic world. Dogged Iranian performance in the bloody war with Iraq (September 1980–?) indicates the likelihood of fanatical and lengthy resistance in the mountains and deserts. Only the Soviets could benefit from the resultant power vacuum in Iran.

In essence, Carter consciously handled the embassy seizure as if it were a short-term diplomatic crisis rather than risk an irreversible break with Iran. In Captain Sick's words: "President Carter never lost sight of the fundamental truth that, painful as it was to have American diplomats held prisoner in Tehran, there were other possible outcomes that were even worse." [16]

Although he rejected an overt declaration of war, President Carter did pursue some military options short of war. As early as 6 November 1979, Carter considered reprisal air strikes and directed increased satellite surveillance of the Iranian defense forces. His concern for the hostages' welfare and the solvency of anti-Soviet Iran guided his thinking. Carter determined to attack in force if the Iranians tried or executed the hostages, and he made this clear to Iran's leaders in his harsh private message shortly after the embassy fell. National security adviser Zbigniew Brzezinski raised the possibility of a rescue, and planning began. But Carter expected a great deal of any military operation attempted. As he recorded in his diary on 10 November: "We want it to be quick, incisive, surgical, no loss of American lives, not involve any other country, minimal suffering of the Iranian people themselves, to increase their reliance on imports, sure of success, and unpredictable."

Carter's overriding interest in bringing the hostages home alive made military means a last resort. The president probably went too far in his even temper and accommodation. As he later wrote: "Although Khomeini was acting insanely, we always behaved as if we were dealing with a rational person. . . . I urged the people in my administration and the members of Congress not to use abusive language about Khomeini or the kidnappers which might provoke violence against the hostages." Carter's diplomats, under Secretary of State Cyrus Vance, pursued every nonmilitary avenue. None of this had any effect on the implacable ayatollah, although he evidently believed Carter's warning about hurting the American prisoners. Behind the hopeless flailing in the impotent courts of world opinion, the military began to prepare for the worst. This took time. When the president reached the end of diplomatic and legal efforts in late March 1980, the armed forces said they were ready.

Brzezinski handled the preparations for military actions. His original suggestions included seizure of the Kharg Island oil facilities, mining Iranian ports with or without a supporting naval blockade, punitive air strikes, and the rescue operation. The Soviet push into Afghanistan ruled out the island assault and the mining option, as both amounted to a declaration of war with attendant risks. Any effort to destroy Iranian commerce or plug Iranian ports could encourage Iran to seek overland trade and succor from its powerful northern neighbor. A blockade effort would alienate Islamic Pakistan, Saudi Arabia, and the lesser gulf states and cause alarm in oil-poor Europe. Bombing remained an option, but principally if Iran killed its captives. Although difficult, Brzezinski favored a retrieval effort. He was willing to include the mission in a larger program of bombing to cover the special operations insertion and to avoid staking U.S. hopes and prestige on the tricky Tehran raid alone.

By 22 March 1980, diplomacy was obviously floundering, and Carter assembled his key political, diplomatic, and military advisers at Camp David. In Brzezinski's opinion, there were only three choices: "negotiating ad infinitum," bombing ("perhaps the worst solution of all"), and the rescue, "a more surgical solution." By 11 April, Carter chose to try Operation EAGLE CLAW as part of an overall series of punitive air bombardments. General David Jones, USAF, chairman of the Joint Chiefs of Staff, told the president that April 24 was the earliest available launch date.

A 16 April meeting with Colonel Beckwith, General Vaught, and other key military officers involved in the operation confirmed Carter's decision. Even Secretary of State Vance's resignation in protest (effective after the rescue operation) did not deter Jimmy Carter. The president canceled the concurrent air attacks, however, to minimize Iranian losses and avoid a casus belli. The chief executive allowed his military subordinates to execute the mission their way: "I made it clear that there would be no interference from the White House while the mission was underway. However, I wanted to be kept constantly informed." [17]

United States Strategic and Operational Objectives for Operation EAGLE CLAW

STRATEGIC OBJECTIVE: Rescue all American hostages in Iran.
OPERATIONAL OBJECTIVES:
1) Secure Desert One refueling/transfer site.
2) Secure Desert Two transfer site.
3) Secure Figbar and wadi hideouts.
4) Assault captured U.S. Embassy to secure fifty hostages.
5) Assault foreign ministry building to secure three hostages.
6) Secure Manzariyeh airfield.
7) Withdraw all forces from Tehran and Manzariyeh.

Carter did not need to interfere; he had already done so, albeit unwittingly. The president's desires to safeguard the hostages and prevent war with Iran apparently blinded him to the realities of using military force. Soldiers, sailors, airmen, and marines smash things and kill people, and that would certainly have occurred in Tehran. Although Carter knew the details of the plans for the violent embassy assault and the potent Spectre flights above Tehran, he avoided consideration of this certain bloodshed. At the 16 April briefing, the president ordered General Jones to devote his personal attention to preventing Iranian casualties. It was as if Carter expected Delta to arrest the Pasdaran sentries.

After the raid miscarried, Carter described the operation as a "humanitarian mission," and even went so far as to say "their goal was not to destroy or injure anyone." Consequently, the Iran raiders received no combat awards, but instead garnered the same sorts of peacetime Department of Defense medals customarily provided for flood assistance or earthquake cleanup. Jimmy Carter evidently believed his own rhetoric. He concluded his memoirs, *Keeping Faith,* with a quote from Thomas Jefferson, who evidently forgot various Indian skirmishes and the 1803–05 Barbary Pirate War: "I have the consolation to reflect that during the period of my administration not a drop of the blood of a single citizen was shed by the sword of war." [18] Both presidents ignored the truth.

President Carter's guidance produced an incursion deep into Iran, relying on extreme secrecy rather than more typical (and destructive) armed diversions. It was a hell of a way to make war, and it had serious effects on the planning and execution of EAGLE CLAW.

Thus, the president of the United States chose a risky military solution, deliberately sacrificing mass and flexibility to insure a supposedly "surgical" rescue mission. Interestingly, there is no evidence that President Carter or his colleagues anticipated a disastrous failure, so well had they crafted EAGLE CLAW. "Careful plans had been made to abort the operation at any time there might be unforeseen problems or a chance of detection," wrote the president. [19] But instead, events took their own tragic course, and Admiral Holloway and his able men were left to sort some sense out of the ruins.

The distinguished Holloway group identified twenty-three separate issues that contributed to the troubles during EAGLE CLAW, and their thorough work forms the basis for any assessment of the failed mission. Adding insights gained since August 1980, it now appears that the demise of EAGLE CLAW involved three major factors: an inflexible plan, helicopter troubles, and a surprising willingness to abort in the face of unforeseen troubles. Basic inflexibility was by far the most serious deficiency, magnifying helicopter problems and encouraging truncation of the mission when things went wrong. Interestingly, although the Holloway Report cautioned "that no one action or lack of action caused the operation to fail," President Carter maintained that everything had gone well, only to be undone by what he called "mechanical difficulties." Brzezinski and Jordan echoed their superior's claims. [20] Blaming inanimate objects seems a bit facile.

The EAGLE CLAW plan involved a very difficult special operation, probably the most daunting ever attempted. American armed forces en-

---

The Holloway Special Operations Review Group

Members: Adm. James L. Holloway, USN, retired; Lt. Gen. Samuel V. Wilson, USA, retired; Lt. Gen. Leroy J. Manor, USAF, retired; Maj. Gen. James C. Smith, USA; Maj. Gen. John L. Piotrowski, USAF; Maj. Gen. Alfred M. Gray, USMC

Issues Affecting Failure of Operation EAGLE CLAW

* * 1. Operational security
* * 2. Organization, command and control, and the applicability of existing JCS plans
* * 3. Centralized and integrated intelligence support external to JTF
* * 4. Independent review of plans
* * 5. Comprehensive readiness evaluation
* * 6. Overall coordination of joint training
* 7. Alterations in JTF composition
* 8. Risk assessment of hostile signals intelligence capabilities
* 9. Abort criteria
* 10. The use of other helicopters
* *11. Helicopter force size
* 12. Alternate helicopter pilots
* 13. Established helicopter unit
* *14. Handling the dust phenomenon
* 15. Weather reconnaissance
* *16. C-130 pathfinders
* 17. Helicopter aborts
* 18. The enemy radar threat
* 19. Helicopter communications
* *20. Alternatives to the Desert One site
* *21. Command and control at Desert One
* 22. Classified material safeguard
* 23. Destruct devices on rescue mission helicopters

* Major contributing factors, as judged by the group.

Source: Special Operations Review Group, "Iran Rescue Mission-1" in *Aviation Week and Space Technology* (15 September 1980), 61–71; "Iran Rescue Mission-2" in *Aviation Week and Space Technology* (22 September 1980), 140–144; "Iran Rescue Mission-3" in *Aviation Week and Space Technology* (29 September 1980), 84–91.

Operation EAGLE CLAW Concept of Operations

PREMISSION PHASE
  1. Initial deployment
     A. Deploy aircraft carriers to Gulf of Oman (Task Force 70)
     B. Infiltrate Tehran (Agents)
     C. Fly to aircraft carriers (MAC, Helicopter Force, Task Force 70)
     D. Prepare trucks and hideouts (Agents)
     E. Survey landing conditions at Desert One (Central Intelligence Agency)
  2. Final deployment
     A. Fly to Qena, Egypt (MAC, JTF HQ, Transport Force, Ground Force, Extraction Force)
     B. Move to eastern Turkey (Python Force)
     C. Fly crews to aircraft carriers (MAC, Helicopter Force, Task Force 70)
     D. Fly to Masirah Island, Oman (Transport Force, Ground Force)

INSERTION PHASE
  1. Flight to Desert One
     A. Fly to Desert One (Transport Force with Ground Force, Helicopter Force)
     B. Secure Desert One (Transport Force)
     C. Prepare Desert Two (Agents)
  2. Desert One Ground Operations
     A. Refuel/Cross-load (Transport Force, Ground Force, Helicopter Force)
     B. Fly to Masirah (Transport Force)
  3. Flight to Desert Two (Helicopter Force with Ground Force)
  4. Desert Two Ground Operations (Agents, Helicopter Force, Ground Force)
  5. Occupation of hide sites
     A. Foot march to wadi (Ground Force)
     B. Fly to Figbar (Helicopter Force)
     C. Secure hideouts until sundown (Helicopter Force, Ground Force)
     D. Final preparations in Tehran (Agents)
  6. Infiltration into Tehran
     A. Drive drivers to warehouse (Agents, Ground Force)
     B. Leaders' reconnaissance of embassy (Agents, Ground Force)
     C. Drive from hideout to embassy (Agents, Ground Force)
     D. Drive from hideout to foreign ministry (Agents, Special Assault Team)
     E. Fly to holding area (Helicopter Force)
  7. Flight to Manzariyeh (Extraction Force)
  8. Flight to Tehran (Spectre Force, Task Force 70 Air Wings, SAC tankers)

Operation EAGLE CLAW Concept of Operations
(continued)

ASSAULT
1. Ground assault
   A. Enter compounds by foot
      1) embassy (Ground Forces, Agents)
      2) foreign ministry (Special Assault Team, Agents)
   B. Secure hostages
      1) embassy (Ground Forces)
      2) foreign ministry (Special Assault Team)
   C. Secure Amjadieh Soccer Stadium (Ground Force)
   D. Destroy Mehrabad military airfield (Spectre Force)
   E. Fly to embassy and foreign ministry (Helicopter Force)
2. Secure Manzariyeh (Extraction Force)
3. Withdrawal
   A. Withdraw embassy hostages (Ground Forces, Helicopter Force)
   B. Withdraw all Americans at foreign ministry (Special Assault Team, Helicopter Force)
   C. Move to Amjadieh Soccer Stadium (Ground Force)
   D. Fly to Amjadieh Soccer Stadium (Helicopter Force)
   E. Withdraw embassy rescue force (Ground Force, Agents, Helicopter Force)

EXTRACTION
1. Manzariyeh operations (Ground Force, Agents, Helicopter Force, Extraction Force)
2. Withdrawal
   A. Destroy helicopters (Helicopter Force, Ground Force)
   B. Fly to Qena, Egypt (Extraction Force, Helicopter Force, Ground Force, Agents)
   C. Depart Manzariyeh (Extraction Force)
   D. Depart Turkey (Python Force)

---

deavored to assemble forces secretly, enter Iran unnoticed, fly almost 1,000 miles undetected, infiltrate an enemy city, swiftly seize a large defended downtown compound, smoothly extricate the hostages from an aroused urban area, and then proceed almost 400 miles through Iran without being destroyed by alerted Iranian military outfits. President

Carter's concern for Iranian casualties did not make it any easier. As the Holloway group proudly noted: "The United States military, alone in the world, had the capability to accomplish what the United States planned to do." [21] The Israeli raid on the Entebbe, Uganda, airport (July 1976) was a similar tough, long-range rescue attempt, but the Israelis attacked a small group of terrorists isolated at an airport. The Israelis landed in fixed wing aircraft, grabbed their countrymen, and took off, spending little time in enemy airspace.

The Iran raid featured one incredibly hard operation within another nearly impossible undertaking: a tricky urban rescue inside a long-range insertion and extraction. Unlike Entebbe, the rescue force intended to sneak into a city of three million people, deep in a paranoid country, without tipping off the Iranian sentinels at the Tehran embassy. The American operation to liberate Son Tay Prison Camp, North Vietnam (November 1970), offers a much more analogous operation, but even this mission focused on a site twenty-three miles from Hanoi. EAGLE CLAW was the equivalent of trying to retrieve American PWs from the downtown Hanoi Hilton.

A small clandestine raid made sense. There probably was no other way to penetrate almost 1,000 miles into a hostile country. But the big question was how to pull it off. When U.S. planners in General Vaught's Joint Task Force 1-79 headquarters began work on 12 November 1979, they immediately faced the troublesome puzzle-box aspect of the Tehran situation. Since the JTF leadership expected to conduct their designed mission themselves, they concentrated on creating the best possible raid. [22] Doing less would imperil their own lives along with those of the hostages.

Rightly, Vaught's officers determined that the actions at the objective (freeing the hostages) keyed the entire U.S. effort. Only the superbly trained counterterrorist soldiers of 1st Special Forces Operations Detachment—Delta, possessed the capability to deal with the beleaguered embassy. The really formidable aspect involved placing Delta in the vicinity of the American legation. Colonel Beckwith formed his unit in 1977 to deal with terrorist takeovers, consciously emulating the renowned British Special Air Service commandos, right down to calling his companies "squadrons," his platoons "troops," and basing his tactics on four-man teams. Prior to 4 November 1979, Beckwith's skilled men expected to do their work in a friendly country, on invitation of an overmatched American ally. Getting Delta into Tehran without killing the hostages was the rub, and that resulted in a complex concept of operations that mandated nearly airtight operational security (OPSEC, concern for secrecy to insure surprise).

One understandable decision early in the planning added most of the mission's intricacies. Faced with settling on a reliable clandestine insertion method, Vaught and his subordinates considered three possibilities: a parachute drop, truck movement from friendly Turkey, and helicopters. The parachute option allowed a fast approach in fixed wing aircraft, and Delta's troops were all qualified jumpers. This sort of raid could be mounted very rapidly. Unfortunately, parachuting almost insured broken ankles and other troublesome drop zone injuries, especially if Delta tried to actually leap into the city. Assuming agents with trucks met Delta at the drop zone and the Iranians did not notice the rain of Americans, they might reach the embassy unseen. But jumping did nothing toward swift removal of the hostages once Delta stormed the embassy. Parachuting rescuers would have to fight their way out of Tehran on the ground to reach a secured pickup zone, and that assumed other Americans could grab a nearby airstrip. Beckwith told Vaught the parachute approach was "ludicrous" and offered "zero" chance of success. Still, this plan remained the designated "emergency" rescue operation in the event Iran began executing hostages. It took months to fashion the more workable helicopter effort.

Trucking in from Turkey was quite possible, because a wide variety of commercial traffic routinely traversed revolutionary Iran. It would take a day or two to navigate the winding mountain roads from the Turkish border to Tehran, but trucks were mechanically reliable and Delta would arrive intact at its objective. Motor vehicles provided excellent concealment for an embassy approach. On the negative side, the trucks again offered the unsavory prospect of slashing out of embattled Tehran toward a secured fixed-wing pickup zone. Worse, a meandering vehicle infiltration risked compromise at the ever-shifting kaleidoscope of Iranian Army, Pasdaran, and national police guard posts, roadblocks, and checkpoints spotted along the likely routes. If compromised, a quick withdrawal seemed impossible. As Beckwith said: "If the Pasdaran opened a refrigerator truck and found it full of Delta operators and not frozen beef, what the hell were we going to do?"

Finally, Vaught turned to helicopters. They were faster than trucks and slower than airplanes, but they could avoid detection on their approach and, most important of all, they had that unique ability to fly straight up and down. Helicopters might escape if detected. Of course, they were much too noisy to bring in the Delta attackers, and the militia at the embassy had spiked the compound lawns to frustrate landings. Trucks certainly seemed the best way to move Delta to the objective. But unlike trucks, helos could lift the freed hostages quickly out of the alerted embassy grounds. As in the other two options, an American force would assault air-land to take a nearby extraction field. The promise of rapidly removing the hostages from Tehran to the withdrawal airhead cinched it for the rotary-wing method.

The choice of clattering helicopters set the tempo, stretching EAGLE CLAW beyond a single night's work. The choppers' sluggish airspeed (135 miles per hour) and short range (750 miles) created problems. They had to refuel en route, and expected to stop just short of Tehran to transfer the ground force to trucks for the final approach. But the slow trucks could not get to downtown Tehran that night, and an assault launched in daylight would likely be detected and repulsed. So the Americans intended to hide more than twenty-four hours to await the next nightfall. The helos were nothing but trouble, except that they alone possessed the critical vertical lift characteristics necessary to whisk the rescued hostages to the extraction airfield. This one key contribution made the slow, balky, short-range choppers essential.[23] But it also doomed EAGLE CLAW to a long operation featuring the Desert One refueling stop, the lengthy hideout, and the entire truck escapade, and adding plenty to the plan's complexity. Using choppers made secrecy all the more critical.

Only the big H-53 series of helos appeared suitable for the operation, and either of the two U.S. Navy aircraft carriers steaming in the Arabian Sea provided a suitable launching platform. Armed, armored U.S. Air Force HH-53C Aerospace Rescue and Recovery Service Jolly Green Giants, of the sort used on the *Mayaguez* mission, could refuel in midair, but did not fold up for carrier stowage and would have looked strange to prying Soviet intelligence collectors. So they were out. Marine Corps CH-53D Sea Stallions had folding tails and rotor blades, but they too might seem out of place on an aircraft carrier.

To serve security, JTF 1-79 selected U.S. Navy RH-53D Sea Stallions from Helicopter Mine Countermeasures Squadron 16 (HM-16), which occasionally flew from carriers. In light of possible mining of Iranian harbors, enemy intelligence probably expected to see these craft. They mounted two .50-caliber heavy machine guns for exploding surfaced mines, which could work handily in hostile Tehran. These choppers might have been fitted for air to air refueling, but Vaught's officers opted to go with ground refueling at an intermediate spot (eventually designated Desert One). So instead of refueling probes, the Sea Stallions received twin auxiliary fuel tanks to extend their 540-mile range to about 750 miles, plus a coat of sand-hued paint to aid in concealment. By 26 December, six RH-53Ds staged through Diego Garcia to USS *Kitty Hawk*. On 23 January, USS *Nimitz* took over in the Arabian Sea, adding the *Kitty Hawk* covey to two of her own RH-53Ds. JTF flight crews trained on similar aircraft in the southwestern United States.[24]

Working under pressure, by 19 November Vaught and his men settled on the long-range helicopter insertion eventually tried, to include the designation of the RH-53D Sea Stallion as the rotary-wing aircraft. This choice underlay the thirty-two-hour-long concept of operations eventually attempted. The severe tasks involved in the Tehran raid insured a challenging mission, but the EAGLE CLAW concept of operations was extremely complicated. JTF 1-79 designed a three-stage operation: insertion, assault, and extraction. Each phase had successive subsegments involving various forces moving in concert, and each portion hinged upon the other.

Especially comforting to President Carter and his top advisers, the plan included provisions for an abort if something went wrong. Certainly, the plan might have been halted without difficulty during the premission deployment, and possibly even up to the refueling stop. In the words of Deputy Secretary of Defense W. Graham Claytor, "We could stop it just before it started if the weather was not right, if there had been a security leak or if there was an indication that surprise was lost—we could terminate at a second point, at Desert One, unless we had what was considered to be the minimum assets needed to carry out the rest of the operation. . . ."[25] Aborts after that point might well be unpleasant and bloody. But as long as the raiders came away clean, the chain of command seemed to think that they could try again the next available night. In brief, keeping it all secret seemed to provide some flexibility in the convoluted plan. As long as America could sneak in and out of Iran, the rescue commanders apparently believed they could attempt the operation more than once.

As Zbigniew Brzezinski rightly noted, the mission depended upon the "essential elements of secrecy and surprise."[26] With more than a day of undetected operations built into the concept of operations and surreptitious withdrawal critical to any repeat efforts, Brzezinski's comment is definitely accurate. President Carter's own insistent denial of resort to military force contributed to the superb concealment effort, as did the passage of months since the seizure. The Iranian guards and military units became careless. The emphasis on operational security succeeded. After all, the Iranians remained unaware of EAGLE CLAW until President Carter announced the raid's failure. But OPSEC also hobbled preparations and execution, particularly affecting the size of the helicopter force, joint training, the flow of weather information, flight altitudes, and communications during the mission.

Brzezinski himself influenced the size of the helicopter force. Despite some initial idea of using as few as forty Delta soldiers and four choppers, by mid-January, the JTF established eight as the number of RH-53Ds aboard *Nimitz*, seven for launch, six at Desert One, and five at Figbar. Although USS *Nimitz* could carry up to eleven Sea Stallions without hurting other air operations, and USS *Coral Sea* was available as well, additional helos were not loaded. Colonel Kyle's planes carried enough fuel to top off ten RH-53Ds. The Holloway group wrote: "It appears that on balance an increase in the size of the helicopter force was warranted." The JTF evidently agreed. Indeed, General Vaught admitted during postmission congressional testimony that a ninth chopper was heading for the Arabian Sea aboard USS *Eisenhower* when EAGLE CLAW started.

So for this most vital mission, why did America commit only eight of its thirty RH-53Ds, not to mention hundreds of other H-53 models available? Here, it appears that the forceful but militarily inexperienced Brzezinski played a role. At the rather late date of 16 April, he finally assented to launching all eight copters on the *Nimitz*, but only after steady military prodding. The national security adviser became obsessed with keeping the operation "as lean and closely honed as possible," to avoid Iranian radar and signal detection. His "gravest concern" revolved around compromise of the mission, and he feared domestic political criticism in that event. Said Brzezinski afterwards, "If the Iranians had discovered the mission because of the size of the air armada penetrating their air space, we all would doubtless be charged with typically excessive American redundancy, with unwillingness to go in hard and lean—the way, for example, the Israelis did at Entebbe." [27] Brzezinski ignored the major differences between Entebbe and Tehran in his zeal to prove that a superpower could pull off the impossible on a shoestring. Thanks to such misguided thinking, it all stayed secret and "lean," but America came up a helicopter short.

Hard, realistic joint training offered the only reasonable way to forge a rescue team capable of executing the involved EAGLE CLAW scheme. This was not an overnight matter. It took from November 1979 until 8 February 1980 to develop even the barest capacity for the helicopter scheme, and until 28 March to achieve a reasonably confident ability to conduct the raid. This lengthy preparation of U.S. rescue forces undoubtedly encouraged President Carter to pursue the diplomatic efforts he favored; he could not launch a raid until April, even had he been so disposed. Given the shrinking length of Iranian nights and decreased helicopter lift caused as the desert heated up, EAGLE CLAW had to go in April or wait until the autumn. So the JTF training rate had a major effect on the president's options. In a very real sense, Carter in April faced a now or never decision.

OPSEC hindered training, because the JTF allowed inordinate concern for Soviet and Iranian detection to limit their exercises. Despite use of remote southwestern desert training areas, mission planners refused to permit a full-scale shakedown, fearing the unwelcome attentions of Soviet agents, electronic eavesdroppers, and spy satellites. Six carefully hidden joint training exercises replicated distinct segments of the mission, particularly the long, low-level helicopter flights, although constant intelligence updates and operational alterations rendered each exercise a bit different from the previous iteration. Some portions of the plan (like the embassy assault) were rehearsed hundreds of times on accurate mock-ups, but even this well-practiced phase was significantly modified by last-minute intelligence from the Pakistani cook. As Gen. David Jones told President Carter on 22 March 1980, he felt better about the viability of each of the parts of the operation than about the entire undertaking.

Even so, not once did the men of JTF 1-79 recreate the entire mission, from carrier lift-off to extraction from Manzariyeh. Nobody practiced certain crucial actions and contingencies such as landing helos inside a soccer stadium or executing an abort withdrawal from Desert One. It resembled an attempt to prepare a football team for a game without a full-contact scrimmage. For example, Holloway's investigators discovered that the vital fuel and personnel transfers at Desert One "had not been fully rehearsed." Instead, only two C-130s and four choppers were used "to validate the Desert One concept" on 13–14 April, scant days prior to force deployment. The resultant confusion and collision at Desert

One, although not a direct cause of EAGLE CLAW's abort, typified some of the training deficiencies. Did similar problems exist in later phases?

Aside from OPSEC, it should be noted that a steady series of alerts also impeded training. At least seven times, Beckwith readied his men to move, only to find that it was a false alarm, and training continued. Every time military and civilian authorities ordered their rescue elements to prepare for action, it disrupted training.[28] These alerts seemed unavoidable, given the nature of the American operation.

Fears that people not directly concerned with EAGLE CLAW might inadvertently leak news of the raid severely affected the flow of weather information. JTF staff officers compartmentalized work, allowing only those with a "need to know" to understand exactly how the fruits of their labors were to be employed. Weathermen knew about the suspended dust phenomenon, and even added relevant comments about haboobs to the written EAGLE CLAW operations plan's weather annex. Because the weather forecasters were not supposed to know what sort of force intended to enter Iran, planners did not permit the meteorologists to brief the transport or helicopter pilots. Weather teams routinely brief Strategic Air Command nuclear alert crews and have participated in many classified missions in Southeast Asia, but JTF 1-79 decided to cut them out as not possessing a vital "need to know." As the Holloway group stated: "The traditional relationship between pilots and weather forecasters was severed. This was done to enhance OPSEC." [29] So the chopper fliers found out about hanging dust clouds the hard way.

Fears of Iranian radar kept flight altitudes low. Transports flew at 400 feet, but Seiffert's crews raced along at only 100 feet, thanks to an offhand comment made by an intelligence officer during premission training. The Holloway group noted that the helicopter pilots probably overdid things. At 100 feet, the dust was much thicker, and the thermal effects of the haboobs on helo number five's guidance avionics insured Colonel Pitman's untimely return to the *Nimitz*. So the 300-foot difference mattered.

Indeed, even Kyle's transports might have erred well on the side of caution. Nearby Soviet radars, other than the single collection ship near Hormuz, could not cover much of Iran. More to the point, by 1980, Iran's radar net leaked like a sieve. Conveniently, the United States Military Assistance Advisory Group in Iran had studied the shah's radar and air defenses intensively in January 1977. The American officers had recommended installation of twelve to twenty-one new Westinghouse ADS-4 ground control intercept radar stations supplemented by seven AWACS aircraft. Since that study, Iran had only received eight of the radars and no AWACS to supplement its ancient airport radar nets around Tehran, Tabriz, and Mashhad. U.S. radar experts in 1977 estimated that without AWACS to fill in low-level gaps on the Soviet and Iraqi borders, twelve to twenty-one radars offered a paltry "10 percent coverage of airspace." The Iranians had eight, and maintenance of those stations could not have been good. EAGLE CLAW planners knew that the radars were in bad shape.

Additionally, American radar specialists enumerated the other problems of using radar in mountainous, undulating Iran. Humidity effects rendered stations along the Persian Gulf "generally ineffective from April to November," the few mountaintop stations provided "limited low altitude coverage," and valley sites "can detect aircraft at only limited ranges, and then only if alerted." Erich von Marbod of the Defense Security Assistance Agency was more blunt: "Iran needs an air defense system. They don't have one."

Khomeini did have a few hundred jets and even four battalions of Improved Hawk American-made surface to air missiles left over from the shah's buildup, although many of the missiles and planes degraded into almost utter disrepair without spare parts. Some high-level Iranian officers appear to have moved the few functioning detection systems to the Iraqi border, a supposition somewhat confirmed by the February 1981 arrest of Gen. Amir Bahman Baqeri, commander of the Iranian Air Force. Khomeini's minions charged Baqeri with cooperating with the U.S. rescue effort by relocating equipment out of the American flight path on 23 April 1980.[30] Given that the apprehension of this key leader occurred during the desperate war with Iraq, the belief that the CIA might have "turned" a few Iranian commanders cannot be discounted.

The upshot of all of this suggests that the U.S. approach routes might have been brought higher, particularly once the chopper crews entered the smothering talc blankets. In 1970, the Son Tay raiders penetrated the elaborate, fully functional North Vietnamese air defense net at 1,000 feet and higher. A willingness to go up might have encouraged Colonel Pitman in helicopter number five to press on to Desert One, which would have placed six operational choppers at the refueling area. Brzezinski's fears of electronic discovery appear greatly exaggerated.

Considering that air to air refueling of helicopters is possible at least as low as 1,000 feet, the sad state of Iranian radars offered an alternative to the whole Desert One situation.[31] Instead, American planners took no risks of detection, went in very low, and vastly increased the dangers of in-flight accidents and mechanical aborts.

Fear of radio interception greatly limited communications, which particularly hurt the helo pilots struggling with the dust. Terrain mitigated the effectiveness of those few Iranian radio direction finders still working in April 1980, but the JTF properly wanted to defeat any Soviet electronic surveillance. By using short, coded, low-power transmissions at close range, secure emergency communications should have been possible. As the Holloway group observed: "There were ways to pass the information to C-130s and helicopters en route that would have small likelihood of compromising the mission."

As with the radar issue, the JTF staff voted for security at the cost of flexibility by simply declaring full radio silence. Once again, the Holloway group found that Lieutenant Colonel Seiffert's unlucky helicopter pilots adhered to stricter standards than the rest of the force. When the choppers entered the unforeseen dust clouds, a few discreet transmissions might have reunited the scattered force or verified clear conditions at Desert One.[32] As with flying higher, this could have kept number five in action. But Seiffert and Pitman stuck with their orders and allowed their helicopter formation to disintegrate, all in the name of secrecy.

All of this OPSEC guaranteed only initial surprise, because once the force entered Iran, enemy forces might have their own ideas about things. When several former hostages were asked about the raid after their return, they expressed reservations that most of the captives could have been saved. They immediately brought up the sort of "fog of war" considerations that could have menaced the raiders in Tehran. *Charge d'affaires* L. Bruce Laingen thought the compound was too large, the city too confused, the streets swollen with random armed groups, and an unopposed extraction unlikely. Political officer Victor L. Tomseth agreed. After Kathryn Koob explained how her isolated location on the chancellery's second floor made her rescue difficult, she concluded dramatically, "Thank God for the sandstorm."[33]

To be honest, chances of compromise increased with every passing hour. At "remote" Desert One, three unexpected Iranian vehicles blundered into the U.S. perimeter within a few minutes. What if a similar event had occurred along the railroad at Desert Two, or during the daylight hours on 25 April, or as Delta's trucks drove toward the embassy? What if the intruders had worn uniforms and fought back? Counting on more than a day of hidden activity deep in a hostile country seemed pretty ambitious. Without armed diversions scheduled, relying on stealth, the small U.S. units could only stick to their script. Discovery equaled failure.

But staying undercover was a means, not an end. Security did not insure mission success. All the OPSEC in the world could not save the hostages. EAGLE CLAW stayed secret, yet it failed, principally because operational security considerations limited deviations from the exceptionally complicated plan. Each element had its orders, and as long as all went well, there would be no need for communications or major changes in flight paths, force composition, or timings. If something went awry, then the Americans intended to abort and try again. Contingencies for catastrophic failure evidently did not exist. In light of the inherently chancy nature of special operations, this trust in the fortunes of war was extraordinary. Even the most skilled soldiers and pilots could only do so much.

Uninformed critics often seize upon helicopter troubles as the reason EAGLE CLAW failed. The somewhat simplistic version attributes the abort at Desert One to aircraft maintenance deficiencies; a more sophisticated variation blames the pilots. Given the severe requirements of the designed plan and OPSEC limits on force size, training, weather data, flight altitudes, and communications, it is amazing that the helicopter force performed as well as it did.

The maintenance deficiency argument is a red herring. The blade failure indication on number six, electronics "brownout" on number five, and broken hydraulic pump on number two had nothing to do with more, less, or improper mechanical work on USS *Nimitz* or elsewhere. Experienced HM-16 squadron mechanics, along with a second set of technicians, civilian technical representatives of Sikorsky Aircraft, and designated test pilots fixed and flew the mission RH-53Ds while they waited for Lieutenant Colonel Seiffert's crews. Seiffert's own maintenance officer checked the helicopters personally three weeks before the operation commenced. He found them to be in excellent condition.

Three popular "inside" accounts are also spurious. True, Pitman ordered the HM-16 maintenance teams to remove the heavy engine air particle separators, filter panels immediately labeled "sandscreens" by journalists searching for an easy explanation. While this removal increased friction damage on the turbine engines, it also increased lift. The haboobs did not even affect the unscreened engines. Perhaps the Sea Stallions might have needed power plant overhauls sooner, but since they were destined for demolition at Manzariyeh, the extra lift was worth the added wear and tear. Reports that a careless sailor sprayed fire-fighting foam on five choppers early on 24 April were also factual, but the external soaking had no subsequent effect thanks to a quick cleanup and thorough inspection. Finally, some reporters thought that helicopter number five carried the spare parts necessary to repair number two's cracked hydraulic pump, and Pitman's abort left the crew of number two without repair items. Although properly ironic, it is completely false. No helo carried a second-stage hydraulic pump; choppers number one, three, and seven had special spare parts kits, and they all arrived at Desert One.[34]

Of the three RH-53Ds that "failed," only number two's mishap seemed to require an abort. Chopper number six's pilots could have probably ignored the blade failure light, given that the cockpit instruments in the RH-53D were notably sensitive. A thorough maintenance analysis prior to launch may have informed Seiffert's pilots that in 38,216 flight hours as of December 1979, the RH-53D had never experienced a spar crack, despite forty-three indications. Indeed, the hundreds of helicopters in the entire H-53 family suffered only three crashes related to rotor spar failure. Sikorsky Aircraft studies indicated that a fully loaded chopper could expect to fly at 120 knots (135 miles per hour) for more than twenty-seven hours with a cracked blade, even if the blade inspection method (BIM) warnings were accurate. A BIM situation arose in training, and it merited some research. But the maintenance staff either ignored the problem or, more likely, simply did not fully brief the pilots. As a result, the number six crew thought things were worse than they probably were.

Colonel Pitman's number five turned back due to severe problems in navigation systems caused by the heating effects of the haboobs. Chopper number five could have continued at higher altitude, in clearer skies, or in tandem with an electronically operational Sea Stallion, if only the marine colonel had violated the flight plan. But he did not realize that number six was down, and assumed that seven other choppers were clattering on to Desert One. Stringent OPSEC rules on flight altitude and communications left Pitman to make his own decision and turn around. As the Holloway group noted, Pitman said that if he had known that he was almost out of the dust and Desert One was clear, he would have continued.

Only number two experienced a definite failure in a key component, and even so, the pilots could have taken the dangerous risk of flying overloaded without a backup hydraulic system. Certainly the bold air force crews at Koh Tang Island in 1975 flew on despite equally hazardous conditions. Instead, like their partners in numbers five and six, the number two fliers opted for an abort, and EAGLE CLAW came to an abrupt end, victimized more by the restrictive flow of key data than by balky machines.[35] Perhaps the often-repeated idea that a clean, secure withdrawal and follow-up effort was quite possible guided the pilots' thinking.

Were the aviators to blame? Colonel Beckwith and his men seemed to think so. Informed of the broken pump on number two, Beckwith mused, "Did these pilots want to go, really want to go?" After the discouraging withdrawal, frustrated by the mission's failures, Beckwith lashed out at the helicopter crews, labeling them "cowards." In 1982, he told *Newsweek* reporter David C. Martin, "If you ask me would I do it again with that crowd, the answer is absolutely no." If other anonymous quotations in Martin's magazine story are accurate, Beckwith spoke for many of his men. Major Logan Fitch summarized the general impressions: "The crews worried us more than the crafts. . . . No one I knew had full confidence in them."

For example, Col. James R. Paschall, USA, who manned the JTF alternate headquarters at Masirah during the raid, strongly believed that selected air force crews might have made a difference. He observed that the United States possessed a superb long-range, rotary wing night penetration force flying in and out of North Vietnam in 1970–71, but that this capability had greatly degenerated by 1979. Even with good air force crews, Paschall believed it would have taken three to four months of tough, realistic training to achieve full readiness. He added that the single air force helo pilot used in EAGLE CLAW made it to Desert One with a sound chopper, and that marine assault pilots "turned back too easily."

Beckwith, too, believed that the marine helicopter crews did not train hard enough before the operation or try hard enough on the mission. He would have preferred to use U.S. Air Force HH-53C search and rescue and special operations pilots. Colonel Beckwith even charged that the Joint Chiefs included marine aviators to "make sure each of the services had a piece of the action." [36]

Beckwith's supposition about some JCS joint service publicity campaign is specious. The sixteen pilots and their crews were a composite group, including thirteen marines from two different units, two naval aviators, and one air force pilot. They were formed in December 1980 after an initially fruitless attempt to convert navy minesweeper fliers into low-level penetrators by pairing marine assault aviators with the mine warfare men. The EAGLE CLAW chopper crews trained quite intensively for their mission, subject to OPSEC limitations. Their dogged flight to Desert One through the baking dust blankets is evidence enough of their determination. More training hours could not right the troubles created by flying at excessively low altitudes, a radio blackout, unexpected haboobs, and a broken hydraulic pump.

To be fair to Beckwith and his disappointed comrades, there were air force pilots available. The Holloway group noted that USAF rolls showed ninety-six HH-53C fliers "current in long-range flight and aerial refuelling," plus an additional eighty-six former Jolly Green Giant pilots with "fairly recent Special Operations Forces or rescue experience." Holloway's investigators agreed that air force crews might have provided an earlier capability to execute the mission or permitted air to air fuel transfers. Holloway's team concluded, however, that by 24 April 1980, Seiffert's men were as ready as any could be to execute the intricate EAGLE CLAW mission. Admiral Holloway might have exaggerated when he said, "The best pilots in uniform were selected for the job," but not by much.[37]

If the chopper pilots were not to blame, was any individual commander at fault? Unfortunately, the weight of evidence points rather clearly at the outspoken Col. "Chargin' Charlie" Beckwith, who had been so quick to blame the "cowards" flying his choppers. When word came that only five flyable RH-53Ds were at Desert One, General Vaught asked his ground force commander to consider a change of plans. The chain of command, right up to President Carter, deferred to Beckwith. Even determined Zbigniew Brzezinski restrained his impulse "to opt for a single daring stroke for the big prize." Instead, it all depended upon a colonel. The plan said to turn back with only five choppers. Would Chargin' Charlie be bound by a plan?

Here was Beckwith's thinking, as recorded in his own words: "He

[Vaught] should have known it will be a disaster if we go forward with five. There isn't any way. I'd have to leave behind twenty men. . . . This is ludicrous. It doesn't make sense. Stay with the plan." Vaught, Jones, Brzezinski, and Carter accepted Beckwith's logic, and EAGLE CLAW aborted. Hamilton Jordan recorded his thoughts at this distressing juncture: "So even Beckwith—a man I knew had believed passionately in the mission and would never give up—had concluded they had to come back." [38]

From that point onward, Colonel Beckwith insisted that he made the correct decision. He even stated that he would have disobeyed an order to proceed.[39] But some of his other actions and comments lead one to think that perhaps the colonel "doth protest too much."

Of course, Beckwith had already changed his assault scheme based upon intelligence placing all hostages in the chancellery, and he decided to proceed even though he would not reach his hide site until after daybreak. The colonel had designed his assault force to search and clear four buildings spread across the compound. Why couldn't he delete some men now that he knew exactly where the hostages were? What would he have done if a chopper had crashed at Desert Two and he lost twenty men? He once said: "Plans are only so good. Sometimes unforeseen events can occur." Beckwith knew this, and prided himself on Delta's flexible structure of four-man teams: "The secret, the key, was modules that could change easily within any situation." Faced with a chance to test by fire what he had tested so often in training, Beckwith demurred.

More damning, Beckwith stated in 1982 that he could have conducted the operation with as few as two helicopters in Tehran: one for the hostages and one to shuttle Delta out to Manzariyeh. He justified his abort decision at Desert One with his general low opinion of Seiffert's pilots, his suspicions about helicopters cranking on the night of 25 April at Figbar, and his fears about Iranian gunnery at the soccer stadium. He said: "If we didn't have six, we wouldn't have ended up with two." [40] Beckwith stuck with his own strange arithmetic, unwilling to take a chance.

Why did this tough-talking, brave old Special Forces soldier insist on an abort at Desert One? Three explanations come to mind. First, perhaps Beckwith was among those who earnestly believed that an undetected withdrawal might lead to a successful attempt a night or two later. Maybe he thought the abort was not final. Even after the fatal crash, Beckwith made a tearful personal request to President Carter on 27 April 1980: "Will you let us go back?"

Second, as noted by strategist and combat veteran Col. Harry G. Summers, USA, Colonel Beckwith exhibited a tendency to deal with pressure rather emotionally. After his resolute "we would go ahead" choice when the choppers reported their late arrival, he seemed to become very agitated when only five helos turned out to be flyable. Some witnesses claimed they saw Beckwith sitting dejected at Desert One, wailing, "I failed, I failed," with his head in his hands. Beckwith described himself grabbing a C-130 pilot after the abort decision but before the collision, hollering, "For God's sake, don't leave." The pilot assured Beckwith that he was not going anywhere without his passengers, and the colonel wrote later: "I wanted to hug him!"

In a review of Beckwith's account of the Iran raid, Summers writes: "It raises the question of why a person of Beckwith's obvious temperament was chosen for such a sensitive assignment. The Army was forewarned how he might react to stress. Beckwith himself describes several instances of how he lost his self-control when things did not go to suit him." So the abort decision at Desert One fell to a tired commander in a dark desert. Maybe his gut reactions got the best of him, and unlike Stonewall Jackson, the Delta commander took counsel of his fears.

The third possible explanation relates to the second. Regardless of his forbidding exterior, Colonel Beckwith was a sensitive person with a deep concern for his Delta soldiers. He had created Delta to his own specifications, ramming the project through numerous bureaucratic obstacles and crafting it to his own high standards. He identified completely with his men—probably too completely. When asked by President Carter on 16 April to describe his mission in Iran, Beckwith had a curious response. He said: "To find and safely extract every American hostage and to bring back alive every one of those beautiful men I have trained." Similarly, when a journalist asked Beckwith why he had not proceeded with only five helicopters, Beckwith snarled in response: "I have been there before. I was not about to be a party to half-assed loading on a bunch of aircraft and going up and murdering a bunch of the finest soldiers in the world. I ain't going to do that." But Beckwith's mission was to rescue hostages, not protect his beloved Delta men.

When Colonel Beckwith stated he had "been there before," he was probably referring to his experiences in the besieged Plei Me Special Forces camp in October 1965. He wrote about what he had learned there, "If you were going to lose lives on an operation, it had better be worth it." [41] Apparently, Beckwith judged that the raid on Tehran was not worth what he assumed to be the likely losses. It is admirable and proper to look out for one's men, but the bottom line is that *the mission comes first*. In the Iranian desert, Colonel Beckwith might have forgotten that iron rule.

There really was a better way to do it, as proven by the brilliant American raid on Son Tay in November 1970. Fuzzy intelligence resulted in a landing at a camp full of Communist soldiers rather than U.S. prisoners, but in a military sense, the mission was a classic. Operation KINGPIN's preparations, approach, actions at the objective, and withdrawal were professionally outstanding. Two distinct differences separated the Son Tay effort from EAGLE CLAW: thorough rehearsals and a range of contingency plans. Close attention to adequate but not stifling operational security did the trick. For example, the raiders carefully dismantled their camp mock-ups when Soviet surveillance satellites passed over their training areas. As far as flexibility, the Son Tay troops and pilots practiced numerous variations, to include flying in fog and rain and conducting the assault with only portions of the raiding force. Indeed, a third of the soldiers landed at the wrong spot at the outset of the actual attack, but a deputy commander immediately switched over to a practiced alternate plan and continued the mission with superb results.[42]

Not only did the KINGPIN commanders press on when a mishap occurred, they opted to run their exceedingly dangerous mission even in the face of data indicating the prisoners might have been moved. Son Tay failed to rescue a single U.S. prisoner, but it showed how it could be done. Colonel Arthur D. "Bull" Simmons, USA, commanded the ground force, and Maj. Gen. Leroy J. Manor, USAF, commanded KINGPIN. By 1980, Simmons was dead of a heart attack. Manor, by then a retired lieutenant general, found out about EAGLE CLAW as a member of the Holloway Special Review Group. Their assault team commander, Richard Meadows, did his part in Tehran. But JTF 1-79 deviated widely from the Son Tay methods. Of course, some of this was due to a different, more challenging situation.

Three other possibilities existed: the Holloway group version of EAGLE CLAW, Zbigniew Brzezinski's direct flight prescription for a second rescue attempt, and an infiltration plan explained by a British Special Air Services veteran who writes under the name Gayle Rivers.

Two U.S. Raids: Son Tay and Iran

	KINGPIN 20–21 November 1970	EAGLE CLAW 24–25 April 1980
Objective	Rescue 61 prisoners from Son Tay, North Vietnam	Rescue 53 hostages from Tehran, Iran
Concept	Direct descent	Staged infiltration
Planned duration in hostile country	Total: 1 hour, 43 minutes Son Tay area: 27 minutes	Total: 32 hours Tehran area: 24 hours
Diversions	Air strikes	None planned
Assault troops	56 soldiers	120 soldiers and volunteers
Intelligence	Overhead imagery	Overhead imagery; covert agents on site
Assault aircraft	6 helicopters 3 transports 5 attack planes	8 helicopters 9 transports (6 in, 3 out) 4 gunships
Flight formation	Helicopters plus transports	Helicopters separated from transports
Flight distance	340 miles from Thailand 340 miles to Thailand	950 miles from Oman area 1,275 miles to Egypt
Aircraft aborts	None	2 helicopters
Aircraft refueling	Air	Ground
Preparation time	6 months	6 months
Rehearsals	170 full-scale practices	6 partial exercises
Training flight hours	1,017	More than 1,000
Results	Mission executed no prisoners found 1 wounded	Mission aborted no hostages rescued 8 killed, 5 wounded

Source: Benjamin Schemmer, *The Raid* (New York: Harper & Row, 1976), 188, 200, 210.

Alternatives to EAGLE CLAW

Holloway Special Review Group Variant to EAGLE CLAW
  Premission
    Full rehearsal of all phases and contingencies
    Independent review of operational plans and readiness
  Insertion
    Transports and 11 helicopters fly together to Desert One
    Alternative Desert One site (away from road)
    Limited air to air communications permitted
  Assault—As per EAGLE CLAW
  Extraction—As per EAGLE CLAW

Zbigniew Brzezinski, 26 April 1980, "Second Shot" Plan
  Premission—Unknown
  Insertion
    Direct fixed wing and rotary wing flight to Tehran area (one night)
    Seizure of nearby airfield (Tehran suburbs)
    Probably diversionary air strikes
  Assault
    Conducted at dawn
    Significantly increased ground force
    Possible crash-landing of helicopters to gain entry
  Extraction
    Use of nearby airfield

Gayle Rivers's Infiltration Plan
  Premission
    As per EAGLE CLAW, plus reconnoiter Tehran embassy sewers and tunnels
  Insertion
    Infiltrate 40-man rescue force as covert agents
    Fly light aircraft with Iranian markings toward embassy
    Rescue force moves into sewers/tunnels that open in embassy grounds
  Assault
    Aircraft drops stun grenades to knock out external guards
    Infiltrated rescuers storm chancellery
    Evacuate hostages in buses to nearby emergency airstrip
  Extraction
    Withdrawal by Iranian-marked C-130 Hercules

Sources: Zbigniew Brzezinski, "The Failed Mission," *New York Times Magazine* (18 April 1982), 79; Gayle Rivers, *The War Against the Terrorists* (New York: Stein & Day, 1986), 55–57.

The Holloway proposal reflected more of the same, only smarter, with major alterations in OPSEC matters. The other two plans would have differed dramatically from EAGLE CLAW by drastically slashing the time on the ground in Iran and simplifying the concept of operations. Interestingly, all three ideas differed very little from the JTF 1-79 plan in their assault and extraction phases. Only the Brzezinski plan ever received much work, and that only as a contingency in the event of hostage executions.[43] No repeat attempt would have been possible until November 1980 or so, when the hostages were reunited in the embassy compound. But by then diplomacy had taken over.

Operation EAGLE CLAW Time Line
4 November 1979–20 January 1981
(Local Iran Time)

4 November   1979—Iranian students and militia seized U.S. Embassy in Teh-
              ran.

6 November   —Rescue mission first proposed in National Security Coun-
              cil.

12 November   —Joint Task Force 1-79 formed.

19 December   —Helicopter force pilots designated.

26 December   —Six RH-53Ds arrived on USS *Kitty Hawk*.

23 January   1980—Two more helicopters arrived aboard USS *Nimitz;* others
              transferred to *Nimitz*.

8 February   —Minimum mission capability existed.

28 March   —Operation judged ready for execution.

31 March   —CIA aircraft surveyed and marked Desert One.

11 April   —President Carter approved mission execution.

19 April   —Unit deployment began.

23 April   —Unit deployment completed.

24 April   (1800)—Lead transport left Masirah Island.

              (1915)—Helicopter force left USS *Nimitz*.

              (2207)—First transport reached Desert One.

25 April   (0015)—First helicopter reached Desert One.

              (0157)—Mission aborted.

              (0222)—Collision occurred.

              (0255)—All U.S. units departed Desert One.

              (1000)—President Carter announced failure.

20 January   1981—Hostages released by diplomatic means.

In fact, maybe the best hostage rescue would have been none at all. As Cyrus Vance explained when he tendered his resignation, a rescue posed more problems than it solved. Aside from rancor in the Islamic world over the certain Iranian casualties, Vance worried about hostage deaths in the potential cross firing. The military guessed that three to fifteen hostages and six to thirty rescuers would be killed or wounded in the raid, so Vance's concerns for his diplomatic staff were hardly idle. But Vance's most telling objection questioned the purpose of the raid. On 24 April 1980, there were more than 200 Americans wandering around Tehran, many of them journalists on assignment.[44] If the U.S. came in with Spectres blazing away and snatched the hostages that united Khomeini's feuding supporters, why wouldn't the Iranians just imprison the other Americans? After a bloody raid, the Iranians might prove to be rather vicious jailers, even by their own low standards. It was a sobering possibility.

There are limits to the utility of armed force, and the Tehran embassy takeover might reflect one of those. The president and his civilian and military subordinates dared a great thing when they dispatched EAGLE CLAW. Had it succeeded, it would have been the greatest feat in the history of special operations. Its tragic end reminds one of the aftermath of Gettysburg. Like Gen. Robert E. Lee of Virginia, President James E. Carter of Georgia might also lament: "It's all my fault. I thought my men were invincible." [45]

Chapter 2 Notes

The epigraphs come from William Conant Church, *Ulysses S. Grant* (New York: Church Co., 1897), 188, 189; Jimmy Carter, "Rescue Attempt for American Hostages in Iran, April 25, 1980" in *Public Papers of the Presidents: Jimmy Carter, 1980–81, Book I* (Washington, D.C.: U.S. Government Printing Office, 1981), 772; and Colonel Charles W. Scott, USA (ret.), *Pieces of the Game* (Atlanta, GA: Peachtree Publishers, Ltd., 1984), 274, 275.

1. Capt. Paul B. Ryan, USN (ret.), *The Iranian Rescue Mission* (Annapolis, MD: U.S. Naval Institute, 1985), 6–10; Jimmy Carter, *Keeping Faith* (New York: Bantam Books, 1982), 456, 457; John D. Stempel, *Inside the Iranian Revolution* (Bloomington, IN: Indiana University Press, 1981), 174, 175, 224, 225. Captain Ryan's book is the finest book-length study of the Iran raid.

2. Col. Charles A. Beckwith, USA (ret.) and Donald Knox, *Delta Force* (New York: Harcourt Brace Jovanovich Publishers, 1983), 227, 255, 256, 261, 264, 265, 267, 268; Jeffrey D. Ethell, "Disaster at Desert One" in *Jane's 1981–82 Military Annual* (New York: Jane's Publishing, Inc., 1981), 21; Richard F. Nyrop, ed., *Iran: A Country Study* (Washington, D.C.: American University Press, 1978), 14, 15; U.S. Congress, House Subcommittee of Appropriations Committee, "Hostage Rescue Mission" in *Department of Defense Appropriations for 1981*, 96th Congress, 2nd Session, 2 June 1980, 627, 637, 640, 662; David C. Martin, "New Light on the Rescue Mission," *Newsweek* (30 June 1980), 18, 19; Special Operations Review Group, "Iran Rescue Mission-3," *Aviation Week and Space Technology* (29 September 1980), 88; "The Iran Raid: Operation Blue Light, An Aircrew Member's Story," *Gung-Ho* (January 1983), 30; Maj. Logan Fitch, USA (ret.) and George Feifer, "Death at Desert One," *Penthouse* (March 1984), 66, 67; Ryan, *The Iranian Rescue Mission*, 66.

3. David C. Martin, "Inside the Rescue Mission," *Newsweek* (12 July 1982), 19; Hamilton Jordan, *Crisis: The Last Year of the Carter Presidency* (New York: G. P. Putnam's Sons, 1982), 278, 279; Beckwith and Knox, *Delta Force*, 247, 248, 267–70; Carter, *Keeping Faith*, 501, 504; Ryan, *The Iranian Rescue Mission*, 48; U.S. Congress, House, "Hostage Rescue Mission," 609, 612, 632; Ethell, "Disaster at Desert One," 23; Fitch and Feifer, "Death at Desert One," 68, 69.

4. Special Operations Review Group, "Iran Rescue Mission-1," *Aviation Week and Space Technology* (15 September 1980), 69; Special Operations Review Group, "Iran Rescue Mission-2," *Aviation Week and Space Technology* (22 September 1980), 144; Special Operations Review Group, "Iran Rescue Mission-3," 84, 85, 88, 90; U.S. Congress, House, "Hostage Rescue

Mission," 635, 636; Ethell, "Disaster at Desert One," 23–25; Martin, "New Light on the Rescue Mission," 18, 19; Ryan, *The Iranian Rescue Mission,* 69–75.

5. Ethell, "Disaster at Desert One," 25, 27; Beckwith and Knox, *Delta Force,* 270, 271, 295; Special Operations Review Group, "Iran Rescue Mission-3," 89, 90; Ryan, *The Iranian Rescue Mission,* 80–83; "The Iran Raid: Operation Blue Light," 30.

6. Carter, *Keeping Faith,* 515; Beckwith and Knox, *Delta Force,* 271.

7. Benjamin F. Schemmer, *The Raid* (New York: Harper & Row, 1976), 87; Benjamin F. Schemmer, "Presidential Courage and the April 1980 Iranian Rescue Mission," *Armed Force Journal,* 61; Beckwith and Knox, *Delta Force,* 239, 253, 254, 271; Martin, "Inside the Rescue Mission," 16–20.

8. Jordan, *Crisis,* 279; Ethell, "Disaster at Desert One," 25; Martin, "Inside the Rescue Mission," 22; Beckwith and Knox, *Delta Force,* 272–74.

9. Beckwith and Knox, *Delta Force,* 276–78; Special Operations Review Group, "Iran Rescue Mission-3," 85–88; U.S. Congress, House, "Hostage Rescue Mission," 621, 654, 655, 657; Fitch and Feifer, "Death at Desert One," 169, 170.

10. Capt. Gary Sick, USN (ret.) "Military Options and Constraints" in *American Hostages in Iran* (New Haven, CT: Yale University Press, 1985), 154; Maj. Robert L. Earl, USMC, "A Matter of Principle," *Proceedings* (February 1983), 30; Jordan, *Crisis,* 280; U.S. Congress, House, "Hostage Rescue Mission," 609; Carter, *Keeping Faith,* 516. Major Earl's article is the best short analysis available of the rescue mission.

11. Ethell, "Disaster at Desert One," 27; Beckwith and Knox, *Delta Force,* 279, 280; Jordan, *Crisis,* 280; Special Operations Group, "Iran Rescue Mission-1," 69; U.S. Congress, House, "Hostage Rescue Mission," 666–68; "The Iran Raid: Operation Blue Light," 30; Fitch and Feifer, "Death at Desert One," 170, 171.

12. Ethell, "Disaster at Desert One," 27; Stempel, *Inside the Iranian Revolution,* 246; Scott, *Pieces of the Game,* 291.

13. The fictionalized account of a successful Tehran rescue was pieced together from the following sources: "Debate Rekindles on Failed Iran Raid," *Washington Post,* 25 April 1982, A1–A14; " 'Gung-ho' Oliver North: Reagan's Man of Action," *New York Times,* 9 November 1986, 9; Leroy Thompson, *The Rescuers* (Boulder, CO: Paladin Press, 1986), 104, 105, 165; Fitch and Feifer, "Death at Desert One," 166–68; Beckwith and Knox, *Delta Force,* 5–9, 145, 200–203, 232, 235, 253–56, 264, 265, 287; Martin, "Inside the Rescue Mission," 19–25; Scott, *Pieces of the Game,* 279; Martin, "New Light on the Rescue Mission," 18, 20; Carter, *Keeping Faith,* 509; Ryan, *The Iranian Rescue Mission,* 65; Jordan, *Crisis,* 261;

Carter, "Rescue Attempt for American Hostages in Iran," 773. Maj. Oliver North, USMC, actually led the Python Force, and later became famous as an energetic member of President Reagan's National Security Council. Captain Butterfield, USN, did indeed accompany the raid as a volunteer driver. Colonel Beckwith's description of room-clearing is a real quote, as is President Carter's line about his duty to launch the raid. All other speeches represent pure conjecture.

14. Special Operations Review Group, "Iran Rescue Mission-3," 90.

15. Capt. Gary Sick, USN (ret.), *All Fall Down* (New York: Random House, 1985), 247, 282; Benjamin F. Schemmer, "Was the US Ready to Resort to Nuclear Weapons for the Persian Gulf in 1980," *Armed Forces Journal* (September 1986), 104, 105; Special Operations Review Group, "Iran Rescue Mission-3," 90; Sick, "Military Options and Constraints," 147, 148, 167–69; Carter, *Keeping Faith,* 4, 457–60; Stempel, *Inside the Iranian Revolution,* 219, 233; Nyrop, *Iran: A Country Study,* 52, 362, 363.

16. Sick, "Military Options and Constraints," 170, 171; Robert Carswell and Richard J. Davis, "Crafting the Financial Settlement," 215.

17. Zbigniew Brzezinski, "The Failed Mission," *New York Times Magazine* (18 April 1982), 28–30, 62, 69; Carter, *Keeping Faith,* 459–61, 507; Sick, "Military Options and Constraints," 145, 146; Sick, *All Fall Down,* 284–87.

18. Jimmy Carter, "The President's News Conference of April 29, 1980" in *Public Papers of the Presidents: Jimmy Carter, 1980–81, Book I* (Washington, D.C.: U.S. Government Printing Office, 1981), 793; Carter, "Rescue Attempt for American Hostages in Iran," 772; Carter, *Keeping Faith,* 596; Benjamin F. Schemmer, "22 Months After Desert One, Some on Iran Rescue Try Still Not Decorated," *Armed Forces Journal* (March 1982), 17; Brzezinski, "The Failed Mission," 64.

19. Carter, *Keeping Faith,* 516.

20. Special Operations Review Group, "Iran Rescue Mission-1," 70; Carter, "Rescue Attempt for American Hostages in Iran," 773; Brzezinski, "The Failed Mission," 79; Jordan, *Crisis,* 272; Earl, "A Matter of Principle," 30.

21. Special Operations Review Group, "Iran Rescue Mission-1," 62; Ryan, *The Iranian Rescue Mission,* 25, 26.

22. Col. Roderick Lenahan, USAF, "Comment and Discussion: A Matter of Principle," *Proceedings* (November 1983), 91.

23. Beckwith and Knox, *Delta Force,* 195, 198, 199, 214–16; Martin, "Inside the Rescue Mission," 17.

24. John W. R. Taylor, editor, *Jane's All the World's Aircraft 1977–78* (London: Jane's Publishing, Ltd., 1977), 404–07; Special Operations Group, "Iran Rescue Mission-2," 143.

25. Carter, "The President's News Conference," 797; U.S. Congress, House, "Hostage Rescue Mission," 609; Earl, "A Matter of Principle," 30.
26. Brzezinski, "The Failed Mission," 30, 31.
27. Brzezinski, "The Failed Mission," 29, 31, 64, 69; Special Operations Review Group, "Iran Rescue Mission-1," 68; Special Operations Review Group, "Iran Rescue Mission-2," 143, 144; U.S. Congress, House, "Hostage Rescue Mission," 664; Ryan, *The Iranian Rescue Mission*, 40. Captain Ryan explained how Brzezinski and the military debated about the proper size of the helicopter force.
28. Special Operations Review Group, "Iran Rescue Mission-1," 68, 69; Special Operations Review Group, "Iran Rescue Mission-3," 89; Sick, *All Fall Down*, 287; Jordan, *Crisis*, 279; Martin, "Inside the Rescue Mission," 22; "The Iran Raid: Operation Blue Light," 28; Fitch and Feifer, "Death at Desert One," 166.
29. Special Operations Review Group, "Iran Rescue Mission-2," 144.
30. U.S. Congress, Senate Committee on Foreign Relations, *Sale of AWACS to Iran*, 95th Congress, 1st Session, 27 July 1977, 34, 57, 96–98; U.S. Congress, House Committee on International Relations, *Prospective Sale of Airborne Warning and Control System (AWACS) Aircraft to Iran*, 95th Congress, 1st Session, 29 June 1977, 11; F. W. E. Fursdon, "The Iraq/Iran War" in *Jane's 1981–82 Military Annual* (New York: Jane's Publishing Inc., 1981), 123; Special Operations Review Group, "Iran Rescue Mission-3," 88; "Debate Rekindles on Failed Iran Raid," A14; Ethell, "Disaster at Desert One," 27; Interview with Maj. Thomas Christianson, USA, 8 January 1987. Major Christianson is an experienced air defense officer familiar with the Improved Hawk system. In his words, "After six weeks without repair parts, a Hawk battery shuts down."
31. Ray L. Bowers, *United States Air Force in Southeast Asia: Tactical Airlift* (Washington, D.C.: U.S. Government Printing Office, 1983), 431; Schemmer, *The Raid*, 108, 200; Special Operations Review Group, "Iran Rescue Mission-3," 84, 85.
32. Special Operations Review Group, "Iran Rescue Mission-2," 142; Special Operations Review Group, "Iran Rescue Mission-3," 88, 89; Ryan, *The Iranian Rescue Mission*, 122, 123.
33. Robert D. McFadden et al., *No Hiding Place* (New York: New York Times Co., 1981), 99.
34. Special Operations Review Group, "Iran Rescue Mission-3," 84, 85; U.S. Congress, House, "Hostage Rescue Mission," 648, 649, 653, 657, 674; Ryan, *The Iranian Rescue Mission*, 57, 69.
35. Special Operations Review Group, "Iran Rescue Mission-3," 84, 85, 88.
36. Beckwith and Knox, *Delta Force*, 225, 276, 283; Ryan, *The Iranian Hostage Rescue Mission*, 128, 129; Martin, "Inside the Rescue Mission," 22; Fitch

and Feifer, "Death at Desert One," 166; Col. James R. Paschall, USA, "Remarks to USMA Department of History," 2 December 1986. Colonel Paschall commanded the Delta unit after the failed Iran mission.

37. Special Operations Review Group, "Iran Rescue Mission-1," 68; Special Operations Review Group, "Iran Rescue Mission-2," 144; Ryan, *The Iranian Rescue Mission,* 128, 129.

38. Beckwith and Knox, *Delta Force,* 277; Brzezinski, "The Failed Mission," 78; Jordan, *Crisis,* 272.

39. Beckwith and Knox, *Delta Force,* 293; Jordan, *Crisis,* 280.

40. Col. Harry G. Summers, USA, "A Review Essay: *Delta Force,*" *Military Review* (November 1983), 24; Philip Keisling, "Desert One: The Wrong Man and the Wrong Plan," *Washington Monthly* (December 1983), 51–58; Beckwith and Knox, *Delta Force,* 103, 261; U.S. Congress, House, "Hostage Rescue Mission," 655; Martin, "Inside the Rescue Mission," 22.

41. Carter, *Keeping Faith,* 519; Summers, "A Review Essay: *Delta Force,*" 26; Martin, "Inside the Rescue Mission," 22; Beckwith and Knox, *Delta Force,* 62–72, 78, 273, 278, 290.

42. Benjamin F. Schemmer's *The Raid* (New York: Harper & Row, 1976) offers a superb description and analysis of Operation KINGPIN.

43. Brzezinski, "The Failed Mission," 79; Gayle Rivers (pseud.), *The War Against the Terrorists* (New York: Stein & Day, 1986), 55–57.

44. Sick, "Military Options and Constraints," 162; Schemmer, "Presidential Courage," 61; Ryan, *The Iranian Rescue Mission,* 11, 50; Martin, "New Light on the Rescue Mission," 20.

45. Douglas Southall Freeman, *Lee's Lieutenants,* Volume 3 (New York: Charles Scribner's Sons, 1944), 166.

CHAPTER 3

BLACK ACES HIGH: AIR BATTLE OVER THE GULF OF SIDRA

19 AUGUST 1981

> *Reporter: "But it sounds like you're saying, no, it wasn't a test, but you aren't sorry you've bloodied Gadhafi's nose."*
> *President Reagan: "This is a rule that has to be followed. If our men are fired upon, they're going to fire."*
> Press conference aboard USS *Constellation*, 20 August 1981

> *"The quality of the box matters little. Success depends upon the man who sits in it."*
> Baron Manfred von Richthofen, the "Red Baron," eighty kills

> *"You fight like you train."*
> Motto, U.S. Navy Fighter Weapons School (Top Gun)

For Americans, freedom of the seas is more than a pleasant phrase. Unlike the Russians, Americans are a traditionally seafaring people, accustomed to trading over water where and when they so desire. The United States has fought for free navigation, skirmishing with the Barbary pirates in 1803–05, battling the mighty Royal Navy in the War of 1812, and joining World War I in 1917 to protest German U-boat attacks on unarmed U.S. neutral shipping. Although it is not well known, American destroyers escorted Lend-Lease shipments to Great Britain beginning in April 1941 and tangled with Nazi submarine wolf packs in the stormy North Atlantic for eight months before America finally declared war on

169

Germany. Since 1945, the powerful fleets and aircraft of the United States Navy have guaranteed the freedom of the seas for American ships and all world oceanic commerce. Unlike the Soviet Union, America and especially its allies depend on sea trade for continued industrial production, to include defense items. The Soviets, like the Germans in the world wars, can bring the whole Western economic engine to a grinding halt by cutting the vital sea-lanes. In recent years, the USSR has developed the deep-water navy necessary for that mission. The Soviets would probably prefer not to fight, so they encourage allies, surrogates, and "socialist brothers" to challenge American claims of free transit. Any blockage in the system, even in peacetime, works against America and the West.

Thus the U.S. Navy takes very seriously its role as guarantor of nautical freedom. Like all naval powers, America routinely exercises its fleets to maintain combat readiness. The continual presence of Soviet "shadows" and pesky Third World interlopers, however, badly blurs the usual line between training and a shooting war. The men of the USN remember what happened at Pearl Harbor, still a major U.S. base. When they sail past the rusted hulk that used to be the battleship USS *Arizona*, the memorial offers a mute testimony against unpreparedness. Today, any deployment might lead to war, ranging from expeditions to World War III. Given this, American fleets regularly maintain a combat regimen. In many ways, America's sailors are already at war.

But what is good can be better, and training continues unabated, day and night, in good weather and bad. U.S. task forces participate in many joint-service and allied nation exercises, honing wartime skills on, above, and below the unforgiving seas. As they train, pursue, and elude the Soviet Navy, the U.S. Navy's ships make a point of sailing in contested waters, providing great gray reminders of the final arbiters of sea control.

Before World War II, most countries claimed and recognized a three-mile limit to their territorial waters. In recent years, twelve miles has become accepted, although several nations insist upon far greater expanses, ranging out to two hundred miles. America confronts these claims during naval movements and exercises. USN warships occasionally sail into the Baltic and Black seas despite Soviet announcements that these are territorial waters. U.S. ships contest questionable assertions of sovereignty by allies as well. In August 1985, for example, an American icebreaker entered the Northwest Passage claimed by Canada. Since

1981, American fighting ships have exercised passage rights against the outlandish proclamations of more than forty countries.

One particular sore spot is the Gulf of Sidra, a 250-mile-wide swath of the Mediterranean Sea carved out of the North African coast. It is tucked conveniently off the major commercial shipping routes, and various nations, including the U.S. and USSR, employ it as a naval and air firing range and sea combat maneuver area. In October 1973, Col. Moammar Gadhafi's grandiosely named Socialist People's Libyan Arab *Jamahiriyah* (state of the masses) declared most of the gulf to be national territory. Besides using his oil income to finance terrorists of every stripe and to buy a panoply of Soviet arms totalling more than $12 billion, Gadhafi has not been shy about pressing his Gulf of Sidra claims. As early as 21 March 1973, two Libyan Arab Air Force (LAAF) jets fired on an unarmed USAF EC-130 electronic reconnaissance plane orbiting more than eighty-three miles from the Libyan coast. After this initial outburst, the Libyans ignored three naval challenges over the next six years. President Jimmy Carter's national security adviser, Zbigniew Brzezinski, intended to prod Gadhafi a few more times in 1979 and after. But then Iran seized the hostages, and Brzezinski's program went on hold.

Carter actually hoped that Libya might aid in freeing the hostages, a rather forlorn trust repaid when Gadhafi's security forces permitted a well-organized sacking of the U.S. Embassy in Tripoli on 2 December 1979. Things got worse. On 16 September 1980, two LAAF MiG-23 Flogger fighters unsuccessfully attacked a USAF RC-135 surveillance craft well beyond the twelve-mile limit. Gadhafi boldly took out an advertisement in the 22 October 1980 *Washington Post,* sternly warning America to stop sending planes "to spy across Libyan borders." Fearful for the Americans in Iran, Carter did nothing.

President Ronald Reagan decided to act differently. In early 1981, he directed an extensive series of freedom of navigation exercises, integrated into ongoing USN operational training. The navy's itinerary included the Gulf of Sidra. There were few illusions about likely Libyan responses.

Coincidentally, the navy published standardized worldwide peacetime rules of engagement (ROE) for seaborne forces. Naval regulations long authorized commanders "to counter either the use of force or an immediate threat of the use of force" with armed action. When Task Force 60 formed for its scheduled training in August 1981, the new ROE were

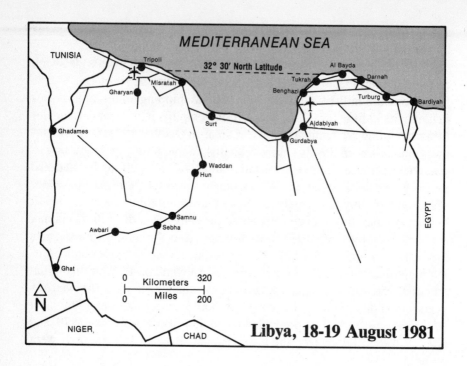

MEDITERRANEAN SEA

TUNISIA

Tripoli

32° 30' North Latitude

Al Bayda

Misratah

Tukrah

Darnah

Gharyan

Benghazi

Turburg

Bardiyah

Ghadames

Surt

Ajdabiyah

Gurdabya

Waddan

Hun

EGYPT

Samnu

Awbari

Sebha

Ghat

0 Kilometers 320

0 Miles 200

N

NIGER

CHAD

Libya, 18-19 August 1981

in full effect. These revised procedures permitted the on-scene commander to reply appropriately to a hostile act, an imminent use of force, and a continuing threat of use of force.[1] The 1981 ROE left no doubt that, in accord with naval tradition, the commander on the spot could take whatever action was necessary to protect his men and ships. Checking with Washington was not required. In an age of instant communications, it was a reassuring vote of confidence in naval professionals.

On 18 August, Rear Adm. James E. Service's Task Force 60 (TF-60) initiated an "Open Ocean Missilex" involving the huge aircraft carriers USS *Nimitz*, USS *Forrestal*, their air wings, and their surface escorts. TF-60 intended to blast drone aircraft targets with Sparrow and Sidewinder air to air missiles from the carrier air wing fighters and Standard surface to air missiles from the cruisers USS *Texas* and USS *Mississippi*. As usual in such training, the United States published notifications to mariners and airmen on 12 and 14 August, warning of missile impacts throughout the 3,200-square-mile irregular hexagon of sea space. Libya's Tripoli flight information region received these notices. Intentionally, a small portion of the designated missile safety area stretched below 32 degrees 30 minutes north latitude, into Gadhafi's touted backyard, the Gulf of Sidra. No American ships planned to cross into the disputed waters.[2]

Although Gadhafi was away in Aden, his associates were not slow in reacting. Throughout 18 August, numerous Libyan aircraft approached the USN exercise area from the west, south, and east, only to turn away when intercepted by *Nimitz* F-14A Tomcats and *Forrestal* F-4J Phantom II jet fighters. Americans met more than thirty-five two-plane sections of Soviet-built MiG-23 Flogger Es, MiG-25 Foxbat A, and French-made Mirage F-1 and 5D variants. The USN aviators closed to fly formation with the intruders and waved off most of them. Six LAAF sections actually entered the exercise zone, closely hounded by American fighters. TF-60 ceased missile firings while the LAAF aircraft transited the range.[3] It was about what the Americans expected: pro forma challenges. Still, the Libyans had fired before, so the U.S. fliers took no chances. Maybe the Libyans were probing, looking for a weak spot.

United States Strategic and Operational Objectives for Sidra Missilex

STRATEGIC OBJECTIVE: Exercise U.S. freedom of navigation in the Gulf of Sidra.
OPERATIONAL OBJECTIVES:
  1) Conduct surface to air and air to air missile firing at target drones.
  2) Intercept and turn away Libyan air, surface, and subsurface intruders.
  3) Defend the fleet.

If the American aviators had eavesdropped on Libyan national television the evening of 18 August 1981, they would have seen a series of hysterical broadcasts by the Jamahiriyah News Agency (JANA). Reporter John K. Cooley of ABC News was in Tripoli that night, and he watched JANA announcers describe an imminent U.S. attack by the steadily advancing Sixth Fleet. Libyan military officers prescribed "a high state of alert" for their forces.[4] The atmosphere in Tripoli promised a strong Libyan response on 19 August. Would the U.S. Navy be ready?

When Gadhafi's pilots flew north at dawn on 19 August, they headed into a multilayered array of sensors and weapons designed specifically

**United States Command Organization
19 August 1981**

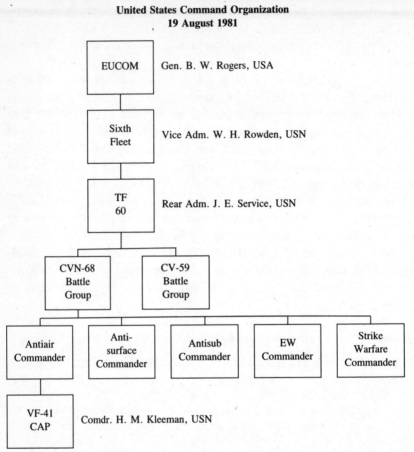

EUCOM's naval deputy, CINCNAVEUR, routinely handled naval affairs in the theater from his London headquarters.

to defend the two U.S. carriers. American seamen had perfected aircraft carrier tactics in the latter stages of the Pacific war of 1941–45, weathering swarms of kamikaze planes as they pressed toward the home islands of Imperial Japan. Carrier-borne bombers had accomplished their missions. But the desperate Japanese suicide squadrons inflicted significant losses and damage, often knocking carriers out of action with their thunderous, blazing impacts. It was a lesson for America's enemies, and the Russians paid attention.

Since 1945, the Soviet Navy has been built to seek and destroy the mighty USN carriers. They have capitalized upon the virtues of a kamikaze barrage, with computers playing the role of diligent young Japanese warriors aboard explosive-packed jet cruise missiles as big as World War II Zero fighters. The cruise systems are the most serious Soviet threat, deliverable by aircraft, surface ships, or submarines. Aside from cruise missiles, Soviet air units confront an American fleet with bombs, strafing, water mines, and electronic jamming to blind and confuse U.S. defense radars. Surface craft ranging from battle cruisers to small patrol boats carry fast torpedoes, rapid-fire cannons, naval mines, and additional jammers, besides their cruise batteries. Finally, the Soviets deploy dozens of stealthy submarines armed with swift, accurate, long-range torpedoes, sea mines, and more cruise missiles. So the dangers can come from above, on, or below the waves.

The United States Navy recognized these multiple hazards. If carrier air wings intended to get close enough to enemy ships and shore facilities to employ their squadrons of fast little A-7E Corsair IIs and powerful A-6E Intruders, the carrier task force had to be well protected. Admiral Service of Task Force 60 controlled two carrier battle groups (CVBGs), both headed by composite warfare commanders (CWCs). In the battle groups, the CWCs delegated key tactical authority and responsibility to five subordinate commands: antiair warfare (AAW), antisurface warfare (ASUW), antisubmarine warfare (ASW), electronic warfare (EW), and strike warfare. Each of the first four deputies concentrated on meeting and defeating hostile units in his unique domain, with full authority to employ the task force's ships and aircraft to engage threats. The strike warfare commander normally handled air and ships' weapons attacks against enemy elements outside the vast carrier defensive bands and on hostile shores. The composite warfare commander integrated and coordinated his five subordinates' activities, sharing information via naval tactical data system down links and ultra-high-frequency radio. When facing fast, jet-powered "bogies," there is little time for time-consuming consultation. Therefore, within certain guidelines from the CVBG, each functional warfare commander had authority to decide and react on his own.

The best defense is a strong offense, and if the strike commander did his job, few enemies would emerge to challenge the American fleet. This aggressive mentality permeated many aspects of battle group defense as well. Leaving aside strike operations for the moment, task force defense involved five aspects: dispersion, detection, deception, destruction, and damage control. American warships routinely practiced these tactics, with real Soviet planes, ships, and subs nearby to lend a sense of urgency to this training.

Dispersion greatly facilitates defense. Attackers cannot hit what they cannot find, and despite capable surveillance satellites, the oceans are still far bigger than the warships that sail them. In 1981, a two-carrier flotilla like Task Force 60 might occupy 56,000 square miles, with wide gaps between ships and extensive use of sensors and long-range missiles to fill in the holes. Carrier battle groups are ringed by three zones: a surveillance area (1,000 to 400 miles out), an outer screen (400 to 40 miles), and an inner screen (the carrier and its escorts). In a multicarrier force on an open ocean, the defense layers could overlap to provide mutual support, but the constituent ships always maintained significant separation. Of course, in the relatively small, shallow Mediterranean, this sort of spread was impossible. TF-60 was cramped in its firing range, with its two-CVBG surveillance area out at only about 100 miles in spots.

Detection varies among warfare types, but each component attempted to locate and identify threats as far out in the surveillance area as possible. Fighter antiair combat air patrols (CAP) normally fly up to 400 miles away, directed by E-2C Hawkeye early warning aircraft, a naval AWACS plane. They intercept and identify approaching air threats. The Hawkeye(s) also direct surface combat air patrol (SUCAP) bombers, attack jets loaded with antishipping munitions that scout advancing surface dangers. Additionally, S-3A Viking jets probe distant waters for hostile submarines, often aided by stalking nuclear-powered attack submarines placed in direct support of the carrier battle group. SH-3H Sea King helicopters search for enemy subs closer to the carriers. All USN ships and planes carry devices to detect and pinpoint enemy search and fire control radars. If the enemy made any electromagnetic "burps," American equipment hoped to notice.

Deception is critical to American defenses, and it involves electronic warfare. Fighting ships in the world wars usually included heavy armor belts; modern warships rarely have any metallic armor. Instead, these strongly built but unarmored craft rely on speed and on electronic devices for protection. Passive detectors are always "listening," so turning on any electronic transmitters advertises the friendly locations. Unfortunately, without emitting energy, a task force cannot effectively search, track, or defeat inbound targets. The key decision in the next sea war

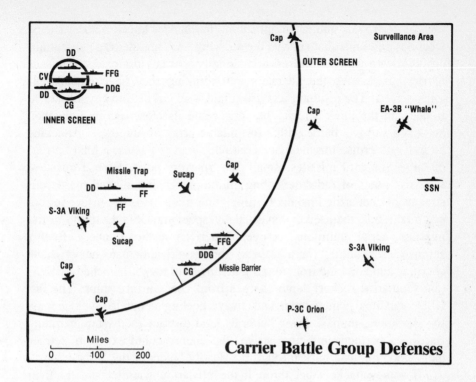

Carrier Battle Group Defenses

might well be when to "light up" the fleet. Once active, fleet electronics can ravage attacking forces. Airborne and ship jammers block enemy weapons radars or paint confusing images on opposing screens, making hostile fire control difficult. Some black boxes can fry and frazzle the electronic chips inside enemy missiles, rendering them inert or sending them spiraling harmlessly away. Small U.S. escorts might even resort to "banzai" jamming, imitating a carrier's electronic blip to attract opposing missiles. Deception continues throughout all USN operations, but grows in intensity as attackers near the battle group.

Destruction provides "hard kills" that complement the "soft kills" achieved by the electronic systems. Functional warfare commanders actively "prosecute" the enemies turned up by detection systems, a rather offensive defense. The air wing engages far out in the surveillance area, endeavoring, as Adm. James Watkins so aptly stated, "to shoot the archer before he releases his arrows," whether that archer is a plane, ship, or sub. At the rim of the outer screen, in the direction of the likely enemy threat, a missile barrier of escorting cruisers and guided-missile destroyers and/or an antisubmarine barrier knock out the enemy weapons and units that survive the air wing. A "missile trap" of antiair-capable destroyers and cruisers occasionally operates just inside the missile barrier, to deceive the attackers into thinking they have reached the inner screen. The resultant ambush might well put paid to any air attack. Finally, in the inner screen, the carrier and its close escorts fight their last-ditch survival battle with a formidable array of firepower. Attacking aircraft and cruise missiles face continued fighter passes, a final barrage of large Standard missiles, small Sea Sparrow point defense missiles, scattered gouts of radar-deflecting aluminum chaff foil, and murderous streams of chattering Phalanx Gatling gun rounds. Hostile surface intruders might find themselves smashed by speeding USN Harpoon cruise missiles, aerial munitions, or even American surface gunnery. Enemy submarines skulking for a torpedo shot could anticipate heavy depth charging and bombing from the air and flurries of rocket-launched ASROC (antisubmarine rocket) depth charges from U.S. surface ships. The fast USN warships plan to spin and sway, heeling about to avoid enemy sea skimmers, unmask firing batteries, and distract enemy bombardiers. Barring a perfectly effective strike, the enemy could expect to retrace their bloody course back through the deadly layers of the USN defense.

If some attackers get through the blistering gauntlet and hit their twisting targets, U.S. Navy damage control teams on the ships hope to minimize the effects of the injuries. American warships are extensively compartmented to limit flooding, and USN crews train regularly to repair their vessels. U.S. carriers are particularly resilient. Several have endured catastrophic crashes and fires during peacetime training and off Vietnam; the tough U.S. sailors literally wiped the mess overboard and restarted flight operations. But without armor, festooned with delicate electronic aerials and radar dishes, all the damage control in the world might not save the electronic nervous systems that really energize a modern fighting craft. Repeated impacts from powerful high-explosive warheads could eviscerate a thin-skinned modern warship. This is why the USN defends its fleets so carefully and fiercely. The first cut could also be the last, particularly for the smaller ships.[5]

Of course, the successive, three-dimensional American defense network was created to blunt a combined Soviet air/sea attack. Although the Libyans posed far less of a threat, the men of Task Force 60 did not alter their tactics. After all, no defense is airtight, and a few mistakes in the surveillance area might allow some Libyan pilots to become heroes.

The Americans had their orders, as did the Libyans. In the final analysis, it would come down to a handful of men already speeding across the Gulf of Sidra by dawn on 19 August 1981.

The bold U.S. naval aviators flying across the Gulf of Sidra allowed Admiral Service to operate with impunity in such restricted waters. Major air operations commenced at 0545, as both carriers launched combat air patrols, surface combat air patrols (SUCAP "Birddog" missions), and antisubmarine flights. A *Nimitz* Hawkeye assumed air controller duties for the U.S. aircraft, although Admiral Service and his CWCs elected to position the early warning plane well in the northern half of the missile-firing region. Service wanted to insure that no lucky LAAF "leakers" might sneak through and shoot up the defenseless turboprop. Based upon the vigorous Libyan air response of 18 April, this was

---

United States Forces Order of Battle
19 August 1981

U.S. Navy/Marine Forces
  Task Force 60, Sixth Fleet
    USS *Nimitz* (CVN-68) with Carrier Air Wing 8 (CVW-8), USS *Texas* (CGN-39), USS *Mississippi* (CGN-40), USS *San Diego* (AFS-6)
    Carrier Air Wing 8
      Fighter Squadron 41 (VF-41): 12 F-14A Tomcats
      Fighter Squadron 84 (VF-84): 12 F-14A Tomcats
      Medium Attack Squadron (VA-35): 10 A-6E Intruders, 4 KA-6D tankers
      Light Attack Squadron (VA-82): 12 A-7E Corsair IIs
      Light Attack Squadron (VA-86): 12 A-7E Corsair IIs
      Tactical Electronic Warfare Squadron (VAQ-135): 4 EA-6B Prowlers
      Airborne Early Warning Squadron (VAW-124): 4 E-2C Hawkeyes
      Antisubmarine Warfare Squadron (VS-24): 10 S-3A Vikings
      Antisubmarine Warfare Squadron (HS-9): 6 SH-3H Sea Kings
    USS *Forrestal* (CV-59) with Carrier Air Wing 17 (CVW-17), USS *Edson* (DD-945), USS *Paul* (FF-1080), USS *Miller* (FF-1091)

Sources: Normal Polmar, "Changing Carrier Air Wings," *Proceedings* (August 1984), 154, 155; Capt. Brent Baker, USN, "Naval and Maritime Events 1981," *Proceedings* (May 1982), 58; Christopher Wright, "U.S. Naval Operations in 1982," *Proceedings* (May 1983), 245.

Libyan Forces Order of Battle
19 August 1981

Libyan Arab Navy
    Osa II class fast attack craft

Libyan Arab Air Force
    2 Su-22 Fitter J fighter-bombers
    8 MiG-23 Flogger E interceptors

Source: Col. W. Hays Parks, USMCR,
"Crossing the Line of Death," *Proceedings*
(November 1986), 43.

---

probably wise. The decision placed a premium upon the fine air search radars of the CAP fighters.

USS *Forrestal* contributed six jets, a mix of four Fighter Squadron 74 (VF-74) F-4J Phantom II fighters and a Birddog Corsair II tandem from Attack Squadron 83 (VA-83). The VF-74 Bedevilers carried radars able to detect enemy aircraft more than 30 miles away. But the most exposed CAP stations went to three two-plane sections of F-14A Tomcats from *Nimitz*'s Fighter Squadron 41 (VF-41) Black Aces. The swing wing Tomcats operated the superb AN/AWG-9 weapons control system, which could search for targets from 75 to 195 miles away. Tomcats had the ability to track up to twenty-four targets and fire at six simultaneously, using the potent AIM-54C Phoenix air to air missile. For their operations over Sidra, however, the Black Aces carried a mix of medium-range AIM-7F Sparrow radar guided missiles and close-in AIM-9L Sidewinder heat-seekers.

By 0715, the American aviators had already enjoyed a busy morning. USN fighters turned back two sets of Libyan MiGs, and the Birddog Corsairs kept watch above a wandering Osa-type missile patrol boat. As two Black Aces and two Bedevilers swung south to intercept two more approaching MiG-23 Flogger Es, USS *Nimitz* began launching the next set of fighters to replace its dawn patrol. Two took off before the Hawkeye and *Nimitz* received another contact message.[6]

This one came from an experienced source. Using their onboard radar, VF-41 skipper Comdr. Henry M. Kleeman and his radar intercept officer, Lt. David J. Venlet, located two unidentified jets flying northeast, apparently from the LAAF's Gurdabya Airfield. Kleeman's wingman, Lt. Lawrence M. Muczynski, and his backseater, Lt. James P. Anderson, confirmed the contact about forty miles to the southwest. Atmospheric conditions, notably temperature and humidity, shielded the Libyans from the big radars on USS *Nimitz* and USS *Forrestal* and their escorts. Even the unusually capable Hawkeye detection radome picked up nothing. The *Nimitz* CVBG antiair warfare commander ordered Kleeman and his partner to investigate the two blips. This would be their last evolution before returning to their carrier. Meanwhile, two Bedevilers from *Forrestal* caught and assumed trailing positions on two MiG-23s.[7] Kleeman and Muczynski planned to conduct what looked to be another standard intercept.

The naval aviators flew almost due south, roughly abreast and spread in the regular USN air combat formation known as the "loose deuce." Muczynski was stacked about 4,000 feet above and two miles to the west, a bit forward of Kleeman. The senior flier bored along at around 18,000 feet. This was a demanding combat formation that only experienced fliers could employ, because both aviators acted offensively, rather than one covering the other. For men in loose deuce, attack is the best defense. U.S. Navy fighter aviators train many hours in this difficult but tactically superior method.

As they flew toward the Libyans, all four aircrewmen craned their heads, scanning for their quarry. Kleeman saw them first about eight miles out, two single-engine Su-22 Fitter J ground attack aircraft whizzing northeast in a tight "welded wing" formation, less than 500 feet apart. That was odd; all previous TF-60 contacts reported MiGs. What were these ground attack planes up to?

Aside from two internal 30-mm cannons apiece, the Libyan Su-22s mounted long silver auxiliary fuel tanks and what appeared to be unsophisticated AA-2 Atoll heat-seeking missiles, useful only when shot straight up the tail pipe. The USN F-14As each carried a single rasping M-61A1 Vulcan 20-mm Gatling cannon and a brace of excellent AIM-9L Sidewinders, an advanced infrared homing missile that could be fired at virtually any angle and still turn in on its prey. Compared to Kleeman's twin-engine Tomcat with its computer-controlled, slatted swing wings, the smaller Su-22 was no dogfighter, slower to turn and at best equal to its bigger rival in climbing and diving. The Libyans had primitive movable wings, to be sure, but Su-22s pivoted only the outer half of their lifting surfaces. Pitting an Su-22 against an F-14A in aerial combat

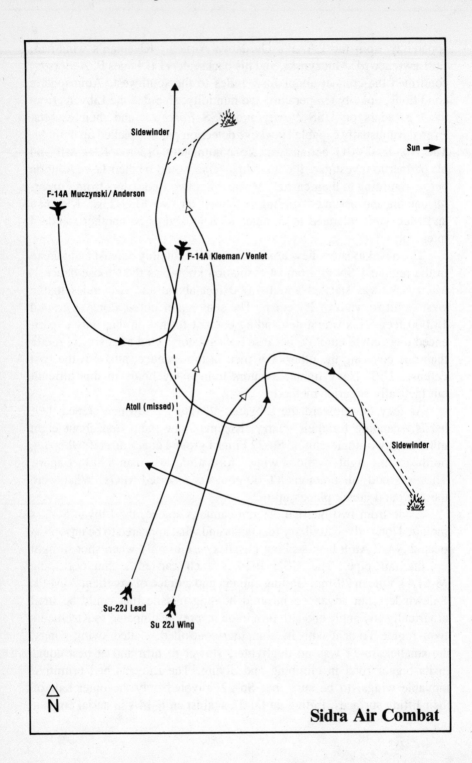

Sidewinder

Sun ➤

F-14A Muczynski/Anderson

F-14A Kleeman/Venlet

Atoll (missed)

Sidewinder

Su-22J Lead

Su 22J Wing

N

Sidra Air Combat

would be akin to entering the family car in the Indianapolis 500. But one could not be too careful; a good technical layout never won a fight. "Unsophisticated" MiG-17s had downed their share of outstanding U.S. aircraft over Southeast Asia. It depended a lot on the pilots, and Kleeman took no foolish risks as he closed in.

Commander Kleeman chose his course carefully to set up a single-offset intercept. By coming in from one flank, Kleeman had the option to head toward the Libyans' noses or swing around to their tails as necessary to guide them out of the maneuver area. The Libyan pilots were evidently inexperienced, as shown by their adherence to the simple welded wing formation, popular throughout the Libyan Arab Air Force. In welded wing, the lead pilot did all the fighting and the wingman merely guarded his leader. For Kleeman and Muczynski in their extended, sophisticated loose deuce, the welded wing was like intercepting a single enemy.[8] Either the LAAF twosome were real "hamburgers" or they were playing possum. Were they sucking the Americans into a trap, or acting as bait for other Libyans lying in ambush? In the back seats, Venlet and Anderson pored over their scopes, trying to be certain that it was really two versus two.

At 0718, Kleeman rolled his plane 90 degrees to the left to come abeam of the forward Fitter J and fly formation. He was about five hundred feet above the Libyans and about a thousand feet away when he glimpsed something very frightening. Slowly at first, then accelerating, an Atoll missile ignited and sped off the Su-22's wing firing rail, zipping right for Kleeman's Tomcat.

Kleeman and Muczynski each called the missile firing, and both broke hard to the left. The Atoll, nearly useless when fired at the American jet's nose, tore harmlessly away beneath Kleeman's roaring fighter. In accord with his aggressive loose deuce role, Muczynski descended to knock out the firing LAAF Fitter, pirouetting inside the climbing Libyan leader. Meanwhile, Kleeman sought the other Libyan.

As the Americans heeled over to avoid the shocking enemy snapshot, the panicky Libyans broke their welded wing and separated widely, the leader soaring to the left to head north, the wingman twisting up and hard right, into the sun rising in the east. Kleeman weaved above the running Libyan wingman, passing over the enemy Fitter twice before settling in on the Su-22's tail. The Black Aces' commander tracked the Libyan into the burning morning sun. Kleeman dared not fire a Sidewinder; it might track the solar disk rather than the Libyan. But the desperate

LAAF wingman accommodated Kleeman and continued his tight turn and shallow climb, moving out of the sun. The American naval officer fired a Sidewinder, which crunched into the enemy's fuselage and sent the stricken aircraft spinning for the sea. The Libyan ejected, and his parachute opened.

As Kleeman polished off the wingman, Lieutenant Muczynski exploited his Tomcat's vaunted maneuverability and his initial altitude advantage to cut close inside the Libyan leader's slow climb, diving onto the enemy jet's tail. The LAAF flier swung left and then right, but Muczynski hung on, closing the range to a half mile. He heard Kleeman report his missile strike just as the Libyan leader started a violent right turn to escape into the sun. Muczynski would have none of that and launched a Sidewinder. The swift projectile slammed right up the Su-22's tail pipe and exploded, blowing the hapless Libyan plane in two. The USN fighter pulled up hard to clear the blossoming cloud of debris and fire from the shattered Libyan jet. The pilot ejected, but Muczynski saw no chute. "We didn't stick around to look for a canopy," he said.[9]

And that was that, all over by 0719. There had been no time for calls back to USS *Nimitz,* let alone to Washington. The chain of command fully supported the aviators. Conveniently, Sixth Fleet commander Vice Adm. William H. Rowden was embarked on USS *Forrestal* to observe training, and he quickly blessed his men's actions: "The aircrews correctly reacted in self-defense. They did not require or ask for any specific authorization from Admiral Service or anyone else." As Kleeman nonchalantly summarized, "I didn't hesitate to fire, although it occurred to me at the time that it might cause a ruckus." [10]

Commander Kleeman was right about the resultant commotion, although there was more smoke than fire. As expected, Gadhafi in Aden said that the "cowardly attack by American imperialists . . . endangered peace." His JANA news organs claimed that LAAF fliers battled eight Tomcats and downed one, an utter fabrication. Despite the bluster, the American fleet completed its missile exercise on schedule without further incident. As for the Libyans, they continued to probe tentatively at the USN exercise area, and mounted a successful rescue effort for their two battered pilots under watchful U.S. surveillance.[11] Both Gadhafi and the Americans would be back for more serious skirmishing five years later.

In Washington, the incident stirred up a little of the usual late summer

Comparative Loss Summary
Personnel

	KIA	MIA	WIA	PW	Nonbattle
U.S. Navy/USMC	0	0	0	0	0
U.S. MILITARY TOTAL	0	0	0	0	0
Libyan Arab Forces *	0	0	0	0	0

Equipment

U.S. Military: none
Libyan Arab Forces: 2 jet fighters

* Both Libyan pilots ejected safely.

Source: David A. Brown, "Libyan Incident Spurs Deployment Shift," *Aviation Week and Space Technology* (31 August 1981), 20, 21.

torpor. Secretary of Defense Caspar Weinberger announced the air scrap, aided by Joint Chiefs of Staff director of operations, Lt. Gen. Philip J. Gast, USAF (deputy commander of the ill-fated EAGLE CLAW raid on Iran). When the reporters asked if President Reagan had authorized the USN aviators to fire, Weinberger responded emphatically, "No, no, that was within the discretion of the commander." Gast, National Military Command Center duty officer, noted that he had received word of the action at 0126 Washington time (0726 Libyan time), and that he knew "nothing in advance, nor did the pilots." Journalists became agitated when they discovered that nobody had awakened President Reagan, although as Reagan observed, "There was no decision to be made or they would have." The president wryly concluded: "If our planes were shot down, yes, they'd wake me up right away; if the other fellow's [planes] were shot down, why wake me up?" [12] Reagan left the fighting to the professionals.

An analysis of the 1981 Sidra incident points up three ideas worthy of consideration. First, the sixty seconds over the Mediterranean constituted the only American aerial combat since 1972 over North Vietnam. There could be few better object lessons in the value of quality planes and, more important, quality fliers. During the first few years over Vietnam, USAF and USN crews suffered one loss for every two to three aerial victories against Hanoi's pilots, as compared to a whopping thirteen victories per loss against Chinese and Russian jet fliers over Korea from 1950 to 1953. What was different? True, Vietnam rules of engagement were restrictive, but so were the regulations over Korea. The Vietnamese pilots were no Red Barons, nor were their planes anything special. The U.S. crews flew good planes, but probably trusted too much in missiles and radars that never quite lived up to manufacturers' brochures. Captain Frank W. Ault of USS *Coral Sea* and some solid naval aviators studied the problem in 1968, and provided the answer: poor U.S. training in basic dogfighting. The result was a thorough aerial fighting school called the U.S. Navy Postgraduate Course in Fighter Weapons, Tactics, and Doctrine, soon known as "Top Gun." When USN planes again went into action over North Vietnam in 1972, they blew away thirteen enemies for every navy jet that fell.[13]

The Top Gun initiative bore fruit over the Gulf of Sidra. The aggressive Black Aces epitomized the stringent level of air to air training introduced by Top Gun, including full exploitation of the loose deuce formation tactics tested at Top Gun and over North Vietnam. Whereas the panicky Libyans fired from a poor angle, broke their simple formation, and buzzed around in near panic, the skilled Americans took charge of the battle and relentlessly and remorselessly eliminated their foes. USAF RED FLAG exercises have brought air force fighter pilots to a level of proficiency equivalent to their naval comrades in arms. It is probably no accident that although U.S. aircraft have participated in every post-Vietnam contingency, only once have they been forced to fight air to air. Most American enemies have air forces, but few enemy airmen have a death wish. So opponents rely instead on ground-based antiaircraft systems.

The Sidra skirmish highlights a second factor. In an era of violent peace, there is no such thing as a routine operation, especially when U.S. forces are deployed in close proximity to potential adversaries. Commander Kleeman and Lieutenant Muczynski rightly regarded their "everyday" assignment as a combat mission. In the best case, they would have gained additional realistic training. In the worst case, which occurred, they were ready to act, even though "nothing like this had ever happened before." But rather than a gradual degeneration into careless laxity, a habitual combat mentality prevailed. The Black Aces and Task Force 60 reflected an awareness of just how dangerous "peacetime" has become.

Finally, the navy and the United States apparently benefited from a

---

Gulf of Sidra Incident Time Line
(Local Libyan Time)
18–19 August 1981

18 August—(0545) United States Navy Task Force 60 commenced missile-firing exercise north of the Gulf of Sidra.
19 August—(0545) Flight operations began.
        (0715) Two Libyan Su-22s acquired by aircraft radar.
        (0718) Lead Libyan fired; both destroyed by U.S. fighters.
        (1900) Exercise ended.

"hands off" attitude in Washington and by intermediate commanders, which communicated itself to the lowest level. Not only did Commander Kleeman not call for authorization to fire, he obviously felt no compunction at all to clear his actions. His orders were clear, and he acted within them. Military and naval professionals can ask for no better support from their chain of command. Moreover, when Monday-morning quarterbacks questioned this delegation of discretionary power, President Ronald Reagan shot back: "We responded as we will respond anywhere when any of our forces are attacked. They're going to defend themselves." [14]

Chapter 3 Notes

Epigraphs come from Ronald Reagan, "Remarks on Board the USS *Constellation*, August 20, 1981," *Public Papers of the Presidents: Ronald Reagan, 1981* (Washington, D.C.: U.S. Government Printing Office, 1982), 723; Comdr. Robert L. Shaw, USNR, *Fighter Combat* (Annapolis, MD: U.S. Naval Institute Press, 1985), 97, 182.

1. Col. W. Hays Parks, USMCR, "Crossing the Line of Death," *Proceedings* (November 1986), 41–43; John K. Cooley, *Libyan Sandstorm* (New York: Holt, Rinehart, and Winston, 1982), 248; Comdr. Lawson W. Brigham, USCG, "U.S. Coast Guard in 1985," *Proceedings* (May 1986), 46; John Wright, *Libya: A Modern History* (Baltimore, MD: The Johns Hopkins University Press, 1982), 214, 215.

2. Lt. Comdr. Frank Marlowe, USN, "Forrestal/CVW-17—Another Successful Med Cruise," *The Hook* (winter 1981), 33; Comdr. Dennis R. Neutze, "The Gulf of Sidra Incident: A Legal Perspective," *Proceedings* (January 1982), 26; "U.S. Planes Attacked by Libyan Aircraft," *Department of State Bulletin* (October 1981), 60; David A. Brown, "Libyan Incident Spurs Deployment Shift," *Aviation Week and Space Technology* (31 August 1981), 19; David A. Brown, "Sixth Fleet F-14s Down Libyan Su-22s," *Aviation Week and Space Technology* (24 August 1981), 20; Parks, "Crossing the Line of Death," 43.

3. Brown, "Libyan Incident Spurs Deployment Shift," 19, 21; Parks, "Crossing the Line of Death," 43; Marlowe, "Forrestal/CVW-17," 34.

4. Cooley, *Libyan Sandstorm,* 265.

5. Capt. P. J. Doerr, USN, "CWC Revisited," *Proceedings* (April 1986), 39–43; Comdr. George Galdorisi, "The Quiet Revolution," *Proceedings* (April 1986), 42, 43; David C. Isby, "Task Force," *Strategy and Tactics,* No. 83 (November/December 1980) 42–44; Adm. James D. Watkins, USN, "The Maritime Strategy" in James A. Barber, Executive Director, *The Maritime Strategy* (Annapolis, MD: U.S. Naval Institute Press, 1986), 12, 13; Capt. Robert C. Powers, USN, "Commanding the Offensive," *Proceedings* (October 1985), 60–64; Ray Bonds, ed. *The US War Machine* (New York: Crown Publishers, Inc., 1983), 115; Comdr. George Galdorisi, "The SH-60F: New Capabilities for the Battle Group," *Proceedings* (February 1987), 88, mentions the use of attack submarines in the outer ASW zone.

6. John W. R. Taylor, ed., *Jane's All the World's Aircraft 1981–82* (New York: Jane's Publishing, Inc., 1981), 369; "Fighter Aircraft Radars," *Strategy and Tactics,* No. 75 (July/August 1979), 24; Marlowe, "Forrestal/

CVW-17,'' 34, 35; Parks, "Crossing the Line of Death,'' 43; Brown, "Libyan Incident Spurs Deployment Shift,'' 19–21.

7. Brown, "Libyan Incident Spurs Deployment Shift,'' 19–20; Brown, "Sixth Fleet F-14s Down Libyan Su-22s,'' 20; Marlowe, "Forrestal/CVW-17,'' 34.

8. Shaw, *Fighter Combat*, 199, 214–23, 353–55; Taylor, *Jane's All the World's Aircraft 1981–82,* 216–19, 368–70; Barrett Tillman, "Black Aces Bag Two,'' *The Hook* (fall 1981), 29, 30.

9. Brown, "Libyan Incident Spurs Deployment Shift,'' 19–21; Brown, "Sixth Fleet F-14s Down Libyan Su-22s,'' 20; Tillman, "Black Aces Bag Two,'' 29, 30.

10. Brown, "Libyan Incident Spurs Deployment Shift,'' 21.

11. Cooley, *Libyan Sandstorm,* 268.

12. Reagan, "Remarks and a Question and Answer Session, August 27, 1981'' in *Public Papers of the President: Ronald Reagan 1981,* 736; "U.S. Planes Attacked by Libyan Aircraft,'' 58, 59.

13. Michael Skinner, *Red Flag* (Novato, CA: Presidio Press, 1984), 11, 12.

14. Reagan, "Remarks on Board the USS *Constellation,* August 20, 1981,'' 722.

Destroyer escort USS *Harold E. Holt* (DE-1074) plies the Gulf of Siam, May 1975. Big USAF helicopters maneuvered over the missile launcher on the fantail in order to use the ship's helipad during the *Mayaguez* operation.

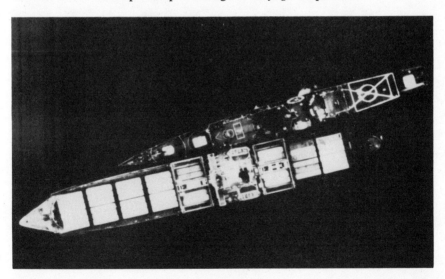

In an action out of the age of sail, destroyer escort *Harold E. Holt* came alongside SS *Mayaguez* early on 15 May 1975 in the treacherous, hostile waters off the Cambodian island of Koh Tang. Skilled U.S. Navy shiphandling allowed American marines to board and secure the abandoned container ship swiftly and efficiently. *AP/WIDE WORLD PHOTOS.*

Clad in chemical protective masks with weapons loaded, men of Company D, 1/4 Marines clamber aboard the *Mayaguez* early on 15 May 1975. Although ready for close combat, the marines met no resistance as they took the ship. *AP/WIDE WORLD PHOTOS.*

The only known photograph taken on Koh Tang Island during the desperate fighting on East Beach. A USAF combat photographer snapped this hazy shot about 1700, 15 May 1975, as Lt. Michael A. Cicere's 3rd Platoon, Company G, 2/9 Marines scrambled aboard the battered USAF helicopter Jolly 11. The men were under heavy fire at the time this picture was taken.

A U.S. Air Force AC-130 Spectre gunship engages targets at dusk, using its internal computer for precision aiming. The big planes provided invaluable support during the *Mayaguez* operation and on Grenada, and stood ready to cover the raid into Iran.

The aircraft carrier USS *Coral Sea* (CV-43), affectionately known as *Coral Maru* and the "ageless warrior," participated in the *Mayaguez* incident, the Iran rescue attempt, the *Achille Lauro* episode, and the 1986 Libyan operations.

Preparing for the Iran hostage rescue: U.S. Navy, Marine, and civilian maintenance and flight crews work on RH-53D Sea Stallion helicopters on the hangar deck of USS *Nimitz* (CVN-68) underway in the Indian Ocean on 23 April 1980. The chopper in the left foreground, #8, completed the torturous flight to Desert One the next evening. Note the upright corrugated cone "sandscreen" pieces standing just behind the forklift. No markings are evident on the helicopters beyond a small number stencilled on the nose panel.

This is it! Prior to leaving the flight deck of *Nimitz*, EAGLE CLAW helicopters start engines early on the evening of 24 April. The helos carry long-range fuel tanks and are painted a dull sand color.

On 26 April 1980, gloating Iranian revolutionaries, soldiers, and religious leaders led western journalists on a grisly tour of the wreckage left behind at Desert One by the ill-fated EAGLE CLAW raiders. The charred, crumbling remains of one unfortunate American dominate this widely publicized commercial photograph. Curious Iranian troops pick through the gutted, twisted aircraft skeletons. *AP/WIDE WORLD PHOTOS.*

A Libyan Arab Air Force Su-22 Fitter J like this one challenged USN F-14A Tomcat fighters early on 19 August 1981 over the Gulf of Sidra. The white missiles on the underbody are AA-2 Atoll infrared types.

Beirut, 1983. A Marine sentry guards one of the better fortified positions around Beirut International Airport during September. Although the perimeter was under fire, this man has no magazine in his M-16A1 rifle. Despite a serious rocket and artillery threat, notice the dearth of true overhead cover, typified by the poncho sunshade to the right rear. The camouflage net appears to be shading equipment; it certainly provides no concealment.

An M-198 155-mm howitzer of Battery C, 1/10 Marines stands ready to fire on enemy elements surrounding the airport. Beirut saw the first operational employment of the new M-198. The placards on the howitzer mount reflect pre-computed firing data for particularly critical target areas.

One of the slablike U.S. Army AN/ TPQ-36 Firefinder radars aligns on a shelling incident in Beirut. These big radars could locate sources of incoming artillery or mortar fires by trajectory analysis. Such locations, accurate to within 10 meters, were forwarded to Marine and Navy gunners for counterbattery efforts. *Photo by Capt. James G. Breckenridge.*

The 24th Marine Amphibious Unit included a significant armored component. Here, three M-60A1 main battle tanks and six LVTP-7 amphibious assault vehicles conduct a firing exercise near Green Beach, Beirut.

Target Acquisition Battery commander Capt. James G. Breckenridge snapped this remarkable photograph while under a barrage on the morning of 4 September 1983. The dirt puff is an enemy shell landing in the combined Army radar and USMC infantry (Company C, 1/8 Marines) position at Combat Post 39, near Khalde. The jeep just right of center is the tail of the Lebanese Army armored column that moved into Khalde that day.

While not all Marine units dug in, soldiers of the Field Artillery School Target Acquisition Battery built deep, sturdy field fortifications following the heavy bombardments of 4 September. *Photo by Capt. James G. Breckenridge.*

The tension is obvious as two Marine jeeps halt enroute to the U.S. Embassy in dangerous downtown Beirut, September 1983. Weapons are loaded, and the men scan their assigned sectors for anything unusual. The Marines wear American flags on their sleeves.

The battered Battalion Landing Team Headquarters building as it appeared on 1 October 1982. Two armed, tracked, armored amphibious assault vehicles are parked to the left.

The wreckage of the Battalion Landing Team Headquarters building as it looked on 15 November 1983, weeks after the truck bombing.

CHAPTER 4

FIRE IN THE LEVANT:
OPERATIONS IN LEBANON

AUGUST 1982–FEBRUARY 1984

Representative C. Robin Britt: "Can you give us insight into the conflict between the presence mission and maximizing security for the Marines?"

Col. Timothy Geraghty: "When we talk in hindsight about the threat being faced there—and to try and put up a hardpoint barricade is what you are talking about—the position where we were, north of the terminal with all that traffic, would be virtually impossible to stop it, and we took moves—and I think a lot of moves—that make a lot of the threats, reduce the vulnerability, but the way of judgment on the calls—and it is a judgment call, it is subjective— is that to provide security for the known threats on the one hand and to provide, you know, an environment that was not reducing our visibility, that we were cowering, particularly with the shelling, it was very adamant that we maintain our visibility."

Representative Britt: "So your sense of that mission, as you understood it, is what proposed that conflict, not anything that the State Department did, but your sense of the mission?"

Colonel Geraghty: "Yes sir; I have to say that in all honesty."

Testimony before the House of Representatives
Armed Services Committee, 9 December 1983

"Digging is not the Marine way."
Gen. Robert E. Cushman, USMC, speaking of Khe Sanh in 1968

"When political objectives are unimportant, motives weak and the passions of the forces slight, a cautious commander may try all sorts of ways by which, without great crises and bloody solutions, he may twist himself into a peace through the weaknesses of his

opponent in the field and in the cabinet. We have no right to find fault with him if the assumptions on which he acts are well founded and promise success, but we must still require him to remember that he is treading a slippery path upon which the God of War may surprise him. He must always keep his eye on the enemy lest he have to defend himself with a dress rapier if the enemy takes up a sharp sword."

Karl von Clausewitz, *On War*

Lebanon is arguably the most dangerous country in the volatile Middle East. Its green hills still feature the famous cedars of biblical lore, and white beaches front on the azure eastern Mediterranean. That very beauty is a cruel deception, a lovely lure that hides the bitter, sputtering struggle for control of a small country not much bigger than Connecticut. The 3 million quarrelsome inhabitants occasionally acknowledge a weak central government and an inexperienced army of at most 20,000 men. But neither the government nor the army is unified. No single authority controls Lebanon, and there is no "safe" district. That is as true today as it was in 1982.

In June 1982, the jewel of the Levant was split among local militias, a Syrian occupation army, vicious Palestinian squatters, and an ineffectual United Nations Interim Force in Lebanon (UNIFIL). Lebanese religious factions also controlled chunks of the small state army. Their private militias squabbled for turf like American ghetto street gangs, but the Muslim Druze Popular Socialist Party (4,000), Maronite Christian Phalange (10,000), Christian South Lebanon Army (3,500), Amal Shiite Muslims (2,000), and numerous smaller splinters employed stolen, borrowed, and bestowed Sagger antitank missiles, 122-mm rockets, 130-mm guns, armored personnel carriers, and even tanks rather than zip guns and switchblades. These groups formed loose alliances on occasion, often crossing religious lines for the sake of expediency. Splits in the militias created new conflicts and reshuffling of this deadly deck.

As if this was not bad enough, foreign forces stirred the pot, forming and playing off the suspicious militias against each other. When Jordan's King Hussein ejected Yasir Arafat's Palestine Liberation Organization

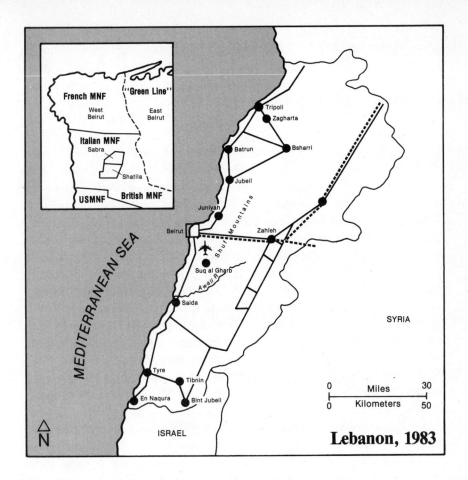

Lebanon, 1983

(PLO) in 1970, the PLO moved to south-central Lebanon, aided by Syrian units. Arafat continued attacks into Israel and manipulated Lebanese Muslim groups; Israel countered by influencing and arming Christian militias. Civil war erupted in 1975, urged by the PLO and Israelis. Fearful that the turmoil might encourage an Israeli military move, Soviet-armed Syrians entered in June 1976 and occupied much of northern and central Lebanon. They actually fought and disarmed many PLO elements. Although Christians, the ruling Lebanese Gemayel clan welcomed the Syrians, then promptly contacted Israel to complain about the Syrian incursion. By the summer of 1982, the Syrians were still there, pressing to install a puppet Lebanese government. Meanwhile, Arafat's heavily armed raiders and rocketeers had long since returned to business as usual, and their strikes took a heavy toll in Israeli Galilee. Israel responded with occasional air bombardment, limited ground raids, and assorted special operations.

Supposedly, UNIFIL existed to prevent the constant Israeli/PLO strife. The United Nations deployed more than 6,000 soldiers from Finland, Fiji, France, Ghana, Ireland, Italy, the Netherlands, Norway, Senegal, and Sweden. The troops patrolled the Israeli/Lebanese border. But the PLO routinely infiltrated these positions, often with UNIFIL approval or at least "official" ignorance.[1] By the summer of 1982, Israeli Prime Minister Menachem Begin, spurred by his pugnacious defense minister, Ariel Sharon (hero of the 1973 Suez Canal counterattack), decided to solve the problems to the north once and for all.

Operation PEACE FOR GALILEE commenced on 6 June 1982, with the stated goal of pushing the PLO fighters at least forty kilometers (about twenty-five miles) into Lebanon, to shove back and destroy Palestinian rocket and gun batteries. This massive operation involved eight division-sized units, and they made short work of the befuddled, unprepared PLO, punching deep into Lebanon on three major axes. The rapid Israeli advance into the Bekáa Valley soon slammed into the Syrians, who fought hard but suffered grievous losses in the air and on the ground. To avoid a major Israeli-Syrian war, a cease-fire went into effect by 11 June 1982, although Israel continued to hunt down and destroy shattered fragments of Arafat's military contingent. Buoyed by their initial successes and having cowed the Syrians, the Israelis pressed well beyond their forty-kilometer limit to the outskirts of Beirut. With Yasir Arafat and the frantic, bedraggled remnants of the PLO trapped in Muslim West Beirut, Begin and Sharon saw an opportunity to smash the PLO utterly. Israeli troops pressed into the populous city of Beirut, bombing and shelling their way toward the desperate Palestinians. Taking advantage of the Beirut operation, the Israeli-backed Christian Phalange entered the Muslim Druze stronghold in the Shuf Mountains to eradicate their rivals.[2]

Supporting the PLO is a knee-jerk Muslim reaction, even in the most moderate Arab states. Faced with the imminent extinction of Arafat's unsavory following, an unlikely pair from pro-American Saudi Arabia and pro-Soviet Syria joined together on 16 July 1982 to ask President Ronald Reagan for U.S. help in arranging a PLO withdrawal. The Arab ministers wanted American troops and warships to insure a safe extraction. Thanks to the efforts of American special envoy Philip Habib, the Israelis grudgingly agreed. Most of the PLO would leave by Greek charter shipping for Tunisia. Considering that some Syrian units had also been trapped in the tightening Israeli noose, the Syrians agreed to permit some of their Palestinian allies to move by highway to Damascus, Syria.[3]

The United States Sixth Fleet landed part of Col. James Mead's 32nd Marine Amphibious Unit (MAU) as early as 23-24 June to evacuate American civilians from Juniyah, Lebanon. From 24 August until 10 September, Battalion Landing Team 2/8 Marines (BLT 2/8) joined with a French Foreign Legion paratroop battalion at the port of Beirut. An Italian unit protected the road to Damascus. Multinational Force (MNF) troops cooperated to escort more than 8,000 PLO soldiers safely out of West Beirut by ship, plus another 6,000 or so over land. The Israelis glowered, rival militias celebrated and demonstrated, and Americans cordoned off the hostile elements. Marines guarded Arafat himself as the PLO leader went aboard a steamer. Intentionally, the marines carried only personal arms. Mortars, tanks, and artillery remained offshore, to avoid any appearance that the Americans had joined the conflict. Given that the United States is Israel's staunch ally, the marines distinctly wanted to appear entirely neutral. It was a risky step, but it worked just as Philip Habib had promised. Everything went well. The Palestinians departed, and Mead reembarked his men without incident. It was just another noncombat evacuation, as at Juniyah. No longer needed, the MNF disbanded.[4]

Four days later, a Syrian-backed assassin blew up Bashir Gemayel, charismatic Phalange chief and duly elected president of Lebanon. Factional eruptions seemed unavoidable. Israeli troops moved into West Beirut to insure order. Vengeful Phalangists took advantage of Israeli negligence (perhaps calculated) and conducted systematic massacres in the Palestinian Sabra and Shatilla refugee camps. The butcher's bill totaled 460, including 15 women; 20 children; and Syrian, Iranian, Algerian, and Pakistani "volunteer" fighters. Bashir's brother Amin Gemayel, chosen as the new Lebanese president, appealed for help from America and Europe. On 20 September 1982, President Reagan joined the French and Italians and announced the reconstitution of the Multinational Force, to replace the Israelis and Phalange in Beirut until the Lebanese Army could take charge.[5] On 29 September, Colonel Mead's men returned to the shattered "Paris of the Middle East." Some marines probably remembered a "temporary" expedition on behalf of Saigon, once known as the "Paris of the Orient." And with that unpleasant analogy noted, the marines dropped into the Lebanese maelstrom.

Colonel Mead's mission on his second insertion into embattled Beirut was not as clear or finite, but it did not seem overly threatening. As President Reagan put it, the marines landed as an "interposition force" to separate the staggering Lebanese government from the feuding religious militias and their powerful Syrian and Israeli associates, at least in the vital capital of Beirut. Obviously, prevention of further factional blood-baths constituted the immediate goal.

But American objectives in Lebanon went beyond a transient sense of order in Beirut. U.S. intentions remained simple and yet maddeningly difficult to achieve: pullout of all foreign forces, restoration of a stable Lebanese government in charge of its own country, and removal of threats to Israel from Lebanese territory. No American leaders were willing to put a time limit on the marine amphibious unit's deployment, but Reagan himself told Congress that the mission would last a "limited period." Finally, the president insisted that "the American force will not engage in combat," although he warned that the marines "may, however, exercise the right of self-defense and will be equipped accordingly." [6]

Real fighting seemed a remote possibility indeed. Reagan told America's legislators that "all armed elements in the area have given assurances" that they would respect the MNF contingents. The first Americans ashore found themselves treated as popular protectors by rejoicing Lebanese Christians and grateful Muslims alike. Having seen Syrian and now Israeli "liberators" overstay their welcome, the locals were fairly certain that the marines and their European allies had no territorial ambitions. Surrounded by a relatively friendly city, the marine commanders agreed with their president's assessment.

Aside from matching conditions on the ground, defining the "interposition" role as a noncombat mission avoided the timetable linked to any congressional War Powers Resolution oversight. For this reason, and to avoid unwelcome comparisons with the lackadaisical UNIFIL elements, American political and military leaders emphasized that the MAU was not in Beirut for "peacekeeping." The marines occupied ground, but the Joint Chiefs of Staff and Gen. Bernard Rogers, USA (commander in chief, European Command) distinctly excused the MAU

United States Strategic and Operational Objectives in Lebanon

1. STRATEGIC OBJECTIVE: Provide an interposition force and contribute to a multinational presence to insure separation of foreign military units preparatory to a full foreign withdrawal.
OPERATIONAL OBJECTIVES:
    1) Occupy and secure assigned positions/section of line.
    2) Conduct combined defensive operations with Multinational Force.
    3) Employ air and naval gunfire support as required.
    4) Protect the force.
    5) Patrol in assigned adjacent areas
       (4 November 1982–31 August 1983).
    6) Perform visibility/presence/peacekeeping tasks.*
    7) Be prepared to withdraw on order.

2. STRATEGIC OBJECTIVE: Reestablish full Lebanese sovereignty over the country.
OPERATIONAL OBJECTIVES:
    1) Conduct combined defensive operations with Lebanese Armed Forces (LAF). Assist LAF to deter passage of hostile armed elements.
    2) Train and assist LAF (13 December 1982).
    3) Provide civic action support to Lebanese population.
    4) Secure Beirut International Airport and keep it operational.*

3. STRATEGIC OBJECTIVE: Insure Lebanese territory would not be used to launch attacks on Israel.
OPERATIONAL OBJECTIVES: None.

ADDITIONAL OPERATIONAL MISSION:
Secure temporary U.S. diplomatic facilities in Beirut (after 18 April 1983).

  * Unclear and assumed missions.

from direct responsibility for any sector of the Lebanese capital. Recalling Vietnam, the U.S. generals and admirals winced at the image of Americans trying to police a restive alien city, fighting as necessary to maintain order. As chief of naval operations Adm. James D. Watkins told a congressional committee, "We are not in a peacekeeping mission. . . . Peacekeeping could well be a combat operation. This is not a combat operation." If things turned sour, U.S. Navy amphibious transports remained just off the beach to withdraw the marines. Intentionally, command never passed ashore; the amphibious squadron commanders remained in overall control throughout the American deployment, just in case an extraction became necessary.[7]

The marines preferred to call their role "presence," seizing upon a line in the JCS mission statement of 23 September 1982 that mandated "a multinational force presence in the Beirut area." The only problem, of course, was succinctly summarized by marine commandant Gen. Paul X. Kelley: "It is not a classic military mission." So Colonel Mead approached his deployment with special care. He directed his men to prominently display the U.S. colors on vehicles and tactical positions, and all marines wore a flag patch on their camouflaged battle dress uniforms. The superbly conditioned and disciplined marines presented a terrific military spectacle, an unmistakable American military presence. Mead might have just as well chosen to emphasize the "occupy and secure" portion of his assignment, or the "combined defensive operations with other MNF contingents" and the Lebanese Army prescribed by CINCEUR (Commander in chief, European command). But the colonel judged that the situation in Beirut hardly necessitated a full-scale defense. So it seemed in those early days.

The Multinational Force divided up troubled Beirut into three sectors. By choice, French paratroopers assumed control over the port and downtown Muslim West Beirut. Colonel Mead wanted access to his amphibious shipping by sea and air, and requested beachfront positions at Beirut International Airport (BIA). This conveniently placed the marines near the wary Israelis, their erstwhile allies. Initially, the MAU commander wanted to expand his outer perimeter to the high ground a few kilometers to the east (the Suq-al-Gharb spur of the Shuf Mountains). The U.S. chain of command said no, probably for fear of involving the marines in the ongoing Druze/Phalange struggle for control of the Shuf. The Italians chose last, and shouldered the unpleasant duties of occupying central Beirut, including the gutted Sabra and Shatilla Palestinian refugee camps.

There was no central MNF command; the French objected to possible American control, and the Americans refused to countenance overall French authority. Instead, the MNF commanders met regularly to exchange information and formulate combined policies, coordinating with their respective ambassadors and the Lebanese government. Each force ran its own area in its own way. Americans maintained their presence, bound by a variant of the same peacetime rules of engagement in use over the Gulf of Sidra in 1981. The Americans avoided combat in an attempt to keep a strictly neutral stance among the squabbling urban factions. The French and to a lesser extent the Italians were much more assertive about keeping order in their more populous areas.[8] In any event, the "temporary" MNF structure persisted long beyond its expected lifetime.

The 32nd MAU's second stop at Beirut went by relatively quickly, marred by one death while marines were clearing unexploded munitions left over by the summer's fighting. Significantly, Colonel Mead and his subordinates chose the basic positions used throughout the Lebanon episode, sending one rifle company south to Khalde, spreading another along the eastern rim of BIA, and placing the third company out at the Lebanese Scientific and Technical University. These units deployed tactically, although they did not prepare major field works.

The marine colonel decided to concentrate his MAU, BLT, and Marine Service Support Group (MSSG) command posts in the airport proper, presumably to facilitate coordination and strengthen rear area security. The MAU commander approved use of the cluster of stout airport buildings for the headquarters and support units. Mead took a risk by putting these key elements within a few hundred meters of each other, but he judged that the threat of serious artillery or ground attack was not great. In any event, the troops assigned to these outfits remained in dispersed bivouacs. The designated BLT command post, destined for a tragic demise, particularly impressed Mead. The blocky, chipped, pocked, battered four-story edifice once served the PLO and Syrians, withstanding heavy bombardments. An Israeli field hospital was set up in the solid building during the summer. Presence had nothing to do with Mead's choices, nor did any political or chain of command pressures. As Colonel Mead said: "It was simply logistics." [9]

Mead's men left on 30 October, replaced by Col. Thomas M. Stokes's 24th MAU. If the 32nd MAU had set the scene, Stokes and his force defined the tactics that came to characterize the U.S. Multinational Force. The only real excitement occurred immediately. On 1 November, a small car bomb blew up harmlessly just beyond the supply parties at work on Black Beach. Which disgruntled faction set the charge remained a mystery. The failed attempt, rated as "clumsy" and "amateurish" by Stokes's intelligence officers, represented the first direct attack on the Americans. It would not be the last.

Within days of his arrival, Stokes received authorization to begin jeep patrols into the Phalange strongholds of Christian East Beirut, a bold move that strengthened the MNF's claims of impartiality among suspicious Muslims. Over time, Battalion Landing Team 3/8 marines instituted foot patrols in Hay-es-Salaam and Khalde, lairs of the Shiite Amal militiamen. These uneventful sweeps showed the flag, and the rifle squads gathered valuable intelligence about activities around the long, fragile marine perimeter. Although the situation remained calm after the freak car explosion, Stokes went beyond his predecessor's restraint. The 24th MAU commander landed his six howitzers and the platoon of five M-60A1 main battle tanks to supplement security arrangements.[10]

During December, 24th MAU began training the Lebanese Army, in coordination with the U.S. Army Office of Military Cooperation (OMC). This had always been an implicit MAU mission, closely tied to the attempt to create a sovereign Lebanese government capable of ruling its own territory. The effort gainfully employed marine expertise, and the Lebanese soldiers received USMC-style camouflage uniforms to mark them as marine products. The significance of this seemingly sensible program cannot be underrated. The Lebanese president, Christian Phalange leader Amin Gemayel, controlled his fragmented Christian/ Muslim army through Gen. Ibrahim Tannous, another Phalangist. Traditionally, Lebanon's army served Christian purposes; Muslims in Beirut thought they endured undue military attentions compared to Christians. Although the Americans encouraged recruitment of Islamic soldiers and trained all Lebanese alike, many Muslims preferred to trust their own militias rather than government forces.[11] By training the Christian-dominated Lebanese Army, the marines inadvertently compromised the neutral image they had tried so hard to build.

Interestingly, Stokes's marines tried to keep their impartiality intact by dealing harshly with an unanticipated source of hostility—the Israeli Defense Forces (IDF). The Israelis pressed regularly at the marine boundaries, challenging U.S. patrols, sending tanks toward American positions, and being rather careless about stray shots and projectiles primarily directed at restive Muslims. Marines stopped patrolling south of Khalde to avoid these unpleasant encounters, but the IDF persisted in its probes and provocations. Despite command conferences and establishment of a USMC/IDF radio link, incidents continued. On 2 February 1983, the bullying went too far. Marine Capt. Charles B. Johnson at the Lebanese University drew his pistol to stop an Israeli tank platoon, announcing that the Israelis could advance at their peril. The confrontation received

**Syrian, Druze, and Other Potentially Hostile Forces Order of Battle
23 October 1983**

Syrian Army in Lebanon: 40,000 men (Bekáa Valley)
  1st Armored Division
    62nd Infantry Brigade, 76th Armored Brigade, 91st Armored Brigade
  3rd Armored Division
    47th Infantry brigade, 51st Armored Brigade, 82nd Armored Brigade
  85th Independent Infantry Brigade
  Palestinian Liberation Army: two brigades—6,000 men
  Air defense forces

Druze Popular Socialist Party Militia: 4,000 men (Shuf Mountains)
  (T-54 tanks, artillery, 122-mm rocket launchers)

Amal Shiite Militia: 2,000 men (Khalde and Hay-es-Salaam)

Numerous additional factional militias (less than 1,000 each)

Iranian Pasdaran Volunteers: 650 men

Christian Phalange: 10,000 men
  (M-48 tanks, artillery)

Israeli Defense Forces in Lebanon: 20,000 men (south of Awali River)
  Two division groups
  Israeli Air Force available on call
  South Lebanon Army: 3,500 men

  Sources: International Institute for Strategic Studies, "Military Balance, 1983–84,"
Air Force (December 1983), 97–100; Chaim Herzog, *The Arab-Israeli Wars* (New York:
Random House, 1982), 387–93.

extensive and favorable coverage in the local Muslim press. It took
direct coordination by Stokes and the Israeli commanders to prevent
more serious scrapes between the Americans and their presumed allies.[12]
Even so, sporadic IDF actions continued to test and endanger the marines,
and American diplomats stayed busy soothing Israeli pride. Apparently,
the IDF expected special treatment by the marines. To Stokes's credit,
he did not deviate from his nonpartisan stance.

On 15 February, Col. James Mead entered Lebanon for the third
time. Mead's 22nd Marine Amphibious Unit (his headquarters had been
renumbered) took over from 24th MAU. The "temporary" expedition
had obviously lasted longer than expected. BLT 2/6 Marines occupied

the usual locations, and Mead trusted that this stay would be as quiet as his previous landings. After all, Stokes's MAU had suffered no casualties despite all of the tussling with the unruly Israelis.

At first, all seemed well. Following a late February blizzard, marines made many friends by using helicopters and amphibious assault vehicles (AAVs) to rescue snowbound villagers, motorists, and even a few Syrian soldiers in the drifting ravines of the Shuf Mountains. In Beirut, Mead's men and U.S. Army Special Forces (Green Berets) of the OMC continued to train the reorganizing Lebanese Army. Shortly after landing, Mead tested his new partners by developing a regular program of joint USMC/ Lebanese Army patrols. At the same time, Mead extended this reconnais-

---

United States Navy Task Forces off Lebanon
25 August 1982–10 April 1984
(approximate arrival and departure dates)

Task Force 60:
USS *Forrestal* (CV-59) Battle Group: 7 July 1982–10 September 1982
USS *Independence* (CV-62) Battle Group: 7 July 1982–1 December 1982
USS *America* (CV-66) Battle Group: 30 September 1982–15 October 1982
USS *Nimitz* (CVN-68) Battle Group: 25 November 1982–1 May 1983
USS *Eisenhower* (CVN-69) Battle Group: 15 April 1983–18 November 1983
USS *New Jersey* (BB-62): 24 September 1983–5 April 1984
USS *John F. Kennedy* (CV-67) Battle Group: 8 November 1983–10 April 1984
USS *Independence* (CV-62) Battle Group: 15 November 1983–15 March 1984

Task Force 61:
USS *Guam* (LPH-9), Amphibious Squadron 4: 25 August 1982–3 November 1982 (Marine Amphibious Unit 32 ashore)
USS *Inchon* (LPH-12), Amphibious Squadron 6: 1 November 1982–15 February 1983 (Marine Amphibious Unit 24 ashore)
USS *Guadalcanal* (LPH-7), Amphibious Squadron 2: 15 February 1983–30 May 1983 (Marine Amphibious Unit 22 ashore)
USS *Iwo Jima* (LPH-2), Amphibious Squadron 8: 28 May 1983–19 November 1983 (Marine Amphibious Unit 24 ashore)
USS *Tarawa* (LHA-1), Amphibious Squadron 1: 12 September 1983–10 October 1983 (Marine Amphibious Unit 31 embarked; not landed)
USS *Guam* (LPH-9), Amphibious Squadron 4: 19 November 1983–26 February 1984 (Marine Amphibious Unit 22 ashore)

United States Marine Forces in Lebanon
25 August 1982–26 February 1984

32nd Marine Amphibious Unit: 25 August–10 September 1982
  Battalion Landing Team 2/8 Marines
  Marine Medium Helicopter Squadron 261 (−) Reinforced
  Marine Service Support Group 32
  CASUALTIES: None

32nd Marine Amphibious Unit: 29 September–30 October 1982
  Battalion Landing Team 2/8 Marines
  Marine Medium Helicopter Squadron 261 (−) Reinforced
  Marine Service Support Group 32
  CASUALTIES: 1 KIA, 3 WIA

24th Marine Amphibious Unit: 30 October 1982–15 February 1983
  Battalion Landing Team 3/8 Marines
  Marine Medium Helicopter Squadron 263 (−) Reinforced
  Marine Service Support Group 24
  CASUALTIES: None

22nd Marine Amphibious Unit: 15 February 1983–30 May 1983
  Battalion Landing Team 2/6 Marines
  Marine Medium Helicopter Squadron 264 (−) Reinforced
  Marine Service Support Group 22
  CASUALTIES: 5 WIA, 2 nonbattle wounded

24th Marine Amphibious Unit: 30 May 1983–19 November 1983
  Battalion Landing Team 1/8 Marines
  Marine Medium Helicopter Squadron 162 (−) Reinforced
  Marine Service Support Group 24
  CASUALTIES: 245 KIA, 136 WIA, 4 nonbattle wounded

31st Marine Amphibious Unit: 12 September 1983–10 October 1983
  Battalion Landing Team 1/3 Marines
  Marine Medium Helicopter Squadron 265 (−) Reinforced
  Marine Service Support Group 31
  CASUALTIES: None

Battalion Landing Team 2/6 Marines: 23 October 1983–19 November 1983
  Headquarters & Service Company, Company E, Company G
  CASUALTIES: None

22nd Marine Amphibious Unit: 19 November 1983–26 February 1984
  Battalion Landing Team 2/8 Marines
  Marine Medium Helicopter Squadron 261 (−) Reinforced
  Marine Service Support Group 22
  CASUALTIES: 10 KIA, 1 DOW, 3 WIA, 1 nonbattle death

sance and "show the flag" effort throughout the neighborhoods of Beirut. The marines and their newly schooled comrades demonstrated their close ties for all to see. Apparently, not everyone was impressed.

The Israelis expressed their discontent with renewed incursions, random rounds, and diplomatic objections about supposed marine slights. The marine corps commandant at the time, Gen. Robert H. Barrow, complained in writing to Secretary of Defense Caspar Weinberger about the incidents, which he suspected were "orchestrated and executed for obtuse Israeli political purposes." Weinberger intentionally released the letter to the U.S. press, and American diplomats expressed serious concern. The fact that America supplied the bulk of Israel's arms, including F-16 fighters embargoed since the Israelis had destroyed an Iraqi reactor site in June 1981, surely played a part. Menachem Begin wanted his fighter jets; the IDF got the message and backed off.[13]

In mid-March, the urban Muslim militias reacted to perceptions that the MNF was getting too friendly with Gemayel's Christian-oriented military. On 15 March, an Italian squad hit a mine field and took sniper fire: one soldier died and two fell wounded. The next day, someone dropped a grenade on a BLT 2/6 Marines fire team in West Beirut, injuring five marines. A day later, a French paratrooper was hit. Mead prudently strengthened his defenses by erecting some concertina wire, adding and reinforcing bunkers, placing snipers on rooftops, and allowing patrols to move through Beirut with loaded magazines and rounds chambered. He accepted some resultant accidental shootings.[14] Mead kept his men dispersed and deployed his patrols carefully, searching for indicators of trouble. But the various enemies of the MNF chose not to test the improved USMC perimeter beyond an odd round or two.

In the early afternoon of 18 April 1983, a pickup truck laden with a ton of high explosives detonated inside the American Embassy compound. The driver parked the vehicle and left before it blew. The resultant explosion shattered the eight-story main building, killing seventeen Americans and forty-four Lebanese. Four marine guards were among the dead.

Colonel Mead reacted forcefully and immediately. He sent all of Foxtrot Company and a rifle platoon from Echo Company, 2/6 Marines, to cordon off the blast site and pick up the numerous classified materials scattered in the disaster. The marines went in loaded for bear, with bullets locked in their rifle chambers. Once the American diplomats had moved to temporary facilities at the Durafourd Building and British

Embassy, a reinforced rifle platoon from the MAU remained on guard to prevent another attack. Barricades, earthen berms, and amtracs (AAVs) with .50-caliber machine guns stiffened the marine defense. There was no room to be polite. At 0220 on 28 April, a Lebanese car ran past a marine AAV, and the American gunner loosed a burst of wicked slugs that sent the light vehicle careening into a barrier. Two drunks emerged, panic-stricken. But Mead refused to compromise the harsh rules of engagement. At the temporary embassy, marines shot first and asked questions later.

At BIA, Mead took further precautions. He increased patrols in frequency to improve his feel for the changing situation in the local slums, doubled the sentries twenty-four hours a day, added observation posts, emplaced AAVs to protect the closely spaced headquarters facilities, and directed the first full-scale field fortifications, to include major wire entanglements and sandbagging efforts around positions and occupied structures. When questioned later about possible political implications, Mead stressed that he considered defensive actions well within his command prerogatives: "I had full authority. I could have put tanks in there, .50 calibers there, and if I needed more weaponry, it would have been flown out from the States." U.S. diplomats stood aside. Special envoy Philip Habib agreed with Mead, because "policymakers at the civilian level don't make the rules of engagement." [15] It evidently worked; 22nd MAU completed its tour without further incident, despite additional random rounds that appeared to be intended for others.

As Colonel Mead prepared to depart Beirut, U.S. Secretary of State George Shultz personally intervened to expedite rambling negotiations for an Israeli troop withdrawal, hoping that Syria would follow. The bilateral Gemayel-Begin agreement, signed on 17 May 1983, favored the Israelis. They were allowed to keep a buffer zone held by client militia, the Christian South Lebanon Army. Moreover, two days later, President Reagan resumed F-16 sales to the IDF, an obvious sweetener for the deal. The Syrians were merely expected to pull out completely, abandoning seven years of effort and leaving numerous Muslim associates to their fate. Aware of Israeli domestic discord, Syria's President Hafiz Assad knew that the IDF would probably leave regardless of Syrian actions. With his Bekáa Valley units refitted from their June 1982 mauling, Assad rebuffed the agreement and dug in to stay in Lebanon.[16] The next marine contingent faced a novel, more deadly situation.

Colonel Timothy J. Geraghty's 24th Marine Amphibious Unit assumed the MNF mission on 30 May 1983. During the relief in place, Colonel Mead explained the local tactical situation, offered views on the Lebanese Army (at least a year to go toward real proficiency), and reminded Geraghty that the Multinational Force commitment was "not open-ended," especially in the face of an increasing threat. Given that Capt. Morgan R. France, USN (aboard USS *Iwo Jima*), and his Amphibious Squadron 8 steamed majestically just off the beach, Geraghty had help on call. Captain France retained overall command in Lebanon, because he might have to pull 24th MAU out any time things got too hot ashore.

Although 24th MAU had just been to Lebanon under Colonel Stokes, few men remained from that recent excursion. The revamped headquarters and assigned subordinate units reflected their new commander, who had worked with Lt. Col. H. L. Gerlach's BLT 1/8 Marines (BLT 1/8), Lt. Col. L. R. Medlin's Marine Helicopter Squadron 162 ($-$) (Reinforced) (HMM-162), and Maj. D. C. Redlich's 24th Marine Service Support Group (MSSG 24) in predeployment training to prepare the marines for Beirut. Like Mead before him, Colonel Geraghty's perceptions of his mission and situation proved critical. On his shoulders rested much of the heavy burden of American foreign policy in Lebanon, and the marine commander thought twice before acting. He was determined to meet the challenge of carrying out his perceived mission in the treacherous Lebanese capital.[17]

Colonel Geraghty was an experienced infantryman, described by a major on his staff as a "poster Marine." He inspired confidence in subordinates, and he demanded high standards. Given the stress on "presence," Geraghty insisted upon a disciplined, combat-ready appearance and proper media relations. During the Atlantic transit, a special duty officer from Headquarters Marine Corps instructed the young men on how to deal with journalists. As Maj. Robert Jordan, MAU Public Affairs Officer, remembered, "The thrust was to prepare them so they wouldn't embarrass themselves by voicing inappropriate or seemingly insensitive comments." Geraghty himself proved adept at handling the press. He wanted his men to do well.

At least one junior enlisted member of the MAU operations staff section sensed something more. "I realized he was a consummate politician. The enlisted troops knew the colonel was bucking for a star," wrote Cpl. Michael Petit, "and being the on-site commander in Lebanon

United States Command Organization
23 October 1983

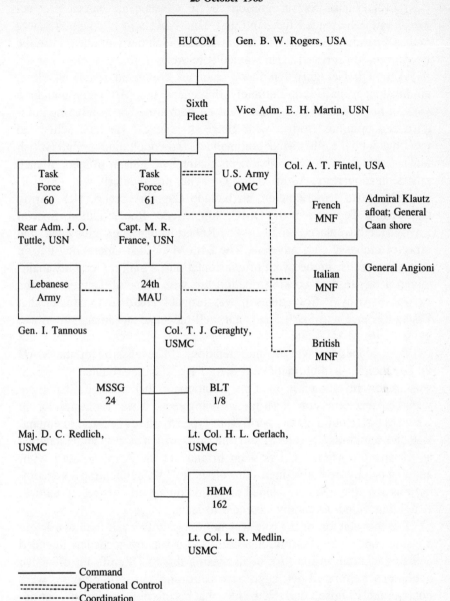

Commanders Sixth Fleet, TF-60, TF-61, and 24th MAU cooperated with the U.S. Embassy in Beirut and the presidential special envoy, although those civilian officials did not exercise any operational authority. Emergency communications with the Israeli Defense Forces also existed.

EUCOM's naval deputy, CINCNAVEUR, routinely handled naval affairs in the theater from his London headquarters.

was a big chance for recognition and to advance his career. Colonel Mead had commanded the 32nd and 22nd MAUs in Lebanon. He was now a brigadier general."[18] In any event, Colonel Geraghty took the Beirut mission seriously. He wanted it to work.

Although Geraghty's military chain of command remained clear, circumstances in Beirut definitely influenced the MAU commander's view of his role. Geraghty found himself bombarded by conflicting guidance and opinions from a wide range of sources. He held scheduled meetings with the other MNF commanders (now including a small British unit). Each of the MNF components maintained liaison officers in each others' headquarters. Additionally, Geraghty met regularly with the U.S. "country team" in Lebanon, to include Captain France, U.S. Army Col. Arthur T. Fintel of the OMC, Ambassador Robert Dillon, Special Envoy Habib (replaced on 27 July by Robert McFarlane), plus a variable array of embassy staff advisers. The 24th MAU had emergency liaison with the Israelis, in the event of confrontations. Finally, Geraghty maintained a day-to-day working relationship with General Tannous of the Lebanese Army.[19] Sometimes it was probably hard to remember that Captain France and Sixth Fleet, not well-meaning diplomats and allies, guided 24th MAU's fate.

By Colonel Geraghty's interpretation, "The mission of the MAU in Lebanon is a diplomatic mission." He elaborated later: ". . . it was important to me, in the interpretation of that mission, that there was a presence mission. That means being seen. It was a mission where we were not to build up any permanent-type structures because to emphasize the temporary nature of our mission, which is my understanding as to why the Marine Corps went in and not the Army to start with, and that is why we maintained ships offshore." By delineating a noncombat mission, the colonel planned to avoid combat and hence, casualties. If fighting flared, Geraghty expected to leave.

But this version of his role was not the only or even the most likely mission concept implicit in his orders, and it was by no means intended to be unalterable in the face of increasing threats. Significant offensive operations were ruled out; aggressive patrolling and solid defenses were not. Geraghty himself derived the idea that his mission precluded "permanent-type structures," based upon his attempt to fulfill a nonmilitary role. After his deployment, the colonel told investigators: "I never felt there was undue influence to retard any type of action I felt necessary for the rules of engagement in the light of the mission." Asked if superiors ever refused greater defensive measures, Geraghty's response was painfully brief: "No, sir." It was up to the commander on the ground.

Because the 24th MAU commander did not think his mission was military in nature, he did not consider standard battlefield defensive tactics applicable, although marine units certainly train on defensive tasks. Like other marines, Geraghty disliked being tied to a static perimeter; he considered it innately nontactical. He stated that he would have acted differently "if we were on a solely military, an offensive mission, more Marine-oriented." Unable to influence his surroundings by the offensive action inculcated into marines (a hollow possibility without significant U.S. reinforcements), Geraghty could either erect sturdy defenses or employ "presence" to try to affect his unwelcome situation.

Geraghty's diplomatic interpretation made him extremely cautious about changing or enforcing the airport perimeter he occupied. Eager to strengthen the Lebanese government's power in accord with American strategic goals, Geraghty deferred to the Lebanese Civil Aviation Administration's desires to keep BIA operational, and ceded official security duties in the area to the Lebanese Army. He thought the marines should be careful not to interfere with Lebanese airport activities, even at the expense of their own security. Geraghty knew this was tricky; he called the tactical situation "terrible," because he was stuck at the active international airport, where "you don't have security." He concluded that vulnerability went with the presence task, "but you accept that."

Like Colonel Mead back in September 1982, Geraghty would have preferred to hold Suq-al-Gharb. Instead he was stuck at the seaside airport, with a reinforced battalion of strung-out, partially dug-in marines. The position was good for resupply or rapid withdrawal; only a prodigious fortification effort could render it suitable for prolonged defense. Geraghty probably figured that a successful defense was unlikely, regardless of the amount of dirt turned or guns sited. As he stated later of the numerous potential factional enemies, the marines conceded the initiative by defending: "Our location has been relatively static . . . and they are going to find vulnerabilities."

Colonel Geraghty believed that the marines' best defense was their visible neutral image. In short, the optimum way to preclude losses was to avoid combat. He trusted that impartiality and showing the flag could accomplish the mission as he understood it. By taking an active, fearless posture and avoiding involvement in militia feuds, the marines might achieve a degree of protection that sandbags could never furnish.

Certainly it had worked previously. As the colonel explained, ''We walked a razor's edge to maintain our neutrality and treated all Lebanese factions alike, showing no favoritism toward one group or another, and it was in this context, I think, that successes were made.'' Despite a steady rise in dangers around BIA, Geraghty did not want to resort to combat actions: ''I was very adamant to maintain that neutrality that I think we had built up—and good will—for over a year.'' [20] The 24th MAU, however, faced trouble trying to show evenhandedness and simultaneously train and operate with the Christian-controlled Lebanese Army.

Colonel Timothy Geraghty had made the conscious choice to eschew defense in favor of presence. He thought it was his mission, and he hoped it would protect his men. Whereas Stokes and Mead had responded to increased threats with beefed-up protection, Geraghty would attempt to alleviate the danger by trying to restore the benign circumstances of early 1983. It was a very risky course of action, a bluff based on the belief that no defense could be airtight. So guts and the U.S. flag replaced interlocking fields of fire, and a marine colonel did his best to handle a tough mission. Presence became defense.

The first weeks of 24th MAU's operations in Beirut passed quietly. The marines dealt with the blazing heat and choking red dust as they moved into 22nd MAU's positions. Battery C, 1/10 Marines, pulled up its new M-198 155-mm howitzers near a knoll just north of the MAU/ BLT/MSSG complex. Marine gunners and Lebanese soldiers manned checkpoint 74 along the main airport access road. Company C established positions at the Lebanese Scientific and Technical University (combat posts 46 and 49) and combined USMC/Lebanese Army combat posts 35 and 69. These isolated posts strung across Hay-es-Salaam, tying the university marines in with Company B. Fronting on Hay-es-Salaam to the north and Ashuefat to the south and east, Company B guarded easterly BIA runways. This unit manned combined American and Lebanese combat posts 11 and 76, almost smack in the center of the slender marine line. Company B's riflemen linked in with the Italians to the north and Company A to the south. Most of Company A held the south end of the airport near Khalde, and a detached rifle platoon protected the temporary U.S. Embassy in downtown Beirut.

Although a few shots echoed through the marine positions, combined USMC/Lebanese patrols came and went without incident. Lebanese officers and guides routinely accompanied USMC jeep patrols, and marine

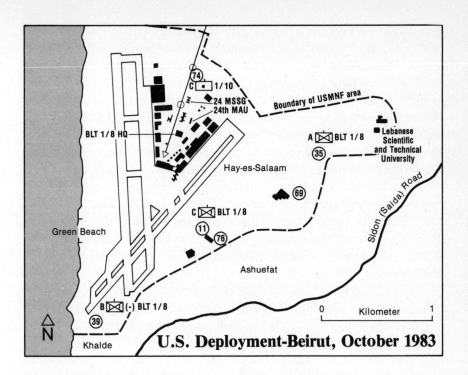

U.S. Deployment-Beirut, October 1983

four-man fire teams joined Lebanese Army squads walking through the Hay-es-Salaam slums. Marines kept busy schooling Lebanese Army units in advanced tactics; conducting their own unit exercises; exchanging special skills training with the French, Italians, and British; and maintaining physical fitness.

Since the immediate threat appeared slight, some of Colonel Mead's security measures were loosened. The amtrac moved away from the BLT building, to join its dozen or so mates as supply and reaction force transports. After a nervous marine shot two Lebanese joggers, Geraghty prohibited insertion of magazines by marines on certain headquarters guard posts and on most patrols. The wartime atmosphere of early May dissipated. In the words of Major Jordan, "Life within the Marine compound varied little from any normal deployment." [21]

Geraghty tried to make the marines' stay bearable and at the same time show his Lebanese friends how Americans lived. Off-duty time provided rather typical military entertainments. Corporal Michael Petit remembered the marines' recreation: "The officers and senior enlisted men were watching a video tape. The tapes came from Habibi's Video in the Shuf, and one of the Arabic-speaking Marines from the Interrogator-Translator Team picked up a supply once a week on 'intelligence gathering' trips. While the enlisted troops were prohibited from drinking hard liquor, the officers' club served both mixed drinks and beer. We weren't allowed to watch just any video tape either. Colonel Geraghty had banned the film *Caligula* as too pornographic for the enlisted troops, and we had to resort to a secret showing. . . ." Junior marines made do with beer, B-movies, and sports. Visits to the other MNF contingents (with the requisite toasts and swapping of memorabilia), relaxing runs out to USS *Iwo Jima,* and occasional liberty trips to Egypt rounded out marine free hours.

Colonel Geraghty insured that even recreation contributed to 24th MAU's mission. On July 4, the marines celebrated Independence Day in a big way, with a combined U.S./Lebanese marathon run and a barbecue, all before a massive press corps. On Sunday mornings, the MAU slept late (except for some sentries). Sunday afternoons, most of the marines enjoyed a pleasant barbecue, often with Lebanese friends and French MNF comrades in attendance. At these parties, intramural sports with the MNF and Lebanese provided diversions, although Colonel Geraghty's subordinates went a bit overboard one day when they created an elaborate wooden and steel regulation basketball court, complete with a scoreboard and proper markings, for a single USMC/Lebanese contest. BLT engineers contributed to the grandiose project. Marine historian Eric Hammel described the scene as Gen. Ibrahim Tannous arrived for the game: "He was seated, as were Colonel Geraghty and other senior American officers, at a table bedecked with a colorful Heineken patio umbrella, the better to shade the Marine retainers detailed to see that the commanders and their staffs were well stuffed with steak and hamburgers and, of course, ice cold beer." [22] It was all in the name of presence.

But even as the marines attempted to make the best of their Beirut routine, the situation around them began to change. On 6 July, Syria formally rejected the Israeli/Lebanese withdrawal plan of 17 May 1983. Their allies of the time, the Muslim Druze, began a major effort to eject the Christian Phalange from the Shuf Mountains. The Syrians expected Israel to withdraw unilaterally; the Druze and Amal Shiites prepared to fill the resultant gap. Unfortunately, so did the Lebanese Army, many resplendent in their new marine-type battle dress uniforms. Their comrades walked, rode, and manned combat posts with the Americans every day.

On 22 July, eleven 122-mm rockets arced into the Beirut International Airport, rattling the marines and chasing them into their hasty fighting holes. The marines went to full alert, but nothing else happened. After ten anxious minutes, the marines emerged to check the damage. One round dug a crater between the BLT and MAU buildings. Fragments injured three Americans. The marines hopefully dismissed the projectiles as a mistake, intended for others.

The supposition was mistaken. On 8 August, two more rockets struck near the USMC bunkers, and Colonel Geraghty's operations log noted: "The rocket attack on 22 July was no longer an aberration, and these impacts signaled that more attacks were likely and, in fact, were becoming standard operating procedure." In agreement with Lieutenant Colonel Gerlach, Geraghty gathered almost all of Gerlach's BLT 1/8 Headquarters and Service Company, Weapons Company, and landing team attachments into the massive BLT command post structure to provide protection from further barrages.[23] Meanwhile, out on the perimeter, the line companies prepared for more trouble. They had rotated on 1 August, with Company B sent to the university, Company A to the eastern BIA line, and Company C to the south end of the runway, less one platoon downtown at the embassy.

Early on 10 August, more than two dozen more rockets smashed into BIA, closing the airport and battering the Lebanese training camp and aircraft flight line directly adjoining the MAU/BLT command post compound. Another marine fell wounded. But this time, the marines found out who was tormenting them. A few days prior, a provisional U.S. Army Target Acquisition Battery (TAB) arrived in Beirut, directly from the Army Field Artillery School at Fort Sill, Oklahoma. The soldiers set up their two new AN/TPQ-36 Firefinder radars, one down near Khalde, the other with the marine artillery battery. Although the army devices could detect mortars and artillery by tracking the rounds as they decelerate after firing, the Firefinders could not trace rockets, which actually speed up after launch. Deprived of electronic help, the dogged army survey section examined the rocket impact points and calculated the enemy locations the old-fashioned way, by crater analysis. Soldiers estimated that the rockets came from Walid Jumblatt's Druze Progressive Socialist Party (PSP) militia area in the Shuf.

Geraghty authorized a unique response. He directed the BLT's 81-mm mortar platoon to fire illumination rounds (parachute flares) above the identified Druze launch site, a clear warning. Lance Corporal Brian Parkin recalled his amazement as he scrambled to conduct his first combat fire mission: "I saw the guys 'half-load' the tubes and then fire. It was only illumination, but I couldn't believe it." [24] The Druze apparently understood, and ceased fire. Although more rounds landed over the next few days, there were no other USMC casualties.

Over the next two weeks, Colonel Geraghty assessed the deteriorating situation. President Reagan's new special envoy and his team arrived. Robert McFarlane (a retired marine lieutenant colonel and a participant in President Ford's planning efforts toward recovery of the *Mayáguez*) took charge dramatically between the 22 July and 8 August shelling incidents. In an attempt to buttress Christian President Amin Gemayel, McFarlane decided to sever all U.S. contacts with Walid Jumblatt's Druze forces, since these militiamen opposed Gemayel's army and government. Gemayel's staff were elated as they schemed to destroy their many enemies with America's supposed blessing. As Gemayel's defense adviser Wadia Haddad remarked, "We have the United States in our pocket."

Although McFarlane later reversed his harsh measure, the damage was done. The wily Jumblatt turned toward his old mentors, the Syrians. Meanwhile, counting on U.S. support, Gemayel and Tannous prepared to send their refurbished brigades into the Shuf when Israel withdrew. The Lebanese Army intended to clear Nabih Berri's Shiite Amal from Hay-es-Salaam as well.[25] The marines, who would undoubtedly have paid anyway, paid more and sooner.

It was a critical time for 24th MAU. Nobody seriously considered withdrawal, certainly no one who spoke to the energetic McFarlane. Colonel Geraghty stressed that the marines could not permit the shellings to stop their presence duties. Major Jordan said that "visibility was still the order of the day." Training of the Lebanese Army increased, to include hand-to-hand combat, repeated combined patrols, artillery drills, and a night infiltration course. Marines jumped with French paratroopers, and hung high over Beirut on special harnesses suspended from clattering CH-46E Sea Knight choppers. It was all very exciting, and the "flying" marines watched the militia skirmishing in the distance. The thoughtful Jordan summarized the mood quite well: "The seriousness of the situation still had not registered on many of the Marines despite several of their mates suffering minor wounds.'' [26] Like it or not, 24th MAU was about to become part of Lebanon's long civil war.

The Israeli Defense Forces planned to withdraw south to the Awali River, largely for their own reasons. At America's request, the Israelis postponed their pullout twice during August, buying time for the Lebanese Army to get ready. But the cacophony of protest in Israel grew louder and louder, demanding an end to the IDF intervention. Phalange elements beefed up to meet the Druze counterattack that would surely follow any IDF withdrawal. The Druze and Amal readied for a finish fight against the Phalangists and their presumed allies, the Lebanese Army. On Sunday, 28 August, long-extant rumors took concrete form as Israel commenced the first parts of their major troop movement. Without warning the marines, the IDF turned over the northern Shuf range and Christian East Beirut to the half-trained Lebanese Army.[27] Within hours, it became evident who had really been providing order around Beirut.

By early afternoon, the marines found themselves in the line of fire as the fighting escalated around them. Most of the marines were at the usual barbecues when the MAU declared a Condition I Alert. Probably, the incoming rounds were not actually aimed at the marines, but Druze and Amal militias must have had a hard time distinguishing between the identically uniformed marines and Lebanese soldiers crouching in their combined force combat posts. As marine Lt. Gregory Balzer aptly explained: ''When the IDF pulled out of the area, the Lebanese Armed Forces began using our lines as protection for movement up and down the coast road, which put us in direct fire of forces hostile to the Lebanese Armed Forces, trying to control the positions that the IDF withdrew from.'' [28]

Regardless of Colonel Geraghty's diplomatic intentions, the marines on the perimeter soon found that mere hunkering down would not suffice. Stray lead ricocheted around the isolated marine positions. About 1610, Amal machine gun fire concentrated on combat post 69, held by 1st Lt. David Hough and his 1st Squad, 2nd Platoon, Company B. As the marines hugged their bunkers, Amal fire grew. Rocket-propelled grenades caromed off the sandbags, 106-mm recoilless rifles punched into the field fortifications, and a half dozen AK-47s blazed away on full automatic. Hough took it for ten minutes as his men pleaded to return fire. ''I knew we had to fire back,'' said Hough. ''The rules of engagement applied, but I called the company headquarters anyway.'' Approval came swiftly. For the first time, the marines shot back, at first to scare, and then to kill. Unfortunately, weeks of complacency had crept up on the Americans. They carried only about 175 rounds per man. Worse, their powerful M-60 machine gun turned out to have a defective bolt, permitting only single shots. Husbanding their precious ammunition, the marines shot back until dark, when the firing slackened.[29]

Lieutenant Hough was merely the first marine leader among many who found himself and his men under direct, intentional attack over the next week. While Hough shot at his fleeting targets, Company A also opened fire with selected marksmen. Unlike Lieutenant Hough in the urban strongpoint of combat post 69, Capt. Paul Roy's Company A occupied sites along the wide-open airfield that marine historian Eric Hammel called "more ceremonial than real." The marines lived in tents that rose high above the sagging knee-high sandbag blast walls intended as shielding. On the morning of 29 August, a mortar barrage killed Roy's 1st Platoon leader and platoon sergeant in their tent. Five marines were wounded. Sporadic 82-mm fire injured three more before Colonel Geraghty authorized Battery C's mighty 155-mm pieces to hit back at the Druze mortar crew spotted by the busy army TAB men. The first 155-mm volley sprinkled illumination rounds over the militia crew near Khalde. The Druze mortar kept shooting. Geraghty authorized a battery sheaf of six high-explosive rounds, and that erased the troublesome militia tube. Meanwhile, the rest of Company A was blazing away, covering the three amphibious assault vehicles sent from the BLT headquarters to retrieve U.S. casualties.[30]

Company C to the south remained unengaged, thanks to the Israelis still in the vicinity. But Company B was not so lucky. Marines at combat post 35 opened fire on their own initiative. Lieutenant Hough's ordeal at combat post 69 continued at dawn on 29 August. Druze officers approached Hough and demanded a surrender. They promised a ground assault. The marine refused, and an extensive 122-mm rocket and artillery barrage rained around the reinforced buildings and trenches, raising a pall of smoke, dust, and splinters. Small arms gunfire kept the marines ducking, and Hough watched with dismay as the Muslim troops of his affiliated Lebanese Army units debated with their Christian officers about returning fire on coreligionists. At least one Lebanese deserted outright. Hough inventoried his slim ammunition stocks: a few hundred rounds; ten M-203 40-mm grenades; and three light antitank weapons (LAWs), unguided rockets in disposable launchers. Fortunately, the Druze threat proved empty, despite heavy fire all afternoon. Perhaps a pair of Cobra attack helicopters that flew over late in the day made a difference. Although ordered not to shoot, Cobra pilot Capt. John Kerr did not hesitate to blast a Druze .50-caliber machine gun that dared to open up on him. Kerr's rocket fire quelled the Druze, at least for the night.

Alarmed by the situation at combat post 69, Colonel Geraghty and BLT commander Gerlach readied a tank and amtrac relief column to rescue the beleaguered outposts. Instead, dawn on 30 August saw the Lebanese Army mount a clumsy armored thrust to protect its forces at combat posts 35 and 69. A great deal of haphazard tank fire and spraying machine gun bullets ripped up Hay-es-Salaam, sending the Amal and Druze scampering for their holes. But as incredulous marines watched and fired at the few militia troops still bothering with the combat posts, the Amal captured one M-113 armored personnel carrier (APC) intact and destroyed two others. Hough tried to hunt down the captured APC over the next few days with his LAWs, but the slippery Amal fired and tore away too quickly. Finally, on 2 September, another platoon from Company B relieved Hough's tired marines, who rotated back to the relative comfort of the university area.[31]

As the fighting slackened, Colonel Geraghty faced an unpleasant quandary. His bluff of presence had been called in a major way. Geraghty and his superior, Captain France, controlled everything ashore, from rifles up to 155-mm shells and Cobra gunships. The commanders devised "a postured response," involving first pointing gun tubes and launching attack choppers, then popping illumination flares over active hostile firing sites, and finally engaging any defiant shooters. As France said, "We were very concerned with remaining neutral. That was the linchpin of our mission and the linchpin of Tim's [Geraghty's] survival." [32]

But the marines had fired small arms, machine guns, grenades, mortars, artillery, and even Cobra rockets at both Amal Shiite and Druze PSP militiamen. Geraghty, Gerlach, and their subordinate commanders tried desperately to control the violence. Even so, things soon spiraled out of hand. Like Captain Kerr in his helicopter, other privates, corporals, sergeants, and lieutenants boldly elected to defend themselves, which was certainly permitted by the rules of engagement.

Although he supported the decisions of the men on the ground, especially after the deaths on 29 August, Geraghty acted as if he thought he could somehow put the lid back on the hideous Pandora's box of indiscriminate shooting and return to the seemingly halcyon days of

June and July. He delayed fire support missions and continued to work through the intimidation and illumination routine even as outlying posts came under heavy fire. As he later explained: "I think a lot of the shelling and the casualties that we took there over the months were really directed to—as bait to force us to have a large response into the village and we didn't do that." He added: "I think we earned the respect of the people." [33]

So what were the American options as they waited for the full Israeli withdrawal and the fire storm sure to accompany it? Planners examined three possibilities: pull out the MAU, reinforce or reposition the MAU, and maintain the status quo. Only Gen. Bernard Rogers at European Command (EUCOM) seriously suggested withdrawal, even though the "noncombat" line was obviously breached. There were those in Washington who wanted to expand the U.S. contingent of the MNF, pushing the enlarged force as far south as the Awali River to fill the gap opened when the Israelis departed. But President Reagan had promised to ask Congress before altering the American role in the MNF or reinforcing the marines. Indeed, Public Law 98-43 (27 June 1983) required such consultation. What if Congress said no? Could Reagan risk a confrontation over the War Powers Resolution, while the ninety-day clock ticked and enemies waited patiently? Where would that leave Gemayel and his fragile army?

Instead, the president decided to retain 24th MAU in place. Encouraged by the forceful McFarlane, Reagan risked the marines as a shield for the Lebanese. The IDF pullout required America to choose between truly neutral interposition and direct support for Gemayel's government. Having already tilted toward Gemayel, the U.S. found its hand forced by the aggressive Shiite Amal and Druze. Every time the marines shot back, they identified themselves as Lebanese Army allies. But rather than admit the changed circumstances, commanders from Washington down to Colonel Geraghty insisted that the marines' mission was unaltered. Reagan emphasized, however, that "U.S. forces will be prepared to exercise their right of self-defense should such attacks recur." [34]

To protect the marines, General Rogers delegated authority to employ carrier reconnaissance jets and naval gunfire to Vice Adm. Edward H. Martin of Sixth Fleet. Offshore, on "Bagel Station," the USS *Eisenhower* and its battle group prepared for action. Additionally, the Pentagon moved USS *Tarawa* and Amphibious Squadron 1, with 31st MAU embarked, toward Lebanon, as potential reinforcements. The French, who also had sustained casualties in the militia skirmishing, readied their air wing aboard the carrier *Foch*. Italian destroyers moved in for fire missions. If the simmering situation blew up again, the militiamen could expect heavy retribution.

Colonel Geraghty's reaction during the lull was quite curious. In order to prevent casualties, he ended all but a few local security patrols on 31 August. Even these were not run when gunfire endangered the marines involved. Concerned about losses, Geraghty intended to close the vulnerable combat posts 35 and 69. He even considered evacuating the university, because if a marine was wounded, "the only way we could have gotten him out is to have an armored force [go] through a hostile village in order to get them." But after consultation with his commanders and McFarlane, who urged him to reconsider, Geraghty found his idea overtaken by events on the ground, and the marines in the combat posts remained fully engaged until the next significant break in the fighting. These initiatives might have cut losses in the short run, but given the suspension of almost all patrols, removing the combat posts from the airport approaches would have torn open 24th MAU's early warning cordon.

But even as the colonel cut his links to the Beirut scene, he clung to the viability of his mission. Geraghty's performance at a memorial service during the first days of September reveals his thinking at the time. With the assembled news media in attendance, Colonel Geraghty went well beyond the traditional eulogy for the dead marines. Geraghty talked very little about the deceased. He said instead that "we must help Lebanon maintain her sovereignty." He ignored the vicious fighting that had flared around the airport. As witness Cpl. Michael Petit said, "This isn't a memorial service to the dead. It's a justification to the press on why we're here." Another marine responded to Petit, "And of course we haven't been in combat. Losey and Ortega dropped dead from boredom, not massive shrapnel wounds to the head." [35] The marine commander was drawing his unit into a shell, but the shell was paper-thin.

On Sunday, 4 September, the Israelis withdrew their main forces. As expected, fierce fighting broke out. Company C, which enjoyed IDF protection until that day, found itself involved in major firefights with the denizens of Khalde. Fortunately, S/Sgt. Joe Curtis woke his 1st Platoon before dawn, suspicious of heavy vehicle noises to the south

United States, Multinational, and Lebanese Forces Order of Battle
10–23 October 1983

United States Sixth Fleet

U.S. Army units

Office of Military Cooperation (Special Forces trainers)

Field Artillery School Provisional Target Acquisition Battery (TAB) *

U.S. Navy/U.S. Marine Corps units

Task Force 60

USS *Eisenhower* (CVN-69) with Carrier Air Wing 7 (CVW-7), USS *New Jersey* (BB-62), USS *Virginia* (CGN-38), USS *Arthur D. Radford* (DD-968), USS *John Rodgers* (DD-983), USS *Bowen* (FF-1079)

Task Force 61 (Amphibious Squadron 8)

USS *Iwo Jima* (LPH-2), USS *Austin* (LPD-4), USS *Portland* (LSD-37), USS *El Paso* (LKA-117), USS *Harlan County* (LST-1196), SEAL Team 4 (−), Beach Group Two (−), Construction Bn. Two (−)

24th Marine Amphibious Unit (24th MAU) **

Battalion Landing Team 1/8 Marines (BLT 1/8), Marine Medium Helicopter Squadron 162 (HMM-162) (−) (+), Marine Service Support Group 24 (MSSG 24)

Amphibious Squadron 1 (forces not landed)

USS *Tarawa* (LHA-1), USS *Duluth* (LPD-6), USS *Frederick* (LST-1184) with Marine Amphibious Unit 31 embarked (BLT 1/3 Marines)

U.S. Air Force Units

Military Airlift Command

Detachment, 375th Aeromedical Airlift Wing (Incirlik Air Base, Turkey)

Multinational Forces

Great Britain: Squadron, Dragoon Guards; RAF Reconnaissance Squadron 87

France: Brigade, 11th Airborne Division; *Foch* (R-99) Task Force 452 (24 attack jets, 8 fighters)

Italy: Infantry Brigade (mechanized battalion, paratroop battalion); Naval Task Force

Lebanese Armed Forces (units in Beirut vicinity)

8th Infantry Brigade (Shuf Mountains), included 85 Field Artillery Battalion

4th Mechanized Brigade (Khalde), included 43 Battalion (Beirut International Airport)

3rd Infantry Brigade, included 31 Battalion (Hay-es-Salaam)

1st Air Assault Battalion

3rd Air Assault Battalion

Air Force: 8 Hawker Hunter F-70 attack jets

* Attached to 24th MAU ashore.
** Also called Task Force 62, U.S. Multinational Force, U.S. Forces Ashore.

Sources: Christopher Wright, "U.S. Naval Operations in 1982," *Proceedings* (May 1983), 225–245; Christopher Wright, "U.S. Naval Operations in 1983," *Proceedings* (May 1984), 291–94; Christopher Wright, "U.S. Naval Operations in 1984," *Proceedings* (May 1985), 44–45; International Institute for Strategic Studies, "The Military Balance 1983/84," *Air Force* (December 1983), 86–88; Michael Petit, *Peacekeepers at War* (Boston: Faber and Faber, 1986), 69, 112, 114, 117, 139; Eric Hammel, *The Root* (New York: Harcourt Brace Jovanovich, 1985), 156, 157, 216.

and east. As historian Eric Hammel recalled: "Curtis had been worried about the platoon's bunkers, which appeared weak in light of the previous week's fighting. There was no end of bitching and moaning. . . ." Even so, the marines were ready when the first Druze shells detonated about 0930.

Surprisingly, two sloppy Lebanese Army armored columns drove south to replace the Israelis. One went down the BIA runway and ran right through Company C; the other went down the coast road. The runway unit planned to clear out Khalde and then swing north through Ashuefat and finally Hay-es-Salaam. Although Tannous never talked to Geraghty, it must have looked as if the marines were providing a base of fire for the Lebanese attack.

By the time Lieutenant Colonel Gerlach authorized Company C to return fire, Curtis's platoon was already in action, shooting up pesky rocket-propelled grenade (RPG) gunners. Heavy supporting fires were not permitted, although S/Sgt. Richard Smith's conveniently placed tank ravaged a noisy 106-mm recoilless rifle position with a "beehive" round. This projectile delivered a brutal cloud of steel flechettes that eliminated the militia crew. Curtis worked with Smith to direct tank machine gun fire onto RPG gunners. The rifle platoon sergeant blew open a building with a precise LAW shot; his men cut down the fleeing enemy with a rasping M-60 machine gun. Captain Roy's Company A on the airfield line received permission from the BLT "to support the LAF [Lebanese Armed Forces] by laying down some screening [suppressive] fire."

The fighting exceeded the late August eruption. At nightfall, 1st Lt. Leo Lachat of 24th MSSG looked south from his supply point at Green Beach (formerly Black Beach). He watched Company C's Khalde position: "Thousands of tracer rounds, the wiggling tracks of RPGs, and the flash of numerous rocket and artillery exchanges blazed through the sky." When Company C called out of this inferno for artillery support, Geraghty okayed only illumination.[36] The fighting smoldered around the southernmost marines, gradually dying down on 5 September. But the Druze gunners were not finished yet, not by a long shot. Perfunctory indirect fire continued to crash into and around the MAU positions.

At 0420 on 6 September, Druze artillery and 122-mm rockets impacted along the BIA perimeter. The airport had been closed by shelling since late August, and Company A expected the irregular clutches of explosives raining down around them. But this particular barrage caught the marines as they were relieving their sentinels: two died and two were hurt. Clanking

AAVs and a tank went out onto the fire-swept runways to retrieve the marines. Company B at the university also took rocket fire. The Army Target Acquisition Battery tracked the sheaf of Druze shots, and Geraghty prepared to strike in force to end the long-range sniping.

The TAB data indicated that the offending pieces squatted behind a ridge. Although Battery C's howitzers used high-angle fire to blast the enemy position, Geraghty and France decided to employ added combat power to eliminate the threat. Attempts to locate the source more precisely led to the commitment on 7 September of *Eisenhower*'s F-14A Tomcat fighters rigged with reconnaissance pods. The French carrier jets were already up, looking for Druze batteries that had shelled their headquarters. Significantly, McFarlane's military aide, Brig. Gen. Carl Stiner, USA, received all intelligence derived from these flights. Along with other information from 24th MAU, Stiner passed this news directly to the Lebanese. F-14As soon flew a few missions specifically for Tannous's fledgling forces.

The American jets quickly found their quarry. The USS *Bowen* sailed slowly south, just past the intervening ridge. When on line with the Druze position, the frigate fired four 127-mm (5-inch) high-explosive rounds, which silenced the site.[37] There could be little doubt that the Americans had intentionally destroyed the Druze battery.

Despite the strong U.S. response, shelling intensified. In the Shuf, the Druze, their Shiite Amal associates of the moment, Syrian advisers, Syrian-backed Palestinians, and even some Iranians cooperated to crush the Phalangists. Fearful of a threat to Beirut, Tannous rushed his shaky Lebanese Army 8th Brigade into the mountains. By 10 September, fighting centered on Suq-al-Gharb, a former resort town on a prominence a few kilometers southeast of BIA. Battered by more than 1,600 artillery rounds, the 8th Brigade barely held on. Robert McFarlane judged that Suq-al-Gharb was a test. If it fell, Gemayel's coalition and U.S. hopes for a sovereign Lebanon might go with it.

On 12 September, General Rogers of EUCOM authorized Sixth Fleet to use carrier planes in strikes to support 24th MAU as necessary. McFarlane and Stiner immediately asked for air support at Suq-al-Gharb, but Captain France and Colonel Geraghty demurred. Geraghty strongly reminded the special envoy that active intervention on behalf of the Lebanese Army "clearly changed our neutral role, our mission, our peacekeeping role, and that our vulnerabilities were not unknown, since we were in static locations and so on." In other words, helping the Lebanese at

Suq-al-Gharb clearly placed the Americans in combat alongside the Gemayel forces and hence, the Christian factions. The militant Muslims
would definitely react.

On 16 September, the cruiser USS *Virginia* and destroyer USS *John
Rodgers* fired to support Geraghty's marines. The ships plastered six
different targets, including suspected Syrian positions, with seventy-two
rounds. The sniping and shelling continued at the airport. But at Suq-
al-Gharb, a Lebanese Army counterattack miscarried, and Walid Jumblatt's Druze tanks and troops menaced the 8th Brigade. Tannous reported
that his men were running out of ammunition, a report verified by U.S.
Special Forces advisers in the mountain stronghold. Given the deteriorating situation, France and Geraghty received orders from Washington
that reinterpreted the ''peacetime'' rules of engagement to add protection
of the Lebanese foothold at Suq-al-Gharb to the marines' self-defense
role. The MAU could help if three things transpired: the mountain spur
was in danger of capture, non-Lebanese forces (Syrians) were attacking,
and the Lebanese asked for the help. Although the change reflected
McFarlane's influence, it came through the chain of command, and it
reserved the final choice to Geraghty.

The desperate hill struggle flared over the next few days. Despite
pressure from McFarlane and Stiner, Geraghty refused to approve fire
support. He expressed concerns that innocent Druze civilians might die.
Tannous screamed for help, claiming his men were under heavy pressure.
One Lebanese officer had been hacked apart by a hatchet in a hand-to-
hand struggle, and the 85th Artillery Battalion ran out of 155-mm ammunition. Geraghty held firm to his three criteria. But when American Green
Berets on the scene reported Syrian tanks closing on Suq-al-Gharb around
0730 on 19 September, Geraghty relented. USS *Virginia* and USS *John
Rodgers* pummeled the Shuf with 368 rounds. Two Syrian or Druze
tanks exploded, and numerous approaching infantrymen died. Geraghty
waved off an orbiting air strike from USS *Eisenhower* as overkill; the
8th Brigade held. Curiously, the Lebanese suffered only eight dead and
twelve wounded in their ''last-ditch'' defense. Perhaps the fog of war
had exaggerated the danger.

Although later analysis keyed on the Suq-al-Gharb incident as the
critical shift in the marines' role in Beirut, the importance of the naval
gunfire is probably overstated. Marines had killed and wounded plenty
of militiamen before 19 September, had employed naval guns twice
before for their own defense, and had intentionally and unintentionally

supported Lebanese Army operations for weeks before Suq-al-Gharb. For the Druze, Amal, and Syrians, telling how or why the marines shot probably mattered little.

Was Geraghty pressured? Yes, he was. But he had the final say, and he made the decision to fire. When he authorized the engagement, he believed in what he was doing: "It would have been unconscionable for us to stand by and not provide support for them at that moment." He thought that if Suq-al-Gharb fell, Lebanon's nearly impotent government would fall.[38] But as he predicted, the marines were now in the fight.

After 19 September, the marines and the militias traded unpleasantries of all varieties and calibers, to include more naval gunnery. Skirmishing erupted along the entire perimeter. But the blunting of their Shuf attack evidently had stymied the Druze and Amal. The arrival on 25 September of the massive battleship USS *New Jersey,* with its nine 406-mm (16-inch) main guns and brace of 127-mm secondary cannons, triggered a cease-fire the next day. In one of the final acts of the "September War," Geraghty ordered Gerlach to withdraw combat posts 35 and 69. Under heavy fire, Company B's men pulled back to the university. A few bold Lebanese engineers began to restore the shell-pocked BIA tarmac. In the words of Major Jordan: "It appeared that presence and a good salvo or more of naval gunfire had indeed made peace a possibility."

On 3 October, BLT 1/8 switched its line company positions for the last time. Company C moved from exposed Khalde to even more exposed combat posts 11 and 76 and the string of airport bunkers. Company A went to the consolidated university site. Company B redeployed to the south end of the runway and sent a reinforced platoon downtown to the embassy. Offshore, USS *Tarawa* and 31st MAU sailed away, seemingly unnecessary. Even USS *Eisenhower* slipped off to Naples for a well-deserved port call. The men of 24th MAU were on the home stretch, grateful for the cease-fire and anticipating their relief at the start of November.

Although Geraghty rightly predicted that there would be retaliation for marine shooting, no serious defensive improvements occurred. Patrolling did not resume, outside a bare minimum of local foot routes. More than 300 marines remained jammed into the stout BLT headquarters. In a gesture of faith in the Lebanese Army, Geraghty removed the USMC guards from checkpoint 74 on the main airport entry road. On 7 October, some subordinate officer pulled the two TOW (tube-launched, optically tracked, wire-guided) antitank missiles out of their rooftop emplacements on the BLT building. Things seemed to be returning to a tense routine similar to late July.

There were indicators that the danger had merely altered, not abated. Frustrated in their attempts to shell or intimidate the stolid marines, the Amal and their comrades resorted to random sniping, particularly in the northeast corner of the marine sector, around the university. Marines noticed some rather hard-looking characters in Soviet camouflage fatigues, sporting red headbands. Two Americans died over the next few weeks, victims of the nerve-racking rifle shots, but USMC snipers eliminated their share of tormentors. On 15 October, 24th MAU proudly announced four confirmed kills, and Geraghty's men demonstrated their precision night sights to interested journalists.

The arrival of the camouflage-uniformed types and the coincident widely publicized sniper dueling might have been the single most critical development leading to the eventual destruction of the BLT building. It appears that the new breed with their red headbands were members of the Islamic Hezballah Amal, a small but fanatical pro-Iranian Shiite splinter group. Marine shooters claimed four dead and fourteen wounded, a significant number for this tiny faction. In the words of Target Acquisition Battery commander Capt. James G. Breckenridge, "There was just no way this act could go unavenged. The problem was that this group did not have the resources like artillery and rockets available to exact but token revenge. To kill the commander responsible for this disaster would be meaningful retribution. When this failed on 19 October, they resorted to a contingency plan or merely pursued an idea that was to supplement Geraghty's death—the bombing of 23 October." Unfortunately, nobody recognized the importance of the sniper struggle at the time.

While the sniping continued, the real harbinger of things to come occurred on 19 October, during a routine supply run to the temporary embassy. Colonel Geraghty rode along, heading for a conference. The sniping incidents encouraged the MAU commander to ride in the back of his jeep, rather than in the front right seat as usual. He carried an M-16 rifle and wore no rank.

The precautions might have saved him. As the American truck and its three escort jeeps passed through the Italian sector, a white Mercedes car parked along the street exploded into a sheet of boiling flame. Geraghty's lead vehicle had just passed. The truck was hit hard, showering chunks of metal into the road as it swerved to a halt. The blast wave threw the trailing jeep into a telephone pole. Four Americans lay dazed and injured. A marine reaction force arrived quickly aboard hulking AAVs, weapons at the ready. All that remained of the car was a smoking chunk of transmission.[39]

Evidently, Geraghty did not let the near-miss shake him. He took no special precautions, nor did he increase security around the marine positions. The car bomb was dismissed as a largely unsuccessful accident, an aberration in the relative calm prevailing after the September outbreaks. On the afternoon of Saturday, 22 October, the United Services Organization (USO) presented two shows by Megaband, a country-western group, right in the BLT compound. A liberty party left for Alexandria, Egypt. Trans-Mediterranean Airlines managed about ten flights from half-repaired Beirut International. A gathering with the French paratroopers was on tap for Sunday, a return to the traditional barbecues of earlier days. Although first light would come at 0524, reveille for marines was set for 0630, typical for a Sunday in 24th MAU.

There were tremors of trouble on 22 October, had anyone noticed. Guards were warned to watch for a blue Opel rigged as a car bomb; American intelligence agencies furnished the marines with many such tips, probably too many. Without patrols, it was the only information available. A remote-controlled mine destroyed a French jeep to the north. Finally, after dark, the routine foot patrol from the BLT headquarters down the runway to Company B at Khalde got pinned in the south by mortar, rocket, and artillery fire. Some rounds sparked off the pavement around the BLT building. Rockets crumped in nearby. After a tense hour or so, the guards relaxed to a lesser alert state. Even that condition was not fully enforced. Although a sentry noticed a suspicious yellow Mercedes truck in the exterior airport parking area about 0500, he made no report. Another marine observed a white Mercedes car stop about 0618. The driver took two photographs of the USMC complex and sped off.

Sergeant Stephen E. Russell, in charge of the guards at the BLT headquarters, had just stopped a jogger from going out to run about 0600. At 0622, he was at his post in the door of the BLT building when he saw, to his horror, a big yellow five-ton truck smash through the concertina wire and head straight for his sandbagged position. The small inside gate was wide open, as usual. Two nearby sentries did not fire; they could not load their magazines fast enough. The truck gunned,

The Increasing Threat in Beirut
29 September 1982–23 October 1983

1 October   1982—One marine killed, three wounded clearing unexploded shells.

, 1 November 1982—Car (300 pounds of explosives) blew up near Black Beach.

2 February   1983—Israel tanks stopped by USMC patrol.

25 February   1983—Two rockets hit airport.

16 March   1983—Five marines wounded on patrol by grenade.

18 April   1983—U.S. Embassy bombed by pickup truck (2,000 pounds of explosives). Sixty-one killed (including seventeen Americans).

28 April   1983—USMC guards fire to halt car at temporary U.S. Embassy.

5 May   1983—USMC helicopter struck by ground fire. Airport shelled.

6 May   1983—Five Druze artillery rounds hit near USS *Fairfax County;* two Druze artillery rounds struck near Black Beach.

14 May   1983—Israeli machine gun fire struck perimeter.

8 June   1983—Company C, 1/8, struck by stray Israeli fire.

22 July   1983—Eleven stray 122-mm rockets struck marine perimeter. Two marines, 1 sailor wounded.

10 August   1983—Twenty-seven Druze artillery rounds fired at airport perimeter; one marine wounded.

11 August   1983—Eight Druze artillery rounds fired into airport.

28 August   1983—Second Platoon, Company B, 1/8, engaged enemy infantry for ninety minutes. First time USMC returned fire.

29 August   1983—Druze rocket, artillery, and mortar barrage and infantry fire killed two marines and wounded fourteen. USMC artillery and Cobras returned fire.

30 August   1983—Lebanese Army and marines engaged hostile elements.

31 August   1983—Druze shelled U.S. ambassador's residence. USMC artillery responded. USMC firefights continued.

4 September 1983—Israelis withdraw to Awali River.

6 September 1983—Druze rocket attack killed two marines and wounded two.

8 September 1983—USS *Bowen* fired on Druze guns, as did USMC artillery.

16 September 1983—USN ships engaged Syrian gun positions.

19 September 1983—USN ships fired in support of Lebanese Army in Shuf area.

20 September 1983—Enemy barrages, firefights, and naval gunfire continued.

21 September 1983—Emeny barrages, firefights, and naval gunfire continued.

23 September 1983—Enemy barrages, firefights, and naval gunfire continued.

24 September 1983—Four marines wounded by Druze barrage.

5 October   1983—Two marine helicopters hit by ground fire.

The Increasing Threat in Beirut
29 September 1982–23 October 1983
(continued)

8 October	1983—Two marines wounded by snipers.
13 October	1983—One marine wounded by grenade.
14 October	1983—One marine killed, three wounded by snipers; firefight.
15 October	1983—One marine killed; marines killed four enemy snipers.
16 October	1983—Five marines wounded by snipers.
19 October	1983—Marine convoy car-bombed; three marines, one navy wounded.
22 October	1983—(2100) BLT compound received small arms and rocket fire.
23 October	1983—(0500) Mercedes truck circled parking lot.
	(0618) Driver of white Mercedes car took photographs.
	(0622) Truck bomb destroyed BLT 1/8 headquarters.

---

the driver smiled, and the speeding vehicle easily careened past the flimsy metal pipes lying in front of the BLT doorway. Russell ran out, screaming, "Hit the dirt!" It was too late.

The truck hit the opening, turned a bright yellow-orange, and a throaty, cracking roar thundered out and up, knocking Russell to the ground. The four-story building lifted up, shrugged apart, and caved in with a tumbling crash.[40] Dust rose like a funeral shroud over the ruins.

Federal Bureau of Investigation (FBI) explosives experts estimated that the truck bomb had delivered the equivalent of up to 12,000 pounds of TNT into the enclosed atrium of the marine BLT building. Even if the bomb had blown well outside the structure, FBI scientist John W. Hicks estimated that "there would be considerable injury and quite possibly loss of life, just simply from the shrapnel, flying glass, and things like that." But the Islamic Hezballah Amal suicide driver had punched home his lethal cargo, and the gas-enhanced detonation utterly wrecked the building. The carnage was tremendous: 218 marines, 18 sailors, 3 soldiers, a visiting French paratrooper, and a Lebanese civilian died. Eighty Americans were wounded and evacuated; 32 other U.S. troops were treated and returned to duty.[41]

Changes to Marine Deployment and Security
29 September 1982–23 October 1983

4 November 1982—USMC patrolling began in East Beirut.

3 December 1982—USMC artillery moved ashore.

10 December 1982—USMC tanks came ashore.

13 December 1982—USMC began training Lebanese soldiers.

14 December 1982—USMC began dismounted patrols near the airport.

24 December 1982—USMC ended Sidon Road patrols to avoid Israelis.

17 February 1983—USMC/Lebanese Army joint patrols began.

19 February 1983—USMC patrols extended throughout Beirut.

1 March 1983—Joint USMC/Lebanese Army combat posts established.*

7 May 1983—USMC rifle platoon sent to temporary U.S. Embassy and Durafourd Building; amphibious assault vehicles blocked entrance to BLT headquarters.

14 June 1983—Local guards at BLT headquarters ordered not to load magazines on certain posts.*

21 June 1983—Amphibious assault vehicles moved from BLT building.

6 August 1983—U.S. Army Target Acquisition Battery deployed.

9 August 1983—Attachments and Headquarters and Service Company centralized in BLT headquarters.

10 August 1983—USMC mortars fired illumination as a warning to enemy gunners.

28 August 1983—USMC returned fire with small arms.

29 August 1983—USMC returned fire with artillery and Cobra helicopters.

31 August 1983—Beirut patrols suspended.

4 September 1983—Israelis pulled back to Awali River; USMC tank engaged Druze recoilless rifle position.

8 September 1983—USN gunfire used to support USMC.

19 September 1983—USN gunfire used to support Lebanese Army; USN carrier air strikes available but not used.

25 September 1983—USMC withdrew from combat posts 35 and 69.

7 October 1983—TOW antitank missile launchers removed from roof; USMC transferred checkpoint 74 (on main airport entry road) to Lebanese Army.*

* Approximate date.

The massive rescue effort involved participants from all MNF contingents, even the French, who suffered a similar bombing that same Sunday. Lebanese, to include Shiite Amal militiamen, assisted in the cleanup and search of the crumpled wreckage. Captain Morgan France immediately executed a well-rehearsed mass casualty plan, employing a USN C-9 Nightingale flying hospital, a United States Air Force C-9 transport and a C-141B Starlifter, and a Royal Air Force (RAF) C-130 Hercules. American casualties were distributed to U.S. bases in Germany, Italy, and the RAF field in Cyprus, following stabilization aboard USS *Iwo Jima* and in local Beirut surgical wards. Curiously, the critically injured Lieutenant Colonel Gerlach ended up in the Shiite Saleh hospital.

Afterward, many reporters and analysts criticized Captain France for not using Israeli assistance offered by cable at 0922 on 23 October. Some, like Eric Hammel, believed that Captain France had been ordered to rebuff the Israelis: "Self-serving explanations later beclouded the essential political nature of the decision." Theoretically, some marines might have gotten treatment more quickly in Israel.

In truth, it appears that Captain France made his decision on purely logistical grounds, without any thought of political repercussions. In the general tumult, he did not even see the offer until 1030 or so. He said: "The basic decisions regarding medevac had already been made and my reply to the Israelis, which I did immediately, was, I thanked them for their offer of assistance and told them that we had an [American] aircraft en route. . . ." Since there had been no previous coordination with the Israelis, let alone training, the American commander stuck to his practiced scheme. Captain France also graciously refused most French and Italian offers, accepting British help only because there had been numerous contacts and exercises with the RAF in Cyprus.[42] Given the likely complexities involved with air traffic control, medical triage, and language troubles, Captain France's choice certainly expedited the evacuation.

The American response to the tragedy took four forms: unit replacements, major alterations in rules of engagement, investigations, and serious reconsideration of the U.S. goals in Lebanon. But the black mushroom cloud that brewed up from the collapsed BLT headquarters marked the funeral pyre of the American military role in Lebanon. Reagan, McFarlane, and Geraghty had gambled and lost. Now it was only a matter of time until the plug was pulled for good.

Within hours of the explosion, 2nd Battalion, 6th Marines, at Camp Lejeune, North Carolina, received an alert order to fly to Beirut and replace the shattered headquarters of BLT 1/8. Some of the men had been in Beirut with Colonel Mead during the spring. Lieutenant Colonel Edwin C. Kelley and his headquarters marines landed about sunset on 24 October, and he became the new battalion commander of BLT 1/8. Although his men brought the 2/6 colors, Kelley wisely elected to retitle his followers as Headquarters and Service Company, 1/8 Marines. Companies E and G soon arrived to supplement the perimeter, freeing Battery C to pull back its guns near Green Beach.

Over time, the marines dug deeply, spread out their forces, and installed massive berms, antitank ditches, and obstacles around their positions. Presence was out; defense became the name of the game. Geraghty shortened his lines to prevent casualties. He and Kelley secured authorization to abandon their most forward post. Captain Roy pulled Company A out of the exposed Lebanese Scientific and Technical University during the night of 7–8 November, fighting his way out without losses in a driving rainstorm. The men gained some catharsis during the savage engagement in the wet darkness. As Major Jordan observed, "Very little personal ammunition remained to be turned in." Roy's exhausted men were moved offshore to the landing ship USS *Harlan County,* joining numerous other 24th MAU service and support troops exfiltrated from the dangerous airport rear area.

The withdrawal of Company A represented Geraghty's last major initiative. On 7 November, he was replaced by Brig. Gen. James R. Joy, USMC. Joy commanded the U.S. Forces Ashore in Lebanon until the final withdrawal in early 1984. The marine colonel remained on the beach; he would bring the battered 24th MAU back to Camp Lejeune when their tour was over.

Even after the truck bombing, Geraghty remained doggedly committed to the mission as he understood it. Asked if he thought the marines had done well in their task, Geraghty responded with vigor: "What we were doing over there I feel was successful, in that what—the main purpose for our mission and for our presence was coming to fruition. There were national reconciliation talks that were getting started." He feared that ". . . we are now doing a lot of things that I think are contrary to our mission when we first came; that is, don't make Fortress America. What we are essentially doing is blockading ourselves into a perfect perimeter, which we said we wouldn't do. . . ." [43] The marines acted deliberately in creating their defensive arrangements.

At least one senior U.S. commander, Gen. Bernard W. Rogers of EUCOM, remarked on Geraghty's reluctance to dig in, even after the truck attack. "We have forced things on the Marines today which they didn't ask for, but which we think they need if they are going to have the kind of position for the security and the safety of their troops that they ought to have." EUCOM officers insisted upon dispersion when they found buildings holding up to seventy-five marines. The visiting staff officers assembled and provided construction materials and equipment that the marines did not want to use. It was an unpleasant task for Rogers, who regretted that he found himself "commanding the battalion" as a theater commander. [44]

Colonel James P. Faulkner's 22nd MAU did not relieve the tired 24th MAU until 19 November. While Geraghty's men pawed through the shifting debris of their BLT building, Faulkner's marines were participating in the triumphant Operation URGENT FURY in Grenada. Within three weeks after their landing, the new arrivals were fully engaged along the BIA line, suffering ten killed and several wounded as they held their bunkers. This far exceeded their losses in the Caribbean.

It all seemed like a mission to nowhere. Faulkner lamented that the list of Lebanese armed elements formed a closely spaced book one quarter inch thick; who could tell anymore which ones were friendly or enemy? As L/Cpl. John McCrey remarked, "We were just something to shoot at when they got tired of shooting at each other." The resultant firefights rivaled and often surpassed the August and September skirmishing. [45]

Major increases in American firepower did little to help the situation. After the barracks bombing, a massive armada gathered on Bagel Station, led by the carriers USS *John F. Kennedy* and USS *Independence*. The latter was fresh from repeated air support missions over Grenada. Syrian and Druze gunners in the Bekáa Valley were unimpressed by the show of force. On 3 December, annoyed enemy soldiers shot about ten Soviet-made SA-7 shoulder-fired infrared homing missiles at two F-14A reconnaissance jets. The pilots were used to gunfire; they flew above that. But the little homers were a new wrinkle. Rear Admiral Jerry O. Tuttle, carrier battle group commander, reported the incident. In Washington, President Reagan authorized a retaliatory air strike aimed at three targets in the Bekáa. The battleship *New Jersey* could have done the job, provided spotters were on hand to view the other side of the Shuf chain. But there were no such observers there.

The carrier aviators had prepared before for a strike into Lebanon's Bekáa Valley, presumably to hit the main Islamic Hezballah Amal camp as a reprisal for the BLT explosion. But that mission never went. During planning, the naval battle group staff compiled plenty of data on other likely objectives for USN air power. Now, their chance was at hand. Tuttle's fliers possessed several completed target folders, and the admiral selected targets Retaliatory Strike (RS) 7, 8, and 16. The first two were hillside gun emplacements; the last was a white building containing a Syrian radar and communications links that coordinated the regional air defenses.

The carrier air wings readied to execute an Alpha Strike (maximum effort) to hit at 1130 on 4 December 1983. The naval fliers might have preferred a night raid, using radar bombing, but RS-7 and RS-8 had almost no radar signature. Hitting these small sites necessitated a visual attack. An 1130 time over target would move the sun above the eastern horizon, clearing the raiders' view and yet allowing for distinguishing shadows on RS-7 and RS-8. Planners intended to use Mark 20 five-hundred-pound Rockeye cluster bombs and a few Mark 83 thousand pounders. Crews were to fly at 10,000 feet to avoid the guns and SA-7 missiles, which could reach only to 8,000 feet. *Kennedy*'s experimental Air Wing 3 featured two medium attack squadrons (A-6E) rather than one, and no light attack (A-7E) elements. So *Kennedy* contributed ten A-6E Intruders, three from Attack Squadron 75 and seven from Attack Squadron 85, under the control of Comdr. John J. Mazach. Commander Edward Andrews of *Independence* led the Carrier Air Wing 6 bombers, a composite force of five A-6E mediums from Attack Squadron 176 and thirteen A-7E Corsair II light attack jets of Attack Squadrons 15 and 87. Tomcat fighters would fly escort, EA-6B Prowlers hoped to blot out enemy radar detection, and an E-2C Hawkeye controlled the raid.

At this point, the murk, muddling, and plain bad luck that dogged the U.S. effort in Lebanon developed again. As chairman of the Joint Chiefs of Staff, John Vessey, USA, said, "There were communications problems—both ways." Tuttle's superiors insisted that all three targets be struck simultaneously to reduce losses from repeated ventures into alerted defenses—a reasonable precaution, although it mandated the tricky cooperative strike by both air wings. The Joint Chiefs inadvertently caused a major problem when they told General Rogers of EUCOM that they *recommended* "an early morning strike," timed to catch the same Syrian gunners in the same places they had been on 3 December. Rogers asked if the navy could hit the targets at 0630. His naval deputy in London, who thought the aircraft were on deck alert, assured him that would be quite possible. With this, a JCS suggestion mutated into an ironclad order "direct from Washington." But somehow, the vital start time fell into a black hole, probably while subordinates at Sixth Fleet tried to alter the "order" from the capital. The carrier aviators slept soundly until about 0400, when they got up to get ready for their 1100 launch.

The execution message reached Tuttle at 0533 on 4 December, specifying a time over target of 0630. His response was blunt: "You've got to be shitting me." It took a half hour just to get from Bagel Station over the Bekáa. Having planned for an 1100 takeoff, Tuttle asked for more time. He got ninety minutes from Vice Adm. Edward H. Martin at Sixth Fleet, but no more. Tuttle sent out the bad news and his men scrambled to react.

Miraculously, the planes were airborne by 0720, and Andrews's *Independence* bombers took the lead. The *Kennedy* planes carried a bizarre, slapdash mix of Mark 83 bombs, Shrike antiradar missiles, and Rockeye cluster munitions. Few bombers carried full loads; most just left with whatever was on the aircraft at launch time. More seriously, the crews had not participated in the detailed preflight briefing necessary to conduct a major air strike, let alone an attack involving two separate air wings.

A shadowing Soviet surveillance trawler probably had warned the Syrians that trouble was coming. They were certainly ready. The first plane across the beach, Andrews's Corsair, took a whizzing SA-7 impact and staggered. Andrews brought the wounded jet over water before ejecting. The navy aviators dipped and weaved in toward their targets, twisting through a blazing curtain of gunfire and wavering missile trails. The rising sun dazzled them and made it hard to pick out aiming points.

The gunners on the ground had better luck, helped as the USN crews slid lower trying to locate their camouflaged objectives. One Syrian missile (probably an SA-7) raced right up the hot tail pipe of one of the few fully loaded Intruders. Lieutenants Mark Lange and Robert Goodman barely ejected before their damaged plane cartwheeled into the flank of a ridge, spilling all six thousand-pound bombs harmlessly into the dirt and sending a sheet of flaming wreckage spinning and rolling down the slope. With his leg severed cleanly, Lange died of massive blood loss on the ground. Goodman survived and was taken as a Syrian prisoner, to be freed later by the unexpected intervention of American black activist Jesse Jackson. The other twenty-six attack jets beat up the nondescript brown hillsides, detonating an ammunition dump, smashing an SA-9 radar, and killing at least two Syrians (and probably many more).[46] Had it not been for American pilot skill, the losses might have been much higher.

The insistence on the stepped-up start time hobbled the attack. General Rogers of EUCOM, already trying to deal with the confusing MNF tasks in Lebanon being conducted under his theater command, found himself and his headquarters widely criticized for the bungled raid. European Command staff officer Col. Ralph A. Hallenbeck, USA, recalled: "General Rogers countered by reminding the JCS, the Chief of Naval Operations [Admiral James D. Watkins]—who had elected to chime in—and Admiral Tuttle, the CVBG [carrier battle group] commander, that they had each concurred in the selection of targets, the concept of operations [as submitted by the CVBG] and the need for a rapid response, all of which had been approved by the President, acknowledged through the chain of command, and ordered executed by CINCEUR [Rogers] well within the planning time constraint all had previously agreed to." The mix-up appeared to lie between Rogers's staff in Belgium, U.S. Naval Forces Europe in London, Sixth Fleet, and Tuttle's battle group. Evidently, Admiral Martin's Sixth Fleet staff and the USN staff in London had differing views about the readiness to launch aboard the U.S. carriers.

Perhaps there was more to the hurried lift-off than meets the eye. At least one special operations expert claimed the raid was merely a cover for a U.S. Green Beret ground action that destroyed Syrian-manned artillery observation posts.[47] If so, perhaps some immediate good came of the undertaking. To those naval fliers involved, who displayed no knowledge of any such concurrent special operation, it hardly seemed worth the effort. Fortunately, the repercussions about the misunderstood launch time paid great dividends the next time the navy conducted a major air raid. The experience over Libya in 1986 would be altogether different, and much more successful.

With their air wings frustrated, American commanders offshore turned to naval gunfire to assist the embattled marines. USS *Claude V. Ricketts* bombarded militia units later on 4 December, after an enemy shell penetrated a bunker and wiped out a U.S. squad. The cruiser USS *Ticonderoga* and destroyer USS *Tattnall* responded to the next Syrian shots at the reconnaissance planes, on 13 December. USS *New Jersey* opened fire with eleven gigantic 406-mm shells for the first time on 14 December, joining *Ticonderoga* and *Tattnall* in missions around the airport. The American ships continued to blast away whenever the marines took heavy fire along their fortified ring. Druze and Amal leaders still claimed it was all really aimed at nearby Lebanese Army units, but as one marine asked, "Are you trying to tell me that they fired more than 150 stray [artillery] rounds?" [48]

Naval gunfire and air strikes protected the marines, but did not convince the Syrians to leave and did very little to support the disintegrating Lebanese Army. One reinforced American battalion, regardless of its floating backup, could not hold off the swelling ranks of Druze and Amal fighters or the powerful Syrians, still chortling over the troubled USN air strike of 4 December. It was time to bring the mission to a close.

Even before the tragedy of 23 October, the agitation to put a time limit on the Lebanon episode produced Public Law 98-119 (12 October 1983). This set the American participation in the MNF at eighteen months without further congressional agreement, mandated regular reports by President Reagan to Congress, and necessitated congressional approval of any increases in the American forces or changes in mission.[49] By 1 January 1984, the standard trio of options faced the Americans: add, stand pat, or go home. But the situation had deteriorated completely.

Two investigations of the BLT truck attack, one by the House Armed Services Committee on 19 December and the other by a Defense Department commission of senior officers on 20 December, reached similar conclusions. Both reports censured the chain of command for errors of omission and commission. More to the point, as Reagan and his advisers pondered American policy in Lebanon, the reports warned of increased vulnerability and further losses. The defense commission stated baldly: "There is an urgent need for reassessment of alternative means to achieve U.S. objectives in Lebanon." [50] In plain English, the two investigations urged Reagan to pull out the marines.

The president held fast in Beirut until early February, while the crumbling Lebanese Army lost its Shuf footholds and most of the outer city defenses to enthusiastic Druze and Amal elements. The Lebanese Army dwindled in strength and capability, and finally lost control of

West Beirut and the areas around BIA on 6 February. With Gemayel's army in tatters, the marines were simply targets. Reagan ordered them withdrawn offshore, a process completed by 26 February. The British and Italians also left, leaving only the French in Beirut. The Multinational Force disbanded. America continued to support the Gemayel government with heavy naval gunfire and one precision night air strike. Sixth Fleet held the marines off Lebanon in a show of force.[51]

Comparative Loss Summary
Personnel

	KIA	DOW	WIA	PW	Nonbattle
U.S. Army	3	0	1	0	0
U.S. Navy/USMC	255	8	168	1*	7 (1 dead)
U.S. Air Force	0	0	0	0	0
U.S. MILITARY TOTAL	258	8	169	1	7 (1 dead)
Syrian Army	2	0	10	0	0
Hostile Militias	85	0	0	0	0
SYRIAN/MILITIA TOTAL	87**	0	10	0	0

Equipment

U.S. Military: 2 jet aircraft, 1 truck, 1 jeep destroyed
Syrian/hostile militias: Syrian surface to air missile radar, 2 Druze or Syrian tanks destroyed

* Repatriated on 3 January 1984.
** Numerous additional Syrian, Druze, and Amal casualties were inflicted. Other equipment losses probably occurred.

KIA = killed in action; DOW = died of wounds; WIA = wounded in action; PW = prisoner of war; Nonbattle = noncombat accidents and illnesses

Marine losses do not include 4 U.S. Embassy guards killed on 18 April 1983.

Sources: U.S. Congress, House Armed Services Committee, *Review of Adequacy of Security Arrangements for Marines in Lebanon,* 98th Congress, 1st Session, 15 December 1983, 75; U.S. Department of Defense Commission on the Beirut International Airport Terrorist Act, October 23, 1983, *Report of the Department of Defense Commission on the Beirut International Terrorist Act, October 23, 1983* (Washington, D.C.: U.S. Government Printing Office, 1984), 119, 120; Ann A. Ferrante and Col. John G. Miller, USMC, "Chronology: Marines in Lebanon," *Proceedings,* 298–303; Christopher Wright, "U.S. Naval Operations in 1983," *Proceedings* (May 1984), 61; Eric Hammel, *The Root* (New York: Harcourt Brace Jovanovich, 1985), 176, 180, 181, 199, 201, 220.

Even this commitment proved hollow. On 5 March 1984, after a trip to Damascus to grovel before Assad, Gemayel abrogated the 17 May agreement with Israel. It was as if the Americans had never even been there. Syria entrenched for the long run; Israel remained watchful in the south with its new buffer strip. And the militias went crazy in the no-man's-land between, presided over by the pathetic shell of Gemayel's impotent government. On 30 March 1984, Reagan broke up the unheeded USN flotilla on Bagel Station, leaving a few wary OMC trainers in Lebanon to patch together the bits of Tannous's army still remaining. Thus ended America's direct role in Lebanon.[52] Bloody, confusing Lebanese civil strife continues unabated to this day.

Like Syria and Israel, America could not exert its will over tumultuous Lebanon. It was overly optimistic to think that the weak Gemayel government would extend sovereignty over the fractured country in a few months or, indeed, ever. The Syrians and Israelis refused to leave unless the mess was sorted out in accord with their contradictory intentions. Although the American goals in Lebanon were probably unattainable from the start, the truck bombing of the marine headquarters precipitated and magnified the eventual U.S. failure. This was the critical event that derailed any remote chance for success, and insured a rather frustrating withdrawal. American influence and prestige in the Levant went up with the blast.

As with the aborted EAGLE CLAW effort in Iran, the Department of Defense established an independent body to investigate the truck attack. A distinguished five-man panel convened on 7 November 1983, and made their report on 20 December. Retired Adm. Robert L. Long chaired the group, which included former state and defense official Robert J. Murray, retired Lt. Gen. Lawrence F. Snowden of the marines, retired USAF Lt. Gen. Eugene F. Tighe, and Lt. Gen. Joseph T. Palastra, a serving army officer.[53] The men had a broad charter to answer a basic question: What went wrong?

For a military professional, there were three possible explanations. The first, associated with Secretary of Defense Caspar Weinberger and marine commandant Gen. Paul X. Kelley, explained the disaster as an unconventional bolt out of the blue, unanticipated by rational men who had done their best to prepare themselves for more ordinary direct and indirect fire threats. These leaders did not think that the marines could have done anything to halt or avoid the mobile bomb. General Kelley told a congressional committee: ''. . . no one that I talked to in Lebanon or anywhere else could ever show me a thread of evidence that would show this kind of massive assault where you are actually penetrating a position with a five-ton truck going sixty miles an hour. This has just never been conceived of before.'' [54] A definite case can be made that the suicide truck bombing was an utter surprise to the marines, and the 24th MAU leadership can be well satisfied with the vigorous support of their chain of command. President Ronald Reagan himself accepted full responsibility for the calamity, and ruled out punitive measures against subordinate officers. In such a view, the exceptional nature of the attack made defense impossible, and hence, no officers were held accountable.

Despite the president's assumption of responsibility, another explanation arose. Not surprisingly, some marines who served in Lebanon believed that their very mission and rules of engagement had turned them into easy marks. As military historian Eric Hammel, who interviewed many of the marine participants, wrote: ''Rather, I believe, the bombing was the direct outgrowth of our leaders' having made available a target of unprecedented magnitude in the center of a chaotic situation. That our combat force was declawed and placed in a static position with no clear mandate or any clear means for eluding the wishes of a maniacal anti-American regime or regimes was a bonus.'' [55] In this interpretation, the MAU leadership had been placed in a hopeless situation, fraught with perils, with both hands tied. Diplomats, civilian security advisers, and other nonmilitary decision makers and staffers supposedly hung the marines out on a limb and then allowed ''terrorists'' to saw off that branch. Most of the popular press critiques of the Lebanon episode reflect this view.

Although each of these versions of the truck bombing have merit, neither goes far enough toward explaining the event. Both the first (blaming the enemy) and the second (blaming the civilian leadership) explanations assign culpability to circumstances external to the MAU command structure. A careful examination of the available facts, buttressed to a large extent by the Department of Defense commission study of the explosion, indicates that a third interpretation is in order. Although the enemy was crafty and circumstances were hardly ideal, it appears that the greatest part of the responsibility for this unfortunate incident rests squarely on the shoulders of the 24th MAU and BLT 1/8 commanders. Their misapprehension of the mission, incomplete deployment and defensive preparations, and permission of deviations from established security regimens certainly exacerbated difficult conditions and expedited the work of a resourceful enemy.

The 24th MAU and BLT 1/8 commanders misinterpreted their assigned mission. This conceptual error produced a misunderstanding of the operational environment in the Beirut area, and placed the marines at risk. How did these capable marine officers make such a mistake? Fundamentally, their misperceptions were a function of a failure to translate diplomatic objectives into military terms. The marine commanders' misapprehensions developed in an atmosphere of what was perceived as tacit consent by the chain of command. Having defined a nonmilitary role in a dangerous urban combat situation and received what they considered passive approval, the marines adhered to outmoded situational assumptions in the face of a deteriorating military situation.

The mission in Lebanon was multifaceted and complex, and the situation on the ground clouded the issue even more. Nevertheless, the Joint Chiefs and USCINCEUR assigned defensive tasks within the military capability of the marines. Combat was not anticipated, but the marines

---

Mission Development

President Ronald W. Reagan, message to Congress, 29 September 1982:
"Their mission is to provide an interposition force at agreed locations and thereby provide the multinational presence requested by the Lebanese government to assist it and the Lebanese Armed Forces. In carrying out this mission, the American force will not engage in combat. It may, however, exercise the right of self-defense and will be equipped accordingly."

Secretary of Defense: guidance incorporated in JCS message.

JCS Alert Order to USCINCEUR (EUCOM), 23 September 1982:
"In order to establish an environment which will permit the Lebanese Armed Forces to carry out their responsibilities in the Beirut area. When directed, US Commander in Chief, Europe, will introduce US forces as part of a multinational force presence in the Beirut area to occupy and secure positions along a designated section of the line from south of the Beirut International Airport to a position in the vicinity of the Presidential Palace; be prepared to protect US forces; and, on order, be prepared to conduct retrograde operations as required."

   Additional guidance:

   U.S. forces would not be engaged in combat.

   Peacetime Rules of Engagement would apply (fire in self-defense and defense
      of collocated LAF units).

Mission Development
(continued)

USCINCEUR would be prepared to extract U.S. forces if required by hostile action.

USCINCEUR OPREP-1 to CINCNAVEUR, 24 September 1982 (as approved and modified by JCS, 25 September 1982):

1. Commander, Task Force 61 (Amphibious Task Force) designated Commander, U.S. Forces Lebanon.
2. ". . . land US Marine Landing Force in Port of Beirut and/or vicinity of Beirut Airport. US forces will move to occupy positions along an assigned section of a line extending from south of Beirut Airport to vicinity of the Presidential Palace. Provide security posts at intersections of assigned sections of line and major avenues of approach into city of Beirut from the south-southeast to assist LAF to deter passage of hostile armed elements in order to provide an environment which will permit LAF to carry out their responsibilities in city of Beirut. Commander US Forces will establish and maintain continuous coordination with other MNF units, EUCOM liaison team and LAF. Commander US Forces will provide air/naval gunfire support as required."

Additional missions:

Conduct combined defensive operations with other MNF contingents and the LAF.

Be prepared to withdraw on order, in event of hostile action.

CINCNAVEUR to Sixth Fleet: defined locations for U.S. positions.

Sixth Fleet to TF-61: designated Commander, TF-61 as On-Scene Commander and MAU Commander as Commander, U.S. Forces Ashore in Lebanon.

Formal modifications: Change 1 altered intelligence data concerning the Israelis; Change 2 (6 October 1982) defined the occupy/secure line; Unnumbered Change (2 November 1982) ordered USMC patrols in East Beirut; Change 3 (7 May 1983) directed the MAU to secure the temporary US embassy facilities in Beirut.

Sources: U.S. Department of Defense Commission on the Beirut International Airport Terrorist Act, October 23, 1983, *Report of the Department of Defense Commission on the Beirut International Airport Terrorist Act, October 23, 1983* (Washington, D.C.: U.S. Government Printing Office, 1984), 35–38; President Ronald Reagan, "Message to Congress: War Powers Resolution and U.S. Troops in Lebanon" in *Department of State Bulletin* (December 1982), 42; U.S. Congress, House Armed Services Committee, *Review of the Adequacy of Security Arrangements for Marines in Lebanon and Plans for Improving that Security,* 98th Congress, 1st Session, 15 December 1983, 605.

---

were explicitly ordered to prepare to defend themselves, other MNF components, and their Lebanese allies. The designated tasks were tactical in nature, not diplomatic.

Although the marines went ashore in support of American diplomatic objectives (a stable Lebanon free of factional and foreign threats), their defense role was described in military terms from the outset. Military units can definitely generate political and diplomatic results, but they accomplish these things by military means. The marines could patrol and defend their positions, but they were neither diplomats nor Peace Corps workers. Senior military, naval, and political officials occasionally described the marines' duties to the American public as "peacekeeping," "interposition," "visibility," or "presence," but the marines' original mission spoke in terms like "occupy," "secure," and "defend." The term "presence" was part of the explanatory guidance on why the marines had gone ashore. Presence influenced *how* the marines were to execute their military mission, but it was never a designated mission.

Unfortunately, the marine commanders allowed State Department rhetoric about "presence" and the symbolic need to keep the airport open to affect military judgments about the tactical situation. This occurred even though such tasks were never assigned to the marines and Department of State personnel were not in the USMC chain of command.

Evidently, the MAU leadership paid too much attention to the desired political-diplomatic effects of their deployment, and not enough attention to military aspects of mission, enemy, terrain, troops available, and time. In Lebanon, the 24th MAU inadvertently allowed national policy ends to pervert the nature of military means. This was not directed; the marines did it on their own and eventually paid for their miscalculation. The marine commanders in Beirut failed in their defense role because they attempted to produce direct diplomatic outcomes that had been intended as second-order consequences of successful marine accomplishment of assigned defense tasks. In the process, the marines jeopardized their military position and eventually undermined the intended diplomatic goals.

The marines slipped into an "administrative" or "quasi-tactical" mode of operations under the full view of their higher headquarters. Superior defense officials, JCS members, commanders and staff officers (from USCINCEUR, USCINCNAVEUR, Sixth Fleet, Amphibious Task Force), and other senior leaders visited the 24th MAU in Beirut, but the marines continued to operate their own way. Admiral Long's group

Uniformed Inspectors and Visitors
18 April–23 October 1983

Gen. John W. Vessey, USA, Chairman, Joint Chiefs of Staff

Adm. James D. Watkins, USN, Chief of Naval Operations

Gen. Paul X. Kelley, USMC, Commandant of the Marine Corps

Gen. Robert H. Barrow, USMC, former Commandant of the Marine Corps

Gen. W. T. Smith, USAF, Deputy CINC, EUCOM (European Command)

Vice Adm. Edward H. Martin, USN, Commander, Sixth Fleet

Lt. Gen. Philip Gast, USAF, Director, Defense Security Assistance Agency

Lt. Gen. B. E. Trainor, USMC, Deputy Chief of Staff for Plans, Policies, and Operations

Lt. Gen. D. M. Babers, USA, Deputy Commander, DARCOM (Material Development and Readiness)

Maj. Gen. Francis J. Toner, USA, Director, J-4, EUCOM

Rear Adm. James S. Elfelt, USN, Director, J-3, EUCOM

Maj. Gen. William E. Odom, USA, Assistant Chief of Staff, Intelligence

Rear Adm. Jerry O. Tuttle, USN, Commander, TF-60

Maj. Gen. A. M. Gray, USMC, Commanding General, 2nd Marine Division

Maj. Gen. K. A. Smith, USMC, Commanding General, 2nd Marine Air Wing

Brig. Gen. Andrew Cooley, USA, Military Representative to Habib mission

Brig. Gen. C. Stiner, USA, Military Representative to McFarlane mission

Brig. Gen. Robert D. Wiegand, USA, Assistant Deputy Chief of Staff, Logistics

Brig. Gen. Joseph P. Lutz, USA, Commander, 1st SOCOM (Special Operations Command)

Brig. Gen. Robert J. Winglass, USMC, Commander, 2nd Force Service Support Group

Brig. Gen. Ernest T. Cook, USMC, Deputy J-3, EUCOM

Brig. Gen. James Mead, USMC, Deputy Chief of Staff, Manpower

Commodore J. S. Cassells, USN, medical officer of the Marine Corps

Brig. Gen. Edward J. Heinz, USAF, Deputy J-2, EUCOM

Source: U.S. Congress, Senate Armed Services Committee, *Situation in Lebanon,* 31 October 1983, 98th Congress, 1st Session, 32.

---

charged a "lack of effective command supervision" throughout the chain of command, and recommended "that the Secretary of Defense take whatever administrative or disciplinary action he deems appropriate." [56]

But there is another way of viewing this situation. These ranking officers allowed the local commanders to assess and react to the situation as they saw fit. There was no interference, nor much in the way of "long-range squad leading." Although the Lebanon commanders were more restricted than U.S. commanders in Sidra or Grenada, the Reagan administration followed their usual policy. They let the MAU perform their professional duties without meddling. The military (and civilian) chain of command approved every marine request for liberalization of rules of engagement, and trusted that the on-scene commanders knew best.[57] Rather than take advantage of the opportunity for local initiative, the marines in Beirut accepted the chain of command's noninterference as a blessing of the MAU's nonmilitary activities.

Until the summer of 1983, the marines' tactical situation remained quiescent and forgiving of lapses in military rigor. This changed in mid-1983, just after 24th MAU arrived. The marines became identified with the largely Christian Lebanese Army. Muslim militias turned against the Americans. Despite a marked increase in automatic weapons skirmishes, barrages, and American casualties, Colonel Geraghty steadfastly stuck to his mission misconceptions. Assumptions in the original deployment orders described a benign environment, Lebanese Army security for the marine units, a limited duration for the deployment, and evacuation if the USMC units were attacked. By September 1983, these assumptions were all invalid, yet Geraghty clung to his usual procedures. The situation had changed; the marines' methods did not.

Throughout August–September 1983, the marines endured regular rocket and mortar barrages and were under direct fire from various Muslim militias. Marines suffered fatalities, exchanged fire, and even employed Cobra gunships and naval gunfire. The Lebanese Army proved incapable of securing itself, let alone the marines. Instead, 24th MAU protected the Lebanese. Marines trained the Lebanese Army, patrolled with them, supported their attacks by direct fire, and even used air reconnaissance and major naval gunfire missions to aid their comrades. There was no indication that the marines would be withdrawn, even though individual marine outposts came under fierce attack.[58] From the start, the 24th MAU did not treat their Beirut deployment as a military mission. Unfortunately, their determined foes were not so accommodating.

The 24th MAU's "semitactical" appreciation of its mission influenced and sustained an incomplete and eventually inadequate defensive perimeter. Although the marines had been in the same positions for more than a year by October 1983, the marine defensive arrangements featured limited dispersion, a dearth of barriers and protective reinforce-

RULES OF ENGAGEMENT
in effect throughout 24th MAU
on 23 October 1983

Summarized 24th MAU Rules of Engagement (derived from EUCOM Directive 55-47A "Peacetime Rules of Engagement" and consistent with 23 September 1982 JCS Alert Order)

1. Action taken by U.S. forces ashore in Lebanon will be for self-defense only. Force will be used only when required for self-defense against a hostile threat, in response to a hostile act, or in defense of Lebanese Armed Forces (LAF) elements operating with the U.S. Multinational Force (USMNF). A "hostile force" will be defined by the offshore commander, Amphibious Task Force 61, who is commander, U.S. Forces, Lebanon. A "hostile act" is defined as an attack or use of force against the U.S. force, or against Multinational Force (MNF) or LAF units operating with the U.S. components, which consisted of releasing, launching, or firing of missiles, bombs, individual weapons, rockets, or any other weapons. A "hostile threat" is the likely imminent execution of the designated hostile acts.

2. Effective 7 May 1983, at the temporary embassy, Durafourd Building, and U.S. ambassador's residency, attempts by personnel or vehicles to breach barriers and roadblocks are also explicitly defined as hostile acts.

3. Reprisals or punitive measures will not be initiated.

4. Commanders are to seek guidance from higher headquarters prior to using armed force, if time and situation allow.

5. If time or the situation does not allow the opportunity to request guidance from higher headquarters, commanders are authorized to use that degree of armed force necessary to protect their forces.

6. Hostile ground forces that have infiltrated and violated U.S. force lines by land, sea, and air will be warned that they cannot proceed and are in a restricted area. If the intruder force fails to leave, the violation will be reported and guidance requested from the MAU commander. The USMNF is authorized to use force only if the intruder committed a hostile act.

7. Riot control agents will not be used unless authorized by the Secretary of Defense.

8. Hostile forces will not be pursued.

Source: U.S. Department of Defense Commission on the Beirut International Airport Terrorist Act, October 23, 1983, *Report of the Department of Defense Commission on the Beirut International Airport Terrorist Act, October 23, 1983* (Washington, D.C.: U.S. Government Printing Office, 1984), 45, 48.

ment, and a contraction of local patrols in the face of an increasing threat. These halfhearted defenses were justified by the allegedly "diplomatic" mission, although complete dispersion, solid defenses, and aggressive patrolling were well within the original concept of operations. Asked if "stronger fortifications" affected diplomatic goals, Special Envoy Philip Habib stated, "It would not have impaired the diplomatic mission." [59] The attempt to perform a self-designated nonmilitary role created unnecessary risk. The failure to prepare adequate defenses heightened the danger.

The marine deployment was not tactically sound, although the rifle companies and some attached units operated from dispersed, sandbagged positions along a lengthy perimeter (about six and a half kilometers fronting on suburban slum areas and small open stretches). Admittedly, the U.S. frontage surpassed the four and a half kilometers prescribed for a marine battalion.[60] The Americans specifically requested the airport sector during Multinational Force planning, since it permitted landing craft and helicopter ingress and egress. The marine area was probably the best of those available, distant from the Palestinian refugee camps and downtown Beirut. The forward USMC locations proved suitable for self-defense, and some position improvement occurred. Given the terrific volume of shooting into these positions, the few losses sustained on the front line reflect favorably on the defenses erected. By and large, the marine combat units performed admirably under trying circumstances.

The real weakness in the marine deployment was in the crowded rear, which was almost a part of the northern perimeter (and hence near the vulnerable U.S./Italian MNF boundary). Here, the majority of the attachments, the service support units, and both the MAU and BLT headquarters elements occupied a few buildings within a 500-meter radius of the Beirut International Airport terminal. By 23 October, the BLT headquarters building alone sheltered 350-odd men. This contingent included engineers, medics (with their aid station), TOW crews, the BLT reconnaissance platoon, part of an army target acquisition battery, air and artillery spotters, sniper teams, and the entire battalion staff and command section. Many of these men could have been profitably employed to bolster the thin, isolated segments of the perimeter or to conduct local security patrols. Critical combat support elements, like engineers, TOWs, snipers, and forward observers, were centralized far to the rear of the embattled rifle companies.

The BLT building epitomized the "business as usual" nature of

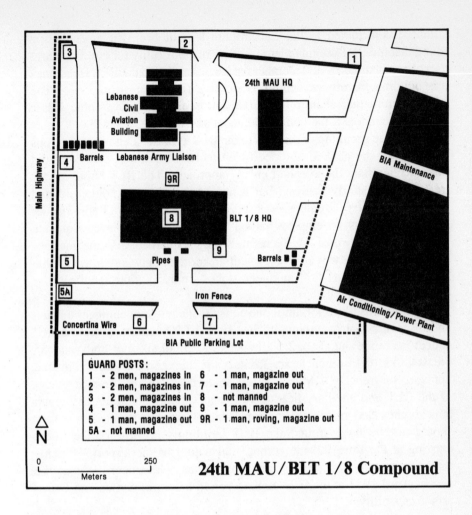

24th MAU HQ

Lebanese
Civil
Aviation
Building

Main Highway

Barrels   Lebanese Army Liaison

BIA Maintenance

9R

8

BLT 1/8 HQ

9

Pipes

Barrels

Iron Fence

Air Conditioning/Power Plant

Concertina Wire

BIA Public Parking Lot

GUARD POSTS:
1 - 2 men, magazines in   6 - 1 man, magazine out
2 - 2 men, magazines in   7 - 1 man, magazine out
3 - 2 men, magazines in   8 - not manned
4 - 1 man, magazine out   9 - 1 man, magazine out
5 - 1 man, magazine out   9R - 1 man, roving, magazine out
5A - not manned

N

0   250

Meters

24th MAU/BLT 1/8 Compound

marine activities in Beirut. Colonel Geraghty and Lieutenant Colonel Gerlach stated that they concentrated their men to protect them from enemy gunfire. Admittedly, the building was solid enough, but it was also the only four-story structure left standing in the area and a perfect landmark for enemy artillerists. Using the edifice as an observation post or even a forward command post was reasonable; employing it as a barracks for hundreds of vital marines in key duty positions was not. In the harsh words of Admiral Long's commission: "While it may have appeared to be an appropriate response to the indirect fire being received, the decision to billet approximately one-quarter of the BLT in a single structure contributed to the catastrophic loss of life. The Commission found that the BLT commander must take responsibility for the concentration of approximately 350 members of his command in the BLT Headquarters building thereby providing a lucrative target for attack. . . . The MAU commander shares the responsibility for the catastrophic losses in that he condoned the concentration of personnel. . . ."[61]

The large grouping of marines in the BIA terminal area was dangerous enough, but the general absence of obstacles throughout the sector did much to facilitate the eventual enemy approach. The BLT building was treated like a sturdy fortress, but it lacked the necessary outworks and redoubts. Secretary Weinberger observed that the marine BLT commander had the authority to employ barbed wire, trenches, or even concrete barriers as he deemed fit. General Kelley explained that the marines used a large quantity of engineer material, more than twenty tons (10,000 feet of concertina, 1,000 engineer stakes, and 500,000 sandbags) by one estimate.[62]

This sounds like a lot, until one consults the relevant engineer manual and discovers that it amounts to just over 1,000 meters of triple-strand concertina fence and about 2.5 kilometers worth of six-foot-high sandbag breastworks (or a much lesser frontage of thicker walls, fully covered bunkers, or trenches). Much of this material went into reinforcement of the BLT and ancillary headquarters and support buildings. Although tank ditches and mines were permissible, Geraghty decided that they should not be used around the BLT building "in view of the threat existing at the time and the commercial nature of the airport."[63] This was despite two experiences with car bombs (November 1982 at the beach, April 1983 at the U.S. Embassy) and a definite Syrian and Druze armor capability.

In truth, the few marine barriers were weak and largely symbolic. Much of the engineer effort was directly devoted to the congested MAU/BLT rear area in the midst of Lebanese airport facilities. The resultant constructions appeared to be mainly for traffic control, not defense. Given the lengthy period ashore, the marine infantry and engineers could have done much more in the way of obstacles. The time was available; 24th MAU engineers spent some of it building an elaborate basketball court. As for defensive wire, General Kelley summarized the USMC building effort: "The wire that was put in, in the estimation of those who put it in, was sufficient to stop a car, not a five ton truck, obviously."[64] The BLT barriers proved incapable of halting a commercial vehicle. Their anticipated effectiveness under determined infantry or armored assault was extremely questionable. In brief, the marines had just enough protection to create a false sense of security.

Finally, the marines intentionally stripped themselves of their organic intelligence-gathering capability in late August 1983. Fearful of possible losses on foot and jeep patrols around Beirut, the MAU contracted marine patrol routes to the immediate vicinity of USMC positions. This was not long after the BLT commander relocated most of his Headquarters and Service Company, Weapons Company, and attached combat forces in the four-story BLT headquarters. In essence, the Americans created a very lucrative target even as they curtailed their early warning network. JCS chairman Gen. John Vessey stated flatly that while he understood Geraghty's desire to cut casualties, "I would have knocked him [Geraghty] for not patrolling for security reasons." [65]

Once the marines largely abandoned infantry patrols and idled their capable reconnaissance platoon, they had to rely on vague national intelligence service reports. There were indicators of what was in store. Numerous intelligence bulletins warned of "shelling, sniping, car bombs, and terrorism" without specifics. Additionally, the marines had firsthand experience with the methods of their Muslim adversaries. The MAU beach had been unsuccessfully car bombed in November 1982, the American Embassy ravaged by a light truck munition in April 1983, and a 24th MAU convoy was near-missed by a car bomb on 19 October 1983. In order to foil the militiamen, the MAU commander thought it necessary to remove his rank insignia and sit in the back seat when traveling by jeep.[66] Though the danger of both conventional and unconventional attack was evident, 24th MAU elected to prevent patrolling casualties at the expense of seeing the battlefield. The final costs of this caution proved to be much higher.

The marines in Lebanon were unprepared for the truck bomb attack when it came. Many marines stress that the nature of the truck strike confounded otherwise adequate defensive works. The question of whether the bombing was "terrorism" or merely an unusual means of delivering a potent explosive is not critical; the MAU defenses were not able to halt a commercial truck.[67] Despite claims to the contrary, it is unlikely that the semitactical marine dispositions in the BLT rear area could have withstood any determined enemy infantry attacks, armor assaults, sapper infiltrations, or concentrated heavy artillery or rocket barrages. The marines were too thick in the airport buildings, and their barriers were too thin. Diplomatic overtures and good intentions proved to be untrustworthy defenses.

Even with their misperception of the military mission and their defensive shortcomings, the marine commanders still had a final means of protection, and a typically capable one: the ingenious, courageous U.S. Marines. Had the established security structure functioned as designed, the resultant American losses might have been markedly reduced. Although a nonmilitary state of mind, lack of dispersion, weak defensive works, and imprecise intelligence increased the scale of the eventual enemy success, intentional and unintentional deviations from security procedures proved to be the immediate causes of the disaster.

The marine rules of engagement were certainly restrictive, although they permitted a wide range of options for self-defense. Individual marines received cards that commenced with these points: "1. When on post, mobile, or foot patrol, keep a loaded magazine in the weapon; weapons will be on safe, with no rounds in the chamber. 2. Do not chamber a round unless told to do so by a commissioned officer unless you must act in immediate self-defense where deadly force is authorized." [68] Vehicular intruders were not addressed. After the U.S. Embassy was bombed in April 1983, MNF marines were sent to guard the temporary facilities. Separate embassy rule of engagement cards specifically labeled as "hostile acts" attempts by vehicles or people to breach the embassy perimeter fence. Unfortunately, the marines around BIA kept their old ROE cards.

Still, the old ROE cards did permit firing in immediate self-defense. The BLT guard force was small but theoretically able to deal with a single vehicle. At full strength, the BLT building guards consisted of a sergeant of the guard, a corporal of the relief, and twenty-two sentries. Two additional reliefs (forty-six men) were off duty but immediately available. Aside from these guards, the building mounted four machine guns on the third floor (the fourth story). Until early October, there were two TOW antitank launchers on the roof. The rooftop offered superb 360-degree observation. A vehicle would have to brave the potentially devastating USMC fires while negotiating a concertina fence, an iron post gate, a lengthwise sewer pipe, and smaller pipes athwart the BLT headquarters entrance. [69] Four alert conditions were prescribed, with Condition I meaning full readiness for imminent enemy attack and Condition II including loading of all weapons, full manning of all positions, and issuance of LAW antitank rockets to sentries on post. The guards were supposedly at Condition II at 0622 on 23 October 1983.

Alert Conditions, BLT 1/8 Marines Compound
(effective 23 October 1983)

CONDITION I: Attack imminent/underway
  Full alert of compound; deployment of all marines
  Cobra attack helicopters on 5-minute standby

CONDITION II: Attack probable
  All positions reinforced to two sentries (off-duty guard force altered; LAW
    antitank rockets issued)
  Machine guns and TOWs manned
  Forward air controllers/artillery observers to roof
  Reaction platoon alerted
  Emergency departures only
  Search of all entering civilian vehicles
  Cobra attack helicopters alerted

CONDITION III: Attack possible
  Physical training suspended
  Patrols suspended; essential movement only (armed escort jeeps required)
  Snipers positioned
  One of five entering civilian vehicles searched

CONDITION IV: Normal operations
  Physical training (jogging) permitted around airport
  Two jeep and seven foot patrols
  One sentry per post (day); two per post (night)—weapons loaded
  Random search of entering civilian vehicles

ACTUAL at 0622 on 23 October 1983: Modified Condition II
  Posts 4, 5, 6, 7—only one sentry, weapons unloaded
  Posts 5A and 8 unmanned
  Off-duty guard force asleep; LAW rockets not issued
  Roof observers asleep
  Reaction platoon asleep
  Machine guns unmanned; TOW launchers removed
  Lebanese searching civilian vehicles
  Cobras not on alert

Sources: Michael Petit, *Peacekeepers at War* (Boston: Faber and Faber, 1986), 109–110; U.S. Department of Defense Commission on the Beirut International Airport Terrorist Act, October 23, 1983, *Report of the Department of Defense Commission on the Beirut International Airport Terrorist Act, October 23, 1983* (Washington, D.C.: U.S. Government Printing Office, 1984), 88–89; U.S. Congress, House Committee on Appropriations, *Situation in Lebanon and Grenada*, 98th Congress, 1st Session, 8 November 1983, 28–29; U.S. Congress, House Armed Services Committee, *Review of Adequacy of Security Arrangements for Marines in Lebanon*, 98th Congress, 1st Session, 15 December 1983, 382–383.

The situation in Beirut by October 1983 was pregnant with known and suspected dangers. The MAU commander, however, made substantial modifications to his security methods, including "a conscious decision not to permit insertion of magazines in weapons on interior posts to preclude accidental discharge and possible injury to innocent civilians." All of the marine sentries interviewed by the Department of Defense (DOD) investigators after the bombing expressed grave reservations about this decision. Only three of the posts were permitted to keep their weapons loaded. Additionally, the interior posts were reduced to one man (with his magazine out) in daylight, and some went unmanned. Finally, LAWs were removed from the guard posts, even when the posts were at Condition II.[70]

As a result, the marines at dawn of 23 October 1983 were operating with a hamstrung, half-strength guard, without LAWs, and largely without loaded weapons. Some of the sentries, in the middle of two-week tours of alternate four-hour stints and eight-hour breaks, had "frankly lost track of what day it is."[71] The Headquarters and Service Company commander, designated the permanent guard officer, was asleep in the barracks, as were the rooftop observers and the reaction force. After many months of duty in Lebanon, the marines had learned that Sunday was the start of the Muslim work week, "Beirut's traditional day of war."[72] But 24th MAU continued to sleep late on Sundays. First light came at 0524, but marine reveille was not scheduled until 0630.

The night of 22–23 October was ripe with approaching trouble. Small arms fire struck inside the BLT compound, several rockets landed nearby. About 0500, a large yellow Mercedes truck was observed circling suspiciously just outside the marine wire. The BLT had gone to Condition I, and was supposedly at Condition II at 0622. Later investigation established that the marines were not even at Condition III. Weapons remained unloaded, LAWs were not issued, posts were not augmented, and the machine gun bunkers apparently were not manned.[73]

The actual attack was over so swiftly that not a shot was fired. The big yellow truck crushed the concertina wire, ran through the open gate (left open for the sake of the Lebanese Army, which used the marine parking lot for training), across the pipes, and into the BLT building.[74] The truck's passage had been eased by the MAU's modifications of the standing guard instructions. It was merely the culmination of a series of understandable small decisions that aggregated to engender a tragedy.

U.S. Multinational Force in Lebanon Time Line
6 June 1982–30 March 1984

6 June	1982	—Israelis began Operation PEACE FOR GALILEE.
9 June		—Israelis destroyed most of Syrian air defense system in Lebanon.
21 August		—French MNF landed; PLO evacuation began.
25 August		—USMC landed to assist in PLO extraction.
10 September		—Marines withdrew.
14 September		—President Bashir Gemayel assassinated.
15 September		—Israelis occupied Muslim West Beirut.
16 September		—Phalange elements began Sabra/Shatilla massacres.
29 September		—USMC returned; occupied positions at Beirut International Airport.
30 September		—First U.S. casualties suffered during removal of dud ordnance.
4 November		—First USMC patrols in East Beirut.
8 November		—U.S. Office of Military Cooperation (OMC) began operations.
13 December		—Marines began to train Lebanese Army.
29 January	1983	—USMC established emergency radio network to Israelis.
2 February		—Israeli tanks stopped by Capt. Charles Johnson, USMC.
10 February		—British MNF unit arrived.
17 February		—Combined USMC/Lebanese patrolling commenced.
25 February		—First stray rounds struck airport.
16 March		—Patrolling marines wounded by grenade.
18 April		—U.S. Embassy bombed.
17 May		—Israeli-Lebanese withdrawal accord signed.
6 July		—Syrians rejected withdrawal plan.
22 July		—Rockets struck airport.
28 August		—First significant firefights occurred. Marines returned fire.
29 August		—Marines employed artillery and attack helicopters.
7 September		—USN and French carrier aircraft flew first reconnaissance missions.
8 September		—USN first fired in support of USMC.
19 September		—USN fired in support of Lebanese Army at Suq-al-Gharb.
22 September		—French carrier jets bombed Druze at Hammana.
25 September		—USS *New Jersey* arrived off Lebanon.
26 September		—Cease-fire announced.
12 October		—President Reagan signed Public Law 98-119, approving an 18-month limit on U.S. MNF operations.
14 October		—Sniper incidents began.
19 October		—Marine truck convoy car-bombed.
23 October		—Marine BLT 1/8 headquarters truck-bombed. French barracks also truck-bombed.
4 November		—Israeli compound at Tyre truck-bombed.
8 November		—USMC withdrew from Lebanese Scientific and Technical University.
17 November		—French air strike attacked Bekáa Valley targets.
4 December		—USN air strike hit 3 Bekáa Valley targets; two planes shot down.
14 December		—USS *New Jersey* engaged targets ashore.
6 February 1984		—USN air strikes hit a Beirut area target. Lebanese Army lost control of most of Beirut to Shiites.
26 February		—USMC withdrew to ships offshore.
30 March		—U.S. concluded Beirut MNF operations; OMC remained.

Did the marines *really* have any alternatives? It appears that they did. The French MNF component suffered a similar incident on 23 October in Beirut and lost fifty-eight men; the Israelis had twenty-nine soldiers killed by a truck explosion in Tyre on 4 November 1983. These injuries were serious, but well short of the toll inflicted on the less numerous U.S. forces. Situational awareness, adequate dispersion, and better security proved to be the major differences.

Yet the Americans need not have looked to foreigners for other approaches to security in Lebanon. Colonel James Mead's actions in late April offered a good model of what the marines might have done as things turned ugly. During the September clashes, the Army Target Acquisition Battery established a solid and secure system of field fortifications. At sea, the carrier battle groups and amphibious ships had maintained a high level of combat vigilance, to include armed sentinels, strict control of local aircraft and boat traffic, and constant, unpredictable motion. In a similar vein, the Office of Military Cooperation (OMC), the joint service advisory element, had reacted strongly to the increased threat following the April embassy bombing. Advisory teams were dispersed in order to reduce the attractiveness of the potential target.[75] While the OMC dispersed, the MAU concentrated.

Admiral Long and his fellow investigators were harsh: "The Commission recommends that the Secretary of Defense take whatever administrative or disciplinary action he deems appropriate, citing the failure of the BLT and MAU commanders to take the security measures necessary to preclude the catastrophic loss of life in the attack on 23 October 1983."[76] But in truth, the marine officers did their duty as they saw it. They guessed wrong, and their men paid. President Reagan spared them, and their superiors, from court-martial proceedings.

The president might have found common cause with Lance Cpl. Gordon Brock of Company E, 2/8 Marines. "When we were in Grenada," said Brock, "I really enjoyed myself. You were out there with your gun, shooting, taking prisoners, doing everything Marines are supposed to do. I felt like Vic Morrow in one of those movies. But you got nothing to brag about from being in Beirut. We were just there, that's all. When I got home, I don't want anyone to ask me about it. I just want to get in my car and drive and forget the whole thing."[77] The expedition to Beirut solved nothing. It just cost.

Chapter 4 Notes

Epigraphs from U.S. Congress, House Armed Services Committee, *Review of the Adequacy of Security Arrangements for Marines in Lebanon*. 98th Congress, 1st Session, 15 December 1983, 578 (hereafter cited as U.S., House Armed Services Committee, *Review of Adequacy*); Michael Herr, *Dispatches*, 105; Karl von Clausewitz, *War, Politics, and Power: Selections from On War and I Believe and Profess*, trans. and ed. Edward M. Collins (Chicago, IL: Regnery Gateway, Inc., 1962), 112.

1. International Institute for Strategic Studies, "The Military Balance 1984–85," *Air Force* (December 1984), 121, 124; International Institute for Strategic Studies, "The Military Balance 1985–86," *Air Force* (February 1986), 108; Ze'ev Schiff and Ehud Ya'ari, *Israel's Lebanon War* (New York: Simon and Schuster, 1984), 19–22, 94; U.S. Department of Defense Commission on the Beirut International Airport Terrorist Act, October 23, 1983, *Report of the Department of Defense Commission on the Beirut International Airport Terrorist Act, October 23, 1983* (Washington, D.C.: U.S. Government Printing Office, 1984), 24–29, hereafter cited as DOD Commission, *DOD Report*.

2. Chaim Herzog, *The Arab-Israeli Wars* (New York: Random House, 1982), 385–93; DOD Commission, *DOD Report*, 29.

3. Schiff and Ya'ari, *Israel's Lebanon War*, 210; DOD Commission, *DOD Report*, 29; Eric Hammel, *The Root: The Marines in Lebanon, August 1982–February 1984* (San Diego, CA: Harcourt Brace Jovanovich, 1985), xxvii. Hammel's account is the definitive story of the daily marine actions in Beirut.

4. Christopher C. Wright, "U.S. Naval Operations in 1982," *Proceedings* (May 1983), 63, 225; Schiff and Ya'ari, *Israel's Lebanon War*, 228; Hammel, *The Root*, 15, 26–28.

5. Schiff and Ya'ari, *Israel's Lebanon War*, 247, 253, 282.

6. President Ronald Reagan, "Message to the Congress, 29 September 1982," *Department of State Bulletin* (December 1982), 42; U.S., House Armed Services Committee, *Review of Adequacy*, 348, 349.

7. U.S. Congress, Senate Armed Services Committee, *Use of U.S. Military Personnel in Lebanon*. 98th Congress, 1st Session, 28 September 1983, 71; Reagan, "Message to the Congress, 29 September 1982," 42; Hammel, *The Root*, 47; U.S., House Armed Services Committee, *Review of Adequacy*, 433, 479; DOD Commission, *DOD Report*, 36, 37, 39.

8. Nathan A. Pelcovits, "The Multinational Force in Beirut: What Went Wrong?" in *International Workshop on the Multinational Force in Beirut* (Oslo, Norway: Norwegian Institute of International Affairs, 30 October

1985), 22, 23; Hammel, *The Root,* 35, 36; DOD Commission, *DOD Report,* 35, 36, 74; U.S., House Armed Services Committee, *Review of Adequacy,* 29, 407, 408, 419, 430.

9. U.S., House Armed Services Committee, *Review of Adequacy,* 408; DOD Commission, *DOD Report,* 72.

10. U.S., House Armed Services Committee, *Review of Adequacy,* 32, 430; Hammel, *The Root,* 54, 55; Ann A. Ferrante and Col. John G. Miller, USMC, "Chronology: Marines in Lebanon," *Proceedings* (May 1984), 300.

11. Thomas L. Friedman, "America's Failure in Lebanon," *New York Times Magazine* (8 April 1984), 37; Michael Petit, *Peacekeepers at War* (Boston, MA: Faber and Faber, Inc., 1986), 92, 93.

12. Friedman, "America's Failure in Lebanon," 37; Ferrante and Miller, "Chronology," 300; Hammel, *The Root,* 62–66.

13. Lt. Col. David Evans, USMC, "Navy-Marine Corps Team in Lebanon," *Proceedings* (May 1984), 135, 136; Hammel, *The Root,* 68–71.

14. U.S., House Armed Services Committee, *Review of Adequacy,* 410–14; Hammel, *The Root,* 74, 75. Col. Ralph A. Hallenbeck, USA, "Force and Diplomacy: The American Strategy in Lebanon." Pennsylvania State University, unpublished dissertation, 1986, 322–24. Hallenbeck provides a most authoritative strategic account of the Lebanon expedition.

15. U.S., House Armed Services Committee, *Review of Adequacy,* 347, 410–12, 416; Evans, "Navy-Marine Corps Team in Lebanon," 136; Hammel, *The Root,* 78–80.

16. Roy Gutman, "Battle Over Lebanon," *Foreign Service Journal* (June 1984), 32; Maj. Robert T. Jordan, USMC, "They Came in Peace," *Marine Corps Gazette* (July 1984), 57; Friedman, "America's Failure in Lebanon," 40; Hallenbeck, "Force and Diplomacy," 324–26.

17. Jordan, "They Came in Peace," 56, 57; Hammel, *The Root,* 89, 90.

18. Jordan, "They Came in Peace," 57, 58; Petit, *Peacekeepers at War,* 65–66.

19. Pelcovits, "The Multinational Force in Beirut," 22; U.S., House Armed Services Committee, *Review of Adequacy,* 358.

20. DOD Commission, *DOD Report,* U.S., House Armed Services Committee, *Review of Adequacy,* 259, 260, 262, 263, 283, 304, 531, 536–38. Colonel Geraghty's testimony offers his views of the mission and the Beirut environment.

21. U.S., House Armed Services Committee, *Review of Adequacy,* 380, 381, 564; Jordan, "They Came in Peace," 58, 59; Petit, *Peacekeepers at War,* 68, 86; DOD Commission, *DOD Report,* 69.

22. Jordan, "They Came in Peace," 59, 62; U.S., House Armed Services

Committee, *Review of Adequacy,* 376, 382, 385, 386; Petit, *Peacekeepers at War,* 71, 74, 75, 84, 85; Hammel, *The Root,* 101, 102.

23. Hallenbeck, "Force and Diplomacy," 326, 327; Ferrante and Miller, "Chronology," 300; Jordan, "They Came in Peace," 59, 60; Petit, *Peacekeepers at War,* 108, 109, 114. Petit quotes the unit operations journal.

24. Jordan, "They Came in Peace," 59, 60; Petit, *Peacekeepers at War,* 113–15; Ferrante and Miller, "Chronology," 300; Eric C. Ludvigsen, "Army Weaponry," *Army* (October 1983), 379, 380; Interview with Capt. James G. Breckenridge, commander, Field Artillery School Target Acquisition Battery, 11 September 1987.

25. Patrick J. Sloyan, "U.S. in Lebanon: Anatomy of a Foreign Policy Failure," *Newsday,* 8 April 1984, 34; Friedman, "America's Failure in Lebanon," 37.

26. Jordan, "They Came in Peace," 60; Petit, *Peacekeepers at War,* 118–20.

27. Schiff and Ya'ari, *Israel's Lebanon War,* 298; Sloyan, "U.S. in Lebanon," 34.

28. U.S., House Armed Services Committee, *Review of Adequacy,* 450.

29. Hammel, *The Root,* 149–52; Jordan, "They Came in Peace," 60.

30. Ferrante and Miller, "Chronology," 300; Hammel, *The Root,* 120, 121, 126, 131, 132, 134, 135.

31. Ferrante and Miller, "Chronology," 300; Hammel, *The Root,* 155, 167.

32. Petit, *Peacekeepers at War,* 137; U.S., House Armed Services Committee, *Review of Adequacy,* 234, 609.

33. U.S., House Armed Services Committee, *Review of Adequacy,* 554.

34. Pelcovits, "The Multinational Force in Beirut," 16; Hallenbeck, "Force and Diplomacy," 327, 328; President Ronald Reagan, "Message to Congress, 30 August 1983," *Department of State Bulletin* (October 1983), 79, 80; U.S., Congressional Research Service, *Digest of Public General Bills and Resolutions, 98th Congress, 1st Session* (Washington, D.C.: Library of Congress, 1983), 17.

35. Ferrante and Miller, "Chronology," 300; U.S., House Armed Services Committee, *Review of Adequacy,* 539, 609; Hallenbeck, "Force and Diplomacy," 327, 328; Petit, *Peacekeepers at War,* 136, 137; DOD Commission, *DOD Report,* 40; Christopher C. Wright, "U.S. Naval Operations in 1983," *Proceedings* (May 1984), 59.

36. Hammel, *The Root,* 173–75, 177, 178, 180–84; Breckenridge interview.

37. Ibid., 191; Evans, "Navy-Marine Corps Team in Lebanon," 136; U.S., House Armed Services Committee, *Review of Adequacy,* 234; Ferrante and Miller, "Chronology," 300; Petit, *Peacekeepers at War,* 138–41; Breckenridge interview.

38. Sloyan, "U.S. in Lebanon," 34, 36, 38; Hallenbeck, "Force and Diplomacy," 328, 329; U.S., House Armed Services Committee, *Review of Adequacy*, 485–87, 529–31, 564, 609; Evans, "Navy-Marine Corps Team in Lebanon," 137; Friedman, "America's Failure in Lebanon," 42; Ferrante and Miller, "Chronology," 303; Petit, *Peacekeepers at War*, 142–46.

39. Hammel, *The Root*, 249, 251, 276, 277, 281; Ferrante and Miller, "Chronology," 303; U.S., House Armed Services Committee, *Review of Adequacy*, 391, 585; Petit, *Peacekeepers at War*, 158–61; Jordan, "They Came in Peace," 61; Hallenbeck, "Force and Diplomacy," 330; Breckenridge interview.

40. U.S., House Armed Services Committee, *Review of Adequacy*, 169, 177, 207–09, 257, 307, 309, 327, 381, 583, 584; Hammel, *The Root*, 292; Petit, *Peacekeepers at War*, 161–64; Jordan, "They Came in Peace," 61, 62.

41. DOD Commission, *DOD Report*, 99, 106; U.S., House Armed Services Committee, *Review of Adequacy*, 75, 402; "Bloody Beirut: Trading in Lives," *U.S. News & World Report* (9 February 1987), 27.

42. DOD Commission, *DOD Report*, 109, 110, 111, 116–18; Hammel, *The Root*, 381, 382; U.S., House Armed Services Committee, *Review of Adequacy*, 219–23, 281.

43. Hammel, *The Root*, 399–401, 403, 405, 418, 419; Jordan, "They Came in Peace," 63; Ferrante and Miller, "Chronology," 303; U.S., House Armed Services Committee, *Review of Adequacy*, 260, 275, 540, 543.

44. U.S., House Armed Services Committee, *Review of Adequacy*, 620, 621.

45. Ferrante and Miller, "Chronology," 303; Friedman, "America's Failure in Lebanon," 62.

46. Evans, "Navy-Marine Corps Team in Lebanon," 139; Wright, "U.S. Naval Operations in 1983," 59–61; Hallenbeck, "Force and Diplomacy," 245–47; George Wilson, *Supercarrier* (New York: Macmillan Publishing Co., 1986), 118, 124–55. George Wilson's eyewitness account is exhaustive.

47. Gayle Rivers (pseudonym), *The Specialist* (New York: Stein and Day, 1985), 20, 21. Rivers also describes other covert actions supposedly conducted by U.S. Army Special Forces in Lebanon.

48. Wright, "U.S. Naval Operations in 1983," 61; Ferrante and Miller, "Chronology," 303; Evans, "Navy-Marine Corps Team in Lebanon," 139.

49. U.S., Congressional Research Service, *Digest of Public General Bills and Resolutions, 98th Congress, 1st Session*, 22.

50. DOD Commission, *DOD Report*, 7; U.S. Congress, House Armed Services Committee, *Full Committee Consideration of Investigations Subcommittee Report on Terrorist Bombing at Beirut International Airport*. 98th Congress, 2nd Session, 31 January 1984, 3.

51. Friedman, "America's Failure in Lebanon," 37; Evans, "Navy-Marine Corps Team in Lebanon," 139; Ferrante and Miller, "Chronology," 303; Hallenbeck, "Force and Diplomacy," 331–35; Christopher C. Wright, "U.S. Naval Operations in 1984," *Proceedings* (May 1985), 45.

52. "Lebanon Cancels Agreement with Israel, 5 March 1984," *Department of State Bulletin* (April 1984), 61; President Ronald Reagan, "Letter to the Congress, 30 March 1984," *Department of State Bulletin* (May 1984), 68.

53. DOD Commission, *DOD Report*, 1, 20, 21.

54. U.S. Congress, House Committee on Appropriations, *Situation in Lebanon and Grenada, Hearings before a Subcommittee of the House Committee on Appropriations*. 98th Congress, 1st Session, 8 November 1983, 19.

55. Hammel, *The Root*, xxvii.

56. DOD Commission, *DOD Report*, 56; U.S. Congress, Senate Committee on Armed Services, *The Situation in Lebanon, Hearings before the Senate Committee on Armed Services*. 98th Congress, 1st Session, 25 and 31 October 1983, 32. Twenty-four flag or general officers visited the 24th MAU, along with numerous civilian leaders.

57. U.S., House Armed Services Committee, *Full Committee Consideration of Investigations Subcommittee Report on Terrorist Bombing at Beirut International Airport*, 3; DOD Commission, *DOD Report*, 44–51.

58. DOD Commission, *DOD Report*, 43.

59. U.S., House Armed Services Committee, *Review of Adequacy*, 358.

60. U.S., Department of the Navy, Headquarters, Marine Corps, *FM 6-2 Marine Infantry Regiment* (Washington, D.C.: U.S. Government Printing Office, 1 February 1978), paragraph 3407.

61. DOD Commission, *DOD Report*, 6, 7.

62. Ibid., 73; U.S., House Appropriations Committee, *Situation in Lebanon and Grenada*, 48, 49; U.S., Senate Armed Services Committee, *Situation in Lebanon*, 11, 12.

63. U.S., House Appropriations Committee, *Situation in Lebanon and Grenada*, 49; U.S., Senate Armed Services Committee, *Situation in Lebanon*, 65; Department of the Army, *FM 5-34, Engineer Field Data* (Washington, D.C.: Department of the Army, 24 September 1976), 93, 109; U.S., Department of the Army, *FM 5-15 Field Fortifications* (Washington, D.C.: U.S. Government Printing Office, June 1972), 4–15.

64. Hammel, *The Root*, 102, 103; U.S., House Appropriations Committee, *Situation in Lebanon and Grenada*, 16.

65. U.S., Senate Armed Services Committee, *Situation in Lebanon*, 51, 52; Hammel, *The Root*, 280; U.S., House Armed Services Committee, *Review of Adequacy*, 611.

66. U.S., House Appropriations Committee, *Situation in Lebanon and Grenada*, 48; Hammel, *The Root*, 281, 282; Evans, "Navy-Marine Corps Team in Lebanon," 136.

67. The view that the Beirut bombing was an act of terrorism is well argued by Maj. Jeffrey W. Wright in his "Terrorism: A Mode of Warfare," *Military Review* (October 1984), 35–45. The opinion that the truck attack was merely an unusual enemy assault method, not a terrorist act, is cogently presented by Lt. Col. Frederic C. Hof in his "The Beirut Bombing of October 1983: An Act of Terrorism?" *Parameters* (summer 1985), 69–74.

68. DOD Commission, *DOD Report*, 49, 50.

69. Ibid., 74, 85–88; U.S., Senate Armed Services Committee, *Situation in Lebanon*, 65, 66.

70. DOD Commission, *DOD Report*, 88, 89; U.S., House Appropriations Committee, *Situation in Lebanon and Grenada*, 28, 29.

71. Hammel, *The Root*, 289.

72. Ibid., 118, 264. Particularly violent Sundays included 28 August 1983, 4 September 1983, and 24 September 1983.

73. Ibid., 292; DOD Commission, *DOD Report*, 88, 89.

74. DOD Commission, *DOD Report*, 94, 95, 99; U.S., Senate Armed Services Committee, *Situation in Lebanon*, 65, 66.

75. DOD Commission, *DOD Report*, 130–32; Capt. Don G. Palen, USN, "Close-in Battle Plan," *Proceedings* (January 1987), 67–73.

76. DOD Commission, *DOD Report*, 10.

77. Friedman, "America's Failure in Lebanon," 33.

CHAPTER 5

ASSAULT ON THE SPICE ISLAND: THE GRENADA CAMPAIGN

OCTOBER–NOVEMBER 1983

"Let us give them the answer that whenever [Sir Eric] Gairy or mercenaries or any other counter-revolutionary elements land on our beaches they will discover the size of our army, how many guns we have, where the guns came from and whether we can use the guns."

Prime Minister Maurice Bishop, 13 March 1980

"That's like the argument of another so-called expert that we shouldn't worry about Castro's control over the island of Grenada—their only important product is nutmeg.

"Well let me just interject right here. Grenada, that tiny little island—with Cuba at the west end of the Caribbean, Grenada at the east end—that tiny little island is building, or having built for it, on its soil and shores, a naval base, a superior air base, storage bases and facilities for the storage of munitions, barracks, and training grounds for the military. I'm sure all of that is simply to encourage the export of nutmeg."

President Ronald W. Reagan, 10 March 1983

"Don't Delay: *The best is the enemy of the good. By this I mean that a good plan violently executed now is better than a perfect plan next week. War is a very simple thing, and the determining characteristics are self-confidence, speed, and audacity. None of these things can ever be perfect, but they can be good."*

Gen. George S. Patton, *War as I Knew It*

The Grenada intervention brewed up unexpectedly, like the potent tropical storms so often born in the warm waters and stiff trade winds of the Lesser Antilles. Even so, just as West Indies inhabitants might view building thunderheads with concern, intelligence and operations officers in the United States Departments of State and Defense examined the political climate in Grenada with increasing consternation in the autumn of 1983. Key American elected officials and strategists knew that something aberrant and potentially dangerous had been percolating along in the southeastern Caribbean for some time. It was simply unfortunate that the Caribbean lid blew off at almost the same time the Beirut roof literally caved in.

At first glance, Grenada seemed an unlikely place for a major American military commitment, let alone the largest joint land, air, and sea operation since the conclusion of the Vietnam War. By mid-October 1983, national attention focused on the tense situation in Lebanon. Fortunately for the hundreds of American medical students and the majority of Grenadians caught up in the island's bloody October, a dedicated coterie of American foreign policy experts, intelligence analysts, and Pentagon staffers saw the trouble explode and initiated actions to meet the challenge. Most American citizens, including the majority of those in uniform, discovered (or remembered) that Grenada existed after army Rangers and marines landed there.

Like many other corners of the world unceremoniously lumped together as trouble spots in routine American intelligence estimates, Grenada had been there all along. Grenada had been placed on the map well before the birth of the United States. Christopher Columbus discovered Grenada in 1498. Following a French presence, the British received Grenada in 1763 after the Seven Years' War (known in America as the French and Indian War). Although a French naval detachment took and held the island during the latter years of the American Revolution, the British regained control by 1783. Grenada inherited Roman Catholicism from France and the English tongue from the British.

Under British rule, the population swelled to more than 12,000 African slaves, under the supervision of 1,250 settlers, officials, and soldiers. Huge sugar plantations generated the island's main export. The slave population on Grenada proved anything but docile. In 1792, a free French-African "colored planter" named Julien Fedon led a successful insurrection of slaves against the outnumbered British colonists. For more than two years, Fedon and his black followers held much of the island, slaughtering the Europeans and repulsing various British military opponents. British and Spanish troops finally crushed the slave revolt in late 1794, but Fedon escaped. Superstitious island blacks remembered Fedon with pride and prayed that he would some day return, a legend exploited by Maurice Bishop during his rise to power in the late 1970s. Not surprisingly, the Fedon heritage created significant black militancy in Grenada. (Years later, the island produced American "Black Power" advocate Malcolm X.) Grenadians long knew that whites were not invincible.

Slavery ended in 1834, but most blacks remained in peonage to the few white islanders. When the sugar market collapsed in 1848, Grenadians shifted to smaller farms, and new nutmeg, banana, and cocoa crops soon joined the familiar sugar fields. The large nutmeg harvests gave Grenada its nickname, the Spice Island. Many of the great estates fragmented into small tenant farms, although a few plantations have remained to the present. Like most of the British crown colonies in the Caribbean, Grenada received its independence rather recently. Grenada maintained a royal appointee as governor general, representing the formal head of state, Queen Elizabeth II. Unlike most of the former colonies, observer M. Hastings observed that "We, the British, had knowingly delivered Grenada into the hands of a lunatic." [1]

Grenadian labor activist Sir Eric M. Gairy had been involved in Grenadian politics since the late 1950s, and he headed the home rule government since 1967. He took over as Grenada's first prime minister on 7 February 1974, and immediately set about proving Hastings's forebodings all too correct. Gairy dabbled in the occult, routinely addressed God for "signs" during political debates, and gradually lost touch with reality. His paranoia grew as time went on. He arrested his opponents (both presumed and real) capriciously, then held them at length. A few random political murders occurred. Sir Eric ruled through the fifteen-seat parliament (his party held nine seats). He ruled around it as well, courtesy of his sixty-five-man army—the Chilean-uniformed "green beasts"—and a group of personally chosen paramilitary thugs known as the "Mongoose Gang." By 1979, Gairy had rigged the 1976 elections, allowed half of the Grenadian work force to languish unemployed, and run up huge trade deficits and a crushing national debt. Infant mortality and illiteracy were higher than in 1974, and per capita income had declined. Unreliable water supplies, neglected street repairs, and nonexistent health care completed the picture. Public discontent with Gairyism grew.

A powerful opposition group craftily focused and exploited the popular discontent in Grenada. Even before independence, Grenada had spawned a leftist anticolonial movement, disaffected with the bizarre, British-backed moderate Gairy. By March 1973, young intellectuals, like London-educated attorney Maurice Bishop and college professor Bernard Coard, united their urban Marxist discussion circles with a mass rural party, the socialist Joint Endeavor for Welfare, Education, and Liberation (JEWEL). The resultant New JEWEL Movement (NJM) favored independence, nationalization of commerce, tourism, factories, land redistribution, and a pronounced anti-American "nonaligned" foreign policy. Although described by ideologist Selwyn Strachan as "a revolutionary democratic party," the democracy part always seemed a bit hazy. The tiny NJM Central Committee, from start to finish, called the shots. Even so, distress with Gairy made the revolutionary faction appealing. Many dissatisfied businessmen and professionals joined with the New JEWEL people for the 1976 elections. The coalition held the six opposition seats in parliament. In June 1977, the alliance dissolved after the disgusted businessmen publicly accused the NJM of communist leanings.

The party leadership denied these charges, even as they systematically gained control of the trade unions and youth organizations. Charismatic Maurice Bishop emerged as the party leader, with the plodding Bernard Coard as his chief theoretician and deputy. Coard was an accomplished student of Marx and especially Lenin, and he intentionally formed the party as a revolutionary vanguard. Coard expelled those unwilling to execute a Leninist coup. With Coard's guidance, Bishop created a paramilitary force and infiltrated Gairy's government, police, and small army. Bishop's operatives in the United States procured old bolt-action rifles, packed them in oil barrels, and conducted a clandestine delivery in September 1978. The NJM prepared to take charge of Grenada.

Up until this time, Cuban and Soviet influence in Grenada had been minimal. Bishop, Coard, and the NJM adopted Marx and Lenin of their own accord. It was the New JEWEL Movement that initiated requests for Cuban and Soviet assistance. Inadvertently, the United States Federal Bureau of Investigation provided the impetus for the eventual NJM coup. The FBI completed a six-month investigation into the Grenadian gun runners and apprehended two of them in February 1979. Post-arrest interrogation clearly pointed to involvement by the upper ranks of the NJM. The FBI was certain to inform the Grenadian police. Fearing arrest and extradition at worst and a significant crackdown by Gairy at best, Bishop elected to make his move. Sir Eric Gairy made Bishop's decision easier. True to his erratic form, Sir Eric reacted to news of the American arrests with sporadic detentions and frantic searches for arms caches. With the situation still very much in flux, Gairy left the Spice Island on 12 March 1979 en route to a long-scheduled visit to the United Nations in New York. Gairy's personal style of rule insured that the government would be paralyzed without its strange overlord. On 13 March, Bishop and his followers assumed control, captured the green beasts and Mongoose Gang, and announced by radio that Gairy had fled the country after ordering the NJM to be massacred (a lie). The populace reacted with relief. Only three of Gairy's troops died. Less than two weeks later, Bishop suspended the 1974 constitution, although he retained Governor General Sir Paul Scoon to mitigate a possible British reaction. In general, it was right out of Lenin's revolutionary doctrine.[2]

Although the United States could not have been gratified by this development in the eastern Caribbean, a socialist revolutionary coup on a distant island did not in itself draw American attention. After all, Michael Manley's Jamaica displayed similar radical tendencies in the late 1970s. Maurice Bishop's opinions and domestic policies, however repugnant to American leaders, caused little stir in President Jimmy Carter's administration. But as time went on, three issues emerged that caused President Ronald Reagan's Departments of State and Defense to look closely at events on the Spice Island. The company Bishop kept, the things his "guests" built, and the presence of a significant American population on the island insured U.S. attention.

It did not take long for the Cubans, the Soviets, and their allies to spring to the aid of the new Grenadian government. Within days after the coup, the Cuban freighter *Matanzas* arrived, chock-full of small arms, mortars, antitank rockets, and ammunition. Allegedly, this was all to ward off an invasion attempt by the befuddled Sir Eric Gairy, who remained in the United States. Cuban military advisers showed up at the same time as the military shipment, even as Bishop and Coard assured U.S. Ambassador Frank Ortiz in Barbados that the New JEWEL Movement had not received any Cuban arms. The steely Grenadians boldly asked for American weapons while the *Matanzas* unloaded at the island's capital, St. George's. A few days later, Bishop broadcast a venomous address in which he accused Ortiz of trying to dictate Grenadian foreign policy in return for American aid. Bishop growled: "We are not in anybody's backyard, and we are definitely not for sale." [3]

That is, unless Fidel Castro ran the yard and offered the goodies. The Cubans led the way, but they were merely the first and largest of other Soviet bloc contingents. Castro gained leverage on Bishop right from the outset. Cuba recognized Bishop's People's Revolutionary Government (PRG) soon after the coup, and established a large, well-staffed embassy at Fort Lucas, immediately south and east of St. George's. Cuban representative Julian Torres-Rizo sat in on PRG and New JEWEL party meetings, offering helpful advice to Maurice Bishop. The Cubans continued to supply arms on a regular basis, and American students later recalled that the island's electrical power shut down on certain nights, followed by the appearance of new military equipment the next day. Under the supervision of the Cubans and Gen. Hudson Austin (a corporal in Gairy's tiny army), the People's Revolutionary Government built a potent regular army and a large militia. Cuban army advisers instructed and drilled the proud new units in Grenada, and Grenadians attended service schools in Cuba. By 1985, the PRG hoped to deploy an army of four regular and fourteen reserve infantry battalions, numbering more than 10,000 soldiers and armed to the teeth with automatic weapons, artillery, and armored vehicles. It was a far cry from a few dozen green beasts. Grenadian troops served in Nicaragua, assisting the Sandinistas against the restive Miskito Indians. Bishop volunteered a battalion of Grenadians for duty in Namibia, against South African forces, although these men did not deploy before the American assault.

The Grenadians received significant military assistance from the Soviets as well. These supplies moved through Cuba, where they were transshipped to Cuban vessels for final delivery. Sometimes, the Soviets split their shipments, sending part to Daniel Ortega's Nicaragua and part to Maurice Bishop. In conformity with a series of secret arms protocols, the Soviets delivered more than $25 million in arms, ammunition, equipment, and armored vehicles, including a small plane. An equal amount was still scheduled for delivery when the U.S. intervened. Several Grenadian officers enrolled in Soviet military schools. By September 1982, the USSR established an embassy just north of the unfinished runway at Salines. Colonel Gennadiy Sazhenev of the Soviet Army GRU (military intelligence and espionage corps) and his twenty-five armed officers conducted military training for the Grenadian Army. Their numbers swelled to forty-nine by October 1983, with thirty-eight men under arms and the remainder male and female civilians.

The Soviet Navy also participated in the Grenadian buildup. The legendary Fleet Adm. Sergei Gorshkov, commander in chief of the Soviet Navy, visited the island in March 1980. He must have liked what he saw. The Soviets offered some fraternal assistance in July 1982. Maurice Bishop happily agreed to Soviet construction of a new deep-water port on the east coast, near Grenville. Soviet warships and merchantmen received full "visiting" privileges. Preliminary engineering studies for the port were completed by September 1983. Soviet naval leaders also arranged to improve the old eighteenth-century Royal Navy anchorage at Tyrell Bay, located on Grenada's offshore possession, Carriacou Island. The Soviets' naval plans had not yet reached the implementation stage by the time of the American intervention.

Seven other minor Soviet allies contributed significant military assistance, based on bilateral secret agreements. The North Koreans, Czechs, and Nicaraguans provided small arms, explosives, uniforms, and personal equipment. East Germany delivered IKA trucks, paramilitary items, and surveillance equipment for the militia and the security forces. Bulgaria and North Vietnam promised military training to Grenadian exchange officers. The North Vietnamese offered detailed information on American air tactics, ground tactics, and equipment. The Libyans sent three small patrol boats. By October 1983, Colonel Sazhenev monitored small detachments of North Korean, East German, Bulgarian, and Libyan advisers on Grenada.

These nations and other Soviet clients (Syria, Iraq, Hungary, Poland) also provided a full range of political/ideological, economic, and health care assistance. To be fair, Cuban medical personnel in particular did a great deal for Grenadian civilians. But this should not obscure the general thrust of all of this activity. The covert military aid transformed Grenada into a Soviet enclave, and provided Bishop and his New JEWEL cronies with a massive combat force relative to his lightly armed island neighbors.[4]

Everything has a price, and even good socialists like the Cubans and Soviets exacted a toll for their largess. The resulting project generated concern at the pinnacle of the United States government. In November 1979, Fidel Castro generously offered to construct a big new airport at Point Salines, supposedly to encourage the long-moribund Grenadian tourist trade. Although the NJM had violently opposed Sir Eric Gairy's plans for a Salines airport before the coup, Bishop changed his mind. In December 1979, Cuban engineers arrived with their Soviet-made heavy equipment to begin construction. Layne Dredging Company of Miami, Florida, helped to fill in the salt ponds.

The airport project raised American suspicions right from the start. Admittedly, the level Salines plain offered a superb runway site, once the salt marshes were addressed. British military officers, British colonists, and Grenadian businessmen had long urged creation of a long runway at Salines, much closer to the capital of St. George's than the cramped, daylight-only runway at Pearls. The small British fighter strip built at Pearls in 1943 could handle only small planes like the forty-eight-passenger Avro 748 air ferry from Bridgetown, Barbados. Air ferry tourists were usually day tourists, spending their lodging dollars and pounds in Barbados. Bernard Coard, deputy prime minister of the PRG and key NJM party officer, pushed especially hard for the Salines development.

There were some obvious holes in the PRG's public case. For one thing, the long landing strip was intended to allow direct flights from North America and Europe, with a resultant rise in lodging revenue. But only one major international carrier showed much interest after the concept was announced. Eastern Airlines demanded a reasonable minimum of 2,100 hotel rooms in order to commence flights; Bishop's island had 437, and even his most grandiose economic plans allotted less than 200 more by 1990. Salines seemed like a runway to nowhere. Second, Grenada could not afford the cost of the new facility, the very point made by Bishop and Coard during their opposition to the Gairy plans for Salines. Estimated building costs exceeded $71 million, and Grenada's gross national product hovered at about $160 million in good years (and the Bishop years were rarely good).

The tourist argument was a half-truth at best, and likely outright disinformation. Certainly, the PRG would have allowed excursion flights to land and they would have gladly accepted the consequent flow of hard currency, had any tourists or airlines showed any inclinations to visit. But the airport was built and paid for by the Cubans, both for their use and for that of their benefactors, the Soviet Union. Libya and Iraq promised money as well, but little of this funding actually arrived in Grenada. The Soviets gave no direct assistance for the airport, but this was not to say that they did not intend to take advantage of it. After all, they subsidized Castro heavily, which automatically entitled them to whatever the Cubans possessed.

Maurice Bishop held no illusions. In March 1980, Bishop had stated directly in a secret Central Committee meeting that the airport was for Soviet and Cuban military use. Later that month, he calmly told a *Newsweek* reporter: "Suppose there's a war next door in Trinidad, where the forces of fascism are about to take control, and the Trinidadians need assistance. Why should we oppose anybody passing through Grenada to assist them?" By May 1980, Bernard Coard signed a treaty with the Soviet Union, which granted Soviet landing rights at Salines. The Soviets intended to land their big Tu-95 Bear long-range reconnaissance aircraft on the 9,800-foot Salines airstrip, although the runway could easily accommodate almost every other combat and transport airplane in the Soviet inventory. The Cubans received formal landing rights in January 1981; they had been using Pearls for some time. Castro's air force could also find the island useful, particularly as a refueling stop on the way to Angola. An American island resident summarized thusly: "It was an awfully big airport, considering the tourist trade they had was almost nil in the last few years. The big joke was that they all believed it was going to be a military base. For anyone on the island, that was pretty much a given." [5]

The Salines airstrip had some uniquely martial features. Although hotel rooms were in short supply, the nearby Calliste/Frequente barracks, infirmary, motor pools, and arms storage sites provided ample accommodations for visiting soldiers. It would have been a short march to firing ranges and maneuver areas. The Cubans built remote, armored jet fuel storage tanks (designed by Norwich Engineering of Fort Lauderdale, Florida), embedded military "hot-refuel" pipes into the parking apron, and added a few reinforced concrete structures that could have served as admirable ammunition bunkers. The Cubans also dictated installation of superb British-made radio, radar, and approach systems, to allow an all-weather capability. Finally, the Soviets conveniently located their embassy just beyond the Calliste complex, well away from the Grenadian capital city. The Soviets convinced the Grenadians of the necessity for an advanced InterSputnik satellite communications station near the Soviet Embassy and the new airport. Similar installations linked the USSR, Nicaragua, and Cuba. Bear turboprop planes can employ the sort of ocean surveillance satellite reports available over such a down link. This station was in the advanced planning stage by late 1983. [6]

The American government viewed the airport construction effort with alarm. Grenada may be a small island, but it is conveniently athwart the shipping routes that carry Venezuelan oil to America. Hostile planes or patrol boats in Grenada could interdict Panama Canal traffic or throttle more than half of the United States' imported petroleum. President Reagan explained this threat as he showed aerial photographs of the Salines facilities in a nationally televised speech on 23 March 1983. The president's comments on Grenada, however, were overshadowed by the first mention of the controversial Strategic Defense Initiative in the same address.[7] Despite the fact that the president and his advisers were well aware of the potential of the Salines building program, no concrete measures were undertaken to meet the challenge. Whether the United States would have permitted Soviet and Cuban aircraft to use the facilities after the proposed opening on 13 March 1984 became a moot point after the American intervention. The airport that so concerned President Reagan now bears his name.

Aside from general worries about the Soviet bloc buildup and the specific concerns about the new airdrome, American interests in Grenada included about six hundred students and faculty at St. George's University Medical School. Founded in 1978, the institution catered to American medical students who had not gained admission to mainland universities. In late 1979, Grenadian PRG functionaries Kenneth Radix and Selwyn Strachan indicated that they supported the Iranian militants' seizure of the Tehran embassy, and opined that the Grenadians might consider capture of the medical campuses in order to force the United States to extradite Gairy for a trial.[8] Nothing came of this loose talk, but it was duly noted in Washington. Whatever transpired in Grenada, the almost wholly white American young people and their instructors would be evident representatives of the superpower to the north, and the U.S. government could not discount the obvious vulnerability of the medical school community. In light of the Iranian debacle, potential hostage situations made American officials very nervous. Arms caches and runways could be bombed; hundreds of civilians might have to be rescued.

It turned out to be personal jealousy as much as ideological strife that changed the American apprehensions into a nightmare. Maurice Bishop's engaging personality made him a truly popular leader, but he enraged the dull, doctrinaire Leninist Bernard Coard. The unimpressive deputy prime minister felt slighted, and carped about Bishop's "cult of personality." Coard declared Bishop another Gairy and charged that the party chief was disregarding the collective leadership of the Central Committee, especially that of Professor Coard. The tension between the two men exploded on 13 October 1983, when Coard surprised Bishop at a Central Committee meeting. While Bishop had been in Hungary and Czechoslovakia, Coard had garnered the support of General Austin's army and militia, the party elite, and, most critically, Soviet Ambassador Colonel Sazhenev for a reassertion of "proper" Leninist collective authority. The Central Committee stripped Bishop of his titles and placed him under house arrest in St. George's, along with a few of his retainers.

But Professor Coard had neglected to line up the group he allegedly worked for: the average people. On the morning of 19 October, a crowd of ten to fifteen thousand Grenadians gathered before Bishop's house, intimidated the small guard force, and carried Bishop to the army headquarters at Fort Rupert. Bishop, stunned at first, rose to the occasion. He denounced Coard, relieved Hudson Austin of army command, and called for followers to arm themselves and march with him against the renegade faction of the Central Committee, then in seclusion up the hill at Fort Frederick. But Coard and Austin still had the big stick. Regulars of the Fort Frederick garrison, mounted in Soviet-made armored personnel carriers and an East German truck, drove toward the assembled citizenry with automatic weapons firing. Pandemonium erupted as the armored column plowed into the frightened, unarmed crowd. The grim Cuban-trained soldiers grabbed Bishop and summarily shot him, along with his personal party. More than fifty innocent civilians died in the hail of bullets and subsequent panic.[9]

Coard had unleashed the armed whirlwind, and it asserted itself. Hudson Austin dissolved the civil government, placed the governor general under house arrest, declared martial law and a twenty-four-hour shoot-on-sight curfew, and established himself as the supreme authority on the island, chief of the Revolutionary Military Council. Coard remained in charge of the party, and perhaps hoped to head the reconstituted civil government once things settled down. The Soviets, under Colonel Sazhenev's urging, recognized and congratulated Austin's new council. Castro was not so certain, and he cabled Austin: "Everything which happened was for us a surprise, and disagreeable." [10] But the Cubans had a tiger by the tail, and they would be along for a very bumpy ride.

General Austin's military forces moved quickly to consolidate their hold on the island nation. They jailed suspect journalists and political foes, increased army and militia patrols, and broadcast a continuing series of emergency declarations over Radio Free Grenada. Coard and his Central Committee supporters faded into the background; was Coard coordinating with Austin or preparing a second coup? Nobody knew for sure.

Most normal activity in Grenada ground to a halt, including classes at the American medical school. At first, it seemed that Austin might permit the frightened American students to leave. He met personally with the Americans on 20 October and told them they could depart whenever they wished. Many students called home to reassure their parents. But then the Revolutionary Military Council severed the off-island phone lines and closed the telegraph office. The worried Americans found themselves trapped in their dormitories with dwindling food supplies. The curfew continued unabated. There was still no word on their departure; in fact, Pearls airport ceased civilian operations and turned away the interisland air ferry. American consular officials from Barbados were denied landing permission on 19 October and for two days thereafter.

All of the turmoil since Bishop's removal from power was reported (in increasingly fragmented form) to U.S. Ambassador Milan Bish at Bridgetown, Barbados, the closest American embassy. On 19 October, Bish reacted to news of Bishop's murder and the declaration of martial rule with a detailed secret transmission to the State Department. He recommended preparations for an immediate noncombat evacuation operation, to be executed should the situation deteriorate further. Ambassador Bish finally inserted two of his foreign service officers on 22 October, but they found the Grenadian officials "obstructionist and uncooperative." There appeared to be "no coherent government" in place or forming. The few American medical students permitted to speak with the envoys wanted very much to depart immediately, and reported similar sentiments among their classmates. Although the Americans met briefly with Governor General Sir Paul Scoon, they were under surveillance and heavily escorted, and Sir Paul made only a few innocuous comments. Ambassador Bish's report on this unproductive visit reached Washington late on 22 October.[11] The American medical students were not allowed to leave, although Austin continued to issue general assurances of their safety.

Why were the Americans being detained? It is hard to know what went through Hudson Austin's mind. One could postulate three good political reasons for keeping the students on the island. First, General Austin had too many other things to do. Security for a large-scale American exodus would stretch his army and militia units from the campuses in the southeast all the way across the island to Pearls airport, where the young people would leave in penny packets of fifty or so on the interisland planes. An extended U.S. departure might permit potential opponents to move against the preoccupied Revolutionary Military Council. Second, the American presence was evidence of Austin's control over the island. If the students left, it would be concrete and obvious proof of Austin's inability to keep order. His authority would be questioned by Grenadians already suspicious after the events of 19 October. Along this same line, his nervous officers (and the touchy Coard) would surely object if he knuckled under to the hated Yankees, especially after the U.S. diplomatic visit of 22 October. Standing up to the U.S. was critical to Austin's political credibility on Grenada and necessary to maintain crucial Cuban and Soviet support. For this reason, he gave no thought to permitting the USN to extract the students peacefully. Austin could not afford to appear weak in the face of American strength.

The third and potentially most dangerous rationale occurred immediately to Washington policymakers—the students were insurance against American reactions. Whether or not Austin really intended to take hostages remains a matter of speculation. But as long as the students stayed on the troubled Spice Island, the possibility existed that Austin, Coard, or some other faction might snatch up some Americans as a focus for national unity. Certainly, that had been a major factor in Iran in 1979. No one could guarantee Austin's intentions; his capability to seize the hundreds of young Americans was unquestionable. As the Grenadian military gradually cut off the flow of communications to the outside and blocked air and sea routes of departure, fears about such hostage-taking speeded American actions. Tehran haunted United States planners.

As Ambassador Bish wrestled with the darkening picture on Grenada, the national security actors in Washington began preparing for the worst. After the initial New JEWEL feuding became public on 13 October, State Department and Defense Department staff officers considered a noncombat evacuation to remove the American students. This alternative became less feasible following the events of 19 October, even as Ambassador Bish urged definite efforts to implement a quick, peaceful extraction. As a precautionary measure, on 20 October, the Department of Defense instructed Adm. Wesley McDonald, commander in chief, U.S. Atlantic Command (LANTCOM), to move the Lebanon-bound USS *Independence* aircraft carrier battle group, along with Amphibious Squadron 4 and its embarked 22nd Marine Amphibious Unit (MAU), south toward Grenada. President Ronald Reagan kept abreast of proposed plans of action.

On 21 October, the small islands of the Organization of Eastern Caribbean States (the OECS—Antigua/Barbuda, Dominica, St. Kitts-Nevis, St. Lucia, St. Vincent/Grenadines, Montserrat), plus representatives of Jamaica and Barbados, asked for U.S. assistance in an intervention to restore order on Grenada. Chief executives Eugenia Charles of Dominica and Tom Adams of Barbados led the conclave that generated the urgent request. The island states intended to deploy their meager forces, but had no illusions. Without U.S. troops in the forefront, the undertaking would be doomed. As a Dominica policeman said after he reached the defended Grenadian shores, an attack by Caribbean police and soldiers alone "would have been mass murder. They [the Cubans and Grenadians] would have walked right through us." [12]

In Washington, the breakdown of diplomatic attempts to remove the students and the insistent tone of the OECS message spurred action. U.S. contingency plans were hastily broadened to include combat seizure of the island. On 22 October, President Reagan approved the National Security Decision Directive for the military option. However, the steady progress toward the Grenada intervention received a major jolt early on the morning of Sunday, 23 October, when the sad news of the Beirut explosion reached the president and the Pentagon. Orders went out to restore the American marine force in Lebanon, rescue survivors, treat the wounded, and identify the dead. But the situation in Grenada would not wait.

President Reagan acted decisively. Around 1900, 23 October 1983, he signed orders for the execution of the attack. Some political opponents later suggested that the president moved against Grenada out of frustration over the marine barracks explosion in Lebanon, but the facts of the decision-making process do not support such allegations. Diplomatic and military initiatives were well advanced by the time of the Lebanon disaster. The naval forces had already repositioned toward Grenada. A few military units had begun alert sequences, and information collection and intelligence analysis proceeded at several levels. Reagan had already approved preliminary military plans the day before, while the marines passed a quiet day in Beirut. Even if the Beirut attack had never occurred, the Grenada assault certainly would have gone ahead.

The American president received confirmation for his decision the next day. A confidential request for immediate U.S. intervention by Governor General Sir Paul Scoon (still under house arrest at the time) reached Bridgetown, Barbados, on 24 October. This missive emphasized the need for speed. President Reagan met with the Joint Chiefs of Staff on the afternoon of Monday, 24 October. He had already informed the armed forces of the strategic objectives: ensuring the safety of U.S. citizens on Grenada, restoration of democratic government, and elimination of Cuban influence on the island.[13] Now it was up to the military.

Translating the presidential decision into a successful military operation was a daunting prospect. Unlike the other American combat actions since Vietnam, the Grenada intervention necessitated a large-scale, rapid concentration of sizable forces. It became evident early on that a few helicopters, some planes, and a battalion of marines would not suffice. Grenada required a real air-land-sea campaign.

Each level of the American defense chain of command contributed to the planning sequence and played a role in the execution and modifica-

---

Formulating Plans for URGENT FURY

STRATEGIC LEVEL: General political/military goals and some guidance
  President Ronald Reagan
    Civilian advisers—Secretary of State George Shultz, Secretary of Defense Caspar Weinberger, CIA director William Casey, and others
    Military advisers
      The Joint Chiefs of Staff—Gen. John Vessey, USA (chairman); Gen. John Wickham, USA; Adm. James Watkins, USN; Gen. Charles Gabriel, USAF; Gen. P. X. Kelley, USMC
  Unified Command (Theater of Operations)
    U.S. Atlantic Command—Adm. Wesley McDonald, USN
OPERATIONAL LEVEL: Concept of Operations
           designation of operational objectives
           assignment of operational missions to units
           commander's intended scheme of maneuver
  Joint Task Force 120—Vice Adm. Joseph Metcalf, USN
           Deputy: Maj. Gen. H. Norman Schwarzkopf, USA
TACTICAL LEVEL: Tactical schemes of maneuver and fire support
  Joint Special Operations Command
  82nd Airborne Division
  Military Airlift Command component
  USS *Independence* carrier battle group
  Amphibious Squadron 4 with Marine Amphibious Unit 22

---

tion of such schemes. The national command authority (President Reagan, advised by his senior civil and military officials) established the general strategic goals and approved the resultant military plans. Admiral Wesley McDonald of LANTCOM was the unified commander responsible for the Grenada region. He created an operational level command, Joint Task Force 120 (JTF 120), to plan and execute the Grenada intervention. Admiral McDonald provided combat forces to execute the strategy and he supervised the military execution of the strategy. In essence, he served as the theater commander, and linked Washington with the fighting echelon. Vice Admiral Joseph Metcalf III, who normally ran the U.S. Navy's Second Fleet, commanded Joint Task Force 120. He designated operational objectives to implement the president's strategy and created a concept of operations to guide the tactical commanders. Largely single service units, like an army division, naval task groups, air wings, a marine amphibious unit, special forces, plus their subordinate outfits, executed the missions identified by Metcalf.

It is important to remember that the aptly named Operation URGENT FURY featured joint, continuous, and concurrent planning. Joint plans involved all four services, plus national intelligence agencies and assets. Continuous planning meant that, right up until the first American combat boots crunched Grenadian soil, army, navy, air force, and marine commanders and staffs refined initial concepts, altered original perceptions, and added intelligence details to fill in the picture. Concurrent planning involved simultaneous efforts at each echelon of command, with each level concentrating on aspects unique to its requirements and coordinating up and down the chain. It all had to be done rapidly, securely, and above all, competently.

In simplest form, the process involved conversion of President Reagan's strategic goals into a military *concept of operations*. This concept of operations combined operational objectives (seizure of key terrain, destruction of enemy forces) with the operational commander's general scheme of maneuver and fire support. The concept of operations gave the tactical commanders (battalions, air squadrons, ships) missions: *what* to do, *when* to do it, *where* to do it, and *why* it was all being done. In other words, the joint task force's concept allocated operational objectives to the appropriate tactical units; these constituted their assigned missions. But the other portion of the concept was just as critical. The concept did not tell the tactical leaders *how* to do things, but it did provide an overall idea of the operational commander's intent and priorities. The lower commanders designed their own plans, shaped by this overarching vision. The JTF commander's scheme and guidance unified the activities of his subordinate units. With their assigned missions and a clear idea of the intent of the higher commander, the fighting units could then design a coherent sequence of tactical actions that satisfied the operational objectives assigned to each component, yet still contributed to the mission of the entire joint task force.

This said, how did the URGENT FURY military planners translate strategic objectives into a concept of operations? Much of the actual planning sequence for Operation URGENT FURY remains classified, but it is quite possible to identify the basic considerations that applied to the October 1983 Grenada contingency. The operational level is particularly interesting, since the crucial conversion of abstract goals into practical objectives occurred in the JTF 120 headquarters. The following account, although presented as fact, represents informed speculation based upon available open sources. It is a likely reconstruction of how the plan evolved in the JTF command.

In brief, the commander and his staff officers analyzed their assigned missions. They gathered information. Then, they had to organize this information into an *estimate of the situation*. More than likely, the American planners applied their usual doctrinal approaches to array the mass of available data. Finally, the staff officers used their estimate of the situation to design possible schemes of maneuver that fulfilled President Reagan's strategy. Vice Admiral Metcalf, closely advised by his army deputy, Maj. Gen. H. Norman Schwarzkopf, judged the possible plans of attack. Metcalf selected the one he thought best as the basis for his concept of operations.

A traditional U.S. Army approach, which allows for a reasonable examination of the Operation URGENT FURY estimate of the situation, is summarized in the military acronym METT-T. METT-T translates into Mission, Enemy, Terrain and weather, Troops available, and Time. The mission came from the president's three strategic objectives, and its initial position in the acronym is not accidental. As in all military efforts, the mission took first priority. All information gathered, estimates made, and maneuver schemes concocted had to accomplish the missions assigned. Mission analysis came first; then the staff fanned out to find information that facilitated completion of the mission.

President Reagan's strategic objectives set the missions of the American forces on Grenada. The safety of the medical students, not the destruction of Cuban and Grenadian units, was the primary, immediate objective. As a result, U.S. forces had to be directed against those hostile units posing the greatest threat to the American citizens on Grenada. The medical students' presence discouraged indiscriminate use of mortar, artillery, and air munitions. The second objective, restoration of legitimate democratic government, necessitated the destruction of Hudson Austin's army and militia, either by military defeat or dissolution. This goal strongly encouraged steps to minimize collateral destruction and civilian casualties. There had to be an island left to restore. Equally important, there had to be enough American soldiers and marines on the ground to physically sweep and control the island to prevent any sort of persistent Cuban/Grenadian guerrilla campaign. The third objective, the elimination of Cuban presence on the island, implied the isolation, destruction or capture, and final removal of the Cubans and their Soviet bloc allies.

In essence, rescue operations had priority. Not surprisingly, the U.S. rules of engagement required minimum force and minimum casualties, both for Americans and Grenadian civilians.[14] With these strategic goals, the concept of operations had to include enough ground troop strength to handle the likely opposition without resort to massive firepower. Vietnam era tactics, in which individual U.S. infantry companies employed devastating supporting fires to defeat North Vietnamese battalions, could not be used.

These clear URGENT FURY strategic objectives certainly steered the JTF planners. In order to develop a practical concept of operations, the JTF staff collected information and intelligence. Mission considerations dictated the priorities in the processing of this potentially vast ocean of data.

What sort of information came to Vice Admiral Metcalf and his staff? It was fairly easy to develop appreciations of missions, troops available, and the likely time schedule for execution. Superior and subordinate American units, agencies, and staffs could provide these items through relatively secure channels of staff coordination. But the situation inside Grenada was not at all clear.

In service parlance, useful knowledge about the enemy, terrain, and weather constitutes intelligence, not just information. Raw data on the enemy, terrain, and weather must be collected, validated, and analyzed to produce reliable military intelligence. Although a cogent summary of the overthrow and death of Maurice Bishop has been presented, not all of these facts were known in the United States at the time. It does not appear that there were any U.S. agents on the island, although the two foreign service officers who visited on 22 October undoubtedly delivered some important impressions. Metcalf's officers had access to various photographs from reconnaissance aircraft and satellites, and these aided in the assessment of both the enemy and the terrain. Nobody had enough maps; some of those available were old or inaccurate. As Metcalf himself said, intelligence was "not what we desired."[15] The JTF officers had to resort to educated guesses to flesh out enemy, terrain, and weather details. In many cases, the blanks just could not be filled in until Americans debarked in Grenada. This was especially true in the case of the opposing forces.

Should American intelligence have been better? It is easy to say yes, but there are only so many national technical assets and personnel available, and a great many countries to cover. Intelligence sources include imagery, electromagnetic surveillance, and men on the ground, and all apparently came into play before the start of the assault. The Americans had not been watching Grenada with special closeness. The U.S. intelligence agencies had rightly assessed the Cubans as the real threat in the area, with the Nicaraguans second, both in service to the most carefully watched adversary of all, the Soviets. Up until October 1983, the Grenadian problem implied a potentially hostile airfield, not a hostage situation. The Americans had plenty of intelligence on the airport, most of which proved worthwhile. Despite the seeming lack of a dedicated intelligence effort aimed at Grenada before October 1983, it turned out that there were enough details available to plan and execute URGENT FURY successfully. Two key tactical commanders, Col. Hugh Hunter (1st Special Operations Wing) and Lt. Col. Ralph Hagler (2-75 Rangers), rated the intelligence as six on a scale of ten.[16] Given time constraints, these evaluations actually reflect some rather decent intelligence work.

The available intelligence on the enemy addressed three distinct enemy components, and the quantity and quality of confirmed data varied for each of these forces. American analysts considered the Cubans, the Grenadian armed forces, and the Soviet military advisers as the likely opposition. In all three cases, commentary on capabilities (what they could do) was more accurate than remarks on intentions (what they would do). Since American military planners base assumptions upon enemy capabilities, not intentions, the forces that intervened on Grenada ably handled the results of information shortfalls.

American planners knew that the Cubans were in charge of the island defenses, although the exact nature of the Cuban forces on Grenada remained unclear. American intelligence estimated 700 Cubans of militia quality, who might or might not fight. Photography from air and space (probably in combination with electronic intercepts and, possibly, agent reports) indicated deployment of the bulk of the Cubans in defensive positions around the Point Salines Airport. U.S. eavesdroppers likely noticed an increase in transmissions from Havana to the Spice Island. A Cuban An-26 Curl transport aircraft (marked in Air Cubana regalia) landed at Pearls on 24 October, although that runway remained formally closed to civil traffic. The Cuban cargo ship *Vietnam Heroico,* a veteran of the Angola run, rode at anchor off St. George's.[17] In summary, the Cubans appeared to be making military preparations.

The intelligence on the Cubans turned out to be close but not quite right. The actual situation was a bit more threatening. Colonel Pedro Tortolo, who arrived on 24 October 1983 aboard the An-26 Curl transport, commanded the Cubans and, evidently, the Grenadian forces. Although he arrived in civilian clothes, he was a professional. The colonel had graduated from the Soviet Army's Frunze Academy and Voroshilov Staff College, and he served as the chief of staff for the Cuban Army of the Center, one of the three Cuban home armies (two others fight in Angola and Ethiopia, respectively). Tortolo knew the situation on Grenada rather

---

**Cuban Armed Forces/Grenadian People's Revolutionary Army
Order of Battle
24 October–2 November 1983**

Cuban Fuerzas Armadas Revolucionarias (FAR), Grenada: 701 men
  Construction Engineer Battalion
  Military Assistance Group, Grenada
  Ministry of Interior (security) Advisory Section
    Vietnam Heroico passenger/cargo ship (cargo unknown) *
  An-26 Curl transport aircraft

Grenadian People's Revolutionary Armed Forces (PRAF)
  People's Revolutionary Army (PRA): 2,179 men
    Calvigny Infantry Battalion (with BTR platoon)
    St. George's Infantry Battalion (with BTR platoon)
    Salines Antiaircraft Battery
    St. George's Antiaircraft Battery (−)
      Pearls Antiaircraft Detachment

**Cuban Armed Forces/Grenadian People's Revolutionary Army
Order of Battle
24 October–2 November 1983
(continued)**

Artillery Battery
Service elements
An-2 Colt transport aircraft
Three Soviet-built coastal patrol craft
People's Revolutionary Militia (PRM): 7,000 men/women
  Seven Militia Infantry battalions
  Service, police, and local security units
East Bloc Embassy Personnel
  Cuba: 83 men/women
    Diplomatic Staff: 18 men/women
    Civil Assistance Personnel: 65 men/women
  Soviet Union: 49 men/women
    Armed Advisory Group: 38 men
    Diplomatic/Civil Assistance Personnel: 11 men/women
  Other Advisory Contingents: 47 men
    Libyans: 17 men
    North Koreans: 15 men
    East Germans: 12 men
    Bulgarians: 3 men
Total East Bloc Personnel: 880 men/women

* This 7,500-ton Cuban merchant ship arrived off the port of St. George's just prior to hostilities. Its passengers, cargo, and crew did not influence the action ashore, though messages to Havana, Cuba, were relayed by the ship's radio. Ship's personnel are not included in FAR or Cuban total figures.

Sources: International Institute for Strategic Studies, "The Military Balance 1983/84," *Air Force,* Vol. 66, No. 12 (December 1983), 125; Timothy Ashby, "Grenada: Soviet Stepping Stone," *Proceedings* (December 1983), 30, 32, 33; Hugh O'Shaugnessy, *Grenada: Revolution, Invasion, and Aftermath* (London: Hamish Hamilton, Ltd., 1984), 9–12, 15–17; Paul L. Seabury and Walter A. McDougall, eds., *The Grenada Papers* (San Francisco: Institute for Contemporary Studies, 1984), 43, 44, 203; David C. Isby, "Military Lessons of the Grenada Campaign," *Jane's Military Review* (London: Jane's Publishing Co., Ltd., 1985), 45–46; U.S. Congress, House Committee on Appropriations, *Situation in Lebanon and Grenada, Hearings before a Subcommittee of the House Committee on Appropriations,* 98th Congress, 1st Session, 8 November 1983, 39; W. T. Leadbetter, Secretary, *Register of Ships, Vol. P-Z* (London: Lloyd's Register of Shipping, 1984), 1,662.

well; previously, he served as commander of the Cuban military advisory team on the island.

After the U.S. attack, Tortolo tried to claim that he had just coincidentally visited the island to clarify the role of the Cubans should the Americans assault.[18] This seems rather unlikely. For one thing, Fidel Castro had already ordered Ambassador Torres-Rizo on 22 October to mobilize his workers. "It is their duty to die fighting," said Castro. He ordered them to "adopt defensive measures . . . fortify their positions as much as possible." Curiously, Castro demanded that the *Vietnam Heroico,* with unknown cargo aboard, "be kept there by all means." He categorically forbade the ambassador to evacuate women and children on the ship, although he authorized these dependents to leave by air when the opportunity arose. Castro told his representative: "Exert as much influence as possible" on the military preparations and operations of the Grenadian forces. Castro repeated these orders on 23 October, warning his troops that reinforcements would not be sent. News of the OECS conference had already leaked to Havana; the Cubans saw the storm clouds boiling.

Instead of reinforcements, Castro inserted Tortolo with a small command group and security team. Tortolo likely had clear orders to take charge on the island; he swiftly dismissed certain suspect Grenadian officers and replaced them with officers from the Cuban military advisory group. The colonel positioned his "construction crew" in accord with Castro's parting guidance: "The Cuban personnel will defend their positions, that is, the runway up to the Hardy Bay filling and the area between Point Salines and Morne Rouge, in case of a large-scale invasion."[19] The Cubans established fighting positions, helped the Grenadians site antiaircraft guns, and blocked the Salines runway.

Tortolo exercised his authority over a significant Cuban force. His forty-three army advisers assisted (and in some cases, commanded) Grenadian Army units. Ten Ministry of the Interior officers provided similar advice to Grenada's militia. The Cuban workers were not a labor unit but a construction engineer battalion, made up of men armed and organized as a military formation. Real Cuban "Labor Army" units are virtually unarmed and include a sizable percentage of women. The Cuban engineers on Grenada, like the construction engineers in most armies, had some infantry training but were certainly not as capable as a true combat engineer unit. Nevertheless, they lived in barracks, used heavy weapons like mortars and machine guns in addition to their automatic rifles, and carried out military orders from Fidel Castro and Colonel Tortolo.[20]

Air reinforcement from mainland Cuba was quite possible (that was how the colonel arrived). Possible sea reinforcement, in the form of the mysterious *Vietnam Heroico,* was already on station, though the ship had not yet off-loaded. In conclusion, the Cubans represented a considerable opponent, and they seemed likely to fight.

Although American intelligence agencies gauged Cuban strength rather nicely and had noted the start of defensive preparations, knowledge of Grenada's People's Revolutionary Armed Forces (PRAF) proved less reliable. The Americans guessed that the People's Revolutionary Army (PRA) had about 1,200 men and estimated the People's Revolutionary Militia (PRM) at anywhere from 2,000 to 5,000 men. Intelligence officers warned of light antiaircraft cannon, heavy machine guns, mortars, and even a few light armored vehicles. But would the PRAF fight? Who was in command—Coard, Austin, both, or neither?

The PRAF proved to be at the same time stronger and weaker than American suppositions. Both components had more personnel than estimated. The PRA disposed two regular infantry battalions, two strong antiaircraft batteries, an artillery battery, and affiliated service units. This entire force had trained to deal with U.S. airborne and amphibious tactics. The PRA requested and used North Vietnamese information on American air and ground equipment and tactics as early as May 1981. Morale, training, and discipline seemed sound, but the Bishop murder had not helped.

PRA armament included eight BTR-60PB (Soviet-made armored personnel carrier) and two BRDM-2 armored vehicles (which are still frontline Soviet equipment), split into a platoon or so per regular infantry battalion. The infantry was stiffened by 82-mm mortars, RPG-7V antitank launchers, 76-mm and 57-mm antitank guns, and heavy machine guns. The air defense units employed eighteen twin 23-mm towed air defense guns, which are simply dismounted versions of the famous ZSU-23-4 Shilka self-propelled air defense gun that performed so well in the 1973 Arab-Israeli War. More than thirty heavy machine guns, both quadruple 14.5-mm ZPU-4 models and single 12.7-mm DshK variants, supplemented the 23-mm systems. Seven 130-mm M-46 field guns and twenty 122-mm rocket launchers constituted the PRA artillery arm.[21] All in all, the PRA formed a capable force, more potent than U.S. expectations.

The PRM, under Lt. Col. Liam James, supplemented the army with seven militia infantry battalions. They had conducted vast anti-invasion maneuvers in April 1983, and possessed well-stocked arms depots. Militia mobilization depended upon a series of alert signals broadcast over Radio Free Grenada, either the primary station at Beauséjour or the alternate facility, conveniently located in the shadow of the Soviet Embassy on Morne Rouge.

Unlike the army, however, the militia had suffered a crippling drop in morale following the execution of Bishop and the St. George's street battle. In rural Grenada, readiness reports included these notes: "4 persons do not believe the threat; 3 persons said that prayers can stop Reagan from coming." One militiaman stated, "I will pray harder; I afraid the gun." Bishop's murder tore out the heart of the popular spirit that drew thousands out for the April 1983 exercises. The Cuban-trained Austin and the dour Coard inspired fear and loathing in the countryside. American missionary Carter Davis observed, "My neighbor said he would have fought anyone who invaded" under Bishop. As for service under Austin, the disillusioned Grenadian replied curtly, "No way." [22] The PRM would prove to be a paper tiger, and as it crumbled, it took most of the PRA with it.

What about the Soviets? They were rather well armed for "diplomats," since in fact, most belonged to the GRU, along with a few KGB types. This much the American intelligence officers suspected. With their small numbers, the Soviet group on Grenada could not create significant armed opposition to any U.S. operations. Provided the Americans avoided the Soviet Embassy, the cautious men in Moscow would certainly order Colonel Sazhenev to stand aside in the face of powerful U.S. action. But even though the Soviet Army contingent disposed few armed officers, it could still influence the action. For one thing, Sazhenev maintained close liaison with General Austin and probably exercised some authority in the Revolutionary Military Council. Not surprisingly, after the intervention the Americans captured two officially unidentified white men (Soviets?) when they seized Hudson Austin's personal group.[23] Another Soviet role centered on their stout embassy facility, which had access to the entire surveillance and early warning network of the USSR. If the Americans neglected this capability, the GRU men would most likely blow the whistle and tell their Cuban and PRA allies about the pending U.S. movements. The proximity of the secondary Radio Free Grenada transmitter to the Soviet Embassy insured that the Soviets could safely sound the alarm if the Americans neglected them entirely.

The intelligence agencies and staffs accurately appraised Soviet capabilities and intentions. Since the Soviets alone possessed serious capacities to interfere with the Americans, this portion of the estimate proved to be critical indeed. Although the small Libyan, North Korean, East German, and Bulgarian contingents could theoretically have provided some assistance to hostile forces, the U.S. intelligence services rightly discounted them as negligible, if curious, participants. The political repercussions of finding these Soviet bloc allies represented on Grenada far outweighed their actual influence.

In total, the possible opposition to URGENT FURY totaled ten battalions, plus combat support and service support units, all under a loose Cuban command and in coordination with cautious Soviet advice. Familiar, uniform equipment and common organization made cooperation easier. On the other hand, various unique languages and different national interests fragmented the hostile forces. Austin had reason to fight to the finish; his allies did not. Nevertheless, American staff planning officers could not arbitrarily determine which elements would fight. They had to plan for the worst case.

Terrain and weather also influenced U.S. plans. Grenada is not a small, flat desert island. Its total area is 119 square miles (311 square kilometers), about half the size of Guam. (By comparison, Iwo Jima covers 7.5 square miles; Saipan is 70 square miles.) Shaped like an uneven lozenge, the island is split by a central massif, topped by a string of burned-out volcanic peaks towering well over 2,000 feet above sea level. Old lava craters like the Grand Etang form hilltop lakes. The summits tumble down toward the thin coastal plain, breaking into steep-sided ridge lines that radiate toward the sea. The island's towns are strung like beads along the narrow coastal flats. Only in the southwest, on a small, level, low-lying Salines "tail" appended to the main oval, does the coastal plain exceed a mile in width. The eastern and northern beaches are rocky, beaten by prevailing winds, and blocked by reefs; the southern beaches are tiny swatches of sand nestled in tortuous coves. The two largest, safest beaches lie north and south of the capital of St. George's.

Grenada's volcanic, hilly terrain would give any soldier pause, and this is compounded by the heavy vegetation. About 12 percent (more than fourteen square miles) of the island is primary rain forest, with most of the rest either secondary forest or cultivated cocoa, sugar, banana, and nutmeg groves. There are few open areas, and many secondary roads are broken and overgrown by the greenery. As Dominican missionary Raymond Devas commented, Grenada offered "one mass of hills, the lower reaches cultivated, the heights thickly wooded."

Weather added to the steep, lushly planted terrain. The mountainous spine and steep slopes cause prevailing northeast trade winds to sheer along the east and west coasts. The surf conditions are progressively more violent farther north and east. Daily rainstorms, often heavy, characterize October and November, and early morning and late evening fogs occur regularly. The hot, humid air averages 82 degrees Fahrenheit, which would affect heavily laden U.S. troops.

Aside from the uniformed enemy, Grenada held a human resource of known quantity but unknown sympathies. The 110,000 inhabitants occupy the landscape at a density greater than that found in Massachusetts or Connecticut. Of the Caribbean islands, only Puerto Rico has more people per square mile than Grenada. Almost 30,000 of the Grenadians live in and around the port city of St. George's, the principal civil and military hub of the island. The rest of the people dwell in small towns and clots of huts under the arching trees that cover Grenada.[24] American planners believed that the islanders might prove supportive, or at worst, neutral. One handy thing separated the Grenadians from the Cubans and Soviets: the English language. If American soldiers heard Spanish or Russian, they knew that their targets were not innocent Grenadian civilians. Additionally, the common language facilitated American interrogation and surveillance of Grenadian resisters.

As for the American citizens on the Spice Island, the True Blue campus of the medical school appeared to be the only certain concentration. The rest of the students were probably nearby, in the populous southwest area, but planners could not be sure. To counter the lack of solid locations for the threatened students, the Americans intended to secure the whole island rapidly, with minimum firepower. In fact, major American communities also existed at Grand Anse and on the Lance aux Epines peninsula. Still, a few dozen other Americans lived at odd spots around the island, and would not have been safe until the entire island had been secured.

In retrospect, some thought that efforts should have been made to contact school officials and parents in the United States for more precise information. Doctor Charles Modica, the chancellor of the school, visited New York in the latter days of October 1983. Doctor Modica had come to address parents at a routine school social gathering on Sunday, 23

October 1983, just as the American military planners hastened to create a concept of operations. Print and electronic journalists, sensing the seriousness of the Grenada situation, queried Modica and several parents about the safety of the young people. Modica knew something was wrong in Grenada, but he and many parents loudly and publicly maintained that all was well. Several parents had spoken to their children before Austin cut off the external Grenadian telephone lines, and honestly believed that their sons and daughters were safe. A group of parents sent a telegram to President Reagan, urging him "not to move too quickly or to take any precipitous action at this time." [25] With the press swarming around the concerned (but misinformed) parents and Doctor Modica, security-conscious American intelligence officers probably made an intentional decision to avoid these lucrative but leaky sources.

The military implications of Grenadian terrain and weather limited the place, pace, and nature of the U.S. assault. Getting ashore looked to be the hardest part. There just were not many military ways into Grenada. To attack an island, the American military had two choices, each with two variants. The main operation could be amphibious (by landing craft or helicopter from offshore ships) or by air (an aircraft assault landing or parachute drop). A seaborne landing faced the shortage of decent beaches, since most beaches were treacherous, even for small boats (let alone landing craft). Only Grand Mal, Grand Anse, and possibly the beach near Pearls looked promising for any serious conventional assaults. As for helicopters, the central rock formations and heavy vegetation limited level open areas necessary for landing zones (LZs). A few helicopters could land at once, but the bare spots did not allow for a rapid, massive insertion. The exceptions, of course, comprised the unfinished Point Salines airstrip (9,800 feet) and the Pearls airport (5,200 feet), which could serve as superb LZs. These facilities could also be employed for air assault landings or parachute drops. Either operation could quickly secure the vital runways for follow-on waves of jet transports (Salines) and turboprops (Pearls). Salines' length made it a better parachute drop zone; Pearls looked to be more suited for helicopters. [26] Other than the two (maybe three) beaches, a smattering of little clearings, and the two airdromes, there was no other quick way of getting onto the rugged slopes and into the thick underbrush of Grenada.

Two other factors influenced force planners. First, the Americans wanted to protect and secure the aid of the large population. This required precision in ground combat actions. Foot reconnaissance would have to replace reconnaissance by fire. Random air strikes, indiscriminate naval gunfire, or unobserved artillery barrages would not work. Second, the stationary enemy defenders had many camouflage advantages. Cover, concealment, and short-range infantry firefights could be counted upon in the successive series of woods, steep hills, valley thickets, and clustered towns. The rampant foliage and precipitous topography would absorb a lot of infantry. Planners discounted ideas of securing Grenada with vehicles or helicopter scouts. Too much could transpire unseen down under the big trees. Grenada was not suitable for large armored units, though armed and transport helicopters would be very useful.

The American intelligence elements combined enemy, terrain, and weather appraisals to forecast the probable enemy dispositions. It was hard to be certain, but the Americans thought that Cubans anchored their defenses on Salines, with something going on at Pearls (as evidenced by the parked An-26 transport plane). The military intelligence officers judged that the Grenadian PRA and PRM had deployed around the significant towns, weighted toward the southwest. The U.S. analysts expected PRA elements at Fort Rupert, Fort Frederick, and the other hilltop forts ringing St. George's. The intelligence officers predicted antiaircraft preparations at both airstrips and noted that the opposition protected the three likely landing beaches.

Even allowing for some variance in estimated enemy strength, the anticipated Cuban and Grenadian positions proved rather close to Colonel Tortolo's deployments. The Cuban engineer battalion held the area north and northeast of the Salines runway. The engineers had barricaded, wired, and staked the macadam strip to block any assault landings. One Grenadian infantry battalion (headquartered originally at Calvigny) defended the thick, rolling jungle hills east of the Point Salines airport, tied in with the Cubans to the north and the sea to the south. The second PRA regular infantry outfit deployed on the chain of ridges around St. George's. PRA regular air defense batteries, supplemented by trained militia, manned 23-mm and lighter weapons around Salines and St. George's. A 14.5-mm detachment protected Pearls. The majority of the militia remained unmobilized, although ample arms caches at Mount Horne to the east, Sauteurs to the north, Fedon's Camp in the central highlands, Carriacou offshore, and the huge Frequente depot in the vital southwest awaited the arrival of the PRM soldiers. In essence, Tortolo defended the critical points in strength and took risks beyond the crowded southwest quadrant.

What troops were available to defeat Tortolo's men? The U.S. armed forces field potent standing elements; the trick was choosing enough to do the job without notifying every Soviet and Cuban spy on Earth, taking forever, or turning the Spice Island into smoking rubble. JTF 120 wanted to employ what they had and what they needed, but not much more. What they had were navy and marine units; what they needed were army and air force outfits to weight the main attack.

The USS *Independence* carrier battle group and navy/marine amphibious group were on hand from the start, steaming north of Grenada by 20 October. Carrier-based A-7E Corsair II and A-6E Intruder attack jets joined with F-14A Tomcat fighters to insure responsive close air support and protection. Three destroyers in the carrier's screen (USS *Caron*, USS *Moosbrugger*, USS *Coontz*) carried 127-mm (5-inch) cannons capable of shore bombardment.

Nearby, the ships of Amphibious Squadron 4, led by the helicopter carrier USS *Guam*, waited to debark their marines. The 22nd Marine Amphibious Unit (MAU) could land its Battalion Landing Team (BLT 2/8 Marines) aboard the MAU's contingent of marine assault helicopters or in amphibious assault vehicles (AAVs). Like its unfortunate twin in Beirut, the BLT included three marine rifle companies, plus powerful attachments: a platoon of M-60 tanks, fourteen AAVs, a 105-mm artillery battery, a TOW antitank missile platoon, and a marine reconnaissance platoon. All in all, the American planners could expect much from the navy and marine force.

The extent of the possible opposition and nature of Grenadian terrain, however, required additional forces. Navy and army special operations forces were allocated to JTF 120 for a few critical tasks, but these small elements could not deal with the three regular and seven militia battalions on the Spice Island. JTF planners had the option to reinforce their BLT two ways: by sea or by air. Sea transport would take a long time, and the dispatch of additional marine amphibious units was ruled out. Air reinforcement allowed quicker entry into the battle area, but it demanded capture of one or more runways. Army paratroopers constituted the logical choice for airstrip seizure; army Rangers had the additional capacity to rescue hostages. Thus, both airborne Ranger battalions were added. These highly trained units, three rifle companies strong, carried light machine guns, 60-mm mortars, and hand-held antitank weapons. They specialized in airfield assaults.

The JTF operations staff wanted additional foot infantry to complete

United States Forces and Caribbean Peacekeeping Force Order of Battle
24 October–2 November 1983

United States Joint Task Force 120

Joint Special Operations Command (JSOC): SEAL Team 6, 1st Special Forces Operations Detachment—Delta, 160th Aviation Battalion

U.S. Army units:

Rangers: 1-75, 2-75 Airborne Ranger infantry battalions *

82nd Airborne Division (−)

2nd Brigade: 2-325,** 3-325, 2-508 airborne infantry battalions

3rd Brigade: 1-505, 2-505, 1-508 airborne infantry battalions

Division Artillery: 1-319, 1-320 airborne artillery battalions

Division Support Command: administration, maintenance, medical, supply

Division Troops: air cavalry, air defense, aviation, engineers, military intelligence, military police, signal

1st Special Operations Command: civil affairs, psychological warfare

Engineer, intelligence, logistics, police, and signal units from XVIIIth Airborne Corps, 1st Corps Support Command; transport units from 7th Transportation Group, 11th and 24th Transportation battalions

U.S. Navy/U.S. Marine Corps units

Carrier Battle Group 20.5

USS *Independence* (CV-62) with Carrier Air Wing 6 (CVW-6), USS *Richmond K. Turner* (CG-20), USS *Coontz* (DDG-40), USS *Caron* (DD-970), USS *Moosbrugger* (DD-980), USS *Clifton Sprague* (FFG-16), USS *Surabachi* (AE-21)

Amphibious Squadron 4

USS *Guam* (LPH-9), USS *Trenton* (LPD-14), USS *Fort Snelling* (LSD-30), USS *Manitowoc* (LST-1180), USS *Barnstable County* (LST-1197), SEAL Team 4, Beach Group Two (−), Construction Bn. Two (−)

22nd Marine Amphibious Unit (22nd MAU)

Battalion Landing Team 2/8 Marines (BLT 2/8); Marine Medium Helicopter Squadron 261 (HMM 261) (−)(+); Marine Service Support Group 22 (MSSG 22)

U.S. Air Force units

Military Airlift Command

1st Special Operations Wing (−): 8th & 16th Special Operations Squadrons

Tactical Airlift Wings: 314th, 317th, 459th, 463rd

Military Airlift Wings: 60th, 62nd, 63rd, 315th,# 437th, 438th, 514th#

United States Forces and Caribbean Peacekeeping Force Order of Battle
24 October–2 November 1983
(continued)

Military Airlift Wings (heavy): 436th, 512th [#]
Groups: 193rd Electronic Combat Group,[#] 913th Tactical Airlift Group [#]
Strategic Air Command
2nd Bombardment Wing (tankers only)
544th Strategic Intelligence Wing
Tactical Air Command
33rd Tactical Fighter Wing [##]
Detachment 1, 507th Tactical Air Control Wing
552nd Airborne Warning and Control Wing

Caribbean Peacekeeping Force (CPF)
Jamaica (infantry company); Barbados (infantry platoon and police)
Organization of Eastern Caribbean States (OECS): Dominica (paramilitary security platoon), Antigua/Barbuda (police platoon), St. Lucia (police platoon), St. Vincent/Grenadines (police platoon), St. Kitts/Nevis (five policemen), Montserrat (British possession—no force contribution)

[*] JSOC controlled both Ranger battalions until about 1900, 25 October 1983.

[**] Company C, 2-325, was left behind at Fort Bragg, N.C. It was a newly formed element and was not considered ready for action. Company B, 2-505 replaced that unit. The 2-505 deployed minus one company and linked up with Company B in Grenada.

[#] Reserve component units.

[##] Additionally, the 23rd Fighter Wing deployed twelve A-10A Thunderbolt IIs to Barbados on 2 November 1983. They never participated in combat on Grenada.

Sources: "Grenada Invasion Units Listed," *Army Times,* 5 December 1983, 23; Lt. Col. Andrew M. Perkins, Jr., "Operation Urgent Fury: An Engineer's View," *Military Engineer* (March–April 1984), 87–88; Henry Zeybel, "Gunships at Grenada," *National Defense* (February 1984), 53, 56; Hugh O'Shaugnessy, *Grenada: Revolution, Invasion, and Aftermath* (London: Hamish Hamilton, Ltd., 1984), 8–9; Roy A. Grossnick, "Year in Review," *Naval Aviation News* (May–June 1984), 30–31; "Units Listed for Armed Forces Expeditionary Medal," *Navy Times,* 8 October 1984, 4; "JCS Reply to Congressional Reform Caucus' Critique of the Grenada Rescue Operation," *Armed Forces Journal International* (July 1984), 99; "Delta Unit's Presence in Grenada Invasion Cause for Lid on Press," *Army Times,* 14 November 1983, 10; "Withdrawal of Troops Begins as Hostilities End on Grenada," *Army Times,* 14 November 1983, 2; James W. Canan, "Blue Christmas Coming Up," *Air Force* (January 1984), 78–81; Maj. James Holden-Rhodes, "The Jamaica Defense Force," *Proceedings* (March 1985), 164–168; Ray Bonds, ed., *The U.S. War Machine (Revised Edition)* (New York: Crown Publishers, Inc., 1983), 136, 138, 141, 142; Lt. Col. Michael J. Byron, "Fury from the Sea: Marines in Grenada," *Proceedings* (May 1984), 124.

the clearance of the steep, vegetated Grenadian countryside. The 82nd Airborne Division was the closest source of nonmechanized army infantry. Airborne infantry battalions also had the ability to parachute into Grenada, and their normal readiness level was well above that of other available army outfits. Like the Rangers, the 82nd paratroopers organized into three rifle companies per battalion, although with significantly heavier 81-mm mortars and capable TOW missile antitank sections.

Of course, employing parachute troops entailed commitment of air force transports to ferry the jumpers and deliver supplies. The soldiers would arrive aboard C-130E Hercules, special purpose MC-130E Combat Talons, and following flights of big C-141B Starlifters and even bigger C-5A Galaxies of Military Airlift Command (MAC). The air force also attached a few AC-130H Spectre gunships, armed with accurate rapid-fire cannons; these promised to provide superb fire support for the unarmed transports. Thanks to permission of Barbados' prime minister, Tom Adams, the smaller American planes could stage through the big Grantley-Adams Airport in Bridgetown. Tankers, command and control aircraft, and even a wing of mighty F-15 Eagle fighters joined the operation. The 33rd Tactical Fighter Wing's Eagles would patrol the airspace around Cuba to discourage Cuban interference with URGENT FURY.

All of these troops, ships, and aircraft could be assembled rapidly, without undue disruption of normal peacetime patterns. The navy and marine forces still appeared to be on their way to Beirut (admittedly on a pretty southerly route by 21 October). The Soviets and Cubans had grown used to watching the Rangers alerted and moved across and around America and the world on short notice; the 82nd Airborne conducted similar exercises. Military Airlift Command regularly carried the Rangers and paratroopers, and the 33rd Wing's Eagles squatted innocently on their alert parking aprons at Eglin Air Force Base, Florida. With the calculated ambiguity of preliminary American movements, surprise remained a strong possibility.

Force planners had one final unit available, the composite Caribbean Peacekeeping Force (CPF). The CPF included the small but well-trained infantry components from Jamaica and Barbados, whose Sandhurst-graduate officers continued the traditions of the venerable British West Indies Regiment. Police platoons from the other islands rounded out the force. Air force MAC planes would pick up the Caribbean Peacekeeping Force at Grantley-Adams Airport on Barbados. The CPF's use was not specified, but its polyglot nature and uneven level of training suited it for rear area duties. Needless to say, the CPF had a political importance that far outweighed its potential military contribution to URGENT FURY. Given the importance of winning over the Grenadian populace, the CPF's arrival could well have definite military benefits. The combined battalion gave proof positive of the English-speaking Caribbean's concern over the trouble in Grenada.

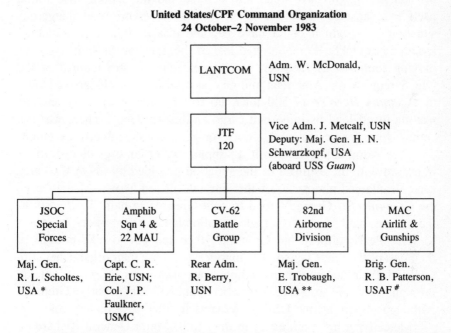

United States/CPF Command Organization
24 October–2 November 1983

LANTCOM	Adm. W. McDonald, USN

JTF 120	Vice Adm. J. Metcalf, USN Deputy: Maj. Gen. H. N. Schwarzkopf, USA (aboard USS *Guam*)

JSOC Special Forces	Amphib Sqn 4 & 22 MAU	CV-62 Battle Group	82nd Airborne Division	MAC Airlift & Gunships
Maj. Gen. R. L. Scholtes, USA *	Capt. C. R. Erie, USN; Col. J. P. Faulkner, USMC	Rear Adm. R. Berry, USN	Maj. Gen. E. Trobaugh, USA **	Brig. Gen. R. B. Patterson, USAF #

* JSOC retained command of the Rangers from early on 24 October 1983 until 1900 on 25 October 1983; special operations concluded at 0712 on 26 October 1983, when the marines relieved SEAL Team 6 at the governor general's residence.

** The Caribbean Peacekeeping Force (Brigadier Rudyard Lewis, Barbados Defense Force, commanding) was attached to the 82nd Airborne. The 82nd had operational control of both Ranger battalions from 1900 on 25 October until 1300 on 28 October.

\# Major General William J. Mall (commander, 23rd Air Force) and Col. Hugh L. Hunter (commander, 1st Special Operations Wing) directed the initial air assault on 25 October 1986.

Time certainly weighed as the most critical factor of all in determination of the eventual American operations in Grenada. U.S. commanders had been directed to conduct URGENT FURY on short notice. There was no time to orchestrate some sort of massive airborne or amphibious attack; the uncertain condition of the American citizens required an immediate response. Diplomacy had been tried and it had stalled out. With regard to the prospect for talks, Deputy Chancellor Doctor Geoffrey Bourne of the medical school said, "Would Bernard Coard . . . have ordered the negotiations stopped? Would the Russians and the Cubans have taken the responsibility to pour in even more troops and arms while diplomatic negotiations were going on? The whole situation with the students might have gone into reverse and the school have found itself in a hostage situation. . . . We had a volatile and dangerous situation . . . which could have become disastrous at any minute." Events ran quickly. Someone had leaked the news of the *Independence* moving south on 21 October; by the next day, Castro learned of the OECS request for American military assistance. Tortolo arrived, and the *Vietnam Heroico* (7,500 tons, up to 218 men) swung at anchor, waiting to off-load its important cargo and passengers.[27] There was not enough time for perfect plans, only for good ones, violently executed.

Vice Admiral Metcalf built a simple, clever concept of operations in accord with the estimate of the situation provided by his staff, which surely contained almost all of the data considered above. Metcalf used the Grenville–St. George's road to split Grenada in half. To the north, the marines held sway. The single battalion landing team received orders to seize Pearls airport and Grenville, then fan out to take control of their part of the Spice Island. The marines could use their organic helicopters and their accompanying amphibious transports to move quickly through, over, and around the sparsely populated northern part of Grenada. Although important, the USMC elements fulfilled a secondary role.

Metcalf put his main effort in the south. Major General Richard L. Scholtes's Joint Special Operations Command (JSOC) inherited this difficult, congested region. JSOC got the tough Salines runway and a few pinpoint sites around St. George's. Scholtes's two army Ranger battalions intended to take the big airport by air landing or by parachute, if necessary. The Rangers expected to employ trained hostage rescue elements to secure the Americans at nearby True Blue. Smaller special warfare units took on such important missions as disabling the Grenadian radio system (thereby crippling militia call-ups), rescuing the trapped governor general, and freeing political detainees in the Richmond Hill prison. JSOC would stay long enough to seize the runway and execute the special raids, then turn over the southern zone to a portion of the army's 82nd Airborne Division. With Salines in hand, the army could reinforce to face the

United States/CPF Strategic and Operational Objectives for
URGENT FURY

1. STRATEGIC OBJECTIVE: Ensuring the safety of American citizens on Grenada.
   OPERATIONAL OBJECTIVES:
   1) Secure and evacuate True Blue campus
   2) Secure and evacuate Grand Anse campus *
   3) Secure and evacuate Lance aux Epines student community *

2. STRATEGIC OBJECTIVE: In conjunction with OECS friendly government participants, restoring of democratic government on Grenada.
   OPERATIONAL OBJECTIVES:
   1) Secure Government House (rescue Governor General Sir Paul Scoon)
   2) Secure or destroy Radio Free Grenada main transmitter: Beauséjour
   3) Secure or destroy Radio Free Grenada auxiliary transmitter: Morne Rouge
   4) Capture or destroy Revolutionary Military Council (Butler House)
   5) Capture or destroy the PRA headquarters element; seize Fort Rupert
   6) Capture or destroy St. George's PRA infantry battalion; seize Fort Frederick
   7) Capture or destroy Calvigny PRA infantry battalion; seize Calvigny barracks *
   8) Secure and evacuate Richmond Hill prison (political prisoners)
   9) Secure other hill forts (Fort Adolphus, Fort Lucas)
   10) Secure arms caches (Frequente, Mount Horne, Fedon's Camp, Sauteurs, Carriacou) *
   11) Search and clear remainder of Grenada; capture or destroy PRA/PRM

3. STRATEGIC OBJECTIVE: Eliminating current, and preventing further, Cuban intervention on Grenada.
   OPERATIONAL OBJECTIVES:
   1) Secure Point Salines Airport; deny Cuban withdrawal or reinforcement
   2) Secure Pearls airport; deny Cuban withdrawal or reinforcement
   3) Capture or destroy Cuban forces:
      a. Capture or destroy Cuban Military Assistance Group; seize Cuban Military Assistance Group barracks south of Morne Rouge
      b. Capture or destroy Cuban Construction Engineer Battalion; seize Calliste barracks *
      c. Secure Frequente arms supply depot *
   4) Secure and evacuate Cuban Embassy
   5) Secure and evacuate Soviet Embassy
   6) Secure and evacuate all other Soviet bloc personnel

4. ADDITIONAL JTF 120 OPERATIONAL OBJECTIVES:
   1) Beach reconnaissance (Grenada and Carriacou)
   2) Point Salines Airport—primary U.S./CPF reinforcement base
   3) Pearls airport—secondary U.S./CPF reinforcement base

* JTF 120 designated these objectives after the start of the operation, based upon clarification of pre-assault intelligence estimates.

sizable, dug-in enemy units expected in the heavily defended area around Salines and St. George's.

Based upon Metcalf's guidance, Scholtes issued especially challenging tasks to his special warfare outfits. The navy's elite SEAL Team 6 detachments planned to eliminate the vital radio transmitter sites and to secure the trapped governor general. In addition, the tough special warfare soldiers of 1st Special Forces Operations Detachment—Delta (aboard the exotic helicopters of the daring, special-purpose 160th Aviation Battalion) hoped to liberate the political prisoners at the inland Richmond Hill penitentiary. For this tricky mission, Scholtes supplemented the hundred or so Deltas with major portions of two Ranger companies (Company C, 1-75, and Company C, 2-75) detached from their parent battalions.

The commitment of these unique units led to one of Metcalf's more controversial decisions of the campaign: the JTF 120 commander excluded print and electronic journalists, with the full agreement of the president and other senior military and civil officials. As one knowledgeable military journalist noted: "Military leaders reportedly wanted to take no chances on the possible spread of knowledge about the Delta unit's operating procedures and techniques. They also wished to avoid public identification of individual members of the unit." [28] As bonuses, the conventional phases of the operation stood a better chance of achieving surprise, and the assault troops avoided the burden of protecting members of the media. Given the unwelcome publication of the naval task group's movement toward Grenada, this censorship provided definite military advantages.

While the special missions could help matters, capture of the airfields keyed the assault phase. Once this occurred, the Cubans and Soviets would be cut off from reinforcements and resupply, the American infantry buildup could begin (led by the 82nd Airborne), and American logistics would be assured. Salines' jetport outweighed the shorter Pearls runway in military value.

Metcalf insisted upon flexibility. The URGENT FURY plan was not written in stone; far from it. The JTF commander knew that things would go wrong, and created (with the help of ground deputy Major General Schwarzkopf) a concept of operations that could be adjusted as the intelligence picture crystallized and the enemy scrambled to react. Always, Metcalf kept his missions in mind. Without complete intelligence, proper rehearsals, or full preparations, he prepared to launch the largest American joint operation since the Vietnam War. Metcalf put his trust in the right people: solid subordinate commanders and innovative, bold American soldiers, sailors, airmen, and marines.

Like an overture for the bigger show to come, the highly trained American special operations units opened URGENT FURY with a series of difficult, precision small unit actions. In and of themselves, these small unit missions would not decide the Grenada campaign. At best, successful accomplishment of the tasks could serve as a catalyst, reducing American losses and saving valuable time. But in the end, the infantry battalions would determine the issue.

The special operations began out at sea just after 2200 on 24 October, with the stealthy dispatch of four distinct groups of navy SEALs. The SEALs are probably the best trained and least advertised of America's special operations forces. Skilled as scouts, scuba divers, small-arms experts, and demolitions operatives, SEALs train to infiltrate enemy oceanside defenses in order to provide surveillance, verify beach conditions, or destroy point targets. A SEAL contingent accompanies every navy/marine amphibious force; scouts from SEAL Team 4 (ST-4) worked for Capt. Carl R. Erie's Amphibious Squadron 4. Their mission comprised beach reconnaissance along the long stretch of sand near Pearls airport.

The other three SEAL units sent ashore operated in the southern zone. They came from SEAL Team 6 (ST-6), under JSOC supervision. This SEAL outfit forms a naval equivalent to the army's Special Operations Detachment, Delta, and operates directly in support of national objectives, such as hostage rescues or counterterrorist actions. SEAL Team 6 would have led the assault on the *Achille Lauro* in October 1985, had that proven necessary. These elite swimmers had three missions: destruction of the Beauséjour radio transmitter, the rescue of Governor General Sir Paul Scoon, and one other unannounced task. The third mission might have been directed against the Cuban military assistance compound or the Radio Free Grenada auxiliary transmitter, both near Morne Rouge.[29]

Off Pearls, a few ST-4 sailors slipped into a small Sea Fox raiding launch and departed from the landing ship USS *Fort Snelling*. Just beyond the beach, four SEALs climbed into a rubber boat and paddled toward Grenada. The pounding surf enabled the clandestine reconnaissance party to get ashore undetected. After securing their raft, the small team began a methodical examination of the Pearls airport area terrain and defenses.

They found two ZPU-4 14.5-mm quadruple-mounted heavy machine guns sited on a small knoll just north of the runway. The gunners slept fitfully near their weapons. The Pearls strip turned out to be very constricted, with wooded high ground on the north, thick jungle to the south, and the lower slopes of the central Grenadian massif to the west, just beyond the end of the runway. The SEALs had to move slowly, and at one point, they ran afoul of some Grenadian militia. The disgruntled PRM infantry had been ordered to dig in along the beach, but the SEALs overheard the English-speaking Grenadians complaining about the rainy weather, and a few PRM troops guessed that the Americans would not really come. The hidden Americans finally crawled off when the hostile soldiers moved on to another location.

By 0300, the SEALs transmitted a short coded message: the beach surf proved "heavy and plunging" and rocks, reefs, wrecks, and sandbars festooned the waterfront and its approach lanes. Landing craft would not work; conditions were marginal for amphibious assault vehicles. The message evidently included key information about the enemy. The SEALs rendered a full report on their findings after their safe return.

These few trained men had a significant impact on the next day's plans. Captain Erie and Col. James P. Faulkner (commander, 22nd MAU) originally planned for Company E to assault vertically by helicopter onto the Pearls strip itself. Just after this, Company G, 2/8 Marines, would attack horizontally, beaching aboard AAVs at the sea end of the Pearls runway, complete with five M-60A1 tanks brought in by landing craft. These two companies could then move south to take Grenville, reinforced by the third rifle company and BLT antitank and recon troops as needed. Even before the SEALs departed on their operation, Faulkner and his marine helicopter commander, Lt. Col. Granville R. Amos, altered Company E's landing site. They picked a new landing zone about 750 meters south of the runway proper, given the likelihood of capable enemy air defenses at the airstrip. The SEALs' observations confirmed this supposition.

Once the SEALs' message came in, the seaborne part of Faulkner's plan went out the window, since everything would have to land by helicopter. Although there were only enough choppers to lift one rifle company at a time, the enemy force seemed small and confused. Colonel Faulkner figured that the marines could probably take Pearls and Grenville rapidly, using one rifle company for each objective. So he took a bold risk. The MAU commander decided to land Company E alone in LZ Buzzard. He depended upon Company E to move out swiftly and seize the airfield unassisted. After the capture of Pearls, Company F would conduct a helicopter assault at LZ Oriole, in the town of Grenville. Company G, with the BLT's tanks and amphibious assault vehicles, remained aboard the landing ship USS *Manitowoc* as a powerful landing force reserve.[30]

Even as the ST-4 sailors crept through the dank undergrowth near Pearls, the three SEAL Team 6 units started their missions. The first element got ashore undetected, and with the help of the destroyer USS *Caron*'s accurate 127-mm gunfire, destroyed the seventy-five-kilowatt Beauséjour transmitter that had been so carefully installed by Soviet and Cuban technicians. The station managed to burp out a single incomplete alert warning to the militia about 0530, then went dead by 0630.

The second ST-6 mission went well, up to a point. Twenty-two of the hardened scout swimmers debouched near St. George's, moved carefully through the darkened city, and arrived unnoticed around the Government House, on the ridge line above the capital. Just as the morning twilight brightened the Spice Island, the SEALs stormed the structure under heavy, if disjointed fire from the shocked PRA guards, and gained control of Sir Paul Scoon and his household. Sir Paul was unharmed and very happy to see the SEALs. Unfortunately, the hostages and their rescuers soon found that getting in was one thing, but getting out was another. PRA regulars, drawn from the St. George's infantry battalion and including BTR armored personnel carriers, surrounded the SEALs and their charges. The situation at Government House amounted to a standoff, but something would have to be done to relieve the SEALs and evacuate the governor general.[31] By daybreak on 25 October, Metcalf had his first problem, even though the main JTF 120 assault was barely underway.

The final SEAL mission never came off; its four-man team drowned in heavy seas off Point Salines, a sobering reminder of the dangers involved in such covert raiding. The two possible targets of this failed operation were dealt with by other American forces, albeit nowhere near as neatly as the SEALs might have done. The Cuban advisory compound remained intact until captured on 26 October, and Cuban officers played major roles in the jungle and hill fights around Salines. Naval aircraft flattened the Morne Rouge transmitter early on 25 October, effectively disconnecting Hudson Austin from his confused militia forces.[32]

Major General Scholtes's forces conducted one other special mission on Grenada. At 0615, after the main American attack commenced, American Delta troopers and supporting Rangers moved to liberate political detainees in Richmond Hill prison, near St. George's. The Delta men roared in aboard fast, low-flying 160th Aviation Battalion UH-60A Blackhawk helicopters, protected by sturdy little egg-shaped Hughes MH-6 Commando gunships. The Delta soldiers, whose last publicly acknowledged role ended in tragedy in the Iranian desert, ran into a deadly barrage of antiaircraft fire. Small arms, machine guns, and twin 23-mm cannons created a brutal cloud of flak. The 160th Aviation's attack formation staggered and fragmented in the face of the violent PRA reaction, although the pilots gamely pressed onward. Given the need for split-second timing, precise locations, and simultaneous landings, the eruption of all of this highly effective antiaircraft gunnery rendered a successful raid impossible. After suffering serious casualties and severe aircraft damage, the Delta commander aborted the mission. The political prisoners remained incarcerated.[33]

The 160th Aviation Battalion pilots struggled to bring their riddled choppers out of the inferno of tracer fire and 23-mm cannon bursts over St. George's. Seven of the Blackhawks endured serious damage, with controls shot away, radios ripped out, fuel leaks, blown engines, and bullet and fragment holes torn everywhere. One Blackhawk limped out to the *Guam,* its pilot shot through the left leg and bleeding profusely. The engine throttle and shut-down systems had been destroyed by 23-mm cannon fire, and the ravaged bird would not shut down. Quick-thinking navy CPO Walter Anderson directed a gushing fire hose into the raging turbines to slow and stop the wild engines.

Amazingly, six of the stout Blackhawks survived the ordeal. Two required major overhauls before they could be used again. Only one crashed and burned, down near Point Salines. American medical student Bill Sabbagh watched a white navy SH-3H Sea King helicopter from the *Independence* recover the crew and passengers from the stricken craft. The cost of the attempted raid had been high: one of the pilots died, and at least eleven fliers and Delta men suffered wounds.[34] Only the protection and resilience of the Blackhawks prevented even greater carnage.

Some speculative reports indicated that the Delta raid actually landed the SEAL element at Government House as well, and that there were related attempts to capture the Revolutionary Military Council intact at Butler House and Fort Rupert.[35] To avoid disclosure of sensitive special operations capabilities, American defense officials refused to confirm or deny such unfounded conjectures. These speculations, while interesting, are not really all that critical to an understanding of the military significance of the Delta defeat. The raid failed; that was the bottom line. Admiral Metcalf had to find other ways to meet Delta's mission in the Grenadian capital.

The special operations phase of Operation URGENT FURY produced some rather good results for small efforts. ST-4's Pearls reconnaissance allowed the marines to recast their attack plans. At Beauséjour, SEAL actions resulted in the destruction of the big radio transmitter, which derailed the Grenadian militia mobilization. These missions had immediate military benefits.

The other special operations also affected the course of URGENT FURY. The partial success at Government House and Delta's rebuff at Richmond Hill influenced later decisions. The point targets in St. George's would have to be taken the hard way, and rescue of the trapped civilians at the Scoon and Richmond Hill sites necessitated speed. Special missions unexecuted became, by necessity, conventional missions that needed attention. By the time the special operations situations became clear, the marines and Rangers had launched the main assault, which created new possibilities and problems.

While the SEALs went about their grim business and Delta helicoptered toward an aerial ambush over St. George's, other young Americans prepared for combat in the predawn gloom off the Spice Island. To the east, Captain Erie's blacked-out amphibious ships stood a few miles offshore, and prepared to launch their brood of green USMC helicopters. Young marines, bright American flags sewn on their left sleeves in anticipation of service in the Lebanon Multinational Force, quietly checked their live ammunition and went over assault plans. To the northwest, army Rangers, bundled aboard noisy, dark C-130 air force transports and laden with bullets and hand grenades, hollered hoarsely over the turboprop howl as they reviewed their attack schemes. Neither the marines nor the Rangers could see much of their eventual destination in the small hours of 25 October 1983.

Both forces intended to arrive simultaneously at 0500, just before dawn broke. For the marines, this meant reveille at 0100. Although the ship's galley prepared breakfast, the assault troops did not eat a great deal. Companies E and F drew their ammunition, marked down

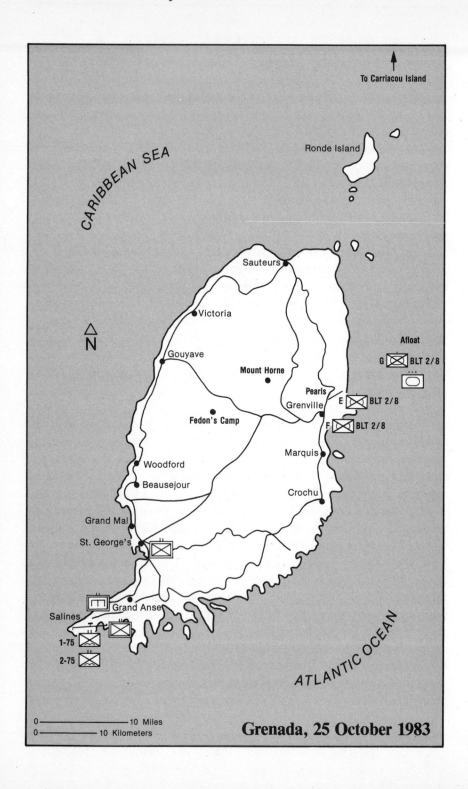

Grenada, 25 October 1983

radio frequencies, and quietly moved out of the *Guam*'s bowels toward the dim flight deck. There was not much banter; a few marines thoughtfully discussed planning details.

On the deck, seven helicopters of marine Medium Helicopter Squadron 261 (HMM-261) squatted, ready to load the first wave. *Guam*'s flight deck had two helo spots to the starboard (right) side (fore and aft of the ship's bridge and funnel island) and five to port (left). Lieutenant Colonel Amos's HMM-261 normally consisted of eighteen CH-46E Sea Knight transport helicopters, ugly twin-rotor beasts known affectionately as "Frogs," capable of ferrying eighteen combat-ready marines. For the MAU deployment, Amos detached six of his Frogs and picked up some useful attachments: four big CH-53D Sea Stallion heavy lifters (fifty-five marines apiece), four nimble twin-engine AH-1T Sea Cobra gunships, and two UH-1N Huey utility choppers. HMM-261 could deliver one combat-ready marine rifle company in a single lift, complete with ammunition and Sea Cobra gunship support.[36] In order to clear the deck for his other craft, Amos launched his first wave at 0320, then brought the next group up from the hangar deck. The second element fueled and embarked its marines, then took off.

Now the real juggling started. The first seven helos returned to top off fuel, then lifted off again. At this point, just prior to 0500, a westward-bound squall line rolled over the *Guam*. This delayed the marine helicopters' form-up, and meant that the USMC missed the 0500 start time. But the storm offered an opportunity as well. Led by two wary Sea Cobras, the rattling Frogs and Sea Stallions followed the moving thunder clouds in to Pearls. The marine fliers used night vision goggles and came in low out of the pink eastern sky, masked by the rain showers. The thunder, pelting rain, and crashing surf muffled the roars of the helicopter engines, and the Grenadian gunners did not open fire until the Sea Cobras swept across the rain-soaked runway.

As the Sea Cobras peeled off to shoot up the enemy ZPU-4 sites north of the airstrip, the transports pressed on toward the half-lit LZ Buzzard. Despite good aerial photographs, the "open" area 750 meters south of Pearls airport turned out to be dotted with sizable palm trees and high scrub. The leading marine pilots, making good use of their night vision goggles, spied a small clearing on the northwest corner of LZ Buzzard. At 0520, the first marine Frog settled down into the tight area, discharged its keyed-up passengers, then lifted off. The other marine choppers followed at two-minute intervals. Grenadian ZPU-4s engaged briefly from their distant hilltop, then succumbed to the pummeling delivered by the active Sea Cobras. The enemy air defenses ceased fire.

Company E, 2/8 Marines, cleared LZ Buzzard rapidly and set off toward the Pearls airport. Despite suspected enemy movement in the brush, the marines did not take any fire until they breached the chain-link fence surrounding the runway. At that point, several nervous Grenadians fired a few wild bursts of AK-47 fire, then melted into the greenery west of the tarmac. The Americans held their fire and moved into the terminal area. While one platoon searched methodically through the air administration buildings, another advanced to clear the knoll used as an antiaircraft site.

Frightened Grenadians saw the burly, sweating, camouflage-clad marines climbing up toward them. The militiamen panicked, dropping AK-47s, abandoning two ZPU-4 quadruple 14.5-mm guns, and leaving behind many pieces of equipment and military documents. Curiously, the marines did not fire but instead attempted to chase down the unencumbered, fleeing enemy. Burdened by heavy ammunition, the marines quickly lost touch with their quarry. As BLT 2/8 commander, Lt. Col. Ray Smith, lamented, "Fire discipline was too good!"

The BLT commander reached Pearls just behind Company E, having landed in the second wave at LZ Buzzard. Lieutenant Colonel Smith ordered his marines to form a perimeter around the airstrip and search two odd-looking aircraft parked nearby. The marines captured and searched the Grenadian An-2 Colt (still with Soviet Aeroflot markings) and Colonel Tortolo's An-26 Curl without a fight. The examination yielded a dozen Cuban airmen.

The Cubans requested permission to depart, but Lieutenant Colonel Smith brusquely rejected their pleas. The time for diplomacy and cajolery had passed long before; the Cubans became prisoners. At 0725, BLT 2/8 declared Pearls secure. The jubilant marines soon renamed their prize "Marine Corps Air Station Douglass," after marine Sgt. Maj. Frederick B. Douglass, a victim of the Beirut truck bombing.[37]

Even as the marines' attack on Pearls proceeded, Lieutenant Colonel Amos led the flight bearing Company F into LZ Oriole, on the southern outskirts of Grenville. By now, the tropical sun brightened the Spice Island. Once again, the chosen LZ was covered with tree stumps and scrub, but Amos quickly elected to put Company F into a nearby soccer field. He based this choice on the paucity of opposition encountered at Pearls. The marines enjoyed an unopposed landing at the new LZ Oriole, and took the town and port area of Grenville by 0728.[38] The marines took no casualties at Pearls or Grenville.

The marines had an unexpectedly easy experience in the north. The army Rangers and their air force transports enjoyed no such luck at Point Salines. The first indication that the enemy desired to contest the Ranger assault came around 0330, when the first of three 16th Special Operations Squadron AC-130H Spectre gunships took up station high above Point Salines.

The enemy did not react as the Spectre assumed a lazy left-turn orbit. The AC-130H stayed just beyond the effective range of Cuban/ PRA 23-mm cannons (6,600 feet). This maneuver exposed the "business side" of the four-engine turboprop. Each Spectre carried two 7.62-mm miniguns, 20-mm Vulcan Gatling-style guns, two long-barreled 40-mm cannons, and a single 105-mm cannon. Low-light television, infrared, and sensitive radar devices provided aiming data to computers, which helped fire this potent gallery of weaponry with uncanny precision. The Spectre crew carefully examined the hostile defensive array portrayed by their diverse bank of sensors. The resultant picture looked uninviting.

As with SEAL Team 4 at Pearls, the lead gunship radioed back findings that altered initial plans. First of all, the Cubans had blocked the runway with construction vehicles, concrete posts, engineer stakes beaten into the hard surface, and an encrustation of razor-sharp barbed wire. This ruled out an assault air landing, in which the planes would touch down and discharge their battle-ready Rangers directly onto the airstrip. Secondly, the gunship crew confirmed earlier aerial photography that showed at least four enemy air defense sites strung along the low ridge just north of the runway. The Cuban/PRA guns looked like twin 23-mm types, just as feared. There was no evidence of any enemy radar detection capacity or surface to air missiles.[39]

This sobering information probably went to an EC-130E Airborne Battlefield Command and Control Center, likely circling just off the projected flight route intended for the Rangers' aircraft. The Joint Special Operations Command battle staff on the EC-130E quickly analyzed the data and forwarded it to JSOC commander Major General Scholtes, aboard the incoming Ranger air mission. Scholtes sought the advice of his competent subordinates, which proved no special problem. In accord with American military tradition, the key commanders were close at hand, leading their tense troops and aircrews by personal example.

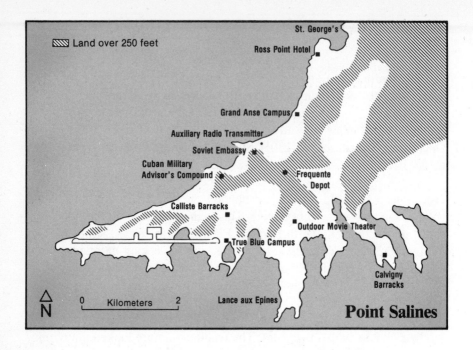

Scholtes consulted with the entire relevant air force chain of command: Lt. Col. James Hobson, commander of the 8th Special Operations Squadron, Col. Hugh Hunter, commander of the 1st Special Operation Wing (1st SOW), and Maj. Gen. William J. Mall, commander of the 23rd Air Force. All of them accompanied on the inbound flight. The impossibility of air landing came as a nasty surprise at the end of a long night flight over water. Airdrops are much harder to pull off. The three experienced USAF commanders expressed concern about the enemy gun batteries and the narrow, seaside drop zone. The prevailing northeast winds, blowing out to sea and the southwest at a treacherous 20 knots, gusted in a steady rhythm, like the breath of a giant. Intermittent rain squalls and the plan to drop in near-darkness at 0500 complicated the scheme. Hobson, Hunter, and Mall seemed uncertain about their ability to place the Rangers on the barricaded airstrip without being shot to bits, dumping jumpers into the ocean, or unloading the soldiers into the trees north and east of the airport. All of the air leaders reassured Scholtes that they would fight through as ordered.

Lieutenant Colonels Wesley Taylor and Ralph Hagler, commanding
1st and 2nd Battalions, 75th Infantry (Airborne, Ranger), recommended
a solution that typified the intensity of the Rangers' devotion to their
mission. Although the enemy antiaircraft mounts dominated the airstrip,
there was a weakness in the Cuban/PRA deployment, evident in some
aerial surveys even before the Spectre reported back. The opposing cannon
crews had picked locations that allowed good observation and clear fields
of fire, but only above 500 feet. After all, Cuban intelligence officers
knew that American paratroopers jumped from 1,000 feet. Unfortunately,
Colonel Tortolo underestimated the cunning and boldness of the 1st
SOW and the Rangers.

Taylor and Hagler insisted that the jump would work, provided the
Rangers came in at 500 feet. This would cut the vulnerable descent
time to thirty seconds or so, insure a more accurate delivery on the
narrow macadam strip, and fly under the big 23-mm twin cannons.
The Rangers would not need reserve parachutes; if the main chutes
failed, time would not permit a reserve to open.[40] Of course, nobody
had done such a thing since Vietnam, particularly none of the young
Ranger privates. But the Rangers and 1st SOW had made the sour incursion
into Iran that had ended in flames at Desert One, and there was definite
determination to press on this time. Scholtes agreed, and the Rangers
prepared to execute the first U.S. combat jump since 1967.

Like the marines, the army attackers found themselves behind schedule. A balky navigation system on the lead plane slowed and scrambled
the inbound formation. With a need for a precision drop, the third MC-
130E took over the lead as the flight approached Salines. The airlifters
had departed over eight hours earlier from Hunter Army Airfield in
Georgia. After a grueling trip at relatively low altitude and in darkness,
excited Rangers struggled to rerig their chutes for a low-level combat
jump. 0500 came and went. Above Salines, the three anxious Spectre
crews on station waited for the transports.[41] Where were the Rangers?

The jump formation approached Grenada from the west in trail along
the main axis of the unfinished Salines runway. The Americans flew in
three groups, split by about thirty minutes flying time. In the lead,
three of Colonel Hunter's dull black MC-130E Combat Talons guided
four camouflaged C-130E Hercules from the 317th Tactical Airlift Wing
(317th TAW). The JSOC command section, USAF Combat Control
Team, and Companies A and B, 1-75 Rangers, rode in this wave. The
next echelon, made up of five more 317th TAW turboprops, carried

Companies A and B, 2-75 Rangers. The last group, nine 317th TAW aircraft, bore additional gun-jeep and motorcycle teams drawn from both battalions, ammunition stocks, and headquarters elements. Only the men on the first seven aircraft expected to jump; the rest hoped to land on a secured tarmac, although they too were ready to parachute in.[42]

On Grenada, nearby U.S. students knew something unusual was underway. Many woke up when they heard the distant drone of the Spectre planes. Young Americans on Lance aux Epines peninsula observed dull gray-black aircraft flying above Salines, staying just out of range. But the Cubans and Grenadians held their fire. Greg Simmons expressed what he and his friends saw: "I was really scared. There wasn't any shooting at first—for about an hour and a half. Just planes flying. And they weren't sightseeing. Then, all of a sudden, all hell broke loose." [43] It was 0536.

The 1st SOW aircraft flew directly into the jaws of death over Salines. For a moment, it was like some low-level variant of a standard drop. Lieutenant Colonel Hobson's black Combat Talon (with General Mall aboard) headed the single file procession as the four-engine transports slid down to 500 feet. The lead plane crossed over the dim coast and the unfinished airport approach lights, then began releasing its men. About a dozen jumpers had left the 1st SOW aircraft when an enemy searchlight flicked on, locked directly on the Combat Talon. The wide-eyed air force loadmaster, standing behind the shuffling parachutists, hollered over the intercom, "They're firing on us." [44]

A mixed clutch of 23-mm, 14.5-mm, and 12.7-mm tracers floated up and around Hobson's aircraft, each hiding three to nine unseen rounds between. Flak proximity fuses popped angry black and orange bursts across the Combat Talon's flight path and tore holes in its thin skin. Muffled booms filled the plane, broken by the sharp pings and clangs as shell fragments and bullets ricocheted into the bucking transport. Hobson gratefully observed that most of the heaviest flak passed just above his MC-130E, exactly as planned.

But one 23-mm site was a little below the others, and these Grenadians had a bead on the Americans. The twin PRA cannons and their nearby lighter machine gun accompanists ripped out a steady stream of accurate fire. Lieutenant Colonel Hobson, with General Mall's reluctant concurrence, ordered his planes to abort the drop and pull up. A second Combat Talon peeled off with slight damage. But Hobson had already spilled Lt. Col. Wesley Taylor and about forty other Rangers into the warm, bullet-filled skies over Point Salines. The other transports backed off and circled over the ocean. On General Mall's urgent orders, Maj. Michael J. Couvillon's AC-130H turned in to deal with the pugnacious ZU-23 battery.

On the ground, the air force combat control team and Taylor's small clot of Rangers struggled to find cover amid the barriers strewn and erected on the runway. Taylor and the USAF men fumbled with radios as the enemy skipped bullets off the runway. One enemy machine gunner pinned the Rangers on the straightaway. The dawn brightened into day, making it easier for the Cuban and PRA defenders to see their targets. Rangers peeped cautiously around obstacles as Cubans and Grenadians shattered the air with steady bursts of automatic fire.[45] Salines hung in the balance for a few very nervous minutes.

Colonel Tortolo's defense put the Americans in a tough position. The U.S. forces had to seize the Salines runway, but the Cubans and their Grenadian allies had laced the area with potent antiaircraft guns. Tortolo's troops drove the Americans down to 500 feet, denied them an air landing attack, and broke up the drop pattern right at the outset. The Rangers and airmen on the tarmac represented potential prisoners, not a military threat. If the Americans turned back at Point Salines, the struggle for Grenada might be decided at a conference table, in the court of world opinion, or in the American news media. For a few minutes before the sun rose on 25 October, Tortolo had a significant victory within his grasp.

Major Couvillon and his Spectre put a quick end to the possibility of a Cuban success at the new airport. Couvillon admitted to natural worries under fire, but his crew knew what to do. The lumbering gunship moved into range of the troublesome enemy gun position, braving an eruption of return fire. The Spectre's Singer-Kearfott computer cut in and out, but it stayed operational long enough to align the two 40-mm cannons on the enemy battery. Two accurate shots sufficed to terminate the gunfire from that position. Couvillon then moved on to smother the rest of the enemy air defense array on the small rise north of the airport, assisted by his fellow gunships. Spectre had reopened the aerial path to the drop zone.

But Couvillon was not finished yet. Two Rangers, trapped by enemy machine gun fire behind a Cuban construction vehicle, called for immediate help. With his computer system relatively ineffective, Couvillon warned the Rangers that the enemy target was too close. The Ranger on the radio replied laconically: "You shoot them or they shoot us. Take your pick." The Spectre pilot turned to navigator Capt. Bryan A. Lasyone to line up the plane's guns. Lasyone and his fellow fliers did the job, pounding the enemy machine gun into impotence with dozens of 40-mm shells and hundreds of 20-mm rotary cannon rounds, all within fifty feet of the embattled Rangers.[46]

The other 1-75 Ranger aircraft dropped quickly at about 0550. Six successive transports filled the sky with light green parachutes as the Cubans and PRA continued their firing. Despite the incredible racket and a real light show of tracers, most of the violent enemy fire missed the heavily laden jumpers. Nevertheless, it was a harrowing descent for many of the soldiers. As 1st Lt. Timothy Sayers said: "I'd made plenty of training jumps before, but it was a bad feeling to look up and see holes in your canopy." [47]

Meanwhile, 2-75 Rangers received the word that they, too, would have to jump. The Rangers wrestled in the jouncing interior of their transports, trying desperately to hook up parachutes, bulky ammunition containers, crew-served weapons, and full rucksacks. They tossed aside their useless reserve chutes. Word came to each plane that their fellow Rangers were on a very hot drop zone. Lieutenant Colonel Hagler yelled back into the clattering interior of his aircraft: "Rangers, be hard. We'll be taking some ground to air fire." Young men clawed at buckles, straps, and slings as the C-130s descended down to 500 feet, rolling and jumping in the stiff island breezes. Then, the jump doors opened, and it was time to go out. It was about 0615.

Hagler's description is illustrative of the fearsome scene around his 2-75 Rangers as the bouncing Hercules crossed the surf line just short of the runway: "I saw 23-mm tracer rounds arching over the C-130s. The west end of the airstrip was under mortar attack, and you could hear the sniper fire over the roar of the engines. There was a lot of fire." Hagler, like Taylor before him, jumped first, and led his battalion down into the maelstrom.

The average Ranger jumped with an incredible load of ammunition; about a hundred pounds was typical. Many Rangers wanted to jump merely to start unloading these huge burdens. As a result, soldiers tumbled out the doors, climbed over those who tripped, and cleared the aircraft in an average of twenty-one seconds (thirty-two seconds would have been normal). The pilots, with adrenaline flowing and enemy flak skittering off their thin-skinned turboprops, sped up to well over the mandated

130 knots. Even so, the skilled Ranger jumpers successfully impacted on the hard, obstacle-covered airstrip. Only one man went into the water, although it lay right at the south edge of the runway. He made it ashore. Another Ranger broke a leg.[48] Overall, the jump was superb.

The Rangers and pilots were not the only servicemen who exhibited exceptional courage that morning. Two USAF jump masters, both of the 317th TAW, leaned out into the hail of enemy fragments and explosives to cut loose jumpers whose parachute deployment static lines had gotten tangled onto the aircraft. In the words of one of them, T. Sgt. Charles H. Tisby: "It looked like the Fourth of July out there." [49] The aircrews put the Rangers right on target; now it was up to the soldiers to clear the runway.

As the Rangers gained strength on the ground, elements moved aggressively toward their objectives. Clearing the airstrip constituted the first priority for the Americans. Furious, if inaccurate, enemy fire made the work tricky. The Rangers had the help of at least two bulldozer drivers of the 618th Engineer Company (Airborne); one of these attached troopers made his first jump since basic airborne school into the Salines drop zone. The Rangers and their helpers hot-wired the Cuban rollers and bulldozers and began to clear the strip. They shoved aside fifty-five-gallon drums, about twenty-five barbed wire fences, concrete posts, and some inoperative equipment. The purloined bulldozers crushed stakes pounded into the runway. By 0740 or so, the final wave of C-130s, bearing the jeeps, motorcycles, their chosen crews, and other supplies and equipment from both battalions, began to land on part of the runway.

While a few Rangers tore down the barriers on the Salines strip, most of the army troops turned to deal with their tormentors. Taylor's 1-75 Rangers assaulted into the Cuban/Grenadian positions with a vengeance. The young Rangers, inexperienced but well trained, advanced under fire with coolness and skill. Taylor's plan was rather elegant: a double envelopment. He put his two available rifle companies on the enemy flanks and turned them loose.

The Cubans and Grenadians had holed up in the building foundations, having built what Taylor termed "pillbox-like fighting positions." The enemy engaged the Americans skillfully, but the Rangers maneuvered and brought effective direct fire to bear. Some Cubans and Grenadians began to run off or surrender, the first signs that Tortolo's defenses were cracking.

Company A, 1-75, pushed boldly toward the eastern part of the antiaircraft ridge. The Rangers employed a Cuban bulldozer to weight their assault, and pressed to the edge of the sprawling Cuban Calliste barracks. The Rangers "borrowed" an enemy antiaircraft gun and used it to support their fires into Calliste.

Company B, 1-75, headed for the western end of the same ridge under an intermittent 82-mm mortar barrage. First Sergeant Rick Cayton led three Rangers into one Cuban platoon, killing two and capturing twenty-eight. Company B snipers silenced the troublesome mortars with sniper fire at ranges up to one kilometer. This company also drove to the edge of the Calliste garrison area. The intrepid first sergeant coerced 175 more Cuban soldiers into capitulation in one corner of Calliste through the threat of an air strike.[50] Salines had been secured from the north and east by 1-75 Rangers.

Inside 1-75's perimeter, 2-75 Rangers moved to clear the runway. Most of Hagler's battalion found itself involved in processing prisoners and removing airfield barricades, although selected elements mixed with their 1st Battalion, 75th Rangers comrades in the ongoing struggle to secure the airport periphery.

Almost as crucial as seizing the runway, Company A, 1-75 Rangers rescued 138 grateful American medical students from the True Blue campus at about 0850. Thanks to careful U.S. fire control, the campus went unscathed in the fierce fighting during the airdrop. Before the attack, the American civilians had watched the Cuban engineers and their PRA comrades set up light antiaircraft weapons alongside the local pathways; now the happy students saw many of these same soldiers marching west, unarmed and under U.S. guard.[51] The Rangers opted to leave the civilians at True Blue for the time being. The withdrawing enemy elements demanded the Rangers' overriding concern.

Within a few hours after the first helicopter touched down at Pearls and the first man jumped at Salines, JTF 120 had achieved its initial objectives. Vice Admiral Metcalf could be well satisfied with the assault phase of URGENT FURY. But by about 1000, the situation in the north differed greatly from that in the south.

In the marine area, BLT 2/8 and its supporting units had secured all initial objectives with little difficulty. The marines successfully blocked Cuban withdrawal or reinforcement and provided an assured secondary source for U.S. supplies and reinforcements. The marines recovered forty-seven more Americans and friendly foreigners up near Pearls. G Company, with its armored AAV carriers and attached tanks, still waited aboard ship, ready for another mission. Given the minimal resistance encountered around Pearls and Grenville, another rifle company and marine helicopters could also be made available to the JTF for new tasks.

To the south, General Scholtes's JSOC had its hands full. Resistance around Salines far exceeded expectations in stubbornness (if not scale), with portions of two hostile battalions identified (Cuban engineers, PRA infantry). The Americans had risen to the challenge. On the positive side, the Rangers controlled Salines airport, although it remained under sporadic mortar and small arms fire. The Americans knocked out about a third of the Cubans in the area. Most important, the Rangers rescued 138 Americans. Thanks to JSOC actions, the Grenadian militia did little. Their vital Radio Free Grenada alert system lay in ruins, replaced by a U.S.-run "Radio Spice Island." SEAL Team 6 elements had reached and secured Governor General Scoon.

The southwest area also featured some serious problems. St. George's remained securely in enemy hands, along with its vital military and political facilities. The special operations units had left work undone at Richmond Hill, and a second, fresh PRA infantry battalion besieged the SEALs at Government House. These conditions rendered an attack toward St. George's by two lightly armed (albeit highly motivated) Ranger battalions rather risky. Nevertheless, the objectives in the Grenadian capital needed to be taken swiftly.

Despite the importance of the goals around St. George's, the Rangers did not push very far north. Hilly, heavily vegetated ground, dotted with many small villages, hamlets, and Cuban/PRA military compounds lay athwart the routes to the Grenadian capital. Most of two enemy battalions occupied defensive positions in this tough terrain. Strong local opposition continued to flare all around the runway, which mitigated against any rapid army advance from Point Salines. The airport had to be kept open, both to insure U.S. reinforcements and to protect the students at True Blue. Airhead security took priority over the need to attack north.

These understandable military challenges were compounded by some unexpected fruits of the Rangers' hard early fighting: more than 200 Cuban prisoners. The Rangers had brought no military police or special medical and logistics elements to watch and care for the dejected Cuban captives. Ranger units have little administrative overhead, so the Americans left most of 2-75 off the thin Salines perimeter just to deal with the massive influx of prisoners. The absence of each battalion's third line company did not help.

Finally, the very nature of the Ranger battalions made it unwise to use them as standard infantry. The Rangers had taken the airhead and secured True Blue, using their extensive training and special skills. But they lacked the weaponry for prolonged slugging. To grind down these lightly armed units in regular combat (as had happened to their predecessors in the infamous drainage ditch at Cisterna, Italy, in 1944) would be wasteful, especially when the 82nd Airborne was already en route. With Delta shot up, Metcalf might need his elite Rangers to save the rest of the American students, wherever they might be. Expending them in meat-grinder terrain against long odds did not seem smart.

But the admiral could not wait forever. The enemy had staked his defenses on the southwestern region. To defeat the Cubans and PRA, the Americans would have to crush the opposition between Salines and St. George's. The longer it took, the more likely it became that the radical Grenadian opposition could turn to guerrilla tactics. Hudson Austin and Colonel Tortolo were still very much at large. With a respectable hostile force concentrated north of Point Salines and in the island capital, Metcalf also had to face the unpleasant fact that he had not yet found and secured the majority of the Americans he had come to rescue. The Cubans and PRA might yet select the hostage option if the Americans moved too slowly.

By 1045 on 25 October, Metcalf began to shift forces to help the embattled JSOC elements.[52] He sent his most responsive units—navy carrier jets and marine helicopter gunships—into the southern zone near St. George's and Point Salines. The jet and chopper pilots joined the fray in force.

USS *Independence* planes added to the air force air power already above Salines. Two Spectre gunships circled overhead at all times while a third flew to Barbados to restock ammunition and fuel. The Spectres ripped apart PRA emplacements, punched holes in Cuban barracks, and caused a few surrenders by their mere presence. Heavily laden A-6E Intruder medium bombers from Attack Squadron 176 joined small, fast A-7E Corsair II light bombers of Attack Squadrons 15 and 87 in repeated strikes around Calliste. The navy pilots crushed the Morne Rouge auxiliary radio transmitter during these sorties.

In St. George's, the SEALs defending Government House received help just in time. The opposing infantry battalion had called in their platoon of Soviet-made BTR-60PB armored personnel carriers. These powerful vehicles rolled up and began slowly pumping bursts of large 14.5-mm machine gun slugs into Governor General Scoon's residence. The masonry facade disintegrated under the impact, and the PRA infantry began to inch forward. But the cavalry arrived in the nick of time, in the form of two AH-1T Sea Cobras. The swift marine gunships spun down to pepper the BTRs, blowing 20-mm rounds through one and driving back the others. The PRA infantry pulled off under the aerial battering, leaving the ruined machine at the mansion's fence.[53]

The marine helicopters did not go unchallenged. Stuttering PRA antiaircraft mounts, which had beaten back the Delta detachment, threw up a fierce barrage from their positions on the arc of ridges around St. George's. Most of the enemy antiaircraft fire came from old British harbor defenses—Fort Rupert, Fort Frederick, and Fort Matthew. British free-lance journalist Hugh O'Shaughnessy, already on Grenada when the fighting started, watched the PRA and PRM gunners in action. He thought them cool and determined, an assessment shared by the U.S. pilots who had to challenge the Grenadian batteries.[54] Continued air support for the SEALs would be needed, and that demanded a solution to the enemy antiaircraft problem.

To avoid civilian casualties in St. George's, the JTF sent in another pair of AH-1Ts to silence the positions near the hill forts. The hovering marine choppers could be more precise than swift navy planes. The Sea Cobras came in low, firing their 20-mm cannons. But the enemy returned a devastating fire that tore open the right side of one marine helo. The engine sputtered, and shell fragments severed pilot Capt. Tim Howard's right arm and holed his right leg. Copilot Capt. Jeb Seagle fell unconscious as the Sea Cobra wobbled down toward a hard landing, guided by the dizzy Captain Howard. The wounded chopper crunched into an open field near the Botanic Gardens, with enemy bullets kicking all around. The wreck caught fire, and Seagle woke up in time to drag Howard out of the inferno. PRA infantry descended from the ridge at a run, closing on the two stricken marines. Howard radioed desperately for help as the Grenadian soldiers advanced. The smoke from the burning helicopter ascended, visible from Salines and well out to sea.

A CH-46E Frog roared in from the *Guam*, seeking to rescue the two pilots. The companion AH-1T, which had turned off to avoid the gunfire, bore in to protect Howard. Seagle began to run off along the harbor beach, drawing a big group of Grenadian troops after him. But about ten continued down toward Howard, stopped momentarily by the 20-mm gunnery of the other Sea Cobra. Howard thought it was all over; he distinctly heard Spanish voices among the enemy troops, indicating Cuban help.

The Frog dropped down to the wave tops, using the anchored Greek freighter *Kronaos* to cover the approach path. The constant suppressive fire from the surviving helicopter allowed the speeding Frog to slip in and grab Howard from the approaching PRA and Cuban soldiers. In a few minutes, Captain Howard entered the sick bay on the *Guam*.

The capable PRA air defenses claimed Howard's guardian angel, blowing the second Sea Cobra into the sea even as the CH-46E rescue craft cleared the harbor mouth. Both marine pilots died. The brave Captain Seagle was killed by the PRA, and his stripped, battered body later appeared in a *Newsweek* photograph, much to the dismay of many Americans.[55]

The marines had lost two Sea Cobras without denting the St. George's antiaircraft situation; indeed, the burning carcass of Tim Howard's chopper no doubt encouraged the confident Grenadian gunners and their Cuban mentors. Metcalf had tried to be careful; now it was evident that some collateral damage would have to be chanced in order to break the back of the seething array of air defense batteries. Metcalf turned to Rear Adm. R. C. Berry in the *Independence*. He sent the attack jets in, loaded for bear.

Nimble Corsair IIs tore across St. George's. They shredded the length of the enemy's antiaircraft ridge. The A-7Es struck at Forts Rupert and Frederick, but the enemy batteries stubbornly kept firing away through the deluge of cannon fire and bombs. Other navy jets plastered the supposed seat of Austin's military junta, Butler House, setting a raging fire. Despite the efforts of the Grenadian fire squads and their East German fire trucks, Butler House burned brightly. But Austin and his staff escaped. The navy planes had wreaked havoc, but the Grenadian gun crews still returned heavy fire. Another series of strikes were needed.

While the navy aviators rearmed, a pair of redoubtable Spectres flew up from Salines to help the SEALs keep the PRA armored vehicles and riflemen at bay. The ungainly gunships stood well away to avoid the hot reception that blackened the tropical skies over St. George's. Fortunately for the Americans, the enemy did not renew their aggressive actions around Scoon's domicile. Finally, around midafternoon, a second flight of heavily laden Corsair IIs bore in low, crossing the harbor to eliminate the stolid PRA air defenses east of St. George's. The small attack planes dumped 500-pound bombs, shot rockets, and strafed the entire ridge with 20-mm cannon shells. This effectively destroyed most of the Grenadian batteries. The scale of the American raids quelled PRA enthusiasm around the battered walls of Scoon's house. For the rest of the daylight hours, Grenada's capital lapsed into exhausted silence, broken by desultory shots and bursts from various small arms and machine guns. O'Shaughnessy and his Grenadian friends thought that perhaps a truce had been arranged. They could not have been more wrong.[56]

Fort Matthew in particular suffered major damage. Americans later learned that the old British installation had been converted into a mental hospital, and that the patients had been present during the strike. Twenty-one died, and many of the rest of the inhabitants of what Grenadians called the "Crazy House" wandered off into the streets of St. George's, half-clad, shocked, and mumbling incoherently. The site was marked on most maps as a hospital; why had it been flattened?

The American action, while regrettable, proved fully understandable. Independent investigations by U.S. Atlantic Command and a congressional committee absolved the navy fliers of any wrongdoing. Fort Matthew looked a lot like the other nearby hill fortifications. It displayed no hospital symbols; far from it. PRA antiaircraft positions dotted the area all around Fort Matthew, and a large Grenadian flag wafted over the structure. There is evidence that PRA troops on the rooftops of Fort Matthew engaged American helicopters and aircraft throughout 25 October.[57] Given the decision to employ fast-moving carrier planes in a heavily populated area, the fact that Fort Matthew was the only such mistake speaks well of the skill of U.S. naval aviators.

Even as the marines and navy dueled with PRA gunners over St. George's, the Rangers anxiously scanned the skies over Point Salines, waiting for the reinforcements of the 82nd Airborne Division to arrive. The Cubans and PRA had backed off; a trickle of quitters continued to dribble out of the low, white Calliste barracks. The Americans used the lull in active combat to send out patrols. A series of gun jeep teams were dispatched by 1-75 Rangers to locate enemy forces; one jeep succeeded all too well. As the wary Rangers entered an outdoor movie theater just northeast of Calliste, they were halted by a fusillade of automatic fire. Four of five Rangers died in the ambush.[58]

The actual runway situation at Point Salines remained marginal at best. The airstrip approach and landing lights had not yet been installed, and a jumble of obstacles and unfinished paving still rendered about a third of the macadam surface unusable. The narrow paved area and lack of true taxiways permitted only two aircraft to be on the runway simultaneously. In front of the unfinished terminal buildings, a maximum of two C-130s and one C-141 could off-load. Occasional mortar and automatic weapons shots impacted on the strip, which made things difficult for thin-skinned aircraft bulging with explosive aviation fuel. Smaller C-130s could and would be diverted to Pearls; big C-141Bs and C-5As had to wait their turn and use Point Salines.[59] Needless to say, this did not make for rapid delivery of sorely needed reinforcements and supplies.

The first group of inbound 82nd Airborne units all flew aboard four-engine jets—twenty-eight Starlifters and six Galaxies. Tension and concern aboard the planes made the four-hour flight unusually quiet. As with the Rangers and marines, many young paratroopers found the whole experience dreamlike and unreal. They had been alerted so many times just for practice. Now, with live rounds in their rifle magazines and fragmentation grenades strapped onto their load-carrying equipment belts and straps, the young "All-Americans" from Fort Bragg faced the possibility of a combat jump. All the C-141B planeloads left Pope Air Force Base, North Carolina, ready to conduct a parachute drop. The intercom crackled with updates: the Rangers had jumped in through heavy flak; the Cubans were putting up a stiff resistance; and most ominous of all, there had been American casualties. URGENT FURY obviously wasn't a training mission. About two hours out, word came that the 82nd Airborne troops would land in their aircraft. The officers and sergeants warned their excited men to expect heavy fire on the runway.[60]

If the paratroopers on the lead Starlifters expected action, they were not disappointed. The Cubans and their Grenadian allies chose to introduce the All-Americans to Grenada the hard way. The first four-engine jet touched down about 1405 in the afternoon. Within twenty minutes, as the initial few planeloads of airborne infantry from the 2nd Battalion, 325th Infantry, ran off the air force transports toward hasty defensive positions, the enemy launched a counterattack.

The paratroopers moved onto the ridge overlooking Calliste. The whistle of bullets and the crump of mortar rounds filled the air. Several unburied enemy bodies sprawled in the path of the All-Americans. Initially, many of the young riflemen did not crouch or zigzag as they moved, but a steady snapping of Cuban fire and shouted warnings from embattled Rangers soon convinced the new arrivals to employ proper crawling and rushing techniques. Just as the men of Company A, 2-325, began to discuss matters with Company A, 1-75 Rangers, the enemy struck.

From the Calliste compound, a fusillade of automatic firing split the air, and rounds thudded into the dirt all around the Rangers and the airborne troops. To their right rear, the men heard the sounds of heavy machine guns and roaring engines. Out of the jungle northeast of the Salines strip appeared three BTR-60 PB wheeled armored personnel carriers, rolling ahead at full tilt. Their big 14.5-mm machine guns blazed away.

Cuban Capt. Sergio Grandales-Nolasco led the PRA mechanized force, drawn from the southern regular Grenadian battalion. Perhaps he recognized that the uncontested arrival of the huge, fully loaded Starlifters marked the end of any realistic chances for a Cuban/PRA victory. So the Cuban armor expert apparently elected to crush the American buildup at the outset, or at least try to do so. If the ploy worked, a snarled runway, blocked American reinforcements, and heavy U.S. casualties might encourage an American turn toward a negotiated settlement. In any event, Grandales-Nolasco started the armored assault, moving directly toward the eastern end of the airstrip.

The Cuban commander chose a very opportune objective. His BTRs drove straight for the young medical students still staying at True Blue campus. Just as dangerous, from the edge of the runway, the wicked 14.5-mm guns could spray heavy slugs into the newly arrived American jet transports and the defenseless refueling equipment. Grandales-Nolasco's drive impacted close to the vulnerable 82nd/Ranger relief activities, a perfect fulcrum to break any military defense. The Cubans in Calliste generated powerful suppressive fires to tie down the Company B, 1-75 troops just north of the airport.

Once again, matters hung in the balance. The only available U.S. armor remained aboard the USS Manitowoc, far to the north. The lightly armed Rangers turned to face the rampaging enemy vehicles. Unlike most American infantry, who depend upon Dragon wire–guided antitank missiles (range 1,000 meters), the Rangers retained the older 90-mm recoilless rifle (range 450 meters). The 90-mm did not promise "one shot, one kill" like the Dragon, but the Dragons rarely lived up to that advertising, anyway. The 90-mm resembled a stovepipe, like the venerable bazooka of World War II. The Dragon, on the other hand, consisted of a small, detachable sight unit and a missile round with case. Only the sight was reusable. After each shot, a Dragon gunner had to get a new missile round. The 90-mm could shoot fast-moving projectiles as rapidly as they could be loaded, whereas each of the slow Dragon missiles had to be tracked for about ten seconds out to maximum range before the next could be mated to the sight and fired. Most useful of all, the 90-mm round armed about thirty meters out from the muzzle, but the Dragon armed at sixty-five meters and came under positive gunner control anywhere from ten to a hundred meters after that. In the small clearing northeast of True Blue, the Rangers had the more appropriate of the two antitank weapons.

The Company A, 1-75 Ranger antitank teams reacted magnificently. Despite skittering PRA machine gun shots, enemy mortar explosions, spinning fragments, and random ricochets, determined Ranger gunners sighted and engaged. The lead BTR slewed to a stop, holes punched into both sides. Ranger M-60 machine gun teams blasted away at the crew and on-board riflemen as they attempted to struggle clear. More 90-mm shots knocked into the second vehicle, which skidded to a halt trailing pieces. When the men inside climbed out, they too were cut down—killed or wounded by Ranger mortars and machine guns. The last BTR slowed and backed off, accelerating toward the tree line. The Rangers fired all their weapons at the withdrawing enemy, but the BTR pulled off, spitting return fire from its cupola 14.5-mm. It crossed the first row of trees, heading east.

By this time, the Rangers' helpers had come on the scene. A-7E Corsair IIs swooped down, 20-mm cannons tearing into the fleeing enemy armored personnel carrier and pumping more destruction into the two wrecked BTRs for good measure. The enemy vehicle swerved and sped up, heading away from the Point Salines runway. A Spectre arrived overhead and went into its trademark left turn. The gunship pivoted its 105-mm cannon and fired four perfectly timed shots into the BTR. That did the trick; the vehicle lurched and bucked, then lay still. A few soldiers fled the battered hull and melted into the jungle.[61]

The enemy counterattack had failed; Captain Grandales-Nolasco lay among the twisted corpses, the highest-ranking Cuban to die in Grenada. The end of this bitter little action saw a tense quiet descend around Salines, which would last until after nightfall. Just as the strong navy air strikes near St. George's had ended active enemy threats to the SEAL team at Government House, the destruction of the PRA armor caused a slackening in enemy resistance around Point Salines. During the lull, the Americans in the south used the interlude to withdraw the Rangers and replace them with the 82nd Airborne Division troops of 2-325. The Rangers would stand by for further special missions, commensurate with their extensive capabilities. Major General Edward Trobaugh, who commanded the 82nd Airborne Division, prepared to take command of southern Grenada.[62] With the assault over and sustained ground operations about to commence, JSOC no longer had a role.

By 1700, the airborne infantrymen displaced the Rangers, who withdrew to reserve positions on the small sand spits south of the runway.[63] Company B, 2-325, held the western half of the ridge overlooking Calliste; Company A, 2-325, defended the eastern portion. Company B, 2-505 (an attachment in place of the newly trained recruits of Company C, 2-325), supplanted 1-75 Rangers along the eastern end of the runway. The first six 105-mm howitzers, of 1-320 Artillery (Airborne), began to set up near the airfield. Although 3-235 Infantry was dribbling into Salines, the slow turnaround on the airstrip delayed their full arrival until 0245 on 26 October. Colonel Steve Silvasy's 2nd Brigade, 82nd Airborne Division, would not reach its full three infantry battalion strength until 2117 on 26 October. Second Brigade would fight on 26 October tired and understrength.

The airlift that brought the All-Americans also delivered the Caribbean Peacekeeping Force (CPF), under the command of Brigadier Rudyard Lewis of Barbados. Brigadier Lewis's men deployed near the runway and went to work processing and securing more than two hundred Cuban and PRA prisoners.[64] The glum Cubans wore disheveled civilian clothes rather than their standard uniforms, probably as part of a conscious Cuban decision to portray the engineer battalion as a civil labor gang. Just as Tortolo's affectation of civilian dress did not conceal his true profession, so the Cuban workers had proven altogether rather familiar with weaponry and tactics. In any case, the CPF provided valuable assistance with the many captives already in hand.

The relief of the austere Ranger command groups by the amply-staffed 82nd Airborne Division headquarters and the appearance of the CPF freed American intelligence interrogators from prisoner duties, and left them time to interview the patient young students at True Blue. Just before nightfall, the Americans discovered that a second student dormitory complex, filled with more than two hundred students, existed on Grand Anse Bay. Alert staff officers telephoned Grand Anse immediately and established communications with these young people, well behind Cuban and PRA lines. The students described the situation at Grand Anse campus as quiet, but noted that there were numerous armed Cubans and Grenadians around their area. A student ham radio operator supplemented the telephone communications and provided regular updates to the 82nd Airborne headquarters.[65] So the Americans had found about another third of the students. But how could they get to them? Imminent nightfall complicated the problem.

Grand Anse became the latest headache of several at JTF headquarters aboard USS *Guam*. Admiral Metcalf and his ground deputy, General Schwarzkopf, had been mulling over the unsettled situation in the south all afternoon. Obviously, some help was necessary, which accounted for the earlier commitment of navy and marine aircraft. Soon after 1200, Metcalf ordered the landing ships USS *Manitowoc* and USS *Fort Snelling*, with Company G, 2/8 Marines and its armor embarked, to start for the western side of Grenada. When the Sea Cobras and carrier air strikes did not break the enemy resistance in and south of St. George's, Metcalf directed the USS *Barnstable County* and his flagship *Guam* to join the move to the western side of the island. Company F, 2/8 Marines, and the helicopters of HMM-261 were told to stand by to fly in to a landing zone in the vicinity of St. George's. By 1400, JTF 120 adjusted the boundary line between the northern and southern zones to place St. George's within the marine area of responsibility. Lieutenant Colonel Ray Smith of 2/8 Marines left his deputy in charge of Company E at Pearls, supported by the landing ship USS *Trenton* and guided missile destroyer USS *Coontz*. The bulk of the BLT and its shipping headed for St. George's.

Moving the uncommitted marines had been the easy part of Metcalf's decision; where to land them remained the question. The helicopters could go almost anywhere, although some sites exceeded others in size and, hence, capacity for choppers. But the tanks had to come ashore by landing craft, and Metcalf wanted to employ his marine armor. Basically, there were three possibilities: land at Salines and join the airborne in an attack toward St. George's, land at Grand Anse and outflank Calliste, or land at Grand Mal and envelop the entire enemy regular force. Whatever the decision, it had to be in motion by dusk on 25 October. Metcalf could not afford to delay, lest the enemy use the breather to seize U.S. citizens as bargaining chips.

Two of the options offered few decisive advantages. Reinforcing Point Salines would be more of the same, and would waste the marines' amphibious capacity by dropping them in beside the air-landed paratroopers. A short hook to Grand Anse might solve the situation at Salines but would do little to take care of the unfinished business in St. George's. The plight of the SEALs at Scoon's home demanded some action; the grim air defense struggle on the afternoon of 25 October indicated the tenacity of the enemy defenders.

The third scheme held promise. The JTF commander envisioned a knockout blow with his five tanks and Company G's thirteen armored AAVs full of marine infantry (one AAV stayed at Pearls, having wallowed ashore in a treacherous confirmation of ST-4's beach reconnaissance). This horizontal push could go in at dusk along Grand Mal Bay, near the Texaco oil pipeline. Metcalf intended to strengthen the horizontal attack with a simultaneous vertical strike by Company F. The company would fly across the Spice Island's spine under cover of darkness, landing in an open area just behind the beach.

This attack could deliver maximum effect on the three enemy battalions congregated in St. George's and the Calliste area. It would amount to a long hook, coming through the back door, saving the SEALs and Scoon, and putting armor in the Cuban/PRA rear as the 82nd pushed hard on the enemy front door through Calliste. Best of all, the envelopment would seize the communications nodes in St. George's and cut off enemy withdrawal. If the concept worked, there would be few PRA or Cubans escaping from the U.S. pincers.

There was no time for proper SEAL reconnaissance; anything less surreptitious endangered tactical surprise. Fortuitously, Comdr. Richard Butler, Amphibious Squadron 4 chief of staff, enjoyed small-boat sailing and had visited Grand Mal Bay on one of his ventures. Commander Butler's detailed recollections allowed reliable plans to be drawn up.[66] Even as the Company G marines staged for the assault, Metcalf received word of the discovery at Grand Anse. Trobaugh thought that the students were safe, and hoped that the planned dawn ground attack by the 82nd Airborne could rescue them. If not, Trobaugh always had the Rangers; the 2nd Battalion, 75th Infantry was largely unscathed and ready for action. Metcalf saw even more cause to hurry.

As night fell, the American forces in Grenada redeployed to meet the following day's ambitious objectives. Although there were still a few viable special missions to be done, General Scholtes's JSOC left the area effective 1900 on 25 October, turning over operational control of both Ranger battalions to Trobaugh. By the next morning, the two

Ranger companies, detached for the 25 October Delta raid, were back with their parent units. The SEALs in St. George's fell under Colonel Faulkner's 22nd MAU, and received word of the intended linkup with the marines of BLT 2/8. Around Point Salines, the paratroopers and Rangers shivered in a driving rain and exchanged nervous gunfire with Cubans down in Calliste. Greenish white enemy tracers mixed with the red American varieties as the fighting flared and died in the steamy night.[67]

Why had JSOC pulled out, with students to rescue and SEALs in peril? The real rationale remains classified, but four potential reasons come to mind. First, the Delta and 160th Aviation elements had been mauled on 25 October and were not really ready for commitment at Grand Anse or St. George's. Other JSOC forces already had missions underway. Second, the remaining "special" missions had major conventional components and were better handled by the airborne and marines. Third, JSOC constituted a national resource, and with Lebanon in turmoil and Central America always a question mark, this unique command element could not get bogged down in a sustained campaign. Terrorist acts in response to the U.S. incursion in Grenada might require a rapid response. Finally, although JSOC left, portions of special operations forces (SEALs, Rangers, 1st SOW) remained near at hand for particular tasks as necessary. JSOC had done what they could. Now it was up to the line battalions.

As for the enemy, they were still full of fight. The PRA, particularly the air defense batteries, had held their own in St. George's. PRA infantry pocketed the little SEAL team in Government House. Near Point Salines, PRA riflemen and Cuban engineers had contained the Americans at the airstrip. Word of their bold armored attack had spread across the island like electricity, at least among the regulars. At Pearls, the Americans seemed content to hold the airport and Grenville. Since midafternoon, the major fighting had died down as the Americans reorganized for their new operations. To the enemy, it looked like hesitancy. But it was merely the calm before the storm.

Hugh O'Shaughnessy described a confident Grenadian soldier on the warm night of 25 October: "The PRA corporal recounted with great pride, though not total accuracy, that the PRA and the Cubans had succeeded in recapturing parts of Point Salines airport and that, with the city of St. George's still in Grenadian hands, the invaders were confined to Pearls airport and the adjacent town of Grenville." [68]

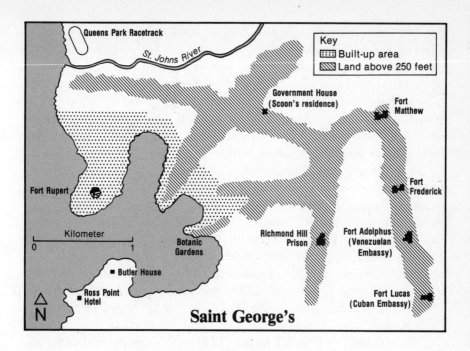

For the Americans—the Rangers collapsed in slumber in their reserve position, the tense paratroopers on the line at Salines, the Company G marines in their plunging amphibious assault vehicles off Grand Anse, or the weary Spectre crews circling lazily overhead—the rainy night of 25 October found them up to their necks in a place most of them had never heard of before. For many, Capt. Jim Zazas of the 317th TAW offered a summary of that eerie evening: "The sight was incredible. You could see Spectre firing down on the hillside and you could see fire coming back up. You could see a building burning and mortar and 105-mm rounds hitting on the hillside. It was kind of dreamlike, but you were not afraid. My own concern was 'Okay, let's get the combat entry checklist complete. Let's get the descent checklist complete, let's keep flying the airplane.' But I was mesmerized by the scene in the hills. I was thinking this is just like a scene out of a movie." [69]

The great envelopment began at about 1900. The *Manitowoc* dropped anchor about a half mile west of Grand Mal Bay and slowly swung its stern toward the beach. The rear ramp opened, and over the next two minutes, thirteen of the bulky, slab-sided AAVs plopped into the water. Dipping and rolling along at seven knots, the big craft crawled onto the glistening sand at about 1930, just as an indigo twilight began to deepen into a muggy, cloudy night. *Fort Snelling* sent her landing craft ashore, with the five throaty, clattering M-60 tanks, by 2000. Even though a few tanks bogged a bit in the soft sand dunes, the marines arrived in good order.[70] Commander Butler's memories of Grand Mal served his amphibious squadron well.

With the tanks and Company G at Grand Mal, the marines prepared to execute the vertical phase of their push into the enemy rear. The marines planned to attack at 0400, so they sent out small patrols to verify their route into St. George's. So far, there had been no opposition and no sign that the PRA knew of the marine landing. Most of the enemy's attention seemed fixed on the sporadic firefights rippling around the Point Salines perimeter. Lieutenant Colonel Ray Smith flew down to join Company G at about 2330, aboard a hedge-hopping UH-1N Huey. Once on the ground, the BLT commander began to refine his tactical plan.

The arrival of Company F by air would serve to reinforce the strength of the marine operation. With the help of HMM-261 aviators, Smith chose a small clearing as Landing Zone Fuel. LZ Fuel lay within the Company G position. Like most Grenadian LZs, this open patch could barely accommodate a single CH-46E Frog at a time. Smith intended to insert Company F into that constricted location, commencing about 0300.[71]

As the marines readied their jab into the Grenadian and Cuban rear, Admiral Metcalf sent a 0200 message to the Joint Chiefs of Staff, explaining the situation on the Spice Island. Metcalf detailed his planned envelopment, then noted that he hoped to begin withdrawing rescued Americans and friendly foreigners as soon as possible. The JTF commander requested another 82nd Airborne brigade.[72]

Metcalf knew that it would take a few days to get the extra All-Americans, especially given the bottleneck at Point Salines. It appears that the JTF commander and his staff had confidence about winning the conventional battle with the forces on hand. Based upon the serious resistance encountered on the first day, however, an enemy retreat into the hills and rain forests seemed a distinct possibility. With the additional army troops, Metcalf could conduct the sort of thorough search for fragments of shattered enemy units that would preclude a long-term insurgency. Coincidentally, deployment of another army brigade would return the Rangers to the United States for future JSOC contingencies and free the marines to continue their journey to relieve their decimated fellows in tumultuous Beirut.

The JTF plan for 26 October amounted to a nutcracker, with the Cubans and Austin's army as the nut. The armored thrust from the north, timed for 0400, would pull enemy attention to the rear. Taking advantage of this, the 2nd Brigade, 82nd Airborne Division (2-325, 3-325, and most of 1-320 Artillery), aimed to attack the Calliste region at 0630, catching the enemy looking backward or at least tying down the bulk of Cuban/PRA forces. With the enemy pulled north to St. George's and south to Calliste, the American students at Grand Anse would remain unmolested in the vacuum created in the middle of the southwestern area. Hopefully, these students could be secured by army ground thrusts. Just to be certain, Metcalf's staff maintained telephone and ham radio contact with the student community. If things did not work out, the JTF could mount a dedicated rescue attempt. Metcalf thought that these ambitious maneuvers would break enemy resistance.

The admiral's high hopes for 26 October proved well-founded. At 0245, the marines of Company F formed in the oppressive humidity of the island night, walking slowly across LZ Oriole in Grenville toward the blacked-out forms of HMM-261's helicopter fleet. The lead Frog lifted off at 0300, skirting low over the Grand Etang lake under scudding clouds. Using night vision goggles, the marine fliers looked for a UH-1N Pathfinder helo that led them into the tiny landing zone. It took until 0530 to get all of Company F into the little clearing.[73]

Meanwhile, Company G pushed rapidly south for St. George's, kicking off right on schedule at 0400. The rumbling marine armored column raced along Grand Mal beach, and the tanks pulled up short at the Queen's Park racetrack to cover Company G's approach to Government House. As the sun rose, marine Sea Cobras came on station in close support.

Only the most scattered sniping hindered the marines. The marines went slowly once they reached the built-up area. They were not exactly sure how to get to Scoon's house, and occasional gunshots echoed in the nearly deserted, twisting streets. When Company G's lead elements reached Government House, they found Sir Paul Scoon, his wife, nine staff members, and twenty-two tired but defiant SEALs. The marines quickly moved the little party to an open area for helicopter withdrawal to the *Guam*.

Company F moved down to Queen's Park, which became the new marine LZ. The marching marines moved forward to Gretna Green, the roll of high ground overlooking Fort Rupert and the harbor. Elated by the dearth of resistance and the early successes, Lieutenant Colonel Smith ordered his reconnaissance platoon to push south to Fort Rupert and Company G (now on foot) to press their attack toward the enemy command post at Fort Frederick.[74]

The men of 2/8 Marines heard few bullets clattering off the streets and buildings of St. George's. As at Grenville and Pearls, the BLT enjoyed good fortune. Most of the enemy fled rather than fought. Staff Sergeant Joseph Covella of Company F described the oddly bloodless marine role: "We haven't fired too many rounds at all. We've just gone from town to town, collecting weapons and prisoners."

The mighty M-60 tanks certainly played a part. As their platoon commander, 1st Lt. Peter M. Walton, remarked: "Tanks are a presence. We fired a couple of rounds when we first got here."[75] Military men often talk about the shock effect of armor; the marines of BLT 2/8 saw it in action.

The marines were not slowed by any enemy; rather, they advanced deliberately due to the joyous welcome that welled into the streets of St. George's. Grenadian civilians treated the marines as liberators. Some of this had been seen in Grenville and in the few villages right near Point Salines, but the marines in St. George's received treatment that rivaled the scenes in 1944 France.

The people of St. George's brought food and drinks, offered information about the PRA, and some volunteered to fight alongside the Americans against the "thugs and criminals" who had murdered Maurice Bishop and dozens of innocent citizens on 19 October. Homemade American flags sprouted everywhere. The happy crowds shouted "God Bless America," and similar sentiments appeared on posters and on wall graffiti. The Grenadians expressed nothing but contempt for the PRA. Almost everyone said that they despised Austin; a popular rumor accused the Cubans of bestiality with the island's sheep flocks.[76] The flood of kindness and gratitude limited the marines' drive toward the hill forts, and the BLT headquarters could barely cope with the long lines of Grenadians who came to identify PRA fugitives and arms cache locations.

What happened to the enemy? The same Grenadians who had fought so well on 25 October disintegrated completely the next day. Hugh O'Shaugnessy watched the PRA unravel. They had held up under the air strikes on the first day, but the reports of marine tanks and amphibious assault vehicles, plus the clatter of helicopters that went on much of the night north of the capital, convinced many PRA soldiers that resistance was hopeless. O'Shaugnessy saw many Grenadian soldiers strip off their uniforms and run away.

American tanks and helicopters alone did not precipitate the collapse. The PRA possessed RPG-7 antitank weapons and Soviet-made antitank guns, not to mention BTR armored fighting vehicles of their own. PRA antiaircraft batteries had already shown great skill and determination. So they had the means of resistance. By the second day, what they lacked was the will.

Three factors generated the PRA collapse. First, and most important, the island population did not support the Grenadian regulars and the Cuban "socialist brothers." When it became obvious that the militia had not mobilized, and that, in truth, the civilians saw the Americans as rescuers, the Grenadian revolutionary leaders knew they were finished. There could be no "people's war" against the Americans. Indeed, the people's war seemed to be aimed directly at Austin's PRA.

Second, the enemy leadership did not exercise much personal influence. The individual soldiers and junior officers of the PRA and Cuban forces displayed competence and courage against powerful U.S. attacks. Captain Grandales-Nolasco showed the potential aggressiveness of boldly led Cubans and Grenadians. But the senior PRA and Cuban commanders deserted their embattled units. General Austin fled for the hills with his staff officers almost as soon at the Americans landed. Colonel Tortolo ran for the Soviet Embassy at Morne Rouge when the Rangers parachuted into Salines. Tortolo's cowardice led to bitter jokes among the Cubans about the Cuban colonel's prospects as an Olympic sprinter for the 1984 games, and some said that Tortolo could endorse a line of running shoes, guaranteed to carry one swiftly to safety.[77] Colonel Sazhenev, who had encouraged Austin's coup, sat calmly in his embassy throughout the invasion. When the going got tough, the enemy commanders got up and left.

Third, the Americans did their best to capitalize on the cracks in Grenadian unity. Military actions, strikes on enemy command facilities, and propaganda all played a part. Metcalf consciously limited the use of indiscriminate firepower, and the Americans used troops, not artillery or air strikes, to clear contested ground. As a result, Americans fought right through the most heavily populated parts of Grenada without devastating these areas. Except for the twenty-one killed at Fort Matthew, only three Grenadian civilians died as a result of stray rounds. Use of Sea Cobras and Spectres to deliver precise fires greatly limited property damage. The Grenadians had suffered much more from Austin's soldiers and the Cubans than from the U.S. forces.

From the outset, the Americans targeted key command installations. They silenced Radio Free Grenada, which truncated the militia activation. American attack jets blasted Butler House, Fort Rupert, and Fort Frederick, derailing enemy attempts to coordinate their defenses. The resultant confusion fueled public distrust of their revolutionary military rulers.

Finally, American psychological warfare units established "Radio Spice Island" to spread news of the U.S. intervention. They printed leaflets to inform the public and safe-conduct passes to encourage defections from the enemy army. The U.S. propaganda cleverly avoided criticism of Maurice Bishop (no friend of America) and instead portrayed the charismatic leader as a martyr to Soviet, Cuban, and radical Grenadian oppression.[78] This approach succeeded far better than a more heavy-handed critique of the Bishop era.

Unpopular, abandoned by their senior commanders, and undermined by calculated American measures, the PRA fell apart. The marine assault from Grand Mal merely hastened the end and accelerated the entropy that shook the enemy defenses.

To the south, the 82nd Airborne met much tougher opposition. Probably, the intermittent communications with the capital precluded knowledge of the marine units loose in St. George's, or the crack-up of the PRA battalion in that area. When the All-Americans began their push into Calliste at 0630, the enemy did not fall apart. Stiffened by the remaining Cubans, the PRA infantry fell back grudgingly. In accord with Metcalf's guidance to General Trobaugh, the paratroopers took care to eliminate enemy pockets before moving north. Nobody wanted a repeat performance of Grandales-Nolasco's armored counterattack.

Caution did not preclude casualties. In the predawn darkness, Captain Michael Ritz of Company B, 2-325 Infantry led a small reconnaissance party forward to establish a good location for his company's base of fire platoon. Moving slowly through the dank, dripping undergrowth,

Ritz and his men topped the ridge directly into the sights of a startled Cuban security post. Green tracers spat into the night, punching Ritz to the ground with a mortal head wound, bowling Sergeant Terry Guinn backward with a hole torn in his chest, and leaving 2nd Lieutenant Mike Seeger alone with a wounded NCO and a missing commander. As medics rushed up to help Guinn, Seeger and his platoon stormed up the blackened hillside. The paratroopers killed the Cubans and took the hill for their base of fire, but Ritz was dead, his body temporarily lost in the lush foliage on the enemy side of the steep incline. Platoon leader 1st Lieutenant Jim Bowen assumed command of the company under the toughest possible conditions.

With their commander lost, lesser troops might well have faltered at the outset of their attack. Despite the costly clash on the high ground, Company B, 2-325 left the western half of the Salines ridge on schedule at 0630 and pushed toward Calliste, overwatched by Company A, 2-325. Almost immediately, the maneuvering company ran into trouble as they came down the vegetated slope toward the low white barracks.

As they came down the ridge toward the barracks, Corporal Raymond Knepper's fire team was in the lead. Knepper recounted his first moments under heavy fire: "We were slowed down even more by automatic fire on a ridge covered with waist-high grass and bushes so dense you couldn't see into them. We couldn't determine the exact location of fire, so our grenadiers began putting M-203 HE [high explosive] rounds 15 to 20 meters in front of us." [79]

Company A opened up from its vantage on the eastern half of the Salines ridge line. The Americans hosed the compound with M-60 machine guns, rifles, grenade launchers, and mortars, which allowed Company B to advance. Cuban return fire and some infiltrators challenged the busy infantrymen of Company A. Sergeant Patrick O'Kelley watched a paratrooper come face to face with the enemy: "A Cuban and he saw each other at the same time. He brought his weapon up, but the Cuban fired first, wounding him in the arm, and knocking him over backwards. He yelled over to a buddy that he was hit. The buddy said, 'You're kidding.' 'No, I'm really hit,' he cried." [80]

American artillery observers began to bring a few 105-mm shells toward the enemy compound. At first, the high explosives popped beyond the enemy barracks; then, gradually, they moved closer and closer. One

sheaf of artillery shells crashed into a warehouse, setting off an ammunition explosion. Soldiers set another storage building afire with M-203
grenade launchers, and more Cuban explosives and cartridge canisters
erupted. Tracers spat crazily into the air, and chunks of the ruined buildings
tumbled up and away, bouncing to uneven landings many feet distant.

Two A-7E Corsair IIs flashed overhead, inbound from the USS *Independence*. The jets' cannons tore up strips of grass and sod in front of
the Cuban structures, then ripped through the cement blocks like chain-
saws. Pieces of buildings collapsed. The American firepower concentrated
on the Cuban compound, and the enemy soldiers in the buildings and
around their foundations started to merely lift their automatic rifles and
spray blindly at the advancing paratroopers. The U.S. infantry pushed
forward under the enemy fire. Fixed bayonets tipped the American rifles.

O'Kelley described the finale of the big firefight, as he shot at a
troublesome Cuban sniper: ''The head came up and I put it down. He
saw the A-7s coming in, and ran for the door. The ground around him
turned into dust and his head disappeared into a red mist as he flew
through the door. The M-60 fired at him, and so did all the snipers.
The next pass [by the A-7s] blew out the side of a building, knocking
down the Cuban flag. B Company (2-325) fired a LAW [light antitank
weapon, a small shoulder-fired rocket] into the side of another building.
A white flag popped out of the window, and the order was given to
cease fire.'' [81] The paratroopers began to round up their prisoners.

One American sergeant died, and eight others in Knepper's platoon
suffered wounds. Knepper noted: ''Seeing them gave me a realistic effect
of the enemy's firepower. It was a little scary.'' But the paratroopers
had given a good account of themselves. In a few hours, they had
taken the infamous Calliste barracks, killing sixteen Cubans and capturing
eighty-six more. Only two U.S. soldiers died, and no American aircraft
were lost. It took most of the rest of the morning to insure that Calliste
was really clear. After all, Cubans had been alternately fighting and
surrendering at the barracks since the Rangers arrived. The paratroopers
were thorough, although regular pops of small arms and snorts of machine
gun fire from the ridges to the north interrupted their search activities.[82]

The smashing U.S. success at St. George's and the hard-won victory
at Calliste did much to deflate the Cuban and PRA resistance. In the
capital, the enemy had fled, pursued by their own people as much as
by the marine tanks. At Calliste, the grim young All-Americans went

in and dug out the Cubans in toe-to-toe close combat. All that remained was to secure the American students at Grand Anse.

Reports from Grand Anse indicated that the American ground attacks had tied up the Cubans and PRA, but that the Calliste operations were pushing the remaining hostile units back toward the campus. Waiting for a ground linkup might be more dangerous than a helicopter-borne rescue. Metcalf, with Schwarzkopf's sound advice, issued orders to Major General Trobaugh at 1100: rescue the students at Grand Anse.[83] The JTF commander gave the 82nd Airborne until 1600 to begin the operation.

The 82nd Airborne Division had been deeply involved in the ground battle around Calliste, and the priority Grand Anse tasking forced Trobaugh to turn most of the ground fighting over to Colonel Silvasy's 2nd Brigade headquarters. Trobaugh's own 82nd Combat Aviation Battalion had not yet arrived, so Metcalf assigned HMM-261 to fly the rescuers to and from Grand Anse. Metcalf promised Trobaugh any other JTF assets needed to conduct the mission. It was up to the 82nd Airborne to design and coordinate the raid. Time, of course, was very short.

Trobaugh and his staff created a scheme that made good use of the various available resources. The 82nd Airborne picked Lt. Col. Ralph Hagler and his 2-75 Rangers to carry out the mission. The 1-75 Rangers led the parachute drop and fought the main engagements near Salines, with 2-75 in a largely supporting role. The 2-75 took no losses on 25 October. Hagler's men itched to make a major contribution to American victory on Grenada. When Trobaugh chose them to conduct the rescue, 2-75 had their big chance. Hagler and his staff selected Company C to bring out the students, with elements of Companies A and B to secure the campus during the extraction.

Trobaugh, with input from Hagler and the marine aviators, planned a surprise air assault. Student radio and phone messages reported about sixty enemy troops (largely PRA) entrenched just south of the campus, with three antiaircraft weapons in view. The enemy units faced south. Corsair II attack jets, Spectres, marine Sea Cobras, and 105-mm barrages from 1-320 Artillery at Point Salines would precede and support the raid. Second Brigade's paratroopers intended to attack north to keep the enemy tied down, and the infantry mortars could also aid in fire support. Once the enemy had been fully engaged, Trobaugh wanted to send in CH-46E Frogs to drop off the Ranger security force and then use the big CH-53D Sea Stallions to remove the students. Direct discussions between Lieutenant Colonel Amos of HMM-261 and Hagler of the Rangers prior to takeoff insured a smooth operation.

The 82nd Airborne staff gave the American students helpful directions to prepare them for the assault. The officers told the students to assemble in a certain building, nearest the narrow beach. They asked the students to gather in one large room on the ocean side, and cautioned them to place mattresses over the windows to block out shell fragments. Warned by ham radio and telephone, the young people complied.

At about 1600, the Ranger/marine assault force lifted off from Salines, heading west over the ocean, then curving back toward Grand Anse. A Sea Cobra escort reluctantly dropped back with a major hydraulic failure. As the raiding force left the Spice Island, two A-7E light bombers raced across the Grand Anse area, strafing the enemy fighting positions just to the south of the campus. The 2-325 Infantry, already embroiled in a stiff action around Morne Rouge, fired mortar shells in support of the air assault. The 1-320 Artillery unloaded a precisely timed cluster of high explosives atop the hapless Grenadians. A lumbering Spectre pumped cannon shells directly into the dug-in PRA troops, and one Sea Cobra peppered the Grenadians with rockets, 20-mm cannon shots, and even TOW antitank missiles employed as bunker busters. The Sea Cobra and Spectre loitered as the HMM-261 choppers slid in just above the surf.

The landing zone, like all the others, proved to be very small. Nine twin-engine Frogs alighted in fairly quick succession, the Rangers ran off, and then the marine helos pulled up and off to a holding orbit out over the water. Two of the long-bodied Frogs damaged their rotor blades on nearby palm trees but kept flying. One CH-46E broke a blade on a tree and took bullet damage, sinking back into the sand, useless. Its crew left on another helicopter.

Sporadic enemy fire rang out across the narrow LZ. The Rangers spread out their security teams, and these men set up Claymore command-detonated mines and prepared LAWs for firing. They soon found themselves hotly engaged with the PRA infantry. A careening pair of Volkswagens spun toward Company B's northern half of the ring, with passengers shooting long, inaccurate bursts of AK-47 rounds into the Ranger positions. Heavy U.S. return firing drove off this odd foray.

Meanwhile, Company C moved to the beachside dormitory and found the students safe, happy, and prepared exactly as the 82nd Airborne had requested. The four huge Sea Stallions popped quickly in and out of the constricted LZ. Cool, watchful Rangers hustled the American civilians aboard each in turn, with PRA bullets pinging all around. The Rangers packed the students into the large helicopters. In the words of Capt. Mark Hanna: "They were crammed in like sardines." One of the transport helos lifted off with angry overload lights blinking all over the instrument panel.

The PRA infantry pressed the Rangers with greater intensity as they saw the evacuation commence. Hostile mortar fire began to fall on the LZ, and the last CH-53D landed in a crooked open spot directly near the dorm building to expedite the withdrawal. Grenadian automatic weapons fire ripped out pieces of the final Sea Stallion. Ranger security platoons and marine door gunners returned fire. The single Sea Cobra and its big brother Spectre beat back the enemy. Nevertheless, the volume of PRA shooting increased dramatically.

With the hostages safe, the eight remaining Frogs came back from their orbit point. The Ranger security elements withdrew deliberately, drawing back by fire and maneuver from their semicircle. Mortar shells burst furiously around the marine aviators, but they and their Ranger passengers stayed calm, finished the loading, and took off. The entire operation lasted twenty-six minutes. Not a single student, Ranger, or marine had been hurt or killed. As Hagler later said, Grand Anse was a "classic Ranger mission." [84] The Rangers saved 224 grateful Americans.

There were postscripts, stemming from the loss of the CH-46E. A dozen Rangers stayed behind, unable to fit in the available helicopters. In accord with their contingency plan, these elite infantrymen exfiltrated out to sea aboard a captured boat after darkness, where they met U.S. Navy elements. As the Rangers headed into the jungle, the AC-130H Spectre shot up the grounded Frog to prevent the use of the equipment by the enemy. Spectre and 1-320 Artillery battered the PRA positions again just for good measure. [85]

Even as Hagler's tough young riflemen snatched the American civilians from under PRA noses, both the marines in St. George's and the paratroopers in Calliste continued their attacks. In both cases, opposition seemed disjointed.

Marines from Company G took Fort Frederick about 1630, and the reconnaissance platoon moved into Fort Rupert by 1700. The marines stopped to search these facilities and began to process the deluge of intelligence data delivered by Grenadian well-wishers. With virtually no sign of the PRA regulars, Smith ordered his men to stop for the night.[86] The marines had been operating continuously for almost two straight days and nights.

The marines did not spend an entirely quiet night. Outside Fort Frederick, the Company G outposts detected movement after midnight. The marine mortars had very few illumination shells, so the company called for illumination from a navy destroyer (probably USS *Caron*). Although the marine spotters could see the ship's silhouette out to the west, they could not get radio contact. The BLT 2/8 naval gunfire liaison officer helped out, and received permission from the 22nd MAU headquarters to shoot. The destroyer double-checked, then fired about six minutes after the original request. The round sighed overhead and hit the dark hills east of Grenada with a dull, distant thud. After this dud, Company G asked for a repeat shot. Once again, the checks and counterchecks ate up about six minutes. Another shot whizzed over, another thud sounded, and still no light. After another six-minute drill, the third round worked. Sometime during this period, an alert marine with a LAW blew out the side of a lurking BTR-60PB, although the PRA squad aboard escaped.[87]

South of the marines, the 2nd Brigade, 82nd Airborne Division, took the sprawling arms storage site at Frequente. The afternoon had been marred by a grueling push up the steep hill north of Calliste. Every man bore heavy rucksacks full of ammunition, and bulky flak jackets slowed movement. Heat began to take its toll, along with a dearth of sleep and a lack of solid food. Many paratroopers had discarded their combat meals to carry more ammunition. Water ran short, and troops searched isolated houses for wells and rain barrels. Sergeant O'Kelley summarized the afternoon: "Move, rest until you could move again, then struggle up the hill some more. We were sucking wind."

The 2-325 Infantry jumped its attached Company B, 2-505, around Sergeant O'Kelley and his friends in Company A. Company A had maneuvered almost north of Frequente, and looked down on the big supply depot. They covered the Company B, 2-505 attack, and watched men of the maneuvering force knock out a menacing BTR with LAW rockets. To the north, they saw and heard the hurricane of fire at Grand Anse. The attached paratroopers of Company B finished their attack after dusk, in a splatter of exploding ammunition and blazing storage sheds.[88] With the Frequente arms and supplies under American control, there was not much chance that enemy resistance could be sustained.

Wary All-Americans, hardened by a long day chasing the enemy in the lush, steamy greenery and backbreaking hills, tied in their lines for the night. The 3-325 Infantry, which had been moving on the eastern flank of 2-325, sent out patrols to prevent infiltration. Young riflemen, like Pfc Gregory L. Kimm of Company C, 3-325 Infantry, walked slowly through the jungle: "My squad was trying to link up with another company at dusk. I kept thinking the road we were on was a great place for snipers or an ambush." [89] By the evening of 26 October, the time for ambushes was nearly over. The Americans didn't know it yet, but the enemy had given up.

Although the PRA rank and file and most of the Cubans knew the end had come, it took the Americans another day to be sure. On 27 October, Metcalf ordered his ground forces to continue their ongoing operations. The marines planned to secure the rest of the St. George's area, to include Richmond Hill prison and the moribund Cuban Embassy near Fort Lucas. The 82nd Airborne, now up to three battalions of infantry, aimed to move north to the outskirts of St. George's. Metcalf shifted the boundary again, just south of St. George's. He hoped for a linkup on 27 October.

There was one possible problem. Company G's seizure of Fort Frederick had yielded a trove of documents, and a few of these papers indicated that Cuban strength on Grenada equaled two engineer battalions, about 1,100 men. When informed of this report, Metcalf and his staff checked with the marines and army, neither of which had seen any evidence of such a large number of active Cubans.[90] Preliminary analysis indicated that the unlocated Cuban battalion might well be at Calvigny barracks, the only major enemy installation as yet untaken. General Trobaugh received the mission to take Calvigny.

Meanwhile, the marines attacked south toward Fort Lucas. Company G took Richmond Hill by 0800 and found it empty. The political prisoners had walked out freely in the mass confusion of 26 October, according to one of the former captives, attorney Lloyd Noel. The marines approached Fort Adolphus, and observed an unfamiliar flag flying. The company commander considered calling for supporting fires and launching an assault, but thought better of it. His scouts confirmed his judgment when Adolphus turned out to be the Venezuelan Embassy. The marines checked to make sure all was well, then moved south around 0900.

At Fort Lucas, the marines found the Cuban Embassy. Despite the protests of Ambassador Julian Torres-Rizo, the Americans eventually removed all the staff and searched the old fortress. They found three RPG launchers, rockets, forty-nine M-16 rifles (courtesy of North Vietnam), and forty AK-47 automatic rifles, plus a million rounds of small arms ammunition, not to mention plenty of sophisticated radio transmission equipment.[91] The marines remained in place after 0950, awaiting the army troops of 3-325 Infantry.

Lieutenant Colonel Ray Smith replaced Company F at Queen's Park with H Battery, 3/10 Marines, organized as infantry. The marine gunners took charge of the swollen marine prisoner camp, freeing Company F to drive along the harbor front toward Ross Point. Company F cleared the Botanic Gardens, aided by numerous Grenadian civilians.

Guided by civilians, Company F apprehended the People's Revolutionary Army chief of operations, who provided some valuable insights. He stated that the scale and ferocity of the initial U.S. landings had shocked the Cuban and PRA commanders. More of interest to the BLT leadership, the PRA officer said that a staff meeting held around midnight on 25 October, with the marines ashore at Grand Mal, had resulted in a general opinion that it would be "suicide to fight the Marines." [92]

At Pearls, Company E stirred from its routine of local patrols and civic action projects to attack enemy facilities at Mount Horne. Based upon interrogation of a captured militia commander, the marines expected to find a large weapons cache. Mounted in jeeps and four borrowed civilian trucks, the marines moved out. The agriculture experimental station turned out to be full of anything but seeds and fertilizer. Instead, it was a battalion arms depot for the local militia. Company E secured the site at 1422. When an enemy patrol attempted to intervene, MAU commander Colonel Faulkner recalled, "The Marines banged up that squad to a point that they headed the other way." [93]

In the south, the lead elements of 3rd Brigade landed at 0930, aboard C-130s staged through the invaluable Grantley-Adams Airport on Barbados. Brigadier General Robert Patterson of USAF Military Airlift Command took charge of the immense air transport effort. Aside from troops heading in, grateful American civilians began to leave Grenada. Air Force Reserve pilot Maj. Charles D. Ethredge flew out the first group of happy American students aboard his 315th Military Airlift Wing Starlifter.[94] While television cameras beamed live pictures all over America, some of these young people kissed the runway at Charleston Air

Force Base, South Carolina, upon their arrival. They had fulsome praise for their deliverers.

Meanwhile, combat operations proceeded north of Frequente. The 2nd Brigade pressed north, with 2-325 near the ocean and 3-325 just inside the north-south valley to the east, in the overgrown Ruth Howard area. As the airborne closed on St. George's, they ran into clusters of small villages. In 2-325's zone, house clearance continued all day long.

The paratroopers had a scare when Company B crossed in front of Company A, 2-325, although it got sorted out. The battalion ground slowly north through successive hamlets. Company A passed the blackened rubble of the auxiliary radio transmission station and the scattered wreckage left from the Grand Anse raid. Meanwhile, the trail element of Company B attracted the unexpected attention of frustrated Russians. Furtive Soviet automatic riflemen emerged from their bypassed embassy and stung the surprised All-Americans, wounding two airborne men. They then retreated into their compound.

Captain Dave Lamm, commander of Headquarters Company, 2-325 Infantry, quickly brought up a security team to clamp down on the aggressive Russians while his battalion pushed onward. Lamm barged into the embassy and warned the Soviets to stay inside. He and his men then took up watch outside the silent compound. Hours passed. Suddenly, an envoy emerged. Could the American send water? Lamm complied immediately, but the wary Soviet would not take the proffered liquid until Lamm drank some first. [94]

An unpleasant event marred 2nd Brigade's generally routine drive to the north. The 2nd Brigade's Tactical Operations Center (TOC) followed behind 3-325 Infantry and coordinated the operation. They occupied a series of small housing areas. Regular reports and orders hummed across the TOC radios, and staff sections posted their battle maps. Suddenly, the headquarters paratroopers found themselves under attack by friendly aircraft. Sixteen airborne soldiers suffered wounds in the erroneous pass. One artillery radio operator lost his legs, and a signalman died months later from severe injuries. Amazingly, the fighting units never knew about the misdirected air strike. As company commander Charles Jacoby (A, 2-325) pointed out: "The brigade TOC never missed a beat; they hung right in there and kept control."

Later investigation disclosed that a combination of faulty map reading by the navy/marine ground spotters and mistaken target identification by A-7E pilots caused the incident. The observers had taken fire from a building close to the brigade TOC area, and called in four Corsair IIs to deal with the enemy position. All friendly units received orders to throw out colored smoke. The TOC, being a headquarters element and not suspecting it was about to become part of the front lines, threw no smoke. When the lead jet rolled in at treetop level, it was traveling at more than 400 knots. The pilot saw the TOC structure first, noted no smoke, and fired away. The spotter, seeing the mistake, called an instant cease-fire. The other three navy jets pulled off. A-6E Intruders later destroyed the actual target with accurate Mark 20 Rockeye high-drag bombs, after a confirming low pass. Naval investigators held no one responsible for the accidental strafing.[96]

Even as Captain Lamm enjoyed his drink and the 2nd Brigade Tactical Operations Center picked up the pieces, General Trobaugh and Lieutenant Colonel Hagler planned their raid on Calvigny. Indicators were vague, but another Cuban unit could be holed up there. The Americans elected to find out once and for all. This time, the 82nd CAB's tough, fast UH-60A Blackhawk helicopters would carry the Rangers. The choppers flew in from Barbados as the officers made their plans. A scant half hour after the last of the rotary wing unit arrived, Trobaugh wanted Hagler to take off, to allow for a daylight battle. A short-fuse operation was bad enough; a "quickie" night raid could spell disaster.

So Company B, 82nd CAB, and Hagler's 2-75 Rangers prepared for their air assault. Company C, 1-75 Rangers, reinforced Hagler's battalion; the rest of the other Ranger battalion stood ready to reinforce 2-75. Things didn't look good.

Opposition promised to be fierce. Some data depicted up to six ZU-23 mounts. First Lieutenant Raymond Thomas recalled that he was briefed to expect "30 Russians and 400 Cubans" at the site. Captain Frank Kearney, commanding Company A, 2-75 Rangers, thought that the helo assault looked to be very difficult. He heard some of his tired men refer to the concept as a "suicide mission." Both Ranger battalions had begun turning in ammunition prior to departure when the word came to prepare for the Calvigny attack, which made the operation doubly unnerving. Who wanted to be the last American to die on Grenada?

The isolated Calvigny compound perched on a bald hill surrounded by lush greenery. Fortunately, it could be plastered without much fear of collateral damage to anything but trees and bushes. Intelligence on the objective indicated a small, four-chopper landing zone (once again) on a narrow street between barracks and warehouses. Getting in without hitting the rows of buildings would require some terrific flying, even without enemy resistance.

Hagler and the army fliers agreed to approach from the south, in flights of four Blackhawks. While the UH-60s held offshore, Hagler intended to shoot the heaviest preparatory fires used in Grenada. Once the firepower lifted, the Ranger commander would insert Company A, Company C, Company B, and the attached Company C, 1-75, in that order. Each company had certain structures to clear en route to a large, circular limit of advance.

The Rangers and their All-American helos lifted off at 1600. As the cramped, worried Rangers flew a lazy loop out across the blue sea, carrier air strikes, AC-130H cannon shots, an artillery barrage, and even a single round of 127-mm naval gunfire from the USS *Moosbrugger* battered the Calvigny camp. The naval shell (or possibly Spectre fire, or both) hit an enemy fuel and ammunition dump, generating a huge fireball and a roaring conflagration. At 1700, the supporting fire lifted and the Blackhawks clattered in from the ocean.

In the lead foursome, the excited 82nd CAB fliers flared to land in column formation, but almost immediately, the pilots recognized that their chosen street was not wide enough for the Blackhawks. Two helos crabbed to the northwest corner of the barracks area into a small open area; the other two dropped off to a similar tight zone in the southeast. As Captain Kearney's landing plan went completely awry, enemy AK automatic rifles opened from about forty meters to the north.

All four choppers landed without any trouble, disgorging their disoriented Rangers. Suddenly, the pilot of a northeast UH-60A took a round through his arm and leg. Other bullets penetrated the Blackhawk's gearbox and cut power to the stabilizing tail rotor. In the close quarters of the makeshift northern Calvigny LZ, the stricken pilot lost control of his damaged craft and plowed directly into his partner and the scrambling infantry on the ground.

Simultaneously, Kearney's helicopter to the southeast had smashed up its tail rotor on a hard landing and flopped wildly as the pilot tried to take off anyway. As the fourth Blackhawk jerked up and away to avoid a collision, the main blade on the injured craft whizzed across the heads of Kearney and his men, who crouched helplessly on the smoldering grass. Kearney recalled: "I was lying on my back. I knew my company was spread all over the place, and I had to gain control of them. Guys were shouting and running in all directions. Shots went everywhere, and I couldn't tell the difference; probably they were mine, but who could tell? I couldn't move because the bird was hanging right over me, wobbling. The big blade kept buzzing right above my head. A guy right near me had just been shot through the neck. The objective was burning, smoke everywhere, and a constant roar of motors, explosions, and gunfire. I felt completely useless.''

After a few scary minutes, the damaged helicopter crashed upright. Most of its disembarked passengers survived, shaken but unhurt. In the two separate chaotic whirls of broken blades and twisting choppers, three Rangers died and fifteen more Americans fell injured. One man lost a leg; a rolling helicopter paralyzed another soldier from the waist down. Ranger medics exhibited skill and valor pulling wounded soldiers from the dangerous wreckage and keeping them alive until they could be evacuated.

The PRA shots had been incredibly lucky, if indeed they were PRA bullets. They could have been stray rounds from exploding ammunition bins or even misaimed U.S. fire. Some Rangers reported fleeing figures, although Kearney saw no enemy on the objective as he reestablished order and secured his part of the barracks. Only a unit with the discipline of the Rangers could have snapped back so quickly from such horrific landing accidents, and their rapid recovery shows the superb fiber of these American troops and their intent leaders.

The rest of the Rangers came in aboard successive single lifts, as careful pilots avoided the hulks and debris that blocked off the northern and half of the southern LZs. Of course, despite a definite desire for vengeance, the Rangers could not find any of the supposed Cubans and Soviets. As Lieutenant Thomas commented, ''We didn't find anything worth shooting at.'' Hagler declared Calvigny secure at 1800. The Rangers guarded the wreckage until marine CH-53Ds winched the three carcasses out the next day. The Rangers departed on Company B Blackhawks at daybreak on 28 October.[97]

The heliborne raid on Calvigny offered a grisly reminder of the dangers of haste and overconfidence. It is an old military maxim that time spent on reconnaissance is seldom wasted. Unlike the initial airfield assaults, Grand Mal, or the Grand Anse rescue, Calvigny featured almost no scouting or reliable on-scene information. A patrol or two earlier on 27 October could have confirmed or denied U.S. suspicions about the area. Instead, fatigued 82nd CAB fliers arrived from Barbados and headed right into combat without much preparation. Stuck with a sketchy plan, distracted by fire and blasts, the chopper crews tried to put too many aircraft into too little space. Given the confused, tragic initial helicopter insertion, the Rangers were fortunate that there was no real resistance.

While remorseless pursuit and destruction of shattered enemy remnants makes perfect sense, flying directly into the maw of a presumed hostile battalion encampment did not. With only four helos landing at a time, General Trobaugh and Lieutenant Colonel Hagler risked the same sort of dribbling attack that cost so heavily on Koh Tang in 1975. Perhaps the earlier Cuban and Grenadian surrenders made the Americans sloppy about basic combat concepts or caused them to place inordinate faith in the preliminary bombardment. Landing 2-75 bit by bit at Calvigny seems reasonable only if the U.S. commanders expected an enemy collapse. But it is always risky to count on hostile intentions. As it was, the enemy had already been beaten, and the rueful Americans escaped with a hard lesson about cutting tactical corners.

The disappointing Calvigny raid amounted to the last significant opposed combat operation on Grenada. While the Rangers dealt with adversity at Calvigny, Company F, 2/8 Marines, received authorization to continue all the way to Ross Point Hotel. A final boundary adjustment designated the hotel as the contact point for army and marine forces. The 2-325 Infantry reached the vicinity just after nightfall, soaked by a driving tropical rainstorm that nearly blotted out all but the immediate surroundings. The army troops wisely decided to wait for morning to effect a juncture. At 0800 on 28 October, the Americans met.[98] Only mopping up remained.

One curious event marked 28 October. During the morning, 82nd Airborne security patrols entered the Lance aux Epines peninsula. Although the area had been under effective U.S. control since very early on 26 October, these paratroopers represented the first direct American entry into the small appendix of land. To their great surprise and gratification, the airborne infantry discovered most of the other American students. The young people said that they had remained in their scattered houses, well aware of what had transpired. There had been general agreement that staying out of the line of fire seemed prudent. No Cubans or PRA entered the peninsula after the American attack commenced, and the students realized that they were in a secure area. "Our area was isolated on a hillside, so we were pretty safe," said Kip Ablin. The steady U.S. pressure on the enemy had paid off; the Cubans and Grenadians proved too busy to bother these U.S. citizens.[99]

Comparative Loss Summary
Personnel

	KIA	DOW	WIA	PW	Nonbattle
U.S. Army	11	1	106	0	23
U.S. Navy/USMC	7	0	7	0	5
U.S. Air Force	0	0	2	0	0
U.S. MILITARY TOTAL	18	1	115	0	28
Cuban FAR *	24	0	59	605	0
Grenadian PRAF **	21	0	337	68	0
FAR/PRAF TOTAL	45	0	396	673	0
Grenadian civilians	24				

Equipment

U.S. Military: 9 helicopters destroyed; # 6 helicopters damaged

FAR/PRAF: 6 BTR-60 PBs destroyed, all other equipment/installations captured

KIA = killed in action; DOW = died of wounds; WIA = wounded in action; PW = prisoner of war; nonbattle = noncombat accidents, illnesses.

* The only FAR soldiers to escape capture were Colonel Tortolo and a dozen others with the Cuban commander. All wounded were also captured. Hugh O'Shaughnessy in *Grenada: Revolution, Invasion, and Aftermath* (London: Hamish Hamilton, Ltd., 1984), 212, mentioned that on 12 November 1983, a Cuban honor guard in Havana removed thirty-seven corpses from the transfer aircraft. As both the U.S. and Cuba agreed that there were twenty-four Cuban KIAs, the identity of the other thirteen has been a subject of some speculation.

** Grenadian wounded total most probably includes some civilian injuries. U.S. reports list only the accidental civilian deaths.

Five of the "destroyed" army helicopters proved repairable.

Sources: "Grenada Casualty List," *Army Times*, 14 November 1983, 66; David C. Isby, "Military Lessons of the Grenada Campaign," *Jane's Military Review* (London: Jane's Publishing Co., Ltd., 1985), 49; U.S. Congress, House Committee on Armed Services, *Lessons Learned as a Result of the U.S. Military Operations in Grenada, Full Committee Hearing of the House Committee on Armed Services*, 98th Congress, Second Session, 24 January 1984, 4; "Target Confusion Blamed in Air Attack on Soldiers," *Army Times*, 23 July 1984, 2; Benjamin F. Schemmer, "JCS Reply to Congressional Reform Caucus' Critique of the Grenada Rescue Operation," *Armed Forces Journal International* (July 1984), 99.

As the rest of the 82nd Airborne's 3rd Brigade arrived, both Ranger units left for dramatic homecomings in the United States. The 82nd Airborne and the marines conducted several unopposed operations. Airborne helicopter raids scoured southern Grenada. Marine armored and amphibious columns secured most of the northern cities, and then the BLT turned over its positions to paratroopers and CPF soldiers and police. A bloodless amphibious attack on Carriacou Island on 1 November, spearheaded by Company G in AAVs and Company F by air, netted nineteen confused PRA prisoners and a battalion equipment cache. Carriacou represented the third navy/marine amphibious attack in seven days.

Aided by the friendly Grenadians, Americans and their Caribbean allies rounded up the fugitive members of the Revolutionary Military Council and the New JEWEL radicals. The marine cannoneers found Bernard Coard on 29 October. Not to be outdone, the army's 2-505 Infantry snatched up Hudson Austin on 30 October. These former rulers found themselves in the Richmond Hill prison, awaiting trial by Sir Paul Scoon's new civil government. Grenadians looked forward to the first scheduled democratic elections since 1976.[100]

The American military officially considered the Grenada campaign to extend until 2 November, but the military struggle really ended on the second day or so. Neither side took excessive losses, although Cuban casualties ran about 12 percent of the total Cuban force engaged. Grenada suffered minimal civilian casualties and collateral damage. All the American students emerged unharmed, democratic government had been restored, and the incursion eradicated the Soviet bloc presence on the Spice Island. American commanders and troops received popular acclaim and military awards. In contrast, Fidel Castro sent Colonel Tortolo and several of his followers to Angola as private soldiers.[101] Colonel Sazhenev's disposition has not been reported.

For the American military, and especially for the army, Operation URGENT FURY represented more than a military victory or a foreign policy signal. Grenada was a vindication of the revitalized American armed forces. Unlike previous post-Vietnam engagements, which featured a few small outfits in action, the Grenada campaign demonstrated joint operations on a large scale. Not every action had been perfect, but the majority had gone very well indeed. Most important of all, command initiative, troop quality, and forceful personal leadership at all echelons turned problems into opportunities. The successful evacuation of more than 600 civilians from a rough, forested island defended by a determined foe represented a significant achievement. The fact that it occurred on short notice made the accomplishment more significant.

URGENT FURY succeeded because President Reagan issued clear strategic goals and some general rules of engagement, then left matters to his competent military commanders. Reagan refused to permit political interference or civilian "micromanagement" in the details of the special and conventional operations. Given the trust of the national commander in chief, the military establishment created a flexible combat organization that created a sound plan and executed it to fulfill the president's objectives.

Professional officers designed a simple command structure with clear lines of authority, then left their subordinates enough latitude to execute assigned missions. As a result, each layer of unit leadership knew what to do, and they themselves determined how to do it. When asked to explain the success of the attack, Vice Adm. Joseph Metcalf told a congressional committee: "I was in charge. There wasn't any doubt about who was involved. I was getting very little guidance from Admiral [Wesley] McDonald [U.S. Atlantic Command]. I felt I had the responsibility. I felt that I could tell the various command elements, whether it was Army, Air Force or anybody else, what I wanted to do. I stayed out of the 'how' just like my seniors stayed out of the 'how' with me. They [superiors] told me what they wanted me to do. They gave me guidelines, very general. I went down there and we had no mucking around from on high." [102]

JTF 120 defeated the Cubans and their Grenadian allies with quality, not quantity. This sounds strange on the face of it, because many evaluators compare the total American force level (nine-and-a-half battalions committed by 28 October) with the regular enemy strength (three battalions). In fact, the Americans fought and won the key engagements at Pearls, Point Salines, St. George's, Calliste, and Grand Anse without any great force preponderance. Most American attacks occurred without the doctrinal three-to-one advantage. Troop quality, not firepower, made up the difference.

Two examples will suffice. At Point Salines, two lightly armed Ranger battalions took a blocked, defended runway from two enemy battalions. The Cubans and PRA had armored vehicles, a potent array of 23-mm and lighter air defense cannons, well-sited mortars, heavy barricades, prepared positions, and some advance warning. The Rangers deployed

---

Ground Unit Force Ratios on Grenada
25 October–2 November 1983

	USA/USMC/CPF	FAR/PRAF
25 OCT 83	1 USMC Battalion (+) 2 USA Ranger Battalions 1 USA Airborne Battalion ½ Battalion CPF	1 Cuban Engineer Battalion 2 PRA Infantry Battalions 7 PRM Infantry Battalions
	4½ Battalions	10 Battalions
26 OCT 83	1 USMC Battalion (+) 2 USA Ranger Battalions 2 USA Airborne Battalions ½ Battalion CPF	⅔ Cuban Engineer Battalion 2 PRA Infantry Battalions PRM (Snipers; fragments)
	5½ Battalions	2⅔ Battalions
27 OCT 83	1 USMC Battalion (+) 2 USA Ranger Battalions 4 USA Airborne Battalions ½ Battalion CPF	⅓ Cuban Engineer Battalion 1 PRA Infantry Battalion PRM (fragments)
	7½ Battalions	1⅓ Battalions
28 OCT 83	1 USMC Battalion (+) 6 USA Airborne Battalions ½ Battalion CPF	1 PRA Infantry Battalion (fragments)
	7½ Battalions	fragments

The 28 October force levels maintained until 2 November, with steady erosion of Grenadian PRA units.

---

no armor, no artillery, and had incomplete information. They drifted in on a narrow runway in daylight, from planes with thin skins and no armament. Fire support available amounted to three lumbering Spectre gunships and hand-carried weapons. Yet the Rangers triumphed.

At Calliste, one airborne battalion assaulted the bulk of an alert, well-armed enemy battalion. Another enemy infantry battalion was nearby, ready to join the fray. The Cuban engineers under attack disposed mortars, prepared positions, and heavy machine guns. Airborne infantry maneuvered across steep slopes, through tall, thick foliage, and into open areas swept by enemy direct fires. The paratroopers' support amounted to a single battery of light artillery, some mortars, and hand-carried weapons. Air power on call consisted of a few A-7E jets firing 20-mm cannons. But the All-Americans crushed the enemy and took the objective.

Cuban and PRA equipment and strength compared favorably to that of the American attackers. They had equivalent small arms, machine guns, mortars, armored fighting vehicles, antitank guns and rockets, and even 130-mm artillery (which never came into use). To offset American air power, the enemy possessed strong air defense gun systems, which did yeoman work against U.S. helicopters. The PRA deployed no tanks; but after all, the American tanks wallowed aboard USS *Manitowoc* throughout the critical daylight hours of 25 October, and played no role at Point Salines or Calliste. The enemy soldiers, with the benefits

---

Operation URGENT FURY Time Line
13 October–2 November 1983

13 October —Grenadian Prime Minister Maurice Bishop deposed and arrested.

17 October —U.S. State/Defense Departments restricted interagency group met; considered noncombat evacuation of U.S. citizens on Grenada.

18 October —USS *Independence* battle group departed for Lebanon.

19 October —Bishop executed; street violence in St. George's. General Hudson Austin assumes control; civil government dissolved. American Joint Chiefs start planning cycle. Amphibious Squadron 4 departed for Lebanon.

20 October —Twenty-four-hour shoot-on-sight curfew announced in Grenada. Vice President George Bush convened Special Situation Group. Prime Minister J. M. G. Adams of Barbados asked for U.S. military intervention. *Independence* and amphibious squadron diverted toward Grenada. Soviets applaud replacement of Bishop; Cubans condemn the move.

21 October —Organization of Eastern Caribbean States, Jamaica, and Barbados request U.S. military participation in a joint intervention. News leaked to Grenada, Cuba, and USSR. American military forces began detailed assault planning.

22 October —American diplomatic mission rebuffed on Grenada. President Ronald Reagan approves preliminary plans. Fidel Castro issued preliminary defense orders to his men on Grenada.

Operation URGENT FURY Time Line
13 October–2 November 1983
(continued)

23 October —U.S. Marine barracks in Lebanon blown up. Captive Grenadian Governor General Sir Paul Scoon secretly requested U.S. armed intervention.

(1900)—President Reagan approved Operation URGENT FURY, with 25 October as D day.

24 October —Cuban Col. Pedro Tortolo took command on Grenada.

(2200)—U.S. Navy SEAL Teams begin preinvasion operations.

25 October —(0500)—Planned H hour (not met).

(0520)—Marines landed at Pearls airport.

(0536)—Rangers parachuted into Point Salines airstrip.

(0850)—U.S. students at True Blue rescued.

(1200)—Marine helicopters diverted to aid SEALs in St. George's.

(1400)—Marines alerted for night attack at Grand Mal Bay. First 82nd Airborne units arrive. PRA/Cuban armored counterattack repulsed.

(1900)—Marines land at Grand Mal Bay.

26 October —(0400)—Marines attack toward St. George's.

(0630)—The 82nd Airborne attacked north and east of Point Salines.

(0712)—Governor General Scoon and SEALs secured.

(1615)—Rangers and marines rescued U.S. students at Grand Anse.

(1700)—Marines took Forts Frederick and Rupert.

27 October —(1220)—Marines secured Richmond Hill prison and Cuban Embassy.

(1600)—Rangers assaulted Calvigny barracks by helicopter.

28 October —(0800)—Army and marines linked up at Ross Point.

(1300)—U.S. students from Lance aux Epines secured: Rangers departed; final 82nd Airborne combat units arrived.

29 October —Marines captured Bernard Coard.

30 October —Marines cleared Sauteurs, Gouyave, and Victoria. Paratroopers seized Hudson Austin.

1 November—(0530)—Marines assaulted and secured Carriacou Island.

2 November—Army relieved marines on Carriacou. Marines back-loaded and prepared to sail to Lebanon.

of the defense, lost their unit cohesion and discipline in the face of spirited American offensives.

The U.S. had much greater firepower potentially available, but intentionally employed only a handful of Spectre gunships, a few tubes of 105-mm light artillery, a smattering of 127-mm naval shots, four Sea Cobras, and less than three dozen carrier attack planes (which usually employed cannons, not bombs). Aggressive soldiers and marines used rifles and machine guns to move in close and kill enemy fighters, determined thrusts that often frightened the rest into submission or flight. As Captain Jacoby commented, "I never gave orders to fix bayonets— my men just knew, and did it on their own." [103] The willingness of American troops to press attacks shattered enemy morale.

The U.S. troops did not resort to massive barrages from distant heavy guns, and Grenadians repaid the American precision with a heartfelt outpouring of gratitude and assistance. Indeed, the restricted American firepower helped cause PRA disintegration because it insured popular support for the American liberators. This effectively separated the revolutionary army from its populace.

Metcalf chose to employ his quality forces for maximum impact. He directed trained, cohesive units against key points. Hence, a few skilled SEALs wrecked the call-up of seven militia battalions. A single Spectre riddled a well-sited enemy antiaircraft gun mount and permitted the parachute operation to go forward. Fewer than 150 Rangers scooped up more than 200 American students from the grip of dug-in PRA riflemen. In the most dramatic maneuver of the campaign, Metcalf pushed the BLT ($-$) ashore behind enemy lines at Grand Mal, an action that ruined the PRA's will to fight. The American pilots, marines, and soldiers operated at night, in foul weather, and in the face of fierce resistance. From start to finish, the tough U.S. regulars went forth to do battle. The enemy gradually collapsed.

With quality to employ, Metcalf had the good sense to use his subordinate units to their best abilities. Each of the services did things essential to its nature. The army seized an airfield by airborne assault and fought the bulk of the enemy ground forces. The navy secured the seas, provided carrier air cover, delivered air and naval fire support, and landed the marines. The marines made their three splendid landings, added punch on the ground, and contributed their hardworking helicopters. The U.S. Air Force watched over the Cuban Air Force, airlifted supplies and reinforcements, and contributed powerful Spectre gunships. Each service freed the others to accomplish their unique missions.

Finally, the upper echelon command initiative and troop quality manifested themselves among the American tactical leadership. Unlike the panicky, inert, or counterproductive actions of many of their enemy counterparts, American officers and sergeants of all services and at all levels exerted the force of personal example essential for success. Amos, Hagler, Hobson, Hunter, Mall, Scholtes, Smith, Taylor, and Trobaugh, to name only a few, could be found at the front when the going got tough. Naturally, their men responded with extraordinary efforts.

The Grenada campaign ended in a clear-cut American victory. For the armed forces, URGENT FURY offered a stark and welcome contrast with the grim images of burned-out helicopters in the Iranian desert or drifting concrete dust over the ravaged Beirut barracks. Just as when Delta Force entered Iran or the marines moved into Lebanon, the mere presence of competent U.S. forces did not automatically insure success. In Grenada, as in other successful operations, American combat leadership made the vital difference.

Chapter 5 Notes

Epigraphs come from Maurice Bishop, *Forward Ever!* (Havana, Cuba: Political Publishers, 1980), 25; Ronald Reagan, "Remarks on Central America and El Salvador, 10 March 1983" in *Public Papers of the Presidents: Ronald Reagan, 1983, Book I* (Washington, D.C.: U.S. Government Printing Office, 1984), 373; George S. Patton, *War as I Knew It* (New York: Pyramid Books, 1970), 305.

1. Hugh O'Shaughnessy, *Grenada: Revolution, Invasion, and Aftermath* (London: Hamish Hamilton, Ltd., 1984), 31, 32; Anthony Payne, Paul Sutton, Tony Thorndike, *Grenada: Revolution and Invasion* (New York: St. Martin's Press, 1984), 1–13; Gregory Sandford, *The New JEWEL Movement: Grenada's Revolution, 1979–1983* (Washington, D.C.: U.S. Government Printing Office, 1985), 4–8.

2. Timothy Ashby, "Grenada: Soviet Stepping Stone," *US Naval Institute Proceedings* (December 1983), 30; Payne et al., *Grenada: Revolution and Invasion*, 10, 14–16; Sandford, *The New JEWEL Movement*, 16, 17, 30–32, 37–40.

3. Ashby, "Grenada," 30; Sandford, *The New JEWEL Movement*, 45, 46.

4. Payne et al., *Grenada: Revolution and Invasion*, 84; Ashby, "Grenada," 30–34; "Rescue from Grenada," *Army Times*, 14 November 1983, 61; Gen. John R. Galvin, "Challenge and Response: On the Southern Flank Three Decades Later," *Military Review* (August 1986), 14; Paul Seabury and Walter A. McDougall, editors, *The Grenada Papers* (San Francisco: Institute for Contemporary Studies, 1984), 17–52, 184, 185; Jiri Valenta and Herbert J. Ellison, editors, *Grenada and Soviet/Cuban Policy* (Boulder, CO: Westview Press, 1986), documents 12, 13, 14, 20, and 21.

5. Ashby, "Grenada," 31; Sandford, *The New JEWEL Movement*, 132–35; Payne et al., *Grenada: Revolution and Invasion*, 31–34; "A Minor League Havana," *Newsweek* (31 March 1980), 22, 23; "Rescue from Grenada," 61; International Institute for Strategic Studies, "The Military Balance 1983/84," *Air Force* (December 1983), 125.

6. Valenta and Ellison, *Grenada and Soviet/Cuban Policy*, 17, 71, document 15; Payne et al., *Grenada: Revolution and Invasion*, 33, 83.

7. Ronald Reagan, "Address to the Nation of Defense and National Security, 23 March 1983" in *Public Papers of the Presidents: Ronald Reagan, 1983, Book I*, 440.

8. Payne et al., *Grenada: Revolution and Invasion*, 29; Sandford, *The New JEWEL Movement*, 130.

9. Sandford, *The New JEWEL Movement*, 176–84; Payne et al., *Grenada: Revolution and Invasion*, 131–36; Ashby, "Grenada," 30, 34.

10. Valenta and Ellison, *Grenada and Soviet/Cuban Policy,* document 18.
11. U.S. Congress, House Committee on Armed Services, *Lessons Learned as a Result of the US Military Operations in Grenada,* 98th Congress, Session, 24 January 1984, 11; Kai P. Schoenhals and Richard A. Melanson, editors, *Revolution and Intervention in Grenada* (Boulder, CO: Westview Press, 1985), 139–46; Stafford Earle, editor, *The Grenada Massacre* (Brown's Town, Jamaica: Earle Publishers, Ltd.), 38.
12. Ralph Kinney Bennett, "Grenada: Anatomy of a 'Go' Decision," *Reader's Digest* (February 1984), 72–75; "Grenadians, Too, Felt Rescued," *Army Times,* 14 November 1983, 26.
13. Bennett, "Grenada," 72–75; Schoenhals and Melanson, *Revolution and Intervention in Grenada,* 145, 146.
14. U.S. Congress, House, *Lessons Learned,* 27; U.S. Congress, Senate, *Hearings on Organization, Structure, and Decision-making Processes of the Department of Defense, Part 8, Hearing before the Senate Armed Services Committee,* 98th Congress, 1st Session, 9 November 1983, 343, 344.
15. Peter M. Dunn and Bruce W. Watson, editors, *American Intervention In Grenada* (Boulder, CO: Westview Press, 1985), 56, 141, 142; Bennett, "Grenada," 73, 74.
16. "Jumping into a Hot DZ at 500 Feet," *Army Times,* 14 November 1983, 10; U.S. Congress, House, *Lessons Learned,* 27, 28; Henry Zeybel, "Gunships at Grenada," *National Defense* (February 1984), 54.
17. Benjamin F. Schemmer, "JCS Reply to Congressional Reform Caucus' Critique of the Grenada Rescue Operation," *Armed Forces Journal International* (July 1984), 12; David C. Isby, "Military Lessons of the Grenada Campaign" in Ian V. Hogg, editor, *Jane's Military Review* (New York: Jane's Publishing Company, 1985), 45, 46.
18. Adrian J. English, "The Cuban Revolutionary Armed Forces" in Hogg, *Jane's Military Review,* 151–53; O'Shaughnessy, *Grenada,* 15, 16.
19. Bruce Marcus and Michael Taber, *Maurice Bishop Speaks: The Grenada Revolution 1979–83* (New York: Pathfinder Press, 1983), 319–23; "Grenada—Will Lessons Learned Be Taught?," *Navy Times,* 5 November 1984, 32. Marcus and Taber reproduced the texts of Castro's orders and statements.
20. English, "The Cuban Revolutionary Armed Forces," 159; U.S. Congress, House Committee on Appropriations, *Situation in Lebanon and Grenada, Hearings Before a Subcommittee of the House Committee on Appropriations,* 98th Congress, 1st Session, 8 November 1983, 39.
21. Valenta and Ellison, *Grenada and Soviet/Cuban Policy,* Documents 12, 13; Seabury and McDougall, *The Grenada Papers,* 43, 44, 184, 185; Ashby, "Grenada," 30, 32, 33; International Institute for Strategic Studies,

"The Military Balance 1983/84," 125; "Grenadian Army Studied US Assault Tactics," *Army Times,* 28 November 1983, 38, recorded the contents of squad leader and soldier notebooks found on 27 October 1983 at Fort Frederick by *Army Times* correspondent Joseph Matera. Detailed descriptions of U.S. paratrooper and marine tactics and equipment were included.

22. O'Shaughnessy, *Grenada,* 13; "Grenadians, Too, Felt Rescued," 26.
23. Dunn and Watson, *American Intervention in Grenada,* 174; U.S. Congress, House, Hon. William Broomfield of Michigan, "Extension of Remarks," 98th Congress, 2nd Session, 26 April 1984, *The Congressional Record,* E1804, E1805. Soviet detainees tried to carry out AKM assault rifles in their luggage. U.S. paratroopers prevented this.
24. Defense Mapping Agency, Hydrographic Center, *Sailing Directions (Enroute) for the Caribbean Sea* (Washington, D.C.: U.S. Government Printing Office, 1976), 219–224; E. Gittens Knight, *Grenada Handbook and Directory* (Bridgetown, Barbados, 1946), 18, 91; Raymund Devas, *Up Hill and Down Dale in Grenada* (St. George's: The Grenadian Guardian, Ltd., 1926), 3, 41, 91, 93; Helmut Blume, *The Caribbean Islands,* trans. Johannes Maczewski and Ann Norton (London: Longman Group, Ltd., 1974), 350–352.
25. Schoenhals and Melanson, *Revolution and Intervention in Grenada,* 144.
26. The possible drop zones were evaluated by use of calculations in accord with Department of the Army, *FM 57–38, Pathfinder Operations (With Change 2)* (Washington, D.C.: Department of the Army, 1973), 39, 40. The arithmetic assumed sixty-four jumpers per C-130, with a dual-door exit at a half second per paratrooper.
27. Schoenhals and Melanson, *Revolution and Intervention in Grenada,* 145; W. T. Leadbetter, Secretary, *Register of Ships, Vol. P–Z* (London: Lloyd's Register of Shipping, 1984), 1,662.
28. Lt. Col. Michael J. Byron, "Fury from the Sea: Marines in Grenada," *US Naval Institute Proceedings* (May 1984), 125; "Delta Unit's Presence in Grenada Invasion Cause for Lid on Press," *Army Times,* 14 November 1983, 10; U.S. Congress, House, *Lessons Learned,* 20.
29. Bennett, "Grenada," 76; Byron, "Fury from the Sea," 125; U.S. Congress, House, 98th Congress, 2nd Session, "Who'll Hold the Reins of Secret Forces?" 21 June 1984, *The Congressional Record,* H6309, H6310.
30. Dunn and Watson, *American Intervention in Grenada,* 91, 92; Byron, "Fury from the Sea," 125; U.S. Marine Corps Development and Education Command Grenada Study Group, *Operational Overview 1-84* (Quantico, VA: U.S. Marine Corps Development and Education Command, 1984), 8.

31. JO1 William Berry et al., "Ten Days of Urgent Fury," *All Hands* (May 1984), 23; O'Shaughnessy, *Grenada*, 202, 211; Schemmer, "JCS Reply," 13, 14.

32. Bennett, *Grenada*, 76; "JCS Reply," 14; O'Shaughnessy, *Grenada*, 211.

33. Leroy Thompson, *The Rescuers* (Boulder, CO: Paladin Press, 1986), 107, 108; "JCS Reply," 14; Stephen Harding, *Air War Grenada* (Missoula, MT: Pictorial Histories Publishing Company, 1984), 19, 26, 27, 30.

34. "Rescue from Grenada," 62; "Ten Days of Urgent Fury," 27; U.S. Congress, House, *Lessons Learned*, 38, 39; "Grenada Casualty List," *Army Times*, 14 November 1983, 66.

35. Harding, *Air War Grenada*, 26, 27.

36. Harding, *Air War Grenada*, 54; John Trotti, *Marine Air* (Novato, CA: Presidio Press, 1985), vii, 108, 136; Ray L. Bonds, ed., *The U.S. War Machine (Revised Edition)* (New York: Crown Publishers, Inc., 1983), 174, 204, 209.

37. Trotti, *Marine Air*, vii, viii; Dunn and Watson, *American Intervention in Grenada*, 92, 93; "Ten Days of Urgent Fury," 19; Byron, "Fury from the Sea," 126; USMC, *Operational Overview 1-84*, 8, 9.

38. Byron, "Fury from the Sea," 126; USMC, *Operational Overview 1-84*, 13, 40; Zeybel, "Gunships at Grenada," 53, 54; "Jumping into a Hot DZ at 500 Feet," 66; Sgt. Cecil Stack, "Grenada," *Soldiers* (January 1984), 39–41.

39. Capt. Bryan A. Lasyone, "Fury in the Spice Islands: A Navigator's Mission," *The Navigator* (Summer 1984), 5.

40. "Jumping into a Hot DZ at 500 Feet," 10; Army Studies Group, "1-75 Rangers in Grenada" (Washington, D.C.: Department of the Army, 1983), 3, 4; CMSgt. Vickie M. Graham, "James Hobson: First to Grenada," *Airman* (September 1987), 50.

41. Lasyone, *Fury in the Spice Islands*, p. 5; Graham, "James Hobson," p. 50.

42. "Grenada: A Special Report," *Airman* (February 1984), 40; "Jumping Into a Hot DZ from 500 Feet," 1; Army Studies Group, "1-75 Rangers in Grenada," 4, 5, 7; Graham, "James Hobson," 50.

43. "Rescue from Grenada," 62.

44. "Grenada: A Special Report," 39; Graham, "James Hobson," 50.

45. Stack, "Grenada," 39; Lasyone, "Fury in the Spice Islands," 5; "Grenada: A Special Report," 37; Graham, "James Hobson," 50.

46. Lasyone, "Fury in the Spice Islands," 5; Zeybel, "Gunships at Grenada," 55, 56.

47. Interview with 1st Lt. Timothy Sayers, platoon leader, Company B, 1-75 Infantry, 21 November 1983.

48. Interview with Capt. Frank Kearney, company commander, Company A, 2-75 Infantry, 24 April 1987; "Jumping into a Hot DZ at 500 Feet," 1, 2, 10.

49. "Grenada: A Special Report," 41.

50. "Paratroopers Get Gratitude, Aid," *Army Times*, 14 November 1983, 26; Schemmer, "JCS Reply," 14, 18; "Jumping into a Hot DZ at 500 Feet," 66; Harding, *Air War Grenada*, 28; Stack, "Grenada," 41; Army Studies Group, "1-75 Rangers in Grenada," 8, 9.

51. Kearney interview; "Jumping into a Hot DZ at 500 Feet," 66; "Rescue from Grenada," 61.

52. Byron, "Fury from the Sea," 127.

53. O'Shaughnessy, *Grenada*, 211; Schemmer, "JCS Reply," 13; Zeybel, "Gunships at Grenada," 55; Harding, *Air War Grenada*, 28, 30.

54. O'Shaughnessy, *Grenada*, 5, 22.

55. "Ten Days of Urgent Fury," 22; Harding, *Air War Grenada*, 33; Trotti, *Marine Air*, vii, viii.

56. Zeybel, "Gunships at Grenada," 55; Harding, *Air War Grenada*, 34; JO2 Timothy J. Christmann, "Tac Air in Grenada," *Naval Aviation News* (November/December 1985), 6–9.

57. Dunn and Watson, *American Intervention in Grenada*, 104; U.S. Congress, House Committee on Armed Services, *Full Committee Consideration of Reports from the Hon. Samuel S. Stratton, Hon. Elwood H. "Bud" Hillis, Hon. Ronald V. Dellums, on their November 5–6, 1983 Fact-Finding Visit to Grenada*, 98th Congress, 1st Session, 15 November 1983, 5.

58. Interview with Capt. Charles Jacoby, company commander, Company A, 2-325 Infantry, 12–13 August 1986; Army Studies Group, "1-75 Rangers in Grenada," 9.

59. Harding, *Air War Grenada*, 33, 34, 39.

60. Sgt. Patrick J. O'Kelley, "So I Gave it a Shot" in Kesaharu Imai, editor, *D-Day in Grenada* (Tokyo: World Photo Press, 1984), 82; Stack, "Grenada," 39.

61. O'Kelley, "So I Gave it a Shot," 82; Harding, *Air War Grenada*, 34; Zeybel, "Gunships at Grenada," 55; O'Shaughnessy, *Grenada*, 17; "Jumping into a Hot DZ at 500 Feet," 66; Army Studies Group, "1-75 Rangers in Grenada," 9–11.

62. O'Kelley, "So I Gave it a Shot," 82; U.S. Congress, House, *Lessons Learned*, 22.

63. Sayers interview.

64. Dunn and Watson, *American Intervention in Grenada*, 104; Byron, "Fury from the Sea," 127; Jacoby interview.

65. U.S. Congress, House, *Lessons Learned*, 22, 23; Dunn and Watson, *Ameri-*

can Intervention in Grenada, 103; U.S. Congress, Senate, *Organization, Structure, and Decision-making, Part 8,* 337.

66. USMC, *Operational Overview 1-84,* 13, 14; Byron, "Fury from the Sea," 127, 128.

67. "Jumping into a Hot DZ at 500 Feet," 66; O'Kelley, "So I Gave it a Shot," 82; Army Studies Group, "1-75 Rangers in Grenada," 12.

68. O'Shaughnessy, *Grenada,* 23.

69. "Grenada: A Special Report," 41.

70. USMC, *Operational Overview 1-84,* 15; Dunn and Watson, *American Intervention in Grenada,* 93, 94.

71. Trotti, *Marine Air,* viii.

72. Harding, *Air War Grenada,* 35.

73. Trotti, *Marine Air,* viii; USMC, *Operational Overview 1-84,* 16.

74. USMC, *Operational Overview 1-84,* 16–18; Byron, "Fury from the Sea," 128; Dunn and Watson, *American Intervention in Grenada,* 94; Harding, *Air War Grenada,* 36.

75. "Despite Grenada Stop, Marines' Mission is Still Beirut," *Army Times,* 14 November 1983, 38, 39; "Marines on Grenada Met Light Resistance," *Army Times,* 28 November 1983, 29.

76. "Grenadians, Too, Felt Rescued," 26; USMC, *Operational Overview 1-84,* 16; Earle, *The Grenada Massacre,* 62.

77. O'Shaughnessy, *Grenada,* 26.

78. Byron, "Fury from the Sea," 119; O'Shaughnessy, *Grenada,* 211; U.S. Congress, Senate Committee on Appropriations, *Special Hearings: Supplemental Appropriations Supporting U.S. Military Actions in and Around Grenada,* 98th Congress, 2nd Session, 21–22 March 1984, 42, 43.

79. Stack, "Grenada," 43; Colonel Steve Silvasy, "Address to Command and General Staff College," Fort Leavenworth, Kansas, December 1983 (private videotape); Silvasy lecture.

80. O'Kelley, "So I Gave it a Shot," 83; Silvasy lecture.

81. Ibid.; Jacoby interview; Christmann, "TacAir in Grenada," 6–9.

82. Stack, "Grenada," 43; Schemmer, "JCS Reply," 14; O'Kelley, "So I Gave it a Shot," 83; Jacoby interview; Interview with Captain David W. Lamm, commander, Headquarters Company, 2-325 Infantry, 12 November 1987.

83. U.S. Congress, House, *Lessons Learned,* 22.

84. Ibid., 22, 23; "Jumping into a Hot DZ at 500 Feet," 66; USMC, *Operational Overview 1-84,* 30; Harding, *Air War Grenada,* 36; Trotti, *Marine Air,* viii, ix; Kearney interview.

85. Schemmer, "JCS Reply," 18; Harding, *Air War Grenada,* 37.

86. USMC, *Operational Overview 1-84,* 16.

87. USMC, *Operational Overview 1-84,* 18; 2nd Lt. James B. Seaton, "NGF Procedures Rusty," *Marine Corps Gazette* (June 1984), 35, 36.
88. O'Kelley, "So I Gave it a Shot," 83, 84; Jacoby interview.
89. Stack, "Grenada," 43.
90. Schemmer, "JCS Reply," 14.
91. U.S. Congress, Senate, *Special Hearings,* 39; USMC, *Operational Overview,* 20; U.S. Congress, House, Broomfield, "Extension of Remarks," E1804, E1805.
92. USMC, *Operational Overview 1-84,* 20–22.
93. USMC, *Operational Overview 1-84,* 20, 22; "Ten Days of Urgent Fury," 26.
94. "Grenada: A Special Report," 38, 42; James W. Canan, "Blue Christmas Coming Up," *Air Force* (January 1984), 78, 79.
95. Dunn and Watson, *American Intervention in Grenada,* 104; O'Kelley, "So I Gave it a Shot," 84, 85; Jacoby interview; Lamm interview.
96. Jacoby interview; "Target Confusion Blamed in Air Attack on Soldiers," *Army Times,* 23 July 1984, 2.
97. "Jumping into a Hot DZ at 500 Feet," 66; Harding, *Air War Grenada,* 41, 42; Imai, *D-Day in Grenada,* 8; U.S. Congress, House, *Lessons Learned,* 31; Dunn and Watson, *American Intervention in Grenada,* 95; Christmann, "TacAir in Grenada," 6–9; Army Studies Group, "1-75 Rangers in Grenada," 12; Kearney interview.
98. USMC, *Operational Overview 1-84,* 22, 23; O'Kelley, "So I Gave it a Shot," 85.
99. Byron, "Fury from the Sea," 129; U.S. Congress, House, *Lessons Learned,* 23; "Rescue from Grenada," 62.
100. "Paratroopers Get Gratitude, Aid," 1; Byron, "Fury from the Sea," 129; USMC, *Operational Overview 1-84,* 25, 26.
101. Harding, *Air War Grenada,* 31.
102. U.S. Congress, House, *Lessons Learned,* 26.
103. Jacoby interview.

CHAPTER 6

THE ELEMENT OF SURPRISE: INTERCEPTION OF THE *ACHILLE LAURO* HIJACKERS

OCTOBER 1985

"It is important to us to emphasize that there is no truth whatsoever to reports that one of the passengers was killed. These reports are designed by the Zionist enemy to exploit the circumstances surrounding the operation in order to cover up its own crimes against the Palestinian people."

Muhammed Abul Abbas, 11 October 1985

"These people don't deserve to live. They are despicable."
Mrs. Marilyn Klinghoffer to President Reagan, 12 October 1985

"These young Americans sent a message to terrorists everywhere. The message: you can run, but you can't hide."

President Ronald W. Reagan, 11 October 1985

In an era of nuclear superpowers, how do the weak influence the strong? They can talk loudly. They can vote in the impotent carnival of the United Nations General Assembly, seek a powerful ally, risk a local war, or resort to terrorism—violent criminal activity used for political purposes. Terrorism has become the favorite weapon of weak states and stateless nationalist and ideological factions. The United States Department of Defense defines terrorism as "the unlawful use or threatened use of force or violence by a revolutionary organization against individuals or property with the intention of coercing or intimidating governments or societies, often for ideological purposes.''[1]

Three portions of this fairly serviceable definition need amplification. First, a revolutionary organization may be just that, such as the Basque separatists in Spain, Yasir Arafat's Palestine Liberation Organization (PLO), or the infamous Irish Republican Army (IRA). But it can also be a state, to include Libya, Syria, Iran, Cuba, Nicaragua, and that helpful friend of all liberation movements, the Soviet Union.

Second, aside from an occasional pinpoint assassination or kidnapping, the individuals attacked tend to be innocent civilians. These defenseless victims are chosen for their nationality or proximity to a political symbol. Nonmilitary structures or means of transportation are typical "property" singled out for strikes. Terror groups hope that the resultant fear will encourage frightened citizens to pressure their government for changes in policy.

Actions against trained, deployed military forces are acts of war, not terrorism, although the means employed and groups involved may be of a terrorist ilk. Strictly speaking, the "terrorists" who blew up the marines in Beirut were nothing more than militiamen resorting to unusual tactics, although Admiral Long and his associates called it "terrorism" and a "new dimension in warfare." In the words of army Middle Eastern expert Lt. Col. Frederic C. Hof, the bombing was "an act which, given the Lebanese scene and American role described by the commission, amounted to nothing more than a military assault against a military installation."[2] The marines had the means to protect themselves. True terrorists target vulnerable innocents; that is what puts the "terror" in terrorism.

Finally, terrorism is not "often for political purposes." It *always* has a political objective, usually something too outlandish for peaceful resolution by legal means. Indeed, this is what distinguishes terrorist acts from random criminal violence. In summary, terrorists represent revolutionary groups or states (typically, but not exclusively, of leftist persuasion); they attack innocent people and undefended property of a symbolic nature in order to dramatize political demands.

Unfortunately, like the Long Commission, many people attempt to identify terrorists by their methods rather than their objectives. Bombing, hijacking, assassination, and hostage-taking are not innately "terrorist"; whether or not they are depends upon the reasons and intended targets.

Bombing Berlin in 1944 or crashing a kamikaze plane into USS *Enterprise* in 1945 were acts of war, targeted upon military forces, although innocents often suffered collateral injuries. Bombing a crowded cafe or crashing a suicide car bomb into an embassy are acts of terrorism, targeted to make a political statement, and aimed intentionally to kill and cow the innocents on the scene.

One particularly virulent strain of terrorism centers on the despondent Palestinians displaced by the foundation of modern Israel in 1948. Yasir Arafat's PLO, financed and encouraged by other Arab and Muslim states, has waged a relentless campaign of military raids and sporadic terror against the tough Israelis. Iran, Syria, and Libya also dispatch and support anti-Israeli cells, alternately cooperating and scrapping with the PLO. The potent Israeli Defense Forces respond harshly and regularly to these random attacks, and Israeli intelligence and security are widely considered to be the best in the world at detecting, preempting, and destroying such threats. As Israel's strongest ally, the United States often finds its citizens, installations, and the private property of its people under attack as well.

The cycle of action and reaction quieted notably once Arafat and most of his minions left Lebanon for Tunisia in 1982, spurred by IDF tank columns and guarded by U.S. Marines. But by 1985, Israel's attempt to create a secure border in Lebanon had completely unraveled, and PLO elements began to prey once again on Israeli military and civilian targets. The Israelis reacted with a brilliant lightning stroke against the new PLO headquarters at Borj Cedria, outside Tunis, Tunisia. Eight American-supplied F-16A Fighting Falcon fighters flew more than 3,000 miles to blast Arafat's command center. IDF chief of staff Maj. Gen. Moshe Levy pulled no punches, claiming the raid was intended to kill Arafat. But the mercurial PLO leader changed his usual routine minutes prior to the raid and was not in his office. Although he escaped, more than seventy-five PLO officials and nearby civilians died.[3] Arafat and his lieutenants planned a major revenge mission.

Muhammed Abul Abbas, chief of the Palestine Liberation Front (PLF) and a member of the PLO Executive Committee, took the lead role in the effort. Abbas designed a military attack on Ashdod, Israel, concentrating on oil and munitions facilities. His operatives had previously scouted the SS *Achille Lauro,* an Italian luxury liner that routinely visited the Israeli port on its Mediterranean circuit. It provided a fine covert means of approach. Conveniently, *Achille Lauro* was leaving from Genoa,

---

Palestine Liberation Front (PLF) Order of Battle
10–11 October 1985

Command Element: Muhammad (Abul) Abbas (PLF factional leader)
                    Ozzudin Badrak Kan (chief, military branch, PLF)

Ashdod Attack Team: Majed Youseff Al-Molky
                       Hallah Abdallah Al-Hassan
                       Hammad Ali Abdallah
                       Abdel Atil Ibrahim

EgyptAir Boeing 737:   2 pilots, 3 flight attendants, 4 Egyptian government
                        officials

Sources: Gayle Rivers (pseudonym), *The War Against the Terrorists* (New York: Stein and Day, 1986), 171; Scott C. Truver, "Maritime Terrorism, 1985," *Proceedings* (May 1986), 167, 169.

Italy, on 3 October. Quickly outfitted with the necessary explosives and firearms, Abbas's four-man team headed for Genoa.[4] Like the Israeli jets, the PLF planned to reach out over many hundreds of miles to conduct a military raid, not a terrorist crime. But something strange happened on the way to Ashdod.

The SS *Achille Lauro* was built in 1947, making her the oldest of the six Italian registry ships active in 1985. At 631 feet long and 23,600 tons displacement, she could carry up to 900 passengers. Although owned by the Italian government's Flotto Lauro Corporation, *Achille Lauro* was under charter to the Greek Chandris Cruise Lines for her October voyage. Aside from her crew of 400 (mostly servers and entertainers), the liner carried 748 people when she weighed anchor from Genoa on 3 October.[5]

As on many such cruises, the majority of those aboard were of middle age or older, enjoying their retirement by vacationing. Passenger Seymour Meskin recalled that "nobody inspected anything" during the boarding period, and that "there were people coming and going at all times." Unlike commercial aircraft, where repeated hijackings have prompted stringent metal detection and baggage screening, ships have been much luckier. The last cruise ship taken by force was the Portuguese *Santa Maria,* way back in 1961. So lax security typified ocean liners.

The Italian officials in Genoa thought nothing strange about the four swarthy young men carrying passports from Argentina, Norway, and Canada, nor did anyone check their bulky attaché cases. The men retired to their cheap cabin. Once the ship left Genoa, the PLF team took their meals in their room and stayed aboard during port calls in Naples, Syracuse in Sicily, and Alexandria, Egypt. The few times anyone saw them outside their compartment, they carried their attaché cases.[6]

At Alexandria all but about a hundred passengers went ashore for a tour of Cairo and the Pyramids. The ship sailed on toward Port Said, where the passengers ashore would reboard. On Monday, 7 October, a waiter brought lunch to the PLF cabin a bit early, discovering the four men busily cleaning their AK-47 assault rifles. The waiter's eyes widened, but he moved too slowly. The PLF team grabbed him and quickly reassembled their weapons. They were not real soldiers, and evidently lacked a contingency plan in the event their indentities were compromised. They panicked. One suggested that they take over the ship and let that be their statement to the world. His three nervous colleagues consented, and a military raid became a terrorist act.

The young men bolted toward the dining room, where Seymour Meskin and his wife had just sat down to eat: "They were carrying what I believe was a submachinegun or automatic weapon. We heard two cracks [gunshots], and then we looked up and the terrorists came in herding before them a number of people from the kitchen crew and some waiters. They came down [to] the dining room and told everybody who was there to get up from the tables and move back further towards the rear of the room." Two passengers and a waiter were hurt in the commotion. All four men carried AK-47s and Soviet-made hand grenades, and two had revolvers.

With the shocked passengers under control, one PLF man went to the bridge and another to the engine room. Meskin commented on their swift, purposeful movements: "We thought there were many more because of the way they were directing their attack." Fully committed to their unexpected course of action, the terrorists began to follow the usual rules of the game.

The two left behind in the dining room sorted out the fourteen Americans, six young female entertainers from Britain, and an Austrian couple with a Jewish-sounding name, herding them into a separate lounge. The PLF agent returned from the engine room with seven containers of gasoline, spotting these here and there among the people seated in silence on the deck. One grinning Arab placed Judge Stanley Kubacki, his wife Sophia, and two other women back to back, handing the two ladies grenades with the pins removed. Anything other than sure grips would release the activating levers and detonate the grenades. Kubacki remembered: "If one of these women fell asleep or fainted, we would all be blown up." The PLF men waved their weapons about, regaling their charges with slogans: "Reagan no good. Arafat good." [7] It would be a long night.

Meanwhile, the remaining PLF man called Capt. Gerardo de Rosa to the bridge. "As soon as I got there," said de Rosa, "I faced the machineguns [an AK-47]. First, they [actually he] fired some shots at the deck, shouting in Arabic. Then they told me to head for Tartus [a Syrian port]." At gunpoint, de Rosa could do little but obey. He thought there were many more terrorists, so he ordered his crew to follow the instructions of the insistent PLF gunmen. In between prodding de Rosa with an AK muzzle and tuning the ship's radio to wailing Arabic music, the PLF broadcast their initial demands. They wanted asylum in Syria and freedom for fifty PLO prisoners held in Israel. [8]

The sketchy initial reports of the hijacking reached Washington by 1000 (1600 Mediterranean time), and President Reagan and his assistants took immediate diplomatic and military measures. Secretary of State George Shultz instructed his subordinates to issue strongly worded requests to Syria, Lebanon, and Cyprus, asking them to close their ports to the ship. Secretary of Defense Caspar Weinberger alerted the Sixth Fleet for possible missions in support of a rescue operation. The guided missile destroyer USS *Scott* left Haifa, Israel, to locate the *Achille Lauro*. Sixth Fleet also readied the USS *Saratoga* battle group, steaming in the northern Ionian Sea, for air action. A U.S. Air Force EC-135 Burning Wind flew toward the hijacked ship to eavesdrop on communications. Finally, Weinberger activated Joint Special Operations Command (JSOC) for a rescue effort. The highly trained swimmers of SEAL Team 6 (ST-6) began movement toward the Mediterranean from their base at Norfolk, Virginia. Selected elements of 1st Special Forces Operations Detachment—Delta, left Fort Bragg, North Carolina. They would assist if America chose to assault the ship. Italian warships also steamed in to shadow the ocean liner, and Italian and Egyptian officials attempted to negotiate with the PLF terrorists. [9]

By Tuesday, 8 October, *Achille Lauro* lay off Tartus, but the Syrians refused to accept the ship. Exhausted by lack of sleep, nervous, and frustrated, the four men decided to demonstrate their seriousness. About noon, the men moved their selected American, British, and Austrian captives up onto the deck above the lounge, all but a wheelchair-bound American Jew, Leon Klinghoffer, whom they kept behind. Following more pleas, demands, and threats, the terrorists radioed Tartus at 1430: "We cannot wait any longer. We will begin killing." No response came. At 1500, the youngest PLF man, Hallah Abdallah Al-Hassan, shot Kling-hoffer in the forehead and chest, splattering blood all over himself. Pushed by the enraged gunmen, frightened ship's waiters helped throw the bullet-ridden corpse overboard. It washed ashore near Tartus on 13 October.

Al-Hassan burst wildly into the ship's bridge, accompanied by one of his associates. "We have killed a man," he exulted to de Rosa, who could not help but see the blood all over the youth's clothes. The older colleague grabbed the radio transmitter and spoke in even tones: "We threw the first body into the water after shooting him in the head. Minutes from now we will follow up with the second one. Don't worry, Tartus, we have a lot of them here." The Syrian voice rumbled back, nonplussed: "Go back where you came from." [10] The PLF bravado had failed, and the men knew that the longer they stayed at sea, the more likely that their bungled escapade would end with a fusillade of deadly SEAL bullets.

The PLF team tried to dock in Beirut, but even that bloody port refused them. For a brief time, the men forced de Rosa to sail for their benefactor Gadhafi's Libyan shores. But in the end, the hijackers gave up their demands for freeing prisoners in Israel, and followed the Syrian advice. They turned back toward Port Said, and the more immediate problem of saving their own skins.

In Egypt, Foreign Minister Esmet Abdel Meguid suggested employing the PLO to mediate a peaceful end to the episode. Egyptian President Hosni Mubarak knew his country was an outcast in the Islamic world for its 1978 accord with Israel, and he was well aware that Arab extremists in his restive country had killed his predecessor, Anwar Sadat. He and Meguid wanted to end the incident without violence, yet avoid a direct affront to Yasir Arafat. So the Egyptians proposed letting the PLO talk its own way out of the fiasco. Mubarak claimed no knowledge of Klinghof-fer's death, and his foreign office spread the word that rumors about a killing aboard the *Achille Lauro* were untrue.

Mubarak and Meguid proposed a rather direct arrangement. The hijackers would be turned over to Arafat's envoys and the ship would be released. On the evening of 8 October, as the ship anchored fifteen miles off Port Said, Meguid encouraged the American, British, Italian, and West German ambassadors to sign the document authorizing the deal. But they refused; they had heard that one man was dead.[11]

American rescue forces were in the area as negotiations commenced. The SEALs debarked at Sigonella Naval Air Station in Sicily, ready to take the ship by force. EC-135 intercepts indicated that one man was dead already, the ritual killing typical to the opening phases of most hostage incidents. During the summer of 1985, U.S. Navy diver Robert Stethem had been murdered in a similar fashion to open the two-and-a-half-week drama of TWA Flight 847. Then, America had been unable to position special operations forces quickly enough. This time, as Caspar Weinberger recounted, "We were prepared to take action against the ship." But with the vessel stationary in Egyptian waters, the Americans decided to let negotiations take their course for one more day.[12] Perhaps it would all end with an arrest, a trial, and no further bloodshed. If not, America's SEALs and Deltas would have another day to size up the ship before storming it on the night of 9 October.

On the morning of 9 October, Muhammed Abul Abbas, of all people, conveniently appeared to lead the PLO mediation effort. He materialized within an hour of being summoned to Port Said, indicating that he had probably been in the area all along. Abbas's "negotiating" sounded a lot more like orders. "Listen to me well," said Abbas, using a code name. "First of all, the passengers should be treated very well. In addition, you must apologize to them and the ship's crew and to the captain, and tell them our objective was not to take control of the ship. Tell them what your main objective was." The tired hijackers complied, assuring the terrified passengers that in fact they meant to kill Israelis and destroy facilities in Ashdod, as if that was just fine.

The crew and those passengers not detained with the Americans proved only too willing to do whatever was needed to end their captivity. After noon on 9 October, the PLF forced Captain de Rosa to broadcast, "Everybody is in good health. Everything is OK," a lie designed to remove suspicion about a murder on 8 October. This was good enough for the Egyptians, who authorized Abbas to go out to the ship and retrieve his men. The Italian and West German ambassadors signed the transfer agreement, confident that de Rosa's statement reflected reality. But the U.S. and British representatives still refused to sign.

Indeed, most of the Europeans aboard the *Achille Lauro* gave their captors a rousing heroes' send-off at 1700 on 9 October. The PLF men crowed to their new friends, "We did not mean to hurt you. We only had an objective. We have a cause." Afterward, when Seymour Meskin confronted Captain de Rosa about his false message and the shameful applause as the PLF departed, de Rosa said, "I would have kissed their toes to get rid of them."

But where was Leon Klinghoffer? Following the few hours of captivity topside on 8 October, his wife Marilyn had been told by the ship's crew and non-American passengers that her invalid husband was resting in the ship's infirmary after a mild heart attack. Meskin opined that "they knew Leon was dead. They were afraid to tell Mrs. Klinghoffer, afraid of any hysterics on her part that might have caused a commotion and put all of the passengers and crew in danger." [13] It was certainly a craven display. Of course, Mrs. Klinghoffer found no trace of her husband in the ship's medical compartments.

The ship docked at Port Said at 2000 on 9 October. After midnight, U.S. Ambassador Nicholas Veliotes arrived from Cairo. He visited the ship, met Mrs. Klinghoffer, and discovered that an American was dead. Veliotes flew into a justified rage. "Tell the [Egyptian] foreign minister," he radioed ashore, "that we demand that they prosecute these sons of bitches."

Around 1000 on 10 October, President Mubarak stated that the PLF team was already gone, in accord with the deal concluded. "We took it upon ourselves," said the Egyptian leader, "to get them out of here so that people would believe us afterwards should there be a similar operation. . . . If the captain had told us that a passenger had been killed, we would have changed our position toward the whole operation." [14] The Egyptians blamed the captain for lying, and the Italians blamed the Egyptians for releasing the hijackers so quickly. But all of this finger-pointing solved nothing. Once again, as during the TWA Flight 847 seizure, it appeared that the terrorists had escaped justice.

Mubarak's blunt assertion seemed to close the case of the *Achille Lauro*. The Egyptians repeated their remarks to Ambassador Veliotes and in other public forums, apparently washing their hands of the entire matter. By the time part of the National Security Council's Crisis Pre-Planning Group met in the White House basement at 0800 (1400 Cairo time) on 10 October, they figured that it would be an after-action review.

President Reagan was en route to a political appearance near Chicago, Illinois, accompanied by National Security adviser Robert McFarlane (one of the special envoys during the ill-fated Lebanon venture). Secretary of Defense Weinberger was resting in Bar Harbor, Maine, a layover before he flew to Ottawa, Canada. NSC deputy staff director Vice Adm. John Poindexter opened the meeting with the dejected words, "It looks like it's all over."

Already, the SEALs and Deltas were redeploying through Gibraltar for home, once again close but not close enough. Preparations were made to stop priority conversion of raw information on the *Achille Lauro* situation into analyzed intelligence. But a committed marine lieutenant colonel, Oliver North, was not ready to give up yet. A veteran of combat and many covert operations (to include a subordinate position in EAGLE CLAW), North and his supervisor Poindexter would soon become notorious for their role in secret arms shipments to Iran. But in October 1985, that was but one of many projects occupying the decisive marine. He pleaded with Poindexter to allow one more review of the latest intercepts and messages from Egypt.

By 0930, North's hunch paid off. A reliable source insisted that Mubarak was lying through his teeth; the PLO had not yet removed its PLF operatives. As the NSC team requested closer scrutiny, further reports came in. The terrorists were sighted with Abbas at the Cairo Sheraton Heliopolis Hotel. North realized that if the Americans moved swiftly, they could still bring the ship hijacking to a successful conclusion. He addressed the admiral: "Do you remember Yamamoto?" (Adm. Isoroku Yamamoto's plane was destroyed in April 1943 by U.S. fighters guided by code breakers.)

"God," said Poindexter, "we can't shoot them down."

"No, but we have two choices. Our friends can shoot them down, or we can force them down somewhere," said North.

"Where?" asked the admiral.

"Sigonella," concluded North. Poindexter nodded, and he gave his energetic assistant clearance to communicate his scheme to Vice Adm. Arthur Moreau, JCS representative on the crisis planning group. Moreau listened intently, then hung up. Ten minutes later, he called back. Sixth Fleet could handle the mission. As the new JCS chairman, Adm. William J. Crowe, briefed Caspar Weinberger: "Our boys are good. I think they can do it. I think we should let them try."

By 1100 Washington time (1700 in Egypt), North, Moreau, JCS

staffers, and intelligence officers had completed preliminary planning. Intelligence revealed that the hijackers intended to leave for Tunis after nightfall. Superb American surveillance pinpointed a Boeing 737 at Al Maza military airfield northeast of Cairo as the PLF's transportation. The Americans learned the EgyptAir plane's tail number, aerial radar transponder code, and its pilot's name, Capt. Ahmed Moneeb.

United States Strategic and Operational Objectives
in the *Achille Lauro* Hijacker Interception

STRATEGIC OBJECTIVE: Capture the PLF hijackers.
OPERATIONAL OBJECTIVES:
  1) Intercept EgyptAir Boeing 737.
  2) Divert EgyptAir Boeing 737 to Sigonella Naval Air Station, Sicily.
  3) Apprehend PLF hijackers upon landing.

North and Moreau concocted a simple but elegant concept of operations. Aided by an Arab linguist aboard a lumbering twin-jet EA-3B Skywarrior (a type nicknamed the "Whale") electronic eavesdropper, USS *Saratoga*'s air wing would conduct a tricky night intercept and force a landing at Sigonella Naval Air Station in Sicily. There, JSOC SEALs and Deltas, reversing their journey home, hoped to nab the culprits and hustle them aboard a Military Airlift Command C-141B Starlifter. Once the operation commenced, State Department officials were to cable the Tunisians, Lebanese, and Greeks, requesting a denial of landing rights. Intentionally, the Italians were not consulted, and the Egyptians remained (at least in any formal sense) uninformed.[15]

The scheme featured two subtle points. First, use of the special operations troops at Sigonella was not accidental. In the event the PLF grabbed their innocent EgyptAir crew in flight or upon touchdown, the SEALs and Delta soldiers could storm the airliner. Second, the Egyptians might well have been part of the operation. Mubarak had to avoid a public stance against the Palestinian terrorists in order to appease Egyptian Arab hard-liners, yet he also was a firm American ally. In theory, surreptitious assistance allowed Mubarak to portray himself as an American victim in his own country and yet assure the United States that Egypt was a faithful ally.[16] If the Egyptians helped, America could never ac-

---

United States and Italian Forces Order of Battle
10–11 October 1985

United States Sixth Fleet

Joint Special Operations Command (JSOC): SEAL Team 6, elements of 1st Special Forces Operations Detachment—Delta

U.S. Navy/Marine Forces

Task Force 60, Sixth Fleet

USS *Saratoga* (CV-60) with Carrier Air Wing 17 (CVW-17), USS *Yorktown* (CG-48), USS *Richmond K. Turner* (CG-20), USS *Scott* (DDG-995), USS *Mahan* (DDG-42), USS *Caron* (DD-970), USS *Seattle* (AOE-3)

Carrier Air Wing 17

Fighter Squadron 74 (VF-74): 12 F-14A Tomcats

Fighter Squadron 103 (VF-103): 12 F-14A Tomcats

Medium Attack Squadron 85 (VA-85): 10 A-6E Intruders, 4 KA-6D tankers

Light Attack Squadron (VA-81): 12 A-7E Corsair IIs

Light Attack Squadron (VA-83): 12 A-7E Corsair IIs

Tactical Electronic Warfare Squadron (VAQ-137): 4 EA-6B Prowlers

Airborne Early Warning Squadron (VAW-125): 4 E-2C Hawkeyes

Antisubmarine Warfare Squadron (VS-30): 10 S-3A Vikings

Antisubmarine Warfare Squadron (HS-3): 6 SH-3H Sea Kings

USS *Coral Sea* (CV-43) with Carrier Air Wing 13 (CVW-13); USS *Wainwright* (CG-28); USS *Biddle* (CG-34)

Electronic Surveillance Squadron 2 (VQ-2), Rota, Spain (EA-3B Skywarrior)

Sigonella Naval Air Station, Sicily

U.S. Air Force Units

Elements, Military Airlift Command

513th Tactical Airlift Wing (EC-135 Burning Wind surveillance aircraft)

Italian Armed Forces

Carabinieri detachment, Sigonella, Sicily

Sources: Norman Polmar, "Changing Carrier Air Wings," *Proceedings* (August 1984), 154–155; Christopher Wright, "U.S. Naval Operations in 1985," *Proceedings* (May 1986), 285–88; "United States Air Forces in Europe," *Air Force* (May 1985), 112.

---

knowledge the aid. But such a possibility certainly explains the extraordinarily accurate intelligence flowing from Cairo.

About 1130 (1730 in Cairo), North contacted McFarlane via a secure net. The marine officer explained the concept of operations to the national security adviser. Within a half hour, McFarlane briefed President Reagan amid the incongruous surroundings of a small cafeteria at the Kitchens of Sara Lee Bakery, just outside Chicago. Reagan agreed in principle, but questioned McFarlane about the exact rules of engagement and potential casualties. The president wanted to insure that America would not repeat (or even appear to imitate) the brutal Soviet destruction of Korean Air Lines Flight 007 of September 1983. Mindful of these legitimate concerns, McFarlane called back to Washington, and North, Poindexter, Moreau, and their planning staff worked out detailed, specific ROE.[17]

While subordinates hashed out rules of engagement designed to prevent injury to innocent Egyptians, Caspar Weinberger reached Reagan to express his reservations. Although Secretary of State George Shultz favored the interception effort, Weinberger objected, saying, "This will destroy our relations with Egypt." The defense secretary warned of the dangerous consequences in the event USN aviators were forced to fire warning shots. Reagan, perhaps aware of covert Egyptian aid, told his distant associate to launch the mission anyway. Amazingly, due to a freakish breakdown in secure radio equipment, a ham radio operator in Chicago monitored a portion of one Reagan/Weinberger exchange. Although a report reached the Columbia Broadcasting System (CBS) offices in New York, the American plan was not compromised.[18]

Regardless, by 1300 on 10 October (1900 in the Mediterranean), the first concrete orders reached the USS *Saratoga* battle group. The big carrier swung south as crews scrambled to prepare for action. In *Saratoga*'s screen, the new Aegis air defense cruiser USS *Yorktown* activated its powerful AN/SPY-1A radar complex and affiliated computer classification system, which allowed superb resolution of air traffic all the way south to the African coast. It was already dark off Albania, but Capt. Kent Ewing, USN, began sending out his first Air Wing 17 aircraft by 2015.

An E-2C Hawkeye turboprop air control plane led the way, followed by a backup to direct combat air patrols over the U.S. battle group. F-14 fighters also took off, with the interceptors from the Fighter Squadron 103 Sluggers and cover courtesy of Fighter Squadron 74, the Bedevilers.

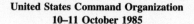

United States Command Organization
10–11 October 1985

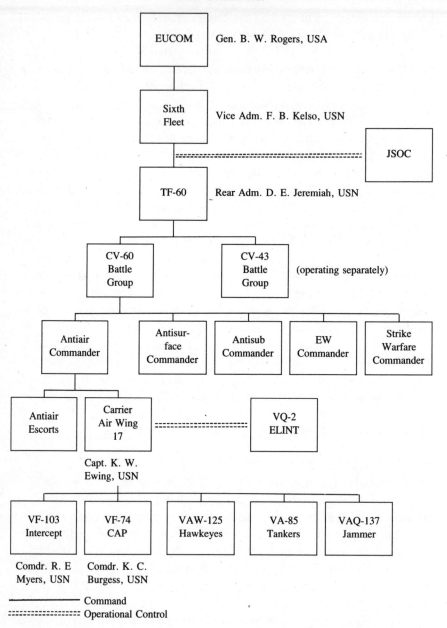

EUCOM — Gen. B. W. Rogers, USA

Sixth Fleet — Vice Adm. F. B. Kelso, USN

JSOC

TF-60 — Rear Adm. D. E. Jeremiah, USN

CV-60 Battle Group

CV-43 Battle Group — (operating separately)

Antiair Commander

Antisurface Commander

Antisub Commander

EW Commander

Strike Warfare Commander

Antiair Escorts

Carrier Air Wing 17

VQ-2 ELINT

Capt. K. W. Ewing, USN

VF-103 Intercept

VF-74 CAP

VAW-125 Hawkeyes

VA-85 Tankers

VAQ-137 Jammer

Comdr. R. E Myers, USN

Comdr. K. C. Burgess, USN

————— Command
::::::::::::::::::: Operational Control

EUCOM's naval deputy, CINCNAVEUR, routinely handled naval affairs in the theater from his London headquarters.

372

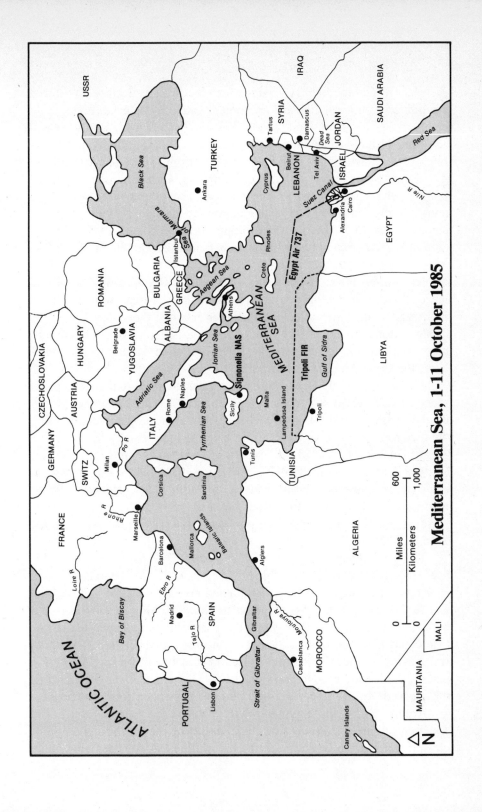

Mediterranean Sea, 1-11 October 1985

A specially configured EA-6B Prowler electronic warfare jet followed the fighters southeast, toward an aerial "gate" to be established about eighty miles south of Crete. Four KA-6D tankers with dimly lighted refueling baskets joined the air element to keep the thirsty jets aloft. Finally, the attached EA-3B Whale from Electronic Surveillance Squadron 2 in Rota, Spain, trailed along, carrying the Arab linguist who would serve as the voice of the intercept force. The planes went south in a ghostly array, all lights out, with electronic data links providing updates automatically to *Yorktown,* the orbiting Hawkeye, and *Saratoga.* [19] Although the Americans were on station before 2100, the PLF still had not left Egypt.

But things began to happen, even as *Saratoga* readied a second wave. American intelligence reported that the terrorists were finally at Al Maza. Shortly thereafter, the PLF men boarded their plane. At 2213, Captain Moneeb filed a flight plan for Algiers, Algeria; American surveillance marked this as a ruse. They were going to Tunis. Two minutes later, the EgyptAir 737 was airborne.

The civil aircraft flew on the expected course, at the anticipated speed of 460 miles per hour and 34,000 feet. The USN Hawkeye picked up the airliner almost immediately, verifying the target identity using the electronic data links back to the battle group. The E-2C was quite an airplane. In the words of experienced Hawkeye flier Lt. Comdr. Clifford Ayer, "One E-2C flying on station during the Battle of Britain could have observed all air activity on both sides, from launch to recovery." [20] Compared to sorting out a massive Soviet cruise missile barrage, locating a Boeing transport on a known course was simple, even at night.

The replacement group from Air Wing 17 launched about 2245, heading south toward the invisible trap zone near Crete. The long-duration Hawkeye and listening Whale maintained contact with the approaching 737 as the seven new F-14s came on station. The Slugger quartet would make the actual interception, while three Bedevilers protected the scene. One could never be too sure about the nearby Libyans. Maybe Gadhafi was paying attention and might elect to join the fray. Air Wing 17's historical files included reports on the 1981 incident over Sidra, when they served aboard USS *Forrestal.* So the navy men took no chances.

Around 2325, the EgyptAir flight entered the ambush zone. The American fighters stole up from behind and below on the lighted 737, closing like swift gray sharks on the tail of the unsuspecting twin-engine jet. After a minute of sizing up their quarry, the USN flight leader made his move. The big twin-engine Tomcats flanked the airliner, two to a side. Stewardess Hala Faham described the event: "We suddenly saw lights flashing so brightly on both sides. We looked out of the windows, and we saw two warplanes on both sides, but we couldn't make out the markings." [21]

The navy crews flew tight formation with the EgyptAir 737. When Moneeb tried to notify Cairo of his plight, the American Prowler jammed the transmission, skipping up and down the airliner's frequency dial to fill Moneeb's headset with blaring static. Then, the Arab linguist on the Whale cut in, speaking like a distant god out of the ether. There was no polite introduction, just a curt demand that the Egyptian pilot follow the "escorts" to Sigonella. "If you do not follow my instructions, we will shoot you," the American concluded.

"Are you serious?" asked Moneeb.

"I think so, yes," stated the calm USN spokesman.

The Egyptian airline captain accepted the inevitable and continued in formation. After about a half hour of silent flight, he tried to call Athens for landing rights. The Prowler let this one go through, and an El Al Israeli plane in the area overheard (and indeed relayed) Moneeb's weak transmission. Israeli First Officer Dror Harish identified "anxiety, tension, and anger" in the Egyptian's tone. "Two military jet fighters are intercepting us and directing us toward Italy," radioed the EgyptAir crew. Athens control acknowledged but refused to offer a safe haven. The Tunisians also rebuffed Moneeb's request for a landing.[22]

Ahmed Moneeb followed his mysterious wingmen despondently. If any Egyptians were part of the U.S. operation, they were not on Moneeb's 737. "I put my lights on," he said, "but they ordered me to put them off. I never thought they were American planes—Italian, maybe, but never American." The Egyptian pilot thought he had no alternative. In the cabin, the PLF men aboard wondered what was going on. The situation did not look promising for them.

The odd aerial procession appeared on Italian radar screens as a complete surprise. Italy ran the eastern approach corridor to their Sicilian airdrome, although U.S. Navy associates assisted. At first, the Sigonella control tower categorically turned away the unanticipated (but obviously politically important) new arrivals. The Italian military flight controllers relented after the accompanying Hawkeye declared a "low fuel emergency" on behalf of the EgyptAir 737. Apparently, directives from

Rome also spurred the Sigonella tower to admit the flight. President Reagan had finally asked Premier Bettino Craxi for help, and the Socialist executive reluctantly agreed to permit the landing at the combined U.S./ Italian base.

Once the 737 braked to a halt on the darkened tarmac, a contingent of Joint Special Operations Command Troops (SEAL Team 6 and some Delta men) surrounded the aircraft. The JSOC commanding general intended to snare his quarry and shovel them aboard a waiting MAC C-141B transport. But the local carabinieri (Italy's elite militarized national police) intervened, taking up stations as well. Later, Americans claimed they were encircled; Craxi alleged that his men showed up first. In any event, some superb fighting men from two old NATO allies stood by while the Italian colonel and American general debated the disposition of their captives. Although the exchanges were noisy (perhaps to be heard above the engines roaring on the airfield), there was no violence or real chance of any sort of fighting. Subsequent wild rumors about drawn weapons and brash threats were greatly overstated.

George Shultz and Italian foreign minister Giulio Andreotti got involved, using satellite hookups to hash out the disposition of the 737 and its passengers. The Americans dropped their objections to Italian custody only after Andreotti promised a murder charge against the terrorists. Shultz insisted upon U.S. extradition rights, and Andreotti agreed to consider that possibility. Around 0300, President Reagan approved orders for the JSOC troops to stand down and turn over their prey to the carabinieri.[23]

The aftermath of the clever interception was rather interesting. The four unlucky hijackers went immediately to jail, facing multiple felony charges, including murder. PLF leader Abbas and his military chief Kan escaped prosecution. Abbas carried Iraqi and PLO diplomatic credentials; Italy recognized both as valid. Good socialist that he was, Craxi let Abbas and Kan slip away, trying to show his domestic critics and Arab allies that he was not an American puppet. Once the two had made it safely to Yugoslavia, Craxi announced that his government would investigate U.S. allegations against the PLF pair. In the end, this double-dealing cost Craxi the support of Defense Minister Giovanni Spadolini, which compelled Craxi to dissolve his government on 17 October 1985.[24] Italy has no death penalty, but the four terrorists received lengthy prison terms for their crimes. In the end, the incident had virtually no effect on U.S./Italian relations or the NATO alliance.

Hosni Mubarak called the U.S. action "air piracy," and he decorated the EgyptAir crew for bravery during the diversion to Sicily. Despite some domestic rhetoric, Mubarak did not alter his generally pro-American foreign policy at all. If he assisted in any way, nobody in Washington or Cairo will admit it. As President Reagan coyly remarked, "We did this all by our little selves." [25]

Finally, in America, the prevailing mood was summarized by Democratic Senator Daniel P. Moynihan: "Thank God we finally won one." [26] Navy Tomcat crews and their assistants had performed a difficult night intercept without firing a shot or hurting anyone. Finally, Carrier Air Wing 17 achieved the dream of decades among national security experts: a truly "surgical" strike.

In analyzing this successful operation in the Mediterranean, three points come to mind. First, the mission made innovative use of available conventional force capabilities to perform a type of task normally handled by special operations units. Considering that it was done at night, on very short notice, and with delicate rules of engagement, the interception looms as a particularly impressive feat. As Navy Secretary John Lehman commented, "First, there was no warning, and what was carried out

---

Comparative Loss Summary
Personnel

	KIA	MIA	WIA	PW	Nonbattle
U.S. Navy/USMC	0	0	0	0	0
U.S. MILITARY TOTAL	0	0	0	0	0
PLF	0	0	0	6*	0

Equipment

U.S. Military: none

One EgyptAir Boeing 737 captured (returned intact)

* Nine Egyptians also detained. Five were in the flight crew, plus four others.

Sources: Scott C. Truver, "Maritime Terrorism, 1985," *Proceedings* (May 1986), 169; Gayle Rivers (pseudonym), *The War Against the Terrorists* (New York: Stein and Day, 1986), 171; "Egyptian Pilot Reports a U.S. Threat to Shoot," *New York Times*, 17 October 1985, A13.

---

was the normal kind of intercept that we train to all the time.'' In short, demanding U.S. naval aviation training paid off handsomely under the stars south of Crete.

Second, although the Tomcats adhered to their rules of engagement and their mere appearance convinced Captain Moneeb to follow orders, would the Americans have shot? Shultz, Weinberger, and Lehman backed away from any detailed discussion of the specific ROE in effect on 10 October, and they cautioned against speculation. They advised journalists to allow prospective terrorists to worry about what might have happened.

Achille Lauro Hijacking Time Line
(Local Egyptian Time)
1–11 October 1985

1 October—Israeli aircraft bomb PLO headquarters in Tunisia.

3 October—PLF team boarded *Achille Lauro* in Genoa, Italy.

7 October—PLF team discovered; *Achille Lauro* hijacked. USS *Scott* departed Haifa, Israel. USS *Saratoga* alerted. American Special Operations forces commenced deployment.

8 October—American Leon Klinghoffer killed; Syria and Lebanon refused to accept hijacked ship.

9 October—Capt. Gerardo de Rosa forced to state that all passengers were alive and well; PLO/PLF negotiator Abul Abbas ended hijacking.

    (1700) *Achille Lauro* freed.

    (2000) Klinghoffer's death confirmed.

10 October—(1000) Egypt reported that PLF team departed their country.

    (1530) Intelligence indicated that PLF men were still in Egypt.

    (1700) Intelligence pinpointed EgyptAir aircraft.

    (1900) President Reagan authorized mission; Sixth Fleet alerted.

    (2000) Final interception plan relayed to USS *Saratoga* Battle Group.

    (2015) USS *Saratoga* launched first set of aircraft.

    (2215) EgyptAir Boeing 737 took off.

    (2245) Second set of USN aircraft launched.

    (2330) Interception completed; Egyptian plane diverted.

11 October—(0030) EgyptAir Boeing 737 landed at Sigonella NAS, Sicily; surrounded by U.S. Special Operations forces and Italian carabinieri.

    (0300) Americans agreed to Italian jurisdiction in case.

Certainly, four fully armed fighter planes could have made short work of an unmaneuverable civil aircraft.

Even so, one can reasonably conclude that further shows of force were probably authorized. As John Lehman said, "Then there are specific procedures to follow, including depending on what the rules of engagement are, the firing of warning shots and so forth." [27] During planning, Weinberger had cautioned Reagan about the risk in such measures, but the president pressed on anyway. In reality, it is unlikely that the Americans would shoot down a plane carrying an innocent flight crew and civilians from a friendly nation. It is easy to say that the Egyptians were part of the plan all along, but if so, nobody bothered to clue in the airline command pilot. The Tomcats had to scare him into obedience or fail in their mission. Had Moneeb run for it, the Tomcats might have pursued, and U.S. JSOC outfits could have been waiting wherever the fleeing 737 touched down. But the brazen USN bluff worked.

Lastly, American political and military leaders could not have been very happy with their Italian and Egyptian allies. The *Achille Lauro* incident underscored once more that even the best of international friends have unique interests and constraints. While alliances can provide strength in numbers, they can also dilute American resolve and hamper American options in situations short of general war. In these dangerous cases, the United States could well expect to act alone. This lesson was not lost on Washington decision makers.

One interception, however brilliant, offered no permanent solution to terrorism. While America celebrated its ingenuity, several sponsors of terrorist groups, most notably Moammar Gadhafi of Libya, plotted retaliation. When American planes again flew in response to terrorism, there would be no nimble surgical strikes. The next round would be for blood.

Chapter 6 Notes

Epigraphs come from Gayle Rivers (pseudonym), *The War Against the Terrorists* (New York; Stein and Day, 1986), 181; "You Can Run But You Can't Hide," *Newsweek* (21 October 1985), 32; President Ronald W. Reagan, "Remarks, 11 October 1985," *Department of State Bulletin* (December 1985), 75.

1. Maj. Jeffrey W. Wright, USA, "Terrorism as a Mode of Warfare," *Military Review* (October 1984), 42.
2. Col. Frederic C. Hof, "The Beirut Bombing of October 1983: An Act of Terrorism?" *Parameters* (summer 1985), 70, 72, 73.
3. "Eight Israeli F-16As in Raid on PLO," *Jane's Defense Weekly* (12 October 1985), 763.
4. Scott C. Truver, "Maritime Terrorism, 1985," *Proceedings* (May 1986), 166, 167; Rivers, *The War Against the Terrorists,* 169–71.
5. U.S. Congress, House Committee on Foreign Affairs, *Overview of International Maritime Security,* 99th Congress, 1st Session, 23 October 1985, 48; U.S. Congress, House Committee on Merchant Marine and Fisheries, *Cruise Ship Industry,* 99th Congress, 1st Session, 22 October 1985, 192, 250.
6. House Committee on Merchant Marine, *Cruise Ship Industry,* 190, 250; "Cruising on a Murderous Course," *Newsweek* (21 October 1985), 34.
7. House Committee on Merchant Marine, *Cruise Ship Industry,* 190, 191; "Cruising on a Murderous Course," 34, 35.
8. "Cruising on a Murderous Course," 35; Truver, "Maritime Terrorism, 1985," 166, 167.
9. Truver, "Maritime Terrorism, 1985," 166; "Fighters Praised for Intercepting Hijackers' Plane," *Air Force Times* (21 October 1985), 4.
10. Truver, "Maritime Terrorism, 1985," 167, 168; "You Can Run, But You Can't Hide," 26; "Cruising on a Murderous Course," 34, 35; "Waiter on the Ship Said He Was Forced to Toss Body into the Sea," *New York Times,* 19 October 1985, L4.
11. "Cruising on a Murderous Course," 35, 37.
12. "Fighters Praised for Intercepting Hijackers' Plane," 4.
13. "Cruising on a Murderous Course," 37; House Committee on Merchant Marine, *Cruise Ship Industry,* 193; "Radio to Hijackers: 'You Must Apologize,' " *New York Times,* 17 October 1985, A12.
14. Truver, "Maritime Terrorism, 1985," 168; "You Can Run, But You Can't Hide," 31.
15. Truver, "Maritime Terrorism, 1985," 168; "You Can Run, But You Can't Hide," 22, 23, 31.

16. "You Can Run, But You Can't Hide," 31; Leroy Thompson, *The Rescuers* (Boulder, CO: Paladin Press, 1986), 108.

17. Truver, "Maritime Terrorism," 168; "You Can Run, But You Can't Hide," 23.

18. Rivers, *The War Against the Terrorists,* 170; "You Can Run, But You Can't Hide," 23, 24; "F-14s Use Latest Electronics in EgyptAir Intercept," *Aviation Week and Space Technology* (21 October 1985), 28.

19. "F-14s Use Latest Electronics in EgyptAir Intercept," 28; "You Can Run, But You Can't Hide," 24, 25; "Fighters Praised for Intercepting Hijackers' Plane," 4; Truver, "Maritime Terrorism, 1985," 168, 169; "New EA-6B Computer Helped Nab Terrorists," *Navy Times* (25 November 1985), 53; Capt. Joseph L. McLane, USN (ret.) and Comdr. James L. McClane, USN, "The *Ticonderoga* Story: Aegis Works," *Proceedings* (May 1985), 118–29.

20. "Airliner Intercept Illustrates E-2C Capability," *Air Force Times* (4 November 1985), 65, 66.

21. "Fighters Praised for Intercepting Hijackers' Plane," 4; "F-14s Use Latest Electronics in EgyptAir Intercept," 28; "You Can Run, But You Can't Hide," 24, 25; "For *Saratoga's* Crew, Big Smiles and Tight Lips," *New York Times,* 13 October 1985, L24; "Egyptian Crew Tells of Incident," *New York Times,* 15 October 1985, A10.

22. "New EA-6B Computer Helped Nab Terrorists," 53; "Fighters Praised for Intercepting Hijackers' Plane," 4; "Egyptian Pilot Reports a U.S. Threat to Shoot," *New York Times,* 17 October 1985, A13; "Israelis Describe Hearing Message of Diverted Jet," *New York Times,* 14 October 1985, A12.

23. "Egyptian Pilot Reports a U.S. Threat to Shoot," A13; Truver, "Maritime Terrorism, 1985," 169; "You Can Run, But You Can't Hide," 25; John Lehman, "This Week With David Brinkley, 13 October 1985," *Department of State Bulletin* (December 1985), 80; "Aides Say Reagan Put End to Troop Stand Off," *New York Times,* 19 October 1985, L4; "Sicilians Won't Pursue Inquiry on U.S. Troops," *New York Times,* 29 October 1985, A12; Lt. E. H. Lundquist, USN, "A Day on the Line," *Naval Aviation News* (March–April 1986), 10, 11.

24. Truver, "Maritime Terrorism, 1985," 169, 170; Rivers, *The War Against the Terrorists,* 171.

25. "Egyptian Pilot Reports a U.S. Threat to Shoot," A13; "You Can Run, But You Can't Hide," 31; Reagan, "Remarks, 11 October 1985," 76.

26. "You Can Run, But You Can't Hide," 32.

27. Lehman, "This Week with David Brinkley, 13 October 1985," 79, 80; George Shultz, "The Today Show, 11 October 1985," *Department of State Bulletin* (December 1985), 76, 77.

Its surface cleared of obstructions, Salines runway, Grenada, glows in the tropical sunlight in October 1983. In the early light of dawn on October 25, USAF pilots threaded a curtain of fire to put Rangers onto this hard, narrow, obstacle-strewn seaside drop zone.

The amphibious assault ship USS *Guam* (LPH-9) steams off Grenada. *Guam* served as headquarters for Joint Task Force 120 during Operation URGENT FURY.

U.S. Army airborne infantrymen search numerous small dwellings as they work their way north from Salines toward St. George's, Grenada. The heavy vegetation and steep hills were typical.

Under a blazing tropical sun, 82d Airborne infantrymen move toward the front. Despite modern high technology, physical fitness is still imperative for ground troops.

Rangers disembark from 82d Combat Aviation Battalion UH-60A Blackhawk helicopters at Point Salines following the frustrating Calvigny raid. The Rangers can be distinguished by their traditional helmet shape; the 82d Airborne wore the coal-scuttle Kevlar variety.

Airborne gunners fire an M-102 105-mm howitzer against enemy targets in Grenada.

A Ranger officer briefs rescued American medical students at True Blue Campus late on the afternoon of 25 October. The civilians wear white armbands to facilitate identification of friend from foe during the actual recovery effort. Note the two hard-looking characters to the right rear sporting bush hats with white headbands; they are probably part of the elite USAF Combat Control Team.

With M-60 7.62-mm machine guns at the ready, two jeeps full of U.S. Army paratroopers escort Soviet Army Colonel Gennadiy Sazhenev's Mercedes sedan to Salines Airport. There, watchful paratroopers insured that Sazhenev and his Soviet Army and KGB comrades departed Grenada. The car is passing the wreck of a Soviet-made BTR-60PB armored personnel carrier knocked out by advancing American forces.

An abandoned Cuban/Grenadian ZU-23-2 overlooks St. George's harbor, Grenada, and a segment of the U.S. Navy's Amphibious Squadron 4.

The aircraft carrier USS *Saratoga* (CV-60). F-14A Tomcats from this ship's Carrier Air Wing 17 snatched the *Achille Lauro* hijackers from mid-air in October 1985 and smashed up Libyan missile radars and corvettes in March 1986. *Saratoga's* aircraft include: F-14As, EA-3B Whales, A-7E Corsairs, A-6E Intruders, S-3A Vikings, SH-3H Sea King helicopters, and E-2C Hawkeyes.

American operations off Libya, 1986: an F-14A Tomcat jet fighter from Fighter Squadron 103 (''Sluggers'') prepares to catapult from *Saratoga* on 22 March.

Alert crews on *Saratoga* rest in fully loaded aircraft during ATTAIN DOCU-
MENT II, 12 February 1986. To the left, an EA-6B Prowler electronic warfare
jet, an F-14A Tomcat fighter, an A-6E Intruder medium attack jet, a second
Intruder (nose just visible), another Tomcat, and a KA-6D tanker. On the right,
an S-3A Viking antisubmarine jet, a Tomcat with AIM-9M Sidewinder missiles,
and an A-7E Corsair II light attack plane with two white munitions cannisters.

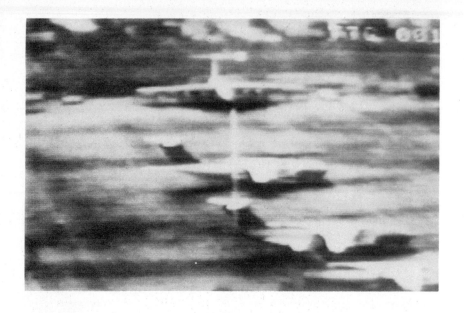

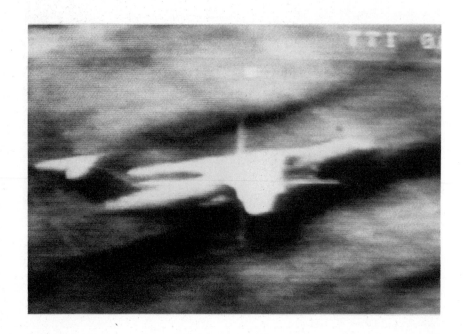

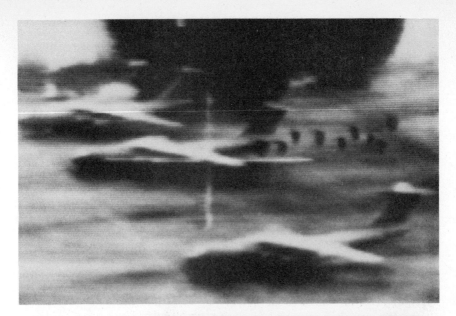

This remarkable sequence of pictures depicts the view through the bombsight of an attacking F-111F jet as it swept down on Tripoli airport. The first two photographs (*opposite page*) show an Il-76 Candid jet transport as the USAF plane approached; the last two shots (*above*) were taken by the Pave Tack system looking backward. "TTG" means time to target (bomb release); "TTI" refers to time to impact once the Mark 82 500-pound munitions dropped. The cross shows the point of aim. These bombs were *not* laser guided, although the Pave Tack allowed precision delivery. Remember that these views were taken about 0200 local time.

This 48th Tactical Fighter Wing F-111F shows its four Mark 84 2,000-pound bombs with Paveway II laser kits affixed. The complex Pave Tack targeting pod is visible on the Aardvark's centerline. F-111s from the 48th TFW participated in the Libyan bombing.

The *Tariq Ibn Ziyad*, a Soviet-built *Nanuchka II* guided-missile corvette of the Libyan Arab Navy, burns fiercely on the morning of 25 March 1986. The two black circles surrounded by flames are launcher tubes for SS-N-2C Styx missiles, which can range out to 25 miles.

CHAPTER 7

TO THE SHORES OF TRIPOLI: OPERATIONS AGAINST LIBYA

MARCH–APRIL 1986

"Every Libyan must take up guns, bombs, and with their guns and bombs they will teach a lesson to America. We will teach a lesson to America greater than the Vietnam lesson. We have fought alongside Nicaragua because they are fighting America. Nicaragua is fighting America near its borders. The American people will be strangled. We are working to build a wide front of people who are against America, Iran revolutionaries, Afghanistan, Nicaragua, Cuba, Namibia, Palestine, South Africa, Northern Ireland—we will form a wide integrated front which encircles imperialism."

Moammar Gadhafi, 1984

Sultan Muley Soliman: "Are you not in fear of being detained?"
Commodore Edward Preble, USN: "No sir. If you presume to do it my squadron in your full view will lay your batteries, your castle, and your city in ruins."

Conversation in Tangier, Morocco, 5 October 1803

The unexpected diversion of the *Achille Lauro* hijackers left the volatile Col. Moammar Gadhafi and his chief terrorist lieutenants in foul humor. Stung by the innovative U.S. action, the Libyan leader turned to the renegade Palestinian Abu Nidal for a violent riposte. Nidal, born Mazen Sabry al-Banna in the British mandate of Palestine, had been forcibly evicted during the establishment of Israel. He never forgot that wrenching boyhood experience. He abandoned the implacable Yasir Arafat as too moderate in 1973, and warred regularly against the mainline PLO structure, using alternate headquarters in Tripoli, Libya, and Damascus, Syria.

The crafty Nidal avoided the potent Americans as he designed retaliatory measures. Instead, he struck at the United States' Mediterranean allies, suspected culprits in *Saratoga's* snatch of the PLF team. Funded and assisted by Gadhafi, Nidal arranged a bloody hijacking to punish the Egyptians and an airport slaughter to injure the Italians, with a side foray into Austria aimed at the Israelis. Nidal's actions were intended to demonstrate that American aerial prowess could not quell Gadhafi and his shadowy associates. In the process, the terrorist chieftain initiated a sequence of dire events that culminated less than six months later in a crushing air raid on Gadhafi's homeland.

The Palestinian Liberation Front's terrorist team had bungled almost their entire operation; not so Abu Nidal's fanatical Fatah Revolutionary Council (FRC). Nidal enjoyed a deserved reputation as one of the more notorious purveyors of political violence, having planned the Black September outrages during the 1972 Munich Olympics. His operatives tracked and murdered Yasir Arafat's associates across the Middle East. The FRC's 1982 execution of Israel's ambassador to Great Britain, Shlomo Argov, helped convince Menachem Begin of the immediate need to "clean out" Lebanon, with tragic consequences for Israelis, Lebanese, and Americans alike. Nidal's staff provided some assistance to their PLF rivals during the *Achille Lauro* episode, but surely took some sardonic pleasure when the plot miscarried.[1] Just over a month later, Nidal sent men to show how such things should be done.

The seizure of EgyptAir Flight 648 occurred on 23 November 1985. Three FRC hijackers took charge of the Boeing 737 as it left Athens bound for Cairo. An Egyptian sky marshal aboard tried to shoot it out and killed a terrorist. The others cut down the brave Egyptian, and the flying bullets punctured the cabin walls, resulting in explosive decompression and a harrowing plunge from altitude. The enraged gunmen diverted Flight 648 to the tiny independent island of Malta, landing late on 23 November on an unlit runway. Over the next few hours, the frenzied hijackers shot three Israelis and two Americans and shoved their bodies out the aircraft door; one person of each nationality died of the wounds inflicted.

Meanwhile, the Maltese government authorized Egypt to stage for a rescue attempt, although the island's leaders denied permission for all but the most minimal U.S. involvement. Malta feared its Libyan neighbors. As 24 November wore on, Egypt's Force 777 commandos flew in and prepared for an assault. USS *Coral Sea* aircraft escorted the rescue team's transport planes and flew vigilant patrols between Malta and unpredictable Libya. Three American officers, including two counterterrorist experts, arrived to offer advice, but the Egyptians did things their way. With Delta Force officers as helpless spectators, Force 777 stormed the plane in an uncoordinated, ill-timed early evening attack. The Egyptians employed too many smoke devices and probably too many operators on the small jet. Of ninety-eight passengers and crew aboard, fifty-seven passengers died, felled by smoke inhalation and accidental wounds in the subsequent aimless firefight. As passenger Marta Diego recounted, "There was smoke everywhere inside the plane. People were shouting and crying. It was worse than hell—worse than you can imagine." [2] The first part of Abu Nidal's *Achille Lauro* revenge had been accomplished.

Two days after Christmas, four dark-skinned men strode nervously through a terminal building in Rome's bustling Leonardo da Vinci airport. The young toughs were dressed in unremarkable attire; two wore blue jeans, one sported an expensive gray suit. But their carry-on baggage was a bit heftier than usual. All four carried AK-47 assault rifles and a few hand grenades. Simultaneously, hundreds of miles north and across the snowy Alps, a similarly equipped trio walked toward an Israeli El Al departure gate in Vienna.

At 0903, one of the four Rome gunmen tossed a grenade into a hamburger cafe, then along with his partners unleashed a hail of bullets directed at the El Al, Trans World Airlines, and Pan American ticket counters. The heavy AK slugs pinged and splattered through more than eight hundred feet of tiled terminal, shattering glass and shredding shocked bystanders. The shooters screamed and laughed like wild men, jumping and firing in a raucous display that, in the words of witness Anna Girometta, "seemed to go on forever." Italian security men gradually gained control of the situation, killing three of the terrorists in a blazing gun battle. One FRC agent died with his bloody fingers raised in a *V* for victory salute. When the shooting stopped, seventeen civilians lay dead, with more than seventy wounded. The corpses crumpled on the reddened tile included Mexican military attaché Gen. Donato Miranda Acosta and his secretary, three Greeks, an Algerian, and five Americans, among them an eleven-year-old girl.

Meanwhile, in Vienna, the other three FRC terrorists struck hard at the passengers on El Al Flight 364. Two died and forty-seven fell injured in a two-minute eruption of firing and grenade explosions. Austrian police killed one of the attackers and captured the other two after a brief chase. But the damage had been done, a grisly masterpiece of criminal coordination at the two airports.

Hours later, a radio station in Malaga, Spain, received a call in Arabic-accented Spanish, claiming the twin strike as the work of the Fatah Revolutionary Council. Police investigators in Austria turned up little, but the Italian authorities found some evidence of Nidal's mentor, Gadhafi. Three of the FRC men possessed Tunisian passports, traced back to a batch stolen from guest laborers by Libyan officials and routinely used by terror cells under Gadhafi's tutelage. Blood analysis indicated that the Rome airport raiders were strung out on copious amounts of amphetamines. Most ominously of all, a note found on one dead gunman read: "Zionists, as you have violated our land, our honor, our people, we in exchange will violate everything, even your children, to make you feel the sadness of our children. The tears we have shed will be exchanged for blood. The war started from this moment."

Moammar Gadhafi praised the killings as "heroic," and publicly announced that he sheltered FRC teams in Tripoli. He had done more than that as well. Nidal's fighters definitely used grenades drawn from Libyan Arab Army stocks; other grenades featuring the same ammunition manufacturing symbols and production lots turned up among captured Libyan positions during the April 1987 combat in Chad.[3] The other weaponry also probably came from Gadhafi's armories. But the Libyans and their Palestinian henchmen were about to find out that wars cut both ways.

The American reaction seemed extraordinarily measured at the time, particularly in the face of what President Reagan called "irrefutable" proof of Gadhafi's hand in the massacres. On 6 January 1986, President Reagan called a full meeting of the National Security Council. Secretary of State Shultz, Secretary of Defense Weinberger, and CIA director William Casey were all there. The subject was Libya: what to do?

The CIA chief warned that the passport connection and Gadhafi's loud pronouncements constituted the only hard links between Abu Nidal and Gadhafi. Nidal was known to frequent Damascus as well, and was sighted now and then in Tehran. Casey also cautioned everyone that the sources involved in U.S. intelligence about Libya were extremely sensitive and should not be exposed lightly. If America needed public and international justification for a harsh reaction, Casey doubted that the available information was sufficiently convincing. Nevertheless, the CIA director correctly judged that if Abu Nidal and Gadhafi attempted further mayhem, America's intelligence agencies were now poised to uncover these activities, perhaps allowing preemption.

As for the Defense Department, Vice Adm. John Poindexter and the Crisis Pre-Planning Group had formulated a series of military options, to include bombing raids by navy jets, F-111Fs based in Britain, or even devastating American-based B-52G and B-52H Stratofortresses. Proposals included pinpoint strikes by BGM-109C Tomahawk turbojet cruise missiles, which featured a digital scene-matching area correlation computer system that guaranteed accuracy over hundreds of miles of low-level flight without exposing pilots to the extensive Libyan air defenses. Finally, it was about time for another USN foray into the disputed Gulf of Sidra, a routine evolution that might provide the sort of diplomatic pressure needed to cow Gadhafi. As usual, Caspar Weinberger advised against committing military forces without clear goals. He remembered Lebanon.

For his part, Secretary of State Shultz laid out a selection of severe economic sanctions, which would end all trade between America and Libya. Additionally, Shultz hoped to garner allied support for U.S. economic strictures, but he doubted that the Europeans would agree to participate. He favored a freedom of navigation exercise near Libya as a means of influencing Gadhafi without resort to massive force. Despite all Gadhafi's loose talk, it would be hard to justify a unilateral U.S. counterattack against him; Syria and Iran were equally implicated, and few wished to launch strikes on these more formidable and strategically important nations. If Gadhafi was the loose cannon everyone suspected, he would overstep prudence again soon. But this time, the U.S. would be ready.

President Reagan agreed with his secretary of state. Although Reagan was certain that Gadhafi was behind Abu Nidal's activities, he needed more direct proof to insure domestic support for any major military effort. Allied backing was unlikely, but he asked Shultz to try. He assented to the total economic cutoff and approved another naval exercise near Libyan-claimed waters. Reagan announced these measures on 7 January 1986.

At the same time, Reagan approved extensive military preparations for more direct action. Tomahawks and B-52s were ruled out; there was no desire to compromise these technologies when other devices could do the job. Both weapons have major nuclear roles, and few relished the prospect of gleeful Libyans presenting pieces of such advanced systems to their Soviet friends. Moving around the cruise missile platforms and Strategic Air Command bombers for pre-attack training and staging might alert the Soviets that something was up, as they maintain careful surveillance of these units. Instead, European Command would devise aerial attack plans using their own resources, under the cover of scheduled peacetime exercises. General Bernard Rogers of EUCOM and his key subordinates began to evaluate target possibilities and Libyan defenses in early January 1986.[4] Meanwhile, Vice Adm. Frank B. Kelso readied his Sixth Fleet for action.

So the first American forces off Libya would be the navy, sailing in pursuit of free navigation in the Gulf of Sidra. In at least one sense, the mightiest sea service in the world returned to the scene of its earliest overseas triumphs. In 1803–05, the fledgling United States Navy and its tiny marine corps conducted a series of punitive amphibious raids against the Muslim pirate pashas of Morocco, Algiers (modern Algeria), Tunis (now Tunisia), and Tripoli (Libya). Several small-scale, bold, violent actions on the Barbary Coast freed American captives and demonstrated U.S. resolve. While the attacks certainly curbed the appetites of local corsairs, like their latter-day terrorist successors, the Barbary folk continued to prey on unwitting travelers. But after 1805, the Muslim buccaneers carefully avoided most U.S. shipping.[5] These North African skirmishes were the first operations in a lengthy tradition of American expeditionary combat, commemorated for posterity in the second line of the United States Marine Corps hymn ("to the shores of Tripoli").

American bluejackets had been this way in recent years as well, heedless of harsh words by Gadhafi. Sidra waters were a regular arena for USN maneuvers by the mid-1980s. Whenever the Libyan Arab Air Force (LAAF) rose to challenge American warships, they were brushed away, hounded, and in that single brief dogfight back in August 1981, destroyed. Since then, Colonel Gadhafi had loudly proclaimed 32 degrees 30 minutes north latitude to be Libya's northern boundary. He called it the "line of death" and vowed bloody mayhem should Americans violate it. Up until 1986, nobody had died in the Gulf of Sidra, although numerous

U.S. ships and aircraft had passed through. With tensions high between America and Libya, the 1986 exercises loomed as particularly dangerous. Even more than usual, the United States Navy would have to be on guard for trouble. A third carrier could be expected by March, which would allow a wider range of retaliatory options if Gadhafi responded. For now, the two in the Sixth Fleet would have to do.

Admiral Kelso personally briefed the aircrews aboard USS *Coral Sea* and USS *Saratoga* in early January. These two carriers planned to spearhead the innocuously labeled Operation ATTAIN DOCUMENT at month's end, flying inside the Tripoli flight information region (FIR) in an announced exercise. Kelso cautioned his aviators: "Do the job professionally, and be ready to defend yourself and your ship—but only within the guidelines of the Rules of Engagement." The peacetime ROE were as in 1981: "Don't fire unless fired upon." Kelso authorized Rear Adm. David E. Jeremiah, commander of Task Force 60, to designate opposing elements as hostile. Sixth Fleet permitted an armed response to three types of danger: actual Libyan use of force, imminent Libyan use of force, and any continuing Libyan threat of use of force. The fleet commander warned his fliers that they could expect difficult close encounters with the Libyans, but that USN aircraft must not open fire first.[6]

Libya claimed the immense Tripoli FIR as its national air defense region, and the U.S. Navy almost immediately discovered that Gadhafi's airmen hoped to enforce that assertion. Even before ATTAIN DOCU-MENT started, Libyan MiG-25 interceptors caught up with a loitering Electronic Surveillance Squadron 2 EA-3B Whale, well north of the FIR. Although the twin-engine Whale escaped unscathed, the incident underscored the seriousness of the LAAF. Evidently, Tripoli was tired of allowing free USN eavesdropping.

On 26 January, the two American carrier battle groups established a combat air patrol (CAP) barrier across the north end of the Tripoli FIR, using F-14A Tomcats from *Saratoga* and new F/A-18 Hornets from *Coral Sea*, both types laden with heat-seeking Sidewinder and radar-guided Sparrow missiles. Deck alert planes stayed ready to supplement the CAPs in the event of a major Libyan response.

Attack jets from both carriers flew surface CAP (SUCAP) missions, armed with Mark 20 Rockeye cluster bombs, capable HARMs (high-speed antiradiation missiles), and AGM-84A Harpoon antiship missiles. The maneuverable SUCAP Hornets disposed air to air weapons as well

Major United States Exercises in the Gulf of Sidra Region
August 1981 to April 1986

Open Ocean Missilex   (18–19 August 1981):   USS *Nimitz* battle group
                                                          USS *Forrestal* battle group
    Two Libyan aircraft shot down during brief engagement.

Freedom of Navigation   (16–17 February 1983):   USS *Nimitz* battle group
    This was a response to Libyan subversion in Sudan.

Joint AWACS MiGCAP   (31 July–1 August 1983):   USS *Eisenhower* battle group
                                                             USS *Coral Sea* battle group
    Joint operations included USAF AWACs and F-15 Eagles monitoring the Libyan invasion of Chad.

Freedom of Navigation   (25–26 July 1984):   USS *Saratoga* battle group
    This was a routine exercise of freedom of the seas.

ATTAIN DOCUMENT   (26–30 January 1986):   USS *Saratoga* battle group
                                                          USS *Coral Sea* battle group
    This exercise responded to Libyan-backed terrorism with a freedom of navigation exercise north of Libyan-claimed waters.

ATTAIN DOCUMENT II   (12–15 February 1986):   USS *Saratoga* battle group
                                                           USS *Coral Sea* battle group

    Forces continued operations near Libya.

ATTAIN DOCUMENT III/   (23–29 March 1986):   USS *Saratoga* battle group
  PRAIRIE FIRE   USS *Coral Sea* battle group
                                                         USS *America* battle group
                                                         Surface Action Group

    Sixteen-hour air/sea engagement resulted.

EL DORADO CANYON   (14–15 April 1986):   USS *Coral Sea* battle group
                                                         USS *America* battle group

    USN aircraft joined with USAF aircraft to strike five targets.

---

as their air to surface munitions. USS *Coral Sea* possessed four squadrons of the dual-role F/A-18 aircraft, replacing her Corsair II light bombers and Phantom fighters. The elderly *Coral Sea* and her sister *Midway* could not operate the big Tomcats, so the Hornets handled air defense for these ships. Eventually, the versatile F/A-18s would replace Corsair II light attack planes throughout the fleet. This operation represented something of an acid test for the new fighter/attack jet.

The Libyans responded quickly. A section of flashing MiG-25 Foxbat interceptors headed directly toward two F/A-18s early on 26 January. A *Coral Sea* E-2C Hawkeye controlled the USN fighters as they rolled onto the enemy's tail pipes in what Lt. Comdr. Robert E. Stumpf (of

Fighter/Attack Squadron 132) called "a classic stern intercept." Stumpf said that his colleagues expected the LAAF to fire during the U.S. approach. The Libyans carried Soviet AA-6 Acrid missiles, able to track targets from all aspects, unlike the rather unsophisticated AA-2 Atolls used back in August 1981. But the two Foxbats remained passive. They flew along with the Hornets on their tails for ten minutes, then split and returned to base independently. Stumpf was unimpressed: "They had displayed only limited maneuvering—nothing approaching what might be considered air combat."

Other Libyan planes also probed the USN combat air patrols. Su-22Js flew in straight and level and turned back quickly. Various Mirage types also appeared. Heavily armed MiG-23 Floggers tested *Saratoga's* Tomcats. The Floggers moved much more aggressively than the others, but failed to reach firing position on the tough USN aviators. Overall, the LAAF proved conspicuous by its absence. After four days, ATTAIN DOCUMENT ended, and Task Force 60 retired north to assess its experiences. As Lieutenant Commander Stumpf recalled, "Most had endured the hours of CAP station maintenance, heavy alert posture, and odd working hours without even as much as a radar contact."

Two weeks later, the two carrier air wings returned to the Tripoli flight information region for ATTAIN DOCUMENT II. This time, the Libyans reacted more vigorously, pressing the American fighters with more than 150 separate sorties. Ground radars in Libya sent the LAAF sections winging right for the CAP stations. On the American side, Hawkeyes picked up the Libyans at long range and vectored Hornets and Tomcats toward the bandits. The early warning allowed U.S. fliers to move quickly to gain firing positions on their opponents' rear quarters. The Libyans reacted by trying to lure the Americans across the line of death, but the carrier pilots disengaged before straying too far south.

The Libyans managed to run a few Foxbats over USS *Coral Sea,* closely followed and dogged by vigilant Hornets. It appeared that a big four-engine I1-76 Candid jet transport (an inferior Soviet version of the C-141) wallowing east and west in the FIR provided maritime surveillance of Task Force 60. It, too, operated with an unwelcome swarm of USN fighters in its vicinity. The Candid was the only Libyan aircraft that routinely flew past sundown; the rest of the LAAF seldom went much beyond their well-lit airdromes during their few night sorties.

Again, the carrier battle groups pulled back after four days. This time, almost all USN fighter sections had the opportunity to chase Libyans.

Generally, the naval aviators found their opposition very weak, with the possible exception of a few Flogger pilots. Apparently, there had been little improvement since 1981. Stumpf noted: "Some made vain attempts to shake the Hornets or Tomcats off their tails. Hard oblique weaves, supersonic accelerations, and decelerations to very slow airspeeds were typical maneuvers, tried mostly by the Flogger pilots. . . . The U.S. pilots could often maneuver at will to arrive at a firing position behind the MiGs." The navy crews began to realize why the Israelis racked up such impressive kills statistics against similarly lame Soviet-trained and -equipped opponents.[7]

Although ATTAIN DOCUMENT and ATTAIN DOCUMENT II definitely confronted Gadhafi, they were not very provocative in nature. No shots were exchanged, and no American planes or ships violated the Libyan line of death. These exercises permitted the navy to gather and confirm valuable information on the capabilities and tendencies of the Libyan Arab Air Force, and allowed time for American intelligence agencies to build a stronger case against Gadhafi's terror network. Most importantly, the maneuvers kept the heat on the desert strongman without turning him into a martyr. International law backed the United States.

Meanwhile, George Shultz twisted arms in Europe, and the Joint Chiefs dispatched a third carrier to the Mediterranean. It all looked perfectly normal as USS *America* steamed east across the Atlantic Ocean, a typical deployment to relieve USS *Saratoga*. Fortunately, from a security aspect, the JCS successfully resisted entreaties by civilian NSC staffers to rush *America* out on some dramatic alert. As a result, the Libyans (and their Soviet "socialist brothers") might have suspected something was up, but they could not be sure.[8] By mid-March, Admiral Kelso believed it was time to cross the line of death.

Admiral Kelso of Sixth Fleet intended to supervise the March maneuvers personally, from his flagship USS *Coronado*. Based upon LAAF activities in February and March, the admiral anticipated a strong Libyan reaction when American planes and ships pointedly crossed Gadhafi's boundary. He wanted to insure that he possessed authority to determine the timing and nature of any military response required from his forces, especially Rear Adm. David E. Jeremiah's Task Force 60. Kelso submitted his request for clarification through General Rogers at EUCOM and the JCS. These officers recommended approval without qualification.

President Reagan authorized Operation ATTAIN DOCUMENT III, with Kelso's amplified rules of engagement, on 14 March 1986. As always, the United States published notifications to airmen and seamen of all nations that the USN would be operating in the Gulf of Sidra as part of ongoing fleet training. While the plans were finalized and announcements made, Task Force 60 integrated USS *America* and her battle group into the established *Coral Sea/Saratoga* tandem.[9]

Kelso directed Jeremiah, a surface warfare officer, to form a surface action group to penetrate beyond the arbitrary Sidra line under air cover from the three carriers. USS *America* planned to operate aircraft from 2400 to 1200 daily, with *Saratoga* to fly from noon to midnight. USS *Coral Sea* overlapped during the daylight hours, flying from 0530 to 1830. The carriers deployed in a defensive arrangement more than 150 miles north of the line of death. From west to east, Jeremiah placed *America, Coral Sea,* and *Saratoga,* accompanied by their strong covey of escorts.

ATTAIN DOCUMENT III included a contingency plan, Operation PRAIRIE FIRE, to be activated in the event of any violent Libyan response. PRAIRIE FIRE would put Task Force 60 on a full wartime footing, free all weapons for task force defense, and permit proportionate preemptive and retaliatory surface and air strikes against Libyan ships, planes, and shore facilities.[10] By 23 March, the Americans were in position to start the naval and air evolution.

Just after midnight local time on 24 March 1986, Jeremiah began sending TF-60 aircraft across 32 degrees 30 minutes north latitude. At 1300, the cruiser USS *Ticonderoga* led the guided missile destroyer USS *Scott* and destroyer USS *Caron* into Gadhafi's claimed waters. *Ticonderoga's* massive AN/SPY-1A Aegis radar system watched and sorted air activity with wide, slablike phased array detectors that did not turn atop a mast but "stared" steadily in all directions out to 230 miles. The Aegis equipment could direct air defense operations for an entire carrier battle group, sending detected data on down links to other ships and planes, tracking and engaging myriad targets, and even automatically employing weapons on other ships in a rapid-fire, fully integrated antiaircraft effort.[11] As the cruiser sped south, its powerful radars and affiliated computers looked deeper and deeper into Gadhafi's homeland. The Aegis ship sent a steady stream of observations back to the trio of carriers to the north, which were accompanied by *Ticonderoga's* equally

United States Strategic and Operational Objectives for
ATTAIN DOCUMENT III/PRAIRIE FIRE

STRATEGIC OBJECTIVES: Exercise U.S. freedom of navigation in the Gulf of Sidra.

OPERATIONAL OBJECTIVES:

1) Conduct flight operations south of 32 degrees 30 minutes north latitude.
2) Deploy surface action group south of 32 degrees 30 minutes north latitude.
3) Defend fleet against Libyan air, surface, or subsurface responses.

United States Command Organization
23 March–18 April 1986

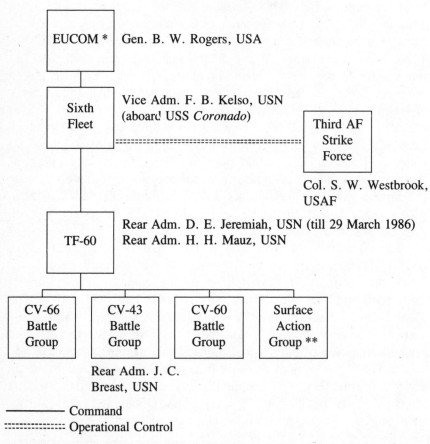

* EUCOM's naval deputy, CINCNAVEUR, routinely handled naval affairs in the theater from his London headquarters.

** The surface action group was formed on 23 March and disbanded on 26 March 1986. The CV-60 Battle Group left Task Force 60 on 29 March 1986.

able sister, USS *Yorktown*. With both surface and flight units across the line of death and defenses primed, the USN waited to see what the Libyans would do.

At 1452, a Libyan Arab Air Force SA-5 Gammon surface to air missile site at Surt activated its Square Pair surveillance and fire direction radar systems. Soviet technicians had finished work on the equipment just months before, and were rumored to still be on hand guiding their Libyan students. American Hawkeyes picked up the illumination of the firing batteries and warned the nearest CAP aircraft. Without warning, the Libyans fired two of the big Gammons, missiles more than 54 feet long with a range out to 185 miles. SA-5s were designed to shoot down high-flying strategic bombers, but TF-60 was ready for them. EA-6B Prowlers confused the Square Pair trackers with spurious signals, and the nimble U.S. Navy fighters easily sidestepped the clumsy shots by a combination of maneuvers and careful use of electronic warfare devices.

Within an hour or so, two LAAF MiG-25 interceptors ventured out across the gulf, although they turned back upon meeting American fighters. The Libyan pilots showed no stomach for dogfighting. Were the Gammon firings accidental? Jeremiah and Kelso thought not, but decided to wait out the Libyans.

At 1700, a bizarre message arrived via commercial teletype from Tripoli. Admiral Kelso was the addressee; it was from the "Commander in Chief of the Libyan Arab Air Force." The missive stated: "Unless the aggressive acts are stopped against Jamahiriyah [Libya] we are bound to destroy the CV carriers /Stop/ In doing that will have the political and military support of the world states /Stop/ Maintain in peace you will leave in peace /Stop/ Best Regards." Did this merit a response? Was it a bluff?

Before the Americans could digest this bluster, the Surt radars came on again, and two more SA-5s took off toward the CAP screen. Once more, USN electronic spoofing and evasive movements foiled the large Gammons. Ten minutes later, as nightfall darkened the seas off Libya, an SA-2 Guideline, famed in Vietnam as the "flying telephone pole," also lifted off from Surt and streaked harmlessly past the watchful American airplanes and their busy electronic deception systems. Less than twenty minutes later, Surt air defenses shot another SA-5, which also fluttered uselessly aside.[12] Even though the missiles went wide, the repeated firings were not accidents. It certainly appeared that the Libyans wanted to fight.

Admiral Kelso had seen enough. He informed all Sixth Fleet units, especially Task Force 60, that any further Libyan warships or aircraft that crossed the twelve-mile limit constituted hostile forces and hence legitimate targets. Kelso also approved Jeremiah's request to knock out the troublesome Surt radars with precision homing weapons. Lieutenant Commander Stumpf remembered how the "Privateers" of Fighter-Attack Squadron 132 reacted to the Libyan SAM launches. "Any previous jocularity was replaced by a firm resolve to respond violently to the Libyan action. In the cockpits, procedures did not change much," said Stumpf, "because the pilots had been ready and waiting for hostilities since January. But there was a new sense of urgency. During this period of hostilities, they knew that any Libyan target encountered would be fair game." [13] It was not long before Libya tested the American fleet.

Despite previous incidents and the teletype threat, the challenge came not by air but by sea. Within an hour of Kelso's decision to implement PRAIRIE FIRE, the Libyan fast attack craft *Waheed* left Libyan territorial waters, proceeding northeast from Misratah. This small vessel was a French export La Combattante II-G 260-ton, 160-foot model, carrying four Italian-made Otomat sea-skimming cruise missiles. The Otomat had the ability to reach out to almost forty miles, so the *Waheed* was nothing to ignore. The 460-pound Otomat warheads could devastate any USN ship they struck. Orbiting E-2C Hawkeye radar planes detected *Waheed* as it left its moorings and moved out to sea. Piercing the cover of night with its Aegis radars, USS *Ticonderoga* also spotted the speedy craft as it heeled east toward the three USN surface ships.

Two SUCAP sections veered through the darkness to deal with the approaching missile boat. A pair of Medium Attack Squadron 34 (VA-34) A-6E Intruders from USS *America* joined a similar duo from Medium Attack Squadron 85 (VA-85) off USS *Saratoga*. The VA-34 Blue Blasters lugged big AGM-84A Harpoon antishipping missiles; the VA-85 Bombing Buckeyes carried Mark 20 Rockeye cluster bombs, each capable of dispensing hundreds of small, potent submunitions. Both teams located the racing La Combattante and engaged before *Waheed* neared Otomat firing range. The formalities of cautionary messages and warning shots were ignored. The Libyans had fired up plenty of SAMs. Now it was the U.S. Navy's turn.

The Harpoon's range of more than sixty miles permitted the navy jets to attack from well beyond the reach of the missile craft's onboard air defense devices. At 2126, a single AGM-84A roared off an Intruder launch rail, zipping with deadly accuracy into the night. Guided by a target image ingrained on its internal radar, the cruise missile dove to just above the wave tops, seeking its unsuspecting quarry. In the words of naval weapons expert Lt. Comdr. James D. Winter, ''The Libyans may have seen Harpoon coming at the last minute. Anyway, I'm sure they figured out what it was.''

The shattering impact and following detonation slammed the fast attack craft to a smoking halt, tearing open the hull with more than a quarter ton of high explosives. Low-flying VA-85 crews finished the job with their deadly cluster bombs, breaking up the disabled hulk and insuring complete destruction of the missile and electronics systems. The fate of the thirty-odd Libyan sailors could not be determined, but *Waheed* sank so rapidly that most probably went down with their luckless boat.[14]

Just over a half hour later, two USS *Saratoga* A-7E Corsair IIs each fired one AGM-88A HARM at the Surt radar site. Again, the USN missile's long range (more than thirty miles) allowed the stealthy Corsairs to stand well out to sea while firing. Specially programmed to seek SA-5 emissions, the swift weapons homed on the Libyan radars, riding the beams right into the surveillance installations. According to U.S. Defense Department spokesmen, the SA-5 Square Pair radars ''ceased to function.'' This was an understatement. The blast and fragments created by the explosion of the two 150-pound HARM warheads probably ripped the radar antennas into jagged, torn debris, severed the power cables, perforated the delicate instrument consoles, and converted the unfortunate crews on duty into very small pieces.[15] Surt's eyes had been poked out.

As the Libyans scrambled to repair their ruined radar site, another Libyan Arab Navy vessel probed at the fringes of the surface action group's defensive screen, at the opposite end from the scene of *Waheed*'s demise. This time, a 780-ton, 197-foot Nanuchka II Soviet-built corvette appeared on American radar screens, westbound from the Benghazi naval base. Armed with four venerable SS-N-2C Styx antiship missiles, the vessel could fire on the U.S. fleet from as far as twenty-five miles away. Again, a surface combat air patrol section from the Bombing Buckeyes responded. Banking in out of the night sky, the two Intruders pummeled the sturdy Libyan warship with Rockeye cluster munitions, blowing off and mutilating communications, tracking, and launching equipment. The listing Nanuchka steered unevenly away, taking refuge near an innocent merchant ship as the VA-85 A-6Es spun about for a second pass. The battered corvette limped into Benghazi early the next morning.[16]

The next contact arose almost directly between the last two, just south of the carriers' outer screen, and not far southwest of the USS *Saratoga*. The vigilant Aegis cruiser USS *Yorktown* began monitoring a small surface return crawling north. It appeared just past midnight on 25 March, and was assumed to be another La Combattante fast attack craft. *Yorktown* was operating in the outer screen, supporting all three carrier battle groups with her high-resolution radar data. The cruiser contacted Admiral Jeremiah's antisurface warfare commander for a SU-CAP flight to check out the suspicious radar image, but the airplanes could not locate the slow-moving, blacked-out missile boat. This seemed very suspicious; it represented a level of tactical skill and deception unseen to this point. USS *Yorktown*'s Aegis radars were extremely capable, and continued to reflect a target closing on the USN task force. Ominously, about 0115, the unidentified boat began to accelerate. *Yorktown*'s warning systems started to indicate activation of missile fire control radars. The mystery craft was closing to attack range on the U.S. carriers.

USS *Yorktown* reacted immediately. At a range of about eleven miles, the big cruiser loosed two RGM-84A shipborne Harpoon missiles, which rose, then dipped down to the black seas, their jet motors twinkling off into the distance. Less than a minute later, *Yorktown* received returns showing two direct hits and the disintegration of the aggressive target. Aircraft vectored to the scene found only debris adrift on the mute waters.

What had *Yorktown* sunk? Initially, Sixth Fleet reported the destruction of a second Libyan La Combattante. Later intelligence indicated that perhaps this was not the case. Armchair critics, recalling the shadowy night actions during the alleged second attack by North Vietnamese torpedo boats in the 1964 Tonkin Gulf incident, wondered if perhaps *Yorktown*'s new radars were playing electronic tricks. If so, it would be out of character for the Aegis. False echoes, particularly those that sped up, emitted fire control signals, and left tangible shards behind, are not routinely encountered by AN/SPY-1A operators. Captain Carl A. Anderson of the cruiser told reporters that he sank his prey; Pentagon officials confirmed that the Aegis ship "hit what she shot at."

Given the controversy, maybe the enemy craft was not Libyan at all. This would certainly account for its stalking tactics. Kelso was sure that it was not part of the Soviet Navy; the four Soviet warships in the vicinity had been under close and constant scrutiny during PRAIRIE FIRE. A helpful Syrian missile craft seems a logical possibility, as they were experienced in scraps with Israel and occasionally visited Libyan ports.[17] Perhaps sinking Syrian boats was not politically palatable. Damascus gave no hint of such an event. In any case, the danger was eradicated, its true nature known only to curious American intelligence specialists.

Even as *Yorktown* dealt harshly with a crafty interloper, the Libyans reactivated their Square Pair system at Surt. American Hawkeyes picked up the strong scan indication and immediately diverted two more USS *Saratoga* A-7Es armed with HARMs. Once again, the USN Corsairs unleashed one slim missile apiece. The twin homing weapons bored unerringly toward Surt. Two direct hits smashed the restored radar. Whether or not the surviving technicians actually cobbled the wreckage together a second time, no Libyan dared turn on the sets until long after the USN ships and aircraft withdrew from the Gulf of Sidra.[18] Task Force 60 had erased Surt as a problem.

Over the next few hours, the Libyans remained quiet. No aircraft, no ships, and no missiles threatened the American battle groups. Toward dawn, observant Hawkeyes spotted a single Nanuchka II corvette moving northwest from Benghazi. A set of A-6E Intruders from USS *Coral Sea* headed to cut off the small vessel as it crossed Libya's twelve-mile limit. Taking advantage of the gloom, the Intruders came in very low to dump Rockeyes on the Libyan missile ship. Unfortunately, the close pass was ineffective, and the hundreds of wicked bomblets scattered into the dark waves. Alerted, the Nanuchka increased speed to twenty-five knots (almost thirty miles an hour) and began to swerve. The Libyans readied their onboard SA-N-4 Ganef surface to air missiles and 57-mm guns for any repeat American attack.

Luckily, two VA-85 Bombing Buckeyes bearing Harpoons entered the fray. Lingering well beyond the Ganef's thirty-five-mile range, the *Saratoga* Intruders locked on. "The Libyans thought they could penetrate the battle group, shoot their missiles, and run like hell. But we didn't give them a chance," said Comdr. Bob Day of VA-85. Instead, one USN bomber fired its lethal payload. The A-6E crews watched the Harpoon on their forward looking infrared (FLIR) displays as it dropped to sea level and raced to its target.

The missile plowed into the Libyan craft dead center, eviscerating the Nanuchka and kindling a hot, oily fire. As the sun rose out of the eastern Mediterranean on 25 March, circling American aviators saw a thick column of dark smoke boiling up from the stricken enemy. VA-85 Intruders used the last remnants of night to roll down and examine the drifting, burning derelict. The Americans watched some of the Nanuchka's seventy sailors scrambling into life rafts. Although TF-60 jets continued to watch later Libyan search and rescue efforts, the Americans made no attempt to interfere.[19] Nobody knew it yet, but the Sidra fighting was over.

Task Force 60 operated its aircraft and surface action group unopposed for two more days, finally pulling the three ships north of the line of death at 1600 on 27 March. This was three days early, but the United States had made its point, and the navy had experienced more than enough live fire training already. Jeremiah's carriers and their escorts left the Sidra area on 29 March, without a single loss. USS *Saratoga* and her escorts turned west, sailing for home after a cruise that featured the *Achille Lauro* episode and a whiff of naval combat.[20] Other task force units, including USS *Coral Sea,* headed for Mediterranean ports for well-earned rests and reprovisioning.

Behind them, the U.S. Navy left two, probably three sunken missile boats, another damaged, and a SAM site reduced to blind impotence. The Libyan Arab Air Force, despite brave blather, stayed on their airfields. Clearly, Libya could not hinder the mighty Sixth Fleet, at least not by any conventional means.

The American victory in the March encounter resulted from three factors: superior organization and training, excellent equipment properly employed, and competent local command. The USN prepared to tangle with the Soviets; the hapless Libyans were no match for the powerful American battle groups. U.S. weapons like HARM, Aegis, Hawkeye, and Harpoon worked as advertised, a tribute to skilled bluejacket operators as well as American technology. America dominated the electromagnetic spectrum, which allowed good intelligence, accurate fire control, and rapid engagements. As a result of good use of advanced systems, the navy hit hard reliably at long range, undeterred by darkness. Finally, Kelso's insistence on firm local command prerogatives allowed Task Force 60 to react quickly and decisively to threats without need to check with higher headquarters. Given the speed and destructive capacity of Otomat and Styx missiles, one slipup while awaiting instructions could have proven fatal. Instead, trained professionals insured that the fatalities were all on Gadhafi's side.

The Libyan armed forces exhibited an utter lack of organization or purpose. Their actions seemed disjointed, utterly uncoordinated, and completely confused. After shooting several SA-5 Gammon SAMs from Surt to trigger a U.S. response and baiting Kelso with an insolent message, the Libyan Arab Air Force played almost no part in hostilities. As shown in January and February, the Libyans simply did not fly missions at night. The unfortunate missile flotilla tried to use the darkness and bore the brunt of the action and the casualties for their troubles. A determined, concerted Libyan attack using deception and air cover might conceivably have damaged or sunk unwary U.S. warships. But Task Force 60 was on guard. Gadhafi's naval leaders sent a few brave, random boats and their crews to their doom without any evident plan. The well-practiced USN carrier defense screens easily brushed aside these aimless forays. To be blunt, Gadhafi's men did not know how to employ their sophisticated weaponry, and they paid for their ignorance.

Excited journalists back in the United States wondered if ATTAIN DOCUMENT/PRAIRIE FIRE was designed specifically to provoke the Libyan dictator. President Reagan rebuffed such speculations: "But it was not a deliberate provocation, not sitting back saying 'Oh goody, he's going to show his hand, and we'll clobber him.' " Reagan reminded critics that American exercises in the Gulf of Sidra were standard procedure, part of long-standing freedom of navigation programs and routine naval training. "So it wasn't an unusual thing we set out to do. And he did open hostilities," noted the president, "and we closed them." [21]

If America wanted an excuse to lash out, the repeated Libyan SAM firings offered plenty of justification. While there were definitely contingency plans afoot for major bombing missions against Libya, it appears that the American goal in ATTAIN DOCUMENT and PRAIRIE FIRE was to frighten Gadhafi, to scare him into quiescence with very big USN sticks. The rapid dispatch of Libya's few aggressive forces merely served to underscore Gadhafi's military weakness and vulnerability to U.S. action. It was hoped this might encourage the colonel to give up his support for terrorist activities rather than face possible consequences. From the time the Sixth Fleet began exercising near Gadhafi's country in January 1986, the Libyans had not engineered any significant terror incidents. Having perhaps taught the desert warlord a lesson about his lack of force to back up his mouth, the Sixth Fleet pulled out and returned to routine operations.

The U.S. president might have also mentioned that Admiral Kelso showed a strict adherence to the idea of proportionality in his conduct of fleet defense operations. The admiral did not seize upon the first Libyan shot to deliver massive retaliatory strikes. After establishing certain Libyan hostile intent, Sixth Fleet replied with carefully chosen shots directed only against clear threats. In short, Kelso justified the faith placed in his judgment. As a result, America did not turn Gadhafi into a victim of heavy-handed U.S. bludgeoning.

A few "inside" sources suggested that the entire U.S. operation was some sort of reconnaissance of Libyan air defenses preparatory to a major aerial bombardment effort. Kelso's reaction to such spurious notions was brief and pointed: "That's completely wrong. There's no way in the world that I, as a military man, would go trolling with my people for SAMs to be shot at them. We were given a job, which I support, to operate our ships in international water and air space. We did that." [22] Of course, the earlier ATTAIN DOCUMENT efforts and regular American transits of the Gulf of Sidra had already permitted Sixth Fleet to gather a plentiful amount of superb intelligence on Libyan air defenses, electronics, and naval capabilities. Modern surface to air missiles are defeated by confusing or breaking their radars; modern radars are beaten by learning and perverting their signals. The navy had no need to get shot at to gain such information. TF-60's evident mastery of Libyan airspace from the outset of the March skirmishes indicated that American seamen already had the majority of the data they needed to penetrate Libyan sanctuaries.

In essence, PRAIRIE FIRE represented not a provocation but a warning shot, a final U.S. attempt to convince Gadhafi to change his ways. But the Libyan leader remained unbowed. He took the defeat as a personal affront, and he raged at the dastardly USN "imperialists." With his vaunted missile boats blasted and his new SA-5s ruined, the vengeful colonel elected to abandon conventional measures. Rather, he turned to his old, familiar ways to hit back at Reagan's countrymen. Across Europe, a few selected terrorist detachments sprung into action.

Just as he did after the interception of the *Achille Lauro* hijackers, Moammar Gadhafi turned to the shady Abu Nidal to produce an appropriately bloody spectacle in reply to America's naval prowess. Nidal's henchmen acted within a few days after Task Force 60 dispersed. Once more, they carefully selected their mark for maximum horror.

On 2 April, Trans World Airlines Flight 840 was twenty minutes outside Athens, heading in to land. The Boeing 727 was passing through

15,000 feet. Aboard the jet, the stewardesses collected the last few used cups and napkins, and the passengers looked out the windows through scudding clouds, glimpsing rocky Greece below. Everything seemed so utterly normal.

Suddenly, a flash lit the plane, followed by a metallic crack and the roaring of air rushing past and through a gaping hole where a row of seats on the right side of the 727 had been. "I saw a sort of green lightning. I thought I was dying," remembered American witness Jane Klingel. The plane lurched and shuddered, oxygen masks sprung loose and dropped from the overhead panels, and the pilots struggled to regain control of their bucking, wounded aircraft. In the confusion, a few horrified passengers noticed that four of their cabin mates were missing, sucked through the screaming maw in the fuselage. Despite the serious damage, the TWA crew brought their plane to a safe landing. Four Americans were missing.

Shocked Greek people far below and behind the damaged plane soon found the mangled remains of a Greek-American grandmother, her grown daughter, and the pitiful corpse of the daughter's eight-month-old baby. A Colombian-American man lay in a twisted heap nearby. Courtesy of a few pounds of Czechoslovakian Semtex plastic explosive, Abu Nidal and his Libyan friends had produced a grisly incident.

Right on schedule, a caller in Beirut told a western news agency that the bombing constituted a response to the American naval and air actions in the Gulf of Sidra. The Arab Revolutionary Cells, a Nidal front group, claimed responsibility. Although done on behalf of the Libyans, the highly disciplined terrorists left few clues. These traces pointed to possible involvement by Syria, if indeed any country could be said to be implicated. Gadhafi appeared conveniently innocent, a beneficiary of some "fraternal revolutionary assistance."

For his part, the Libyan colonel praised the terrorists as bold freedom fighters, and warned, "We shall escalate the violence against American targets, civilian and non-civilian, throughout the world." [23] Even as Gadhafi spouted venom, his own revolutionaries prepared for an additional mission.

Unfortunately for the unpredictable Libyan leader, the U.S. National Security Agency (NSA) had webbed Gadhafi's communications links with eavesdropping platforms ranging from sensitive satellites to armed forces aircraft to implanted "bugs." American monitors were particularly attentive, because they already had an alarming message from Tripoli to Libyan agents in Paris, Belgrade, Rome, and Madrid, warning each local People's Bureau (embassies) "to prepare to carry out the plan." Energized by the TWA 840 blast, U.S. intelligence agencies worldwide attempted to isolate the details of "the plan."

In the wee hours of 5 April, a large bomb gutted La Belle Club discotheque, a popular gathering place for black troops from the U.S. Army Berlin Brigade. Sergeant Kenneth Ford, an infantryman, and his Turkish girlfriend died almost instantly, ripped to bits by the force of the bomb. Another 79 American soldiers, relatives, and retirees were hurt, along with more than 150 other bystanders.[24]

This time, though, American electronic surveillance intercepted two key messages from the East Berlin Libyan People's Bureau. A few hours prior to the detonation, the Libyans in East Berlin had alerted Gadhafi: "We have something planned that will make you happy." European Command intelligence staffs and units tried vainly to identify the "something." Before dawn on 5 April, the analysts had narrowed their suspicions to La Belle Club. Unfortunately, the researchers arrived at their conclusions a mere fifteen minutes too late for Sergeant Ford.

But the watchful NSA remained very interested in the circuits from Berlin to Tripoli. Their diligence was rewarded. Even as West Berlin police and paramedics clawed through the smoking rubble of La Belle Club, the East Berlin Libyan People's Bureau signaled home: "An event occurred. You will be pleased with the result." The message noted the precise time of the discotheque explosion.[25] By handling the deed through his own people, Gadhafi provided what President Reagan asked for so often: clear, direct proof of responsibility for terrorism.

Unaware of the U.S. electronic intercepts, Moammar Gadhafi attempted to feign ignorance of the Berlin attack. He quickly pointed to his "exoneration" by the thorough Germans, just because they were not willing to limit their investigation to the Libyans. German police gathered their own intelligence, and it was somewhat cloudy at the lower levels. The local authorities received a call claiming the bombing as the work of a familiar domestic nemesis, the Holger Mein Red Army faction. When West Berlin forensic scientists and detectives tracked the demolitions to their source, they discovered that the stuff had come through the Arab-German Friendship League, a Syrian-run organization often involved as a purchasing agent for terrorists. Significantly, the Germans did not clear the Libyans of culpability. They were simply unwilling to stop their examination at that point. After all, the Germans were trying to apprehend and try the perpetrators in a court of law, not deal with distant Gadhafi.

The Libyan colonel met rumors of possible U.S. retaliatory strikes with characteristic bravado. On 8 April, he boasted: "If there is an American attack, American security will be threatened in American cities and American targets all over the world. From now on, it should be clear that this is the [Reagan] administration's responsibility. It is not us." [26]

Reagan and his subordinates, buttressed by the fine work of the NSA, refuted Gadhafi's dissembling and faced his veiled threats squarely. America's ambassador to West Germany, Richard R. Burt, told journalists that the link from the La Belle tragedy to Libya was "very, very clear." On 9 April, the president reminded assembled journalists that Gadhafi had already declared war on the United States. Reagan definitely considered the Libyan leader responsible for the Berlin incident. The president closed the issue with these pregnant lines: "No, it's as I say, we're going to defend ourselves, and we're certainly going to take action in the face of specific terrorist threats." [27]

Around the room, the reporters nodded knowingly. They had heard Reagan promise action before, but nothing much had come of such assertions. He had not gone after the captors of TWA 847, or the directors of the Rome and Vienna airport massacres, or even the Iranian-sponsored maniacs who had killed the marines in their bunks in Beirut.

But this time would be different, thanks to the convincing signal intercepts. Before meeting the press on 9 April, President Reagan met his closest advisers in a secret session. The president authorized the military to carry out a series of air strikes on Libya, Operation EL DORADO CANYON. After a lot of talk, it was time to use the big stick.

Almost as soon as President Reagan saw the damning Berlin-to-Tripoli message traffic, he had initiated concrete steps to implement long-standing American contingency plans, although the president reserved final authority to execute the mission. On 6 April, Gen. Bernard Rogers of EUCOM ordered his operations and intelligence staff sections to revise plans concocted as early as the last days of December 1985. Thus, Operation EL DORADO CANYON was born.

Reagan's goal was very direct: destroy as much of Libya's terrorist infrastructure as possible. The president specifically mandated minimum collateral damage to Libyan civilians and, although this seemed obvious, minimum risk to U.S. forces involved. Other than that, Ronald Reagan gave his commanders fairly free reign.

Reagan's mission offered some intriguing possibilities. For one thing, it provided a direct reprisal to Gadhafi's Berlin escapade, although this was not the primary purpose of EL DORADO CANYON. The president wanted to do more than deliver retribution. Indeed, by concentrating on terrorist facilities, the U.S. operation endeavored to disrupt and destroy impending Libyan-sponsored terrorist acts. Diverse United States intelligence assets indicated an extensive series of imminent kidnappings, assassinations, and bombings designed by Libya and aimed at American civilians and embassies in Latin America, Africa, and the Middle East. These undertakings were already programmed, mainly in response to the March naval scraps. La Belle and TWA 840 looked like the opening shots in a lengthy terror campaign. But that was not the only danger.

United States Strategic and Operational Objectives for EL DORADO CANYON

STRATEGIC OBJECTIVE: Destroy major elements of Libya's terrorist command, training, and support infrastructure.

OPERATIONAL OBJECTIVES:

1) Bomb terrorist facilities in Tripoli: Aziziyah barracks, Murat Sidi Bilal Training Camp, Tripoli military airfield.
2) Bomb terrorist facility in Benghazi: Jamahiriyah barracks.
3) Suppress Libyan air defenses: bomb Benina military airfield, destroy air defense radar network.

Reacting to press rumors of potential U.S. air attacks, Gadhafi raised the possibility of seizing Europeans and Americans in his country and moving these hostages onto likely U.S. strike objectives. Loose talk about hostage-taking generated two images in American planners' minds: 444 miserably impotent days in Tehran and more than 600 medical students saved by a bold stroke in Grenada. The stark difference seemed obvious. So preemption loomed as the principal goal for the Americans, and Kelso had to act swiftly.

Finally, a careful and intentional effort to distinguish Gadhafi's personal cadres and terror cells from the Libyan Arab Armed Forces and civil populace might bear fruit in serious unrest, coup attempts, or perhaps even insurrection in the desert country. Any or all of these developments would serve to keep the excitable colonel too busy to dabble in international terrorism efforts.[28]

With their mission in hand, General Rogers's officers updated their original proposed schemes. Rogers designated Vice Adm. Frank Kelso of Sixth Fleet as the commander for EL DORADO CANYON. Aided by EUCOM's extensive staff and joint service components, Kelso and his subordinates got ready to challenge Gadhafi once more. Sixth Fleet evaluated Libyan defenses, possible targets, forces available, and time allotted to mount the effort. Time drove the train; EUCOM wanted Sixth Fleet to act before the Libyans started their worldwide mayhem or policed up stray foreigners as "insurance."

If Sixth Fleet intelligence officers knew anything, they knew all about Libya's military strengths and weaknesses. The army looked like an opportunity rather than a threat, mainly because some influential Libyan ground officers distrusted the erratic Gadhafi. Rumors spread that the desert chieftain planned to replace his shaky army with a loose, paramilitary mob collected from his poorly trained but eminently loyal Popular Resistance Forces. Regular Libyan soldiers showed little stomach for Gadhafi's aimless external wars and incursions. Mutinies, combat refusals, serious losses, and depressing performances in Uganda and Chad marred the army's lackluster record. Few Libyan commanders appreciated Gadhafi's preposterous communiques describing nonexistent "victories" across Africa and against the redoubtable Sixth Fleet. Now and then, the army showed real signs that it might fight much better against its own capricious master.

Gadhafi responded to the dangers posed by his untrustworthy (but well-armed) ground units by forming special "revolutionary" elements to do his bidding. Informers and toadies occupied critical arsenals and supply depots in order to separate possibly rebellious troops from their potent arsenal of modern weapons. The Popular Resistance Forces cheered energetically, if little else. Colonel Gadhafi also controlled three motley (but impressively named) "Pan-African Legion" brigades recruited from all over the continent to carry out the Libyan leader's foreign adventures. For personal protection and covert missions, the colonel deployed a "deterrent battalion" drawn solely from his own tribe, plus a coterie of fanatic Jamahiriyah Guards. An efficient East German security battalion

---

Libyan Forces Order of Battle
23 March–18 April 1986

Revolutionary Command Council Forces
  Al-Gadhaf Deterrent Battalion
  Jamahiriyah Guards Battalion
  3 Pan-African Legion Brigades
  East German Security Battalion
  Popular Resistance Forces (militia)

Libyan Arab Army
  20 tank battalions
  30 motorized rifle battalions
  10 artillery battalions
  10 special forces battalions
  2 antiaircraft (gun) battalions
  2 surface to surface missile brigades (48 FROG-7, SS-1 Scud B)
  9 surface to air missile battalions (SA-6, SA-8, SA-9)

Libyan Arab Navy
  6 Foxtrot class diesel submarines
  1 Vosper Mark 7 Frigate (*Asawari*)
  1 Vosper Mark 1B corvette
  4 Assad class corvettes
  4 Nanuchka II class corvettes
  3 Susa class first attack craft
  10 La Combattante II-G class fast attack craft
  12 Osa II class fast attack craft

Libyan Arab Air Force
  1 bomber squadron: 7 Tu-22 Blinder A bombers
  3 interceptor squadrons: 32 Mirage F-1ED/BD; 143 MiG-23 Flogger E; 55 MiG-25 Foxbat A; 55 MiG-21 Fishbed
  5 fighter-bomber squadrons: 58 Mirage 5D/DE/5DD; 14 Mirage F-1/AD; 32 MiG-23BM Flogger F; 100 Su-20/22 Fitter E/F/J
  3 surface to air missile brigades (SA-2, SA-3, SA-5, Crotale)

Sources: International Institute for Strategic Studies, "The Military Balance 1985/86," *Air Force* (February 1986), 108–109; David James Ritchie, "To the Shores of Tripoli," *Strategy and Tactics,* 109 (September–October 1986), 14–24.

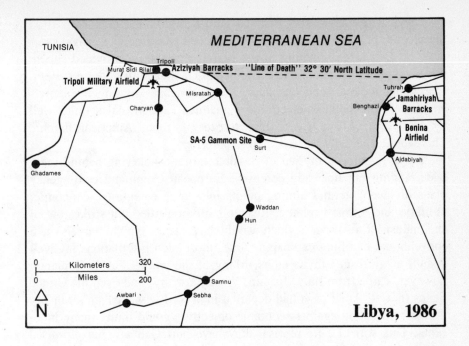

TUNISIA

MEDITERRANEAN SEA

Tripoli
Murat Sidi Bilal • •Aziziyah Barracks   "Line of Death" 32° 30' North Latitude
Tripoli Military Airfield

Misratah

Charyan

Tuhrah
Benghazi   •Jamahiriyah
            Barracks

Benina
Airfield

SA-5 Gammon Site •
Surt

Ajdabiyah

Ghadames

Waddan
Hun

0
├──────────┤
Kilometers   320
0
├──────────┤
Miles   200

Samnu
Awbari •   • Sebha

△
N

Libya, 1986

provided a final guarantor of safety. If Kelso struck at the Libyan ground forces, it would make sense to concentrate on these personal contingents. The fact that almost all of them participated in terrorist training and operations made them all the more attractive targets for U.S. planners.

As for the Libyan Arab Navy, it appeared to be a floating sham, likely to stay in port and cower. It certainly posed a minimal threat to any prepared USN battle groups. The Libyan Arab Air Force had plenty of good equipment and plenty of bad pilots, all quite familiar to the Sixth Fleet and hence, EUCOM. The Libyans flew only in fair weather during daylight hours. After sunset, the skies over Libya were open to incursions.

Libya disposed only two outfits likely to disturb American night operations. About twelve night-capable MiG-23 Flogger E interceptors squatted on the apron at Benina airfield near Benghazi. Some reports stated that pilots from North Korea, Syria, Pakistan, the PLO, and even the Soviet Union flew for this crack squadron. In any case, these planes had to be nullified.

Libya's extensive array of radar-guided SAMs and guns comprised the second threat to air operations in darkness. Routine U.S. naval exercises off Libya, culminating in the March skirmishes, provided superb information on the nature and capacities of Gadhafi's air defense system. Everything looked good on paper, but Americans knew their enemy's antiaircraft procedures, electronic signatures, and missiles quite well by April 1986. Libya was familiar territory to many American fliers.[29] This would markedly assist suppression efforts.

Libya featured a myriad of possible targets sheltering behind these wide-ranging but unsteady defenses. European Command contingency plans divided potential aiming points into three categories: economic, military, and terrorist related. Reagan's mission ruled out strikes on oil and industrial facilities, which would have been typical targets in a conventional bombing campaign. True, most such installations lay well inland, away from Libyan cities. Many of the workers at these plants, however, came from Italy, Britain, West Germany, and even the United States (not all Americans had departed in accord with Reagan's January decree). So acting against economic objectives could injure many innocents. This sort of pure reprisal may have hurt Gadhafi, but promised no effects on Libyan terrorism.

The Libyan military had to be hit, but only to force open clear paths to get at terrorist-related targets. General Rogers and Admiral Kelso agreed that those sites blocking U.S. entry and exit would be hit, but no others. For example, the Benina Flogger jets and the SAM systems required attention. Given the touchy relations between Gadhafi and his armed forces, discrimination in this portion of EL DORADO CANYON allowed for vigorous repercussions by the largely untouched Libyan military.

Finally, Reagan's orders steered EUCOM and Sixth Fleet to a thorough consideration of locations directly related to Gadhafi's ongoing terrorist efforts. With more than two dozen worthwhile points identified, Kelso and Rogers agreed on four particularly important targets: Aziziyah barracks and the military portion of the airfield in Tripoli, Murat Sidi Bilal Training Camp on the coast near Tripoli, and the Jamahiriyah barracks in Benghazi. Each of these places displayed distinctive visual, radar, and infrared silhouettes. There would be no confusion about finding them, regardless of lighting conditions or weather.

If these four locations were eliminated, the loss of the people and facilities appeared quite likely to cripple Libya's terror network. Each target was important. Along with Libya's main terrorist command center, Aziziyah held part of the Jamahiriyah Guard, the Al-Gadhaf Deterrent Battalion, and some of the tough East Germans. An unknown number of terrorist "guests" were probably on hand. Gadhafi himself occasionally frequented the immediate area in one of his houses or his quaint nomad's tent. Unfortunately, civilian housing surrounded the barracks; there was plenty of evidence that Gadhafi desired to use his population as a protective screen. This one would be hard to attack.

The military side of Tripoli's airport housed the big Il-76 Candid jet transports used to carry terrorists on their international forays. Some specialized equipment and supplies might have been stored in the immediate vicinity, perhaps watched by sentries from terrorist militias. This target was more isolated, but it required some care to avoid the civilian side of the airport.

Murat Sidi Bilal schooled the PLO and other unsavory types in waterborne raids, ship seizures, port assaults, and underwater demolitions work. Terrorists in training occupied the barracks here. Located on the water's edge but encircled by civilian apartments, the site would be hard to bomb, although not so bad as Aziziyah.

Finally, the Jamahiriyah barracks in Benghazi featured an alternate command headquarters, another large chunk of Gadhafi's anticoup troops, and visiting cadres from various terrorist groups. A MiG fighter warehouse on the grounds provided an additional incentive to plaster this target. As at Aziziyah and the swimmers' school, civilian buildings surrounded this downtown compound, making it a difficult place to take out.[30]

Kelso's available forces shaped the design to address his Libyan objectives. Though the four chosen targets were within range of mammoth battleship main guns, none of these leviathans were on duty with Sixth Fleet in April 1986. But Kelso enjoyed three other alternatives. He could employ highly trained SEALs or Green Berets from Special Operations Task Force Europe to conduct coordinated raids by helicopter, infiltration, surfboat, or scuba approach. Or, he might choose to fire highly accurate BGM-109C Tomahawk high-explosive cruise missiles from offshore nuclear submarines. Finally, Kelso still had two of his three carrier battle groups from PRAIRIE FIRE in the Mediterranean, and Rogers at EUCOM assured him that U.S. Air Force F-111F Aardvark long-range bombers in Great Britain stood ready to back up any naval air strike.

Sixth Fleet's USS *America* and USS *Coral Sea* carrier battle groups

United States Forces Order of Battle
23 March–18 April 1986

United States Sixth Fleet: USS *Coronado* (AGF-11)

U.S. Navy/U.S. Marine Corps units

Task Force 60

USS *America* (CV-66) with Carrier Air Wing 1 (CVW-1); USS *Ticonderoga* (CG-47); USS *Dale* (CG-19); USS *Farragut* (DDG-37); USS *King* (DDG-41); USS *Peterson* (DD-969); USS *Halyburton* (FFG-40); USS *Vreeland* (FF-1068); USS *Ainsworth* (FF-1090); USS *Donald B. Beary* (FF-1085); USS *Pharris* (FF-1094); USS *Garcia* (FF-1040); USS *Aylwin* (FF-1081)

USS *Coral Sea* (CV-43) with Carrier Air Wing 13 (CVW-13); USS *Biddle* (CG-34); USS *DeWert* (FFG-45); USS *Jack Williams* (FFG-24); USS *Capodanno* (FF-1093); USS *Jesse L. Brown* (FF-1089); USS *Mount Baker* (AE-34); USS *Monongahela* (AO-178)

USS *Saratoga* (CV-60) with Carrier Air Wing 17 (CVW-17); USS *Yorktown* (CG-48); USS *Richmond K. Turner* (CG-20); USS *Scott* (DDG-995); USS *Mahan* (DDG-42); USS *Caron* (DD-970); USS *Paul* (FF-1080); USS *Seattle* (AOE-3)

Surface Action Group (drawn from CV-60 and CV-66 battle groups): USS *Ticonderoga* (CG-47), USS *Scott* (DDG-995), USS *Caron* (DD-970) (active 23–27 March 1986 only)

Electronic Surveillance Squadron 2 (VQ-2)

U.S. Air Force units (available 9–18 April 1986)

Third Air Force EL DORADO CANYON Strike Contingent

Elements, 48th Tactical Fighter Wing

Elements, 20th Tactical Fighter Wing

Strategic Air Command

European Tanker Force: 306th Strategic Wing

11th Strategic Group

2nd Bombardment Wing (tankers only)

22nd Air Refueling Wing

68th Air Refueling Group

513th Tactical Airlift Wing (SR-71 strategic reconnaissance aircraft)

Sources: Col. W. Hays Park, USMCR, "Crossing the Line," *Proceedings* (November 1986), 44–45; "U.S. 6th Fleet," *Washington Post,* 26 March 1986, A22; "Pride, Joy as Ships Come Home," *Navy Times,* 28 April 1986, 1, 32, 60; Christopher Wright, "U.S. Naval Operations in 1985," *Proceedings* (May 1986), 285–88; Christopher Wright, "U.S. Naval Operations in 1986," *Proceedings* (May 1987), 43, 221–225; "Strategic Air Command," *Air Force* (May 1986), 101–102; "Planes Launch from Four Bases," *Air Force Times,* 28 April 1987, 4, 10.

deployed ninety-two potential attack planes between them. These included *America*'s twenty-four familiar A-7E Corsair IIs, which worked best in daylight, and *Coral Sea*'s forty-eight new dual-role F/A-18 Hornets, also fair-weather light bombers. Some *Coral Sea* F/A-18s (up to half) would perform fighter missions to protect their floating air base and the strike aircraft. For heavier work, each carrier controlled ten A-6E Intruders, sturdy all-weather medium bombers. Intruders sported a little target recognition and attack multisensor (TRAM) turret under their noses. With TRAM, an A-6E could employ forward looking infrared electronics to pick up targets from the powerful onboard search radar. The TRAM also permitted laser designation for accurate bombing. Despite night, clouds, rain, or fog, Intruders possessed the ability to go in low and dump up to 15,000 pounds of bombs dead on the bull's-eye.

Along with their attack planes, the two carriers also disposed superior fighters (twenty-four Tomcats on *America,* plus a percentage of *Coral Sea*'s swarm of Hornets) and four EA-6B Prowler electronic warfare jets apiece. Four indispensable Hawkeye radar control planes aboard each flattop facilitated command of any proposed strike operations.

If Kelso turned to the air force, he had available the best low-level medium bomber in the world, the F-111F. The U.S. Third Air Force's 48th Tactical Fighter Wing (TFW), stationed at RAF Lakenheath in Britain, flew the long-nosed Aardvark. The F-111F was the latest version of a fighter that had mutated into a bomber. The F-111 arose from a typically misbegotten Robert McNamara attempt to compel the design of a common USAF/USN fighter, known as the tactical fighter experimental (TFX). The navy balked at the immense bastard offspring of this shotgun marriage, but the air force found a use for the swing wing plane that resulted. Packing tremendously accurate terrain-following radar, adjustable wings for stomach-lurching maneuvers across rugged land, two big engines to race along at nearly supersonic speeds just above the uneven ground, and a deadly precise bombing computer, early F-111 models regularly punctured the vaunted North Vietnamese air defenses to deliver well over 25,000 pounds of munitions. The big jets flew at night, in bad weather, and alone, plowing through jungle canyons at an average of 200 feet above the ground. Sardonic fliers labeled this hair-raising approach "skiing." Bereft of a flashy official nickname, the pilots called their ungainly planes Aardvarks, after the large burrowing nocturnal anteaters of Africa. Respectful North Vietnamese gunners, who rarely caught the lone F-111s, called the bomber "whispering death."

The Lakenheath F-111Fs featured additional capabilities, including better, more powerful engines and an electronics package called Pave Tack. The Pave Tack targeting pod, mounted on a rotatable cradle in the Aardvark's internal weapons bay, included low-light television, infrared, and laser sensors and designators. Like the A-6E, the F-111F used its search radar to identify targets. Then, as Pave Tack expert Maj. Robert Rudiger explained, "The radar tells the pod where to look, and the laser allows us to put the weapon precisely on target." The Aardvarks flew by night; they were well trained for deep strikes at long range, high speeds, and low altitude.

Aside from the bombers, Third Air Force could also contribute some key supporting aircraft. EF-111A Ravens (invariably nicknamed "Spark Varks" by their crews) of 20th TFW's 42nd Electronic Combat Squadron occupied RAF Upper Heyford. These planes carried slightly reworked EA-6B Prowler jammer devices, and hence operated rather easily in harness with the navy electronic warfare jets. Last, but in some ways most important of all, Third Air Force had access to the European Tanker Force, an expandable contingent of aerial refueling craft flown in from the United States. Although in Britain, Third Air Force commanded the means to reach Libya and hit hard.

Given all this, Admiral Kelso selected his forces rapidly. Special operations teams would not do. They required covert delivery and extraction, needed significant preparation time, insured unavoidably complex ground maneuvers, and risked serious casualties. Tomahawks had been ruled out during initial planning back in January, and since strategic considerations remained the same, Sixth Fleet officers spurned this option. Understandably, Kelso turned to his air power arsenal to ravage Gadhafi's terror network. Aircraft could hit the targets with precision munitions and get in and out quickly.[31]

Time considerations encouraged a rapid launch for EL DORADO CANYON. Any hesitation could allow Moammar Gadhafi's terrorist allies to carry out their extensive sequence of anti-American plots. General Rogers gave Admiral Kelso about a week to create and implement his final plan.

Kelso and his subordinates, with Rogers's assistance and approval, devised a shrewd operation employing both USN and USAF aircraft. A single raid would strike all four targets in a simultaneous night attack, inundating and overwhelming Libyan defenses. American pilots and aircraft were prepared to take advantage of the same darkness that hobbled their opponents. To ease the bombers' passage, carrier planes intended to eliminate the Libyan strip alert fighters at Benina airfield (adding a fifth target) with bombs and slash apart the Tripoli and Benghazi air defense grids with homing missiles.

The U.S. raid employed two strike groups against the five Libyan targets. Eighteen USAF 48th TFW Aardvarks formed EL DORADO CANYON's primary punch. The air force anticipated a lengthy flight from their British bases, much of it across friendly France. They aimed at the three Tripoli targets, with nine F-111Fs going in against Aziziyah barracks with 2,000-pound laser-guided Paveway II Mark 84s and three similarly armed jets sliding over to hit Sidi Bilal. Skillful use of Pave Tack pods would allow the jets to identify targets and guide their own munitions past crowded civilian neighborhoods in the immediate vicinity. The other six Aardvarks intended to complete the Tripoli attack by smashing up the military airfield with 500-pound Snakeye retarded delivery Mark 82 bombs. These bombs popped out ballute (balloon/parachute) stabilizers to slow their descent. This permitted the air force crews to make very high-speed passes "on the deck" without risking blast damage from their own weapons' explosions.

In a supporting attack, seven VA-34 Blue Blasters planned a concurrent bombardment of Benghazi's Jamahiriyah barracks. These Intruders expected to drop Snakeyes from rooftop altitude, using their TRAM modules to insure accuracy. In direct support of the four antiterrorist strikes, eight VA-55 Warhorses from USS *Coral Sea* prepared to pummel the Libyan interceptors on alert at Benina airfield. They carried more Snakeyes and lighter Mark 20 Rockeye cluster munitions chock-full of lethal bomblets to wreck the airdrome.

Admiral Kelso realized that bombing in congested urban areas required strict rules of engagement in order to minimize exposure of U.S. aircraft, destroy assigned targets, and reduce or avoid civilian casualties. The admiral limited his aircrews to a single run on their targets, mainly for their own safety in the midst of alarmed Libyan defenders. He insisted upon positive identification of all targets on radar, infrared, low-light television, and, if applicable, laser sensors. This reduced the chance of stray drops, but it just as surely promised to place explosives on the crucial places, which buttressed mission accomplishment. Finally, air force and navy fliers received strict orders to abort their attacks if their Pave Tack and TRAM systems experienced any sort of difficulty. Without these alignment devices, the planes would have to resort to cruder night attacks using estimated data, leaving little chance of hitting their aiming points. America fully intended to kill terrorists, but nobody wanted a sloppy bloodbath in Libya's streets. Bombs off the mark contributed nothing to EL DORADO CANYON's goals. Kelso demanded hits from his well-honed crews and gave them the tools to get these hits.

Two other carrier-based forces prepared to assist the joint USAF/ USN bombing mission. The suppression group expected to clear holes in the enemy defenses, either with high explosives or high technology "black boxes." USS *America* readied a half dozen Corsair IIs for anti-SAM duties around Tripoli, aided by the electronic spoofers on *America*'s Prowlers and three Spark Varks that would accompany the USAF bombers. USS *Coral Sea*'s Hornets and Prowlers would handle similar tasks around Benghazi. As far as the fighter escort group, *America*'s Tomcats had responsibility for the joint air missions around Tripoli. *Coral Sea* Hornets planned to protect the Benghazi raiders. All told, EL DORADO CANYON endeavored to bring together more than a hundred strike and support aircraft from across Europe and the Mediterranean in utter darkness for a raid expected to last just about fifteen minutes.

Three alternate variations on the basic concept gave the Americans some operational flexibility. In the event France refused overflight rights for a nearly 3000-mile round trip, the U.S. would ask Spain, making for a slightly longer route. If Spain said no, the European Tanker Force planned a maximum effort to fuel the F-111s on a nearly 6,000-mile round trip. Should Britain undercut use of the USAF jets, or if sufficient tankers failed to arrive in time, Kelso could revert to an all-navy strike, cutting out one target. The Sixth Fleet commander and General Rogers at EUCOM hoped that the U.S. Department of State could convince the sometimes truculent French to cooperate.

Although President Reagan retained the authority to cancel the undertaking, he insisted that Kelso control the timing and details of any attack. Nobody wanted a repetition of the confusion during the December 1983 Lebanon air strike.[32] So the admiral and his air force deputies created their own brand of raid with the full support of the president. It promised to be arduous, but the operation would be built on American strengths and would exploit Libyan weaknesses.

Tactical surprise keyed Kelso's thinking for EL DORADO CANYON. One big, fast attack avoided the need to test alerted Libyan antiaircraft belts with follow-up sorties. Hitting at night limited Libya's response and took advantage of American technology and flight crew abilities.

Using the British-based 48th TFW for the main effort allowed Kelso to indulge in a rather good deception. The Sixth Fleet commander knew that press speculations ran high over an American response to the La Belle attack. Rather than try to clap a vain lid on some pretty significant ship movements, Kelso apparently elected to use the hubbub to his advantage.

As he finalized plans, the admiral flaunted his carriers. Journalists watched as USS *Coral Sea* slipped anchor from Malaga, Spain, on 10 April, officially to sail for the United States. But the press reported the carrier and several escorts steaming east into the Mediterranean. In Genoa, the media noticed USS *Ticonderoga* head out to sea and made similar observations.[33] Kelso allowed leaky Washington to fix its attentions on his warships, and perhaps even scared Libya into illuminating its air defenses a few more times to allow some final confirmatory eavesdropping. Libyan SAM and flight crews grew exhausted from irregular, confusing false alarms. Yet while Gadhafi and the world pondered the maneuvers of the carrier battle groups, Third Air Force in distant Britain quietly marshaled its tankers on "routine" exercises and prepared the powerful F-111Fs. The Libyans thought they knew what was coming. The only problem was that they would be looking seaward toward the Sixth Fleet, only to be blindsided by the racing Aardvarks.

It took only a few days to finalize the American attack plans. EL DORADO CANYON might have been launched even earlier, but France refused overflight rights, as did Spain. Both nations belong to NATO, but neither participates in the unified military command. France and Spain support antiterrorist actions (and have cooperated with the U.S. on many other occasions). Frustrating America, however, seems to entertain certain domestic constituencies in these states. Despite closed flight routes, the two countries (and NATO ally Portugal) evidently chose to overlook the eventual passage of USAF planes just beyond their territorial waters, although such a movement must have clearly shown on coastal radars. Prime Minister Margaret Thatcher of Great Britain rendered far firmer assistance, heedless of certain backlash from her own parliamentary opponents. Recalling Reagan's aid in the 1982 Falklands War, she authorized American strikes against Libya from British air bases.[34] Thanks to inscrutable French and Spanish behavior, the 48th Tactical Fighter Wing faced an even longer mission than anticipated.

Between 10 and 14 April, the U.S. Air Force scrambled to implement the long flight option. The European Tanker Force grew rapidly as tanker jets flew in from America. Most of the air refuelers arrived on 13 April. By 14 April, a dozen wide-bodied KC-10A Extenders joined nine KC-135R Stratotankers at RAF Mildenhall. Five more KC-10As and four KC-135Rs staged at RAF Fairford.

At the same time, Col. Sam W. Westbrook of 48th TFW readied two dozen of his F-111Fs and five attached EF-111As for the mission. The air force pilots worked out attack profiles, target engagement details, and defensive procedures. Westbrook's men, not Washington or EUCOM, selected the final munitions loadings and established their operational timetable in accord with Sixth Fleet's guidance. The USAF crews coordinated with their naval suppression group and fighter cover. Some limited rehearsals were conducted. After a few very busy days, Maj. Gen. Thomas G. McInerney of Third Air Force signaled Admiral Kelso, already at sea aboard USS *Coronado*.[35] By 14 April, Westbrook's air force fliers were ready.

Task Force 60, minus the departed *Saratoga* and her brood, conducted similar prebattle preparations. Rear Admiral Henry H. Mauz, who had arrived with *America* in March, assumed command of the armada. Air officers selected and confirmed approach routes, chose aiming points, checked electronic countermeasures, and insured that their plans meshed with those of the USAF Aardvarks. Some local flying provided practice, but these crews were veterans of PRAIRIE FIRE. They knew their quarry well. As the aviators completed their activities, ordnance handlers on the flight decks marked the chosen Rockeye cluster bombs and Snakeye high-drag munitions with typically defiant slogans, including, "I'd fly 10,000 miles to smoke a camel" and "To Moammar: For all you do, this bomb's for you."

Mauz commanded the USS *Coral Sea* and USS *America* carrier groups from aboard the all-seeing Aegis cruiser USS *Ticonderoga*. Once in position in the Gulf of Sidra, *Ticonderoga*'s mighty radars would allow Mauz to "see" the entire Libyan coastline and the airspace above it. During the preliminaries, the admiral dispersed Task Force 60 across the central Mediterranean, ready to unite his two flattops once the final attack orders went out. The *Coral Sea* and her escorts, for example, steamed north of Sicily.[36] Mauz was set before 14 April, waiting on the air force.

Admiral Frank Kelso already had authority to launch when he was satisfied with preparations. Upon receipt of Third Air Force's message, the Sixth Fleet commander relayed the order to Third Air Force and Task Force 60: execute EL DORADO CANYON. Kelso established a time over target of 0200 on 15 April, Tripoli time. In Britain and in the blue Mediterranean, planes and ships sprang into action. After drills, alerts, shows of force, endless frustrations, and several near misses, this one was going all the way.

The tankers took off first, rumbling slowly into the late afternoon haze over Mildenhall and Fairford at 1713 (1913 Tripoli time) on 14 April. Twenty-eight launched in all, brimming with volatile aviation fuel. The big jets attracted some attention, but with NATO exercises almost always in progress, none of the local press organs connected the procession of departing KC-10As and KC-135Rs with the heightened tensions regarding Libya. Largely ignored (until after the raid, when press agencies would suddenly remember their takeoff), the tankers headed south toward the first refueling area.

By 1736 (1936 Libyan time), the F-111Fs lifted into the sky from Lakenheath. To the southwest, the Spark Varks left Upper Heyford. All of these swing wing aircraft slipped aloft virtually unnoticed, although again, some observers later understood and described the significance of the rapid sortie sequence they had witnessed. These strike planes also swung south toward the first tanker linkup.[37]

With the air force portion of EL DORADO CANYON underway, Task Force 60 moved to its designated rendezvous about 150 miles off the Libyan coast. Even as the sun flattened and reddened on the western horizon, USS *Coral Sea* and her accompanying warships suddenly accelerated to flank speed and pounded south. The battle group tore through the Strait of Messina so quickly that a trailing Soviet Navy destroyer dropped far astern, lost in the gathering gloom. USS *America* and her escorts also dodged their Soviet snooper with a similar coordinated high-speed evolution. Many naval aviation experts believed that other Soviet surveillance vessels betrayed the ill-fated 4 December 1983 air strike to Syrian air defenders ashore in Lebanon. This time, Mauz's fast ships obviated that possibility. The Soviets did not catch up until the next day.[38]

With the western sky streaked by the last light of 14 April, Colonel Westbrook's Aardvark formation found their tankers and sucked in the first of four refuelings en route to Tripoli. The planes maintained total radio silence during the tricky junctures. As his comrades hooked onto the Extenders and Stratotankers, Westbrook watched an EF-111A and six F-111Fs turn back for green England. They were unneeded spares. The remaining air force bombers droned on into the night, struggling with blustery head winds in the Bay of Biscay. Aboard each jet, the pilot and weapons systems officer sat side by side before the dim, crowded instrument consoles, following their spectral running mates on a roller coaster of high and low legs. Perhaps the EF-111A Spark Varks confused an allied radar or two as they raced along the European coast. Westbrook's men met their tankers twice more before midnight.[39]

While the air force pushed toward Libya, the two aircraft carriers took their places just north of the Tripoli flight information region, with *America* and its screen ships to the west and the *Coral Sea* group to the east on a rough line abreast. Both flight decks filled as elevators brought the "go birds" up from the hangar decks for spotting and final checks. Maintenance teams tested engines and control surfaces, electronics technicians tweaked the delicate target recognition attack multisensor pimples beneath the chins of the A-6Es, and fuel handlers topped off their charges. Thanks to Kelso's scheme, each flight crew concentrated on a single job: strike, combat air patrol, or SAM suppression.

Unfortunately, the naval aviators overheard some alarming excerpts from speculative news reports as they met in their ready rooms. Aboard *Coral Sea*, an alarmed Lieutenant Commander Stumpf recalled, "These broadcasts listed target areas and proposed target times which coincided almost exactly with the actual missions. Many believed chances for success without significant losses had been seriously jeopardized, since a major tactical feature of the strikes was the element of surprise. There was talk of postponing everything until whoever was compromising this vital information could be throttled." Had enthusiastic news teams doomed the navy jets?

It appears that the electronic media picked up tremors of Reagan's meeting with congressional leaders (1600 Washington time, 2300 in Tripoli) and jumped to likely conclusions. The reporters pieced together various snippets of guesswork and assumptions generated during the previous tense week, when almost every major media organ explained possible American military options. Almost all of the rumors focused on the carriers, and that fell right in line with the EL DORADO CANYON plan. Despite the fears of Stumpf and his fellows, the uninformed press commentary only tangentially addressed the actual U.S. mission outline. Most broadcasts summarized the USN's capabilities and the locations

of Libya's major cities, hardly classified information. As JCS chairman
Adm. William J. Crowe said, "While there was a great deal of talk in
the newspapers about the raid and so forth, we went to some effort,
and I think we were successful in concealing the time of the raids and
the actual targets." [40] To be blunt, Stumpf and company learned that a
good deception offers small comfort to the deceiving force. Luckily,
the steady sequence of building pressure from 3 to 14 April did not
produce increased Libyan vigilance but fatigue. Tripoli evidently ignored
the flurry of late afternoon and early evening conjectures as the American
forces assembled.

Just after midnight, the blacked-out USN carriers swung into the
wind and started catapulting their aircraft into the moonless darkness.
Without marker lights, with minimal radio chatter, the Hawkeyes, Tomcats, Hornets, Corsairs, and Intruders bounded off the hot metal slabs
and arranged themselves into distinct elements. Fighters formed a combat
air patrol over the U.S. flotillas and joined strike planes to ride shotgun.
Coral Sea's six F/A-18 Hornet antiradar shooters and EA-6B Prowlers
circled well off Benghazi; *America* Corsairs and jamming jets with equivalent loads puttered back and forth beyond Tripoli. By 0120, all navy
planes were airborne, with the exception of an A-6E deck abort on
USS *America*. Two more *Coral Sea* A-6Es turned away with TRAM
malfunctions before reaching Benina. [41]

Over the Mediterranean, Colonel Westbrook's approaching Aardvarks
made their final tanker connection just prior to heading toward the Libyan
shoreline. The eighteen F-111Fs anticipated splitting into three elements:
three for Murat Sidi Bilal, nine for the Aziziyah barracks, and six for
the Tripoli airport. In three bombers programmed for Aziziyah, however,
final electronics inspections revealed problems with the Pave Tack targeting modules, terrain-following radars, or both. Kelso's guidance forbade
use of these electronically degraded planes in crowded Tripoli. In other
combat circumstances, these F-111Fs could have engaged their targets
using less accurate alternate methods, or even diverted to other objectives.
But for this raid, they were out of the picture.

Exhaustion picked off two other Aardvarks. Strained by flying at
varying speeds and altitudes through several hours of darkness, two
crews became misoriented. One 48th TFW jet dropped off its tanker
and headed in the exact opposite direction from its mates. By the time
the chagrined crew figured out their mistake, they were well behind
schedule and completely off course to their airport target. They aborted

their run and headed for the postmission refueling area. Another Aardvark was not so lucky. After leaving its tanker, the F-111F dropped toward the water for its low-level approach to Aziziyah. On a nearby Corsair inbound to hit Libyan radars, a horrified navy pilot watched the long-nosed air force jet fall too fast, smack water, and cartwheel into a shattering yellow fireball. Only fragments survived the catastrophe.[42] Westbrook's Aziziyah group was down to five strike craft and not a single Libyan shot had been fired.

Indeed, excited navy and air force fliers racing toward Tripoli and Benghazi saw both cities shining with their usual lights, completely oblivious to the menace emerging from the Mediterranean. Most Libyan radars remained quiescent, finally stirring to frantic life at 0154 in disjointed response to a barrage of heavy jamming from the EF-111As and carrier-launched Prowlers. As the Libyan SA-2, SA-3, SA-6, SA-8, and French-made Crotale batteries illuminated their search sets, pouncing Corsairs and Hornets gunned them down. The navy jets pumped HARMs into the more advanced sites and loosed Vietnam-era Shrikes against their old Hanoi nemesis, the SA-2s. Screaming homing weapons decapitated active radar antennas with bursting explosives, shredding the delicate dishes and stanchions and raining hot chunks and speeding fragments into nearby control facilities. Not surprisingly, the SA-5 launcher at Surt elected not to engage at all; those soldiers had learned hard lessons back in March. As the navy tore gaps in the enemy radar system, USS *Ticonderoga* and the orbiting Hawkeyes updated their inbound air force colleagues on the situation.

At the same time, Lieutenant Commander Stumpf and his *Coral Sea* partners closed on Benghazi. They "saw the incoming HARMs' orange cones of destruction, smothering SAM sites in their paths. SAMs that were launched created a sensational effect in the night sky, but none guided effectively." [43] With random missile shots lacing the heavens, the U.S. strikes thundered in at a hundred feet or so. The first bombs hit Benghazi and Tripoli exactly at 0200. At sea on USS *Coronado,* Vice Adm. Frank Kelso could be well pleased with such terrific synchronization and complete surprise. Rear Admiral Mauz aboard *Ticonderoga* relayed regular messages describing the chaotic Libyan defensive effort and the cool, methodical U.S. attack.

In Benghazi, *America*'s six Intruders skipped low over the city neighborhoods and plastered the Jamahiriyah barracks with 500-pounders, ravaging the adjacent MiG assembly warehouse in the general devastation.

Operation EL DORADO CANYON
Attack Profile

Target	Planned planes over target	Planned bombing *	Actual planes over target	Actual bombing
Aziziyah Barracks	9 F-111F(48 TFW) 4 × 2,000 lb. each	36 Mk 84 2,000-lb. LGBs	3 F-111F bombed 1 F-111F missed 4 aborts; 1 lost	13 hits 3 misses
Murat Sidi Bilal Camp	3 F-111F(48 TFW) 4 × 2,000 lb. each	12 Mk 84 2,000-lb. LGBs	3 F-111F bombed	12 hits
Tripoli Airfield	6 F-111F(48 TFW) 12 × 500 lb. each	72 Mk 82 500-lb. RDBs	5 F-111F bombed 1 abort	60 hits
Jamahiriyah Barracks	7 A-6E (VA-34) 12 × 500 lb. each	84 Mk 82 500-lb. RDBs	6 A-6E bombed 1 aborted on deck	70 hits 2 misses
Benina Airfield	8 A-6E (VA-55) 12 × 500 lb. each	72 Mk 20 500-lb. CBUs; 24 Mk 82 500-lb. RDBs	6 A-6E bombed 2 aborts	60 Mk 20 hits; 12 Mk 82 hits
Tripoli Air Defense Network	6 A-7E (CVW-1) 4 × Shrike/HARM each	8 Shrikes 16 HARMS	6 A-7E fired	8 Shrikes 16 HARMS
Benghazi Air Defense Network	6 F/A-18 (CVW-13) 4 × Shrike/HARM each	4 Shrikes 20 HARMS	6 F/A-18 fired	4 Shrikes 20 HARMS
TOTALS	45 aircraft	300 bombs 48 homing missiles	35 bombed 1 missed 1 lost 8 aborts	227 hits 5 misses 48 homing missiles

* LGB, Paveway family laser-guided bomb; RDB, Snakeye retarded delivery (high-drag) bomb; CBU, Rockeye cluster bomb unit—a container with hundreds of submunitions; Shrike, older, short range (about 10 miles) antiradiation missile; HARM, newer, longer range (about 30 miles) antiradiation missile.

Sources: Col. W. Hays Parks, USMCR, "Crossing the Line," *Proceedings* (November 1986), 51–52; Lt. Comdr. Robert E. Stumpf, USN, "Air War with Libya," *Proceedings* (August 1986), 48; "U.S. Demonstrates Advanced Technology in Libya," *Aviation Week and Space Technology* (21 April 1986), 18–21; "UK-Based F-111Fs the Best for Strike," *Jane's Defense Weekly* (26 April 1986), 737.

Two Mark 82s went wide of the mark and crushed two civilian houses. Brick dust, flickering little fires, and a gentle rain of debris marked the wake of the VA-34 Blue Blasters.

Simultaneously, VA-55 Warhorses of *Coral Sea* wrecked Benina airfield, cratering the runway apron, igniting the alert MiG-23s, and scattering a thick carpet of bouncing, blasting Rockeye submunitions across the battered parking apron and among the overturned, stricken, and fiery carcasses of Libyan aircraft. The runway lights at Benina stayed lit throughout the raid. There was no Libyan air response; in fact, when ordered by Tripoli to pursue departing USN jets, the local Benina commander refused.[44]

As the Intruders gutted their Benghazi targets, Colonel Westbrook's F-111Fs rushed over Tripoli at a dizzying nine miles a minute barely a hundred feet up. Overhead, wild SAM and antiaircraft fire arced and crossed in impotence, sending huge unexploded missiles tumbling down on the Libyan capital to burst upon impact. Heedless, the USAF Aardvarks bored in. Three used their Pave Tack devices to pick out the Murat Sidi Bilal maritime terrorist facility. Big Paveway one-ton bombs glided right down their laser paths and into the combat swimmers' training camp. The string of hits crumpled administration buildings, ruined neat rows of boats, and inflicted casualties on the faculty and their fanatic students.

Of five American aircraft left to hit Aziziyah barracks, three bombed dead on target, threading their heavy munitions right through the dense civilian housing abutting the compound. The laser-guided Paveways slammed into the billets and the headquarters complex and erupted, tearing down walls, blowing open roofs, and collapsing part of one of Gadhafi's many houses. Several terrorist "guests" and Gadhafi's anticoup cohorts no doubt suffered greatly as portions of their stronghold were reduced to rubble. A fourth F-111F failed to identify the radar offset point and did not bomb, pulling away after a twisting trip among Tripoli's roofs and walls. But a fifth Aardvark used the wrong radar offset mark and lobbed three of four massive 2,000-pound laser bombs into some slums near the French Embassy, riddling the diplomatic building in a bit of unintentionally poetic justice.

At 0206, the last five F-111Fs swept across the military end of Tripoli airfield. Using their precise Pave Tack pods, the bombers slung Mark 82 Snakeyes across the runways, focusing on a group of huge transports parked at one end. The soaring weapons were not laser guided, but they left their Aardvarks at exactly the proper split seconds. Numerous hits caved in the thin sides of parked Il-76 Candid four-engine transports, touching off spasmodic explosions and spewing flames and hot metal across the area and into neighboring planes. The strike left two Candids in flames and eviscerated three more. No more terrorists would depart Libya on the broken, flaming skeletons left behind. By 0211, all F-111Fs were clear of their targets and on their way to their refueling point.[45]

As both strike elements reported "feet wet" at 0213, the fountains of Libyan gunfire and SAMs continued astern. Over the eastern targets, Stumpf's Hornet fighters pulled out once the bombers were safe. The lieutenant commander remarked, "The last view of Benghazi was a skyline ablaze with secondary fires from the downtown areas, backdropped by a softer glow from fires burning at the airfield which was several miles inland."[46] The entire raid lasted nineteen minutes. Other than the single unlucky air force twosome, there had been no U.S. losses.

By 0253, all navy planes were back on deck, to the immense relief of the many tense sailors left behind. It took two refuelings and six and a half hours, but the weary Third Air Force attack group reached its bases by 0830 (0630 in England) on 15 April. One F-111F diverted to Rota Naval Air Station with an overheated engine; it was repaired and the aircraft flew back to Lakenheath the next day.[47] Admiral Kelso and his men had done it. They had avenged Sergeant Ford and saved many potential victims from Libyan terrorism.

Behind them, the Americans left utter confusion, far out of proportion to the damage incurred. The Libyans completely avoided powerful Task Force 60, although the Americans sailed just beyond the contested Gulf of Sidra for three more days. In a weird, bungled attempt at retaliation on 15 April, the Libyan Arab Army fired two SS-1 Scud B missiles at the tiny U.S. Coast Guard long-range navigation (LORAN) beacon on the Italian island of Lampedusa, 170 miles from Libya. The two rockets zoomed into the ocean more than 2 miles from the shore, detonating with two loud, metallic, and totally harmless bangs. In some ways, the aimless Lampedusa shots typified Libya's military impotence. That seemed to be about all they could manage. The night after the U.S. attack, Tripoli rocked with explosions and gunfire and sparkled with the trails of SAMs and tracers reaching for nonexistent American raiders.[48]

As for Colonel Gadhafi, he disappeared in the pandemonium that gripped his capital after the U.S. jets wheeled off. Rumors of military mutinies, coup attempts, and possible injuries surfaced from the paranoid Libyan whispering network. Although Gadhafi was alive (if not quite well), he ordered no response, preferring to portray himself as the victim of dastardly imperialist warmongers. He muted his fiery rhetoric and seemed dazed and dreamy for months thereafter. A year later, as a sparse crowd gathered near the unrepaired ruins of Gadhafi's Aziziyah abode to commemorate and condemn "barbaric, aborted American aggressions," the colonel pointedly backed out of the disorganized rally. He evidently had learned something from the bombing.

Despite the most strident warnings and hand-wringing panic in some American and European circles following the raid, there were no Libyan-sponsored terrorist reprisals linked to the air strike. In fact, the only incident even related to EL DORADO CANYON involved the deposit of three British corpses in Lebanon's war-torn Shuf Mountains on 18 April, supposedly on behalf of Tripoli. Given the horrendous situation around Beirut, these killings might well have had nothing to do with the U.S. attack other than an unfortunate coincidence in timing.[49] Far from unleashing a terrorist spree, the air operation apparently smashed both Gadhafi's instruments of terror and his will to use them.

Even as his aircraft headed home from their harsh work on the African coast, President Ronald Reagan addressed the American people to explain EL DORADO CANYON. After reminding his audience of the "irrefutable" La Belle evidence, he summarized in measured tones: "We Americans are slow to anger. We always seek peaceful avenues before resorting to the use of force—and we did. We tried quiet diplomacy, public condemnation, economic sanctions, and demonstrations of military force. None succeeded. Despite our repeated warnings, Gadhafi continued his reckless policy of intimidation, his relentless pursuit of terror. He counted on America to be passive. He counted wrong." [50]

Why did EL DORADO CANYON succeed? America massed capable forces, flexibly organized for a surprise attack that exploited Libyan weaknesses, and left command decisions to the professionals on the scene. All the ingredients for an effective expedition came together on that dark night in April 1986.

The joint use of carrier jets and air force F-111Fs massed combat power on the chosen targets. Self-appointed experts remarked that the Third Air Force units had been introduced in order to give the USAF a piece of the pie over Libya, as a sop to that favorite whipping boy of

Comparative Loss Summary
Personnel

	KIA	MIA	WIA	PW	Nonbattle
U.S. Navy/USMC	0	0	0	0	0
U.S. Air Force	2	0	0	0	0
U.S. MILITARY TOTAL	2	0	0	0	0
Libyan Arab Forces *	93	0	93	0	0

Equipment

U.S. Military: 1 jet fighter

Libyan Arab Forces: 1 corvette destroyed, 1 fast attack craft destroyed, 1 fast attack craft probably destroyed, 1 corvette damaged, Surt/Tripoli/Benghazi air defense radars destroyed,** 4 jet fighters destroyed on ground, 1 turboprop transport destroyed on ground, 2 helicopters destroyed on ground, 2 jet transports destroyed on ground, 3 jet transports damaged on ground, 2 military jet airliners damaged on ground, 1 helicopter damaged on ground, 1 turboprop transport damaged on ground, 4 fighter shipping crates destroyed on ground, 1 fighter shipping crate damaged on ground, fighter assembly warehouse damaged, Aziziyah barracks damaged, Murat Sidi Bilal complex damaged, Jamahiriyah barracks damaged, Benina military airfield cratered

* The Libyan losses from EL DORADO CANYON raids totaled 37 killed and 93 injured, supposedly all civilians except one. Libya admitted 56 dead from the March naval actions. These figures are highly suspect.

** Some of these were later repaired.

Sources: Col. W. Hays Parks, USMCR, "Crossing the Line," *Proceedings* (November 1986), 51–52; "DoD Details Civilian Damage in Libya Raid," *Air Force Times*, 26 May 1986, 12; "Targeting Gadhafi," *Time* (21 April 1986), 20.

many armchair generals, "interservice rivalry." General Bernard Rogers of EUCOM dismissed this suggestion as "baloney." He had specifically elected to use the swing wing airplanes to insure he could hit all his targets in one stroke. With only two carriers in the Mediterranean and Libya already watching the flattops carefully after the March skirmishing, Admiral Kelso agreed wholeheartedly. In truth, joint service cooperation on the Libyan attack was thorough and effective. Far from being harmed by interservice bickering, the joint strike made EL DORADO CANYON work.

So the Aardvarks delivered the really heavy punches in Tripoli, shielded and aided by the navy. Their ability to race along belly-scraping attack routes, carry heavy payloads over great distances, and engage difficult targets with extremely accurate night bombing all made the F-111Fs ideal for the Libyan mission. In training, the air force bombers regularly replicated the sort of demanding long-range effort they provided on 14–15 April 1986. With naval aircraft running interference, the 48th TFW and their electronic warfare consorts focused attention on doing one thing right: putting steel on target. Despite an epic, trying, 6,400-mile flight over monotonous black water capped by maddening mistakes and equipment trouble, Colonel Westbrook's men kept their minds on Tripoli and took out their objectives with dispassionate skill. Few other pilots could have done so well. Additionally, reliance on this new component altered the situation developed during months of USN maneuvers off Libya. As Adm. William J. Crowe noted, "While they [the Libyans] were concentrating on the carriers, we wanted to throw [in] an element we didn't believe they were ready for or anticipated." [51] Thanks to air force skill, the F-111Fs crossed thousands of unforgiving miles to appear over Tripoli right on time.

Flexibility keyed the American effort. Although the air force exhibited determination and courage, carrier aviation contributed the truly impressive lion's share of the night's many necessary aerial tasks. Along with protecting their own ships, the navy guarded the strike planes, erased Libya's early warning and SAM radar system with agile missiles and blaring electronic noise, commanded and coordinated the multitude of air movements, and stationed search and rescue elements just offshore. Aside from securing the air over Tripoli and Benghazi, USN aviation also knocked out a tough urban target and smashed the enemy fighter alert outfit on its runway. Finally, the navy fulfilled the thankless role of decoy force with ingenuity, employing tactical expertise to surprise and bewilder the Libyans, even though the defenders expected the carrier strikes.

The positive outcome over Tripoli and Benghazi related directly to the disappointing, mixed-up daylight attack against Syrian gunners in Lebanon back in 1983. The recriminations after that miscarried mission led to the establishment of the Naval Strike Warfare Center at Lemoore Naval Air Station (NAS), California, in May 1984. The center moved to the wide open spaces of Fallon NAS, Nevada, in 1985. Navy fliers trained in a full free play environment, and the curriculum allowed for intensive practice on raids under strict political rules of engagement.

High tempos of operation, small concealed targets, and wily opposing forces complicated the environment.[52] When the navy flew over Libya in the spring of 1986, they knew their business. Given that Sixth Fleet planned the mission, the new Fallon mentality (and familiar naval common sense) permeated the operation.

As always, firm local command proved decisive. Encouraged by General Rogers of EUCOM, Vice Admiral Kelso and his subordinates, Rear Admiral Mauz and Colonel Westbrook, designed the attack plan and implemented it when they were ready. The flight commanders, their staffs, and the combat fliers worked out the details.[53] Their effort speaks for itself: USAF units from four English bases thousands of miles distant and air wings of two carriers underway on the dark Mediterranean Sea united more than one hundred diverse, high-performance aircraft in the dead of night over a hostile country, struck five targets successfully, and then dispersed safely, with the loss of only a single jet.

With regard to the Libyans, they were if anything even more inept than in previous confrontations. The entire world witnessed the futile bankruptcy of Gadhafi's vaunted defense buildup and his nation's obvious vulnerability to American actions. Libya took inadequate precautions despite plenty of warning. The voluminous deluge of burned-out rounds vomited aloft by the befuddled, pointless SAM and gunfire barrages over Tripoli and Benghazi probably injured more Libyans than the U.S. bombers. As a final insult, it appears that at least part of Gadhafi's armed forces revolted in the aftermath of the air attack. Unable to hurt the hated Americans, frustrated Libyan troops turned on their boisterous leader.

Although EL DORADO CANYON was a military victory that certainly calmed Moammar Gadhafi's fervor for terrorism, it was not without controversy. Three interesting debates developed almost before the last American plane touched down. Military reformers and critics almost instantly seized upon the large number of aborted U.S. bombing runs as proof that complicated weapons do not work. Libyan propagandists, unable to salvage any shred of military pride from the air raid, instead dwelled on the allegedly wanton collateral damage. Finally, both immediately and over time, half-informed marginal participants and investigative journalists proposed the idea that the entire operation was a ruse, a giant cover for a failed attempt to assassinate Gadhafi and his family using laser-guided bombs.

There were six air force bombers out of eighteen (33 percent) and three navy attack jets of fifteen (20 percent) that failed to engage their aiming points. Although these figures sound alarming, in reality, six of the nine aircraft involved suffered degradation of their targeting and tracking devices sufficient to make accurate night strikes in crowded cities very uncertain. The F-111Fs bucked and rolled for more than six hours at several altitudes and through four fuel couplings; that some microchips jarred loose should come as no surprise. The jolting effects of carrier catapultings also took an understandable toll on the A-6Es.

In any other circumstances, these airplanes would have and could have bombed with less accurate backup methods. Three other USAF jet crews, laboring under the pressure and fatigue of their long night journey, made flying errors that botched their only permitted pass over target; in one case, the results proved tragic. The other two Aardvarks that failed to line up on their initial run might have gone around again. But in this particular mission, the certainty that planners had programmed some additional air power against each site allowed all of these fliers to turn away without jeopardizing the overall mission.[54]

The Aziziyah barracks benefited from five of these mishaps, although four other Aardvarks planted thirteen one-ton bombs squarely into the compound, which more than did the job. All other targets underwent effective attack despite the missing planes, a tribute to Kelso's thorough planning and insistence upon a large strike group, especially that portion contributed by the remote USAF units. He and his subordinates anticipated such mechanical lapses on a lengthy, challenging low-level night operation. Unlike the delicate Iranian rescue mission, EL DORADO CANYON permitted the friction of war full reign, yet still provided forces powerful enough to accomplish the difficult mission. In any event, without Pave Tack, TRAM, and guided weapons, the entire operation would have been impossible. A few aborts did not detract from the advantages created by American technology.

The high abort rate related directly to stringent U.S. rules of engagement intended to protect innocent civilians. Nevertheless, Libyan officials and the JANA press personnel spun lurid tales that implied reckless American carpet bombing of Tripoli and Benghazi. Jamahiriyah News Agency (JANA) releases focused on civilian deaths and injuries; Libya admitted thirty-seven dead and ninety-three wounded, with only one soldier supposedly among the corpses. The Libyans referred to "devastation" in their neighborhoods, and the French, Swiss, Austrian, Finnish, and Iranian embassies all suffered blast and fragmentation effects.

In Tripoli, embittered JANA guides led foreign journalists on crudely choreographed tours of ''representative examples'' of the wreckage caused by the raid. The press saw workers' quarters, portions of the Aziziyah area, and a naval cadet secondary school, all allegedly ruined by American explosives. Some diligent observers later discovered that the school had been torched by an unrelated butane canister fire, not F-111Fs. When curious members of the media asked to see the Murat Sidi Bilal complex, the JANA people denied any knowledge of such a facility. Instead, the Libyans showed off examples of United States devilry. Reporters examined a few unexploded Rockeye bomblets as their tour leaders reminded them that international law prohibited the use of such devices, a ''fact'' duly relayed to ''CBS Evening News'' audiences on 21 April 1986. The foreign newsmen also viewed a chunk of what their hosts called ''Yankee jet debris'' exhumed from a collapsed house.

Had the EL DORADO CANYON raiders inadvertently wreaked havoc across two Libyan cities? Most journalists agreed that the JANA evidence seemed shady, and clumsy Libyan attempts at information manipulation impressed few. But would the Department of Defense answer Tripoli's allegations or take shelter behind security considerations and leave the floor to Gadhafi's mouthpieces?

American bomb damage assessments, to include footage from Pave Tack cameras, allowed thorough poststrike debriefings. Cloud cover delayed and impeded photoreconnaissance, but Caspar Weinberger's Department of Defense chose to confront the Libyan allegations forcefully. Assistant secretary of defense for public affairs, Robert B. Sims, announced that, in fact, about 2 percent of the American munitions impacted off-target in civilian areas. Due to a pilot mistake, three one-ton bombs flew wide in Tripoli; two 500-pounders missed Jamahiriyah barracks in Benghazi. Combined with crew interviews and graphic films of the low-level attack sequences, Sims's statements left no doubt that great care had been taken to avoid collateral injury.

But the American official went beyond mere explanation. He pointed out obvious inconsistencies in the Libyans' stories. For one, the announced Libyan casualties looked suspicious; HARM shots alone likely killed more than one soldier. Perhaps Gadhafi was generously lumping his personal bodyguards and terrorist allies under a civilian heading. Second, Sims and naval aviators who flew the mission reminded the press that the big SAM missiles whizzing above Libyan roofs had to come down somewhere, at high velocity and often with resounding detonations. Considering that much of the Libyan fire occurred after the U.S. planes departed, not to mention the unprovoked fireworks the next night, the air defenders ended up bombarding their own unfortunate countrymen. Except for the admitted U.S. misfires near the French Embassy, Tripoli's self-inflicted shower of rocket pieces caused the trouble at the other legations.

The weapons display also prompted American responses. Defense Department lawyers quoted the minutes of the 1979–80 United Nations Conventional Weapons Conference to refute the inane claim that cluster bombs were illegal weapons; North Vietnam had once made similar false charges. Finally, Sims pointed out that the battered tube portrayed as American aircraft wreckage was in actuality part of an SA-3 booster stage that made an uninvited descent through a Libyan home.[55] The exhaustive, forthcoming U.S. public admissions and press conferences contrasted mightily with Libya's stage-managed excursions and did much to discredit the ludicrous JANA diatribes.

EL DORADO CANYON was not perfect. It definitely did not constitute a "surgical" strike, despite Secretary Weinberger's remarks to the contrary on 14 April, unless one normally does precision medical work with one-ton munitions.[56] Bombing Libya with laser-guided weapons was akin to doing oral surgery with a drill press; it was better than a chain saw, but not as precise as a finely honed dentist's drill. Even so, the number of bombs on the aiming points offered a quantum improvement over the average World War II daylight raid and surely bettered the record of early guided-weapon attacks in Vietnam.[57] The Libyan attack effectiveness and consequent lack of random dispersion are even more impressive given the effects of darkness and the fast, low-approach lanes.

The collateral damage issue was minor compared to the belief in certain government and press circles that the raid was crafted to "get Gadhafi." While F-111Fs winged homeward, Caspar Weinberger and George Shultz met the press in Washington. One of the first questioners asked if there was a plan to kill the Libyan colonel. Weinberger responded curtly: "No, there was not."

News out of Libya seemed to show that, intentionally or not, Gadhafi and his clan were in the line of fire. The injured, at least according to JANA sources, included Gadhafi's wife and children. The colonel's adopted daughter, fifteen-month-old Hana, died in the hospital; it appears, however, that the colonel or his retainers probably adopted the unfortunate child *after* the bombing raid in a propaganda ploy. The sight of children swathed in bandages played on Western emotions, though the thick dressings made definite identification of the young victims very tentative. The JANA propagandists certainly never allowed truth to get in the way of good imagery before, so who could be sure? As his "children" suffered on the world's television screens, the erratic Gadhafi's uncharacteristic absence suggested that he too had been wounded by American weaponry. It certainly looked like an assassination attempt.

EL DORADO CANYON, FRANTIC VI, and LINEBACKER I:
A Comparison

	EL DORADO CANYON (15 April 1986)	FRANTIC VI (11 September 1944)	LINEBACKER I (10 May 1972)
Target(s)	Tripoli (3) and Benghazi (2), Libya	Auto Union A.G. Chemnitz, Germany	Paul Doumer Bridge North Vietnam
Type	Night low level	Day high level	Day medium level
Bombers launched	33	51	16
Aborts	8	2	0
Lost	1	0	0
Bombs Dropped	232 (79 tons)	467 (176 tons)	29 (29 tons)
Bomb Hits	227 (75.5 tons)	12 (3 tons)	12 (12 tons)
Percentage of hits	98	3	41

Sources: Col. Dewey Waddell, USAF, ed., "The Tale of Two Bridges" in *Air War Vietnam* (New York: Arno Press, 1978), 88–90; United States Strategic Bombing Survey, *Auto Union A.G. Chemnitz and Zwickau* (Washington, D.C.: U.S. Government Printing Office, 1947), 15.

In light of the pitiful scenes from Tripoli, Weinberger's early denial did not quiet speculation. On 21 April 1986, Weinberger faced the House of Representatives Appropriations Committee for scheduled testimony on the defense budget. Attention turned to the recent Libyan action. At one juncture, Representative Norman Dicks remarked on the heavy pounding near Gadhafi's Aziziyah barracks home and tent, then queried the secretary: "Can you characterize this in any other way than an attempt to eliminate a foreign leader?"

Weinberger replied confidently. "Oh yes, Mr. Dicks, we sure can. His living quarters is a loose term. This is a command and control building. His living quarters vary from night to night. He never spends two nights in the same place. His actual living quarters are a big Bedouin sort of tent. We are not targeting him individually. You are going to see a lot of unauthorized comments and a lot of people who don't know talking to the press to show how much they know.'' The secretary concluded by noting that all indications argued against Gadhafi's presence in the building at 0200 on an average night.[58]

JCS Chairman Adm. William J. Crowe echoed his superior. He stated that there had been ''loose talk,'' but that such targeting was ''never part of the plan.'' Secretary of State Shultz agreed: ''We are not trying to go after Gadhafi.'' [59] But conspiracy theorists merely grew more excited. The more the main actors denied, the more certain investigative journalists and self-appointed insiders convinced themselves that the mission was, in fact, a failed assassination.

Probably the most full-blown version of the ''get Gadhafi'' school came out in the *New York Times* in February 1987. In a feature Sunday magazine article, Pulitzer Prize winner Seymour Hersh concluded: ''The assassination of Gadhafi was the primary goal of the Libyan bombing.'' Written in light of the covert Iranian arms scandal, Hersh wove an elaborate, convoluted tale in which Lt. Col. Oliver North, USMC, and his dark minions had concocted and conducted the assassination plan with the approval of a detached president. Much of Hersh's article offered perfectly reasonable (and well-stated) pieces of the story of EL DORADO CANYON and related events. But the author's speculations hurt the worthwhile portions of his explanation. As if to remind his readers of Lieutenant Colonel North's duplicity, Hersh punctuated his account with repeated irrelevant references to the marine's questionable dealings with Iran.

With regard to the supposed assassination scheme, Hersh based his argument on these ''facts'': ''There was no executive order to kill . . . there was no written record. . . . Even the official bombing orders supplied by the White House to the Pentagon did not cite as targets the tent where Gadhafi worked. . . . The shielded orders explain a series of strong denials.'' [60] In other words, because there was no proof, it must have been so.

Hersh developed his findings after extensive interviews with more than seventy ''current and former'' White House, State Department, CIA, NSA, and military officials, who ''agreed to talk only if their names were not used.'' [61] Weinberger had warned that people who knew

U.S. Operations Against Libya Time Line
November 1985–18 April 1986

23 November 1985—Abu Nidal's terrorists seized EgyptAir plane; sixty killed during the episode, most during a failed rescue attempt.

27 December 1985—Abu Nidal's terrorists attacked Rome and Vienna airports; five Americans killed. Libya implicated.

7 January 1986—President Reagan ordered all U.S. citizens to leave Libya; complete severance of U.S./Libyan economic ties.

14 January —Libyans intercepted USN EA-3B surveillance aircraft.

26 January —ATTAIN DOCUMENT exercise commenced.

30 January —ATTAIN DOCUMENT concluded.

12 February —ATTAIN DOCUMENT II commenced.

15 Feburary —ATTAIN DOCUMENT II concluded.

14 March —President Reagan approved crossing on 32 degrees 30 minutes north latitude in the Gulf of Sidra (the "line of death").

24 March —(0001) USN aircraft crossed line of death. ATTAIN DOCUMENT III/PRAIRIE FIRE commenced.

(1300) Surface Action Group crossed line.

(1452) Surt SA-5 site engaged USN aircraft.

(1945) Surt SA-5 site engaged USN aircraft.

(1955) SA-2 site engaged USN aircraft.

(2014) SA-5 site engaged USN aircraft.

(2126) USN aircraft sunk *Waheed*.

(2206) USN aircraft shot HARMs at Surt radars.

(2315) USN aircraft damaged Nanuchka corvette.

25 March —(0115) USS *Yorktown* sank fast attack craft.

(0154) USN aircraft shot HARMs at Surt radars.

(0807) USN aircraft sank Nanuchka corvette.

27 March —(1600) Surface Action Group retired across line of death.

29 March —Task Force 60 withdrew from Sidra area.

3 April —Bomb on TWA Flight 840 killed four Americans; Gadhafi praised Syrian-sponsored action.

5 April —Bomb in Berlin discotheque killed one American soldier; Libya clearly implicated.

9 April —President Reagan authorized EL DORADO CANYON.

14 April —(1913) USAF tankers launched from British bases.

(1936) USAF F-111s launched from British bases.

15 April —(0020) USS *Coral Sea* launched aircraft.

(0045) USS *America* launched aircraft.

(0154) U.S. aircraft began to suppress Libyan air defenses.

(0200) Simultaneous attacks on five Libyan targets started.

(0213) Attack completed; one USAF F-111 missing.

(0253) All USN aircraft recovered.

(0830) USAF aircraft returned to bases.

15 April —Libyans fired two Scud B missiles at U.S. Coast Guard station on Lampedusa Island.

18 April —Task Force 60 withdrew from Sidra area.

very little would talk as if they understood everything; Hersh was ready to listen to them.

Of course, the entire "get Gadhafi" line of thinking is patently silly and reflects a misapprehension of the capabilities of conventional bombing, not to mention a dismal view of American government ethics. There are three major flaws in the assassination thesis. First, the majority of the raid struck other targets related to terrorist activities; it is asking a bit much to believe that these dangerous, demanding attacks were conducted merely to camouflage a murder. Second, the targets were chosen ten days before the bombs dropped; who could be sure which house Gadhafi would be using when the bombs fell? Admiral Kelso, not Oliver North or anyone else in the White House, controlled the timing and most of the operational framework of EL DORADO CAN-YON; like the president himself, the admiral even had authority to cancel the operation if he so chose. He ran the mission as soon as enough USAF tankers marshaled in Great Britain, and without any evident regard for Gadhafi's whereabouts.[62] Finally, granting for the sake of argument that killing Gadhafi constituted Reagan administration policy, use of more than a hundred expensive aircraft dropping big, not wholly precise weapons is equivalent to trying to exterminate an ant with a pile driver. American intelligence and counterterrorist elements could have done the deed with much more certainty, perhaps under the diversion of an air raid, as with somewhat similar, although wholly legitimate, combat activities in Lebanon.

It is hard to imagine that anyone in Washington would have been greatly upset had the Libyan strongman perished, but such was not the goal of EL DORADO CANYON. In the final analysis, scaring Gadhafi and tearing strips out of his terrorist infrastructure might well have worked better than eliminating him. A dead colonel could have been a martyr to Libyan nationalism and a spur for newer, more virulent strains of terrorism. Alive and shaken, the desert chieftain has apparently thought better of his worldwide adventures in factional violence. In the bitter twilight struggle against terrorism, that is victory enough for now.

Chapter 7 Notes

Epigraphs come from U.S. Congress, House of Representatives, Armed Services Committee, *State Sponsored Terrorism,* 99th Congress, 2nd Session, 28 January 1986, 5, 6, and Glenn Tucker, *Dawn Like Thunder* (Indianapolis: Bobbs-Merrill, 1963), 206.

1. Gayle Rivers, *The War Against the Terrorists* (New York: Stein and Day, 1986), 96–98, 168.
2. Ibid., 83; "To Shoot or Not to Shoot," *Newsweek* (9 December 1985), 36–39; "Maltese Reported to Have Barred Role for U.S. Officers in Jet Raid," *New York Times,* 3 December 1985, A1; "U.S. May Move Anti-Hijacking Experts," *New York Times,* 5 December 1985, A3; Leroy Thompson, *The Rescuers* (Boulder, CO: Paladin Press, 1986), 154–56.
3. Col. W. Hays Parks, USMCR, "Crossing the Line," *Proceedings* (November 1986), 44; "Ten Minutes of Horror," *Time* (6 January 1986), 74–76; Seymour Hersh, "Target Qaddafi," *New York Times Magazine* (22 February 1987), 48; "A Libyan Missile May Be In Works," *Middletown, NY Times Herald Record,* 30 April 1987, 50. This last piece, summarized from Associated Press wire stories, includes details of matching grenade lot numbers from Chadian war trophies and residue at the Malta, Rome, and Vienna sites.
4. Hersh, "Target Qaddafi," 48, 71; Parks, "Crossing the Line," 44; Ray Bonds, ed., *The U.S. War Machine* (New York: Crown Publishers, 1983), 250, 251; Lt. Comdr. Robert E. Stumpf, USN, "Air War with Libya," *Proceedings* (August 1986), 42.
5. Robert Leckie, *The Wars of America* (New York: Harper & Row, 1981), 226–28.
6. Stumpf, "Air War with Libya," 43, 44; Parks, "Crossing the Line," 43, 44.
7. Stumpf, "Air War with Libya," 44–46.
8. Hersh, "Target Qaddafi," 71.
9. Norman Friedman, "The Sixth Fleet at Forty," *Proceedings* (May 1987), 151–61; Stumpf, "Air War with Libya," 46; Parks, "Crossing the Line," 44.
10. Stumpf, "Air War with Libya," 46; Parks, "Crossing the Line," 44.
11. Michael Skinner, *USN* (Novato, CA: Presidio Press, 1986), 68, 69.
12. Stumpf, "Air War with Libya," 46; David M. North, "Merits of U.S., Soviet Weapons Explored in Libyan Conflict," *Aviation Week and Space Technology* (31 March 1986), 20; "Showdown in the Gulf of Sidra," *Washington Post,* 26 March 1986, A22; "Best Regards," *Washington Post,* 26 March 1986, A22.

13. Stumpf, "Air War with Libya," 47.
14. Ibid.; Parks, "Crossing the Line," 45; "U.S. Reports a Libyan Ship 10 Miles From Americans," *New York Times,* 26 March 1986, A8; "Shooting Match Provided Equipment Test," *Navy Times,* 7 April 1986, 39, 40; JO2 Timothy J. Christmann, USN, "Harpoon Proves Its Tenacity," *Naval Aviation News* (July/August 1986), 13; Michael Vlahos, "Middle Eastern, North African, and South Asian Navies," *Proceedings* (March 1987), 52, 53.
15. North, "Merits of U.S., Soviet Weapons Explored in Libyan Conflict," 20; "Shooting Match Provided Equipment Test," 39.
16. "Showdown in the Gulf of Sidra," A22; Christmann, "Harpoon Proves Its Tenacity," 13.
17. "U.S. Asserts Right of Free Navigation," *Navy Times,* 7 April 1986, 37; "Pride, Joy, as Ships Come Home," *Navy Times,* 28 April 1986, 50; "Shooting Match Provided Equipment Test," 40; "Showdown in Gulf of Sidra," A22; "U.S. Reports Libyan Ship 10 Miles From Americans," A8; North, "Merits of U.S., Soviet Weapons Explored in Libyan Conflict," 21.
18. "Showdown in the Gulf of Sidra," A22; "Shooting Match Provided Equipment Test," 30; Stumpf, "Air War with Libya," 47; North, "Merits of U.S., Soviet Weapons Explored in Libyan Conflict," 30.
19. North, "Merits of U.S., Soviet Weapons Explored in Libyan Conflict," 21; "U.S. Reports Libyan Ship 10 Miles From Americans," A8; Christmann, "Harpoon Proves Its Tenacity," 12–14; Parks, "Crossing the Line," 45.
20. "U.S. Asserts Right of Free Navigation," 37; Stumpf, "Air War with Libya," 47; Parks, "Crossing the Line," 45.
21. President Ronald Reagan, "News Conference of April 9, 1986," *Department of State Bulletin* (June 1986), 25.
22. "U.S. Asserts Right of Free Navigation," 37.
23. "Explosion on Flight 840," *Time* (14 April 1986), 34–37; Parks, "Crossing the Line," 45.
24. "Targeting Gaddafi," *Time* (21 April 1986), 20; Hersh, "Target Qaddafi," 74; "Med Forces Move; Security Tightens," *Navy Times,* 21 April 1986, 4.
25. "Joint News Conference by Secretary Shultz and Secretary Weinberger of April 14, 1986," *Department of State Bulletin* (June 1986), 5; "Worldnet with Secretary Shultz of April 16, 1986," *Department of State Bulletin* (June 1986), 8–11; Hersh, "Target Qaddafi," 74.
26. Parks, "Crossing the Line," 44; "Med Forces Move; Security Tightens," 4; "A Syrian Connection," *Newsweek* (12 May 1986), 54.

27. Hersh, "Target Qaddafi," 74; Reagan, "News Conference of April 9, 1986," 25, 26.
28. Parks, "Crossing the Line," 50; U.S. Department of Defense, *Annual Report to the Congress* (Washington, D.C.: U.S. Government Printing Office, 1987), 61; "Reagan Ordered Air Strikes to Preempt Libyan Terrorists," *Aviation Week and Space Technology* (21 April 1986), 22, 23.
29. "American-Libyan Tensions Span Almost 2 Centuries," *Navy Times,* 21 April 1986, 18; International Institute for Strategic Studies, "The Military Balance 1985/86," *Air Force* (February 1986), 108, 109; John K. Cooley, *Libyan Sandstorm* (New York: Holt, Rinehart and Winston, 1982), 282; John Wright, *Libya: A Modern History* (Baltimore: Johns Hopkins University Press, 1982), 210–12.
30. Parks, "Crossing the Line," 46–48; Hersh, "Target Qaddafi," 74, 84; "American-Libyan Tensions Span Almost 2 Centuries," 18; "Training, Skill Used to Hilt in Raid on Libya," *Navy Times,* 28 April 1986, 18; U.S. Congress, House of Representatives, Committee on Appropriations, *Department of Defense Appropriations for 1987,* 99th Congress, 2nd Session, 21 April 1986, 696.
31. Parks, "Crossing the Line," 47–49; Hersh, "Target Qaddafi," 84; Bonds, *The U.S. War Machine,* 180, 181, 198, 204, 205; "U.S. Demonstrates Advanced Weapons Technology in Libya," *Aviation Week and Space Technology* (21 April 1986), 21; John Morrocco and the editors, *Rain of Fire* (Boston MA: Boston Publishing Company, 1985), 153, 154.
32. U.S. Congress, House Appropriations Committee, *DOD Appropriations for 1987,* 692–96; Stumpf, "Air War with Libya," 48; "U.S. Demonstrates Advanced Weapons Technology in Libya," 18–21; Parks, "Crossing the Line," 49; "Countdown to Operation EL DORADO CANYON," *Jane's Defence Weekly* (26 April 1986), 736; "USAF's Role in Libyan Raid," *Air Force* (November 1986), 26, 29.
33. Christopher Wright, "U.S. Naval Operations in 1986," *Proceedings* (May 1987), 43; Stumpf, "Air War with Libya," 47.
34. Ibid., 29; U.S. Congress, House Appropriations Committee, *DOD Appropriations for 1987,* 692.
35. "Training, Skill Used to Hilt in Raid on Libya," 4; "Countdown to Operation EL DORADO CANYON," 736; Hersh, "Target Qaddafi," 20; Parks, "Crossing the Line," 50; "United States Air Forces in Europe," *Air Force* (May 1986), 108, 111.
36. Parks, "Crossing the Line," 50; Stumpf, "Air War with Libya," 48; JO2 Timothy J. Christmann, USN, "The Navy Strikes Tripoli's Terrorist," *Naval Aviation News* (July/August 1986), 17; JOC Dave Lee and PH2 Chris Holmes, "Operation EL DORADO: The Men Behind the Headlines," *All Hands* (June 1986), 27.

37. U.S. Congress, House Appropriations Committee, *DOD Appropriations for 1987*, 692; "Countdown to Operation EL DORADO CANYON," 736.

38. Stumpf, "Air War with Libya," 48; Christmann, "The Navy Strikes Tripoli's Terrorist," 17.

39. "U.S. Demonstrates Advanced Weapons Technology in Libya," 19; Hersh, "Target Qaddafi," 22; "Countdown to Operation EL DORADO CANYON," 736.

40. Parks, "Crossing the Line," 51; Stumpf, "Air War with Libya," 48; U.S. Congress, House Appropriations Committee, *DOD Appropriations for 1987*, 701, 702, 719.

41. U.S. Congress, House Appropriations Committee, *DOD Appropriations for 1987*, 719; "Countdown to Operation EL DORADO CANYON," 736; Stumpf, "Air War with Libya," 48.

42. U.S. Congress, House Appropriations Committee, *DOD Appropriations for 1987*, 693, 707; "USAF's Role in Libya Raid," 26, 29; "Training, Skill Used to Hilt in Raid on Libya," 4; "F-111 Most Capable Aircraft for Libya Raid," *Air Force Times*, 28 April 1986, 4; "Libya May Have F-111 Parts," *Air Force Times*, 5 May 1986, 28.

43. Stumpf, "Air War with Libya," 48; Parks, "Crossing the Line," 51; Christmann, "The Navy Strikes Tripoli's Terrorist," 16, 17.

44. Stumpf, "Air War with Libya," 48; "Libyan SAM Missiles Hit Civilian Areas, Says USA," *Jane's Defence Weekly* (26 April 1986), 737; "DOD Details Civilian Damage in Libya Raid," *Air Force Times*, 26 May 1986, 12.

45. "DOD Details Civilian Damage in Libya Raid," 12; "Libyan SAM Missiles Hit Civilian Areas, Says USA," 737; "USAF's Role in Libya Raid," 26, 29; "Countdown to Operation EL DORADO CANYON," 736.

46. Stumpf, "Air War with Libya," 48.

47. Lee and Holmes, "Operation EL DORADO," 28, 29; "Countdown to Operation EL DORADO CANYON," 736.

48. "Station Attacked," *Navy Times*, 28 April 1986, 18; "Libyan Scud B Attack on Lampedusa Island," *Jane's Defence Weekly* (26 April 1986), 739.

49. "Reagan Ordered Air Strikes to Preempt Libyan Terrorists," 23; "Libya Marks Anniversary of U.S. Raid," *New York Times*, 16 April 1987, A3.

50. President Ronald Reagan, "Address to the Nation of April 14, 1986," *Department of State Bulletin* (June 1986), 1, 2.

51. "F-111 Most Capable Aircraft for Libya Raid," 4; "USAF's Role in Libya Raid," 26, 29; U.S. Congress, House Appropriations Committee, *DOD Appropriations for 1987*, 691; "UK-Based F-111Fs Best for Strike," *Jane's Defence Weekly* (26 April 1986), 737.

52. Parks, "Crossing the Line," 48; Barrett Tilman, "Strike U," *Proceedings*

(January 1987), 81, 84; "Perspectives on Naval Aviation," *Proceedings* (February 1987), 10.

53. Parks, "Crossing the Line," 49, 50; David M. North, "Air Force, Navy Brief Congress on Lessons from Libyan Strikes," *Aviation Week and Space Technology* (2 June 1986), 63.

54. U.S. Congress, House Appropriations Committee, *DOD Appropriations for 1987,* 692, 693, 719.

55. "DOD Details Civilian Damage in Libya Raid," 12; "Libyan SAM Missiles Hit Civilian Areas, Says USA," 737; Parks, "Crossing the Line," 51, 52.

56. "Joint News Conference by Secretary Shultz and Secretary Weinberger of April 14, 1986," 3–6.

57. Col. Dewey Wadell, USAF, ed., "The Tale of Two Bridges" in *Air War Vietnam* (New York: Arno Press, 1978), 88, 89; United States Strategic Bombing Survey, *Auto Union A.G. Chemnitz and Zwickau* (Washington, D.C.: U.S. Government Printing Office, 1947), 15.

58. "Joint News Conference by Secretary Shultz and Secretary Weinberger of April 14, 1986," 4; U.S. Congress, House Appropriations Committee, *DOD Appropriations for 1987,* 697; Hersh, "Target Qaddafi," 19, 22; "DOD Details Civilian Damage in Libya Raid," 12; Parks, "Crossing the Line," 52.

59. Hersh, "Target Qaddafi," 22.

60. Ibid., 17, 19, 20.

61. Ibid., 19.

62. North, "Air Force, Navy Brief Congress on Lessons from Libyan Strikes," 63; "Washington Whispers," *U.S. News & World Report* (9 March 1987), 12.

CHAPTER 8

FORCE AND FRICTION: A RECKONING
1975–1986

"Everything is very simple in war, but the simplest thing is difficult. These difficulties accumulate and produce a friction beyond the imagination of those who have not seen war. . . . Friction is the only conception which, in a fairly general way, corresponds to the distinction between real war and war on paper."

Karl von Clausewitz, *On War*

"When things went wrong at the Pentagon, really wrong, you'd always hear some bright guy in a business suit complaining that a country able to land a man on the moon should be able to carry out any operations on earth: raid Hanoi, drop into Tehran, whatever. I always pointed out to these smart alecks that as I recalled, the moon didn't hide, move around under its own steam, or shoot back."

Col. John R. Boyd, USAF (retired)

The seven major U.S. expeditions since the evacuation of Saigon resulted in five successes and two failures. Armed interventions exacted a price. American casualties in these actions totaled 712, with 337 dead, missing, or died of wounds. More than two-thirds of those killed fell in a single searing second in Beirut. To put these losses in perspective, in Vietnam the 1st Cavalry Division (Airmobile) suffered 334 dead and 736 wounded in its first major engagement in the Ia Drang Valley during October and November of 1965. In Normandy, American assault units staging for Operation COBRA (24–25 July 1944) lost 757 men to misdirected "friendly" bombing.[1] Of course, statistics are cold comfort to those who paid in blood.

What did the U.S. get for these efforts? Americans secured *Mayaguez* and its crew unhurt, brushed back a Libyan air challenge, rescued more than 600 students unharmed from the midst of a defended island, snatched brigands from midair over a dark sea, and blew holes in Colonel Gadhafi's terrorist schemes. All of these victories came far from American shores, in hostile skies, on disputed ground, and upon unfriendly waters. U.S. forces crushed their opposition in almost every instance in which combat occurred. In addition, American military prowess enforced national strategies in many other situations short of conflict. Far from being the hobbled giant portrayed in so many dire predictions of 1973–74, the United States reasserted its traditional role as keeper of the peace. Having recovered from the doldrums of the Vietnam era, capable armed forces once again gave the president the big stick needed to back up U.S. policy worldwide.

The dismal outcomes of EAGLE CLAW and the marine deployment in Beirut reflected individual, political, and organizational problems. Although U.S. citizens can be proud of troop performance, neither of these episodes offered comfort to American military leaders. The Defense Department's forthright insistence on learning what went wrong, and why, stands in marked contrast to the inordinate focus on "good news only, please" that led the country down the road to ruin in Indochina in the 1960s. Reviews of the failed expeditions were hard-nosed, uncompromising, and thorough. Evidently, the military paid attention. In consequence, the two defeats provided valuable, sobering lessons that were not lost on U.S. planners during later operations. For example, American special operations forces reorganized after Desert One played a major, and far more fruitful, role in the Grenada campaign. Similarly, U.S. troops in Honduras have avoided the marines' mistakes in Lebanon; they routinely guard strong defensive perimeters in order to frustrate local insurrectionaries. Finally, in a less celebrated case, determined naval aviators studied the mistakes of the bungled December 1983 strike near Beirut. The USN jet crews functioned far more effectively when they bombed Gadhafi's Libya in 1986. This willingness to admit errors and correct them bodes well for the future.

Amazingly, many self-appointed military experts have been highly critical of not only the defeats but the victories as well. Journalists have given much credence to such thinking, and in almost any piece on defense matters, one will encounter assertions of allegedly severe flaws in post-Vietnam actions. William Lind wrote *America Can Win,* suggesting that recent battles were anything but successful. Richard Gabriel, a college professor and reserve army intelligence officer, penned the venomous *Military Incompetence*—the title summarizes Gabriel's assessment of America's armed forces. In *The Pentagon and the Art of War,* Edward Luttwak also complains that the U.S. military does not know how to fight. In each case, these authors recount the American expeditions after the second Indochina war, dissecting every miscue and accident and inventing or distorting more than a few events for good measure.

A bit of Luttwak will suffice to set the tone. The *Mayaguez* rescue was "clumsy," the Sidra air battle of 1981 a "most feeble" triumph, and Grenada supposedly featured "gross failures of planning and command." In his key diatribe, Luttwak echoes the other critics as he derides U.S. errors in URGENT FURY. He describes a version of Grenada in which "each engagement should have been swiftly victorious. It was not." Instead, "the Grenadian leaders and the Cubans were left undisturbed to organize resistance" from St. George's, in "the central part of the island." Luttwak judged most of the Cubans as "only construction workers" and found that "not more than 43 were professional soldiers," numbers derived from press reports based upon, of all things, Fidel Castro's somewhat suspect postinvasion protest speeches. Luttwak concludes: "The most disheartening aspect of the entire Grenada episode was the ease with which the performance of the armed forces was accepted as satisfactory, even praiseworthy." [2] If the American military did as poorly on Grenada and in other expeditions as Luttwak, Lind, and Gabriel indicated, there would be cause for real alarm.

These men want drastic reforms in American military structure and practice, and look for anecdotal evidence that buttresses their ideas. Lind wants "maneuver warfare," rather than what he sees as an American dependence on material superiority and "attrition." Gabriel decries "managers in uniform," and Luttwak denigrates "interservice rivalry." They cite real and half-real problems since Vietnam to "prove" their cases. In Washington budget battles, this all may make some sense, and probably impresses civilian lawmakers and executives. But these vague prescriptions offer little for the professional soldier, even in the few cases where the reformers' descriptive case studies coincide with actual events. It is the military analog to sports writing—entertaining "inside" stories based vaguely on real occurrences and penned by "experts" who never played the game.

Lacking any significant military experience, these writers have seized upon what military theorist Karl von Clausewitz called "friction," that compendium of self-sustaining, nagging confusion peculiar to the danger, physical exertion, incomplete information, and other annoying situational pitfalls of warfare. Expeditions are dangerous by nature, small snippets cut from the likely canvas of full-scale war. Even among the most hardened professionals, nobody wants to die or be maimed. This is especially clear when one notes that most post-Vietnam actions featured troops new to combat. Consider the plight of the marines on Koh Tang as the sun went down, or Captain Kearney's frightening initiation at Calvigny. Only training, discipline, and forceful leadership can counter the effects of danger.

Physical exertion in combat cannot be neglected. War saps strength and spirit, and expeditions are no different for those involved. It was easy to say afterward that Grenada always looked like a short mission; the marines in Beirut were once told the same thing. Thirst, lack of sleep, and exposure to weather played a part on Grenada. But not all exertion occurs on the ground. Pilots exhausted by low-level flight over long distances do not always function at full efficiency, as seen in Iran, at Calvigny, and over Libya. Commanders must know when to call for that last full measure from their men; when leaders guess incorrectly and press beyond human capacities, mishaps, aborts, and even failures result.

Clausewitz warned that "a great part of the information in war is contradictory, a still greater part is false, and by far the greatest part is doubtful." Despite satellites, signal intercepts, infrared photography, and other modern wizardry, intelligence still turns out to be inadequate, especially on short-notice expeditionary missions. The marines found plenty of Khmers and no American merchant seamen on Koh Tang; JTF 120 had to scour Grenada to find the bulk of the young people they had been sent to rescue. All one can do is weigh the possibilities and bring enough extra fighting power, or units with a wide range of abilities, to exploit unforeseen surprises rather than be exploited by them.

Finally, there are what Clausewitz called "innumerable trifling circumstances." Since humans make war, they make errors. The more complex the operation, the more likely that parts will break down or go awry.[3] Perceptions can prove false, as for the 24th MAU in Lebanon. Snarled and missed communications played major roles in the Desert One failure, the muddled December 1983 air raid on Syrian air defenses, and the hasty helicopter assault on Calvigny barracks. Finally, odd phenomena and unexpected elements enter the fray: dust clouds in Iran or uninvited carabinieri at Sigonella. Simple, shrewd plans, flexibly executed, can beat back some of these frustrations.

Friction is equivalent to Murphy's Law, and neglect of this factor risks a major disaster. It was fully present during the seven American combat actions after the Indochina war, and when the participants accommodated friction, victory followed. Unfortunately, by scrutinizing minor military operations through highly focused lenses, the critics fault any action that falls short of perfection. But as Clausewitz warned, military operations cannot be perfect—it is not in their nature. One cannot remedy friction.

That realization, in essence, is what is lacking in many critiques of U.S. performances in these small conflicts. There is a feeling that somehow, because these engagements involve only a fraction of American might against Third World opposition, they should be textbook affairs. Armchair generals are not satisfied with a quick victory or low casualties; it should be quicker, and casualties of any kind are unacceptable. For these experts, every weapon, every commander, and every unit should enjoy unsurpassed success, because they are participating in "easy" little squabbles. But for those men under fire, the dogfight over Sidra or the defense of the marines' Beirut perimeter were not insignificant skirmishes. And, of course, the local adversaries might well be like the Khmer Rouge on Koh Tang, and fail to recognize their evident inferiority with a handy capitulation in the face of U.S. power.

In sum, Clausewitz cautioned against overreliance on the views of inexperienced thinkers: "Action in war is movement in a resistant medium. Just as a man immersed in water is unable to perform with ease and regularity the simplest and most natural of movements, that of walking, so in war, with ordinary powers one cannot keep even the line of mediocrity. This is why the correct theorist is like a swimming master, who teaches on dry land movements which are required in water, which must appear ludicrous to those who forget about the water. This is also why theorists who have never plunged in themselves, or who cannot deduce any generalizations from their experience, are impractical and even absurd, because they teach only what everyone knows—how to walk.'' [4] Winning in expeditionary combat, or any warfare, is never a walkover, especially for those involved.

Having considered expeditionary battles since Vietnam with allowances for the influences of friction, are there any conclusions to be drawn from the U.S. experience? In recent missions, air strikes and special operations were the most prevalent types of combat, followed by amphibious assaults and ground defensive operations. Mass, flexibility, and command keyed the victories.

Since even the United States has finite military resources, what sort of forces provide the mass and flexibility that allow for success by imagina-

Types of U.S. Expeditionary Combat Operations 1975–1986

Operation	*Mayaguez*	Iran	Sidra	Lebanon	Grenada	*Achille Lauro*	Libya
Air to air combat			X				
Air strike vs. ship	X						· X
Air strike vs. ground	X			X	X		X
Close air support	X				X		
Naval surface combat							X
Naval gunfire support	X			X	X		
Amphibious sea assault					X		
Amphibious air assault *	X				X		
Airborne drop					X		
Helicopter raid		X			X		
Ground attack	X				X		
Ground defense	X			X	X		
Special operations	X	X		?	X	X	

* Assaults to gain a lodgement versus limited objective, short-duration helicopter raids.

tive local commanders? Aircraft carrier battle groups, special operations forces, and marines exhibited a terrific amount of versatility, and proved useful in a majority of the situations. These are the muscles and sinews of American power projection.

The aircraft carrier battle group is often criticized as an overly expensive relic of the Pacific war of 1941–45, and commentators speculate on the short lives these leviathans might lead in a nuclear war. Barring Armageddon, the carriers have been well suited for a variety of missions, including air strikes at sea or ashore, cover for amphibious landings, sea control, and even odd jobs like launching the Iran helicopter contingent or snatching terrorists from midair. The power concentrated in the flattop, its brood of planes, and its brace of escorting warships has many aspects, from the subtlety of electronic eavesdropping to the screaming lances of Harpoon missiles or the mighty hammer of air bombardment. Not surprisingly, the Reagan administration has built up fourteen of these carrier battle groups, with provisions for a fifteenth.[5] These floating airfields and their sea and air outriders constitute a principal American advantage in the global balance of power. U.S. naval intelligence indicates that the Soviets are finally about to commission their first aircraft carrier. But for now, the USN sets the standard for large-deck flight operations and ancillary combat capabilities. America's superbly trained carrier groups have been ready whenever called upon.

Whereas aircraft carriers have clearly contributed to American successes, special operations forces have a more ambiguous record, although their services are in equal or perhaps even greater demand. The USAF 1st Special Operations Wing has always performed well, with yeoman service in the Iran rescue attempt and during URGENT FURY. Navy SEAL Team 6 accomplished most of its difficult tasks on Grenada. The army's 160th Aviation Battalion trains very hard, but it took a terrible beating over the Spice Island. As for America's highly trained premier hostage rescue unit, Delta still awaits its first publicly acknowledged triumph to balance the sad images of the Desert One debacle and the disheartening repulse at Richmond Hill prison. Although hardly glamorous and largely neglected, Green Berets in Lebanon and psychological operations units in Grenada performed valuable, unique tasks in support of the conventional missions in progress. In the shadow of the expeditionary conflicts, Green Beret advisory teams served with distinction throughout the Third World, and with notable promise in El Salvador, a Vietnam on the verge of being won. In sum, the U.S. special warfare

U.S. Armed Forces Expeditionary Participation
1975–1986

Force	Mayaguez	Iran	Sidra	Lebanon	Grenada	Achille Lauro	Libya
USN							
Carriers	X	X	X	X	X	X	X
Surface	X	X	X	X	X	X	X
Amphibs				X	X		
USAF							
Tactical	X						X
Airlift	X	X		X	X	X	
Tankers	X	X			X		X
Recon	X	X			X	X	X
USMC							
Ground	X			X	X		
Air		X		X	X		
USA							
Ground				X	X		
Air	X				X		
Special Ops							
Delta		X			X	X	
ST-6					X	X	
1st SOW		X			X		
ALLIES				X	X	X	

troops have evidenced plenty of skill and combat potential in many efforts, but their few significant failures show that there is still room for improvement.

Planners agree that much is expected from these units, but so far, they have yet to pull off an American equivalent of Entebbe. Recognizing the myriad of possible threats, the Department of Defense, under strong congressional prodding, has taken major measures to strengthen national special warfare capabilities. New equipment coming on line includes improved USAF MH-53J Pave Low, Army MH-60X Blackhawk, and Army MH-47E Chinook long-range helicopters, new MC-130H Combat Talon II transports, and refurbished AC-130U Spectre gunships. By 1992, these modified models will be supplemented by the truly unique MV-

22 Osprey, a propeller plane with a tilting wing to permit vertical takeoff and landing. Ospreys might make a future version of EAGLE CLAW more viable. All services have taken steps to attract, recognize, and retain high-quality special troopers and commanders; for example, the army has established a distinct special operations branch for the officers and men traditionally seconded from other arms of the service. Finally, the somewhat ad hoc JSOC has been replaced by the unified U.S. Special Operations Command, a major organization on par with such regional headquarters as PACOM and EUCOM.[6]

Curiously, despite much ink spilled on the supposedly arcane nature of special warfare, the most effective American special efforts since Vietnam have been carried out by conventional forces or special warfare units working conventionally. These include the convoluted but victorious *Mayaguez* recovery, the Rangers' and marines' swift Grand Anse raid, and the brilliantly executed interception of the *Achille Lauro* hijackers. American defense officials acknowledge that their strategy for dealing with demanding special warfare contingencies includes both dedicated special operations elements and general purpose forces.[7] Simpler, regularly exercised conventional actions offer a useful complement that can offset the innate riskiness of special missions; Grenada offers the best example of such a concept in practice.

Along with the carriers and special units, the U.S. Marine Corps played a role in those expeditions necessitating land combat. With their own armor, artillery, engineers, sealift, helilift, and service support, backed up by powerful naval task forces, USMC battalion landing teams can deal with many unexpected situations, from handling civilian evacuations to conducting outright invasions. Without the full BLT, as at Koh Tang Island, the marines lose some of their intrinsic flexibility and much of their combat power. Marines regularly point out that they do their best work as assault troops. But their varied capabilities and availability offshore from trouble spots make them likely actors in any crisis requiring a ground force. Only Grenada, however, featured a traditional "hit the beach" situation; the Koh Tang rescue attempt and the confusing Lebanon deployment stretched marine ingenuity to the limit and, in Beirut, beyond. Like the carrier battle groups, the marines exist to project power. They, too, represent a major U.S. edge in comparison to the USSR. Of all the marines and naval infantry in the world, almost half wear the globe and anchor of the USMC.[8]

If any element of the armed forces could be said to have disappointed

American hopes after Vietnam, it is that darling of Southeast Asia, the helicopter. Many proponents warned that these ungainly aircraft were not panaceas for tactical problems, and recent U.S. experiences have proven that with a vengeance. Yes, they could go straight down, hover, and lift straight up. But when damaged, helicopters enjoy all the aerodynamic stability of a chipped brick. Finicky, complicated, fatiguing to fly and fly in, and vulnerable to the most unsophisticated air defenses, choppers have shown a wide panoply of definite limitations. Koh Tang, the bleak journey to Desert One, Richmond Hill, and Calvigny might well be warnings. The days of direct helicopter air assaults may be numbered. Like horse cavalry in the American Civil War, they may have to eschew shock action in favor of reconnaissance, flank security, and utility roles, not to mention their important logistic and transport assignments behind the main battle area. The U.S. Army recently established a new aviation branch to direct the many initiatives of its vast rotary wing fleet, and these aviators and their marine and USAF special operations colleagues would do well to consider the sobering performance of helicopters under direct fire during post-Vietnam combat.

In the final analysis, the real reason for the overall record of American success since the fall of Saigon does not revolve around arms or organizations, but people. U.S. unit quality has been uniformly good, a marked contrast from the ragged, dispirited remnants of the later Vietnam era. The leaders, especially those at the lower and middle level, have made a difference. Their insistence on quality paid off in battle. Even the setbacks were normally the result of misjudgments, not incompetence and never malice. Brigadier General S. L. A. Marshall aptly described the ethos of the men who inspired America's post-Vietnam expeditionary forces: "In any situation of extreme pressure or moral exhaustion, where the men cannot otherwise be rallied and led forward, officers are expected to do the actual, physical act of leading, such as performing the first scout or point." [9] Lieutenant Colonel Randall Austin on the smoking green hell of Koh Tang, Sgt. Maj. Don Linkey in the burning transport plane at Desert One, Comdr. Henry Kleeman rolling into action over the Gulf of Sidra, Lt. Dave Hough on the firing line in wild Beirut, Capt. Frank Kearney among the exploding inferno of Calvigny barracks, and Col. Sam Westbrook under the streaking SAMs of Tripoli—they and many like them took charge when the going got tough. In the final reckoning, wars are won by men, not weapons. Fortunately, the United States has the right sort of men.

Chapter 8 Notes

Epigraphs come from Karl von Clausewitz, *War, Politics, and Power*, trans. and ed. Edward M. Collins (Chicago, IL: Regnery Gateway, Inc., 1962), 131, 132, and Col. John R. Boyd, USAF (ret.), "Remarks to USMA Department of History/Department of Military Instruction Art of War Symposium," 29 April 1987.

1. Shelby L. Stanton, *Anatomy of a Division* (Novato, CA: Presidio Press, 1987), 65; Russell F. Weigley, *Eisenhower's Lieutenants* (Bloomington, IN: Indiana University Press, 1981), 152, 153.
2. Edward N. Luttwak, *The Pentagon and the Art of War* (New York: Simon and Schuster, 1984), 17, 51, 57.
3. Clausewitz, *War, Politics, and Power*, 126–37.
4. Ibid., 133.
5. U.S. Department of Defense, *Annual Report to the Congress: Fiscal Year 1988* (Washington, D.C.: U.S. Government Printing Office, 1987), 171.
6. Ibid., 293–96; U.S. Joint Chiefs of Staff, *Military Posture FY 1988* (Washington, D.C.: U.S. Government Printing Office, 1987), 64.
7. U.S. DOD, *Annual Report 1988*, 61.
8. James F. Dunnigan, *How to Make War* (New York: William Morrow Company, 1982), 200.
9. Brig. Gen. S. L. A. Marshall, *The Armed Forces Officer* (Washington, D.C.: U.S. Government Printing Office, 1975), 188.

Selected Bibliography

The many sources used in the compilation of this book are acknowledged in the chapter endnotes. For the reader who wishes a more in-depth account of particular actions, the following list of selected sources is provided.

PROLOGUE: An Era of Violent Peace (Saigon 1975)

Butler, David. *The Fall of Saigon*. New York: Simon and Schuster, 1985.

Herrington, Lt. Col. Stuart. *Peace with Honor?* Novato, CA: Presidio Press, 1983.

Snepp, Frank. *Decent Interval*. New York: Random House, 1977.

Watkins, Adm. James D. "The Maritime Strategy" in James A. Barber, executive director, *The Maritime Strategy*. Annapolis, MD: U.S. Naval Institute Press, 1986.

CHAPTER 1: "Marines Over the Side!" (*Mayaguez* 1975)

Comptroller General, "The Seizure of the *Mayaguez*" in U.S. Congress, House of Representatives, Committee on International Affairs. *Seizure of the Mayaguez: Part IV*. 94th Congress, 2nd Session, 4 October 1976.

Des Brisay, Capt. Thomas D. "Fourteen Hours at Koh Tang" in *USAF Southeast Asia Monograph Series, Volume 3*. Washington, D.C.: U.S. Government Printing Office, 1977.

Ford, Gerald. *A Time to Heal*. New York: Harper & Row, 1977.

Head, Richard G., Frisco W. Short, and Robert C. McFarlane. *Crisis Resolution: Presidential Decision-making in the Mayaguez and Korean Confrontations*. Boulder, CO: Westview Press, 1978.

Johnson, Col. John M., Lt. Col. Randall W. Austin, and Maj. D. A. Quinlan, "Individual Heroism Overcame Awkward Command Relationships, Confusion, and Bad Information Off the Cambodian Coast." *Marine Corps Gazette* (October 1977).

"Mayday for the *Mayaguez:* the Patrol Squadron Skipper, the Battalion Operations Officer, the Company Commander, the Guided Missile Destroyer's Skipper, the Destroyer Escort's Skipper." *Proceedings* (November 1976).

Taylor, Capt. John. "Air Mission *Mayaguez*." *Airman* (February 1976).

CHAPTER 2: Dust and Ashes (Iran 1980)

Beckwith, Col. Charles A. with Donald Knox. *Delta Force*. New York: Harcourt, Brace Jovanovich, Publishers, 1983.

Brzezinski, Zbigniew. "The Failed Mission," *New York Times Magazine* (18 April 1982).

Carter, Jimmy. *Keeping Faith*. New York: Bantam Books, 1982.

Earl, Maj. Robert L. "A Matter of Principle," *Proceedings* (February 1983).

Ethell, Jeffrey D. "Disaster at Desert One" in *Jane's 1981–82 Military Annual*. New York: Jane's Publishing Co., 1981.

Fitch, Maj. Logan with George Feifer. "Death at Desert One," *Penthouse* (March 1984).

"The Iran Raid: Operation Blue Light, An Aircrew Member's Story," *Gung Ho* (January 1983).

Jordan, Hamilton. *Crisis: The Last Year of the Carter Presidency*. New York: G. P. Putnam's Sons, 1982.

Martin, David C. "Inside the Rescue Mission," *Newsweek* (12 July 1982).

Ryan, Capt. Paul B. *The Iranian Rescue Mission*. Annapolis, MD: U.S. Naval Institute Press, 1985.

Sick, Capt. Gary. *All Fall Down*. New York: Random House, 1985.

_____. "Military Options and Constraints" in *American Hostages in Iran*. New Haven, CT: Yale University Press, 1985.

Special Operations Review Group, "Iran Rescue Mission," *Aviation Week and Space Technology* (15 September 1980, 22 September 1980, 29 September 1980).

Summers, Col. Harry G. "A Review Essay: *Delta Force*," *Military Review* (November 1983).

U.S. Congress, House of Representatives, Subcommittee of Appropriations Committee, "Hostage Rescue Mission" in *Department of Defense Appropriations for 1981*. 96th Congress, 2nd Session, 2 June 1980.

CHAPTER 3: Black Aces High (Sidra 1981)

Brown, David A. "Sixth Fleet F-14s Down Libyan Su-22s," *Aviation Week and Space Technology* (24 August 1981).

_____. "Libyan Incident Spurs Deployment Shift," *Aviation Week and Space Technology* (31 August 1981).

Cooley, John K. *Libyan Sandstorm*. New York: Holt, Rinehart, and Winston, 1982.

Isby, David. "Task Force," *Strategy and Tactics*, No. 83 (November/December 1980).

Shaw, Comdr. Robert L. *Fighter Combat*. Annapolis, MD: U.S. Naval Institute Press, 1985.

Tillman, Barrett. "Black Aces Bag Two," *The Hook* (fall 1981).

CHAPTER 4: Fire in the Levant (Lebanon 1982–1984)

Evans, Lt. Col. David, "Navy-Marine Corps Team in Lebanon," *Proceedings* (May 1984).

Friedman, Thomas L., "America's Failure in Lebanon," *New York Times Magazine* (8 April 1984).

Hallenback, Col. Ralph A. "Force and Diplomacy: The American Strategy in Lebanon." Pennsylvania State University, unpublished dissertation, 1986.

Hammel, Eric. *The Root: The Marines in Lebanon August 1982–February 1984*. New York: Harcourt Brace Jovanovich, 1985.

Jordan, Maj. Robert T. "They Came in Peace," *Marine Corps Gazette* (July 1984).

Petit, Michael. *Peacekeepers at War*. Boston, MA: Faber and Faber, Inc., 1986.

Sloyan, Patrick J. "U.S. in Lebanon: Anatomy of a Foreign Policy Failure," *Newsday*, 8 April 1984.

U.S. Congress, House of Representatives, Armed Services Committee. *Review of the Adequacy of Security Arrangements for Marines in Lebanon*. 98th Congress, 1st Session, 15 December 1983.

U.S. Department of Defense Commission on the Beirut International Terrorist Act, October 23, 1983. *Report of the Department of Defense Commission on the Beirut International Airport Terrorist Act, October 23, 1983*. Washington, D.C.: U.S. Government Printing Office, 1984.

Wilson, George. *Supercarrier*. New York: Macmillan Publishing Co., 1986.

CHAPTER 5: Assault on the Spice Island (Grenada 1983)

Army Studies Group, "1-75 Rangers in Grenada." Washington, D.C.: Department of the Army, 1983.

Ashby, Timothy. "Grenada: Soviet Stepping Stone," *Proceedings* (December 1983).

Bennett, Ralph Kinney. "Grenada: Anatomy of a 'Go' Decision," *Reader's Digest* (February 1984).

Berry, JO1 William et al. "Ten Days of Urgent Fury," *All Hands* (May 1984).

Byron, Lt. Col. Michael J. "Fury from the Sea: Marines in Grenada," *Proceedings* (May 1984).

Canan, James W. "Blue Christmas Coming Up," *Air Force* (January 1984).

Christmann, JO2 Timothy J. "Tac Air in Grenada." *Naval Aviation News* (November/December 1985).

Dunn, Peter M. and Bruce W. Watson, editors. *American Intervention in Grenada*. Boulder, CO: Westview Press, 1985.

"Grenada: A Special Report." *Airman* (February 1984).

Harding, Stephen. *Air War Grenada*. Missoula, MT: Pictorial Histories Publishing Company, 1984.

Lasyone, Capt. Bryan A. "Fury in the Spice Islands: A Navigator's Mission." *The Navigator* (summer 1984).

Marcus, Bruce and Michael Taber. *Maurice Bishop Speaks: The Grenada Revolution 1979–83*. New York: Pathfinder Press, 1983.

O'Kelley, Sgt. Patrick J. "So I Gave It a Shot" in Kesharu Imai, editor, *D-Day in Grenada*. Tokyo: World Photo Press, 1984.

O'Shaughnessy, Hugh. *Grenada: Revolution, Invasion, and Aftermath*. London: Hamish Hamilton, Ltd., 1984.

Sandford, Gregory. *The New JEWEL Movement: Grenada's Revolution 1979–1983*. Washington, D.C.: U.S. Government Printing Office, 1985.

Schemmer, Benjamin F. "JCS Reply to Congressional Reform Caucus' Critique of the Grenada Rescue Operation." *Armed Forces Journal International* (July 1984).

Schoenhals, Kai and Richard A. Melanson, editors. *Revolution and Intervention in Grenada*. Boulder, CO: Westview Press, 1985.

Seabury, Paul and Walter McDougall, editors. *The Grenada Papers*. San Francisco, CA: Institute for Contemporary Studies, 1984.

Stack, Sgt. Cecil. "Grenada," *Soldiers* (January 1984).

Trotti, John. *Marine Air*. Novato, CA: Presidio Press, 1985.

U.S. Congress, House of Representatives, Committee on Armed Services, *Lessons Learned as a Result of the U.S. Military Operations in Grenada*. 98th Congress, 2nd Session, 24 January 1984.

U.S. Marine Corps Development and Education Command Grenada Study Group. *Operational Overview 1-84*. Quantico, VA: U.S. Marine Corps Development and Education Command, 1984.

Valenta, Jiri and Herbert J. Ellison. *Grenada and Soviet/Cuban Policy*. Boulder, CO: Westview Press, 1986.

Zeybel, Henry. "Gunships at Grenada," *National Defense* (February 1984).

CHAPTER 6: The Element of Surprise (*Achille Lauro* 1985)

"F-14s Used Latest Electronics in EgyptAir Intercept," *Aviation Week and Space Technology* (21 October 1985).

Truver, Scott C. "Maritime Terrorism," *Proceedings* (May 1986).

"You Can Run, But You Can't Hide," *Newsweek* (21 October 1985).

CHAPTER 7: To the Shores of Tripoli (Libya 1986)

Christmann, JO2 Timothy J. "Harpoon Proves Its Tenacity," *Naval Aviation News* (July/August 1986).

————. "The Navy Strikes Tripoli's Terrorist," *Naval Aviation News* (July/August 1986).

"Countdown to Operation EL DORADO CANYON," *Jane's Defence Weekly* (26 April 1986).

Hersh, Seymour. "Target Qaddafi," *New York Times Magazine* (22 February 1987).

Lee, JOC Dave and PH2 Chris Holmes, "Operation EL DORADO: The Men Behind the Headlines," *All Hands* (June 1986).

North, David M. "Merits of U.S., Soviet Weapons Explored in Libyan Conflict," *Aviation Week and Space Technology* (31 March 1986).

Parks, Col. W. Hays. "Crossing the Line," *Proceedings* (November 1986).

"Reagan Ordered Airstrikes to Preempt Libyan Terrorists," *Aviation Week and Space Technology* (21 April 1986).

Stumpf, Lt. Comdr. Robert E. "Air War with Libya," *Proceedings* (August 1986).

"USAF's Role in Libyan Raid," *Air Force* (November 1986).

U.S. Congress, House of Representatives, Committee on Appropriations. *Department of Defense Appropriations for 1987*. 99th Congress, 2nd Session, 21 April 1986 (segment on air attack, 680–725).

"U.S. Demonstrates Advanced Weapons Technology in Libya," *Aviation Week and Space Technology* (21 April 1987).

CHAPTER 8: Force and Friction: A Reckoning

U.S. Department of Defense, *Annual Report to the Congress: Fiscal Year 1988*. Washington, D.C.: U.S. Government Printing Office, 1987.

U.S. Joint Chiefs of Staff, *Military Posture FY 1988*. Washington, D.C.: U.S. Government Printing Office, 1987.

In addition to the specific works cited above, readers are referred to back issues of the professional and trade journals listed below.

Air Force (Air Force Association)
Air Force Times
Airman (USAF)
All Hands (USN)
Armed Forces Journal International Army (Association of the U.S. Army)
Army Times
Aviation Week and Space Technology
Department of State Bulletin
The Hook (USN carrier aviation)
Jane's Defence Weekly
Marine Corps Gazette
Military Review (USA Command and General Staff College)
National Defense
Naval Aviation News
The Navigator (USAF flight navigators)
Navy Times
Parameters (USA War College)
Proceedings (U.S. Naval Institute)
Soldiers (USA)
Strategy and Tactics (wargamers' magazine)

General accounts of recent events can be found in appropriate editions of these periodicals.

New York Times
Newsday
Newsweek
Reader's Digest

Time
U.S. News & World Report
Washington Post

Finally, and most importantly, these officers aided research immensely with candid speeches and interviews.

Col. John R. Boyd, USAF (ret.), 29 April 1987.

Capt. James G. Breckenridge, USA, 11 September 1987.

Maj. Thomas Christianson, USA, 8 January 1987.

Capt. Charles Jacoby, USA, 12–13 August 1986.

Capt. Frank Kearney, USA, 24 April 1987.

Captain David W. Lamm, USA, 12 November 1987.

Col. James R. Paschall, USA, 2 December 1986.

1st Lt. Timothy Sayers, USA, 21 November 1983.

Colonel Steve Silvasy, USA, December 1983 (private videotape).

INDEX

NORTH
ATLANTIC OCEAN

SOUTH
PACIFIC OCEAN

⑤

SOUTH
ATLANTIC OCEAN

N